WITHDRAWN

Environmental Conflict in Alaska

Ken Ross

UNIVERSITY PRESS OF COLORADO

Published by the University Press of Colorado
5589 Arapahoe Avenue, Suite 206C
Boulder, Colorado 80303

The University Press of Colorado is a cooperative publishing enterprise supported, in part, by Adams State College, Colorado State University, Fort Lewis College, Mesa State College, Metropolitan State College of Denver, University of Colorado, University of Northern Colorado, University of Southern Colorado, and Western State College of Colorado.

The paper used in this publication meets the minimum requirements of the American National Standard for Information Sciences—Permanence of Paper for Printed Library Materials. ANSI Z39.48-1992

Library of Congress Cataloging-in-Publication Data

Ross, Ken, 1937–
    Environmental Conflict in Alaska / Ken Ross.
      p. cm.
    Includes bibliographical references and index.
    ISBN 0-87081-588-1 (alk. paper) — ISBN 0-87081-589-X (alk. paper)
      1. Environmental policy—Alaska—History. 2. Environmental protection—Alaska—History. I. Title.

GE185.A4 R67 2000
363.7'009798—dc21

                                          00-064831

Design by Laura Furney
Typesetting by Daniel Pratt

09 08 07 06 05 04 03 02 01 00 10 9 8 7 6 5 4 3 2 1

Environmental Conflict in Alaska

Contents

Illustrations

MAPS

Tables

Acknowledgments

Thanks to the following for chapter reviews and information: Lauri Adams, Judy Alderson, David L. Allison, Stan Ashmore, Dixie Baade, Warren Ballard, Kim Behrens, Laverne R. Beier, Cynthia Bily, Ed Bovy, Pamela Brodie, Jim Brooks, Valerie Brown, Margaret Calvin, Ray Cameron, Cathy Campbell, Michael Carey, Alex Carter, Bob Childers, David Cline, Serena Down, Tom Edgerton, Richard Fineberg, Becky Gay, Joe Geldhof, Richard Gordon, Bev Grafel, Gordon Haber, Lisa Harbo, David Harkness, Daniel Henry, Jack Hession, John Hodges, Vicky Hoover, Celia Hunter, John Hyde, Ronald K. Inouye, Chuck Joy, Steve Kallick, Roger Kaye, Pamela Khiani, James G. King, Matthew D. Kirchhoff, Chuck Kleeschulte, Philip S. Koehl, Bart Koehler, Julie Kelly Koehler, Dean Kohlhoff, K. Koski, Jerry Landgrebe, Robert Leedy, Calvin R. Lensink, Jack Lentfer, Sue Libenson, Buck Lindekugel, Clifford Lobaugh, Leon Lynch, Ellen Maling, Mary C. Mangusso, Margo Matthews, George Matz, Fran Mauer, Michael McGrath, Carol McIntyre, Donald E. McKnight, Steve McMains, Joe Mehrkens, Herbert R. Melchior, Wyn Menefee, Ted Merrell, Debbie S. Miller, Glenn Miller, Pamela A. Miller, Wilbur Mills, Thomas A. Morehouse, Jack Moseby, Eric Myers, John Myers, J. Richard Myren, Jay Nelson, Jon Nickles, Sheila Nickerson, Russ Oates, Karl Ohls, Dan O'Neill, Walter B. Parker, Clare Pavia, Susan Peck, Anna Phillip, Paula Phillips, Anna Plager, Janet D. Platt, Robert Polasky, Robert E. Price, John Quigley, Jim Rearden, Penny Rennick, Peter Richter, Dan Roby, Don Ross, Deborah D. Rudis, Alfred Runte, Jeanne Schaaf, Scott Schliebe, Bill Schneider, Karl Schneider, John W. Schoen, Peter Scholes, Joe Sebastian, Kirsten Shelton, Terry Simmons, Maryli Sisson, Allen Smith, Eric Smith, Andy Spear, David L. Spencer, Robert O. Stephenson, Jim Stratton, Ken Taylor, Averill Thayer, Nancy Tileston, Peg Tileston, Will Troyer, Doug Vandegraft, Leslie A. Viereck, R. T. Wallen, Sylvia Ward, Ed Wayburn, Robert B. Weeden, Maureen Weeks, Steve Wells, Gail Welsh, Michael Wenig, Cynthia Wentworth, Denny Wilcher, Deborah Williams, Kenton Wohl, Ginny Wood, Steven T. Zimmerman, Mary Zalar. Apologies to others who may have been forgotten.

Special thanks to the following for full-text editing: Cynthia Bily, Neil Davis, Erwina Godfrey, Laura Furney, and Scott Vickers of the University Press of Colorado.

Able assistance from many librarians in Alaska and the Lower 48 is appreciated. Thanks also to Adrian College for providing two sabbatical leaves in support of this project.

"You *can't write* how bad an idea that was," the old professor told me. He didn't know me, but noticed my research on the Rampart Dam. A truly stupendous scheme of the 1960s, Rampart aimed to put a chunk of Alaska the size of Lake Erie under water in a speculative attempt to boost the state's economy. More realistically, it promised temporary prosperity for the construction industry. The fight over whether or not to build it is one telling episode in the story of Alaska, the environmental movement, and evolving national values.

Rampart typifies the patterns of resource disposal that have characterized Alaska. They are born of the state's image, held by residents and outsiders alike, as a realm of freedom to exploit and experiment. Gold Rush stories fashioned a highly romantic myth of plucky individuals braving a forbidding environment in search of adventure or profit. As machines grew more powerful, profit waxed and adventure waned, but the myth refused to die. Alaska loomed larger than life, a land of superlatives, a place of escape, a lure for impulses of freedom and greed.

Such an image invited plunder reminiscent of pioneer days in the Lower 48. But several conditions limited the scope of environmentally destructive behavior in pre-statehood Alaska. Remoteness and cold discouraged immigration and commercial enterprise. Less than a quarter-million people lived there before 1959, at modest consumption levels, primarily in three cities. Little private industry existed onshore, and not much advanced technology. Even the Alcan Highway, opened to the public in 1948, afforded but inconvenient access from the outside. Territorial government possessed few powers to promote the economy, and the federal government owned nearly all the real estate. Excepting military operations, the land incurred only minor damage. Americans had no feeling that Alaska needed to be saved.

World War II set in motion profound changes through the influx of thousands of people, construction of the Alcan Highway, and heightened visibility of the territory. In the Lower 48, postwar industrial expansion called for more oil, and prospectors soon identified Alaska as a source. They succeeded in 1957, propelling the land on a course of economic development and paving the way for statehood. Adventurers, newly affluent and freed from the constraints of the Great Depression and the war, gravitated northward. Cold War responsibilities reinforced the territory's strategic value and led to buildup of navy, air force, and army facilities, in turn amplifying popular interest in Alaska. Airplanes and other implements of modern technology hastened the erosion of wilderness before the advent of statehood on January 3, 1959.

Momentous social change swept the nation during the 1960s. Affluence translated into demands for lifestyle amenities including outdoor recreation and living close to nature, and multiplied the negative effects on the environment through accelerated production and consumption. Swelling numbers attended college, advancing public understanding of social problems. Having never known hardship and easily able to find employment, students registered opposition to traditional institutions and pursued alternate philosophies, careers, and lifestyles. They composed a driving force in the civil rights movement. Goaded by the Vietnam War and its draft, they rebelled against the military-industrial complex. Their reaction to environmental pollution events such as the 1969 Santa Barbara oil spill led to Earth Day in 1970, a milestone of environmentalism. Many saw racism, sexism, militarism, corporate power, and environmental destruction as interrelated exponents of an outmoded social system. Some of their views enjoyed support in the media, the academic community, the Kennedy and Johnson administrations, and the public at large.

Television and other media stimulated nature appreciation and awareness of environmental abuses in the 1960s and early 1970s. Above all, people saw pollution as a threat to their own well-being. Conservation values shifted from management by natural-resource professionals for human material consumption toward "environmental" values, centering on pursuit of a sustainable relationship between humans and the natural world. By fusing nature protection, pollution control, and other social issues, the new environmentalism quickly gained public approval and political influence.

Americans began to perceive the natural environment as a vital public resource, and Alaska as the crown jewel of their wildlands. The state's environmental image shifted from a wonderland of wildlife and endless open space—some called it wasteland—to a land needing protection. Awareness of the extent and rapidity of environmental degradation in the Lower 48 flowed from the publication of Rachel Carson's book *Silent Spring*, building of the Glen Canyon Dam, cutting of the Texas Big Thicket, and other such events. Reaction to the losses fed a determination that these mistakes must not be repeated in Alaska. Improved access to the state gave outsiders a more direct stake in the quality of its environment and its potential for outdoor recreation. An emerging environmental movement increasingly made its presence felt in Washington, D.C., and turned its attention to prominent Alaskan issues.

In the early years of Alaska's statehood, a dispute over polar bear hunting by aircraft measured the relative power of the new state government, desiring to maintain management of wildlife, and the federal government, pushed by public sentiment favoring the bears and by Natives seeking exclusive hunting access. Contests over migratory waterfowl and bowhead whales helped clarify rules of subsistence resource use and define the status of Alaska Natives. The state's bounty system ended in a clash between the traditional view of predators as varmints and a broader perspective based on ecological science and philosophy. Project Chariot, a Cold War spinoff featuring proposed nuclear explosions in the Arctic, matched the power of the military-industrial complex against conservationists, environmentalists, and early advocates of Native rights. The Rampart Dam project pitted economic boosters against wildlife enthusiasts and Natives scheduled to lose their villages. Nuclear explosions at Amchitka brought the Atomic Energy Commission and Department of Defense into confrontation with a growing list of interests: environmentalists, Aleuts, Alaskan officials, Canadians, and Japanese. These early disputes served to strengthen the legitimacy of cardinal environmental values: governmental accountability, public access to relevant information, the necessity for adequate research, holistic perspectives in ecosystem management, public participation in resource management, biological sustainability in wildlife use, and economic sustainability in industrial enterprises.

Through the 1970s the modern environmental movement flowered and diversified. It drew strength from a widespread feeling that government, business, and other large institutions had lost touch with evolving problems and needs. Collectively, its concerns encompassed wildlife and wildland protection, animal rights, pollution and population control, energy policy, recycling and resource limits, environmental health, local community control and quality of life, and some civil rights and peace aspects. Environmentalists tended to see these elements, and all social and economic questions, as part of an integral whole. Human lifestyles, they believed, should be ecologically and economically sustainable. As key means of achieving these goals, they advocated public involvement in resource management and government and corporate openness and accountability. They pursued these goals through a variety of tactics. When possible, they participated in public hearings and other points of access to legislative and regulatory processes. The National Environmental Policy Act of 1969 and its requirement of environmental impact statements served as a valuable tool for groups able to provide expert testimony or mount lawsuits. The communications media conveyed ecological perspectives to an awakening public, and government policies from national to local levels began to respond.

National public opinion increasingly adopted modern environmental values, providing they did not appear to threaten a comfortable lifestyle. The Arab oil embargo instilled, at least temporarily, a sense of limits to growth. Repeated and heavily publicized toxic-chemical incidents (e.g., Love Canal and the PBB misfortune in Michigan) convinced the public that pollution must be controlled and the quality of their surroundings maintained or restored. Continued affluence whetted appetites for outdoor recreation and closeness to nature, though hunting declined as a sport. People grew less inclined to leave crucial judgments to managerial experts, and pressed government for many forms of action. Thousands of groups, often ad hoc, took action to ward off threats or enhance the livability of their communities. Numerically, at least, they made up much of the bulk of the movement. Many joined established environmental organizations or assisted in creating new ones. Their endeavors broadened and deepened American environmentalism, helping to ensure its legitimacy as a political institution.

History's timing of the Alaska oil pipeline and the lands ("d-2") settlement blessed the advocates of preservation. Both issues coincided with the national value shift toward natural amenities, and with the upswing of environmentalism. Both held the national spotlight when they peaked. Forces of development, including the Alaska government and powerful oil companies somewhat tainted by oil spills and the energy crisis, lined up against a movement enjoying firm media, congressional, and national public support. National environmental organizations stepped up their activity in Alaska, supplementing local groups. In resolution of the land status question in 1980, the Carter administration rendered vital assistance to conservation values. The lands competition ended in a draw, and defenders of exploitation values prevailed in the case of the oil pipeline.

Reagan and Bush policies nearly halted environmental progress in the 1980s, employing administrative measures to promote development over conservation. National and Alaskan environmental groups responded through appeal processes and lawsuits. Reform of Tongass National Forest policy called for reversing a dogmatic Forest Service commitment to logging. Defense of the Arctic National Wildlife Refuge offered the nation a classic choice between wilderness and oil. The *Exxon Valdez* oil spill, perhaps the world's most visible environmental catastrophe, served as a reminder of the public's perennial interest in Alaska and its outrage at the destruction of nature. National opinion also made its presence felt when the State of Alaska undertook wolf control to supply more moose and caribou for hunters.

Haltingly, but cumulatively, the conflicts of the statehood period moved state and national policy in the direction of environmental responsibility. Wildlife disputes applied the principle of sustainable use, and generated models of public participation in resource management. The *Exxon Valdez* oil spill settlement affirmed, belatedly, the principle of corporate accountability. Increasing pressure from environmental groups, the media, and the public forced logging and mining operations toward greater ecological and economic sustainability. At the same time, rising population and conservative political leadership worked to undo the gains in environmental protection. At the millenium, the future of Alaskan environmental quality remained in doubt.

Alaska's recent environmental experience differs from that of the Lower 48 not only because the stakes are higher, the land more legendary, and the scenes more beauteous. Unlike any other state, Alaska retained most of its wildness until that in the Lower 48 had nearly disappeared, national values had evolved toward preservation, and the environmental movement had emerged. Alaska Natives, most of them never conquered, maintained claims on the land that could not be ignored in an era of civil rights. The great northern land imparted a unique opportunity to protect wilderness on a grand scale. For more than four decades, Alaska put the nation's values to trial.

This work presents an overview of the salient environmental contests of the statehood period, illustrating the gradual implementation of environmental values in the management of Alaskan natural resources. The reader is offered a moderately preservationist interpretation of events—though not, it is hoped, at the expense of accuracy. Other writers will explore in greater depth some of the topics treated here in relative brevity. In doing so, they will add to a fascinating record that deserves an eminent place in American environmental history.

1867	United States purchases Alaska
1912	Alaska designated a territory
1925	Alaska Game Law
1947	Tongass Timber Sales Act
1954	Ketchikan Pulp Company mill opens
1957	Alaska Department of Fish and Game organized
1957	Oil discovered on Kenai Peninsula
1958	Project Chariot proposed
1958–1959	Alaska Statehood Act; statehood
1959	Alaska Pulp Company mill opens at Sitka
1959	Rampart Dam proposed
1960	Alaska assumes control of fish and game
1960	Alaska Conservation Society organized
1960	Multiple Use-Sustained Yield Act defines national forest uses
1960	Kuskokwim, Izembek, and Arctic National Wildlife Ranges created
1964	National Wilderness Preservation Act
1964	Good Friday earthquake
1965, 1969, 1971	Atomic tests at Amchitka
1966	Endangered Species Preservation Act
1966	Alaska Federation of Natives organized
1967	Fairbanks flood
1967	Oil discovered at Prudhoe Bay
1968	Most predator bounties ended
1968	National Wild and Scenic Rivers Act
1969	Hickel Highway built
1969	Southeast Alaska Conservation Council organized

1969	Friends of the Earth organized
1969	Greenpeace organized
1969	National Environmental Policy Act
1971	Alaska Department of Environmental Conservation created
1971	Alaska Coalition organized
1971	Alaska Center for the Environment organized
1971	Fairbanks Environmental Center organized
1971	Alaska Native Claims Settlement Act (ANCSA)
1972	Marine Mammal Protection Act
1972	Coastal Zone Management Act
1972	Clean Water Act
1973	International Agreement on Conservation of Polar Bears
1973	Endangered Species Act
1973	Congress authorizes Trans-Alaska Pipeline
1974	Trustees for Alaska organized
1974	Legislature supports Susitna Dam
1976	National Forest Management Act
1976	Fisheries Conservation and Management Act sets U.S. jurisdiction at 200 nautical miles
1977	Trans-Alaska Pipeline begins operation
1977	Alaska Eskimo Whaling Commission organized
1978	Sierra Club Legal Defense Fund organized in Alaska
1978	Carter creates 17 national monuments in Alaska
1980	Alaska Conservation Foundation begins operation
1980	Alaska National Interest Lands Conservation Act (ANILCA), or Alaska Lands Act
1981	Alaska Environmental Assembly, Alaska Environmental Lobby, and Alaska Environmental Political Action Committee begin operation
1982	Alaska Chilkat Bald Eagle Preserve created
1986	Yukon-Kuskokwim Delta Goose Management Plan
1989	*Exxon Valdez* oil spill
1990	Oil Pollution Act
1990	Tongass Timber Reform Act
1990	Federal government takes control of subsistence wildlife on federal lands
1993	Alaska Pulp Company mill closed
1996	Louisiana Pacific Ketchikan mill closed
1999	Federal government takes control of subsistence fisheries on federal land

Environmental Conflict in Alaska

PART I

Wildlife Disputes

A laska's early years left a record of unshackled and often violent exploitation of natural resources. A remote repository of rich if rather sparsely distributed treasures, the
territory attracted fringe elements of society—adventurers and entrepreneurs—who dared
defy the harsh conditions of the north. Directly or indirectly, wildlife bore the brunt of their
assault. Russian fur seekers decimated the sea otters and fur seals, in the process enslaving
the Aleuts and drastically altering their culture. Americans then took up the quest for fur
profits, driving the two sea mammals to the brink of extinction. Whalers scoured the seas,
nearly eradicating the right whale and gravely diminishing other species. Natives collaborated in the commercial whaling and walrus ivory industries, thereby hastening destruction of their own food sources. Added to liquor, disease, and modern implements,
commercial hunting further disintegrated Native lifestyles. Walruses and coastal caribou
populations grew scarce, and the few remaining Alaskan musk oxen disappeared. Salmon
canners raided the coastal streams, aggravating periodic collapses of one of Alaska's prime
natural assets. Gold seekers ravaged river valleys by fire and depleted game and fur mammals.
All of these endeavors speeded the introduction of a cash economy that dismantled Native
culture and encouraged excessive killing of wildlife. The territorial legislature manifested the
exploitation ethic, badgering the federal government for ever greater access to natural resources. It placed bounties on the wolf, the bald eagle, and other creatures considered threats
to human economic advantage. It acted upon the dominant notion that no controllable aspect
of nature must be permitted to impede the momentum of human (particularly Euro-American)
settlement and industry. In the most salient bone of contention in territorial-federal relations,
Alaskan politicians echoed the popular view that the federal government favored outside
interests in the commercial competition for valuable salmon fisheries. Some early Alaskan
visitors introduced a different agenda. Seeing the land and its wildlife as beautiful and
valuable in itself, they sought to prevent its destruction. Educated and politically sophisticated sport hunters, notably members of the Boone and Crockett Club, succeeded in effecting
federal laws and executive orders to protect wildlife and to lay the basis for a system of
national and Alaskan wildlife preserves. Their efforts supplemented the work of naturalists
and scientists, both private and governmental, and of federal wildlife managers. Game laws
passed in 1902, 1908, and 1925 brought some rapacious behavior under control. Fur seals,
sea otters, walruses, and whales received protection, as did a broad array of wildlands
including the Tongass and Chugach National Forests (1902–1909), Aleutian Islands Reserve (1913), Mount McKinley National Park (1917), Katmai and Glacier Bay National
Monuments (1918, 1925), Kenai National Moose Range (1941), Kodiak National Wildlife
Range (1941), and in 1960 the Kuskokwim, Izembek, and Arctic National Wildlife Ranges.

Changes prior to statehood in 1959 shaped the future of the environment. World War II
caused a great population infusion, elevating demands on fish and game species and open

space. New technology, particularly the chain saw, bulldozer, and all-season and multi-terrain aircraft, magnified the damage potential. Slowdown of Cold War–related spending in the late 1950s led Alaskans to adopt any scheme appearing to further economic progress. Discovery of oil on the Kenai Peninsula in 1957 stimulated investment and further exploration, invigorating the movement for statehood and bearing the promise of permanently altering Alaskan life. Although the frontier had in large measure disappeared, the myth of Alaska as a limitless, uninhabited land tempted its residents and some federal agencies to treat it as an opportunity for aggressive consumption and an experimentation ground for poorly conceived projects.

Thanks in part to the 1925 Alaska Game Law and its Game Commission, the territory suffered no loss or serious endangerment of any species of terrestrial wildlife. But the territory experienced a rough transition to state control: rivalry and resentment between state and federal wildlife officials accompanied the transfer of jurisdiction over fish and game. Mutual distrust reinforced accusations by territorial politicians and game officials of federal mismanagement of natural resources, and prompted a decision to extend its wildlife management for one year beyond statehood.

The federal government maintained jurisdiction over migratory birds, and consolidated control over marine mammals in 1972. Thus it occupied center stage in the clashes over geese in the Yukon-Kuskokwim Delta (Chapter 3), bald eagles in the Chilkat Valley (Chapter 4), and the hunting of bowhead whales (Chapter 2). Polar bears (Chapter 1), initially under state jurisdiction, passed to the federal government in the wake of a controversy over aerial hunting. The 1972 Marine Mammal Protection Act also limited taking of marine mammals to subsistence use by Natives. Wolves (Chapter 5), by contrast, remained a state responsibility as did other land mammals. A heated and ongoing struggle over wolf control pushed state policy back and forth in response to evolving public opinion and the demands of hunters and trappers. The wolf, outnumbered 100 to 1 by humans, emerged a symbolic figure in the debate over natural resources, and its most vocal protector, Alaska Wildlife Alliance, gained rapidly in membership.

Several parties—the state and federal governments, Natives, sport hunters and fishers, environmentalists, and others—engaged in an emotionally loaded tug-of-war over "subsistence" use of wildlife (Chapter 6). Natives claimed special rights based on cultural and economic needs, while many non-Natives expected equal access. The political-philosophical differences could not easily be settled by law or by the application of environmental principles, and endured throughout the latter half of the century.

Advancing technology, human population growth, and public involvement all affected wildlife policy. Highly visible species such as bears, wolves, eagles, and whales evoked strong feelings among their sympathizers and their persecutors. State and federal wildlife managers had to balance the demands of many contending parties: resource extractors, sport hunters, Natives, local residents, the Alaskan and national publics, and increasingly numerous and sophisticated environmentalists. To a large extent, the outcomes of wildlife disputes depended on the quality of ecological research, seldom adequately funded. In the process of resolving the controversies, wildlife management evolved toward sustainable use through cooperative arrangements among government overseers, user groups, and other interested parties, including environmentalists.

Polar Bear's Passage

One of the earliest clashes over wildlife in Alaska's statehood period involved the polar bear, a circumpolar carnivore spending most of its life on the sea ice. Government officials, sport hunters, conservationists, and Natives contended over who would have hunting rights to the bear, and by what methods. The issue illustrated the nation's changing attitudes toward wildlife protection and its crystallizing view of Alaska as a national environmental treasure. Resolution of the polar bear issue in turn advanced the principle of sustainable use through cooperative resource management.

Inaccessibility helped protect the polar bear until the 1950s. Yet the bears did not escape the predations of the whaling era, when whalers and Eskimo hunters killed many for hides to be sold in the States. Evidence suggests that overwintering whalers drove out polar bears denning in the Canning River vicinity. Bears once lived all year on St. Matthew Island, but fell before the guns of commercial whale and walrus hunters. Other intruders hastened the decline: biologist G. Dallas Hanna, who surveyed the island in 1916, noted that "in 1874, when Elliott and Maynard landed on St. Matthew in midsummer, polar bears were very abundant. . . . Captain Lane told me that the bears were found up until sometime in the 90s when a party from the revenue cutter *Corwin* landed and shot 16. The old trails Elliott mentioned are still plainly seen; worn deep into the tundra. Skulls of several animals were found, all with bullet holes in them."[1]

THE HUNTING CONTROVERSY

During the first half of the twentieth century, Eskimos did nearly all the polar bear hunting, primarily by dogsled and for subsistence purposes. Successful hunts reinforced cultural traditions through stories, dances, and ceremonies, and won high social standing for the hunters. Air travel signaled a change by introducing trophy hunters in the late 1940s.[2]

By 1960 disquiet grew over increased killing by the airborne sport hunters. Four coastal towns (Teller, Kotzebue, Point Hope, and Barrow) functioned as jump-off points. In most cases, two planes flew in search of a bear. Experienced pilots could distinguish the tracks of the larger and preferred male bears from those of the normally smaller females and cubs. Tracks could be followed to the quarry. One plane landed close to the bear and the other circled, often herding the bear back to the hunter, who needed hardly any skill and faced

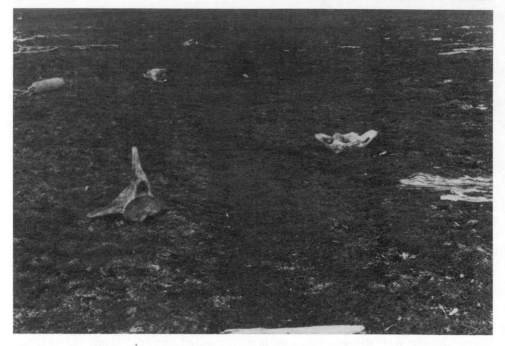

1.1. Polar bear trail on St. Matthew Island, ca. 1950s. Courtesy Alaska Resources Library and Information Services, Anchorage. Sixty years after extermination in the 1890s, bear trails wind among ancient whalebones.

minimal danger or inconvenience. After being shot, the bear would be skinned and its hide flown back, the rest left.[3] Guides often guaranteed their clients a kill and flew an average of 85 miles offshore to find bears. By the mid-1960s, each of the expensive hunts added around $1,500 to the Alaskan economy. A few guides who tried to interest clients in hunting by dogsled—an arduous, time-consuming, and uncertain venture—did not succeed.[4] About 30 pairs of airborne guides participated in the spring trophy hunts, engendering a half-million-dollar industry.[5]

Several objections arose. One centered on fear of depletion of the species; no one knew how many polar bears existed. Excessive killing of its bears, some of them living partly in Alaska, induced the USSR to ban hunting in 1956 and classify parts of Wrangel Island as denning sanctuaries in 1960.[6] Alaska had instituted bag limits in 1948, and by the time of statehood each hunter could take one bear per year, and no mothers or cubs.[7]

A second complaint related to the Natives. Prior to the 1950s, Eskimos killed an average of about 100 bears annually. From 1960 to 1972 the yearly total averaged 260, mostly by trophy hunters and only 13 percent by Eskimos.[8] Bears grew scarce near villages, where they could be reached by surface transportation, and harvest by Natives declined by 70 percent while the toll by aircraft hunters doubled. Eskimo hunters lost prestige when villagers noticed how easily the white hunters could kill bears.[9] Point Hope villagers incurred a significant economic loss by reduced sales of skins, and critics leveled the familiar charge that hunters brought liquor to the Natives.[10]

1.2. Sport hunter poses with polar bear she has just killed, near Kotzebue, 1957. By Steve McCutcheon. Courtesy Anchorage Museum of History and Art. Success required negligible skill on the part of the hunters.

A third criticism involved sportsmanship. The trophy-hunting procedure could scarcely be considered fair chase, and the commercial element made it seem even more distasteful. Former Alaska wildlife manager Frank Dufresne and other sporting writers voiced their opposition, as did preservation groups. Some Alaska Department of Fish and Game (ADF&G) biologists agreed, warning that aerial hunting could jeopardize state control of polar bear management. A *New York Times* editor penned:

> The polar bear is a victim of a peculiar—and peculiarly repulsive—expression of man's egotism. Wealthy men have taken to hunting bears in Alaska from airplanes. . . . This kind of hunt is about as sporting as machine-gunning a cow. Its only purpose is to obtain the bear's fur as a trophy for the floor or wall of someone's den. . . . The polar bear maintains a higher standard than some humans. He kills for food, never for pleasure.

Only Norway and Alaska "encourage this degraded 'sport' as a tourist promotion." In 1966 the National Rifle Association terminated its annual polar bear trophy award following the Boone and Crockett Club's decision to remove the bear from its big game list.[11]

Polar bear hunting sometimes involved risk for the pursuers. On one occasion a plane took off from the icepack, striking a ski on the top of an ice pressure ridge. The ski tip flipped

Bowhead Whales and Eskimos

Bowhead whales, rich in oil and baleen, ranked as the main prize of the Yankee whalers during their heyday in the North Pacific. A fleet of more than a hundred ships in the early 1850s expedited the termination of Russian dominion in Alaska. The Russians preferred control by the United States to that by Great Britain. Substitutes for whale oil and baleen, and shrinkage of whale concentrations, ended commercial bowhead whaling in the early twentieth century. Following more than a half-century of quietude, bowheads resurfaced in the 1970s as a subject of contention. The whales now encountered only Inupiat Eskimo hunters, but had won reluctant defenders among state, national, and international officials, and some environmentalists. Millions of people opposed any slaughter of whales, yet Eskimos hunted the animals for food. Resolution of the conflict would set new balances between nature preservation and human use values, force consideration of new mechanisms for wildlife management, and test the relationship between Natives and the environmental community.

Reduced to a small fraction of its premodern total of perhaps 50,000, by the mid-twentieth century the world's bowheads existed in five locations: Svalbard, Davis Strait, Hudson's Bay, the Sea of Okhotsk, and the western Arctic (Bering, Chukchi, and Beaufort Seas). Only the western Arctic stock, by far the largest, still provided food for humans.[1]

TRADITIONAL AND COMMERCIAL WHALING

Eskimos, predominantly Inupiat, had pursued the bowhead and other whales for more than 2,000 years at St. Lawrence Island and for over 1,000 years on the northwest Alaska coast. Whaling supplied a high proportion of the year's protein for several villages. Point Hope, Kivalina, Wainwright, and Barrow relied most on the animals in the 1970s; less whaling took place at other villages, including Gambell, Savoonga, Wales, Diomede, Kaktovik, and Nuiksut.[2]

As the ice goes out in late spring, the western Arctic population of bowhead whales migrates from the Bering Sea up the Alaska coast and eventually to the Canadian Arctic, returning in the fall. In the precommercial era, crews from coastal villages prepared for the migrations and scanned the leads of open water for bowheads. From a walrus-skin or bearded sealskin *umiak*, the crew quietly approached a surfacing whale and, wielding harpoons tipped by bone, stone, or ivory, struck it. At the end of a rawhide line tied to the spearhead

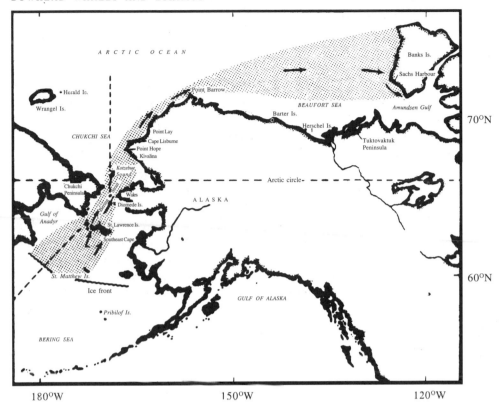

2.1. Spring Migration Route of Bowhead Whales, 1970s. Courtesy Braham, Fruker, and Krogman, "Spring Migration of the Western Arctic Population of Bowhead Whales," Marine Fisheries Review nos. 9–10 (1980), 42.

rode sealskin or walrus-skin floats. Attempting to dive and escape, the whale tired from efforts to pull down the floats that forced it to surface ever more frequently. If not able to escape under the ice, the whale suffered repeated spearings and the burden of as many as 15 floats. Eventually the team came alongside the exhausted whale, lanced it in the lungs and cut the tendons in its tail.[3]

News of a whale kill sparked excitement and celebration among the villagers. They hauled the body up on the ice by a cooperative effort. According to custom, villagers butchered it and apportioned the meat and blubber to the various families. Whaling in this traditional form entailed mortal danger, and the organization and completion of a victorious expedition depended on great skill. Successful captains earned high status in the community, and religion, songs, stories, dances, and seasonal activities revolved around whale hunting. Year-round preparation for and celebration of the hunts, sharing of meat, and leadership roles of the organizers fostered identity and solidarity in the community. As Martha Aiken of Barrow testified in the hearings for the Marine Mammal Protection Act (MMPA), "If our livelihood and diet of centuries are taken away from us, what's the use of being called an Eskimo?"[4]

Far less prestige, though sometimes much profit, accompanied the search for the "ice whale" by commercial whalers who entered the western Arctic in 1848. Captain Charles Melville Scammon related: "Soon after the ships' arrival, the whales avoid their pursuers by going under the main body of ice, situated in the middle of the bay, finding breathing-holes among the conglomerate flow. The boats cruise along the edge of this barrier, watching for them to emerge from their cover, which occasionally they do, and are given chase to instantly." Whales broke through ice at least four inches thick to breathe, and could be heard at long distances. Repeated attacks made the whales shy. Later in the summer, "although there are frequently seen large numbers of whales spouting among the numerous boats scattered across the water, not a single animal could be approached near enough to dart at it with the hand harpoon."[5]

Yankee whalers visited traumatic changes upon the Natives' livelihood. They harvested as many as 20,000 bowheads.[6] By the late 1860s whale scarcity drove the whalers to killing walruses, in turn hard to find by the late 1870s. Hired Natives decimated caribou herds to supply food to the whalers. For the Eskimos, periods of starvation, interspersed with deaths from influenza, measles, tuberculosis, venereal disease, and alcohol, ensued.[7] Influenza took the lives of 200 inland Eskimos at Barrow in 1900, and another 100 Barrow residents in 1902.[8]

To exploit whales migrating along the shore, land-based stations sprang up in the 1880s, employing Eskimos as hunters. Having acquired whale guns and bomb lances, the Eskimos grew careless and lost many wounded whales, worsening their own food supply shortage. The whaler *West Shore* reported in 1890 that Natives fired hundreds of missiles and secured only eight whales. Vilhjalmur Stefansson noted six or eight Eskimo whaling crews operating in 1908 in competition with whites, each member being paid $200 for the six-week season. By the time ship-based whaling ended in the Arctic in 1916, both Eskimo and bowhead populations had been reduced to fractions of their former levels. Reindeer imported by the federal government helped tide some of the Eskimos over until the revival of game mammal populations and fox trapping in the 1920s.[9]

WHALE PROTECTION EFFORTS

Awareness of the losses of whale populations gave rise to remedial action. A Convention for the Regulation of Whaling outlawed commercial killing of bowheads and other right whales in 1931, as did 1946 rules of the International Whaling Commission (IWC), to which the United States acceded in 1949. These agreements exempted traditional use by aboriginal people. The 1931 convention allowed Natives to take the whales if they used hand or sail-propelled traditional boats and no firearms. In 1946 the IWC forbade killing "except when the meat and products of such whales are to be used exclusively for local consumption by the aborigines." However, Eskimos had abandoned traditional killing methods in the 1880s by adopting hand-held harpoon guns, and persisted in employing them despite international agreements. A 1964 IWC amendment deleted any mention of methods or weapons.[10] The Endangered Species Acts of 1966 and 1969 identified great whales as endangered, and banned importation of whale products. The MMPA of 1972 outlawed both sport and commercial hunting of marine mammals, excepting Natives provided they killed for subsistence and not in a wasteful manner. Sale and trading of crafts made of bone, ivory, and baleen had been practiced before the commercial whaling era, and MMPA regulations interpreted them as subsistence activities. In 1973 the Endangered Species Act prohibited domestic and international trafficking in products of endangered species, exempting Alaska Natives as had MMPA.[11]

Modern conditions altered the terms of bowhead whaling. Between 1910 and 1969, Eskimos obtained an annual average of approximately 13 bowheads for subsistence (Table 2.1).[12] Then a radical change arrived. Money from oil exploration and pipeline construction jobs entered the villages, enabling many more, but far less qualified, men to finance whaling expeditions. The number of crews doubled from the normal 45 in 1973 to 99 in 1980. Landed whales shot up to 48 in 1976. A year later, hunters brought home 29 bowheads but wounded or lost as many as 84, apparently through inexperience.[13] Harpooners often used shoulder guns without provision for attaching ropes and floats. They fired at whales from excessive distances, and bombs regularly misfired from poor maintenance.[14]

Members of the IWC Scientific Committee voiced concern to the U.S. government as early as 1972. In addition to the high mortality figures, rumors circulated that much of the

Table 2.1—Bowhead Whales Landed and Struck but Lost by Eskimo Hunters, 1960–1999

Year	Landed	Struck and Lost	Year	Landed	Struck and Lost
1960	22	11	1980	16	28
1961	10	9	1981	17	11
1962	12	9	1982	8	11
1963	10	6	1983	9	9
1964	16	7	1984	12	13
1965	9	2	1985	11	6
1966	16	17	1986	20	8
1967	8	—	1987	22	9
1968	17	5	1988	23	6
1969	21	18	1989	18	8
1970	26	42	1990	30	14
1971	22	9	1991	28	19
1972	40	5	1992	38	12
1973	39	20	1993	41	11
1974	20	34	1994	34	12
1975	15	28	1995	43	14
1976	48	43	1996	39	5
1977	29	82	1997	48	18
1978	12	6	1998	41	13
1979	12	15	1999	42	5
Totals				944	600
Annual Avg.				23	15

Source: L. Michael Philo, Emmett B. Shotts Jr., and John C. George, "Morbidity and Mortality," in John J.Burns, J. Jerome Montague, and Cleveland J. Cowles, eds., *The Bowhead Whale*, Society for Marine Mammalogy. Special Pub. No. 2 (Lawrence, KS: Allen Press, 1993), pp. 276–277; Sam W. Stoker and Igor I. Krupnik, "Subsistence Whaling," in Burns, Montague, and Cowles, p. 619; and National Marine Fisheries Service, Marine Mammal Commission, *Annual Report, 1999*, Table 2.

2.1. *Inupiat hunter prepares for whale hunt, Point Hope, 1969. Courtesy Victor Fischer collection, University of Alaska Fairbanks, Alaska and Polar Regions Archives. Whale meat made up an important part of the diet in some villages throughout the twentieth century.*

2.2. *Umiak crews search for whales, Point Hope, April 1960. Courtesy Don C. Foote collection, University of Alaska Fairbanks, Alaska and Polar Regions Archives. Successful whaling expeditions won social status for the hunters.*

2.3. Point Hope villagers pull bowhead whale ashore, 1969. Courtesy Victor Fischer collection, University of Alaska Fairbanks, Alaska and Polar Regions Archives. Whaling is a source of cultural identity for the Inupiat in several villages.

meat and blubber taken in 1976 had been left on the beach, or removed from the permafrost storage caverns and thrown away to make room for that acquired in 1977. Eskimos flew meat and blubber to families and friends living in Fairbanks and Anchorage. Moreover, urban-dwelling Eskimos took time off from work to fly back to the villages for whaling.[15] Critics deemed such activities misuse of endangered whales for manhood and other rituals in violation of the spirit or letter of MMPA.

According to IWC's limited information, only 600 to 2,000 of an original population of 12,000 to 18,000 bowheads existed in the western Arctic, and the current mortality rate might carry them to extinction. Thus in June 1977 the IWC Scientific Committee recommended total

2.4. Villagers processing two bowheads. Courtesy Arctic Environmental Information and Data Center, Anchorage. Concern for the bowhead population set off an environmental dispute in the late 1970s.

protection for bowheads.[16] IWC officials expressed alarm at the spring 1977 statistics. They knew the populations of whaling villages had doubled between 1950 and 1975,[17] and that the crash of the western Arctic caribou herd had prompted a sharp cutback of caribou bag limits in 1977. But could these factors explain or justify the number of whales being killed, much less the loss ratio?

National public opinion favored both civil rights and endangered-species preservation. Alaskan environmentalists and the U.S. government found themselves in the middle; they wanted guarantees for both the whales and Eskimo subsistence. Alaska Conservation Society, Fairbanks Environmental Center, and Alaska Center for the Environment called for the United States to object to a total ban. Friends of the Earth in Anchorage supported the government's intention not to object, but urged negotiations to gain a special dispensation for the Eskimos.[18] Having led the world's whale preservation effort for years, the United States now found itself reduced to the role of special pleader. Behind closed doors, it obtained a 1978 quota of 12 bowheads killed or 18 struck, whichever came first. In what looked like a quid pro quo, the Japanese and Russians had their sperm whale quotas raised from 743 to 6,444. Following a 1978 survey estimating a bowhead population of 2,265, the United States received 1979 and 1980 quotas of 18 killed and 27 struck.[19]

Eskimos, incensed by the ban recommendation, also disputed the quotas. They charged that officials had underestimated the whale population and endangered the Native economy and culture. Whereas non-Natives tended to view the whaling as a search for meat supply,

Eskimos perceived it as preeminently an affirmation of their cultural identity, essential to the welfare of their communities.[20] North Slope Borough produced two films, *Hunger Knows No Law: A Whaling Film* and *The Last Anchor*, to be used in a public-relations campaign.[21] Barrow militant Charles (Etok) Edwardsen, an active leader in the Native land claims lobbying effort, observed, "[Whites are] very selective about which species they preserve. . . . Evidently, [the Eskimos] are among the species they have destined for extinction."[22] Several Inupiat groups sued the government and lost. The Justice Department investigated a report that five more than the quota of whales had been struck in the spring of 1980. The Reagan administration dropped the investigation in 1981.[23]

Claims that Eskimo cultural identity relied on bowhead harvest had a basis in fact. The upsurge of whaling activity in the 1970s coincided with a national revival of Native culture, and drew strength from the Native claims settlement process in Alaska. Although cash from the oil boom apparently lessened the need for subsistence living, three villages (Barrow, Kaktovik, and Point Hope) relied on the bowhead for more than 20 percent of their food supply. Whaling success still earned social status and bolstered communal ties. The chase itself followed a pattern quite similar to that of a century earlier, except for such technological additions as radios, outboard motors, aluminum boats, and plastic floats.[24] In the future, should the oil money disappear, whale hunting might be elevated as an economic and cultural necessity.

Confrontation over whale quotas turned toward accommodation. An Alaska Eskimo Whaling Commission, created by the Inupiat in 1977 in response to the IWC restrictions, pled the Native cause and undertook research and cooperation for more efficient hunting methods. It worked out a formal cooperative agreement with the National Marine Fisheries Service in 1981. Given responsibility for management within the quotas, the commission worked effectively. Compared to an estimated recovery rate of one-fourth of the whales struck in 1977, hunters recovered two-thirds in 1978.[25] Despite threats to ignore the quotas, compliance prevailed. A 1981 count placed the number of bowheads at 3,865,[26] the harvest quotas increased, and the controversy died away.

As a result of improved counting methods and coordination between Eskimos and scientific observers, the bowhead tally continued to rise. Researchers compiled estimates by visual observation and acoustical devices north of Point Barrow, where nearly all the whales passed during spring migration. A 1983 survey estimated 8,200; since 1978 the stock had increased by slightly more than 3 percent per year.[27] During 1990–1999, a reported average of 38 whales were harvested, and 13 struck and lost (Table 2.1). For the years 1996–1998, IWC set kill quotas of 51 for the ten villages, well below the sustainable maximum of 75.[28] Since 1977, harvests had seldom reached the permitted levels. For the time being, circumstances favored both consumers and defenders of the bowhead whales.

Beginning in 1997 the United States and Russia entered into a series of agreements for cooperative management of the western Arctic bowheads. The IWC set a total quota of 280 whales to be harvested between 1998 and 2002. Alaskan Eskimos would be allotted 67 strikes per year and Chukotka Natives, 7. Unused strikes could be carried over to the following year. Alaskans landed 41 whales in 1998 and 42 in 1999. Chukotkans, who had been forbidden to pursue whales since the 1960s, took one in 1998 and another in 1999. The two nations continued to confer on whale management within the quota guidelines set by the IWC.[29]

Hunting by Eskimos accounted for by far the greatest number of known bowhead whale deaths. Between 1981 and 1989, an estimated five escaped each year and died of wounds. Beyond hunting data, biologists knew little of bowhead mortality. A few probably succumbed to disease and being hit by ships. Some got trapped in ice, and some eaten by killer whales. Oil spills or other toxic materials and habitat disturbances could pose hazards if industrial growth proliferated in the Arctic.[30] Calving every three to four years and not reproducing until perhaps 20 years of age, the whales exhibited slow growth rates; the Svalbard, Okhotsk, and Davis Strait herds retained small remnants of their former strength.[31] Yet the Bering Sea population of bowheads continued to prosper and to fulfill an ecological role that sustained Inupiaq ties to ancient traditions.

The bowhead experience furthered changes in the terms of wildlife policy in Alaska. It strengthened Natives as players in the Alaskan environmental drama, particularly in the realm of cooperative wildlife management. It generated a firm commitment to science-based sustainability as the key objective. Protection of marine mammals called for ever more sophisticated coordination among state, national, and foreign governments, user groups, scientists, and concerned citizens. Bowhead management remained in the hands of the federal government and Eskimos, an arrangement that might prove inadequate to reflect future involvement of tourism, industry, or others. Yet the Whaling Commission represented gains in environmentally viable resource use. Old-style top-down management no longer fit the realities of Native empowerment; enforcement would be ineffective in the absence of cooperation. Natives could no longer ignore ecological science in their exploitation of bowhead whales or other threatened species. Evolving environmental values and laws meant lawsuits or other sanctions against those who mistreated natural resources. And all parties interested in preserving wildlife stocks owned a stake in avoiding degradation of ecosystems by ever-encroaching human population and development.

NOTES

1. Hill, DeMaster, and Small, *Alaska Marine Mammal Stock Assessments*, 138.
2. Bockstoce, "Eskimo Whaling," 4; Davidson, *Eskimo Hunting*, 8.
3. Durham, "Historical Perspective," 5.
4. Davidson, *Eskimo Hunting*, 16–17, 24; Liebhardt, "Among the Bowheads," 282–283.
5. Scammon, "Northern Whaling," 550–551, 554.
6. International Whaling Commission, "Report of the Cultural Anthropology Panel," 36–37.
7. Burch, *Traditional Eskimo Hunters of Point Hope, Alaska: 1800–1875*, 16.
8. Chance, *The Eskimo of North Alaska*, 15.
9. Ibid., 13–16; Hinckley, *Americanization of Alaska*, 198.
10. Durham, "Historical Perspective," 6.
11. Davidson, *Eskimo Hunting*, 4–7; U.S. National Marine Fisheries Service, *International Whaling Commission's Deletion*, 1–8; 80 Stat. 926, October 15, 1966; 83 Stat. 275, December 5, 1969; 86 Stat. 1027, October 21, 1972; 87 Stat. 884, December 28, 1973.
12. Stoker and Krupnik, "Subsistence Whaling," 604.
13. McClung, *Hunted Mammals*, 135; Morgan, "Politics of Whaling," 8–9; Bockstoce, "Eskimo Whaling," 5.
14. Boeri, *People of the Ice Whale*, 124–129; Gambell, "Bowhead Whale Problem," 1.

15. McVay, "Another Perspective," 13.
17. Gambell, "Bowhead Whale Problem," 2; Conrad, "Bioeconomics and the Bowhead Whale," 975.
16. U.S. National Marine Fisheries Service, *International Whaling Commission's Deletion*, 38.
18. Weeden, "Bowhead Hunting Stopped," 8; C. Smith, "ACE Objects," 1.
19. McClung, *Hunted Mammals*, 136–137; Morgan, "Politics of Whaling," 8.
20. Liebhardt, "Among the Bowheads," 278–279, 292–296.
21. *Orca*, "Editorial Perspective," March 1979, 18.
22. Boeri, *People of the Ice Whale*, 109.
23. Ibid., 279; Morgan, "Politics of Whaling," 9.
24. Stoker and Krupnik, "Subsistence Whaling," 606–616.
25. Liebhardt, "Among the Bowheads," 292, 295; J. Adams, "The IWC," 11.
26. Boeri, *People of the Ice Whale*, 280.
27. Hill, DeMaster, and Small, *Alaska Marine Mammal Stock Assessments*, 138–140.
28. Shelden and Rugh, "The Bowhead Whale," *16–17*.
29. National Marine Fisheries Service, Marine Mammal Commission, *Annual Report, 1999*, 24–25.
30. Philo, Shotts, and George, "Morbidity and Mortality," 275–306.
31. Shelden and Rugh, "The Bowhead Whale," 16–17.

3

Yukon-Kuskokwim Geese

A decades-old quarrel over one of Alaska's premier wildlife resources—the waterfowl of the Yukon-Kuskokwim Delta—neared resolution in the 1980s. It crafted a model of cooperative wildlife management being applied to several other species and regions in the state. The issue came to public notice in the spring of 1961, shortly after the designation of Clarence Rhode National Wildlife Range on the fringes of the delta. A series of politically loaded incidents transpired, forcing into the open some fundamental questions about the status of wildlife management in Alaska, and contributing materially to a historic shift in power and land use patterns.

On orders from Washington in 1960, U.S. Fish and Wildlife Service agents initiated a stepped-up enforcement of laws prohibiting the hunting of migratory waterfowl during the spring and summer nesting season. They began by employing films, discussions, and posters in targeted Yup'ik Eskimo villages. In April 1961 they commenced to apprehend violators. On May Day, airborne agents Jim Branson and Milstead Zahn spotted hunters in blinds on the Kuskokwim River above Bethel. When they landed, the hunters fired at the agents at least 16 times using shotguns and .22 rifles at a distance of 150 yards. The agents called in teammates Ray Tremblay and Neil Argy, who circled over the suspects, taking fire a minimum of 30 times. In a sequence of exchanges, Branson and Zahn fired warning shots and killed a dog accompanying the suspects, who fled through creeks and snowdrifts. Tremblay and Argy flew the two planes back to Bethel to give the impression that the chase had ended. Branson and Zahn then arrested a young Eskimo who returned. They confiscated the bodies of 50 pintail ducks, 6 white-fronted and 3 Canada geese, a black-bellied plover, a pair of lesser sandhill crane wings, and 11 gyrfalcons. When apprehended, the 23-year-old ringleader pleaded "starvation" but displayed a large roll of cash. The local magistrate, an Eskimo woman, sentenced him to 30 days in jail and forfeiture of his shotgun. Another defendant, a 15-year-old, assaulted three FBI agents with a chair and showered obscenities on the magistrate, who committed him to a reform school. The shooting incident appeared to be more youthful misadventure than test of subsistence hunting laws, but it stimulated racial and political tensions over the utilization of waterfowl.

A few days after the shooting episode, upon attempting to arrest another suspect for duck shooting, Tremblay and Argy found themselves confronted by 15 or 20 angry Eskimos. In a tense altercation, they taxied their plane for takeoff while the villagers attempted to hold it back. In their report the four agents summed up the situation:

There is currently a great deal of resentment against the Fish and Wildlife Service and its waterfowl enforcement program among the native inhabitants of the District. They feel the birds are theirs and their use of them should not be curtailed. For the first time in the history of the Alaska Game Law enforcement, it appears it will be necessary to be armed and take precautions against physical violence when working in the field and communities of this area.[1]

On May 20 the action shifted to the north. Near Barrow, agent Harry Pinkham arrested an Eskimo in possession of three geese. Nine days later, Pinkham and John Klingbiel arrested Barrow residents Tom Pikok and State Representative John Nusunginya walking down a Barrow street carrying an eider duck. Their action ignited a mass protest on the following day, when 138 villagers appeared at the Top of the World Hotel where the agents lodged. Each held a duck and each had signed a statement that he had shot the bird.[2] The Barrow engagements won media attention, centering on questions of Native rights. Who could take waterfowl in Alaska? Was enforcement of the laws proper or feasible? Who owned Alaska and who could make the rules? Natives, wildlife managers, sporting groups, and newspapers jumped into the fray.

Barrow residents claimed scarcity of other wild game that spring, but insisted in any case they had a right to the waterfowl. State Senator Eben Hopson, a Barrow father of seven, explained, "When God . . . placed the white people, the Indians, the colored people or other people in parts of the world where it was warm, he made sure they could survive from the land by growing crops for food. When he placed us in the far north he made sure we could survive from the land by hunting game and birds for food. It's as simple as that."[3] Letters to the editors proliferated, many siding with the Eskimos against the U.S. government or the sport hunters in the Lower 48, who could shoot the migratory birds in the fall after they left Alaska. Senator Ernest Gruening vowed to go to jail with the Eskimos to assert their claims. The Justice Department declined to prosecute the Barrow defendants, and the Fish and Wildlife Service backed off.[4] Meanwhile, the controversy, supplemented by Project Chariot, inadvertently caused the first political unification of the Eskimos.

Under pressure from Gruening, the Fish and Wildlife Service ordered its agents to notify villages before visiting. State Representative Raymond Christensen advised Yukon-Kuskokwim villagers to hunt where planes couldn't land, and to evade arrest. He assured them they had the right to hunt. Reinforcing his message, Gruening issued a statement implying that agents had misinterpreted the law and acted without authority.[5] A lid settled on the long-simmering matter pending future legal or legislative action. Jim King, manager of Clarence Rhode National Wildlife Range, analyzed the problem in a 1963 report:

Modern rifles and shotguns have replaced the old weapons and larger dog teams; motorized sleds and motorboats have enabled the hunters to range more widely and fetch home bigger loads. . . . In order to purchase guns, ammunition, motors, gasoline and other paraphernalia, cash money must be diverted from welfare payments, trapping

3.1. Jim Geertz, Joe Punuyaka, and Jim King banding brant, Clarence Rhode National Wildlife Range, 1964. Courtesy Alaska Resources Library and Information Services, Anchorage. The Yukon-Kuskokwim Delta is one of the nation's top waterfowl breeding areas.

income, etc. Fishing is neglected during the spring bird migration although fish are readily available in many places. Any sign of hunger in the villages is quickly averted by shipments of surplus food. In view of these changes in the economy it can only be assumed that the taking of birds out of season by unlawful methods is rapidly making the transition from a necessity to a sport, even if a useful sport. Damage to the breeding stock of some species may be of significant proportions.[6]

The issue resurfaced in 1978 when refuge manager Don Frickie arrested Eskimos who had chartered a plane and killed a number of geese.[7] Again the question arose whether special "subsistence" hunting rights should be available to those apparently not pursuing a subsistence lifestyle.

ORIGINS OF THE REFUGE

Federal officials had long been interested in the Yukon-Kuskokwim Delta, one of the world's topmost waterfowl nesting sites. Formed by silt carried down the Yukon River and molded by wind and frost action, the delta is a fan-shaped, mostly flat region of some 26,600 square miles. Its vast, nearly treeless plains are dotted by an estimated 86,000 lakes and ponds, and drained by countless sloughs and streams. More than 170 species of birds could be seen on the delta in the 1970s; over 200 million birds might pass through it in a given year. It provided the prime nesting ground for tundra swans, spectacled eiders, black brant, and cackling Canada, white-fronted, and emperor geese. Shorebirds and songbirds wintering on Pacific Islands and the Asian continent mingled with species known only in the Americas. Harsh winters on the outer delta discouraged mammalian predators, creating a safe refuge for ground-nesting colonies of birds. Mammals most commonly found in the region included moose, wolverines, lynx, red and Arctic foxes, beavers, varying and Arctic hares, river otters, muskrats, mink, and weasels. Salmon ascended the delta's rivers and marine life abounded in its shallow offshore waters.

European and Euro-American exploration got underway in 1818 when Russian naval officer P. Korsakovskij led an expedition to the delta coast. Adolph Etolin, a Finn serving in the Russian navy, sailed up the Kuskokwim River in 1821.[8] Russians built the first fur-trading post in the region in 1833 at St. Michael, just north of the delta. A second, at Nulato, twice underwent destruction by Indians. American scientist William H. Dall studied the lower and middle Yukon during the Kennicott expedition of 1865–1866.[9] Biologist Lucien Turner served at St. Michael from 1874 to 1877 in the U.S. Army Signal Corps, succeeded in 1877–1881 by Edward W. Nelson, who carried out an extensive biological and ethnographic survey of the region including the Yukon-Kuskokwim Delta. Through his ornithological and ethnological work, and his tenure as chief of the Bureau of Biological Survey, Nelson exerted a permanent influence on Alaska.

Dall, Turner, Nelson, and Fish and Wildlife Service chief Ira Gabrielson, among others, expressed concern for the great colonies of nesting ducks and geese. Writing in the 1880s, Turner observed, "At St. Michael's the geese and ducks have greatly decreased in number, if we may believe the reports of the hunters of former days who bagged many times the quantity which may be obtained." He pinpointed the cause as "immense quantities of cheap shotguns."[10] Nelson described thousands of emperor geese driven into fishnet traps during molting season: "The slaughter in this way was very great, for the young were killed at the same time and thrown away in order to get them out of the way of the next drive. The Eskimos of this region also gather large numbers of eggs of the breeding water-fowl for food; and this practice, with the demand for eggs at the mining-camps, has constituted a serious menace to the existence of these and other water-fowl."[11]

St. Michael operated as a way station for the Klondike, then for gold seekers descending the Yukon for another gold rush in Nome. Bureau of Biological Survey agent Frank Dufresne noticed that "a herd of domestic reindeer, driven in to feed the miners during the gold rush, had trampled into extinction the colony of rare, black-beaked Aleutian terns discovered by Dr. Nelson on adjacent Stuart Island."[12] Except for the introduction of guns, incursions by Euro-Americans did not materially affect goose and duck populations or the lives of delta Natives. Villagers continued to harvest large quantities of ducks, geese, and eggs, in large measure to change the diet of fish that sustained them over the winters. Nelson and other federal officials hoped to designate the nesting territory a wildlife refuge, but the Yup'ik Eskimos possessed a much longer-standing claim to the waterfowl harvest as a traditional activity and biological necessity.

Events in the Lower 48 moved toward greater protection for birds. Reacting to the widespread slaughter of wild birds for meat and plumes, and the unrestricted gathering of eggs, the American Ornithologists' Union and Audubon chapters lobbied for protective legislation. The Lacey Act of 1900 outlawed interstate transportation of wildlife taken in violation of state game laws, and empowered the secretary of agriculture to adopt measures to restore populations of game birds. Three other statutes forbade the gathering of eggs in Alaska, though the 1902 Alaska game law permitted subsistence hunting by Natives. None of these laws measurably altered Native behavior, especially on the Yukon-Kuskokwim Delta. The American Ornithologists' Union lobbied successfully for the withdrawal by Theodore Roosevelt in 1909 of a large part of the delta as a wildlife preserve. Despite his interest in safeguarding the delta, Bureau of Biological Survey chief Edward W. Nelson later recommended abolition of the reserve. Alaskan politicians interpreted all reserved lands as evidence of federal interference in local affairs, and Nelson needed their support for passage of the 1925 Game Law. He also realized that enforcement of game laws on the delta would be next to impossible. An executive order revoked the reserve's status, offering no explanation, in 1922.[13]

Nelson revisited the delta in the summer of 1920, accompanying Olaus Murie up the Yukon to the young biologist's first Bureau of Biological Survey assignment in Fairbanks.[14] Murie returned to the delta in 1924 on an expedition jointly sponsored by the bureau and ornithologist Herbert W. Brandt. It constituted the first well-equipped ornithological expedition to the region, an event Nelson had long envisioned. Brandt, Murie, and H. Boardman Conover of the Chicago Field Museum traveled by dogsled 850 miles from Nenana to spend the late spring and summer studying and banding birds and collecting specimens. Agent Frank Dufresne, a guide for the party, recorded their visit to a delta Eskimo igloo where they stayed the night:

> I could hear the men of science gasping and gagging as dirt enscaled brown hands dipped into a pot, snicked fish heads off with their teeth, loudly sucked the flesh loose and tossed the bones on the floor, now and then reaching sticky fingers under their goose-skin tunics to scratch flea bites. . . . I heard Brandt turn to his partner H. Boardman Conover and propound the question, "I say, Connie, isn't that chief's shirt made from the skins of *Philacte carnagica* [emperor goose]?"

Nelson had described the Bering seacoast climate as one of the worst to be found anywhere. As the party crossed the snow-covered tundra toward Hooper Bay, they encountered constantly blowing snow. Dufresne and Murie had to be left behind at a trading post to recover from snow blindness. When the snow melted, the tundra exploded in bird life, though the party enjoyed only one sunny day during June.[15] Brandt's ensuing book, *Alaska Bird Trails*, drew stateside attention to the ecological significance of the delta.

Step by step, the delta region regained refuge status. Presidential directives set aside Nunivak Island in 1929 for reindeer breeding, and the 6,800-acre Hazen Bay islands in 1937 for birds. Secretary of the Interior Fred Seaton reserved the Kuskokwim National Wildlife Range in 1960 for nesting waterfowl, and the department renamed it for Fish and Wildlife Service regional director Clarence Rhode in 1961. Through the Alaska National Interest Lands Conservation Act (ANILCA) of 1980, all the selected lands became part of the

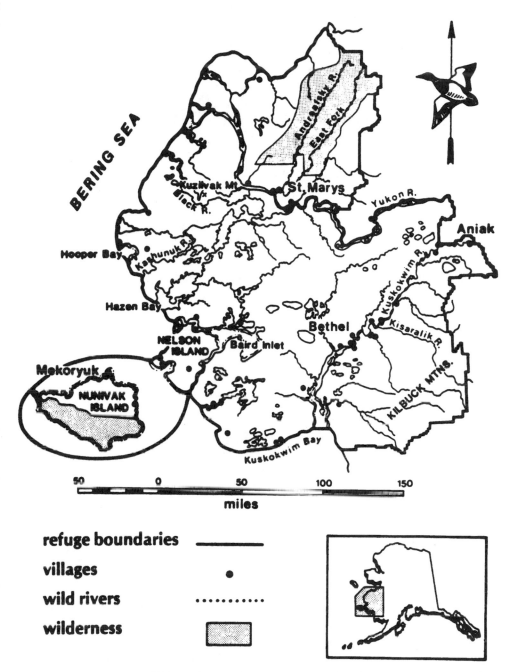

BERING SEA

Kuzilvak Mt
Black R.
St. Marys
Yukon R.
Aniak

Hooper Bay
Kashunuk R.
Kuskokwim R.

Hazen Bay
Kisaralik R.
Bethel

NELSON
ISLAND
Baird Inlet

Mekoryuk
NUNIVAK
ISLAND
KILBUCK MTNS.

Kuskokwim Bay

Andreafsky R.
East Fork

| 50 | 0 | 50 | 100 | 150 |

miles

refuge boundaries ——————
villages •
wild rivers ....
wilderness

3.1. Yukon Delta National Wildlife Refuge, 1992. Courtesy U.S. Fish and Wildlife Service, Division of Realty, Anchorage.

19.6-million-acre Yukon Delta National Wildlife Refuge.[16] Some of the best nesting grounds, however, remained in Native ownership, scattered among refuge lands.

TOWARD RESOLUTION OF THE CONFLICT

Bird protection laws and treaties, more than land designations, expressed the differences over waterfowl management. As newly appointed director of the Bureau of Biological Survey, Nelson facilitated the passage of the Migratory Bird Treaty of 1916 and the Migratory Bird Treaty Act of 1918, building upon the 1913 Federal Migratory Bird Act to fashion a U.S.-Canada agreement protecting North American birds. To shield nesting populations, the laws prohibited spring and summer hunting. The United States concluded similar treaties with Mexico in 1936, Japan in 1972, and the USSR in 1976. The 1925 Alaska Game Law, in large part the work of Nelson, allowed for subsistence hunting and specifically reaffirmed the provisions of the Migratory Bird Treaty Act.[18] Collectively, the treaties contained mandates to protect and restore ecosystems and nesting colonies, and to permit some regulated subsistence harvest of birds and eggs by Native residents. ANILCA in 1980 provided for "continued subsistence uses by local residents" of the delta, subject to wildlife conservation and treaty obligations. It stipulated that none of its subsistence provisions could modify or supersede the Migratory Bird Treaty Act. For all federal lands, ANILCA required that subsistence use be "nonwasteful" and "consistent with management of fish and wildlife in accordance with recognized scientific principles and the purposes of each unit." Rural residents would be given a "meaningful role" in management of local fish and wildlife and their subsistence uses.[18]

Migratory bird legislation and management left room for disagreement. The 1925 Game Law guaranteed Indians and Eskimos access to game birds when "in absolute need of food and other food is not available...nor shall any such measure contravene any of the provisions of the Migratory Act and regulations." In 1940 Congress softened the law to allow harvest by Natives when "other sufficient food is not available." The Fish and Wildlife Service adopted a regulation in 1944 that excluded migratory birds from harvest, but did not systematically enforce it against Alaska Natives until 1960. The 1979 U.S.-USSR treaty permitted spring and summer subsistence hunting of migratory birds pending corresponding modification of the U.S.-Canada treaty. Pressure from sport hunting interests held up the change through the 1980s. Critics argued that state and federal wildlife management agencies had failed to recognize the legitimate interests of Natives and non-hunters, and by denying the legality of spring and summer subsistence hunting, had neglected effective regulation and thereby endangered goose populations.[19]

University of California Davis biologist Dennis Raveling, who had conducted goose research on the delta, noted that agents had voiced concern about goose declines since the early 1970s, and that harvests on the delta appeared to be a prime cause. He described "large-scale shooting when geese arrive in spring, flushing geese on nests with snowmachines in order to drive them to hunters, shooting geese on nests, taking of eggs, and shooting or capture of geese with broods." He noted that "a decrease of knowledge of wildlife and skills in hunting and survival skills by young natives has long been obvious. Many hunts have taken on a sport character when one considers the costs of machines and fuel and amazing waste of costly ammunition in relation to some harvests. Failure to deal with these issues will result in collapse of the resource bases which form the goal of subsistence policy to maintain productivity for humans." Raveling characterized Fish and wildlife Service and Alaska Department of Fish and Game management efforts as weak and inconsistent. He recommended improved understanding between sport hunters and Natives, and effective data gathering on harvests to support legalized but regulated subsistence hunting.[20]

Waterfowl on the Yukon-Kuskokwim Delta took off on their southward migration at the end of the summer and none stayed beyond freeze-up about the second week in October; hence by the terms of the 1916 treaty, relatively few fowl could be gotten by the Eskimos after the opening of sport hunting on September 1. In practice, spring and summer hunts persisted, wildlife officials tolerating them as traditional practice and/or conforming to an interpretation of the 1925 Game Law. Some enforcement of the law had occurred in the 1940s and 1950s, but Clarence Rhode directed his energy toward the more pressing issues of hunting by military construction personnel and by others arriving on the Alcan Highway and by airlines, invading the wilds in an array of modern machines. Rhode also sensed that vigorous enforcement might touch off a storm of controversy, as it did in 1961.[21]

The issue went unresolved partly because no waterfowl species neared extinction, but conditions changed. Egg-taking and harvest of molting birds lost their urgency as living standards rose, yet hunting persevered, and a fast-growing Native population called for more food. The delta, rated as one of the most economically depressed regions of Alaska, featured high reliance on hunting, fishing, and gathering. Hunters aggressively pursued waterfowl using boats, snowmobiles, off-road vehicles, and aircraft. By the early 1980s, three of four species of geese nesting predominantly on the delta had lost half or more of their Pacific flyway strength. Comparable total population estimates for 1965 and 1985 stood at: cackling Canada goose 384,000 and 32,000; Pacific white-fronted 303,000 and 94,000; Pacific black brant 167,000 and 144,000; and emperor goose 139,000 (1964) and 59,000. Wildlife officials reacted in consternation over the figures. Surveys in 1980 had indicated a disproportionately high kill on the delta. Scientists believed hunting to be the major cause of the downward trend.[22]

A running argument ensued over responsibility for the declines, and about what should be done. Some Eskimos blamed sport hunters in California, where most cackling Canada geese and some brant wintered. California hunters shot large numbers of geese in the 1960s and 1970s, likely including many from the Yukon-Kuskokwim Delta. Liberal bag limits existed until 1979, and gunners could bag cacklers until 1984. Loss of habitat to agriculture, and chemical pollution and lead shot, probably added to waterfowl losses. For their part, sport hunters placed most blame on the 15,000 Eskimos of 50 or so delta villages. They cited the fact that emperor geese wintered in the unpopulated Aleutians as evidence that the main hunting pressure took place on the delta.

Cultural differences also lay behind the dispute. Anthropologist Ann Fienup-Riordan found that Yup'ik people believed wild creatures would continue to present themselves for the sustenance of hunters who behaved in a proper, respectful manner. Thus hunters and other community members thought they bore the responsibility for the abundance of wild food in any given season. Extinction of species could not occur in this perspective, though

3.2. Panel from Yukon-Kuskokwim goose educational pamphlet, late 1980s. Courtesy U.S. Fish and Wildlife Service. Use of delta waterfowl reflected a gap between Native and Euro-American concepts of game harvest.

animals might remain hidden. The harvesting, sharing, and consumption of local foods comprised an integral part of Yup'ik identity.[23] The Yup'ik regarded sport hunting as illegitimate, and found it difficult to understand the scientific view of wildlife biologists that emphasized human causes of extinction, and controls through hunting seasons and bag limits.[24]

Attempting to bridge the cultural and political gaps, Alaska Department of Fish and Game (ADF&G) and the Fish and Wildlife Service organized 1983 meetings of several interested parties: Alaska and California hunters, landowners, wildlife management groups, and Native organizations and conservation groups including Nunam Kitlutsisti and Audubon/Alaska. A resulting 1984 Hooper Bay Agreement promised better protection for geese, and extensive cooperation and research. Audubon/Alaska initiated a congressional lobbying effort yielding an additional $750,000 for scientific investigations, and participated in the interagency educational task force working with the villagers.[25] Stringent hunting regulations went into effect south of the delta and down the Pacific flyway through California. Delta Natives agreed to reduce their spring goose harvest on the condition that they be allowed to shoot other waterfowl.

Following the January 1984 agreement, two sporting groups, the Alaska Fish and Wildlife Federation and Outdoor Council Inc. and Alaska Wildlife Conservation Fund, sued in

3.3. Entry by Don Sagmoen, Yukon-Kuskokwim goose poster contest, 1988. Courtesy U.S. Fish and Wildlife Service. Federal officials and delta Eskimos cooperatively devised educational programs in waterfowl ecology.

federal court on grounds that any spring or summer hunting violated the Migratory Bird Treaty. They contended that killing waterfowl preoccupied with nesting is far more destructive than shooting into a bumper crop of young in the fall and winter. Their suit called for a ban on the use of aircraft in hunting, for accessible public hearings, and for an environmental impact statement to clarify the costs and benefits of alternative courses of action.[26] A January 1986 ruling dismissed their argument, and upheld subsistence use as authorized by the 1925 Alaska Game Law.[27]

In 1985 the Fish and Wildlife Service and ADF&G had drafted a Yukon-Kuskokwim Delta Goose Management Plan involving coordination, research, and educational efforts among the interested parties. A Waterfowl Conservation Committee of Yup'ik elders would negotiate ongoing management provisions with the Fish and Wildlife Service and the Alaska and California Departments of Fish and Game. A new approach, it won appreciation and cooperation from the Eskimos. "They couldn't believe what the interpreters were telling them," recalled ADF&G director Lew Pamplin of the first meeting. "I saw eighty-year-old men crying. We had come to them open and non-accusatory."[28] The plan spelled out protective measures for the four goose species: no gathering of eggs; a ban on hunting cackling Canada or emperor geese anywhere in the flyway; no killing of brant or white-fronted geese

Table 3.1—Estimated Management Plan Goose Harvests, Yukon-Kuskokwim Delta, 1985–1999

	Pacific White-Fronted	Cackling Canada	Emperor	Pacific Black Brant	Total
1985	3,803	1,485	4,031	2,168	11,487
1986	2,806	2,067	3,091	1,483	9,447
1987	3,722	3,218	1,352	1,030	9,322
1989	5,324	3,584	1,616	2,372	12,896
1990	8,287	5,903	3,440	3,133	20,763
1991	5,709	4,926	2,394	2,258	15,287
1992	9,237	4,490	2,669	2,798	19,194
1993	8,207	7,087	2,602	2,502	20,398
1994	9,570	9,780	1,493	2,326	23,169
1995	11,388	13,799	2,041	4,995	32,223
1996	14,582	14,983	2,374	3,302	35,241
1997	8,528	9,921	1,469	3,572	23,490
1998	12,359	15,173	1,899	4,100	33,531
1999	13,320	11,145	818	2,721	28,004

Source: Cynthia Wentworth, "Subsistence Waterfowl Harvest Survey, Yukon-Kuskokwim Delta: 1994 Results and Comparative Data, 1985–1994," U.S. Fish and Wildlife Service, Division of Migratory Bird Management (Anchorage, June 1995), Table 1; Wentworth, *1987–1997* (December 1998), Table 4; *1990–1999* (May 2000), Table 1.

Note: No available 1988 figures. Estimates based on household surveys in 38 villages. Emperor and brant figures least reliable because of disproportionate harvest in villages refusing to report.

during nesting, rearing, or molting; and no use of aircraft in pursuing the four species. These restrictions applied outside Alaska also, though only white-fronts and cacklers wintered in the Lower 48. Most brant wintered in Mexico, and emperors in the Aleutians and Asia.[29]

An October 1987 circuit court ruling jeopardized the management plan by reversing the district court and affirming precedence of the Migratory Bird Treaty. But the court left wildlife managers a way out: it ruled enforcement of the treaty discretionary and not subject to judicial review. It remanded the case to the district court, which approved a slightly revised plan in June 1988. In a Solomonic decision, the district court ruled that the 1984 and 1985 agreements violated the Migratory Bird Treaty Act by explicitly legalizing hunting during the March 10 to September 1 closed season, but judged the revised 1988 plan legal in that it acknowledged the closed season. In effect, the approved plan permitted spring and summer hunting by the Eskimos, accompanied by measures for protection of the four threatened species of geese.[30]

The Yukon-Kuskokwim goose plan progressed in a revised form in 1989. It met indications of cooperation by the Yup'ik Eskimos, some of whom accepted the need for conservation in Euro-American terms. Many others, especially elders, disagreed with biologists. Some blamed goose declines on lack of appropriate behavior toward the animals: loose social behavior of young people, prohibition of egg-taking and its attendant ceremonies, and the activities of researchers studying the geese. Beyond traditional cultural perspectives, anthropologist Fienup-Riordan identified other barriers to Yup'ik acceptance of game regulations:

Table 3.2—Pacific Flyway Goose Population Counts, 1965–2000

	Pacific White-Fronted	Emperor	Cackling Canada	Pacific Black Brant
Y-K Plan Goal:	300,000	150,000	250,000	185,000
1965	303,000	139,000 (1964)	384,000	167,000
1985	93,800	58,833	32,100	144,803
1986	107,100	42,231	51,400	128,570
1987	130,600	51,655	54,800	—
1988	161,500	53,784	69,900	138,578
1989	218,800	45,800	76,800	128,163
1990	240,800	67,581	110,200	146,012
1991	236,500	70,972	104,500	128,378
1992	230,900	71,319	149,300	116,500
1993	295,100	52,478	164,300	124,105
1994	325,000	57,267	152,500	130,046
1995	277,500	51,200	161,400	133,700
1996	344,075	80,300	—	126,900
1997	319,000	57,060	205,100	158,000
1998	413,050	39,700	191,120	138,500
1999	—	54,600	214,659	129,300
2000	—	62,565	210,441	135,044

Source: U.S. Fish and Wildlife Service, Division of Migratory Bird Management, Anchorage.

Note: Estimates of total populations, some not nesting on the delta. Counts are done by aerial surveys in spring (emperor, and cackling Canada after 1998), fall (cackling Canada to 1998), and midwinter (white-fronted and brant).

resistance to change, lack of prior law enforcement, the perceived unfairness of the fall hunting rule, self-interest, and the high recreational value of waterfowl hunting.[31]

To further the conservation effort, hundreds of delta children took part in poster contests featuring the endangered geese. Nevertheless, surveys estimated an annual average harvest of 6,296 white-fronted, 4,811 cackling Canada, 2,521 emperor geese, and 2,230 brant between 1985 and 1994.[32] A 1994 addendum to the management plan permitted limited hunting of cackling Canada geese, at a level designed to maintain a population increase.[33] Between 1994 and 1999, average harvests stood at: white-fronted, 12,035; cackling Canada, 13,035; emperor, 1,720; and brant, 3,738 (Table 3.1). By 2000, judging by total numbers and nesting success rates, the Pacific white-fronted and cackling Canada geese appeared to be recovering. Emperor geese and Pacific black brant showed no significant change (Table 3.2).[34]

A mid-1990s study of the delta village of Scammon Bay by anthropologist Erika Zavaleta found evidence of adherence to conservation practices by a substantial number of hunters. Elders tended to limit their take of waterfowl in deference to the law, though they held to the traditional and majority belief that humans could not limit wildlife populations. Those aged 18 to 49 generally accepted harvest limits as necessary for maintenance of wildlife stocks. Teenagers exhibited little or no regard for conservation, apparently because they did not envision subsistence living as part of their future. Zavaleta found scant evidence of Yup'ik

conservation patterns prior to European contact, and attributed much of the recent conservation behavior to the collaborative and educational efforts of the goose management plan.
She concluded that in contrast to the costly and unworkable enforcement approach, the
voluntary, educational method could be "creating over time a partially self-perpetuating
system of attitudes and practices that promote sustainable resource use."[35] Credit for success belonged in part to Ray Christensen, formerly an adversary of federal enforcement
efforts, who spent years on the Waterfowl Conservation Committee urging support for the
goose management plan.

By use of a flexible interpretation of the law and by giving local residents and other
interested parties a role in the formation and enforcement of the plan, wildlife officials found
a partial solution to a 70-year-old problem of law enforcement and wildlife conservation. In
doing so, they created a model of cooperative wildlife management. Such a model could be
particularly useful in Canada or in Alaska, whose 10,000 to 13,000 subsistence waterfowl
hunters harvested an estimated 307,000 waterbirds annually in the mid-1980s. More than half
this total involved spring and summer hunting, still a debated practice despite its incorporation into the goose management plan. In April 1995, Canadian and U.S. wildlife officials
signed a protocol, subject to legislative ratification, to amend the 1916 Migratory Bird Treaty.
The agreement, approved by the U.S. Senate in 1997, legalized subsistence use through
regulated spring and summer hunts by permanent indigenous residents of designated villages, and sought improved cooperative management of migratory birds.[36]

Several questions lingered, however. Management plans called for total populations
varying from 150,000 (emperors) to 300,000 (white-fronts), and for resumption of hunting
upon attainment of about half the maximum historical levels.[37] Would there be no attempt to
regain the original populations? Based on observations for more than a century, far greater
numbers of geese once existed, and colony nesting extended as far north as Kotzebue
Sound. Fish and Wildlife Service officer David Spencer, who initiated aerial surveys of
nesting geese on the Yukon-Kuskokwim Delta in 1949, reported seeing a colony of brant
stretching over 100 miles; by the 1980s he found the area largely unoccupied.[38] Few geese
frequented the Yukon River islands, once prime nesting territory and favorite foraging sites
for early travelers seeking eggs or geese.

Other questions related to the long-term sustainability of goose and duck populations.
Colony nesting functioned as a survival strategy for birds against natural predators, especially the Arctic fox. Given a rapidly increasing and mobile Native population, would it be
possible for colony nesting to continue in the twenty-first century? On the other hand, might
some delta villages, not economically viable in modern times, be abandoned? Should nesting
sanctuaries be set aside and protected from predation and human disturbance, to determine
whether high-density nesting can be restored? What caused the disappearance of the once-
common Steller's eider and catastrophic decline of the spectacled eider as delta nesting
species? What should be done to ensure the survival of the spectacled eider, now listed as
threatened?[39]

Attempts to rescue the spectacled eider, a large duck, in some ways paralleled those for
the delta geese. An estimated 100,000 of this species nested on the delta in the 1970s; the
count plummeted to about 5,000 in the late 1990s. A similar-sized concentration nested on

the North Slope, and a far larger number in eastern Siberia. Very little information existed on the causes of decline of the delta flocks. Radio-tagging led to the 1995 discovery of their wintering-grounds on the Bering Sea ice; no hunters molested them there. In addition to delta hunting and possible egg-taking by Eskimos, evidence suggested lead poisoning as a factor in the losses. Predation by foxes and gulls, or pollution in the Bering Sea, might add to mortality. The Fish and Wildlife Service liaison team persuaded most of the delta village councils to pass resolutions recommending the use of steel shot in place of lead pellets.[40]

In 1997 the Fish and Wildlife Service, Association of Village Council Presidents, U.S. Geological Survey, and Alaska Department of Fish and Game signed an amendment to the goose management plan, to protect the Steller's and spectacled eiders, both listed as threatened species. As of spring 1998, killing of the eiders or taking their eggs became illegal, as did the use of lead shot on the delta. Parties would cooperate on enforcement, monitoring, and research. At the millenium, susistence use contributed to the decline in an unknown but worrisome degree. During the combined 1998–1999 seasons, hunters reported killing 186 Steller's and 180 spectacled eiders. Few still nested on the delta.[41]

Management of Yukon-Kuskokwim Delta waterfowl illustrated and molded advancing environmental values through its openly participatory approach. Participants reached a compromise that retained some traditional Yup'ik practices while incorporating science-based measures to ensure sustainability of waterfowl populations. Environmentalists represented by Audubon/Alaska and Nunam Kitlutsisti played useful roles in shaping the delta plan, a pattern of natural-resource management applicable to other species (walrus, polar bear, sea otter, caribou) and locales of Alaska. Audubon Society involvement incorporated interests of nonconsumptive users, and sport hunters tested their position by a lawsuit. Research on subsistence use as well as goose numbers helped build the trust necessary for intercultural cooperation. Beyond its potential for maintenance of biological diversity and resource sustainability, cooperative management served to strengthen the integrity of Yup'ik culture. Yet the near-disappearance of the spectacled and Steller's eiders on the delta suggested limits to the effectiveness of cooperative management. The difficulty of any kind of enforcement in a vast and remote region, and the rapid growth of the human population, left open the question of whether subsistence use of wildlife on the delta could be ecologically sustainable.

NOTES

1. Tremblay et al., "Memo to Regional Director"; James G. King, interview by author, June 30, 1989; letter to author, September 7, 1993.

2. *Fairbanks Daily News-Miner*, June 7, 1961; Daley and James, "An Authentic Voice," 22.

3. *Fairbanks Daily News-Miner*, June 17, 1961.

4. Laycock, "Doing What's Right," 126–128.

5. King, "Refuge Narrative Report," 20–21.

6. Ibid., 21.

7. *Alaska*, "Alaska Sportsman," August 1978, 34; James G. King, interview by author, June 30, 1989.

8. Simmerman, *Alaska's Parklands*, 285–286; *Alaska Geographic*, "The Yukon-Kuskokwim Delta," 9, 12, 36; James G. King, letter to author, September 7, 1993.

9. USDOI, *Final Environmental Impact Statement, Proposed Yukon Delta*, 24.

10. Gabrielson and Lincoln, *Birds of Alaska*, 9, 22.

11. E. Nelson, "The Emperor Goose," 61.

12. Dufresne, *My Way Was North*, 96–98.

13. J. Cameron, *Bureau of Biological Survey*, 92, 110; Sherwood, *Big Game in Alaska*, 22–24, 43; Theodore Roosevelt, *Executive Order No. 1041*, February 27, 1909; Warren Harding, *Executive Order No. 3642*, February 27, 1922, both in *CIS Presidential Executive Orders*, Microfiche (Washington, DC: GPO).

14. Gabrielson and Lincoln, *Birds of Alaska*, 22.

15. Dufresne, *My Way Was North*, 113; Brandt, *Alaska Bird Trails*, 71–75, 81.

16. U.S. Fish and Wildlife Service (USFWS), *Yukon Delta Comprehensive Plan*, 1988, 1–4. By the mid-1990s, refuge acreage stood at 21.9 million acres.

17. C. Hunter, "This Our Land," September 1985, 28; 40 Stat. 755, July 3, 1918; 43 Stat. 749, January 13, 1925; James G. King, interview by author, July 13, 1989.

18. USFWS, *Yukon Delta Comprehensive Plan*, 1988, 4–6; 94 Stat. 2371, December 2, 1980, Sections 801(5), 802(1,2), 815(4).

19. 43 Stat. 744, Sec. 10; 29 UST 4647, Nov. 19, 1976; D. Mitchell, "Native Subsistence Hunting," 527-532.

20. Raveling, "Geese and Hunters," 555, 564-569.

21. James G. King, interview by author, July 13, 1989; letter to author, September 7, 1993.

22. Pamplin, *Cooperative Efforts*, 7, 39–41; Laycock, "Doing What's Right," 125, 128.

23. Fienup-Riordan, *When Our Bad Season Comes*, 28–29, 321–324.

24. Steinhart, "Can We Solve the Great Goose Mystery?" 4–8.

25. Pamplin, *Cooperative Efforts*, 2; Laycock, "Doing What's Right," 129–130.

26. James G. King, interview by author, June 30, 1989; letter to author, September 7, 1993.

27. Pamplin, *Cooperative Efforts*, 13–15, 29–30; *Alaska Fish and Wildlife Federation v. Dunkle* 829 F. 2d, 933 (9th Cir. 1987).

28. Laycock, "Doing What's Right," 129; Association of Village Council Presidents, "Goose Conservation," 6–7.

29. USFWS, *Guide to Yukon-Kuskokwim Delta Goose Management Plan*.

30. USFWS, *Environmental Assessment: Yukon-Kuskokwim Delta, 1989*, 1–3; *Alaska Fish and Wildlife Federation v. Dunkle* 829 F. 2d 933 (9th Cir. 1987).

31. Fienup-Riordan, *Eskimo Essays*, 177–178, 189–190.

32. Laycock, "Doing What's Right," 130–133; Wentworth, "Subsistence Waterfowl Harvest Survey," Table 1.

33. USFWS, *Yukon-Kuskokwim Delta Goose Management Plan, 1994 Addendum*.

34. Stehn, et al., *Population Size and Production of Geese*; Bartonek, *1992 Pacific Flyway Briefing Material*, 82. Emperor numbers are based on spring counts in Alaska Peninsula and Bristol Bay; others on fall and winter counts in Washington, Oregon, California, and Mexico. Brant counts include a few thousand wintering in Alaska.

35. Zavaleta, "Emergence of Waterfowl Conservation," 233, 253, 256–257, 262–264.

36. Wentworth, *Subsistence Waterfowl Harvest, 1987–1997*, "Dedication," 8, 10, 14.

37. Ibid., 5–6, 31–34.

38. USFWS, *Amending the Migratory Bird Treaty*, 3–5; News release, USFWS, May 8, 1995; *Alaska Report*, "Migratory Bird Treaty," 7.

39. USFWS, *Yukon-Kuskokwim Delta Goose Management Plan*, 1989, 3–4.

40. King and Derksen, "Alaska Goose Populations," 465–473.

41. Ibid., 473–476; James G. King, Calvin R. Lensink, and David L. Spencer, interviews by author, June 30, July 28, and July 30, 1989; James G. King, letter to author, September 7, 1993.

42. Dunkel, "Eyeballing Eiders," 49–54.

43. Wentworth, *Subsistence Waterfowl Harvest Survey: Yukon-Kuskokwim Delta, 1987–1997*, 32, 88–96; *Subsistence Waterfowl Harvest Survey: Yukon-Kuskokwim Delta, 1990–1999*, Table 1. Russ Oates, personal communication, May 17, 2000.

4

Chilkat Eagles

A confrontation between environmentalists and economic interests erupted in the Alaskan Southeast during the late 1970s, inspiring an exercise in civil-conflict resolution. A unique feature—the national bird—lent intensity to the dispute and urgency to efforts at settlement. Private and government participants demonstrated that in at least some cases, the wide gap between preservationists and exploitation-oriented Alaskans could be spanned.

Bald eagles in Alaska recovered from the predator-control efforts of the territorial years to approximately 30,000 in the 1970s. No longer perceived as threats to the salmon supply, they nevertheless encountered indirect hazards. Concentrated in the Southeast, they subsist primarily on fish. Their best-known feeding spot is the scenic Chilkat River Valley north of Haines, bordered by 7,000-foot peaks and hanging glaciers. The 52-mile-long Chilkat is one of the most productive salmon rivers in Southeast Alaska; over 3,000 eagles gather there in the fall and early winter months for the salmon runs. Upwellings keep the water unfrozen longer than in most rivers in the region. The eagles perch in large cottonwood trees lining the riverbanks, and also use them as nesting trees; 90 nests existed in 1980.[1]

More than 280 other species of birds visited the Chilkat Valley in the 1970s, including nesting trumpeter swans. Moose, mountain goats, brown bears, black (and glacier variety) bears, wolves, coyotes, wolverines, lynx, river otters, mink, muskrats, and snowshoe hares could be found there. Dolly Varden char, steelhead, grayling, cutthroat and brook trout, and all five species of Alaskan salmon inhabited its waters.

"Chilkat" in Tlingit means "salmon storehouse," referring to a local tribe. Indians traveled the valley for centuries as a trade route to the interior. Yukon Indians offered moose and caribou hides, furs, moccasins, jade tools, and copper in exchange for fish oil, and later for blankets, gunpowder and shot, flour, and tobacco. Two salmon canneries opened in 1882 and 1883. Gold seekers ascended the Chilkat Valley enroute to the Klondike. The notorious Oklahoman Jack Dalton set up a travel route in the 1890s, built bridges and way stations, and charged toll as the Indians had traditionally done. Prospectors found gold in 1898 at Porcupine Creek and extracted 60,000 ounces from the vicinity before mining receded in the mid-1950s.[2]

4.1. Mature bald eagle at 22°, Chilkat River, December 1977. By Steve McCutcheon. Courtesy Anchorage Museum of History and Art. The Chilkat River is the world's foremost gathering place for bald eagles.

EAGLES AND INDUSTRY

Human activities spelled danger for the Chilkat eagles. Adjacent to the feeding area lay a low-grade iron deposit the Columbia Mining Company considered stripping in the late 1950s. Columbia proposed to reroute the Chilkat River and spread mine tailings over six square miles of the valley. This prospect moved the U.S. Fish and Wildlife Service to undertake studies aimed at protection for the eagles. Agent Fred C. Robards, long interested in the birds, initiated a banding effort on the Chilkat in the early 1960s. He spent years trying to generate local support for the eagles.[3]

Shortly after statehood, Alaska selected as state land the Chilkat River Valley, ignoring conflicting claims by the Tlingit Indians in the nearby village of Klukwan. In 1972 the legislature marked out a segment of the riverside as the Chilkat River Critical Habitat Area. The Fish and Wildlife Service had recommended that 128,000 acres be reserved, but Haines and Klukwan residents succeeded in scaling down the figure to 4,800 acres. A petition to the governor bore signatures of 211 people, nearly half the adult population of 1,500-resident Haines. Opposing the sanctuary bill, it exhorted: "Let's create a refuge for the people in this area, as the people represent the minority group and not the eagles! Let's get back to the people, the economy and proper development of the great State of Alaska."[4] A 4,800-acre tract afforded minimal protection for wildlife, and eagle defenders grew increasingly anxious about the effects of mining and logging in the area. Working through a local group named Lynn Canal Conservation, Steve Waste and two other graduate students in biology conducted largely voluntary research during 1976–1978, receiving support from the Wildlife Research Institute.[5]

By the mid-1970s, lumber companies in the Haines vicinity had exhausted the timber under contracts let by the state in 1969. Uncertainty of access to their main supply source in the Tongass National Forest far to the south, and fluctuating world markets, forced one sawmill to close and set off a local recession. John Schnabel, a sawmill owner in Haines since 1939, organized a movement to gain rights to state timber in the Chilkat Valley through long-term contracts such as the Forest Service had given to Alaska Pulp Corporation and Ketchikan Pulp Company. In 1976 the state suggested a land use plan; Haines area groups rejected it and formed a coalition to draw up one of their own. Businesses, sporting groups, miners, commercial fishers, Natives, the City of Haines, and the borough joined the coalition.[6]

When Governor Jay Hammond's administration proposed a state park along the river in 1977, it encountered vigorous resistance in Haines; people worried that it would limit mining, logging, or personal entry. Environmentalists tried to insert protective language in "d-2" (Alaska lands) bills; Haines residents managed to have it removed. Klukwan Tlingits rejected the park as further encroachment on their land claims. A struggle took shape, bald eagles the symbol and center of it. In December 1978 a spokesperson for the Haines Independent Business Association warned: "Preservationists could use manipulation to tie up a vast area. . . . People in Haines might be so frustrated they would vent their anger in a wholesale slaughter of the Haines eagles. There's no question but what these eagles could be destroyed in a very short period. It would take a platoon of Army to protect those eagles."[7] Steve Waste discovered 20 dead eagles during 1977–1978, most of them shot.[8]

In June 1978, state officials had visited Haines to propose a revised land use plan for the area. The Haines Coalition drafted a more growth-oriented alternative. They persuaded the legislature to pass a bill in 1979 facilitating long-term timber sales in areas experiencing high unemployment. The state's June 1979 Haines-Skagway Area Land Use Plan incorporated most provisions desired by the Haines Coalition. In August the state and Schnabel Lumber Company signed a 15-year timber contract, extendable to 25 years. It committed 83 percent of the valley's old-growth forest to clear-cutting.[9]

A month later Southeast Alaska Conservation Council (SEACC), assisted by the newly-established regional office of the Sierra Club Legal Defense Fund, filed suit against the state, claiming the sale violated resource management provisions of the state constitution and laws. SEACC contended that contrary to the state's claims of environmental responsibility during the d-2 deliberations, "this contract instead demonstrates the extent to which the State is willing to sacrifice environmental protection for the sake of local and immediate economic exploitation of State-owned resources." SEACC noted the contract even encouraged Schnabel to find a market for the cottonwoods used for eagle perching and nesting. Environmentalists argued that post-oil construction recessions happened all over Alaska, that Schnabel had overbuilt his sawmill capacity and wanted to be bailed out by the taxpayers, that the cutting rate of the contract would take a nonsustaining 90 percent of the commercial timber in 100 years, and that the contract put salmon and eagles in jeopardy.[10]

The logging arrangement appeared to be economically marginal at best, and likely a loss for the state. It effectively guaranteed Schnabel a profit, even if the costs of roads exceeded the receipts from timber. Schnabel had designed his mill in the mid-1960s so that it needed 30 million board feet annually to make a profit; the contract promised only 10.2 million. Schnabel hoped to get the remaining timber from elsewhere in the Southeast. He did not want the cottonwoods, he said, but the state required that some be cut to facilitate replanting, as it had in an earlier contract.

More than 600 citizens signed a petition asking the City of Haines to join the state as a defendant in the lawsuit. Klukwan residents endorsed the contract, as did local commercial fishers, but United Southeast Gillnetters Association did not. A rare neutral Haines resident observed, "I don't see what all the fuss is about. This always happens in Haines. The mill closes and the workers go back to Oregon. It opens and they come back. What is so different this time?"[11]

The lawsuit revived the bumper-sticker industry: "Sierra Club: Kiss My Axe" and "Improve the Forest—Plant a Sierra Clubber" sprouted. Merrill Palmer, member of Alaska Miners Association and leader of the Haines Coalition explained, "Right here is what's at stake. This country is being denied the right to develop its natural resources. We're just one little redneck community but this thing is going on all over the country. These environmentalists, this minority, either through design or ignorance, is going to bring this country to its knees. SEACC is using the environmental symbol against the very thing for which it stands." Opponents labeled environmentalists "enemies of liberty and justice." Richard Folta, a leader of Lynn Canal Conservation, watched his law business wither away and his children being harassed in school. Others lost jobs or received warnings to quit conservation work.[12] Superior court ruled against SEACC in June 1980 and ordered it to pay $25,000 in costs. The state supreme court later concurred but struck down the payment.[13]

SEARCH FOR A SOLUTION

The conflict had reached a serious point, and efforts to defuse the situation proceeded. The National Audubon Society, first alerted in 1970 by Haines resident Vivian Menaker, took up the issue. Audubon and the Fish and Wildlife Service launched a 1979–1982 cooperative study of the eagles and effort to find a political consensus. Retired Fish and Wildlife Service biologist Erwin Boeker, a friendly man who had extensive eagle experience, and Andrew J. Hansen, an ecologist at Oak Ridge National Laboratory, represented Audubon. Joel Bennett's film *Last Stronghold of the Eagles* played nationwide through its Audubon sponsors. Alaskan officials received a record-breaking flood of letters demanding protection for eagles. The

4.2. National Audubon Society consultant Andy Hansen (left) and assistant conducting bald eagle research, Chilkat River Valley, November 1979. By Steve McCutcheon. Courtesy Anchorage Museum of History and Art. Cooperation among many groups wrote a successful chapter in wildlife protection.

letters reminded them of the depth of public support for wildlife conservation, the more so for the national bird, an endangered species in the Lower 48.

Effective July 1980, Governor Hammond declared a moratorium on the logging and appointed a problem-solving committee representing Haines, Klukwan, the commercial fishers, the miners, Schnabel, the Fish and Wildlife Service, Alaska Department of Fish and Game, the Department of Natural Resources, the legislature, and the environmental community represented by David Cline of Audubon's Alaska office. Assisted by information from federal, state, and Audubon studies, the parties (except Klukwan who refused to sign) reached agreement in February 1982. A 49,000-acre Alaska Chilkat Bald Eagle Preserve surrounded by a Haines State Forest became law in June 1982. Cline's evaluation of the decision emphasized its success: "I know of no other resource controversy in Alaska where loggers, miners, commercial fishermen, conservationists and borough, city, state, and federal officials all signed a page-and-a-half agreement that settled the issue."[14]

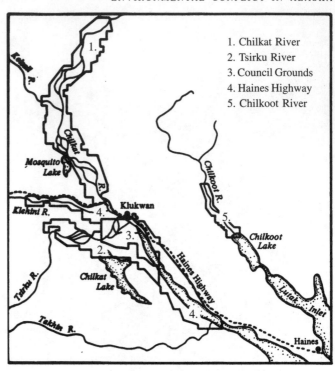

1. Chilkat River
2. Tsirku River
3. Council Grounds
4. Haines Highway
5. Chilkoot River

4.1. Alaska Chilkat Bald Eagle Reserve, 1985.
Courtesy Alaska Dept. of Natural Resources,
Division of Parks and Recreation.

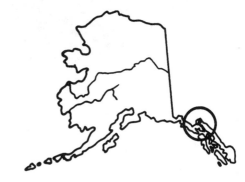

Research by the Audubon–Fish and Wildlife Service team yielded extensive data on eagle behavior in the region. Chilkat attracted many of the bald eagles of the Canadian and Southeast Alaskan coast during September through January, a time of relative food scarcity elsewhere. Birds flew north to feed and returned south for the nesting season. Adults tended to remain in Alaska; young ones continued southward as far as Washington. Large cottonwoods along the Chilkat afforded daytime perches and night roosting sites during the early fall. Later in the year, and during storms, eagles roosted in evergreens on nearby ridges. Those nesting in the valley chose old-growth cottonwoods or spruces. Authors of the study recommended management to avoid activities harming the runs of salmon or disrupting the feeding behavior of eagles. Among the most intrusive potential activities would be

logging or mining near the preserve, especially removal of nesting, roosting, and perching trees; excessive use of motorized craft during the feeding period; disturbance of the 5,000-acre counciling grounds near Klukwan where eagles did the bulk of their feeding; and further transfers of public land to private control. Interpretive centers might be constructed in Haines and Klukwan, the authors suggested, and an observation platform near miles 20 or 21 of the Haines Highway.[15]

Following completion of the revised logging contract, Schnabel Lumber Company once again shut down. Battered by the conflict over the Tongass (Chapter 15) that choked off its timber supply, the last large sawmill closed in 1990. Disney filmed *White Fang* in the valley in 1991, spending a lot of money. Tourism swelled during the decade, shifting the economic base by degrees. Yet bitter recriminations divided the community of Haines, pitting those who demanded open access to natural resources against those advocating a more moderate course. A *Chilkat Valley News* reporter eventually left town in frustration, citing "the impossibility of reason—because of a culture that celebrates dissent in defiance of the law, historical fact and any other coherent value system outside of self-interest." Haines had not solved the identity crisis over its relationship to the land.[16]

Valley residents had hoped the eagles could engender a viable tourist industry, and people came from around the world. Eagles reached a peak of 3,998 in 1984 and photographers numbered 650 in 1986. Nature guide Dan Egolf related that on one occasion "there were so many [human] tracks out on the flats, it looked like a migrating herd of caribou had passed through. One bird trying to feed was surrounded by tripods." Protective regulations had to be implemented.[17] But the lateness of the gathering season—late October through January—deterred eagle enthusiasts from coming in sufficient numbers to exert much of a year-round influence on the economy. The preserve nevertheless won acceptance by the people of Haines. Klukwan Tlingits continued to insist their claim to the land preceded its selection by the state. However, they vowed not to log the forest if they should gain ownership.[18] Although periodic shootings occurred, valley residents came to see themselves as guardians of the Chilkat eagles.

The Chilkat episode served to advance sustainable use of Alaskan resources in several ways. It generated experience in cooperative problem solving, strengthened the roles of the national public and environmental groups as interested parties, demonstrated the essentiality of scientific research, gave permanent protection to a unique wildlife population and, not least, left most participants feeling good about the outcome. Several conditions made the success possible, including the patriotic symbolism of the bald eagle, the lack of high financial stakes, sympathy from important elements of the state and federal governments, and the skill of negotiators. Rarely would such a favorable array of circumstances be found in an Alaskan environmental dispute.

NOTES

1. Waste, "Gathering of Eagles," 4; Cline, "To Band a Bald Eagle," 48; Rearden, "Chilkat Miracle," 43.

2. *Alaska Geographic*, "The Chilkat River Valley," 15, 18–19, 38–43, 55, 62–71; Orth, *Dictionary of Alaska Place Names*, 209.

3. Cline, "Conflict on the Counciling Grounds," 7; Hansen et al., *Bald Eagles*, 8.

4. Macy and Steinberg, "A Feast of Eagles," 28; Dorothy E. Fossman, letter to the editor, *Chilkat Valley News*, letter dated January 31, 1972. The letter doubled as a petition to the governor. Among the environmentalists active in establishing the Habitat Area were Jerry Deppa, Richard Folta, Karl Lane, Margaret Piggott and R. T. "Skip" Wallen.

5. Cline, "Conflict on the Counciling Grounds," 6.

6. Henry, "Allowable Cut," 170–172; Rearden, "Chilkat Miracle," 49.

7. Cline, "Conflict on the Counciling Grounds," 7; Rau, "Valley of the Eagles," 78.

8. Waste, "Gathering of Eagles," 85.

9. Macy and Steinberg, "A Feast of Eagles," 28; Cline, "Conflict on the Counciling Grounds," 7, 77; *Ravencall*, "O'Haines," 10.

10. Macy and Steinberg, "Conservationists Sue," 13; Rau, "Valley of the Eagles," 85, 88, 90.

11. Rau, "Valley of the Eagles," 80, 82, 85, 88, 90.

12. Rearden, "Chilkat Miracle," 50; Rau, "Valley of the Eagles," 80, 82, 88, 90.

13. Stratton and Peale, "Haines Lawsuit," 2.

14. Rearden, "Chilkat Miracle," 44, 50–54; *Alaska*, "Alaska Sportsman," December 1982, 94–96; *Alaska Session Laws, 1982*, Chapter 95.

15. Hansen et al., *Bald Eagles*, 7, 17–25.

16. Henry, "Allowable Cut," 177–182.

17. *Anchorage Times*, December 28, 1986, D1.

18. *Alaska Report*, "Chilkat Eagles Threatened," 5.

5

Wolf Control

Attempts to achieve sustainable use of the wolf, or to reach consensus on the animal's status, proved far more difficult than for any other wildlife species. Distinctive, perhaps mysterious qualities helped single out the creature for special treatment as a predator. As preservation values spread in the 1970s, some of those same qualities earned the wolf an appreciative audience willing to confront its persecutors—a recipe for lengthy, emotional strife. Hunters, trappers, and their allies on the Board of Game relentlessly strove to limit wolf consumption of moose and caribou. Environmentalists in Alaska and the Lower 48, especially those more oriented to animal rights, spearheaded the opposition to wolf control. Unable to force the issue to a favorable conclusion, they nevertheless placed state policy on trial before a state and national public uneasy about the killing of wolves.

EARLY PREDATOR POLICY

Wolf control in Alaska has deep historical roots. Before the era of ecological awareness, Americans labeled any wild creature interfering with human activities a varmint or predator, and attacked it through private and public efforts. They seldom pondered or investigated the side effects of its disappearance. This legacy of pioneer days found virile form in Alaska, where it lasted throughout the century. Acting on antipredator sentiments, the new legislature placed a bounty on the wolf in 1915. Over the next 38 years bald eagles, hair seals, coyotes, Dolly Varden char, and wolverines joined the wolf. Alaskans regarded them as menaces to other wildlife, or to hunting, trapping, or salmon fishing. The territory withdrew the Dolly Varden bounty in 1941 and the bald eagle gained protection by national legislation in 1952. But the federal assistance in wolf and coyote control that originated in the 1920s reached a high point through the use of aircraft and poison in the 1950s.

Predator-control politics in Alaska entered a new phase after statehood, shifting its emphasis from organized control programs to the bounty system. Public opinion swung in favor of the wolf as widening awareness and such literature as Lois Crisler's 1958 book *Arctic Wild* took hold. The new state gained wildlife management jurisdiction on January 1, 1960. Its game officials had opposed the federal wolf control program, especially the use of poison, and made their views known to the public. Except for a limited reindeer protection effort resumed by federal authorities in 1963, the Alaska Department of Fish and Game

(ADF&G) ended most organized wolf control in 1960. In 1963 the Board of Fish and Game elevated the wolf to big game and furbearer status, and invited nonresidents to hunt it as a trophy. The board lowered bag limits, instituted year-round protection in some sectors, and ceased issuing off-season kill permits.[1] It outlawed wolf hunting and trapping on the Kenai Peninsula. Kenai wolves, once considered among the largest of the species, had been exterminated by 1915, and excepting a few wanderers, none returned until 1968.[2]

ADF&G ended nearly all use of poisons by 1962, but conducted temporary wolf control programs in 1963 and 1964 at Neets Bay and the Chickamin River in the Southeast to facilitate elk and moose calf transplants. As a result of pressure and funding from the legislature's House Finance Committee in response to deer-hunting interests, ADF&G engaged in wolf control in the Petersburg-Wrangell vicinity in 1968. Traps and strychnine effected a known kill of nine wolves and two wolverines. As for other species, fishing interests induced the slaughter of 4,000 sea lions at Sugarloaf Island in 1963. Programmed elimination of hair seals and belukhas ended in 1959 and 1965, respectively. Federal authorities took action against cattle-killing black bears in the Little Susitna River valley in 1961–1962. Grizzly bear control, following the "Kodiak Bear War" of 1963 wherein ADF&G secretly killed 35 bears near the cattle ranches, phased out in 1969.

Bounties, having stirred controversy in the Lower 48, eventually spread to Alaska. Before the turn of the century, critics such as Bureau of Biological Survey officials C. Hart Merriam and T. S. Palmer had disputed the effectiveness of bounties, showing that Pennsylvania had spent $90,000 to kill economically beneficial hawks and owls to save $1,875 worth of poultry.[3] In 1938 Bureau of Biological Survey director Ira Gabrielson termed Alaska's bounty system a failure, recommending the use of paid government hunters.[4] Nineteen years later, ADF&G adopted an official stand against bounties.[5] ADF&G biologist Calvin Lensink articulated the new agency's position. He favored predator control but regarded the bounty system as driven by welfare politics to be "at its best ineffective and wasteful," and at worst "harmful to the very animals that we are trying to protect." Bounties didn't significantly affect wolf numbers, he said, and about half those bountied would have been killed anyway. Individual wolverines could be nuisances to property, but it made no sense to go after all of them and waste valuable fur in off-seasons. Only in the heavy salmon run areas did seals eat salmon. In the north, bounties applied primarily to ringed and bearded seals, species not eating commercially valuable fish of any kind. Lensink called for more selective control and expanded research.[6]

Alaska Conservation Society (ACS) leaders enthusiastically seized the bounty issue. They endorsed Lensink's ideas, publicized them, and called for repeal of all bounties. Pointing out proof that well-to-do white gunners got most of the money, Celia Hunter argued that the "antiquated and costly system" did not even function well as a welfare program.[7] Early attempts at repeal failed—ACS once persuaded a Fairbanks legislator to introduce a bounty repeal bill; he and every one of his colleagues then voted against it.[8]

As the wolf population recovered from the federal control program, citizens multiplied their complaints about loss of game. In 1965 the Alaska Senate spoke:

> Whereas in the not-too-distant future a reactionary Legislature listening to a long-suffering public ignored and abused by the Division of Game, will rise up against the

5.1. *Guides skin wolves taken in aerial hunt, 1963. By Gordon Henning. Courtesy Anchorage Museum of History and Art. Between 1915 and 1972, Alaska paid bounties on wolves.*

Department and remove its vicious dictatorial powers and slash the game budget to a skeleton force . . . Be it resolved that the Senate reaffirms its belief in the bounty system as the proper predator control for wolves; that under the law the wolf is a predator and not a trophy animal and the Department of Fish and Game is directed to discontinue any closed season for wolves and to end any area protection.[9]

No agency could long stand such pressure, and ADF&G lacked research data to fortify its position. A political contest ensued, centering on the Nelchina wolves in south-central Alaska. By the late 1960s the Nelchina caribou herd had swelled to 80,000 as an apparent consequence of the 1948–1951 wolf control program of the U.S. Fish and Wildlife Service. Using poison and firing shotguns from aircraft, agents had killed more than 200 wolves in one part of the Nelchina Basin; only 12 remained there in 1953. Beginning in 1957, the agency declared the basin off-limits to wolf hunting, and initiated a long-term predator-prey study that continued under ADF&G after statehood. By 1964–1965, the Nechina wolf population exceeded 200.[10] Wolf numbers then dropped off as many followed caribou out of the area and a minimum of 64 fell to poachers in 1965. A fall 1967 count estimated about 200 wolves in the district. Nevertheless, hunters appealed to the legislature and Board of Fish and Game for access to the wolves. In early 1968 the politically appointed board overrode the game professionals and ordered a Nelchina wolf hunt for the winter of 1968. It authorized a kill of up to 10 wolves per hunter, for a

5.2. Aerial wolf hunters and their kill, spring 1972. Prior to mid-1972, hunters could shoot wolves from the air. Courtesy Alaska Department of Fish and Game, Fairbanks.

possible total of 300.[11] The hunt proceeded, accounting for 120 wolves.[12] But it touched off a strong public reaction among Alaskans; many letters to the editors objected to the slaughter. Others took the opposite view: farmer Paul Elbert in a letter to the *Fairbanks Daily News-Miner* asserted, "To me, the campaign to preserve wolves unlimited smacks of foreign sabotage, and seems to fit right in with the demoralization of our youth, our judicial system, our financial structure, etc. . . . Remember a wolf eats $5 worth of meat a day, $2,000 worth a year. He hunts and eats 365 days a year. Wolves get most of the game every year."[13]

Outside environmentalists kept quiet during the bounty controversy; ACS led the opposition. Celia Hunter summarized the society's view: "Alaska's present attitude toward the wolf is still a mixture of folklore, witchhunting and scapegoating, leavened with an awakening of ecological awareness. It is disheartening to find the outmoded bounty system still firmly entrenched in Alaska's laws . . . and to find the legislature vigorously dictating our game management policy on the basis of emotional public demands."[14]

But time grew short for the bounty system. In 1967 the Board of Fish and Game restricted seal bounties to north and northwest Alaska. This action cut the number of seals taken for bounty from 70,462 in fiscal year 1966 to 7,147 in fiscal year 1968.[15] Charles Lindbergh, who had not spoken in public for ten years, delivered a conservation address to the legislature in March 1968, advising,

The action you take here . . . is something that affects people all over the world, particularly in what you people call the 'Lower 48.' The people down there are fascinated with

Table 5.1—Wolves and Wolverines Bountied in Alaska, 1959–1972

Year	Wolves	Wolverines	Year	Wolves	Wolverines
1959	227	213	1967	1,679	694
1960	520	420	1968	1,714	578
1961	725	441	1969	1,008	242
1962	869	383	1970	225	0
1963	757	445	1971	179	0
1964	818	551	1972	179	0
1965	825	420			
1966	1,360	659	Total	11,105+	5,046+

Source: Donald E. McKnight, *The History of Predator Control in Alaska* (Juneau: Alaska Dept. of Fish and Game, 1973), 9.

Note: Bounty records incomplete for 1969.

Alaska—you can get great numbers of tourists and others coming up here, an opportunity that has hardly been touched. . . . there is nothing more important than preserving our natural environment.[16]

Senator Lowell Thomas Jr. pushed for a repeal of the bounty. The legislature responded. It outlawed the use of poison by state agencies except by written permission of the Board of Fish and Game, and ceased wolf, wolverine, and coyote bounty payments except for residents taking wolves in their local management areas.[17] The number of bountied wolves dropped from about 1,700 in 1968 to 225 in 1970. Bounty payments for wolverines and coyotes ended in 1969. Between 1959 and 1969, payments had been made on at least 5,046 wolverines (Table 5.1).[18]

Game officials soon came under attack from another quarter. A film titled *The Wolf Men*, depicting aerial hunting unfavorably, appeared on national television in 1969. In one of its memorable scenes a guide appeared to eat raw wolf meat. The film incensed a generation brought up on nature films. Thousands of letters poured in to ADF&G and Governor Keith Miller's office, more than ever before on any subject. People sent copies of Farley Mowat's *Never Cry Wolf,* demanding, "Read this!" Game managers regarded the book, critical of Canadian wolf control policy and decidedly solicitous of the wolf, as less than accurate.[19] But the people had spoken clearly. In 1970 the Board of Fish and Game suspended wolf bounties in most districts, and in 1972 the legislature ended bounties on wolves and hair seals by ceasing to budget money for payments. Near-complete records showed a total since 1959 of 11,105 wolves taken for bounty (Table 5.1).[20]

Events in Washington, D.C., affected the changes in Alaska. A panel headed by ecologist A. Starker Leopold examined predator control on Department of the Interior lands. It concluded in 1964 that far too many wild animals had been needlessly killed, and except for western grazing lands, all use of poison should be stopped. Resistance from grazing interests forestalled a policy change. A 1971 panel headed by biologist Stanley A. Cain, including Starker Leopold and Richard Cooley, also recommended the termination of poison. It further requested a halt to nearly all shooting of animals from aircraft. Coming at a high point of the environmental movement, the panel's work helped bring about an executive order banning use of poison on federal and state lands, and contributed to passage of the October 1972 Airborne Hunting Act prohibiting aerial shooting of birds, mammals, or fish except by state permit.[21] Earlier in 1972, Alaska Fish and Game Commissioner Jim Brooks had banned aerial shooting in Alaska "to bring conservation practice out of the pioneer era and into accord with conditions and attitudes that generally prevail today."[22]

RETURN OF WOLF CONTROL

In its wolf management policy adopted in 1973, ADF&G acknowledged that "traditionally, game management has emphasized maximum production of ungulates for man's use, but . . . [ADF&G] recognizes the Constitutional mandate of the State of Alaska to manage wolves on the sustained yield principle for the benefit of the resource and the people of the state, and also recognizes that national and international interests must be considered." Multiple uses of the wolf meant recreational observation and maintenance of wilderness quality as well as hunting and trapping. "Aerial sport hunting of wolves generally is not considered a desirable use of the resource," the policy stated, and "control will be implemented only after an investigation by Department personnel has determined a valid need exists." Scientific research, it asserted, should be the basis for management policy.[23]

Declarations of policy often carried less weight than did political influence. Not long after the bounty controversy died down, another sprang up to place the wolf on center stage. Again, wolf competed with human for moose and caribou, and again outsiders questioned Alaskans' ability to treat resources wisely. As a likely result of the federal and territorial efforts of the 1950s, wolves had been severely diminished in some areas, and moose and caribou proliferated. In Game Management Unit 20A, a 6,560-square-mile region northeast of Mt. McKinley (later Denali) National Park, moose numbered 23,000 in the mid-1960s. Fairbanks moose hunters favored 20A, but by 1971 the population of moose had dropped to 9,000. Game biologists conjectured that a combination of hunting, hard winters, and wolf predation caused the loss. Mild winters and ample food supply in the early 1970s did not revive moose levels. Biologists attributed the low incidence of calf survival to predation by wolves, now thought to be too numerous for the moose.[24] Hunters demanded permission to pursue wolves by aircraft. Hunting pressure on moose had risen rapidly through the use of snowmobiles, jetboats, and all-terrain vehicles. Pipeline workers and military personnel, inexperienced and in many cases wasteful of meat, made up a high percentage of hunters. Despite the relative scarcity of moose, the amount shot by hunters in 20A rose from 350 in 1971 to 710 in 1973—a toll beyond the ability of the population to sustain. The Board of Fish and Game reacted to the kill figures by shortening the season for 1974, though 350 moose fell in that year, and by severely curtailing the season in 1975.[25] Only 3,000 moose remained in 20A.

A similar pattern applied to the Delta caribou herd frequenting 20A. It also peaked in the 1960s, and experienced a steep slide from 5,000 in 1970 to 2,000 in 1975. Following closure of hunting in 1973, no recovery occurred, and calf survival stayed below normal. As in the case of 20A moose, biologists believed wolf predation to be the cause. The Board of Fish and Game decided to institute an aerial wolf hunt beginning in 1974–1975 to eliminate 80 percent of the

5.3. Alpha wolf feeding on caribou, North Slope, 1974. By Dan Roby. Often the leading predators of caribou, wolves evoked resentment among hunters.

estimated 175 wolves in 20A. Game officials planned to employ fixed-wing aircraft and helicopters, and also to permit private fliers in fixed-wing aircraft, to shoot the wolves from the air. This would help moose and caribou recover, and participation by private parties would ease the burden on the ADF&G budget.[26] The Board of Game (formed by division of the Board of Fish and Game in 1975) also planned a predator-prey experiment for Unit 13 in the Nelchina sector southeast of McKinley Park. The Nelchina experiment aimed to remove all of the 35 to 40 Unit 13 wolves in 1975–1976 and study the effects on ungulates over an extended period.

Opposition to the plans quickly materialized. Lee Harrison of the Committee for Wildlife on the Last Frontier (WOLF) in Anchorage expressed a common theme: "The wolves are being used as a scapegoat by the Alaska Department of Fish and Game for years of mismanagement in section 20A." Similarly, the *New York Times* accused the state of permitting overhunting and catering to sport hunters who brought money into the state. Defenders of Wildlife member Jim Hunter of Fairbanks articulated a preservationist position: "[T]he hunting public by and large believes predators must not be allowed to flourish lest they reduce the human share of that good red meat out there or kill a cow moose which might have given birth to a bull with a Boone and Crockett rack . . . man has *no* right to extinguish predators in favor of increased hunting pleasures for himself."[27]

Fairbanks Environmental Center, Friends of the Earth, Defenders of Wildlife, Friends of Animals, Canadian and American Wolf Defenders, and private individuals filed suit against the 20A plan, contending that only state employees should be allowed to kill wolves. They

5.4. Alaska Dept. of Fish and Game biologists Bob Stephenson and Victor van Ballenberghe with tranquilized wolves, Nelchina district, 1975. Courtesy ADF&G, Fairbanks. Lack of information on predator-prey relations aggravated conflict over wolf control.

won an injunction delaying the plan for a year while the state changed its permit arrangement. A lawsuit filed in Washington by Defenders of Wildlife against the Unit 13 and 20A plans, on grounds that they required environmental impact statements, failed.[28] ACS recommended a postponement of the 20A plan in 1975, calling it an "ad hoc decision" in response to "human mismanagement" that "sets a poor precedent for professional game management within the State of Alaska." It argued that "in the present instance, consumptive uses are completely dominating the management posture, to the detriment of those whose primary interest lies in seeing a well-balanced population of wildlife of all sorts." It cautioned that national reaction could jeopardize Alaskan jurisdiction over wildlife. A year later the society adopted a more noncommittal stance on 20A, asking for proper research if the project were to go ahead, and more careful monitoring of hunting in the future. It approved the Unit 13 plan, providing an adequate multiyear study be carried through.[29]

As the controversy heated, thousands more letters arrived from outside, the vast majority castigating the plans. Governor Jay Hammond warned that the dispute could hurt the state's position in the d-2 lands deliberations. The 1976 legislature entertained a resolution suggesting cynically that the wolves be relocated to the Lower 48. The committee chair who

5.5. Grizzly bear and downed yearling moose, Nanushuk River, 1971. By Lynn Crook. Courtesy ADF&G, Fairbanks. Grizzlies often killed more moose than did wolves.

introduced it explained, "I am sick and tired of the eco-freaks in the Lower 48 criticizing our treatment of the wolf. So now we are giving them a chance to help us with the overabundance. Now they can put up, or shut up." University of Alaska professor Sarkis Atamian ventured that "the hunter, who was once the hero is now the villain. The wolf, once the villain, is now the hero. It is the hallmark of a society that is coming apart."[30]

ADF&G started up its programs in 1975–1976. Following elimination of most wolves in 20A, the adult moose death rate dropped from 20 percent to 6 percent, and calf survival more than doubled. Caribou survival also increased, and biologists concluded that wolf control made the difference.[31] In Unit 13 the project continued for five years, adding a new dimension. Contrary to expectations, after wolf removal the moose calf losses persisted. Further research identified grizzly bears as the source. Much more numerous than wolves in the game unit, they accounted for nearly 80 percent of the predated calves; wolves got about 10 percent. Tranquilization and transfer of 60 percent of the bears appeared to have minimal effect, but after the targeting of three problem bears, calf numbers increased rapidly. But in Unit 13A, by 1980, two years after wolf control ceased, it recovered nearly 90 percent of its precontrol wolf population.[32] A later study in east-central Alaska, where wolves had not been systematically removed, determined that of about 600 moose born each year, grizzlies took about 300, wolves 90, and accidents and miscellaneous causes 90.[33]

The predator-prey debate evolved to a more sophisticated level. Several conclusions seemed warranted by the studies done on wolf-prey relationships in the 1960s and 1970s.

Each situation and thus each study is made unique by variations in climate, habitat, predator and prey ratios and numbers, proximity to other wildlife populations, harvest by hunters, disease, and other factors.[34] The wolf normally takes the path of least resistance but kills healthy as well as weak prey. Wolves sometimes kill more than they can eat immediately, but the remains supply food for later use and for other animals. Wolves may or may not be the prime predators of an ungulate species in a particular location; when wolves are scarce, more prey may be taken by grizzlies or black bears. Following reduction, wolves may recover quickly through migration and reproduction. They control their own populations to a degree and can limit prey populations, but not evenly; great fluctuations take place, resulting in abundance or starvation for either wolf or prey. Many researchers and most game managers agreed with leading wolf expert L. David Mech that properly conducted wolf control could in some circumstances benefit both predator and prey by moderating population highs and lows.[35] Few took the preservationist position that the ecosystem should be allowed to function naturally; most accepted wolf control as a means of maintaining larger stocks of ungulates, primarily moose and caribou. Sport and subsistence hunters, the prime beneficiaries of ungulate abundance, exercised the most political influence on the wildlife management process.

As the 20A and 13 unit studies progressed in the mid-1970s, a crisis unfolded in the western Brooks Range: the western Arctic caribou herd crashed. From a peak of at least 250,000 in the late 1960s it fell to 90,000 to 100,000 by early 1976. Considering that Natives killed about 25,000 to 30,000 per year and an estimated wolf population of 1,200 to 1,400 pulled down as many as 12,000 more, the news shocked game officials. Speculation and accusation flourished, and rumors spread of piles of gutted caribou left on the tundra by Eskimos. Sympathizers of the Natives accused the critics of racism. Why, others asked, had ADF&G allowed it to happen? ADF&G cited the difficulty and expense of aerial surveys, and conceded it had assumed that transition to snowmobiles would eliminate the need for large amounts of meat to feed sled dogs. Possibly the use of snowmobiles greatly increased the kill, but the dogs had been kept and fed much of the meat.[36]

August 1976 introduced worse news: a new survey recorded the herd at 52,000—two years' normal kill. Alarmed, the Board of Game devised a plan. A quota of 3,000 bull permits would be allocated annually to and by the various villages. No caribou could be wasted or fed to dogs. To supplement the plan, up to 80 percent of the 1,000 wolves on the South Slope would be eliminated by airborne government-licensed private hunters. At the hearings, reactions to the plan varied. The expected flood of indignant letters did not materialize, because environmentalists took no unified stand. Most villagers accepted the plan; others threatened to ignore the caribou bag limits. Tanana Valley Sportsmen's Association filed suit against the Natives-only permit system. As a result, officials closed the caribou season for 1976–1977. Defenders of Wildlife, Friends of the Earth, and six other environmental and animal rights groups sued to stop the wolf kill, and won a preliminary injunction. Jim Kowalsky, Friends of the Earth representative in Alaska, argued that if Alaskans really cared about the caribou they should not only end wolf control but restrict mineral extraction and highway construction in the caribou ranges.[37] Sierra Club/Alaska declined to challenge the plan, based on its concern for Native subsistence and the caribou population.[38]

5.6. *Alaska Department of Fish and Game agent setting wolf traps in Southeast tidal pool, as used in 1970s wolf control. Courtesy LaVerne Beier. Alaska ended wolf control in 1960, then revived it in the 1970s as moose and caribou declined.*

Alaska Conservation Society executive director Tina Stonorov voiced reluctant approval of the plan, including wolf control. Society members cared not only for the viability of the Native lifestyle but, as Bob Weeden explained, "If the western Arctic caribou decline further and remain scarce for very long, their range will be taken over *permanently* by coal miners, reindeer, copper miners, oilfields and pipelines."[39] State and federal officials in fact made a brief attempt in the late 1970s to extend reindeer grazing into the North Slope caribou range. And decades earlier, reindeer herding had been introduced to the northeast coast to provide sustenance for Eskimos following the decimation of caribou herds in the whaling era. Severe winters in 1935 and 1936 caused most of the reindeer and some of the Eskimos to starve, ending the experiment.[40]

Defenders of Wildlife et al. succeeded in curtailing ADF&G's western Arctic program. Only 48 wolves fell to aerial permit shooting, but hunters and trappers killed another 157 in the area during 1976–1977. Disease may also have contributed to the wolf toll. Hunting restrictions in place, the caribou began to recover. For this reason, and given the sensitive nature of d-2 lands legislation, the Board of Game did not revive Arctic wolf control when the injunction ended in 1980. Plans for reindeer grazing on the North Slope faded as the caribou herd rebounded.

Results of the 20A program encouraged demands for wolf control in other districts. The Board of Game chose three districts in 1979 and once more, challengers filed suits: private parties in the state superior court and Defenders of Wildlife and its co-plaintiffs in federal court. Superior court dismissed the state suit; the federal case ended in a ruling affirming the right of the state to manage wildlife within its borders. Wolf control efforts continued, more selective and limited. A candid admission appeared in a 1979 ADF&G position paper: "The Department of Fish and Game acknowledges, as a basic proposition, that wolf-reduction programs which are intended to rehabilitate depressed ungulate populations are not needed to increase the population of either predator or prey species, but are for the sole purpose of providing more animals for human consumption."[41]

Numerous studies in Alaska and Canada convinced game managers that predation by wolves, grizzly bears, and black bears can hold prey (specifically moose or caribou) populations at low levels for lengthy periods of time; that predator control can increase prey so that hunters can harvest more, and the increased prey numbers can feed a substantial population of predators as well.[42] Some scientists and environmentalists challenged these conclusions, but most debate focused directly on the propriety of wolf control. Environmentalists questioned its ethics, aesthetics, and effects on the tourist trade. Some criticized it as narrow, single-species management. Most believed that wolf management stemmed from the influence of hunting groups on the Board of Game and ADF&G. Hunters and some game managers tended to view activist opponents of wolf control as sentimentalists lacking knowledge or respect for biological facts.

Turmoil over wolf control spanned the 1980s, building toward one of the most acrimonious natural-resource fights of the statehood period. It distanced Alaskan environmentalists from their erstwhile allies in the utilitarian conservationist game management community and its constituent hunting groups. It stimulated the involvement of outside experts and activists, reinforcing Alaskan antipathy toward outside influence. Conversely, it revived suspicions of outsiders that Alaskans abused wildlife belonging to the nation. Debate centered on two immediate questions: Is wolf control desirable? How should aircraft be used, if at all, in taking wolves? More fundamentally, the dispute aired long-standing differences about the purposes of game management and the proper role of Alaskan and outside public opinion. For whose benefit should Alaska's wildlife be managed? Hunters and sport fishers who generated a high percentage of the ADF&G budget through license fees? A broader range of user groups including tourists and nonhunting outdoor recreationists? The Alaskan public as a whole? The American public? The integrity of the ecosystem per se? And who should participate in the decisionmaking process?

Between 1980 and 1986, ADF&G pruned wolf populations in selected areas (Table 5.2), primarily to increase moose. In 1981 the Board of Game officially declared that its wolf control policy sought to restore low ungulate populations.[43] As board member and wildlife management professor Sam Harbo justified it, "I think what we're doing in some of these areas is recognizing that the consumption of prey by humans is the priority wildlife use, and we're managing accordingly."[44] Game officials encountered implacable opposition in Wayne Hall of the Alaska Wildlife Alliance (AWA), who had worked at the issue since 1978, Greenpeace Alaska representative Cindy Lowry, and the Defenders of Wildlife national office. Sierra Club/Alaska objected to wolf control in wild and scenic river areas. Other Alaskan environmental groups, absorbed in other matters or less oriented to animal rights, took low-key positions if any.[45]

Table 5.2—Wolves Taken in Control Programs by ADF&G and Aerial Permit, 1976–1986

Year	Agent	Wolves Taken	Year	Agent	Wolves Taken
1975–1976	ADF&G	67	1982–1983	ADF&G	61
				Permit	25
1976–1977	ADF&G	27	1983–1984	ADF&G	9
	Permit	48			
1977–1978	ADF&G	39	1984–1985	ADF&G	24
1978–1979	ADF&G	18	1985–1986	ADF&G	29
	Permit	45			
1979–1980	ADF&G	30			
	Permit	46	*Subtotals*	ADF&G	441
1980–1981	ADF&G	68		Permit	225
	Permit	45	*Unit 13, 1975–1978*		60
1981–1982	ADF&G	69			
	Permit	16	*Total*		726

Sources: Alaska Department of Fish and Game, "Wolf Management Programs in Alaska, 1975–1983" (Juneau, November 1983), Appendices 3, 3a; Robert O. Stephenson et al., "Wolf Biology and Management in Alaska, 1981–91." *Proceedings of 2nd International Wolf Symposium.* Canadian Wildlife Service Series. (Edmonton, August 1992), 22–30.

When the Board of Game adopted wolf control plans without significantly involving the public, AWA complained to the state Ombudsman office. In March 1983 the Ombudsman advised the board that its policy and programs constituted regulations under law, necessitating proper public notice and hearings. In November 1983 AWA sued in superior court, winning an injunction against wolf control pending public-involvement procedures. In its March 1984 meeting the board adopted measures for public review and for basing wolf control plans on scientific evidence, taking into account long-term objectives for both wolves and prey species. These objectives were to include both consumptive and nonconsumptive uses of wildlife.[46]

For its 1984–1985 wolf control programs, the state obtained a Federal Communications Commission (FCC) permit for radio telemetry to track the wolves. Critics discovered the permit had been granted for research purposes, and requested it be withdrawn. In late 1984, FCC ordered the state to cease using the radio collars. ADF&G obtained a different permit for the collars in 1985–1986. AWA failed in a legal action to stop the use of telemetry.[47]

The Board of Game authorized wolf control in one game management unit, 20B (Minto Flats), in the winters of 1985 and 1986. Employing methods begun in 1982, agents flew fixed-wing aircraft and helicopters to shoot wolves. Adding a new measure to increase efficiency, game officials first tranquilized and radio-collared a wolf, then followed it to kill the rest of the pack.[48] Besides stirring public resentment, the program proved expensive—$44,000 in the winter of 1986 to kill about 34 wolves. It accounted for a total kill of about 58 wolves in 1985 and 1986 combined. Outside the realm of formal wolf control, hunters and trappers took about 1,600 in the same two-year period. ADF&G estimated the 1985–1986 statewide pre-pupping wolf population at 4,933 to 6,212.[49] In spring 1987 Governor Steve Cowper ordered

Table 5.3—Alaska Statewide Private Wolf Harvests, 1970–2000

Year	Wolves Taken	Year	Wolves Taken
1970–1971	635	1985–1986	669
1971–1972	1,335	1986–1987	806
1972–1973	1,071	1987–1988	1,099
1973–1974	970	1988–1989	858
1974–1975	1,090	1989–1990	941
1975–1976	1,243	1990–1991	1,089
1976–1977	1,076	1991–1992	1,162
1977–1978	917	1992–1993	1,051
1978–1979	905	1993–1994	1,583
1979–1980	643	1994–1995	1,457
1980–1981	667	1995–1996	1,251
1981–1982	686	1996–1997	1,280
1982–1983	754	1997–1998	1,061
1983–1984	745	1998–1999	1,324
1984–1985	1,054	1999–2000	1,609

Source: Alaska Department of Fish and Game, Division of Wildlife Conservation, Juneau.

an end to state-funded aerial wolf control, remarking that whenever the state does it "there is a great howl from all over the place . . . I've got enough things to attend to without having to become a party to 12 or 15 lawsuits."[50]

Meanwhile, in the mid-1980s wolves on the Kenai faced a problem of lice picked up from dogs. Louse infestation caused a loss of hair, endangering winter survival. Some game officials thought it best to kill the infested individuals; AWA and Greenpeace disagreed. ADF&G brought the problem temporarily under control by immobilization and injection and by setting out meat containing the drug Invermectin, though reinfestation from dogs could occur at any time.[51] The apparent migration of some wolves off the peninsula, however, jeopardized the entire Alaskan wolf population.[52]

In the absence of ADF&G funding for wolf control, private hunting served as a means of paring wolf populations. Between 1986 and 1992, hunters and trappers killed an average of 1,000 wolves annually (Table 5.3), not much different from the previous 15 years, but greatly in excess of the number taken in directed wolf control programs.[53]

ADF&G tested a new technique in 1989–1990 to alleviate wolf and bear predation by obtaining moose carcasses from the railroad, where trains killed about 300 in the fall and early winter. They placed the meat in selected areas during the spring, feeding wolves and bears to determine whether the attrition of calf moose and caribou would stop.[54] The feeding program may have effected a slight increase in survival of calf moose, but made no noticeable change in abundance of caribou calves.[55]

"LAND-AND-SHOOT"

Alaska Wildlife Alliance and Greenpeace initiated unsuccessful legal efforts in 1986 against the "land-and-shoot" or "same-day" regulation allowing private hunters to land and kill wolves after stepping out of the plane. Difficult to enforce in practice, the regulation

5.7. Remains of five wolves (lower right) killed by snowmobilers, Deadman Creek, April 1993. By Gordon Haber. Courtesy Alaska Wildlife Alliance. High-speed, long-range snow machines or aircraft can easily run down wildlife in open country, and protective laws are difficult to enforce.

invited violations such as shooting while still airborne, and using aircraft to herd or tire wolves before or after landing. Driving of wolves could most easily be done on tundra or lightly wooded terrain. At the 1989 Board of Game hearing, a trapper testified, "I have landed and shot wolves same-day-airborne. Very occasionally you can catch a wolf unaware, in a landable, shootable position. However, most wolves are driven, harassed from where they are to where they can be shot. A totally unsportsmanly act, which leaves the wolf worn out and stressed if it does get away."[56]

A widely publicized case involving misuse of aircraft arose from a March 1989 incident on Kanuti National Wildlife Refuge near the Koyukuk River. National Park Service rangers Bruce Collins and Judy Alderson, flying overhead, recorded the dialogue of two fliers pursuing wolves on the refuge. Inspection of snow markings confirmed that wolves had been illegally chased and killed by use of aircraft above and on the ground. Anchorage guide Charles J. "Chuck" Wirschen forfeited his aircraft, wolf hides, and a Dall sheep taken illegally, paid a $10,000 fine and spent 15 days in jail. Anchorage surgeon John D. "Jack" Frost, an outspoken advocate of land-and-shoot hunting, reached a similar plea bargain but spent no time in jail.[57]

AWA and Greenpeace argued that same-day or land-and-shoot killing amounted to another form of wolf control that should be subject to adopted regulatory guidelines. They believed that a ban, if enforced, would end most of the abuses. The two organizations lost their case in the Alaska Supreme Court in December 1987. That same fall the Board of Game circumscribed the land-and-shoot practice by classifying it as hunting rather than trapping, and restricting it to seven game management units. These provisions somewhat limited the wolf kill, but induced a protest from National Park Service officials, who considered land-and-shoot a violation of fair-chase guidelines employed in its preserves (national park units open to sport hunting). Lacking a response from the Board of Game, the Park Service instituted a one-year ban in November 1988, and initiated proceedings for a permanent ban through federal regulation. In November 1989 the board, anticipating a loss of management control, acceded to the Park Service proposal, whereupon the Park Service halted its pursuit of a regulation. The board extended land-and-shoot to a total of ten state management units. In 1996, environmentalists succeeded in placing on the ballot a proposal to prohibit land-and-shoot. It passed by 58–42 percent.[58]

CONFLICT IN THE 1990s

Research on predation yielded steadily improving results. By the early 1990s it had been determined that when grizzly bears are abundant, they can be the prime cause of moose calf mortality. Black bears, if about ten times as numerous as grizzlies, may be the leading calf predators. Grizzly bears can also take down significant numbers of adult moose, as can wolves, but black bears cannot. Grizzly bear, black bear, and wolf predation can separately or collectively limit moose population growth. However, knowledge about the interrelationships of predation, hunting and other human disturbances, weather, food supplies, and other factors, still existed in an early stage.[59]

Studies appeared to be building an ever-stronger case for some form of wolf control, yet opposition continued to grow in Alaska and the Lower 48. Lawsuits, letters, and other expressions of disapproval accompanied every attempt to implement wolf control. Some ADF&G officers believed that part of the problem lay in a breakdown of trust and communication, and that ADF&G and the Board of Game had lost touch with evolving public opinion. The officers drafted a proposal to broaden public participation in the decision-making process. Endorsed by the board in 1989, it authorized ADF&G to select representatives of Alaskan groups most interested in predator-prey management.[60] Biologists, hunters, trappers, ecotourism representatives, environmentalists (including delegates from Alaska Wildlife Alliance, Audubon/Alaska, and Northern Alaska Environmental Center), other citizens, an ADF&G official, and a Board of Game member made up the Alaska Wolf Management Planning Team formed in 1990.[61] The team solicited written and verbal public input, and professional mediators led the diverse group through a series of six two- or three-day meetings. The team adopted guidelines for habitat conservation, for consumptive and nonconsumptive uses of the wolf, and for a system of identified zones in which various degrees of wolf protection or control might exist under specified conditions. An unusually civil process, given the background of the issue, fashioned a consensus reported to ADF&G in June 1991. The agency drafted a plan based on the team's guidelines, held a public hearing, and presented the plan to the Board of Game.

At the November 1992 Board of Game meeting, Alaska Wildlife Alliance and Northern Alaska Environmental Center voiced acceptance of what they believed to be the consensus developed by the team—a conservative guideline for wolf control on an infrequent and emergency basis. In closed session, the board approved wolf control for three areas.[62] The plan called for an effort that could kill 300 to 400 wolves in 1992–1993 and 100 to 300 annually in later years. It provoked indignation among members of the environmental community, who regarded it as essentially a rejection of the team recommendations.[63]

A postmortem by ADF&G officers and a Board of Game member identified several shortcomings in the attempt to increase involvement of the public. Election of Walter Hickel to the governorship in 1990 had shifted policy emphasis toward more intensive wolf control and away from wide consultation of the public. Neither the tourist industry nor groups outside Alaska had been meaningfully involved, nor had the public in general been adequately informed. The Board of Game had been too hasty in taking control of the planning process and promoting its own agenda. As a result, the review determined, trust had been damaged and the fragile consensus shattered.[64]

Negative reaction to the new wolf control plan spread rapidly. Governor Hickel's office received 20,000 messages, nearly all in protest.[65] Communications from the Lower 48 had been triggered by critical newspaper articles and by a television appearance wherein Hickel declared, "You can't let nature just run wild."[66] Defenders of Wildlife, Fund for Animals, and other environmental groups called for a tourism boycott.[67] Alaskan environmentalists publicized the results of a 1992 Dittman survey of state public opinion on wolf management (Table 5.4). Of 641 adults polled, 43 percent preferred that the proposed wolf kill be reduced, and 8 percent wanted it increased. Two-thirds thought aircraft should not be used in wolf hunting, 74 percent disapproved of killing by state agents from aircraft, and 57 percent objected to the use of snowmobiles to hunt wolves. By 55 to 26 percent, respondents believed wolf reduction would not result in more moose and caribou. One-third had hunted Alaskan big game in the preceding five years. Big game hunters, rural residents, and those in Alaska for less than one year most strongly favored wolf killing.[68] A December poll conducted for the tourist industry indicated that 55 percent of Alaskans opposed aerial wolf hunting and 30 percent approved.[69] A 1991 survey by ADF&G, not mentioning aircraft in its question, had indicated that 47.5 percent of Alaskans favored wolf control and 36.9 percent opposed it.[70]

Governor Hickel, moved in part by the prospect of lost tourist dollars, postponed the wolf management plan pending a January 1993 "Wolf Summit" to be held in Fairbanks. Later in December the Fish and Game commissioner announced that no wolf control would be conducted in winter 1993. Invitations to the January summit went to 125 experts and representatives of interested groups nationwide. Audiences of up to 1,500 at a time also attended. Biologists, game managers, environmentalists, politicians, Natives, hunters, trappers, tourist business owners, and others aired their views on various aspects of wolf management. In small discussion groups, they generally subscribed to: (1) wider public participation in the planning process; (2) an expanded public education effort by ADF&G; (3) incorporation of the guidelines of the International Union for Conservation of Nature into any wolf management plan; and (4) broader public representation on the Board of Game and its advisory committee.[71]

Presentations and audience testimonials at the summit ranged from the dry and scholarly to the contentious and emotional. Speaking for the Alaska Outdoor Council, Sam Harbo reasoned that managing wildlife for a human food supply entailed less energy use and

Table 5.4—Alaskan Public Opinion Responses Regarding Wolf Hunting, 1992

Question	Response	
"Last year we killed over one thousand wolves out of	24%	Greatly reduced
a total population of approximately 6,000 to 7,000.	19%	Moderately reduced
Do you think the number of wolves killed for	28%	Current level
population control should be reduced, increased,	6%	Moderately increased
or remain at the current level?	2%	Greatly increased
	21%	Unsure
"Do you feel the shooting of wolves by the public should	1%	From aircraft
be allowed from aircraft or from the ground, after	21%	From ground
spotting from aircraft?"	7%	Both
	66%	Neither
	4%	Unsure

	Support	Oppose	Unsure
"Do you support or oppose hunting wolves by trapping			
and snaring?"	48%	43%	9%
"Do you support or oppose hunting wolves by snowmobile?"	35%	57%	8%
"Do you support or oppose state agency personnel shooting			
wolves from helicopters or airplanes?"	19%	74%	7%
"Do you support or oppose hunting wolves in national parks			
in Alaska?"	29%	57%	14%

Source: Dittman Research Corp., *Survey Among Alaska Residents Regarding Wolf Hunting* (Anchorage, 1992), 3–6.

environmental impact than did cattle ranching. Native trapper Gilbert Huntington described banning of wolf control as "a threat to the survival of our people . . . Our job is to put meat in the pot." Al Manville of Defenders of Wildlife termed wolf control "a case of single-species management at its worst," insisting that ecosystem management should replace game management. Representing Greenpeace/Alaska, Cindy Lowry held that ADF&G, now dominated by wolf control promoters, needed to be more representative of public opinion. For AWA, Nicole Evans warned that since most Alaskans opposed aerial wolf control, they might have to seek outside support to change the hunter-controlled policy. David Cline of Audubon/ Alaska proposed that the Board of Game be replaced by professional wildlife commissioners less subject to conflict of interest.[72] Alaska Discovery's Tom Garrett expressed widely held fears of a negative impact on the tourist industry. He disputed the notion of some hunters that wildlife belonged to them: "The assertion that tourism somehow has nothing to do with game management couldn't be further from the truth." Ralph Seekins, on behalf of the recently formed Alaska Wildlife Conservation Association backing wolf control, held that increased numbers of moose and caribou would benefit the tourist industry: "I believe abundance of wildlife is the answer."[73] Governor Hickel appealed to the hunter groups and states'-rights partisans who had helped elect him: "I will not be a part of Alaska giving away its sovereignty over fish and game."[74]

The summit took place in an atmosphere of attitudes repolarized since the November Board of Game meeting. A division appeared among environmentalists: The Northern Alaska Environmental Center underwent criticism for its position supporting wolf control in one of the three sectors scheduled by the board. A message faxed to the center read, "Greenies don't kill wolves, compromises do."[75] A vastly wider gap opened between proponents of wolf control on the one hand, and most environmentalists on the other. Barbara Beckman of Wasilla lamented the influence of "pinko, whining" outsiders on wildlife management: "Allow the Outsiders to manage it their way and Alaska will end up like their states with not enough fish and game to allow them to enjoy the independent lifestyles we so cherish here as Alaskans."[76] Celia Hunter objected to the ADF&G plan, later implemented, to shift $100,000 from its nongame budget to pay for the wolf control program. She suggested that hunter dominance of wildlife management be moderated by funding ADF&G through the legislature rather than hunting and fishing fees, and that ADF&G be renamed the Department of Fish and Wildlife.[77]

Outside the summit meeting, Joe Vogler pronounced, "Unless you live in Alaska, you have absolutely no right to make any input into our fish and game rules." Nearby, Rob Mulford's sign concurred: "Right on, Joe Vogler; Posy Sniffer, Get a Life." Mulford added that "these forces behind this 'Don't kill a wolf,' 'Love Mother Earth' . . . stuff are basically antihuman, earth-worshipping pagans." A counterpart held a sign reading, "I will share with Brother Wolf"; another wore a button mocking development extremists: "Kill it! Drill it! Fill it! Spill it!"[78] A wolf control enthusiast's sign accompanied by a wolf skin: "Good Wolf. Good Wolf." Another beside a pile of moose and sheep heads read: "Timber wolf's eat only the old and the weak is a Damn Lie."[79]

In its June 1993 meeting the Board of Game adopted a revised wolf control plan based on what it assumed to be consensus findings at the January summit. Wolf control would be confined to a 4,030-square-mile segment of Game Unit 20A south of Fairbanks. Over a three-year period the wolf population of 150 to 200 would be scaled down by 50 to 75 percent, to allow the Delta caribou herd to reach 6,000 to 8,000. Wolf kills would be undertaken by ADF&G and trappers under its supervision. ADF&G would give trappers information on wolf territories and locations of moose and caribou kills, but neither aerial shooting nor radio-collaring would be employed. However, persons holding trapper licenses could use aircraft in all areas open to hunting, providing they did not violate federal law forbidding herding or harassment of animals. They would have to travel 100 yards from the airplane before legally shooting a wolf.[80]

Upon learning of the new plan, Fund For Animals initiated a second tourism boycott. Most Alaskan environmental organizations did not join it.[81] Tourist industry leaders decided not to contest the wolf control plan, having seen the legislature cut the Alaska Tourism Marketing Council budget by $500,000 in retaliation for their earlier opposition.[82] Alaskan environmentalists generally repudiated renewed wolf control. They expected that use of aircraft would mean widespread abuse, as in the past. They objected to the removal of bag limits on wolves, and lack of controls on hunting by snowmobiles, capable of overtaking any pack of wolves in open terrain. They sought federal legislation to further restrict the use of aircraft in hunting.[83]

5.8. Prowolf protester at Wolf Summit, Fairbanks, January 1993. Courtesy ADF&G, Fairbanks. Alaska's attempts to control wolf populations drew international attention.

In fall 1993 the new control program went into effect. Owing to late snowfall, ADF&G initially brought in train- and road-killed moose to attract wolves, and later used natural kills. Two full-time agents set 1,080 snares and 24 leg-hold traps at 82 sites. During the October 1993–April 1994 season they caught 98 wolves: 84 by snares, 12 shot, and 2 by leg-hold traps. Also in the 20A unit, private trappers got 61 wolves. The 84 snares accidentally caught and killed 12 moose, 2 caribou, 6 coyotes, 13 foxes, a snowshoe hare, and a wolverine. The operation cost $100,000.[84]

Fate delivered a stiff blow to the wolf control program in fall 1994. Three wildlife advocacy groups—AWA, Friends of Animals, and Wolf Haven International—sponsored a monitoring effort by wildlife ecologist Gordon Haber. On November 29, accompanied by *Anchorage Daily News* journalists, Haber visited a snare site in the 20A district. They videotaped four

5.9. Antiwolf protester at Wolf Summit, Fairbanks, January 1993. By
Steve Wells. Wolf control persisted as one of the most passionate and
intractable issues in Alaskan politics.

ensnared wolves. One of the three still alive, a young one, had chewed off the lower half of
its leg in an attempt to escape. An ADF&G biologist arrived and enriched the photographic
record by taking five shots (four by .22 pistol and one by a rifle) to dispatch one of the
wolves. Friends of Animals immediately released the videotape; the story appeared on CNN,
NBC, the Internet, and in the *New York Times*. Within days the state called a halt to the 20A
program.[85]

An avalanche of public reaction followed the videotaped airing. In letters to the *Anchorage Daily News*, some defended wolf control. Robbie Carroll of Kasilof wrote, "I believe the
wolf represents everything I love about Alaska. But I'm sorry, I won't put him above any of
the other wildlife—including bats, shrews and mice. There is no room for emotions in managing wildlife." Larry Kaniut presented a traditional view of the wolf as predator: "For all you

readers who want to save Old Yellow Eyes, I hope you consider the fact that Mr. Wolf is not a cuddly critter—Mr. Wolf is a killing machine with a potential to eradicate big game in his environment." Harold Dale of Kenai took the newspaper's editor, Howard Weaver, to task for biased coverage: "Why don't you print some picture of a wolf killing a moose or some other animals?" Dick Bradford of Palmer suggested, "I would like to see the State of Alaska implement a method of Mr. Haber minding his own business, whatever that is."[86]

Far more numerous critics of wolf control offered a variety of perspectives. Thirteen-year-old Marci Pederson wrote, "Wolves are so beautiful. Why would anyone even think of killing them?" Gabe Wheeler, 14, thought "it is wrong to kill wolves just because they eat too much caribou or moose. Anything they eat is their natural prey because Mother Nature made them that way. Fish and Game and Fairbanks don't understand that. I think they're selfish." Management officials incurred a lot of wrath: "My worst fears about this incompetent, barbaric, so-called wolf program have been realized" (Penelope Wells). Andrea Saunders asked, "Why must so-called civilized man destroy the lesser animals, nature and everything else in his path? Are we still so primitive?" Sheila Mourer-Woodcock questioned the economic wisdom of the program: "Does the revenue from hunting benefit the state more than the tourist dollar?"[87]

Newly elected governor Tony Knowles cancelled the program in February 1995, commenting that it "was professionally mismanaged, caused indiscriminate killing of other wildlife, and was an unacceptable way to treat any animal." He announced that, to receive his sanction, any wolf control program would have to pass tests of public support, economic soundness, and scientific validity. He appointed a citizen advisory panel to review wolf control policy.[88]

Conservative legislators and other wolf control adherents launched a variety of attempts to increase the moose and caribou supply. A private group paid $400 bounties for wolves taken in the Fortymile district of east-central Alaska. To restore the Fortymile caribou herd, which had fallen well below historic levels, ADF&G initiated a five-year plan in fall 1997 to permit increased hunting and trapping, sterilize the Alpha wolves, and translocate pups to the Kenai Peninsula and part of the Brooks Range. A planning team representing a wide range of interested parties, including environmentalists and the ecotourism industry, had devised the plan. Northern Alaska Environmental Center accepted it as a workable compromise, but Alaska Wildlife Alliance rejected it as unnecessary and harmful, in part because of the ongoing louse infection suffered by wolves on the Kenai. The Alaska Trappers Association disparaged the plan as too restrictive of their freedom to hunt wolves.[89]

Wolf sympathizers placed a proposal on the 1998 ballot to ban snaring of wolves and possession of wolf furs acquired by snaring. Another impassioned debate ensued. To combat the ban, a Coalition for the Alaskan Way of Life enlisted Native and sporting groups, including the Alaska Airboat Association, Alaska Outdoor Council, Alaska Trappers Association, National Rifle Association, and Safari Club International. The coalition's TV ad claimed that if the measure passed, "parkas, mittens, children's dolls—anything made of wolf fur—if you own it today, Measure 9 says it's a crime . . . Associated federal law could lead to a felony conviction and may result in your loss of right to possess a firearm . . . Don't let outside groups dictate policy here in Alaska. Protect your gun rights and Alaska's Way of Life." Coalition co-chair and president of Indigenous Survival International Ben Hopson Jr. declared that "whaling, sealing and many other traditional uses of wildlife have been destroyed by the same Lower 48 animal-rights groups behind Ballot Measure No. 9 . . . It should be defeated because of its destructive impact on Native cultures."

Kneeland Taylor, a Fairbanks attorney and chair of Alaskans Against Snaring Wolves, contended that furs would be illegal only if taken after the effective date of the law, which would have no significant impact on subsistence because most snared wolves came from areas near highways rather than rural Native villages. Snares accounted for only a third of the wolf kill, he said, and other species would be caught in them. His coalition's TV ad highlighted the suffering of snared creatures, depicting the wolf that had chewed off its leg in the 1994 wolf control program.[90] On November 3, Measure 9 went down to defeat.

In its 1998 session, the legislature passed and Governor Knowles signed a bill mandating the maximization of moose and caribou as a primary goal of wildlife management. A year later, overriding a veto, the legislature authorized ADF&G to shoot wolves, bears, and other predators from aircraft, should moose or caribou populations decline. In March 2000, reacting to complaints of fewer moose and caribou, the Board of Game authorized hunters to shoot wolves from moving snowmobiles in parts of Game Units 13 (Nelchina Basin), 19D (McGrath), 20A (Alaska Range foothills), and 20D (Delta Junction).[91] The move, a substitute for formal wolf control but contravening state public opinion, ensured more rounds in the fight over wolf control.

DIRECTIONS IN WOLF MANAGEMENT

A few biologists dissented from official interpretations of wolf predation studies. Researcher Victor Van Ballenberghe believed wolf numbers in the Nelchina Basin had been pared to levels lower than necessary to produce high ungulate harvests for hunters. One result, he said, could be an excessive growth of the moose population, resulting in a starvation-induced decline to the point where wolves and bears could again hold down the population.[92] Gordon Haber, in a study sanctioned by the Alaska Wildlife Alliance, challenged assumptions behind the wolf control plan. Caribou and moose in 20A did not need wolf control, he claimed; caribou had returned to recently held numbers from an unusual high. Moreover, he said, the wanderings of caribou undermined the validity of attempts to maintain fixed numbers in specific locations.[93] Haber had studied wolves in Alaska since the mid-1960s and come to the conclusion that wolf control methods disrupted the social structure of wolf packs. He believed that caribou should be understood and managed on an ecosystem or statewide basis, a perspective that would greatly lessen the need for wolf control. Some ADF&G biologists believed that Haber's theories lacked scientific evidence.[94]

Longer-range and more-inclusive studies offered an improved basis for wolf management. ADF&G reported on a 1975–1994 study of predator-prey relationships in the Tanana Flats and Alaska Range foothills northeast of Denali National Park. Wolf control had been conducted during nine of the twenty years, and private taking went on throughout. The study confirmed assumptions that "wolf predation can and often does reduce abundance of primary ungulate prey." It found that scaling down the wolf population increased prey (moose and caribou) and eventually, wolves as well. Thus wolf control represented a gain for hunters and ungulates, and "a clear benefit to wolf conservation and to recreational use of wolves, wolf sign, and wolf sounds." The authors prescribed periodic wolf control to avoid the decline of moose and caribou. Restriction of hunting could not by itself maintain ungulate stocks, they stated, because it amounted to only about 5 percent of the kill rate by predators.[95]

Haber labeled the ADF&G approach "farming" based on maintenance of numbers rather than "true sustained-yield management." Research had shown that killing of more than 15 to 20 percent of a wolf population caused less selective breeding (normally only the Alpha pair breeds), and tended to increase the size of wolf packs, at least in the short run. Haber contended that unlike ungulates, wolves are an intensely social species dependent on complex patterns of interrelationship for effective functioning as packs. High harvest rates of wolves, especially by private hunters and trappers under the sanction of ADF&G, would probably cut short learning by the young (dependent on their elders for a proportionately longer period than are humans) and impair genetic transmission. Effects could include alteration of life patterns and possibly long-term attrition of populations. Haber urged more investigation of the qualitative effects of wolf killing, and considered wolf control justified only in cases of steep ungulate recession. Moreover, he judged that the advanced social characteristics of wolves, as in apes and whales, "provides an ethical reason for them not to be harvested and for considering short-term remedial control only in the rarest of circumstances, when there are solid, irrefutable biological and cost-benefit arguments and no other reasonable alternatives."[96]

In fall 1997 the National Academy of Sciences, through its National Research Council (NRC), released an analysis of predator control in Alaska in response to a request by Governor Knowles. The NRC evaluated the adequacy of scientific knowledge, including biological and social aspects, of predator control in the state. It made recommendations for improving research to the end of increasing public confidence in the fairness of the predator control decisionmaking process. It did not offer final judgments about the advisability of predator control, a matter subsuming important ethical and political components.[97]

Surveying predator control programs carried out in Alaska and Canada over the past half-century, the NRC found that wolves and bears in combination may lower caribou and moose populations and hold them below carrying capacity, but that evidence did not support the existence of extended high levels of both predators and prey, which promoters of predator control hoped to achieve. For wolf control to substantially increase prey stocks, wolves would have to be reduced to 55 percent or less of their precontrol level over an area of at least 10,000 square kilometers, for a minimum of four years and perhaps continuously. Partly because of lack of data on habitat quality, said the council, scant evidence existed that prey might maintain high numbers long after predator control, nor is it known whether they might exceed the land's carrying capacity. In any case, it would be difficult or impossible to keep constantly fluctuating populations of moose or caribou at stable levels to fulfill user expectations. The NRC recommended that more complete data be collected on habitat, predators, prey, and alternative control methods; that management and research be integrated; that programs be designed to more effectively evaluate outcomes; and that ADF&G coordinate its studies with other agencies affecting wildlife policy.[98]

The NRC concluded that Alaskan predator control programs had not been based on relevant economic and social information, and that the public had not been sufficiently involved in policymaking and implementation. It recommended more baseline research and the application of modern cost-benefit calculation methods to measure the values of hunters, Natives, viewers, passive users (those valuing the existence of predators without seeing them), and others interested in both predators and prey. The public, it suggested, should participate in all phases of policymaking, and the process should be somewhat more decentralized in order to fit the needs and make use of the knowledge of rural citizens. A permanent conflict resolution process should deal with disputes such as those marking past predator control programs. The state should develop a long-range plan for wildlife management, cooperating with Natives and federal agencies holding land in Alaska.[99]

The NRC advised that an effective model for considering a predator control program would include (1) clarification of goals: e.g., to preserve an ungulate herd, to satisfy subsistence needs, to provide recreational hunting or viewing, etc.; (2) quantification of cost versus benefits; (3) study of predator and prey population history and current trends, movements, habitat condition, predator-prey-habitat interaction, and ecological side-effects of control; (4) consideration of alternatives such as habitat manipulation by fire, diversionary feeding, sterilization, or various methods of removal; and (5) adequate monitoring of results.[100]

The NRC team recognized that Alaska posed a number of barriers to rational predator-prey policy, including the patchwork pattern of land ownership, the intense emotions of pro and con contestants, and political pressures from the legislature. Yet the team believed that if interest groups perceived a fair process, they would be less likely to attack it through lawsuits, tourism boycotts, and other disruptive means. The team acknowledged that properly conducted predator control, by means acceptable to the public, would be more expensive than previous programs.[101]

Environmental values related to predator control during the statehood period have, generally and belatedly, illustrated the national shifts in values. Predators, especially bears and wolves, have won the appreciation of the public. Correspondingly, nonconsumptive uses of wildlife including viewing and existence valuing have grown in recognition and practice. Environmental organizations, many advocating animal rights or specifically protective of the wolf, have become more numerous and active. Interest groups have increasingly resorted to the courts and communications media, and have demanded greater participation in the wildlife management decisionmaking process.

Alaskan wildlife managers have responded to the value shifts by gradually widening the scope of research toward a more ecological perspective, though limited by resistance from the legislature and by the traditional focus on species accounts. Alaska has a modest nongame wildlife program and bear-viewing sites, but no such arrangement for wolves. The "Wolf Summit" and Wolf Management Planning Team temporarily involved the public, but predator-prey policy remains hunter-dominated.

Recommendations of the NRC team would, if adopted, advance ecologically viable wildlife management through wider public participation, broader-based research, and more realistic means of calculating nonconsumptive values of wildlife. But no study or scientific process could remove the emotions from the wolf control issue and, as the NRC team pointed out, science could not fully resolve the value questions. The controversy extended well beyond how to maintain a stable number of animals. It embraced complex questions of predator-prey-habitat relationships and of ethical-political aspects of "game farming" versus maintenance of more natural conditions. In the political realm, it demonstrated the politically loaded nature of equitable representation of interested groups in management policy.

Long-term trends toward environmental values promised to eventually change predator management in Alaska, notwithstanding the entrenched conservatism of the legislature and hunting-trapping interests. Economics, in the form of rapidly rising tourism and the gradual abatement of hunting and trapping, would play a part. So would modern communications media, poised to broadcast nationwide any perceived abuse of wildlife species. Curbs on the use of aircraft would likely be followed by restrictions on such devices as snares and snowmobiles in hunting wolves or bears. Advancing research would expand awareness of ecosystem complexity and introduce more caution into management processes. Yet the intricacy of its biological and ethical aspects, and the intensity of the feelings of the many participants, permitted little chance of early resolution of the differences over how, or whether, wolves should be managed.

NOTES

1. Rausch, "Progress in Management," 43.
2. Peterson and Woolington, "The Apparent Extirpation," 338–342.
3. Sherwood, *Big Game in Alaska*, 88.
4. Gabrielson et al., "Wildlife Resources," 86–90.
5. McKnight, *History of Predator Control*, 4–8; Laycock, "Alaska's Wildlife," 84.
6. Lensink, "Predator Control," 95–99.
7. *Alaska Conservation Society (ACS) News Bulletin*, August 1960, 5–7; January 1961, 4; May 1961, 9–10.
8. Robert B. Weeden, interview by author, August 15, 1989.
9. *ACS News Bulletin*, May 1965, 5; *Alaska Session Laws, 1965*, SR 13.
10. Van Ballenberghe, "Forty Years of Wolf Management," 562–563.
11. Laycock, "Alaska's Wildlife," 81–82.
12. Van Ballenberghe, "Forty Years of Wolf Management," 562.
13. Fortier, "Year of the Wolf," 7–9.
14. C. Hunter, "Big Wolf Witch Hunt," 16.
15. McKnight, *History of Predator Control*, 8–9.
16. L. Thomas, "Giant State," 33.
17. *New York Times*, March 20, 1968, 30; *ACR*, Summer 1968, 11; *Alaska Session Laws, 1968*, Chapters 81, 113.
18. McKnight, *History of Predator Control*, 9–10; Harper, "Wolf Management," 27.
19. *New York Times*, December 28, 1969, 34; Donald E. McKnight, interview by author, March 9, 1988. According to Booton Herndon, *The Great Land*, 183–185, a camera crew had hired bush pilot Howard J. Knutson to do a kill for "Wolf Men" and asked him to raise a bloody knife to his lips "as a joke," implying it would not be shown. Knutson claimed to be personally opposed to bounty hunting and aerial wolf hunting.
20. McKnight, *History of Predator Control*, 9.
21. Rearden, "An End to Poisoning?" 13; Trefethen, *An American Crusade*, 285–288; Richard Nixon, *Executive Order No. 11643*, February 8, 1972, *CIS Presidential Executive Orders*, Microfiche, Washington, DC: GPO; 86 Stat. 905, October 18, 1972.

22. J. Mitchell, "Fear and Loathing," 31.

23. Alaska Dept. of Fish and Game (ADF&G), *Alaska Game Management Policies*, 37–39.

24. Gasaway et al., *Interrelationships of Wolves,* 1, 16.

25. J. Mitchell, "Fear and Loathing," 28–34; Rearden, "Wolves, Moose, Airplanes and Man," 30–31.

26. Harbo and Dean, "Historical and Current Perspectives," 56–57.

27. *New York Times*, March 24, 1975, 30; February 23, 1975, IV, 12; article by Jim Hunter, *Sierra Club Alaska Newsletter*, 11.

28. *New York Times*, March 5, 1975, 78; January 16, 1977, 33; J. Mitchell, "Fear and Loathing," 35; Tileston, "Temporary Restraining Order," 2; Harbo and Dean, "Historical and Current Perspectives," 57–58.

29. *ACR*, Spring 1975, 10; *ACR*, "ACS Policy on Wolf Management," 8–9.

30. J. Mitchell, "Fear and Loathing," 36–39: The resolution did not pass.

31. Gasaway et al., *Interrelationships of Wolves*, 1, 30–31.

32. Ballard, "Case of the Disappearing Moose," I, 24; II, 36–39; III, 40–42.

33. *Alaska*, "Alaska Sportsman," August 1986, 58.

34. Haber, "Eight Years of Wolf Research," II, 50; Ballard, "Case of the Disappearing Moose," II, 42.

35. Mech, *The Wolf*, 194–195, 264–271; M. Fox, *The Wild Canids*, 283–284; Mech, "How Delicate," 83; Gasaway et al., *Interrelationships of Wolves*, 1, 46; ADF&G, "Wolf Management Programs," 1–4.

36. Wood, "Where Have All the Caribou Gone?" 6–7; Greiner, "Tomorrow Came Too Soon," 4–6; Rearden, "The Arctic Caribou Herd," 4–6. Subsequent review cast doubt on the certainty of caribou herd counts and causes for decline (Flanders, "Native American Sovereignty," 442–444).

37. Rearden, "The Arctic Caribou Herd," 4, 76; *Alaska*, "Alaska Sportsman," May 1977, 68; November 1977, 28; Wood, "Where Have All the Caribou Gone?" 6; J. Mitchell, "Where Have All the Tuttu Gone?" 13.

38. *Sierra Club Alaska Newsletter*, June 1977, 6.

39. Weeden, "ACS and Western Arctic," 6.

40. Klein, "Caribou: Alaska's Nomads," 202; D. Miller, *Midnight Wilderness*, 46–47.

41. ADF&G, "Wolf Management Programs," 8–9, Appendix 3; Harbo and Dean, "Historical and Current Perspectives," 60–63.

42. Gasaway et al., *Role of Predation in Limiting Moose*, 6, 7, 50.

43. Stephenson et al., "Wolf Biology," 24.

44. Mlot, "Wolf Hunts Resume," 279.

45. *Center News*, October/November 1983, 5; Kabisch, "ADF&G vs. Wolves," 7.

46. Stephenson et al., "Wolf Biology," 25–27.

47. *Science News*, "FCC Stops Wolf Hunt," 57; *AWA Newsletter*, March-April 1985, 1; March-April 1986, 1; January-February 1987, 1–2.

48. Stephenson et al., "Wolf Biology," 24, 29–30.

49. *New York Times*, March 1, 1987, 26; *AWA Newsletter*, March-April-May 1987, 1.

50. *New York Times*, March 1, 1987, 26; *AWA Newsletter*, March-April-May 1987, 2.

51. W. Hall, "Kenai National Wildlife Refuge," 3; *AWA Newsletter*, January-February 1984, 4; *AWA Newsletter*, "Kenai Wolf Louse Update," 4–5.

52. Warren B. Ballard, interview by author, August 12, 1992.

53. Philip S. Koehl, letter to author, June 12, 1994.

54. *AWA Newsletter*, January-February 1990, 1–2.

55. Stephenson et al., "Wolf Biology," 19.

56. *AWA Newsletter*, January-February 1990, 6.

57. Laycock, "How to Kill a Wolf," 48; *Anchorage Daily News*, July 31, 1991, B1.

58. Stephenson et al., "Wolf Biology," 32–35; Landry, "Wolves Lose," 11; *AWA Newsletter*, September-November 1989, 1; *Alaska Report*, March 1990, 8; Lowry, "Ballot Measure," 1.

59. Ballard, "Bear Predation on Moose," 10, 17.

60. Haggstrom et al., "Citizen Participation," 105.

61. *The Spirit*, "ADF&G Appointed Citizen Planning Team," 1–2.

62. Haggstrom et al., "Citizen Participation," 5–12; National Research Council, *Wolves, Bears and Their Prey*, 17–18.

63. Van den Berg, "Center Condemns Wolf Control," 3.

64. Haggstrom et al., "Citizen Participation," 12–13, 15–20.

65. *Los Angeles Times*, February 25, 1993, A5.

66. T. Williams, "Alaska's War on the Wolves," 44.

67. *Los Angeles Times*, June 15, 1993, C1.

68. Dittman Research Corp., *Survey Among Alaska Residents*, 1–6, unpaginated tables.

69. *Fairbanks Daily News-Miner*, January 18, 1993.

70. S. Miller and McCollum, *Alaska Voters*, table A-33. The question was, "I support killing wolves in some areas of Alaska to increase the numbers of moose and caribou."

71. Haggstrom et al., "Citizen Participation," 14–15.

72. *Fairbanks Daily News-Miner*, January 17, 1993.

73. Ibid., Jan 18, 1993.

74. T. Williams, "Alaska's War on the Wolves," 47.

75. *Fairbanks Daily News-Miner*, January 15-16, 1993, A1.

76. *Anchorage Times*, January 4, 1993.

77. *Fairbanks Daily News-Miner*, December 31, 1992.

78. *Christian Science Monitor*, February 25, 1993, 9.

79. *Los Angeles Times*, February 25, 1993, A5.

80. ADF&G, "Questions and Answers," 1–4.

81. *Anchorage Daily News*, July 2, 1993, B1.

82. *Fairbanks Daily News-Miner*, June 24, 1993, A1.

83. Wells, "Alaska Moves Ahead," 1, 7.

84. ADF&G, "Preliminary Results," 1–3; Ken Taylor, interview by author, August 30, 1994.

85. "TV Pictures Lead Alaska to Suspend Wolf Killing," *New York Times*, December 3, 1994, I8; Steve Reinhart, "Maverick Biologist Defends the Packs," *Anchorage Daily News*, December 11, 1994, A6.

86. "Letters," *Anchorage Daily News*, December 15, 1994.

87. Ibid.

88. *New York Times*, February 5, 1995, 29; *The Spirit*, "Always Cry Wolf," 3.

89. Lowry, "Fortymile Wolf Sterilization," 1, 4; Van den Berg, "An Improvement," 3, 5.

90. Kate Ripley, "Emotions Boil in Campaign Over Snaring Ballot Measure," *Fairbanks Daily News-Miner*, October 10, 1998; Ripley, "Natives Unite Against Proposed Wolf Snare Ban," *Fairbanks Daily News-Miner*, October 23, 1998; "Measure No. 9: Wolf Snaring Bites Both Ways," *Fairbanks Daily News-Miner*, October 17, 1998.

91. *The Spirit*, "Gunning for Predators," Fall 1999, 1, 4; Tom Mowry, "Game Board Allows Shooting of Wolves From Snowmobiles," *Fairbanks Daily News-Miner*, March 15, 2000, A1, 9.

92. Van Ballenberghe, "Forty Years of Wolf Management," 464–465.

93. W. Hall, "Alliance Helps Commission Wolf Research," 3, 6.

94. Reinhart, "Maverick Biologist," *Anchorage Daily News*, Dec 11, 1994, A6.

95. Boertje et al., "Increases in Moose, Caribou, and Wolves," 475, 487.

96. Haber, "Biological, Conservation and Ethical Implications," 1068–1075.

97. National Research Council (NRC), *Wolves, Bears and Their Prey*, 182–83, 189. NRC's 13-member Committee on Management of Wolf and Bear Populations in Alaska included three Alaskans: Patricia A. Corcoran, Alaska Native Science Commission; David Klein, University of Alaska; and George Yaska, Tanana Chiefs Conference.

98. Ibid., 183–188.

99. Ibid., 189–193.
100. Ibid., 128–129.
101. Ibid., 122, 140, 176–177.

6

Subsistence

Asked in a 1998 opinion poll to identify "the most important issue right now that you'd want your elected officials working on," 30 percent of Alaskans named subsistence—more than three times as many as for the runner-up, education.[1] Conflict over the subsistence use of natural resources, especially fish and game, had intensified since the 1970s. Every major environmental controversy in statehood Alaska embodied subsistence aspects, commonly involving rights to fish and game by Natives and non-Natives. Closely related to access disputes lay questions of jurisdiction over natural resources and rules of disposal. Outcomes of subsistence contests promised to be determining factors in the well-being of Native communities, as well as in the balance of power among state, federal, and private players. Environmental principles inhered in the disputes, and the integrity of the environment also depended in part on the outcomes.

SUBSISTENCE RULES

Roots of subsistence disputes extend back to prehistoric Native cultures and to the beginnings of visitation by outsiders. Aboriginal Alaska Natives lived as hunter-gatherers, engaging minimally, if at all, in agriculture. Early Europeans and Euro-Americans—whalers, fur traders, salmon fishers, explorers, miners, and settlers—also relied on wildlife, exhausting stocks of some species. In the first decades of the twentieth century, the federal government took steps to control the exploitation of wildlife. Several Alaska game laws and migratory bird treaties contained subsistence provisions, and subsistence guarantees for both Natives and non-Natives became confirmed in law and tradition. Low human population levels during the territorial period enabled all parties, given moderate regulation, to sustainably consume fish, birds, and mammals.

Scholars debate whether the maintenance of nearly all wildlife stocks prior to Euro-American influence resulted from primitive technology, low Native populations, or conservation practices. In any case, Native subsistence customs, maintained in part to the present, often clashed with Euro-American methods of fish and game management. Lack of political power and clear legal standing by Native decisionmaking groups allowed Euro-American values to prevail in the form of statutes and regulations such as hunting and fishing seasons and bag limits. But the greater the Native majority and the more remote the village, the less likely that legislated rules would be honored in practice.[2]

6.1. Inupiat woman harvesting whitefish by gillnet set beneath the ice, Kobuk River, October 1966. By Ken Ross. Natives in several rural areas retained substantial reliance on natural resources for subsistence.

Although not conquered militarily, Alaska Natives lacked the means to assert control over natural resources until the 1960s. In the context of the civil rights movement, and catalyzed by the Project Chariot (Chapter 7) and waterfowl hunting (Chapter 3) crises, they organized for action through the Alaska Federation of Natives. Having become a political force enjoying national political support, they successfully pressed for ownership of lands, granted in the Alaska Native Claims Settlement Act (ANCSA) of 1971 (Chapter 13). ANCSA itself did not address the subsistence issue, but its conference committee report called on the secretary of the interior and State of Alaska to protect the subsistence rights of Natives.[3]

Surges of non-Native population spurred by oil activity turned up the pressure on wildlife. Following the crash of the western Arctic caribou herd in the mid-1970s, the Alaska Department of Fish and Game (ADF&G), responsible for managing wildlife on state, federal, and Native lands, gave preferential access to rural subsistence consumers of fish and game. A successful lawsuit by outdoor sporting groups declared the regulations in violation of the state's constitutional provision of equal access. The state legislature codified subsistence rights in the 1978 Subsistence Hunting and Fishing Act, but omitted the requirement of rural residence except in emergencies. The Alaska Federation of Natives lobbied Congress in pursuit of subsistence rights.[4]

In 1980 the Alaska National Interest Lands Conservation Act (ANILCA) recognized subsistence rights on federal lands, guaranteeing a priority for "nonwasteful subsistence uses" by rural residents in case of shortages of fish, mammals, waterfowl, timber, and other resources traditionally relied upon. Eligibility for subsistence use would depend on "(1) customary and direct dependence on the [wildlife] populations as the mainstay of livelihood, (2) local residency, and (3) the availability of alternate natural resources." The act defined subsistence use as "customary and traditional uses by rural Alaska residents of wild, renewable resources for direct personal or family consumption as food, shelter, fuel, clothing, tools, or transportation, for the making and selling of handicraft articles . . . for barter, or sharing for personal or family consumption, and for customary trade." These activities applied predominantly to Natives.[5] In addition to Native and state lands, Natives and some rural non-Native residents could hunt and fish on national wildlife refuges, national parks and preserves (except the pre-ANILCA segments of Denali, Glacier Bay, and Katmai), and other federal lands. The Marine Mammal Protection Act gave Natives exclusive hunting rights to polar bears, whales, walruses, seals, sea lions, and sea otters.

Differences over subsistence rights intensified in the 1980s. ANILCA gave the state management authority over fish and wildlife on federal lands provided the state legalize rural subsistence preference, but an attempt to pass state legislation fell short in 1981. The Boards of Fisheries and Game then incorporated rural preference into their regulations. Perceiving their share of fish and game to be at stake, urban and outdoor sporting interests introduced a ballot measure in 1982 to prohibit all wildlife access preferences; it went down by 42 to 58 percent. They took the Alaska Department of Fish and Game (ADF&G) to state court over its rural preference regulations, and won in 1985. A year later, the legislature passed a rural preference provision corresponding to ANILCA. Opponents challenged the law in federal court, winning decisions in 1989 and 1992 that declared rural residence preference a violation of the Alaska constitutional requirement of equal access to natural resources. An effort to amend the state constitution missed by one vote in a special 1990 legislative session. As a result, jurisdiction over subsistence use of wildlife on federal lands reverted to the federal government. ADF&G continued to manage fish and wildlife on state and Native lands, and federal agencies oversaw federal lands, employing regulations similar to those used by the state prior to 1990. A 1995 case extended federal responsibility to all navigable waters involving subsistence rights under ANILCA. Further attempts to amend the state constitution fell through, and the federal government took full control of its inland waters in October 1999.[6] Given the migratory nature of most fish, federal jurisdiction would probably apply to many waters on state and Native lands as well.

SUBSISTENCE PRACTICES

Natives—Eskimos, Aleuts, and Indians—comprised 16 percent of Alaska's population in the mid-1990s. About 93 percent lived in the 270 rural communities whose residents qualified for subsistence rights under federal law. Natives made up half the total of these communities. In northern and western regions, Natives constituted higher proportions of the population and pursued more of a subsistence lifestyle. Yup'ik Eskimos in the Yukon-Kuskokwim Delta, Inupiat in the Arctic and near the Seward Peninsula, and Athabaskans in the Yukon and Koyukuk River valleys relied heavily on food from the wild. All villages mingled sporting and subsistence activities in various degrees, depending on the region and resource.[7] Most research data did not distinguish between Native and non-Native subsis-

Table 6.1—Subsistence Harvests of Wild Foods, Alaska, Early 1990s

	Urban Areas (79% of 1990 pop.)	Rural Areas (21% of 1990 pop.)
Total annual harvest	9.8 million lbs.	43.7 million lbs.
Per capita annual harvest	22 lbs.	376 lbs.
Composition		
Fish	68%	59%
Land mammals	30%	20%
Marine Mammals	0%	14%
Shellfish	< 1%	2%
Birds	1%	2%
Plants	< 1%	2%

Annual per capita harvest by location			
Fairbanks/Delta	16 lbs.	Kodiak Island	276 lbs.
Anchorage	19 lbs.	Southwest/Aleutian	505 lbs.
Matanuska/Susitna	27 lbs.	Arctic	662 lbs.
Juneau	35 lbs.	Rural Interior	704 lbs.
Rural Southcentral	197 lbs.	Western	767 lbs.
Rural Southeast	248 lbs.		

Source: Robert J. Wolfe and Robert G. Bosworth, "Subsistence in Alaska: 1994 Update." Alaska Dept. of Fish and Game, Division of Subsistence (Juneau: March 1, 1994.)

tence harvests. Rural residents took a much greater total volume of wildlife, and in the 1990s consumed an annual average of 376 pounds of wild foods as compared to 22 pounds for urban residents (Table 6.1).

Harvesting of inland fish and wildlife threatened, eventually, to reach a saturation point. Richard Cooley observed that the dispute over access to wildlife could become "one of the most divisive in Alaska's history" and could jeopardize the future of wildlife populations:

> Beyond the racial, cultural, and rural overtones of the controversy lies a basic physical fact: the controlling element is the very low biotic carrying capacity of much of the land and interior waters of the state. . . . [T]here are not enough big game animals to meet the expectations of either today's growing urban population of sport hunters, or those of an enlarged, cash-holding Native population with rifles, motorboats, and snow machines— much less the expectations of both groups.[8]

Cooley might have added that mounting numbers of tourists, photographers, and other nonconsumptive users would also lay claim to the animals.

In the view of some observers, changes in Native life lessened the vulnerability of wildlife stocks. School, sports, television, and other cultural influences effected a shift in values and behavior. Youths devoted less time to hunting, fishing, and trapping skills, and the economy progressively shifted to a monetary basis. Cash made it possible to import more agricultural food, and lack of interest in trapping reduced activity except near the towns. But many Natives valued their ties to the land, and a rapidly rising rural population employing modern implements and priority subsistence-use rights embodied a potential for environ-mental harm.[9]

In some cases, Natives undermined their subsistence benefits through the behavior of their village or regional corporations, intended to make profits according to the vision of ANCSA. Corporations in the Southeast selected land covered by the largest old-growth trees, and logged them with virtually no concern for the environment. In doing so, they diminished wildlife resources important to the material and spiritual sustenance of both Native and non-Native villagers. Inexperienced in business, several corporations lost money on the ventures. Most of the shareholders and nearly all the leaders lived in urban areas; hence they overrode the wishes of the more traditional villagers to avoid logging in their backyards. Rather than selecting nearby land for preservation, Hoonah's village corpora-tion chose and logged part of faraway Prince of Wales Island, while other Native corpora-tions and Forest Service clients logged prized wildlife habitat near Hoonah on Chichagof Island.[10]

Commercial or sport fishing and hunting impinged on subsistence utilization of some resources, especially moose, caribou, and salmon. Growing urban populations generated more licenses and thus more regulations and enforcement of game laws, gradually constrain-ing local subsistence use. To participate in the Euro-American–dominated legal and admin-istrative systems, Natives formed political organizations at the local, regional, state, and international levels. Mainly through lawsuits, they won some concessions to local resource needs. In several regions (e.g., the Yukon-Kuskokwim Delta), cooperative wildlife manage-ment systems controlled harvest of game mammals or birds. Such arrangements were modest in scope; they tended to be species-specific rather than ecosystem-oriented, and applied only to a small fraction of disputed resources. Yet they combined the viability of local knowledge and needs with the scientific expertise, conservation interests, and consumption claims of wider state and national communities.[11]

DIMENSIONS OF SUBSISTENCE

Legal and legislative struggles revolved around several questions: (1) Who should have subsistence rights? Natives only, rural residents only, those in need, those customarily living off the land, or everyone? How would those eligible be identified? (2) What applica-tions should qualify as subsistence? Food and clothing only, limited cash commerce, cul-tural affirmation, recreation, any and all uses by those eligible? (3) What methods of harvest should be allowed; e.g., what weapons and transportation vehicles? (4) How should fish and wildlife be managed for subsistence? Seasons and bag limits, or customary practices? (4) Who should control subsistence resources on Native, state, and federal lands, and by what procedures should regulations be set?

The multifaceted character of the subsistence matter rendered it difficult to solve. Defin-ing the term itself proved contentious; each variation carried implications for who would get what benefits or restrictions. ANILCA did not clearly spell out what it meant by "customary" and "traditional" purposes. In practice, various groups and individuals spent different amounts of time in rural areas, engaged in a wide variety of activities. Some had lived in rural areas all their lives, others for a few months or years. People differed in their reliance on local natural

6.2. Inupiat wolf hunter, Brooks Range, April 1995. By Ken Ross. A wolf pelt could sell for $500 or more. Controversy over subsistence rights involved wolves as well as moose, caribou, and fish.

resources, either by preference or necessity. Some hunted and fished frequently, others seldom. Of the hunters and fishers, some shared their harvests. Some reportedly wasted wildlife, others practiced conservation. Some relied on modern technology including aircraft, others more modest means. Some maintained a substantial cash flow, others not. Some appeared to take wildlife primarily for food, some for cash, others for cultural identity, and yet others for recreation. Moreover, changes in population, economics, and technology continually altered the behavior patterns of groups and individuals. Who then should qualify for preferential subsistence rights? How could status be proved and rules enforced? Wherever the lines might be drawn, a disinterested observer could readily identify parties who appeared to be granted too much or too little.

A central aspect of the controversy had to do with cultural differences. Natives traditionally, and to some extent through the 1990s, valued natural-resource use as integral to their identity and way of life. Gathering, distribution, processing, and consumption of wild goods gave them a sense of well-being and invigorated their communities. Many viewed a Natives-only subsistence preference as fair and proper. An August 1997 "subsistence summit" attended by 900 Alaska Natives called for "recognition that subsistence is a basic indigenous right," "co-management with equal state, federal, and tribal involvement," and "a subsistence priority based on Alaska Native, community, religious/spiritual, nutritional, medicinal, and cultural practices rather than an individualized or needs-based system."[12] In

6.3. Caribou hunters, Nelchina district, August 1990. By Kim Behrens. Courtesy Alaska Wildlife Alliance. A three-day "subsistence" hunt in the district drew several thousand urban and rural hunters. Highly mechanized hunting practices called into question notions of both "subsistence" and "sport" hunting.

essence, they wanted exclusive and permanent subsistence rights, and a near-veto over management of subsistence resources.

Euro-Americans, by contrast, tended to approach natural resource management from an individual rather than a communal perspective. They perceived appropriation of resources as more of a material or recreational than a social or cultural benefit. Sport hunters, sport fishers, guides, and many urban residents interpreted their own activities as the legitimate pursuit of recreational or economic values. They perceived much hunting and fishing by Natives as sporting behavior comparable to their own, thus not deserving preferential status. They contended that hunting expeditions (by power boat, aircraft, etc.) that cost more than the value of the harvest should not be termed "subsistence" activity. Many believed Natives to be assimilating into modern culture, making claims of reliance on the land less true or relevant. Debaters often talked past one another. Even if they did not, some questions inherently arose: How could the relative merits of material, spiritual, social, or recreational values be weighed? How could it be proved what values a group or individual derived from natural-resource use? Would it be rational or fair to assign exclusive rights to a group based on race or residence, and if not, how could special needs be met? At what point, if any, should modernization invalidate preferential subsistence rights?

Anthropologists, sociologists, subsistence agency officials, and many environmentalists generally accepted the Natives' argument and subscribed to a Native subsistence preference, or at minimum a rural preference designed to assist Natives. Outdoor sporting groups, guides, and many urban Alaskans rejected even a rural preference, which could reduce their portions of fish and game. Large numbers of people, including many environmentalists and the vast majority of rural residents, wanted a rural preference.

Questions of who should manage subsistence resources, and how, added to the definitional aspects. State officials desired to control fish and wildlife within their borders. The legislature and Boards of Game and Fisheries strongly reflected the will of outdoor sporting interests, commercial fisheries, and urban residents. By tradition, ADF&G regulated by seasons and individual bag limits, and made moderate efforts to involve rural residents in cooperative management. Following the court decisions declaring its rural preference unconstitutional, the state tried to conserve fish stocks by establishing subsistence fisheries, an approach that worked fairly well because subsistence fishing could normally be distinguished from commercial operations by the types of gear employed. Considering that large numbers of Alaskans now qualified for subsistence hunting on state lands, the Board of Game sought to protect mammals and maintain rural subsistence benefits by tightening seasons and bag limits, and setting up special subsistence hunts. Urban participants increasingly dominated advisory proceedings, criticized the subsistence hunts, and promoted decisions and regulations that restricted hunting by rural residents.[13]

By contrast, the federal government, given responsibility for Native affairs and implementing ANILCA, leaned toward generous rules and cooperative management involving Natives. After assuming subsistence responsibility for federal lands in 1990, under ANILCA guidelines, it established an interagency Federal Subsistence Board, and regional advisory councils staffed by coordinators, biologists, and anthropologists. The councils included well-known and experienced Native leaders. ANILCA had directed the secretary of the interior to override an advisory council recommendation only if "not supported by sufficient evidence, [it] violates recognized principles of fish and wildlife conservation, or would be detrimental to the satisfaction of subsistence needs." During the first five years of operation, the board accepted 90 percent of council recommendations.[14]

The subsistence question, then, bore a number of dimensions: (1) a fight over resources, principally among Natives, rural non-Natives, and urban non-Natives; (2) a cultural disagreement, largely between communal and individual orientations; (3) a management challenge, involving many options for monitoring and enforcement; (4) a conceptual problem, of defining subsistence use; (5) a justice issue, of determining eligibility; and therefore (6) a political challenge, of how to achieve a mutually agreeable resolution.[15]

OPTIONS FOR RESOLUTION

At the turn of the century, participants discussed possible solutions to the subsistence question: (1) a Natives-only preference; (2) "Natives plus" (all Natives, plus non-Natives meeting specified criteria); (3) individualized eligibility only; (4) rural residence plus customary need, as per ANILCA; (5) all residents of designated rural areas; and (6) dual management, by state and federal governments on their respective lands. "Natives-only" and "Natives plus" would probably be rejected in Alaska and likely in Washington as well, in part because of reluctance to revisit the sensitive compromises written into ANILCA. Individual eligibility would be exceedingly difficult to prove and enforce. Amendment of the state constitution for rural preference might still come to pass. Eligibility by area only might be politically impossible to achieve. In the interim, dual management, though not preferred by either the state or the Clinton administration, might prove workable. It could be expected to involve local populations in management, but it complicated the already problematic nature of management in a maze of jurisdictional areas.[16]

Some Natives demanded "sovereignty," or full self-government for tribal areas, which would mean complete control of wildlife and other natural resources on tribal lands. Several major barriers made sovereignty unlikely. Opposition from state and federal officials and numerous interest groups kept legislation from Congress. Federal courts did not mandate sovereignty. Full governance of a possible 200 or more tribal units could be prohibitively costly and burdensome. Jurisdiction over ecosystems would be further fragmented, frustrating sustainable management. And Natives could fulfill subsistence needs more easily through other means.[17]

Various forms of cooperation appeared to be a trend in fish and wildlife policy. Some, exemplified by bowhead whale management, strengthened both wildlife conservation and Native culture. For other areas and resources, a more complete form of local involvement might work. Athabaskans on the Koyukuk River traditionally practiced a form of regulation in salmon fishing that had the effect of sustainability. They continued the conservative practices into the 1980s, enforcing taboos against waste of fish stocks. They differentiated between the subsistence fishery, employing gillnets, and the fish wheel–based commercial industry, in which they also engaged. Overfishing by commercial interests earlier in the century had given rise to regulations encompassing both fisheries. To the extent that the two operations could be separated, local control of subsistence fishing might reap multiple benefits of resource sustainability and maintenance of indigenous culture.[18]

Yup'ik educator A. Oscar Kawagley proposed a supplementary means of alleviating both the problems of carrying capacity and enhancement of Native culture. He suggested that modern science be combined with traditional Native ecological perspectives in the classroom. The result could be a renewed faith in indigenous belief systems and a move toward "soft technology"—styles of living less dependent on cash and outside control, and designed to sustain the environment. More broadly, he believed that a holistic view incorporating the best of both cultures is "necessitated by a deteriorating world situation."[19]

Some elements of modern environmentalism have attended the subsistence controversy. Many phases, from legislation to regulation to litigation, involved public participation. Social science helped document and interpret Native subsistence patterns. Biological science undergirded rules of management, whether cooperative or not, and the complexity of the issue pushed policymakers in the direction of a more holistic, interdisciplinary approach. Economic and social sustainability of Native cultures received high attention, and resource sustainability remained an explicit goal regardless of eligibility decisions.

Resolution has been difficult in part because neither exploitation nor sustainability values clearly imply which groups should have what rights to which resources. To the extent that Natives or rural residents are traditionally or continually reliant on a resource, fairness has suggested that a sustainable supply be available to them. As Natives and other rural residents have become more cash-wealthy and modernized, especially if increasing natural-resource consumption is needed to maintain the cash flow, the fairness claims have lost some of their strength. If rural residents voluntarily continue to increase their populations and their consumption of local resources, they will put resource stocks at risk and magnify the question of fairness to the other claimants being progressively excluded. They will also contribute to their own impoverishment and undermine the identity and self-esteem many Natives and some others derive from subsistence ties to the land.

Consumptive-use rights have dominated the discussion of subsistence; accordingly, Natives and non-Native hunters and fishers have been the main contestants. Tourism interests and other nonconsumptive users have not yet been significantly involved. Their concern is likely to emerge as tourism grows, distances shrink, and species populations are diminished. Environmentalists have displayed ambivalence. While normally emphasizing nonconsumptive treatment of wildlife, many have endorsed some form of Native subsistence rights. But others see a potential for abuse by Natives as well as other groups; e.g., they dislike hunting in wildlife refuges and national park preserves, especially when done by snowmobile or aircraft. Some dislike sport hunting, whether by Natives or non-Natives. Many object to the environmentally destructive ventures of some Native corporations. Some have been concerned about potential conflicts between subsistence use and biological sustainability, as in the case of geese and eiders on the Yukon-Kuskokwim Delta.

Governments, subject to an array of pressures, formulate and implement usage rules. They have attempted to achieve biological sustainability through cooperative management of single species in geographically limited areas. In such cases as bowhead whales and polar bears, both the wildlife populations and the subsistence traditions have been maintained. But statewide management of subsistence rights to widespread species such as moose, wolves, or bears poses a more complex problem. Numerous jurisdictional boundaries further magnify the task, in addition to the many political obstacles. Research on species population trends and subsistence use of wildlife has assisted management. Yet greater knowledge, integrating the natural and social sciences, is needed to oversee multiple, interrelated, fluctuating, often mobile wildlife populations affected by increasing numbers of humans who appropriate them in various and contested ways.

NOTES

1. Ivan Moore Research, "Statewide Public Opinion," 2.

2. Wolfe, "Subsistence and Politics," 14–18.

3. Kancewick and Smith, "Subsistence in Alaska," 655, 658–662.

4. Berman, "Renewable Resources," 127; Flanders, "Native American Sovereignty," 439; *Alaska Session Laws, 1978*, Ch. 151.

5. Kancewick and Smith, "Subsistence in Alaska," 655, 658–662; 94 Stat. 2371, December 2, 1980, Sec. 803-4.

6. Thornton, "Subsistence," 207–210; Caulfield, "Alaska's Subsistence Management Regimes," 26–31; Kancewick and Smith, "Subsistence in Alaska," 662–664, 671–674; *McDowell v. Alaska* 785 P. 2d. 1 (Alaska 1989); *State v. Morry*, 836 P. 2d 358 (Alaska 1992).

7. ADF&G, "Subsistence in Alaska: 1998 Update," 1–4.

8. Cooley, "Evolution of Alaska Land Policy," 42.

9. Author interviews of James W. Brooks, June 30, 1988; Chuck Kleeschulte, June 27, 1988; Herbert R. Melchior and Robert B. Weeden, July 12, 1988.

10. Durbin, *Tongass*, 294–301.

11. Wolfe, "Subsistence and Politics," 16, 19–23, 25–26.

12. Alaska Natives Commission, *Final Report: Vol. III*, 40–42; Worl, "Competition, Confrontation, and Compromise," 78.

13. Behnke, *How Alaska's Subsistence Law Is Working*, 5–16.

14. Brelsford, "A Meaningful Voice," 72; 93 Stat 2371, December 2, 1980, Sec. 805.

15. Schneider, "Subsistence in Alaska," discusses dimensions of the issue.

16. Thornton, "Subsistence," 216–219.

17. Flanders, "Native American Sovereignty," 441, 446, advocates comanagement as the preferred option.

18. Wheeler, "State and Indigenous Fisheries Management," 38–44.

19. Kawagley, *Yupiaq Worldview*, 105–107, 122–123, 132–133, 136–139.

PART II

Use of the Land

*S*tatehood thrust forward the question of what would happen to Alaska's far-flung lands. Which should be owned by the U.S. government, the state, the Natives, or private individuals, and under what rules of use? Land decisions would in large measure shape the future of Alaska's mammals, fish, birds, forests, waters, scenery, and wilderness. Alaskan public opinion, though by no means the controlling element, would be very influential in the direction of these decisions. In the absence of greater support for environmental values, forces of exploitation would prevail. Alaska could go the way of the Lower 48, its vast realms of wilderness vanished forever.

And which interest groups would steer the land disposal process? Mining, an extractive industry exerting powerfully negative impacts on environmental quality, enjoyed a prominent position in Alaskan public opinion and politics, as well as clout in Washington. Beginning in the 1950s, logging and oil gained equal or greater power in Alaskan affairs. Sport hunters held firm standing in Alaska, but environmentalists were scarce and poorly organized. If an "environmental" organization is defined as a private group whose dominant concern is protection of natural resources, no such statewide nor any influential local body existed in Alaska before statehood. The only effective statewide conservation group, the utilitarian conservationist Alaska Sportsmen's Council, originated in 1954.

Alaska reflected the conservative and growth-oriented era of the 1950s that diverted the nation's attention from conservation concerns. At the same time, appreciation for nature and outdoor recreation found expression in acquisition of national parklands, and in the beginnings of resistance to environmentally injurious projects on public lands. Civil rights consciousness, another legacy of the 1950s, reached Alaska Natives by the early 1960s.

Excepting the Simeonof National Wildlife Refuge for sea otters named in 1958, no Alaskan federal land had been set aside between 1941 and statehood. Native claims remained unsettled, and state land selections would soon be made. A half-million square miles lay at stake; groups and conditions destined to make the choices had yet to be identified. Two land issues surfaced in the 1950s to form and test the competing elements. One, the proposed Arctic National Wildlife Range (ANWR), involved caribou, wilderness, and minerals. National environmental organizations, led by Olaus Murie's Wilderness Society, launched an effort culminating in the establishment of ANWR in 1960. An unresolved question of whether to allow oil drilling in the refuge (Chapter 16) simmered for another 40 years.

The second early issue, Project Chariot (Chapter 7), featured caribou, Eskimos, and nuclear bombs in a battle over appropriate use of land and technology. The ANWR and Chariot debates captured the interest and involvement of environmental activists in the Lower 48, few in number prior to the emergence of the environmental movement at the end of the 1960s. Chariot furthered the national shift toward environmental values. ANWR and Chariot also gave birth to a pioneer Alaskan environmental organization, the Alaska

Conservation Society, that fostered others and laid the groundwork for a statewide environmental community.

Like Project Chariot, the Amchitka controversy (Chapter 8) started as a government attempt to find a location for a questionable project, and ended by helping to shape national environmentalism. Similarly, the Rampart Dam project (Chapter 9) mobilized conservationists on a national scale. More than a decade later, a proposed Susitna Dam (Chapter 10) echoed Rampart by stimulating action among environmental defenders and yielding them another victory.

Development fever reached a new peak following the late 1967 discovery of oil at Prudhoe Bay. Impending construction of the oil pipeline (Chapter 11) attracted fortune seekers to Alaska early in the 1970s. Oil companies urged settlement of Native claims so they could get on with their work. Identification of Native lands in turn awaited permanent decisions about which parts of Alaska would belong to the state or nation. Accordingly, a mammoth land-status conflict (Chapter 13) ensued. Pipeline construction and the money flowing from oil leases and royalties fueled a strong push for additional resource exploitation. Zeal for profits dramatically displayed its shortcomings in the Exxon Valdez oil spill (Chapter 12). To augment the economy of the Southeast, the Forest Service executed its plans to log off much of the virgin Tongass rainforest (Chapter 15). Industrial activity placed heightened stress on wildlife and on the integrity of wilderness areas. In their role as counsels of restraint, environmentalists succeeded only in moderating the impacts.

Alaskan society itself changed in the boom period. Oil money expanded social services and increased material wealth, quickening the pace of life and raising the expectations of citizens. Traditional lifestyles of relative tranquillity and simplicity grew increasingly rare and difficult to sustain for both Natives and non-Natives. Disagreements over land and resources convertible to personal profit, and over subsistence rights to fish and wildlife, created tensions among ethnic groups and communities.

Environmentalists (Chapter 17) stepped up their activity in resource controversies. In the 1970s they emphasized the new social and technical concerns of political openness, social responsibility, and pollution control. They employed more aggressive political tactics, especially lawsuits, and a somewhat preservationist approach to wilderness and wildlife. Above all, they pushed for ecologically and economically sustainable use of resources. By contrast, conservationists, most prominently sport hunters and fishers, adopted a more utilitarian position on wilderness and wildlife, and often rejected the social agenda and tactics of the environmentalists. The difference in values caused Alaskan outdoor sporting groups to repudiate the leadership of the National Wildlife Federation and to counter the environmentalists on core aspects of the lands settlement. Alaskan and national environmental groups, despite some value disagreements, for the most part worked together. Economic boosters and their allies in the media and legislature attacked environmentalists as enemies of progress.

Federal biologists and other agents participated actively in Alaskan environmental issues. Many engaged in the effort to designate lands as national parks and wildlife refuges. A few openly cooperated with environmental groups; many others did so more covertly and in lesser degrees. Among the land management agencies, the National Park

Service and Fish and Wildlife Service lent the most support to environmental protection values. The Bureau of Land Management, sympathetic to the oil and mining interests, and the Forest Service, closely tied to the timber industry, characteristically stood against protective measures.

Alaska state government attitudes toward environmental values ranged from mildly tolerant to firmly negative. The state's environmentalists worked for the 1974 and 1978 elections of Governor Jay Hammond, whom they preferred to prodevelopment candidates William Egan, Walter Hickel, and Keith Miller. Beset by the insistent demands for growth strongly registered in the legislature, Hammond chose a moderately prodevelopment stance on the lands issue. Otherwise the administration looked favorably on environmental protection. Alaska Department of Fish and Game (ADF&G) biologists vitally influenced the lands legislation by working for a conservative prohunting position regarding parks and wildlife refuges. Individually, some state officials subscribed to a protectionist agenda.

To effectively engage the oil, timber, and lands issues, environmentalists intensified and coordinated their efforts. The 1969 National Environmental Policy Act lent them a potent weapon: lawsuits to demand adequate environmental impact statements as means to relevant information and government accountability. Alaska became a battleground and a test site for environmental law. Fears of interruption of the Mideast oil supply, culminating in the OPEC embargo, helped precipitate an oil boom that both overwhelmed the resources of the environmentalists and drove their movement toward maturity. A sympathetic Carter administration (1977–1981) gave Alaskan environmentalists some relief from the oil-connected, proindustry policies of Presidents Nixon and Ford.

The Alaska National Interest Lands Conservation Act (ANILCA) in 1980 climaxed the exhaustive contest for formal ownership of large land tracts in Alaska. In doing so, it triggered less-intensive but crucial encounters over rules for management of federal lands (Chapter 14), and over the selection and disposal of state and Native lands. Exploitation and sustainability advocates each realized part of what they sought. As memories of the ANILCA and pipeline controversies faded, the public showed less antagonism toward environmental protection.

Politics of the 1980s changed working conditions for environmentalists. Reversing a slack period of the mid to late 1970s, national popular approval of environmentalism experienced a second surge. Alaska offices of national environmental organizations, more numerous and active, nonetheless allowed the state groups to take the lead on some issues. Divisions arose among economic interests, typically arraying tourist-oriented and subsistence users against large commercial resource extractors. State environmental groups could therefore join broader, if temporary, coalitions for the pursuit of legislation and administrative and legal decisions.

Forces of resource exploitation predominated in Alaska during the first half of the 1980s. Oil revenues boosted state spending, encouraged subsidized investment, and invited immigration. Interest groups multiplied, intensifying demands on state government and deepening dependency on government and oil money. Then state income suffered a reversal from falling world oil prices, precipitating a recession in the second half of the decade. No gas pipeline or similar project materialized to perpetuate growth, and the *population temporarily underwent one of the few declines in its history. Harder times induced legislative backing for economically unsustainable resource development, such as concessions to loggers and miners on state land. At the same time, lack of funds helped spell doom for grandiose projects.*

Counterbalancing some emigration during the recession, Alaska's population grew at one of the highest rates in the nation during the 1980s. Television and other modernizing influences hastened the transition from subsistence to product-consumption economies, and aggravated social stresses in rural villages. Tourism shot upward and high gold prices engendered a revival of mining. Oil drilling, commercial fishing, and timbering intensified the strain on Arctic, ocean, and rainforest ecosystems. Cumulatively, these trends eroded wilderness values and gave environmentalists and wildlife managers far more work than they could handle.

At the national level, environmental values met powerful hostility in the 1981–1989 Reagan years. Backed by Alaska's congressional delegation and in most cases its legislature, Reagan appointees employed means of dubious legality to maximize acquisition of Alaskan resources by mining, timber, and especially oil interests. Federal officials amenable to environmental protection felt constrained to keep a low profile. Bush administration (1989–1993) policies did not change much from those of Reagan. Both strove for deregulation and other cutbacks in environmental safeguards, and sought to bypass protective legislation through administrative means. Consequently, environmentalists resorted to lawsuits much more frequently than during the 1970s. Their tenacious efforts, often finding sympathy in Congress, held in check many moves of the Republican administrations. Clinton (1993–2001) policies tended to lighten the load of the environmentalists if not openly sanction their agenda, but could make only modest headway against a Republican-controlled Congress.

In the state government, Governors Bill Sheffield (for half his 1982–1986 term) and Steve Cowper (1986–1990) responded moderately to environmental appeals. The legislature exhibited a cool but not hostile attitude toward environmentalists, and gained respect for their increasing ability to form alliances and stop legislation they opposed. A variety of conservation measures emerged. ADF&G became less openly protective of the environment, reacting to the more conservative atmosphere and the growing capacity of environmentalists to carry the fight on issues with which ADF&G officers sympathized. The Department of Environmental Conservation remained relatively weak and underfunded, and the Department of Natural Resources functioned as an effective arm of the business community. Upon the inauguration of Governor Walter Hickel in 1990 and a rigidly conservative legislature shortly thereafter, state resource policies turned back a quarter-century to aggressive attempts to cut forests, promote mining and oil drilling, and drive roads into wilderness. Governor Tony Knowles, elected in 1994 and again in 1998, displayed far more acceptance of environmental values, but the legislature maintained stoutly exploitative attitudes.

Paralleling the national trend, Alaska's environmental community progressed in numbers, organization, and sophistication after 1980. Numerous units sprang up to tackle local problems or to specialize—in air and water quality, toxics, recycling, energy, envi-

ronmental education, historic preservation, coastal study, birds, or bears. Advancing technology and demands on resources forced both wildlife managers and environmentalists to broaden their frames of reference in ecological, cultural, and economic dimensions. Government, especially national agencies, by the 1990s became more accountable to the public in its use of resources, conceding greater access to information on environmental and social impacts. Resource management increasingly involved users and other interested groups in advisory and regulatory roles. Ocean research and management necessitated ever closer consultation among Pacific nations, and for the Arctic, European nations as well. Environmentalists moved to develop strategy and encourage planning on the basis of ecosystems—Arctic, ocean, and rainforest.

By 2000, Alaska's environmental glass stood half full; extractive industry and growing population continued to tear at the fabric of ecosystems, but much had been sheltered in the form of parklands. Rules of land use had tightened to curb some of the more destructive practices. Low gold prices slowed mining activity, and the gradual fall-off of oil revenues forced the state to begin reining in expenditures. Tourism continued to escalate, adding to the pressure on wilderness quality yet affirming the nation's interest in natural areas. National government commitment to environmental values ebbed and flowed, and industry showed faint signs of cooperation with environmentalists. Patterns of resource use had edged toward the goals of ecological and economic sustainability. As national and international awareness of environmental problems broadened, Alaska continued to attract the nation's attention and serve as its prime ecological preserve.

7

Ancient Village, Modern Bomb: Project Chariot

Alaska's pioneer environmental organization, the Alaska Conservation Society, formed in 1960 to work for the Arctic National Wildlife Range, soon found itself amid a nuclear controversy. Unbeknownst to any of its early participants, the so-called Chariot episode would trigger far-reaching changes in the environmental and Native-rights movements both in Alaska and nationwide.

Project Chariot originated in the Lawrence Radiation Laboratory (LRL) of the Atomic Energy Commission (AEC), which had been assigned to conduct underground nuclear explosions. Beginning in February 1957, LRL administrators promoted industrial applications of nuclear explosives, as momentum gathered toward peace talks that might put an end to nuclear weapons testing. In June, the AEC, much of whose technical work went to LRL, approved Operation Plowshare, part of an effort to find nonmilitary purposes for nuclear explosives, authorized by the Atomic Energy Act of 1954. The AEC and LRL planned to explore such possibilities as excavation of harbors and canals, most prominently a sea-level Panama Canal. Scientists feared property damage from blasts larger than one megaton in the Nevada test range. Looking for a site in a remote area where larger-scale experiments could be conducted,[1] LRL chose a spot on the northwest coast of Alaska: Ogotoruk Creek, 30 miles southeast of Point Hope and 40 miles northwest of Kivalina. The 300-person Inupiat Eskimo village of Point Hope, one of the oldest and most self-sufficient in North America, survived largely by hunting on land and sea.

LRL contracted for preliminary geological and mineral surveys, neither done on site, and reported good prospects for extraction of coal, oil, and other minerals.[2] The AEC, then, in a classified action, petitioned the Interior Department's Bureau of Land Management for release of a 40-mile-square tract (one million acres) of land. LRL planned to use thermonuclear explosives to carve out a harbor, declaring its value for fishing, mineral extraction, and stimulation of the Alaskan economy. A 2.4-million-ton explosion—of two one-megaton and two 200-kiloton hydrogen bombs—would take place in the summer of 1959.[3]

Dr. Edward Teller, "Father of the H-Bomb" and director of LRL, appeared in Alaska on July 14, 1958, accompanied by a group of scientists to solicit support for the project, code-named Chariot. Teller, an ardent believer in nuclear excavation possibilities, served as tech-

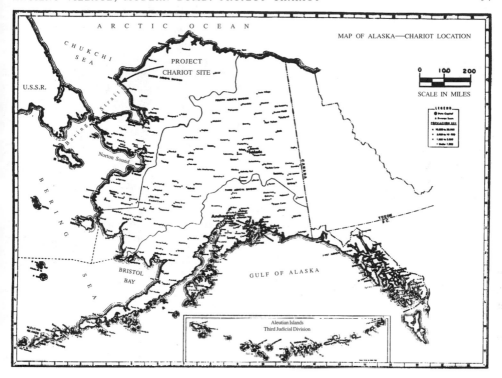

7.1. Project Chariot site. Courtesy Atomic Energy Commission.

nical advisor for Chariot. He assured audiences the project would not be undertaken unless economically viable, and promised that two-thirds of the $5-million cost of harbor construction would be spent in Alaska. Military spending had tapered off after the completion of the Distant Early Warning radar system (DEW Line), and the recession of the fur, fishing, and gold-mining industries had further weakened the economy. Oil could not yet take their place. Project Chariot tempted some growth-oriented interests.[4] The *Fairbanks Daily News-Miner* editorialized: "We think the holding of a huge nuclear blast in Alaska would be a fitting overture to the new era which is opening for our state."[5]

A number of academic and business leaders felt less enthusiastic. At a meeting with Teller at Juneau, economist George Rogers questioned the economic viability of the plan for extracting minerals. He pointed out that the coal to be mined lay far across the mountains from the harbor site, itself ice-bound for nine months of the year. Teller replied that the AEC would build a railroad and storage facilities for the minerals to be extracted. Asked about financing of this infrastructure, Teller switched the subject to souvenirs. Rogers acquired the impression that no assessment of cost-effectiveness had been done and that project planners had already determined to proceed. In various discussions Teller encouraged consideration of alternative ventures. He reacted favorably to suggestions for harbors at Nome or the Naval Petroleum Reserve, damming of major rivers, a canal across the Alaska Peninsula, and other projects. But two months before Teller departed for Alaska, LRL had requested the

7.1. Edward Teller at Kotzebue, 1959. Courtesy Lawrence Livermore Laboratory. "Father of the H-Bomb" Teller led the public relations for a plan to test explosive characteristics of hydrogen and atomic bombs in Alaska.

land set-aside at Ogotoruk Creek. Based on its mineral assessment report from E. J. Longyear Co., LRL had narrowed its choice for the test site to a 20-mile stretch between Cape Thompson and Cape Seppings. Location any farther north would mean extremely difficult ice conditions, and farther south would be too remote from coal and oil deposits. While Teller spoke in Fairbanks, surveyors walked the Ogotoruk Creek site. LRL test division chief Gerald Johnson held press conferences at the site on July 17–19, announcing the laboratory's choice for the Chariot Project.[6]

LRL planners did not make known the depths at which they planned to bury the explosives. However, the film they showed at the September 1958 Geneva conference, modeling Chariot, specified depths of 98 feet for two atomic bombs and 164 feet for a hydrogen bomb. No H-bomb had yet been exploded underground. Two previous Nevada atomic tests, situated 16 and 63 feet down and using small charges of 1,200 tons, nevertheless blew their crater debris and up to 90 percent of their radioactivity into the atmosphere. Chariot's blast, 2,000 times greater, might throw up 70 million cubic yards of earth as high as the stratosphere, broadcasting virtually all of its radioactive material. LRL changed the plan after the fall of 1958 when a Nevada shot called Neptune, set 210 feet down, unexpectedly broke the surface and released 1 to 2 percent of its radioactivity. Neptune also demonstrated that larger craters could be made by placing explosives deeper underground, permitting less radiation release. Thus the Atomic Energy Commission wanted more testing to determine the optimal depth for a given size of explosives.[7]

On another front, the nuclear powers moved toward a test ban agreement. September 1958 deliberations at Geneva aired considerable negative feeling about Plowshare. Soviet delegates labeled it an excuse to perpetuate bomb testing, doubly objectionable in light of Chariot's proximity to Soviet territory. Teller had criticized a test ban treaty as an obstacle to the search for peaceful uses for nuclear explosives, and served on a U.S. delegation at Geneva that argued that Plowshare should be exempted from any treaty. AEC leaders viewed testing as essential for weapons design, their main interest. They treated Operation Plowshare as a public relations device to put a better face on their weapons program. They opposed a nuclear test ban, and as an agreement neared, they adopted Plowshare as a way of continuing testing. A June 1957 visit to President Eisenhower by Teller and AEC chairman Lewis Strauss had dissuaded the president from agreeing to a comprehensive (including underground) nuclear test ban. Eisenhower eventually changed his mind, however, and the United States, United Kingdom, and USSR began observing an informal testing moratorium in November 1958. The Nevada event and the test ban progress added to public skepticism, and the economic unfeasibility of the harbor idea caused the AEC to rethink Project Chariot.[8]

Additional resistance came from University of Alaska professors critical of the lack of provisions for environmental assessment of the project. No decision to proceed, they reasoned, should be made without a thorough understanding of the ecology of the affected areas. In late February 1959, the AEC presented Alaskans a new plan. Chariot would now be an experiment in nuclear excavation, they said, to advance research on canal and harbor construction elsewhere. It would also measure effects of blast and fallout. The size of the blast would be reduced to 460,000 tons, using atomic rather than hydrogen explosives. By March they had received the endorsement of the Alaska legislature and the backing of nearly every Alaska chapter of the Chamber of Commerce. Responding to the requests from the University of Alaska, the AEC assembled a seven member environmental studies committee of scientists to oversee a one-year program of research to determine the optimal timing and fallout pattern, and do a pre- and postdetonation study of the biota. One Alaskan served on the committee: Alaska Conservation Society board member Robert L. Rausch of the Arctic Health Research Center in Anchorage. The Alaska Department of Fish and Game (ADF&G) raised questions about the viability of the harbor project, but AEC refused to fund an ADF&G liaison person. Governor William Egan chose the commissioner of the development-oriented Department of Natural Resources to coordinate the state's participation in the project. In April the Bureau of Land Management announced withdrawal of the 1,600 square miles AEC had requested, though the bureau had asked for public comment on only 40 square miles in September 1958.[9]

Critics attacked the new proposal. Carl Hamlin of Matanuska Valley organized a Committee for the Study of Atomic Testing in Alaska, an affiliate of a St. Louis-based group of scientists attempting to inform the public on nuclear issues, known as the Committee for Nuclear Information. In mid-February 1959, AEC chairman John McCone had told a congressional committee that the agency tabled Chariot because "we couldn't find a customer for the harbor," and that the AEC would have to find a more suitable location.[10] Shortly afterward, the AEC reversed its position. Senator Bob Bartlett, who had spoken in favor of the plan in early February, withdrew his endorsement, explaining that "no one on the commission concerned with this believed for a minute private capital could, in the foreseeable future, invest money in this area merely because an artificial harbor had been created. . . . I have now been completely disillusioned."[11] Bartlett remained sanguine about the possibilities for a similar project, such as construction of a canal across the Alaska Peninsula.[12]

Out of synchronization with the new design, Teller's *Reader's Digest* article in May 1959 claimed the harbor "would open the way to the development of vast coal deposits near the coast as well as valuable oil resources inland."[13] In a May graduation speech at the University of Alaska, Teller appealed to the desire for economic expansion and the can-do frontier spirit: "Anything new that is big needs big people to get it going . . . and big people are found in big states." Standing to gain most from Chariot, he speculated, would be the Eskimos, who could become coal miners. At Nome he added the Japanese to the list: they would be customers for the coal and oil. "The Japanese were the first to suffer by atomic blast," he suggested. "How wonderful it would be if they might be the first to benefit." In response to an Anchorage audience question about other possible projects, he quipped, "If your mountain is not in the right place, just drop us a card."[14]

Enthusiasm for an economic venture gained a life of its own. Reporter Albro Gregory, in an article in the *Fairbanks Daily News-Miner*, maintained hope for a harbor at Ogotoruk Creek to accommodate the largest oceangoing ships. He judged environmental studies unnecessary because "most scientists . . . already believe [the project] to be feasible," and the danger to humans as minimal because "only a few Natives pass by."[15] In a letter to John McCone, Arctic Circle Chamber of Commerce president William T. McIntyre declared,

> Alaskans, who are all pioneers, if not in fact then in heart, should feel proud that our state has been singled out to play yet another leading role in the Drama of the Century. We who live in this [Nome-Kotzebue] part of the state . . . feel this project will be the means of paving the way for the future development of this area . . . possessing vast potentialities in the mineral, coal, oil and hydroelectric fields, indeed, want the original harbor plan rather than [the] scaled down experiment.[16]

In June, AEC Environmental Studies Committee chairman Dr. John N. Wolfe reiterated the intent as excavation experimentation, adding that it would be the first opportunity to examine the effects of such an explosion on life in a region.[17] Confusion persisted over the true purpose of the environmental investigation. In part, it existed to mollify public opinion. AEC spokespersons made repeated assurances that no explosion would take place unless the studies determined it would be safe. Yet the research program had not been designed to answer questions about danger to humans. Whereas most safety concerns revolved around radiation, the agenda contained no effort to measure existing levels of radioactivity in humans, or to calculate the likelihood of radiation injury to humans through the food chain. When biologist William Pruitt addressed the question of contamination by consumption of caribou, Wolfe edited the material out of his report, and the AEC refused Pruitt's request for evaluation of the risks involved.[18] Lack of clarity of intent also shadowed Chariot itself: statements by Teller conveyed the impression that beyond keeping the Lawrence laboratory in business, the testing program embodied a political motive: to sustain a nuclear weapons development lead over the Soviet Union during a period of test bans.[19]

7.2. Dog team at Angmakroq Mountain, April 1960. By William O. Pruitt. Courtesy Project Chariot collection, University of Alaska Fairbanks, Alaska and Polar Regions Archives. Biologist Pruitt, a key figure in the Chariot controversy, engaged team owner Lawrence Sage of Kivalina to help conduct research.

Once again, by early 1960 the AEC scaled the blast down—to 280,000 tons, one-eighth of the original explosive power. Two 100-kiloton bombs buried 800 feet deep and four 20-kiloton bombs at 400 feet would leave a channel 1,800 by 750 feet, and an inner harbor a mile long and a half-mile wide. Debris would rise to 30,000 feet and cover the earth six feet deep near the site and a half-inch deep five miles away. Estimates of the proportion of radioactive material to be released into the atmosphere varied from 1 percent to 30 percent.[20] No one knew because no experiment had been carried out using multiple charges or in an area featuring similar soil, wind, and temperature conditions.

The AEC's environmental studies commenced in late spring 1959 and lasted into 1962. Politics immediately carried over into the research process. Albert W. Johnson received appointment as chief scientist, and Leslie A. Viereck as his assistant. They and two other biologists at the University of Alaska, L. Gerard Swartz and William O. Pruitt, had been among Chariot's leading skeptics. Viereck later conceded they accepted the posts "with the idea that we could do more to oppose the project in this way than we could if we sat on the sidelines." The four viewed their efforts as a counterbalance against those who had made up their minds in favor of Chariot.

Concern began to form among the Eskimos, who obtained material from the Committee for Nuclear Information. Aware of some unfortunate results of nuclear testing in the Pacific, the Point Hope village council voted unanimously in November 1959 to stand against

7.3. Seabird cliffs at Cape Thompson, ca. 1959. Courtesy Project Chariot collection, University of Alaska Fairbanks, Alaska and Polar Regions Archives. Some observers feared that nuclear explosions would damage the cliffs, a nesting site for murres, kittiwakes and other birds.

Chariot.[21] Pressured by Senator Bartlett, AEC representatives arrived in March 1960 at Point Hope to formally meet the Eskimos for the first time. They faced a difficult task; the Eskimos worried about radiation and resented the land reservation blocking their selections under the Native Allotment Act. Claims had been filed on part of the Ogotoruk Creek site in 1950. In the AEC presentation, Eskimos heard on the one hand that no harm would be done to their lifestyles, and on the other about fences, guards, and airplanes to keep people out of restricted areas for an unspecified period. They had read a statement by a leading AEC official that the Ogotoruk Creek area had not been utilized by Eskimo hunters for many years, a claim they knew to be untrue. After the meeting the village council again voted to repudiate the project.[22] Villager Kitty Kinneeveauk told the AEC representatives, "We really don't want to see the Cape Thompson blasted because it is our home, homeland. I'm pretty much sure you don't like to see your home blasted by some other people who don't live in your place like we live in Point Hope."[23] Village president David Frankson later commented, "I haven't been to the colleges, but I'm against it."[24] Eskimos facilitated their opposition by tape-recording their council meetings, and made certain to record the remarks of AEC representatives. They sent the tapes to other villages to raise awareness and help organize resistance.[25]

Early in January 1960, the AEC's environmental studies committee had released a preliminary statement recommending that if the detonation take place, it be in March or April of the (unspecified) test year, when negative effects would be minimal.[26] Environmental Studies chief Wolfe announced in August 1960 that "there are no biological objections to the shooting based on our investigations." Later that year he issued the statement, "We now know that the excavation won't affect the health, food sources and general livelihood of the Natives. . . . [T]here is no evidence that the damage will be widespread or will have any long-range effect on the environment."[27] In fact, researchers had identified several problems. Nearby cliffs, possibly subject to crumbling, hosted thousands of nesting Arctic birds that Eskimos caught for food. Contrary to the AEC's assumptions, Eskimos frequently traveled and hunted in the test area during March and April. The AEC also assumed the snow cover would enable most of the radioactive fallout to decay before spring melting deposited it on the lichens. These plants, reliant on airborne nutrients, absorbed the carcinogen strontium 90 that in turn concentrated in the caribou that ate them. In the wake of previous atomic tests, herds of caribou in the region already exhibited up to 20 times the contamination level of cattle in Fairbanks. Some Natives, reliant on caribou, registered four to five times the normal level of strontium 90 in their bodies. William Pruitt revealed that partly because of high winds, much of the fallout site lay bare of snow during the winter. Caribou wintered there, providing sustenance for Eskimos. Fallout would directly contaminate the lichens. Pruitt's protests to the AEC received no response.[28]

Researcher Don C. Foote, assigned to study human geography, charged that the environmental studies committee had gone beyond the bounds of propriety in prematurely approving the project. Upon inquiry by Senator Bartlett, general manager A. R. Luedecke of the AEC replied that "of 85 investigators employed in those surveys, Mr. Foote is the only member to develop this extreme attitude."[29] Four other scientists—Pruitt, Viereck, Johnson, and Swartz—publicly protested the go-ahead statements of Wolfe. Viereck wrote the committee in December 1960 pointing out that on January 7, 1960, it had cited weather considerations, recommending March or April as the best time for the nuclear blast. These were the months known to be desired by the AEC, but no weather data had been gathered to justify the January 7 statement. When Viereck and his three colleagues had protested, Wolfe responded in July that weather readings had been taken, but failed to mention it had been done since January. "This," stated Viereck, "was the first indication that any of us had that the Environmental Committee was merely going along with the predetermined policy of the AEC and was not using reports of the investigators to formulate their decisions." Noting other indications, he announced: "Because of the repeated inference that all of the biologists are in favor of the shot and that it has been proved that there will be no biological damage [and] because the Project Chariot study is not a purely biological study but one intimately connected with AEC politics and directed by an Environmental Committee that is biased in its decisions and membership, I wish to resign from the project."[30]

Mounting criticism and concern, especially about nuclear fallout, eroded the momentum of Chariot. The Alaska legislature shifted its position in 1960, urging that Cape Thompson residents be informed of plans and possible effects of the project.[31] A June 1961 report by the Committee for Nuclear Information calculated that fallout could be five or ten times higher than AEC public estimates, and could contaminate the entire food chain.[32] The United States and Soviet Union still observed a moratorium on testing.

More than two years after the AEC abandoned its economic rationale, Robert Atwood's *Anchorage Daily Times* kept the hope alive: "The harbor would create an economic value by encouraging the development of resources now latent." Acknowledging criticism of the project, it pronounced, "Premature judging of the project shows prejudice, which is a poor basis for decision. Until the scientific studies are complete no decision is in order. . . . It would be better to approach the project with a positive attitude. Man must progress. . . . Nuclear power opens amazing new avenues for greater achievements. Mankind must explore them and the Alaska experiment may be the key."[33] The Governor's Advisory Committee on Economic Development proposed legislation in spring 1962 to move the people of Point Hope, Kivalina, and Noatak, to Nome for the duration of the nuclear test. Committee member Frances P. Walker explained to the Point Hope council that Chariot "would provide the United States with extremely valuable scientific information" and that "such a nuclear explosion at this particular site would be of tremendous economic value to Alaska."[34]

Meanwhile, the Lawrence Radiation Laboratory encountered further difficulties over Chariot. Permafrost limited the comparability of cratering results in other regions. Prevailing winds would probably not carry the fallout over the tundra, where radioactivity effects could be measured. Seawater might melt the permafrost, caving in the harbor walls. Resumption of nuclear testing in Nevada in August 1961 yielded more cratering information, and LRL wrote the AEC confidentially in April 1962 recommending cancellation of Chariot. Both agencies strove to avoid the impression that they had capitulated to local pressures, lest future projects be put in jeopardy. Then the AEC set off a Nevada explosion named Sedan in July 1962, 635 feet below the surface. Publicly, the agency claimed that Sedan had released 5 percent of its radioactivity; secretly, they estimated 25 percent. Winds blew material into the Dakotas and probably into Canada. By comparison, the third Chariot plan would have released almost three times the energy of Sedan and 17 to 38 times the radiation of the later Chernobyl meltdown. The initial Chariot configuration could have equaled 314 to 675 Chernobyls.[35]

Sanctioning of Project Chariot by Presidents Eisenhower or Kennedy never materialized. The AEC announced in August it would "defer, for the present, any recommendations to the President on whether to conduct the experiment." The AEC and LRL still denied Chariot's potential for significant bioenvironmental damage. They made no mention of disagreement by the Interior Department. Point Hope villagers had contacted Interior Secretary Stewart Udall, asking how land could be made available to the AEC in apparent violation of laws protecting Native land claims in Alaska. Udall wrote to AEC chairman Glenn Seaborg in January 1962, requesting Interior Department participation in review of Chariot environmental studies and in any further deliberations involving the Natives. An aide to Udall observed,

> Those involved with the project at AEC and at Livermore knew that Interior was prepared to exercise severe judgment in the matter of Project Chariot. Rather than have us issue a counter-report to the President which we would have publicized, and which

would have been most embarrassing to the AEC, they withdrew early in the fray, and in the most face-saving manner.

In January 1963, the AEC relinquished its control of 90 percent of the withdrawn acreage, and on September 2 returned the remainder to the Department of the Interior.[36]

A second round involving nuclear weapons and the defense establishment soon came to pass at Amchitka (Chapter 8), and a possible third round sprang up in 1987. Edward Teller, an originator of Ronald Reagan's Strategic Defense Initiative ("Star Wars"), returned to Alaska to promote the idea. Speaking to the business group Commonwealth North, he proposed Alaska as the best location for laser antiballistic missile defenses. As he had a quarter-century earlier, he appealed to the Alaskans as "reasonable" people who would want to help the nation "find out what weapons are possible" and "make a great contribution to the nation's defense." He plumped for oil drilling in the Arctic Refuge, remarking that before Prudhoe Bay "the North Slope was not yet there—or, to be more accurate, nobody was there except the North Slope." Chariot, he reflected, "should have been done." In an unintended compliment to the environmentalists whose movement he had stimulated, he asserted they had stopped Chariot "with no good reason."[37]

FALLOUT FROM PROJECT CHARIOT

Chariot boosted the political experience of the Alaska Conservation Society (ACS) and, as a signal victory, lifted morale. The society elected Leslie Viereck its first president; Pruitt, Johnson, and Swartz also held early memberships. ACS took the position that "there is sufficient basis to seriously question the advisability" of the project, and that full and unbiased studies should be done and opened to public scrutiny. Extensive coverage of the issue in the March 1961 *ACS News Bulletin*, repeated in the May *Sierra Club Bulletin*, alerted a national audience. Copies went to selected groups and individuals all over the nation, and attracted the notice of Barry Commoner and Interior Secretary Udall.[38] Consulted by and quoted in national media, ACS abetted the demise of Project Chariot.

Dissenters paid a price for their actions. University of Alaska President William R. Wood, recently arrived from the University of Nevada, openly touted Chariot. Agreeing with Robert Atwood of the *Anchorage Daily Times* and C. W. Snedden and George Sundborg of the *Fairbanks Daily News-Miner*, he judged, "If the United States government decides that the project is a safe one, there is no reason for concern." Of the critics, he suggested, "Perhaps it is not in the University's best interest to rehire members of the staff if they feel strongly against the activities of the agency that is providing money for their research." When William Pruitt's dispute with the AEC became known to him, Wood contended that whether the bias on the part of the AEC be valid or not, it discredited Pruitt and thereby the university. Chariot involved the university's own financial interest, in Wood's view, and one should not jeopardize opportunities for funding from government organizations by criticizing the way in which they apply the research data.[39] Pruitt charged that his department chairperson, Brina Kessel, altered his final report to make it more palatable to the AEC. The university did not renew contracts for Viereck and Pruitt, and Albert Johnson later left as a result of dissatisfaction with Wood and Kessel. Montana State University, despite the unanimous approval of its biology department, rejected an application from Pruitt. Wood had allegedly intervened by suggesting MSU's president contact the AEC. An investigation by the American Civil Liberties Union did not find sufficient basis for a lawsuit.[40] Chariot's scientists became the first political casualties among Alaska's environmentalists.

Three decades after Chariot's demise, a pair of events signaled the gradual shift toward Alaskan acceptance of environmental protection and the work of environmentalists. Chariot recaptured the public spotlight when researcher Dan O'Neill discovered that the AEC had transported some radioactive material from Nevada to the Chariot site in 1962 to test its dispersal in tundra soil and water. Energy Department officials acknowledged that the test had been conducted and that following deactivation of the site, the soil had been scooped up into a mound 40 feet square by 5 feet high, and abandoned. They claimed that only a small amount of radioactive material (26 millicuries) had been involved, posing no danger. North Slope Borough, Point Hope residents, and others demanded a cleanup. In a $5-million effort, the Department of Energy completed the task in August 1993, transporting the material to Nevada for burial.[41]

Earlier in 1993 William Pruitt and Leslie Viereck won belated recognition from the University of Alaska Fairbanks. Tacitly acknowledging their contributions in the Chariot controversy in addition to their later achievements, the university awarded honorary degrees to both. And in a generosity of spirit rare for any public body, the legislature paid its tribute to the two: "Gentlemen, you were right, and we, the people of Alaska, owe you a debt of gratitude for holding strong to your principles. The members of the Eighteenth Alaska State Legislature humbly thank you."[49]

Chariot's environmental research advanced the principle of accountability through identification of social and environmental effects. Although motivated partly by the AEC's desire to measure the before-and-after characteristics of a nuclear explosion, it constituted probably the most complete survey of any location in the American Arctic. Nearly 100 scientists produced 41 studies of the geology, flora, and fauna of the land and Chukchi Sea, and of the coastal Eskimos. The AEC Committee on Environmental Studies published its 1,200-page report in 1966.[42] Its work significantly forwarded biological science in Alaska.

Chariot left a legacy in the evolution of political awareness in Native communities. Supplementing a crisis over waterfowl hunting (Chapter 3), Chariot triggered a historic autumn 1961 meeting at Barrow on Native rights. Under sponsorship of the American Association of Indian Affairs (AAIA), the conference took a stand against the land withdrawal for Chariot, and asserted Native subsistence rights. Calls for a public forum for Native concerns culminated in publication of the newspaper *Tundra Times* as of October 1962. Initial funding came from AAIA member Henry S. Forbes. Howard Rock, an Inupiat Eskimo artist raised in Point Hope, returned from Seattle and assumed the editorship. Thomas Snapp, a *Fairbanks Daily News-Miner* reporter who covered the Barrow conference and rejected his paper's stance on Chariot, assisted Rock. Snapp and Rock also facilitated a June 1962 meeting of the Tanana Chiefs Conference, an Athabaskan body that had not convened since 1915. Worried about encroachments on their traditional hunting and fishing grounds, Athabaskans joined the Eskimos in requesting protection by the Interior Department. *Tundra Times* became the most prominent voice of Alaska Natives, who held their first statewide conference in June 1964, leading to creation of the Alaska Federation of Natives two years later.[43] Taking readily

7.4. Leslie Viereck, pressing plants, Ogotoruk Creek, 1959. Courtesy Les Viereck. Project Chariot produced one of the most complete bioenvironmental surveys in any Arctic region, and foreshadowed the environmental impact statement.

to politics, Natives made their needs felt in the Rampart controversy, the Alaska Native Claims Settlement Act of 1971, and the Alaska National Interest Lands Conservation Act of 1980.

Chariot affected national affairs as well. It marked a transitional phase in the growth of environmental philosophy and politics: toward greater public participation and a broader ecological orientation, including social and political aspects. A decade before the emergence of the national environmental movement in 1970, activists focused on preservation of wild lands and wildlife species. Ogotoruk Creek and the surrounding region, however, possessed only slight scenic value and did not contain recognized wildlife populations threatened by the project. One of the first national environmental leaders to question Chariot, Wilderness Society leader Olaus Murie belonged to the small number knowledgeable about the Arctic. Pointing out the beauty and ecological richness of the region, he objected to its use as a "dump-ground" for schemes not welcome elsewhere. His organization adopted its stand in February 1960, followed by the Sierra Club in March.[44] Other conservation publications and organizations voicing skepticism toward Chariot included *Outdoor Life*, *National Wildland News*, Alaska Sportsmen's Council, Defenders of Wildlife, and National Parks and Conservation Association.[45]

Reluctance to challenge Chariot revolved in part around the nuclear element. In the fear-laden atmosphere of the Cold War, only a few dared criticize the defense or nuclear establishments. Those who did might find themselves unemployed or followed by intelligence agents. Moreover, in a decade of economic and technical progress, Americans revered

technology and looked suspiciously on social dissent. Alaska, immersed in its frontier entrepreneurship and far removed from the fine-tuned political thinking of Washington, naturally
fostered strong support for and opposition to the AEC and Chariot.

As a potential menace to the interrelationship of human lifestyles and natural ecosystems, Chariot necessitated a broad framework of reference. Evaluation of such a proposal
required an integrated knowledge of sociological, economic, technical, biological, and political factors, tempered by philosophy—a holistic approach. No single interested group could
operate holistically. Yet many issues gained clarification through Chariot's environmental
study program and the efforts of groups and individuals focusing on nuclear technology,
Native rights, Arctic ecology, and the proper role of government. Chariot heralded modern
environmental issues and significantly shaped the environmental movement.[46] Barry Commoner, founder of the Committee for Nuclear Information and a leading writer on technology
and pollution, said of his start as an environmentalist, "It is absolutely certain that it began
when I went to the library to look up the behavior of lichen in connection with the Chariot
program . . . I realized that we're dealing with an ecosystem here." His broadening focus
eventuated in his prominent role in the 1970 Earth Week, and "Chariot can be regarded as the
ancestral birthplace of at least a large segment of the environmental movement." Commoner
also regarded Chariot research as the prototype of the environmental impact statement,
written into national law in 1969.[47]

In addition to furthering principles of biological sustainability, Chariot represented a
first, if modest and temporary, citizen victory over the defense-nuclear technocracy. It gave
force to fundamental notions of democracy: that lying and excessive secrecy by government
undermine freedom; that institutional power must not go unchecked; that government and
other actors should be accountable for the effects of their behavior; and that freedom
depends on vigilance by an informed citizenry. Through its studies, Chariot deepened scientific understanding of Arctic ecology. The affair elevated public awareness of the Arctic as
a functioning ecosystem, a perspective informing later conflicts over the oil pipeline and the
status of the Arctic National Wildlife Refuge.

NOTES

1. G. Johnson, "New Explosions," 155–158; O'Neill, "Project Chariot: How Alaska Escaped," 28.

2. Brooks and Foote, "Disturbing Story," 61–62.

3. O'Neill, "Project Chariot: Thoughts," 1. According to Walter Sullivan ("H-Bombs May Dig
Harbor in Alaska," *New York Times*, June 5, 1959, 1), hydrogen bombs offered the advantage of less
release of radioactive material than atomic bombs. Gerald W. Johnson, former Alaskan Project technical director, confirmed in a 1989 interview that thermonuclear explosions had been planned (O'Neill,
Project Chariot: A Collection, vol. I, 235).

4. Coates, "Project Chariot: Alaskan Roots," 3.

5. Brooks and Foote, "Disturbing Story," 62.

6. Coates, "Project Chariot: Alaskan Roots," 3–5; O'Neill, "Project Chariot: How Alaska Escaped," 30–31; O'Neill, *Firecracker Boys*, 29, 34–35, 38.

7. *Sierra Club Bulletin*, "Project Chariot: The Long Look," 8–9; O'Neill, *Firecracker Boys*, 41–
43, 55–58.

8. Coates, "Project Chariot: Alaskan Roots," 5, 26 n.15, 16; O'Neill,"Project Chariot:How
Alaska Escaped," 33; O'Neill, *Firecracker Boys*, 25, 38–40, 48–54.

9. Coates, *Trans-Alaska Pipeline*, 117–120, 361 n.43; Grahame, "A-Test Alaska Threat?" 10–11;

Alaska Session Laws, 1959, HJR 9. Coates (p. 118) reports that the AEC explained the withdrawal discrepancy as a "mistake" (presumably a confusion of 40 square miles and 40 miles square).

10. Coates, "Project Chariot: Alaskan Roots," 5–6.

11. Brooks and Foote, "Disturbing Story," 65.

12. Coates, "Project Chariot: Alaskan Roots," 27 n.22.

13. Teller, "How Nuclear Blasts Could Be Used," 109.

14. Coates, "Project Chariot: Alaskan Roots," 9–12, 28 n.30.

15. *Fairbanks Daily News-Miner*, August 25, 1959.

16. Coates, "Project Chariot: Alaskan Roots," 9.

17. *New York Times*, June 5, 1959, 8.

18. O'Neill, *Firecracker Boys*, 157–159, 211–212.

19. O'Neill, "Project Chariot: How Alaska Escaped," 31.

20. *Sierra Club Bulletin*, "Project Chariot: The Long Look," 9, 12; Teller, "We're Going to Work Miracles," 97–99; Grahame, "A-Test Alaska Threat?" 137.

21. Coates, "Project Chariot: Alaskan Roots," 9, 13, 15.

22. Foote, "Project Chariot and the Eskimo," 9–11; Morgan, *Art and Eskimo Power*, 168, 173.

23. Coates, "Project Chariot: Alaskan Roots," 13.

24. *New York Times*, August 17, 1960, 4.

25. O'Neill, *Project Chariot: A Collection*, vol. 2, 627–628 (interview of Ginny Wood, November 8, 1988).

26. Coates, "Project Chariot: Alaskan Roots," 12.

27. *New York Times*, August 17, 1960, 4; December 4, 1960, 55.

28. Ibid., May 13, 1962, 71; Foote, "Project Chariot and the Eskimo," 5–7; Herbert R. Melchior, interview by author, July 12, 1988.

29. *Sierra Club Bulletin*, "Project Chariot: The Long Look," 6.

30. Ibid., 6–7.

31. *Alaska Session Laws, 1960*, SJR 13.

32. *Science News Letter*, "High Alaska Fallout Risk," 375; Margolis, "Project Chariot: Two Groups," 2000–2001.

33. *Anchorage Daily Times*, June 29, 1961, 4.

34. Morgan, *Art and Eskimo Power*, 189–190.

35. O'Neill, "Project Chariot: How Alaska Escaped," 36–37; O'Neill, *Firecracker Boys*, 146–147, 248–253.

36. Coates, "Project Chariot: Alaskan Roots," 16–17; O'Neill, *Firecracker Boys*, 229–231, 243–246, 250, 253–254.

37. Coates, "Project Chariot: Alaskan Roots," 24; O'Neill, "Project Chariot: Thoughts," 11.

38. *Alaska Conservation Society News Bulletin*, March 1961, 6; Coates, "Project Chariot: Alaskan Roots," 15; Celia Hunter and Ginny Wood, interview by author, July 28, 1992.

39. O'Neill, "Project Chariot: Thoughts," 8, 10.

40. *New York Times*, October 27, 1963, 84; Herbert R. Melchior, interview by author, July 12, 1988; Coates, "Project Chariot: Alaskan Roots," 28–29 n.41. Wood, interviewed in 1988 by a reporter from the University of Alaska Fairbanks newspaper *Polar Star*, acknowledged having advised the president of Montana State University to contact John Wolfe at the AEC about Pruitt, but justified it as a normal reference for informational purposes (see O'Neill, *Project Chariot: A Collection*, vol. 2, 442–443).

41. *Anchorage Daily Times*, August 13, 1993, C1.

42. O'Neill, *Firecracker Boys*, 266.

43. Wilimovsky and Wolfe, *Environment of Cape Thompson*, vi, xiii–xvi.

44. Daley and James, "An Authentic Voice," 23–29.

45. Coates, "Project Chariot: Alaskan Roots," 10, 17, 20.

46. Coates, *Trans-Alaska Pipeline*, 125; O'Neill, *Firecracker Boys*, 215–217.

47. Coates, "Project Chariot: Alaskan Roots," 20; O'Neill, "Project Chariot: Thoughts," 10.

48. O'Neill, *Project Chariot: A Collection*, vol. 1, 283–284, 288, 291.

8

Return to Amchitka

For a second time in the first decade of statehood, Alaskan environmental advocates encountered nuclear and space-age politics of the great powers. And for the second time, they took part in an episode whose effects rippled far beyond the state's borders, adding to the nation's commitment to environmental values. Amchitka, an island in the western Aleutians, provided the stage.

Amchitka is a low, rainy, foggy, windy, 42-mile-long by 4.5-mile-wide strip of land, mountainous at the northwest end. Residents in the 1960s included sea mammals, introduced rats, more than 100 species of local or migrating birds including bald eagles and peregrine falcons, and a half-dozen little spruce trees only nine inches taller than when planted around an officer's mess in 1943.[1] For 200 years after the Russians first raided the sea otters, no one resided permanently on the island, and few visited or cared much about it. Then the Japanese seized Attu and Kiska in 1942. Needing a base from which to strike back, the Americans built an airfield and stationed more than 10,000 GIs on Amchitka. B-24 and B-25 crews and fighter pilots flew their missions in some of the world's most unpleasant weather. In August 1950 the military left the island. Early in 1951 the Atomic Energy Commission and Defense Department investigated Amchitka as a possible site for surface and underground nuclear explosions. After drilling 34 test holes, officials decided to carry out the tests in Nevada. Near the site of the test holes, Department of Defense crews operated a communications antenna during 1959–1961 as part of the Distant Early Warning radar system (DEW Line).[2]

Amchitka's sojourn into the nuclear age took shape in late 1963 or early 1964 when the Atomic Energy Commission (AEC) and Defense Department chose a remote location for nuclear testing. Since the signing of the Nuclear Test Ban Treaty in 1963, weapons could be exploded only underground. The AEC found the geology of Amchitka Island favorable, the nearest people lived 200 miles away, abandoned airstrips could be rehabilitated, and a clause in the executive order creating the Aleutian Islands Reserve permitted its use for military purposes.

Any intrusive undertaking on Amchitka necessarily violated its integrity as a wildlife refuge, and military operations had not been the first. As part of an effort to make economic use of undeveloped lands, the Interior Department had permitted Natives to import Arctic foxes from a nearby island. Seven freed in 1921 multiplied rapidly, feeding on eggs and birds

8.1. "Amchitka National Forest"—spruce trees planted at officers' mess in 1943, ca. 1965. Courtesy J. Sheldon collection, University of Alaska Anchorage Archives. World War II left hundreds of military buildings and facilities.

and exterminating a nesting population of Aleutian Canada geese. Fur trapping lasted from 1925 to 1936, when the market fell off. Fish and Wildlife Service agents eradicated the foxes in the 1950s by dropping poisoned bait from aircraft.[3] But Norway rats, brought in ships during World War II, survived to menace the birds. Song sparrows and winter wrens ceased nesting on the island.

To wildlife managers who knew the Aleutians, the sea otter stood out as the most interesting and valuable of Amchitka's wildlife assets. Proposals for nuclear tests, therefore, would have to contain assurances against harm to these animals. Once the most prized commodity of the fur trade, sea otters again rose to prominence in the statehood era. Ignored by public opinion when they neared extinction at the turn of the century, they evolved into symbols of conservation in Alaska. Few had existed at the time of designation of the Aleutian Islands Reserve by William Howard Taft in 1913. They eluded public attention until 1956 when officers arrested a saloon operator in Valdez for possession of otter pelts. Reviving an old free-enterprise tradition, he had been trading a gallon of whiskey for each pelt, rumored to be worth $5,000 in China. He paid a fine of $500.[4] Otters repopulated Amchitka and by the 1950s numbered an estimated 3,000, the world's largest concentration. High mortality and low reproduction rates suggested Amchitka otters had in fact become too numerous.[5]

8.2. Sea otters, Amchitka Island, 1967. By David L. Spencer. Courtesy Alaska Resources Library and Information Services, Anchorage. Sea otters played the most prominent wildlife role in the Amchitka controversy.

During the Kennedy administration, AEC and Defense Department officials planned for testing on Amchitka. Not wanting to provoke the Soviet Union, the administration shelved the idea, but it resurfaced during the Johnson years.[6] Preparations advanced for Long Shot, an 80-kiloton blast 2,300 feet below the surface, and the AEC and Defense Department announced the project in early 1965. They identified its purpose as improving detection of man-made (Soviet or Chinese) blasts in contradistinction to earthquakes.

Among the first environmental organizations to voice uneasiness about the testing plan, the Alaska Conservation Society (ACS) spoke cautiously. "We don't want to block a step toward world peace," President Fred Dean said, but why had a wildlife refuge been chosen? Would there be proper environmental safeguards and public notification? The society lacked resources to investigate the matter and mobilize public opinion if necessary, and granted its qualified approval of the project.[7] National Audubon Society officials, expressing the society's interest in wildlife refuges, charged that the AEC and Defense Department kept the matter secret to avoid critical examination by the Interior Department or the public. The AEC conducted no pretest biological review, and relegated refuge managers Karl Kenyon and David Spencer to a subordinate role in a posttest survey contracted to the

University of Washington's Laboratory of Radiation Biology. The agency scheduled no cleanup of debris.

Long Shot went off on October 29, 1965, doing virtually no apparent damage to wildlife. Researchers found two dead seabirds and no mammals. Some radioactive tritium escaped into mud pits near ground zero.[8] Calvin Lensink, manager of Clarence Rhode National Wildlife Range, remained on the island when the detonation occurred, and reported, "Habitat destruction resulting from Project Longshot was extensive. In the vicinity of ground zero an area of approximately 200 acres was denuded of vegetation." The explosion broke an earthen dam and released drilling muds and oils from a holding pond. Lensink observed that there had been meager healing of the extensive World War II damage.[9]

A year later the AEC announced a search for another test site. The Pentagon planned for an antiballistic missile called Spartan to carry a hydrogen warhead. No explosion this large had been conducted underground, and scientists judged the risk of radiation leakage or building damage too great to justify such a test in Nevada or elsewhere in the Lower 48.[10] Accordingly, the search focused on Amchitka and a more northerly site. The latter turned out to be near the Utukok River on the North Slope, a prime caribou calving ground and a more remote and costly location to supply than Amchitka. The AEC reviewed the site in apparent response to a request by Governor Walter Hickel, who believed that a nuclear testing program would help develop the North Slope. Eventually, the AEC abandoned the northern option.[11] Of the two sites, the ACS preferred Amchitka, but it went on record against further nuclear testing on any wildlife refuge.[12]

Amchitka's ecosystem had already been compromised by its military service, and each test added new insults. Visitors in 1968 could see vehicle tracks and trails in the tundra leading to hundreds of aging quonset huts and other buildings. Several huge dumps of barrels and junked equipment lay by the roads. Adding to the impact left by Long Shot, preparations for the next test put heavy equipment to work digging pits and constructing a two-lane road 20 miles long. The world's largest drilling machines dug several mile-deep holes, one of them ten feet in diameter. Spoils went to settling ponds and burial pits. Shops, service buildings, an airport, and 255 vehicles supplied a town of 480 workers, to be doubled in 1969.[13]

For the Spartan program, the AEC specified parallel tests in Nevada (Faultless, carried out in 1968) and Milrow (on Amchitka, for 1969). Exploratory drilling and biological-impact studies had commenced at Amchitka in mid-1967. Project Milrow would be much larger than Long Shot: 1.2 million tons set 4,000 feet deep, its purpose identified as "calibration"— exploration of the feasibility of exploding the larger Spartan warhead. It received a mixed reaction in Alaska. Aware that Amchitka sat close to a fault zone known for seismic activity, critics aired fears of earthquakes, tidal waves, radiation contamination, and environmental damage. Former governor William Egan, who had approved of Long Shot, now expressed doubt. Senator Mike Gravel objected to Milrow, as did the *Anchorage Daily News*. The *Anchorage Daily Times* labeled opponents "either outsiders or newcomers to Alaska backed by outside agitators."[14] In a telegram sent to three state senators criticizing Milrow, Governor Keith Miller declared, "I am becoming increasingly convinced that the sudden surge of

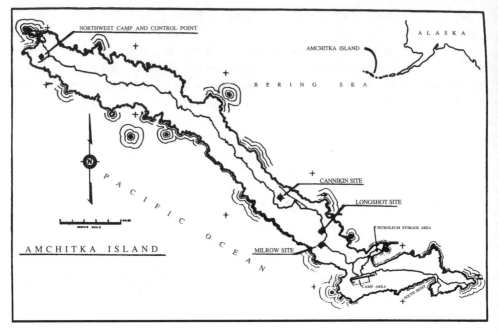

8.1. Amchitka Island, 1971. Courtesy Atomic Energy Commission.

outcry against the Amchitka test is a result of a well-financed, highly organized international movement."[15] The government of Japan formally protested the plan.[16]

Milrow climaxed on October 2, 1969 and as predicted by the AEC, only moderate damage resulted. Minor amounts, if any, of radiation escaped. Ground movement of six inches along the shoreline triggered slides of rock and topsoil. Subsidence of the surface above the explosion created a small lake, and sticklebacks died and water levels fell in several other small lakes. A sea otter died in a study pen and a dead porpoise lay on the beach, neither apparently having been killed by shock waves. Site preparation activities generated more impact than did the blast. Milrow's results might have dampened dissent and public involvement, but Project Baneberry (Nevada, 1970) went awry and leaked radiation, causing public concern. Also, the 1969 National Environmental Policy Act now required an environmental impact statement for all such projects.

Next at Amchitka, the AEC scheduled Cannikin, the test of a 5-megaton Spartan hydrogen bomb buried 5,875 feet deep, to take place in fall 1971.[17] This time the resistance grew much stiffer. Senator Daniel Inouye pointed out that a tidal wave from a 1946 earthquake originating in the Aleutians killed 159 Hawaiians and did $25 million damage. Some top nuclear scientists doubted the Spartan system would work.[18] Skeptics pointed to the Office of Technology Assessment judgment of Spartan as obsolete and the test as unnecessary. Spartan had been designed as a limited-capacity defense of targets in East Asia from Chinese attack. Supporters later promoted it as protection for U.S.-based Minuteman missile sites, but an improved, lower-yield warhead would be ready in time to meet a potential Soviet threat. Five of the seven agency chiefs consulted by President Richard Nixon on the matter

8.3. Project Cannikin drill rig, 1971. Courtesy Atomic Energy Commission. Cannikin involved the underground detonation of a 5-megaton hydrogen bomb.

disapproved of Cannikin; only the Defense Department and AEC favored it.[19] Japan and Canada protested; 100 members of the Canadian Parliament signed a telegram to Nixon, asking for a halt.[20] Thirty-five U.S. Senators petitioned against it.[21] A group of eight environmental, peace, and Native organizations including Sierra Club and Friends of the Earth sued on grounds of inadequate environmental impact statement, losing their appeal by 4-3 in the U.S. Supreme Court.[22] The Aleut League filed a similar suit against the AEC in district court. They feared damage from shocks, radiation, earthquakes, or tsunamis. The court refused their request for an injunction, and they opted not to appeal.[23]

Anti-Cannikin protesters greeted Nixon when he arrived in Anchorage on October 26. He came to meet Emperor Hirohito, who broke 2,600 years of tradition in leaving his native Japan.[24] Less than six weeks later Nixon gave the go-ahead to Cannikin, assuring the public there would be no "substantial" damage to the environment. On November 6 the $200-million blast, unleashing the power of 500 Hiroshimas, forced the ground to roll 200 miles away at Adak and registered in Japan, prompting another strong protest.[25]

The AEC's environmental impact statement, issued in June, had stated, "Like Milrow, Cannikin is expected to have only a minimal long-term impact on the environment," and the principal disturbance would be from the activities of several hundred workers. Cannikin, Milrow, and Long Shot each occupied a different site. Addressing the most sensitive question, the impact statement ventured that "some sea otters, estimated at as many as 20 to 100, could suffer adverse impacts due to overpressure." [26] A dozen had died during tests conducted in 1968 to determine the effects of shock.[27]

Following Cannikin, AEC and Defense officials declared satisfaction and announced no more testing for Spartan would be necessary; they prepared to clean up their leavings and vacate the island. The AEC's followup reports admitted damage. Earth dams had cracked and spilled 5,000 cubic yards of drilling muds. Some cliff faces collapsed, four lakes drained, and another about 25 feet deep appeared where the earth had subsided. The blast killed at least four seals, some ocean fish, and several thousand freshwater fish. A small amount of radioactive material seeped into the lake above the detonation site. More than a mile of beach rose as much as three feet, causing local ecological disruption. Rock and turf slides knocked down six bald eagle and two peregrine falcon nest sites. No detectable waves appeared except in the water closest to the detonation site. Following a strong ground shock and aftershocks, regional seismic activity did not change. Site preparation had disturbed slightly more than 1,000 acres of land. As for the sea otters, the AEC estimated that 700 perished.[28] A later study by the Alaska Department of Fish and Game placed the number at 900 to 1,350.[29]

AMCHITKA'S AFTERMATH

Amchitka nuclear testing took place in an era of growing suspicion about the military-industrial complex, fostered in large part by the Vietnam War. The public had grown less willing to sacrifice nature for the designs of powerful corporations and bureaucracies. *New York Times* editorials castigated the AEC and the Defense Department for using "national security" as an excuse to avoid environmental protection requirements, and for endangering national security by escalating the arms race through unnecessary weapons tests. "The whole experiment was a gamble with nature. How many more Amchitkas before the gambler and the victim are one?" they asked.[30] A year after Cannikin, the Anti Ballistic Missile Treaty prohibited the deployment of more than one Soviet and one American battery of antiballistic missiles. The United States chose not to complete its battery.

Amchitka's physical and psychological remoteness, and the technical and political dimensions of the controversy, made it far too difficult an issue for Alaskan conservation groups to manage. They participated as best they could, and lost the contest. They gained experience and some stature by restricting their claims and concerns to possibilities of damage to wildlife—proven valid, as it turned out, by the results of Cannikin.

Some benefits to wildlife and ecological restoration flowed from the Amchitka nuclear testing program. For public relations purposes and to remove animals from the danger zone, the AEC funded the translocation of several hundred otters to repopulate parts of their original habitat. During 1965 and 1966, the Alaska Department of Fish and Game had moved 53 otters from Amchitka to Prince William Sound. Between 1967 and 1972, AEC funding enabled the transfer of more than 700 from Amchitka to coastal locations between Prince William Sound and Oregon. About 350 additional otters died during the operations. Meanwhile, between 1962 and 1972 the state investigated the economic potential of sea otters by harvesting and selling the pelts of 2,431. State agents took them from Amchitka, Tanaga, Kanaga, Adak, and Delarof Islands.[31]

Amchitka testing also bequeathed gifts in the form of cleanup and scientific knowledge. After Cannikin, the AEC launched a restoration effort lasting until late 1973. Crews sealed 34 drill holes and seeded about 190 acres. They cleaned up many World War II sites and removed, buried, or burned equipment and about 400 buildings.[32] Although not initially required by law to do so, the AEC followed the precedent of Project Chariot and contracted for extensive bioenvironmental studies beginning in 1967. Carried out by Battelle Memorial Institute, the research sought to describe the environment in order to predict, limit, and measure the impacts of nuclear tests. Battelle applied much of the design and implementation experience gained in Chariot. In addition to strictly physiological assessments, at least 26 life-science studies covered history and geography, hydrology and weather, geomorphology and soils, land and sea flora and fauna, environmental contaminants, and ecological effects of the testing. Like the Chariot investigations, they possessed the value of a broad-based survey done at a specific time and place. The Amchitka studies ranked among the most advanced and comprehensive done in northern regions.[33]

Another of Amchitka's chapters had a long-term effect on Alaska and the world as well; it grew out of Project Milrow in 1969. A group of Canadians and Americans in Vancouver organized a border demonstration by 7,000 people against the test. Shortly after Milrow, the AEC announced plans for Cannikin in 1971. Some of the Milrow protestors set up a Don't Make A Wave Committee—recalling the 1964 Alaska earthquake tsunami that hit Vancouver Island—to oppose Cannikin. Most of the group belonged to the British Columbia chapter of Sierra Club, but chose a new name because the Sierra Club did not want to divide its efforts and membership by involvement in the peace movement. Based on the precedent of the Quaker peace ships *Phoenix* and *Golden Rule* protesting atomic tests in the Pacific, the group resolved to sail a vessel to Amchitka. They intended to publicize opposition to the test by radio broadcasts, and to lie three miles offshore at the time of the blast. The committee embarked on a lengthy quest to locate a boat. In 1971 they found one: the rusty, 30-year-old, 80-foot halibut seiner *Phyllis Cormack*, piloted by owner John Cormack. Rental money from small donations, a rock concert featuring Joni Mitchell and James Taylor, and a generous donation from the Palo Alto Society of Friends, sent the expedition to sea on September 15. Eight Canadians and four Americans made up the crew. One, political scientist Richard Fineberg, held Alaska residence. Peace and ecology symbols adorned the sail, and sign-boards on the wheelhouse read "Greenpeace." Coined by Canadian social worker Bill Darnell, "Greenpeace" became the informal name of the ship and the group's identification in the media.

A long, cramped, and rough ride across the Gulf of Alaska put the crew into Akutan. They had been refused permission to stop at the naval port of Dutch Harbor to obtain supplies. At Akutan they encountered the Coast Guard Cutter *Confidence*, whose captain advised them they had violated the law requiring notification of the Anchorage customs

8.4. Phyllis Cormack ("Greenpeace") at Akutan, ca. September 1971. Courtesy Greenpeace. The environmental organization evolved directly from the Amchitka issue.

office within 24 hours of arrival. Customs at Anchorage directed them to its nearest office; that meant backtracking 200 miles to Sand Point in the Shumagins. While the captain visited the wheelhouse to serve notice on Captain Cormack, a Coast Guard crewman handed the "Greenpeace" members a written statement: "Due to the situation we are in, the crew of the *Confidence* feel that what you are doing is for the good of all mankind. If our hands weren't tied by these military bonds, we would be in the same position you are in if it was at all possible. Good luck. We are behind you one hundred per cent." Eighteen signatures, of nearly the entire crew, followed. The "Greenpeace" radio operator immediately broadcasted news of the "mutiny," and Alaskan Mothers' Campaign Against Cannikin paid the $100 fines incurred by the crew members for their actions.

Discouraged and imperiled by fall weather, the "Greenpeace" crew debated at Sand Point whether to go forward to Amchitka or back to Vancouver. After long and sometimes acrimonious deliberations they voted to return home. They had begun to accomplish their goals, however. Detainment in Akutan won the "Greenpeace" and her crew the attention of the American news. Sympathetic receptions greeted the crew in Kodiak, Juneau, and Prince Rupert. Canadians sent the world's longest telegram, bearing 188,000 signatures, to the White House in protest of Cannikin. A second vessel, the *Edgewater Fortune*, dubbed "Greenpeace Too," left Vancouver for Amchitka. A day out, it met the "Greenpeace," four of

8.5. *"Greenpeace" crew, 1971. Courtesy Greenpeace. Left to right (top): Robert Hunter, Patrick Moore, Bob Cummings, Ben Metcalfe, Dave Birmingham; (bottom): Richard Fineberg, Lyle Thurston, Jim Bohlen, Terry Simmons, Bill Darnell, Capt. John Cormack. Photographer (not pictured): Bob Keziere.*

whose crew (Dave Birmingham, Bob Cummings, Rod Marining and Terry Simmons) transferred to it carrying the "Greenpeace" flag. But the "Greenpeace Too" ran into heavy seas; it got no closer than 700 miles from Amchitka when the bomb exploded.[34]

By carrying out nuclear experiments in an environmentally sensitive area in an age of active protests, the AEC and Defense Departments touched off a reaction helping to fuse environmental and peace issues. They also sired Greenpeace, among the most daring of all environmental-protection groups. Formally named in 1972, it soon gained international fame for its skillful engagement of the media to motivate the public, most noticeably against whale killing and marine pollution. In 1978 it opened a branch office in Alaska.

Amchitka testing coincided with the birth of the modern environmental movement. Building on the Chariot experience, Amchitka bolstered the notion that potentially damaging projects must be justified through proper scientific investigation. It put government on notice that the media, the public, and environmental groups would be watching and would demand a voice in the use of public funds for projects inimical to safety or ecosystem integrity.

NOTES

1. McCutcheon, "Atomic Blast vs. Otter?" 376–377; *New York Times*, July 21, 1971, 30.
2. Merritt and Fuller, *Environment of Amchitka Island*, 124–134.
3. Laycock "The Beautiful, Sad Face," 12, 16.
4. McCutcheon, "Atomic Blast vs. Otter?" 378–380.

5. Lensink, "History and Status of Sea Otters," 121–122.

6. Laycock, "The Beautiful, Sad Face," 14.

7. Dean, "Amchitka," 2–3; McCutcheon, "Atomic Blast vs. Otter?" 376.

8. Buckheister, "Duplicity and Destruction," 371; Merritt and Fuller, *Environment of Amchitka Island*, 133–134; *New York Times*, November 2, 1965, 10.

9. Lensink, "Memo to Wildlife Administrator."

10. Merritt and Fuller, *Environment of Amchitka Island*, iii–vi; U.S. Atomic Energy Commission (AEC), *Background Information Regarding AEC Activities*, 1–2.

11. *New York Times*, May 29, 1967, 15; O'Neill, *Firecracker Boys*, 274–275.

12. *Alaska Conservation Society (ACS) News Bulletin*, May 29, 1967, 15.

13. U.S. Fish and Wildlife Service (USFWS), *Aleutian Islands National Wildlife Refuge*, 1969, 11.

14. Merritt, *Physical and Biological Effects: Milrow*, 6; *New York Times*, July 14, 1969, 38; September 30, 1969. Luther Carter ("Earthquakes and Nuclear Tests") discussed the concerns of scientists about possible seismological effects of Milrow or larger blasts.

15. USFWS, *Aleutian Islands National Wildlife Refuge*, 1969.

16. *New York Times*, September 17, 1969, 11.

17. Merritt, *Physical and Biological Effects:Milrow*, 47, 70–71, 106; Merritt, *Physical and Biological Effects: Cannikin*, 1; New *York Times*, April 18, 1971, IV, 6; June 13, 1971, 30.

18. Peter, "Cannikin," 955; *New York Times*, July 21, 1971, 30.

19. Peter, "Cannikin," 956–958.

20. *New York Times*, October 23, 1971, 78; November 5, 1971, 20.

21. *New York Times*, November 6, 1971.

22. *New York Times*, November 8, 1971, 38; *Committee for Nuclear Responsibility v. Seaborg*, (71–1732) D.C. Cir. (1971). Amchitka Two, American Association of Indian Affairs, National Parks and Conservation Association, SANE Inc., and the Wilderness Society also filed as plaintiffs.

23. *Anchorage Daily News*, September 3, 1971, 1; *Aleut League v. Atomic Energy Commission* 337 F. Supp. 534 (1971); Terry Simmons, interview by author, July 26, 1989.

24. *New York Times*, September 27, 1971, 1.

25. *New York Times*, November 7, 1971, 64.

26. AEC, *Environmental Impact Statement, Cannikin*, 1–3.

27. Laycock, "The Beautiful, Sad Face," 19.

28. AEC, *Project Cannikin: D + 30 Day Report*, 20–26; Merritt, *Physical and Biological Effects: Cannikin*, 44, 49, 55–58, 62, 72–73, 89, 97.

29. Burns, Frost, and Lowry, *Marine Mammals Species Accounts*, 42.

30. *New York Times*, November 7, 1971, IV, 10; November 8, 1971, 38; December 23, 1971, 24.

31. Calkins and Schneider, "The Sea Otter," 42–43.

32. AEC, *Summary Report: Amchitka Demobilization*, 10–11, 16, 36–37.

33. Merritt and Fuller, *Environment of Amchitka Island*, iii–xii; J. Reed, "Ecological Investigation," 322.

34. Keziere and Hunter, *Greenpeace*; R. Hunter, *Warriors of the Rainbow*, 3, 7–8, 11–13, 42, 52–61, 74, 80; *Greenpeace Examiner*, "Fifteen Years," 8; Brown and May, *Greenpeace Story*, 7–15; Terry Simmons and Denny Wilcher, interviews by author, July 26 and August 3, 1989.

9

Rampart:
Developer's Dream, Nature Lover's Nightmare

A drama of grand proportions unfolded in Alaska during the 1960s, uniting preservationists and utilitarian conservationists in defense of wildlife and wildlands. Fortuitously, it strengthened the local and national environmental communities, spurred Native land-rights efforts in Alaska, and informed the lands settlement of 1980. It centered on the merits of a colossal dam project.

Long before Alaskan statehood, travelers noticed a narrow passage on the upper Yukon River, and named it Rampart Canyon for its steep walls. In 1948 the Department of the Interior's Bureau of Reclamation initiated surveys of potential hydropower sites in Alaska; the Army Corps of Engineers followed suit in 1954. The Bureau of Reclamation built a small dam at Eklutna in 1950, and hoped by the end of the decade to start work on others at Snettisham near Juneau and at Devil Canyon on the Susitna River north of Anchorage. The corps favored the Rampart site 130 miles northwest of Fairbanks on the Yukon, and one of modest size at Bradley Lake on the Kenai Peninsula. U.S. Senator Ernest Gruening took up the issue from his seat on the Public Works Committee when he entered Congress in 1959. He conducted hearings on hydropower needs in Alaska in 1960, finding Juneau, Anchorage, and Fairbanks speakers in favor of projects nearest to their respective cities. He concluded that Snettisham and Bradley Lake should be built as temporary measures, and that a Rampart Dam best suited long-range economic needs. Given money for a feasibility review of Rampart, the Corps of Engineers appointed a three-member Alaskan advisory board to oversee the contracted study: state senator Irene Ryan, University of Alaska president William R. Wood, and former legislator Stanley McCutcheon. The corps and its advisory board enthusiastically promoted a Rampart Canyon Dam and Reservoir Project.[1] It would be an enormous undertaking: a dam 530 feet high and 4,700 feet across; its lake 280 miles long and up to 80 miles wide, larger than Lake Erie. It would cost an estimated $1.3 billion and generate 5 million kilowatts of electricity—comparable to that of Grand Coulee Dam.[2]

Political timing did not favor Rampart. The nation had begun to express its newfound affluence in love of nature and outdoor recreation. Environmentalists had defeated a proposed dam at Dinosaur National Monument in the late 1950s. A few years later, damage wrought by the Glen Canyon Dam again called into question the wisdom of such megaprojects, inspiring critics to be more active. Outdoor sporting groups, including duck hunters, had

9.1. Athabaskan woman softening moose skin, upper Yukon region, ca. 1916. Courtesy Phillips collection, University of Alaska Fairbanks, Alaska and Polar Regions Archives. Countless generations of Natives relied on the rich wildlife resources of the Yukon Valley.

grown more politically aware. In both Washington and Alaska, Democratic administrations permitted wildlife managers relative freedom to speak out on controversies. Travel and communications gave Alaska more visibility as a national asset. And early in the 1960s, the civil rights movement began to make its presence felt in Alaska. Rampart's pursuit engendered a struggle that would alter the fate of government agencies, the environmental movement, Natives, and even its leading proponent, Senator Gruening.

The site of the proposed Rampart lake, Yukon Flats, is a large, relatively level bowl in north central Alaska, bisected by sweeping bends of the Yukon River. Covered by oxbow marshes, small lakes, tundra, and forest, the region is rich in wildlife. It hosts one of the world's largest gatherings of nesting ducks and geese. For over 10,000 years, Gwitch'in Athabaskan Indians lived off the moose, caribou, rabbits, ducks, geese, and ptarmigans, and caught the king (or chinook), dog (or chum) and silver (or coho) salmon ascending the Yukon. The river carried trade in moose hides, furs, porcupine quills, copper, jade, and shells.[3]

Life began to change in the eighteenth century as Western trade goods entered the interior to be exchanged for furs, and later when Europeans and Euro-Americans arrived. Russians erected trading forts at St. Michael in 1833 and Nulato in 1839. Before they could extend their reach into the upper Yukon, Hudson's Bay Company arrived. First known of the Westerners on the Yukon Flats, trader John Bell, descended the Porcupine to its mouth on the Yukon in 1846. Alexander Murray followed, and built Fort Yukon in 1847. He designed the fort, a Hudson's Bay trading post, to defend against Russians as much as Indians; but thanks to an 1839 treaty no direct conflict took place. Trading flourished; the company considered Fort Yukon its most lucrative post west of the Rockies.[4] The location itself often failed to inspire. Murray reflected on his first year at the post:

> As I sat smoking my pipe and my face besmirched with tobacco juice to keep at bay the d—d mosquitoes still hovering in clouds around me . . . my first impressions of the Youcan were anything but favorable. . . . I never saw an uglier river, everywhere low banks, apparently lately overflowed, with lakes and swamps behind, the trees too small for building, the water abominably dirty, and the current furious.[5]

Murray participated in a colorful history. Robert Kennicott, later to head the Western Union Telegraph expedition exploring the feasibility of a line to Russia, first visited the upper Yukon in 1860–1861. After his death at Nulato, fellow expedition members Frank Ketchum, Michael Lebarge, and William Dall arrived in 1866 and 1867. As the first paddle-wheeler *Youcan* made its way up the river in 1869 to take possession of Fort Yukon for the United States, Army Corps of Engineers Captain Charles Raymond reported that it sparked great excitement among the Natives, and "appeared to them as a huge monster, breathing fire and smoke."[6] Gold seekers first entered the upper Yukon in 1873, and worked up a minor gold rush by the mid-1880s. Selling supplies to prospectors replaced fur trading in the local economy. A strike at Birch Creek in 1893 gave birth to Circle City, for a few frantic years the hub of life on the upper Yukon.[7] Arthur T. Walden, who freighted supplies among the gold fields, described the overland travel conditions faced by the sourdoughs packing to the Birch Creek mines as far as 80 miles south of Circle City:

> The trail across was over a swampy plateau, covered with shallow ponds and muskeg, and a few stunted spruces. In summer there was absolutely no game of any kind on these flats, on account of the mosquitoes which are simply impossible to describe. Not a particle of the body could be exposed, and the sun was actually obliterated. . . . Men have been known to go raving mad; the mosquitoes never let you alone day or night.

Walden rated the mosquitoes "the worst hardship we had to bear when traveling in Alaska, and I have known men who had readily braved all previous hardships, but who gave up when it came to facing that pest."[8]

Life in the Rampart basin donated generously to the lore of the Far North. Jack London and Rex Beach spent the winter of 1898–1899 at Rampart, absorbing material for their novels. Beach stayed through the following winter. When the Gold Rush passed in the early twentieth century, the Yukon Flats again functioned as a fur-trading center, reaching its peak in the late 1920s. Travel by aircraft, and declining fur prices, drained the upper Yukon towns (Fort Yukon, Beaver, Circle City, Eagle, and Rampart) of vitality by the 1940s.[9]

Events of the nineteenth and twentieth centuries had a powerful impact on the Indians of the upper Yukon. Large numbers died of introduced diseases. Their economy shifted from hunting and fishing to commercial fur trapping in the 1850s. Cash and its resultant social changes appeared as they sold moccasins and other goods to the gold seekers. After the Gold Rush, Indians lost control of much of the fur trapping to former gold prospectors. Wildlife also paid a price during the gold era; moose and some furbearers grew scarce. Hunting by aircraft beginning in the 1930s kept moose and caribou numbers low.[10] The upper Yukon remained an economic backwater through the territorial period.

9.2. Rex Beach's cabin at Rampart, ca. 1904. Courtesy R. K. Woods collection, University of Alaska Fairbanks, Alaska and Polar Regions Archives. The Yukon served as a transportation route for gold-seekers and for writers who romanticized them.

Like the Yukon Flats, Alaska endured a depressed economy at the time of statehood, and its legislature embraced nearly any proposal for economic growth. Two power-source options received most attention: the high-profile Rampart Dam and a smaller dam at Devil Canyon on the Susitna River. Most observers believed the federal government unlikely to fund both. The legislature issued a qualified endorsement of Rampart, calling for more investigation. Alaska's congressional delegation chose a panel that authorized a preliminary evaluation by Arthur D. Little Inc. of Cambridge, Massachusetts. Little's report, appearing in January 1962, expressed doubt about the project's viability. Rampart Dam, it noted, would generate power "many times the ability of Alaskan industry, commerce and population to absorb."[11] A Corps of Engineers–sponsored review then predicted that "the power output of Rampart can be marketed" and the market growth "will create a demand within that area for low-cost power in addition to Rampart soon after Rampart is in full operation."[12] A lengthy battle-of-the-studies ensued. The Senate Public Works Committee favored the corps-sponsored assessment.[13]

An unusual turn of bureaucratic politics intervened. The Interior Department and the Corps of Engineers, rivals for control over federal lands, agreed in 1962 to separate their functions. Interior would conduct economic and environmental analyses for dam projects in Alaska; the corps would finish its Rampart examination but thereafter do only engineering and construction. Interior embarked on its studies of Rampart. Congress appropriated insufficient money for a full environmental impact assessment, and Fish and Wildlife Service officials maintained they needed six years or more to determine such elements as the migratory patterns of salmon and waterfowl. Given only two years, they made the most of it. At a

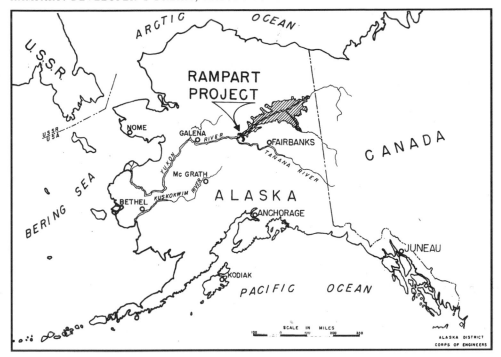

9.1. Rampart Dam site. Courtesy Gruening collection, University of Alaska Fairbanks, Alaska and Polar Regions Archives.

meeting of Alaska Sportsmen's Council in January 1963 they released preliminary estimates, projecting huge wildlife losses. Word spread, alarming sportsmen in the Lower 48. Wildlife Management Institute director Ira Gabrielson termed Rampart "a massive and irreparable threat to fish and wildlife," and organized a campaign to combat it.[14]

Alaskan business groups split over the two dam options. Rampart backers met in September 1963 to organize. They formed Operation Rampart, soon to be renamed Yukon Power for America (YPA) and presided over by *Fairbanks Daily News-Miner* publisher C. W. Snedden. William R. Wood acted as vice president, Irene Ryan as executive secretary, and *Anchorage Daily Times* publisher Robert Atwood sat on the executive committee. Most members held positions in government or business. Ted Stevens, a trustee, termed the organization "not a lobby group," only "a group of public-spirited citizens." YPA sought unsuccessfully to insert funding for Rampart in the Rivers and Harbors bill of 1964.[15]

YPA's multicolor brochure compared Rampart to the Panama Canal and the Golden Gate, and spoke of "the American way of getting things done" and "almost incalculable dividends." Industry, aluminum in particular, would be attracted and "Alaska's dependence on seasonal construction activity and military spending [would be] replaced by a stable and growing economy." Boating, sailing, hunting and fishing camps, and access to the nearby Arctic National Wildlife Range would ensue; "thus a sprawling land area, barren, virtually inaccessible, offering no foreseeable opportunity for development, would be converted into a physical and scenic asset with untold commercial and recreational promise." There would be "no significant effects" on wildlife, and "ample time to relocate game in areas bordering the lake." Hinting that Russia might be getting ahead in its dam construction, it proclaimed Rampart "a need which must be met."[16]

YPA set about fund raising and received $10,000 from the Anchorage City Council and a matching amount from the Fairbanks Public Utilities Board. The legislature voted amounts totaling nearly $50,000, overriding objections by a minority led by Senator Jay Hammond.[17] YPA hired Ivan Bloch and Associates, a hydropower consulting firm, to do a feasibility study. Bloch's report, though not completed, appeared on December 7, 1963 (Pearl Harbor day and two weeks after JFK's assassination). Its introduction quoted Kennedy from a 1960 campaign speech in Anchorage: "I see a land of over 1 million people. I see a giant electric grid stretching from Juneau to Anchorage and beyond. I see the greatest dam in the free world at Rampart Canyon, producing twice the power of TVA to light mills and cities and farms all over Alaska." However, Kennedy had reportedly switched to the Devil Canyon option in 1961.[18]

Ernest Gruening, the prime mover of Rampart, delivered the keynote speech at YPA's organizing meeting. The senator, a former editor of *The Nation*, viewed himself as a committed New Dealer and conservationist. He believed in the use of government, as in the Tennessee Valley Authority experiment, to stimulate economic production and raise standards of living. His notion of conservation echoed that articulated in Theodore Roosevelt's administration: the planned appropriation of natural resources, controlled by government for national well-being, as distinct from random and unrestricted exploitation by private interests. Unlike Roosevelt's, his belief left scant room for preservation of wildlife, land, ecosystems, or even Native or other traditional lifestyles, all points of contention in the Rampart controversy, raising barriers between Gruening and others calling themselves conservationists. The Rampart debate clarified differences between economically-oriented utilitarian conservation and the wildlife protection values of the outdoor sporting groups and the budding environmental movement.

Rampart Dam bid fair to be a spectacular monument to Gruening's public service, and he strove doggedly for the goal. He believed cheap power would bring in people and industry and solve the state's economic problems. Yukon Flats, the area to be flooded, "is a mammoth swamp," judged the senator, and "from the standpoint of human habitability is about as worthless and useless an area as can be found in the path of any hydroelectric development. Scenically it is zero." As the lake waters rose the moose could just walk away, he asserted, and so could the furbearers.[19] Calling himself "a fervent conservationist," he considered it "folly to allow waters of the Yukon to flow wastefully to the sea when this can be an unparalleled source of power."[20] He visited six of the seven small Indian villages to be flooded out and found them in favor of the project. Villagers mostly relied on welfare and stood to benefit more than anyone else, he said. "Their children do not have a future such as every American child should rightfully expect."[21]

For a brief period there seemed to be Native approval. On April 16, 1963, a letter from "Sam John of Rampart" appeared in the *Fairbanks Daily News-Miner*: "Alaska big. Lots

9.3. Senator Ernest Gruening, Army Corps of Engineers Colonel Christian Hanburger, and U.S. Rep. Ralph Rivers at Rampart Dam site, early 1960s. Courtesy Gruening collection, University of Alaska Fairbanks, Alaska and Polar Regions Archives. Senator and former Alaska Governor Gruening championed the Rampart project.

land. Who cares about little piece flooded? I for Rampart. Peoples against Rampart don't look into future." The editors incorporated it into a pro-Rampart editorial and ran it again. At length it became clear that no such Sam John existed.[22]

The Bureau of Land Management (BLM) held hearings in Fairbanks and Fort Yukon in February 1964 to consider reservation by the U.S. Geological Survey of 8.9 million acres for a dam site. At least 80 percent of those testifying at Fairbanks, primarily from business interests, wanted the reservation. They included the Fairbanks Chamber of Commerce and William R. Wood. Correlating water and ducks, Mayor Darrell Brewington asserted that Rampart Lake would "enhance the duck picture." Native leader Howard Rock of the *Tundra Times* editorialized against the withdrawal. Celia Hunter, speaking for the Alaska Conservation Society, criticized it as a foot in the door for Rampart over other options.[23]

The next day's hearing at Fort Yukon revealed anxiety and confusion among the Indians over the prospective obliteration of their homeland. Paul Solomon Sr. presented one view of the trade-offs and uncertainties they faced: "I lived here for 50 years. . . . My children, seven of them went through high school. When they come back . . . they don't know how to set snare, they don't know how to set trap, they don't know how to hunt. What they going to do? Most of them high school education come back they are in jail now. What's the matter with them? Just because they have no job. That's why I am for Rampart Dam. There's lots of jobs." During the 50 years, said Solomon, "we going ahead a million year. We go too fast in that 50 year—all our children, going to school they can't see nothing, we go too fast." He reflected on the mixed benefits of modernization: "I think the United States don't want to cheat nobody. We just ask for good living and modern place to live after we flood it off. . . . Money is no good to us. Most of us got a few thousand dollars, we'd die. I know that. Because I am an Indian [word obscured], when I make a lot of money, I went crazy and when I broke then I start to think again."

Peter Simple interpreted for elder Philip Peter, who said he had never attended school and considered himself "not much better than an animal." Said Philip Peter, "This land is dear. There has been a day in the past that our grandfather has made a living in this land with a bow and arrow . . . [M]illions and millions of dollars wouldn't mean a thing to us, wouldn't do us no good. If they take those millions and millions of dollars and distribute them among men, women and children, they would only be shortening their lives." The true basis of Indian life, he said, is the wildlife of the region. Mr. Peter then posed the question of how people in the Lower 48 would feel if Indians with money arrived to build a dam and flood them out: "Would you say 'Yes, go ahead' without a fight?" Speaking for himself, Peter Simple expressed a fundamental fear: "We have no judgment whatever in our future. We are afraid we might put our children up against something they don't know." Johnathan Solomon read the official statement of the Gwitchya Gwitchin Ginkhye ("Yukon Flats People Speaks") organization opposing the reservation and the dam: "We believe it to be a violation of the rights of the legal owners. . . . [This land] is the resting place of our loved ones that are dead. It is worth more than money to us."[24]

OPPOSITION GAINS STRENGTH

Votes in the 13 villages most affected by the project revealed 11 against it, 1 in favor, and 1 neutral. All 7 to be submerged—Beaver, Birch Creek, Chalkyitsik, Rampart, Stevens Village, Venetie, and Fort Yukon—containing 1,200 people total, voted no.[25] *Tundra Times*, alluding to Gruening, commented, "We emphatically object to public officials making hurried trips to the areas affected and then expounding in the press false statements of what they did, or did not learn on the trip."[26] During one meeting in Fort Yukon, attended by Gruening, the proceedings evolved into a conversation in the local language. At length the moderator, an elder, turned to Gruening and explained: "We were discussing what to do with a dog when it gets too old to pull."[27] In March 1964, Alaska Native Brotherhood announced its opposition to Rampart.[28]

The Fish and Wildlife Service then struck a telling blow. Exercising Interior's environmental impact study prerogative, its April 1964 report addressed what lay *below* Rampart's

Table 9.1—Projected Wildlife and Habitat Losses in Rampart Dam Project, 1964

	In Reservoir Area	Downstream	Total
Ducks	1,500,000	5,000	1,500,000
Loons	—	—	20,000
Grebes	—	—	20,000
Canada/white-fronted geese	12,500	300	12,800
Little brown cranes	10,000	—	10,000
Shorebirds and songbirds	—	—	"Countless numbers"
Moose	12,500	500	13,000
Furbearers (except hares)	3,550,000	10,500	3,560,500
Waterfowl habitat degraded	10,500 sq. mi.	5,000 sq. mi.	15,500 sq. mi.
Lakes and ponds	36,000	—	36,000
Major streams	5,000 mi.	—	5,000 mi.
Minor streams	7,600 mi.	—	7,600 mi.

Source: U.S. Fish and Wildlife Service. *A Report on Fish and Wildlife Resources Affected by Rampart Dam and Reservoir Project, Yukon River, Alaska.* (Juneau: USFWS, April 1964), 2–10, 91–98, 120.

waterline (Table 9.1). Drowned, it calculated, would be 36,000 ponds, 400 miles of river, and 2.4 million acres of prime waterfowl nesting area. Lost would be 200,000 to 400,000 salmon, a vital subsistence food for Native villages, as well as 1.5 million ducks, 12,500 geese, 10,000 cranes, 20,000 loons, and 10,000 grebes, plus grouse and ptarmigan. Mammals, too, would be lost: 12,500 moose plus black and grizzly bears, beaver, otter, mink, muskrat, red fox, marten, lynx, wolverine, and weasel in the thousands. These figures did not fully count downriver areas to be dried up by the reduced and evened water flow, eliminating more wetland habitat. On the positive side, the reservoir would eventually host populations of lake trout and whitefish. The piece de resistance of the document appeared in a judgment destined to be repeatedly cited in articles and editorials on the subject: "Nowhere in the history of water development in America have the fish and wildlife losses anticipated to result from a single project been so overwhelming." No feasible way existed to avoid the losses, said the report. "Accordingly, we strongly oppose authorization of the Rampart Canyon Dam and Reservoir Project." In an act of bureaucratic courage, given the vulnerability of agency budgets to political pressures, it bore the signatures of regional directors J. T. Barnaby of the Bureau of Sport Fisheries and Wildlife and Harry T. Rietze of the Bureau of Commercial Fisheries.[29]

Outdoor sporting and environmental groups reacted to the Fish and Wildlife assessment. Practically every such organization of national standing went on record against Rampart. Former Alaska game manager Frank Dufresne penned in *Field and Stream*: "Long before Rampart's turbines spun a single kilowatt of power, the most damaging single blow ever struck against America's waterfowl would have landed." He ventured that "Rampart Dam is not Alaska's private game of roulette, but the personal concern of every U.S. citizen. There is much more at issue, too, than a deeper tax bite for all of us. There's a wholesale sacrifice of natural resources, some of which in the name of fair play belong to not only Alaska but to neighboring Canada, the remaining states, even Mexico and Central America."

9.4. Rampart Dam site. Courtesy J. Sheldon collection, University of Alaska Anchorage Archives. The proposed dam would flood an area the size of Lake Erie on the Upper Yukon River.

Canada objected to the dam, in part because it violated the 1871 boundary treaty guaranteeing navigational access to the Pacific.[30]

Alaska Sportsmen's Council voted against Rampart in early 1964, and the Sierra Club ran boating trips down the Yukon in 1965 to highlight the issue.[31] Tanana Valley Sportsmen's Association raised the specter of "an industrialized Alaska of highly commercialized areas with plants that discharge air and water-polluting gases and wastes, and a landscape bound with a network of high tension power lines." Dam enthusiasts, by contrast, held that Alaska needed more population, and that economic expansion posed no threat to the natural character of so vast a land. Some argued that release of urban tensions, even the health of democracy itself, required movement into open land.[32]

The Natural Resources Council, a coalition of conservation groups, funded an investigatory team headed by Stephen H. Spurr, a resource economist and graduate dean at the University of Michigan. The council included the Audubon Society, Sierra Club, Isaac Walton League, Boone and Crockett, and National Wildlife Federation.[33] Released in 1966, Spurr's report identified the barriers to development in Alaska as "lack of raw materials, unsuitable terrain, poor climate, distance from markets, high labor costs, [and] high costs of living," and judged that low energy costs could not overcome them. Aluminum, the projected major industrial application of the power, allotted only 13 percent of its costs to energy. The analysis concluded, "Present indications are that future Alaskan markets in themselves will not be sufficient to absorb Rampart power even when it becomes available many years in the future. . . . In short, Rampart is an expensive gamble—the most expensive gamble ever suggested in hydroelectric development—and there is little evidence on hand to suggest that the probability of success is high." It recommended as alternatives natural-gas-generated electricity and a diversion of some Yukon water to the Taiya River for power in the Southeast. It rated Rampart "by far the most destructive" to wildlife of the various options.[34] Team ecologists A. Starker Leopold and Justin Leonard calculated the project would destroy 2.4 million acres of prime wildfowl habitat—more than had been rehabilitated and purchased in all federal efforts since 1936. It would also exterminate the upper-Yukon strains of coho, chum, and chinook salmon, the longest river migrators (nearly 2,000 miles for the chinook) of any salmon in the world.[35] Closely monitoring the story, the *New York Times* commented, "Even if it would create an impoundment larger than Lake Erie and surpass in size any hydroelectric project yet undertaken by the Soviet Union, will it benefit the United States if it turns out also to be the world's biggest sinkhole for public funds?"[36]

Proponents felt temporarily heartened by the issuance of Interior's power marketing study in 1965, even though it estimated the cost of power at 5 to 11 mils per watt compared to YPA's claim of 3, and the total cost had risen from $1.6 billion to $2.3–$2.8 billion. As a technical work, however, it made no recommendations.[37] Interior's summary statement of June 1967 effectively demolished YPA's position. Seconding the Spurr and Fish and Wildlife Service evaluations, it termed Rampart "inappropriate to satisfy Alaska's limited power requirements," adding that power could not be sent economically to the Lower 48. It repeated the familiar projection of "overwhelming" losses of wildlife and called for smaller-scale power alternatives.[38]

Gruening vented his anger at the critical studies and the *New York Times* editorials endorsing them. Attacking the Spurr report for its connection to conservation groups, he labeled the studies "nothing but propaganda for a highly specialized point of view." As for the groups, he suggested that "all of them are notably more concerned with the conservation of wildlife than of the species known as *homo sapiens* which would be the chief beneficiary of the Rampart Dam project."[39] He directed his heaviest fire at Gabrielson, whom he accused of allowing the salmon to decline while serving as Fish and Wildlife Service director, and of trying to keep oil drilling out of the Kenai Moose Range that Gabrielson had persuaded Interior Secretary Harold Ickes to reserve in 1941. Gruening bestowed on Gabrielson the extraordinary title of "the principal factor in Alaska's plight and problems, past, present and future."[40] His dream nearly finished, Gruening vowed to fight on. But Congress members did not relish spending so much in one district and taxing their own constituents for the privilege.

The Corps of Engineers, having maintained a low profile since its pact with Interior, released its final report in 1971. At best, it concluded, the plan had a 0.96-to-1 benefit-to-cost ratio, and rising costs could worsen it. "Fish and wildlife losses would be significant"; thus it advised that Rampart "not be undertaken at this time." Adding insult to injury, an appended letter to the corps from the Bureau of Outdoor Recreation pronounced, "The Rampart reservoir would not constitute a recreational opportunity of national or state significance because of the absence of outstanding scenic attractions, probably unattractive shorelines, unfavorable conditions for swimming and bathing, and hazardous conditions for small boat operations over most of the reservoir."[41]

Disunity of dam adherents and outsized damage potential placed Alaskan environmentalists in a strong position to combat the project. Alaska Conservation Society (ACS) leaders adopted a restrained approach. Rather than directly attacking Rampart, they questioned its economics and called for more thorough assessment. They avoided the "wildlife versus people" terms in which proponents tried to cast the debate. Vice President Daniel W. Swift announced the society would withhold approval "until it is shown to be a good thing for Alaska's economic development and its further long-run interest."[42] Ginny Hill Wood took off the gloves in the Wilderness Society's magazine: "It was perhaps inevitable that the Yukon River could not continue to flow unnoticed by the Corps of Engineers, which looks upon any free-running stream of consequence as a loss to mankind unless converted into kilowatts with concrete. And it was also inevitable that the imaginations of Alaska businessmen, politicians, and labor leaders would be fired by visions of what a gigantic hydroelectric project would do for a wobbly economy."[43] ACS publicized the controversy, backing the Fish and Wildlife Service. They participated in radio and TV presentations and spoke in favor of nuclear power and Devil Canyon on the Susitna River as alternatives—positions they would later regret.[44] National media consulted and quoted their spokespersons. As in the case of Project Chariot, they augmented the winning position while maintaining their reputation as a responsible organization to which Alaskans could comfortably relate.

Rampart spun off more than one ironic twist of fate. Reaching for their dream, boosters invigorated both the Alaskan and national environmental communities, who widened their constituent bases and their experience in contravening large industrial schemes. Following on the heels of Project Chariot and coinciding with the emerging land settlement conflict, Rampart helped consolidate Native political power. Controversy over the dam called national attention to Alaska and to the duck and goose banding and research undertaken by the Fish and Wildlife Service. This awareness strengthened the agency, elevated interest in Alaska by Lower 48 environmentalists, and laid groundwork for the 1980 designation and expansion of many Alaskan national wildlife refuges, including Yukon Flats.[45] It demonstrated the wide common ground between environmental and utilitarian wildlife conservationists in the realm of land and wildlife protection. Investing solely in Rampart rather than accepting the lesser Susitna option, Rampart subscribers ended up getting neither. By his treatment of the Natives, Ernest Gruening assisted his own defeat in the 1968 primary. The local political defender of the Natives against Rampart, Fort Yukon schoolteacher Don Young, won election to the legislature in 1966 opposing Rampart. Sent to Congress in 1973,[46] Young endured for decades as a consistent adversary of environmentalists.

Rampart died in large part because it arose at a time when the magic of large dam projects as symbols of American progress had begun to wear off. It also coincided with the early stages of modern environmentalism, which had erected a victory marker in its triumph over the Dinosaur National Monument dam. The vast scope of Rampart's threat to sustainability of wildlife populations incensed the outdoor sporting community as well as environmentalists. Scientific investigation, albeit hasty and incomplete, succeeded in alerting the public to some of the costs of the project. Both in and outside Alaska, the Rampart affair advanced several fundamental principles of modern environmentalism: sustainable use of natural resources, accountability of government for the effects of its actions, appropriate research, and public access to relevant information.

NOTES

1. Coates, *Trans-Alaska Pipeline Controversy*, 134–146.

2. U. S. Army, Corps of Engineers, *Rampart Study*.

3. King, *Alaska's Yukon Flats*, 16–17; Drucker, "Alaska's Upper Yukon," 1982, 80–85; Grauman, *Yukon Frontiers*, 16.

4. Grauman, *Yukon Frontiers*, 20–22; U.S. Dept. of the Interior (USDOI), *Final EIS: Proposed Yukon Flats*, 32.

5. Grauman, *Yukon Frontiers*, 24–26.

6. Ibid., 27–31.

7. USDOI, *Final EIS: Proposed Yukon Flats*, 32; Drucker, "Alaska's Upper Yukon," 51.

8. Walden, *Dog-Puncher*, 25–26.

9. Ricks, *Alaska Bibliography*, 37; USDOI, *Final EIS: Proposed Yukun Flats*, 32; Drucker, "Alaska's Upper Yukon," 95.

10. King, *Alaska's Yukon Flats*, 17, 22; Drucker, "Alaska's Upper Yukon," 87, 90, 94; Grauman, *Yukon Frontiers*, 27, 89–90.

11. P. Brooks, "Plot to Drown Alaska," 58; *Alaska Session Laws, 1973*, SJR 11.

12. U.S. Army, Corps of Engineers, *Market for Rampart Power*, introductory letter.

13. *New York Times*, August 22, 1965, 30.

14. Coates, *Trans-Alaska Pipeline*, 141; August, "Political History," 5–6; Gillelan, "Rampart Dam," 15.

15. Coates, *Trans-Alaska Pipeline*, 143.

16. Yukon Power for America, "The Rampart Story," (brochure).

17. *Alaska Conservation Society (ACS) News Bulletin*, October 1963, 2; Coates, *Trans-Alaska Pipeline*, 146, 153.

18. Bloch and Associates, *Rampart Project*, "Introduction"; Naske and Hunt, *Politics of Hydroelectric Power*, 12.

19. Coates, *Trans-Alaska Pipeline*, 156–157; Gruening, "Plot to Strangle Alaska," 58–59.

20. *New York Times*, September 15, 1964, 18.

21. Gruening, "Plot to Strangle Alaska," 58.

22. *ACS News Bulletin*, December 1963, 9–10; *Fairbanks Daily News-Miner*, April 16, 1963, 4.

23. U.S. Bureau of Land Management (BLM), *Hearings on Proposed Rampart*, February 15, 1964.

24. Ibid., February 15, 1964, 14, 17–18, 25–28, 42.

25. Coates, *Trans-Alaska Pipeline*, 148–149.

26. Corso, "Benefit-Cost Considerations," 8.

27. Calvin R. Lensink, interview by author, July 28, 1989.

28. Naske and Hunt, *Politics of Hydroelectric Power*, 16.

29. U.S. Fish and Wildlife Service (USFWS), *A Report on Fish and Wildlife*, 2–13, 91–98, 120–122.

30. Dufresne, "Rampart Roulette," 10, 12.

31. *Alaska Conservation Society (ACS) News Bulletin*, December 1964, 13; *New York Times*, July 11, 1965, 44.

32. Coates, *Trans-Alaska Pipeline*, 155–156.

33. *New York Times*, April 20, 1966, 46.

34. Spurr, *Rampart Dam*, 28, 43, 55–59; *New York Times*, April 11, 1966, 24.

35. Leopold and Leonard, "Alaska Dam," 177–178.

36. *New York Times*, March 8, 1965, 28.

37. Ibid., February 28, 1965, 54; USDOI, *Field Report: Rampart Project*; Wood, "Rampart: Foolish Dam," 4.

38. USDOI, *Alaska Natural Resources*, 35–36.

39. *New York Times*, April 20, 1966, 46.

40. Gruening, "Plot to Strangle Alaska," 57–58.

41. U.S. Army, Corps of Engineers, *A Report on the Rampart Canyon*, 30–32.

42. *ACS News Bulletin*, February 1964 (attached resolution dated February 11, 1964); *New York Times*, August 22, 1965, 25.

43. Wood, "Foolish Dam," 4.

44. *ACS News Bulletin*, May 1965, 6–7; Naske and Hunt, *Politics of Hydroelectric Power*, 16.

45. James G. King and Calvin R. Lensink, interviews by author, July 13 and 28, 1989.

46. Coates, *Trans-Alaska Pipeline*, 148; Barone and Ujifusa, *Almanac of American Politics*, 35.

10

Susitna: An Exercise in Power Politics

Hopes and dreams of the big dam enthusiasts, dashed by the downfall of Rampart Dam, returned in the Susitna River project and set off another altercation between development and conservation. In playing their part, Alaskan environmentalists defended both nature and the public treasury. Although economic sustainability proved to be the deciding principle, the endeavor reinforced the values of government accountability, and of public participation based on availability of relevant information.

Susitna's origins related closely to the Rampart controversy. The late 1940s Bureau of Reclamation survey listed Susitna's Devil Canyon as a potential damsite, and a followup review by the agency in the 1950s produced a favorable rating in 1961. However, consideration of the Rampart project caused the Interior Department to defer the Susitna option even though Devil Canyon possessed some superior characteristics. The canyon, a deep 50-mile-long gorge, embraced the 275-mile Susitna River on its way from the Alaska Range and the Talkeetna Mountains to the sea. Nineteenth-century explorers headed north to the Yukon drainage could see no value in the canyon, impassible by water and located on an 80-mile stretch of the river running east to west. Army Lieutenant E. F. Glenn, in charge of one of the earliest such expeditions in 1898, carried out orders to scout a route from Cook Inlet and appraise the economic potential of the southern interior. Glenn found a successful route by ascending the Susitna 80 miles until it split into three branches (Chulitna, main branch, and Talkeetna), then following the Chulitna northward rather than taking the main branch eastward through the canyon.[1]

Except for dam builders, only kayakers showed interest in Devil Canyon, where the rapids throw up waves 20 feet high. A kayak team headed by Walt Blackadar, a medical doctor from Salmon, Idaho, first ran the canyon. Alaskan John Spencer first soloed it, except for a 300-yard portage, on Memorial Day 1975. Spencer's father Dave circled overhead during the passage, then flew to Talkeetna to refuel. When he landed, the current seized his float plane and forced its wingtip under some logs. Thinking the plane lost, Dave walked to town for help. Wingtip extracted, he took off and reached the canyon to find his exhausted and triumphant son on a sandbar.[2] But the canyon gained more notoriety as a site for a gigantic dam.

10.1. Susitna River and Mt. McKinley (left background), 1983. Courtesy Alaska Power Authority collection, University of Alaska Fairbanks, Alaska and Polar Regions Archives. In the 1970s, projected growth revived interest in an electricity megaproject.

Susitna's location, 125 miles north of Anchorage, bested Rampart for delivering power to population centers. Dam advocates perceived Susitna as a way to convert temporary oil wealth into permanent, cheap energy, generating less excess power and flooding far less acreage than Rampart. In the 1960s, environmentalists, some of the business community, Governor William Egan, and the *Anchorage Daily News* all endorsed it in contrast to Rampart.[3] State and federal wildlife officials strongly preferred it, citing its relatively small projected environmental impact.[4] But Rampart, the choice of Senator Gruening, the Army Corps of Engineers, and powerful Alaskan business interests, enjoyed greater momentum than did Susitna. Unable to agree on Susitna as superior to Rampart, Alaskans lost an opportunity to build it. Rampart adherents gambled everything on the bigger scheme. The noisy fight over Rampart and the increasing availability of oil pushed Susitna out of the picture. The Interior Department dropped Susitna from its list of options in 1966.[5]

OPEC's oil price hikes of the mid- and late 1970s revived interest in Susitna. A 1974 Federal Power Commission review judged a Susitna venture appropriate for Alaska's future power needs. It projected annual Railbelt (Fairbanks to Kenai Peninsula) electricity demand at nearly 10 billion kilowatt-hours for 1990 as compared to 2 billion in 1972. It estimated the cost of Devil Canyon and Denali dams (two of the four envisioned for the project) at $682 million in 1974 dollars. Devil Canyon alone would save 4.9 million barrels of oil annually; the four-dam project would save 11.9 million barrels and generate 7 billion kilowatt-hours annu-

10.2. Devil Canyon, Susitna River, 1982. Courtesy Alaska Power Authority collection, University of Alaska Fairbanks, Alaska and Polar Regions Archives. The deep, 50-mile-long canyon drew the attention of dam builders.

ally. Acknowledging that Healy coal might be marginally cheaper, the commission concluded that "there is little question that economic justification exists for the project."[6]

Kaiser Aluminum expressed an interest in Susitna in 1974 as a basis for an aluminum industry.[7] In that same year the legislature backed the dam, declaring it "the catalyst to spark the economic expansion of the Railbelt area," and "of great importance not only to Alaska, but the nation as a whole, especially in these times of energy needs which are likely to be increased in the future." Congress, to pay the bill, and the secretary of the interior were "urgently requested to make the Devil Canyon project one of the highest priority" and to start construction "at the earliest possible time." The resolution noted that the dams' fish ladders would benefit the salmon having difficulty ascending the gorge.[8]

Responding to a 1972 request from the Senate Public Works Committee, the Army Corps of Engineers reassessed the 1960s Susitna configuration. The Federal Power Commission,

Department of the Interior, and University of Alaska Institute for Social, Economic, and Governmental Research all conducted evaluations of power needs. All regarded Susitna as economically viable and preferable to alternatives, the most prominent being natural gas and oil. The corps rejected the earlier four-dam scheme in favor of two large dams at Devil Canyon and Watana. Shortly after the release of the 1976 corps document, Congress authorized $25 million for preliminary work.[9]

Susitna, according to the vision of the late 1970s and 1980s, would be a big undertaking: two of the highest dams in the world. Devil Canyon dam, a 645-foot high structure, would back up the river for 26 miles. Just above this lake at Watana would stand an earthen dam 885 feet high and 4,100 feet wide, creating a lake 48 miles long. Total surface of the lakes would be 75 square miles. The 6.2 billion kilowatt-hours generated annually could power the entire Railbelt.[10]

Although the corps had estimated a 1.3-to-1 cost-benefit ratio, the Carter administration looked with disfavor on large water projects and refused to sanction funding for engineering design. In 1978 the state created an Alaska Power Authority (APA), granting it dual promotional and decisionmaking power. The APA quickly demonstrated its commitment to Susitna,[11] while Washington gave the idea an increasingly cool reception. Senator Mike Gravel, whose election had been made possible partly by Gruening's devotion to Rampart, twice in a single day attempted to insert an additional congressional appropriation for Susitna into unrelated bills. Colleagues noticed the moves and defeated them.[12] APA assumed responsibility for feasibility assessment in 1979, after the corps withdrew from the project. APA's preliminary power market analysis, released in mid-1979, rated Susitna superior to the other options.[13]

Studies, often conflicting, played a central part in the Susitna debate. A 1976 review by the Institute for Social and Economic Research (ISER) had projected substantial growth in Alaska's power needs. A 1980 evaluation completed for APA by Acres American drew a similar conclusion. Soon thereafter a Tussing Associates analysis, done for a legislative committee, articulated suspicions about the assumptions of the ISER and Acres. It predicted a peaking out and declining of Alaska's population in the late 1980s or early 1990s. It charged that Acres' recommendations "strongly imply that Acres and possibly the Power Authority have already decided that Susitna is in fact the best generation alternative for the Railbelt and that the project should go ahead," and if the recommendations were followed, "the decision regarding Susitna's feasibility will not be based on either its economic or financial feasibility."[14]

Notwithstanding the lack of federal financing for Susitna and the skepticism expressed in the Tussing estimate, considerable momentum and enthusiasm existed for Susitna. Most commentators assumed that like the Alaska pipeline, it would be built. The legislature shared the "Build Susitna Now!" spirit of the construction industry, and by 1980 had appropriated $31 million for studies.[15] A year later it went much further, passing bills creating $5 billion or more in financial commitments—about $50,000 for each Alaskan household. Payment would come through statewide uniform electricity rates set by APA. A "Susitna blackmail clause" required all smaller power projects to pay a stiff financial penalty (their state grants would be converted to loans repayable at 10 percent per year) unless the legislature appropriated the

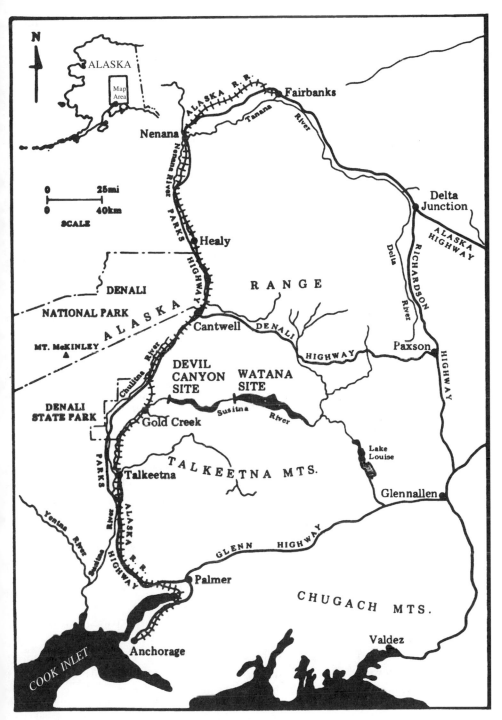

10.1. Susitna Hydro Project Site. Courtesy Neil Davis.

$5 billion for Susitna within five years. This arrangement would ensure the construction of Susitna by committing the state to unprecedented high expenditures and no return to the treasury, and would place APA in a commanding position over the development priorities of the state and the funds of its citizens. Governor Jay Hammond signed the bills in 1981, reportedly reluctant and vowing to seek reform the following year.[16] He had also secured 1980 legislation that specified cost-benefit analyses for large construction projects, and had reorganized the APA board before leaving office. These changes laid the basis for more critical scrutiny of the hydro project, increasing the likelihood that its economic unfeasibility would be exposed in the public examination process, causing it to fall of its own weight.[17]

COUNTERVAILING FORCES

Susitna faced a lengthy list of problems and critics. One of the reservoirs would sit literally on a fault zone, and geologists knew reservoirs could cause earthquakes. The surrounding area produced 20 percent of the state's moose harvest and hosted black bears making their winter dens. The Nelchina caribou herd used the vicinity as calving grounds. Wolves, wolverines, mountain sheep, beavers, otters, and salmon would also decline. Critics questioned the proponents' assumptions. The projected annual output far exceeded the Railbelt use level of the early 1980s. The Corps of Engineers had assumed an Alaskan population increase of up to 200 percent in 20 years, and an annual electricity use rate increase of 3 percent. Population seemed unlikely to grow at that pace, as it had in the oil pipeline boom period. Moreover, oil price increases in the 1970s lowered consumption of electricity; Fairbanks home use dropped at rates as high as 12 percent per year. When the oil price fell in the early 1980s, state revenues accordingly shrank and slowed growth in the state, reducing power needs and making fossil fuel power generation relatively more economical. According to a 1978 calculation by the federal Office of Management and Budget, given a cost overrun of 30 percent, Susitna would not be feasible. Both the corps and the federal Alaska Power Administraton had poor records for cost containment. The corps' Snettisham Dam cost 36 percent more than its projected amount, the Alaska Power Administraton's Terror Lake dam 90 percent, and its Tyee dam over 200 percent. The corps' 1976 estimate of $2.6 billion for Susitna reached about $5 billion in real dollars by 1981.[18] An investment in Susitna could become a deep financial trap and jeopardize the state's credit rating.

Future oil prices, more than any other single factor, would determine the economic viability of Susitna. High prices generated more money for Alaska to fund capital projects, and made hydroelectric and other alternatives relatively desirable. The 1979–1980 Iranian crisis, adding to the effects of the earlier OPEC oil price hikes, drove world oil prices to an all-time high. In February 1981, North Slope crude oil peaked at $36.90 per barrel. Acres American and Battelle Pacific Northwest feasibility studies, released in 1982, projected very high oil revenues for Alaska. Thus it appeared that sufficient money would be available to fund Susitna. By 1982, however, oil prices had entered a steady decline, forcing APA to consider state funding options other than full cash financing for construction.[19]

The Alaska Center for the Environment, Northern Alaska Environmental Center, and Trustees for Alaska (TfA) manifested a strong interest in and critical attitude toward Susitna. TfA brought suit against the funding legislation in 1982. Soon afterward, the legislature

10.3. Protest against Susitna power project, Talkeetna, May 1982. Courtesy Alaska Power Authority collection, University of Alaska Fairbanks, Alaska and Polar Regions Archives. A potential financial disaster, the project lacked enthusiastic support from the public and the Hammond administration.

repealed the uniform rate arrangement and appropriated $26 million more for investigation of technical feasibility, environmental impact, and alternative power sources.[20] Spring 1982 reports by Acres American and Battelle Northwestern (advocate and moderate supporter, respectively, of Susitna) and the state House Energy Research Agency, all described the Bradley Lake proposal as cheaper than Susitna. The APA expressed optimism about Susitna, providing oil prices did not maintain their downhill trend. The Northern Alaska Environmental Center, leader of the environmental adversaries, opened a Susitna project office in Anchorage and demanded that more current data be used in decisionmaking.[21] Alaska Environmental Lobby director Dave Allison, later appointed to the APA by Governor Bill Sheffield, derided Susitna as costing "$12,500 for every man, woman, and child in the state to build a project that's going to produce excess power we don't need." Senator Ed Dankworth of Anchorage, the dam's leading patron and author of the "Susitna blackmail clause," dismissed the complaints of the environmentalists as "frivolous."[22]

An unexpected event transpired in Spring 1982: Senator Dankworth announced a new plan for Susitna. The entire state Permanent Fund would be cashed for 3.1 trillion pennies to be used in construction of the dams. "With the cost of rebar and steel reinforcements skyrocketing, this is a common sense way to hold the cost of the project down," declared Dankworth. When the dams lost their usefulness they could be converted to copper mines. "It's a concrete investment. Those pennies aren't going anywhere. And think of all the jobs it will create." In an attempt to avoid Greenie burnout, the Northern Alaska Environmental Center staff had crafted a special edition of their *Northern Line* on April Fool's Day.[23]

In February 1983, APA applied for a construction license from the Federal Energy Regulatory Commission (FERC). APA's enthusiasm for Susitna survived undiminished, though it knew the means of financing had become problematic. A House Energy Research Agency analysis had calculated that without a $2.5 billion cash subsidy for construction, Susitna power would be more than twice as costly as the alternatives. The Northern Alaska Environmental Center held a workshop to train people for testimony at the FERC hearings, and won official intervenor status in the FERC process. Hearings proceeded in 1983, resulting in a ruling that APA seek updated economic forecasts. In the following year, the FERC released its seven-volume environmental impact statement. One of the efforts not controlled by APA, it did not flatter Susitna. It recommended a mixture of fossil fuel and smaller-scale power projects.[24]

In early 1984, position papers released by APA, and by Kentco for the Anchorage Chamber of Commerce, persisted in showing optimism over the project, but proposed financing less by construction cash subsidies and more by bonds and electricity rate subsidies after the beginning of operation. The legislature approved construction of the $3.75 billion Watana dam but committed only $1.3 billion over a period of seven years. Susitna's funding problem had yet to be solved.[25] Moreover, the outlook for Alaskan energy needs appeared even less favorable for Susitna. World oil prices could not be counted on to rise again in the near future. Therefore, warned economist Arlon Tussing, building Susitna instead of using Alaskan fossil fuels would be "taking the risk of replacing the lowest-price thermal energy in North America with about the highest-cost large-scale electrical generation in the world." He added, "One element continually missing from the Power Authority's Susitna assessments is . . . a clear explanation of the consequences for Railbelt taxpayers, the state's fiscal position, and Alaska's economy if the demand and fuel-price projections of its carefully selected forecasters turn out to be wrong." For years to come, said Tussing, Cook Inlet gas and other sources could meet Anchorage area needs. An undertaking the size of Susitna would not be needed for a decade or two if at all.

Tussing offered up a candid description of the politics of economic development in Alaska:

> The big thrust for Susitna indeed arises not so much because there is a respectable case for it as an investment in Alaska's distant future, but rather because it involves enormous spending in the near term. The more costly it is, the more jobs it would "create," and the more popular it becomes with everyone who perceives it will be built with someone else's money. Susitna is the most popular project in the neighborhood precisely because it is the biggest. In this context, the forces that select these projects can be expected to undermine any will on the part of a community's political system to control costs. . . . Cost overruns will be the norm as long as state-funded projects and particularly hydro projects, are advocated largely as public works programs to keep the construction industry in business and growing.[26]

During the 1984 session the legislature passed, and Governor Sheffield signed, measures for continuing annual appropriations of $200 million for Susitna until 1991, $50 million for Bradley Lake Dam, and $21.7 million for power cost equalization. These appropriations would not be subject to legislative or gubernatorial review. Trustees for Alaska and Alaska Public Interest Research Group challenged in court the constitutionality of the provisions. In August 1985, superior court ruled the funding arrangement "null and void," and barred the state from spending any more of the money. The Sheffield administration chose not to appeal the decision.[27]

The Alaska Department of Fish and Game found evidence that 10–15 percent of the Susitna salmon run would be lost if the dams were built. But financing still constituted the central deterrent. The legislature had spent $145 million by 1985; another $1.4 billion would be needed by 1991 and a total of $3.5 billion by 2005. Many other programs would have to be foregone to build Susitna.[28] In a belated attempt to hold down initial construction costs and production of electricity beyond growth demand, APA proposed in early 1985 to construct Watana dam in two stages: half prior to Devil Canyon Dam and half subsequently. Financing would be acquired primarily through revenue bonds. A total debt load of over $20 billion, however, might exceed the capacity of the state and the utility companies. No greater cash outlays could be expected from the state, and electricity rates might be forced so high as to negate the purposes of the project. Given the additional uncertainties of future oil prices, possible construction cost overruns, and electricity demand in Alaska, APA officials realized by early 1986 that Susitna would not be funded.[29]

Prospects for Susitna ran into an insurmountable barrier as a recession struck in late 1985. Governor Sheffield announced in March 1986 that he would not sanction further funding for the project; it "had no future." The legislature established a Railbelt Energy Fund, removing the large pool of power development money from the control of the Alaska Power Authority.[30] For the time being, and perhaps forever, Susitna was dead. Long after environmental concerns had brought about a reversal of public enthusiasm for big dams in the Lower 48, and 20 years after Rampart, another dream of an Alaskan megaproject collapsed.

Alaska's environmental groups made their significant contribution by identifying and publicizing weaknesses in the economics of Susitna, and through court action. The Northern Alaska Environmental Center produced a 40-page treatise on "Alaska's Energy Needs" for distribution to the legislature, recommending conservation measures and electricity generation by North Slope gas.[31]

Susitna represented a gain for environmental values. Its timing facilitated the national government's refusal to fund it. It could not meet the test of economic sustainability, and research demonstrated some cost to wildlife sustainability. The opportunity for public participation in the debate enabled environmentalists and other critics to advertise its shortcomings and demand government accountability. As in the case of Rampart, Susitna reiterated the lesson that experts and interested parties, government or private, could not necessarily be trusted to act in the best interests of the public. Susitna's undoing heartened the state's environmental community, strengthened its claim to be a public service institution, and gave it experience to be applied in future trials.

NOTES

1. U.S. Department of the Interior (USDOI), Alaska Power Administration, *Devil Canyon Project*, 5; Ray, *Compilation of Narratives*, 629, 656, 665–669.

2. David L. Spencer, interview by author, July 30, 1989.

3. Tussing, Kramer, and Morse, "Susitna Hydropower," 1–3.

4. Weeden, "Fish and Wildlife Service Issues Report," 5.

5. *Alaska Conservation Society (ACS) News Bulletin*, October 1966, 8.

6. USDOI, Alaska Power Administration, *Devil Canyon Project*, 10–11, 61, 72–73.

7. Yould, "Susitna Hydroelectric Project," 14; Tussing, Kramer, and Morse, "Susitna Hydropower," 5.

8. *Alaska Session Laws, 1974*, HJR 72.

9. Yould, "Susitna Hydroelectric Project," 14–15.

10. Harrison, "Susitna Hydroelectric," 22.

11. Connors, "Corps Finally Takes Susitna Plans," 1.

12. Bratton, "Descent Into Devil's Canyon," 32.

13. Tileston, "New Susitna Report," 4.

14. Tussing, Kramer, and Morse, "Susitna Hydropower," 12, 15, 21.

15. Nerz, "Susitna Dam Proposal," 8.

16. Weltzin, "Alaska Legislature Goes Home," 1,3; C. Hunter, "This Our Land," March 1983, 36; *Center News*, April 1982, 2, 9, 11.

17. George Matz, letter to author, July 8, 1994.

18. Motyka and Reichardt, "Concerns About the Susitna," 6–8; C. Hunter, "This Our Land," March 1983, 36; Weltzin, "Susitna River," 6–7.

19. Harrison, "Susitna Hydroelectric," 25–26.

20. *Center News*, June-July 1982, 4; Hartle, "Summing Up," 9; *Alaska Session Laws, 1982*, Chapter 133.

21. *Center News*, October-November 1982, 3; Zimiski, "Bradley Lake Hydro Project," 1–2.

22. *Anchorage Daily News*, April 3, 1982.

23. *Northern Line*, "Permanent Pennies," 3.

24. Myers, "Susitna Update," 6; Myers, "Federal Commission Continues," 10.

25. Harrison, "Susitna Hydroelectric," 26–27.

26. Tussing, "Alaska's Energy Policy," 30–33.

27. *Trustees for Alaska v. State of Alaska* No. 84-12053 CIV; No. 3AN-84-12053 CIV; *Northern Line*, September-October 1985, 10; Highleyman, "Lobby Gears Up," 3; *Trustees for Alaska*, Fall 1985, 2; Winter 1985–1986, 1.

28. *Alaska Economic Report*, March 17, 1985, 3; *Alaska Economic Report*, "Searching for a Future," 3, 6.

29. Harrison, "Susitna Hydroelectric," 27–31.

31. Colt, "Devil Canyon Dam," 4.

30. G. Matz, "Susitna Hydropower," 4–5, 7.

11

An Oil Pipeline Changes Everything

Nothing in Alaska's experience did more to make it a subject of national environmental concern, or to foster the growth of Alaskan and national environmentalism, than did oil. Discovery of the Kenai Peninsula deposits in 1957 ushered in statehood, boosting the economy and the population. But North Slope finds dwarfed all others in the state, vastly accelerating the pace of modernization. Oil became the most potent driving force behind environmental degradation and, indirectly, environmental activism in Alaska. It sharpened national awareness of the principle of environmental sustainability, and provided a medium for growth of the related values of governmental and corporate accountability, public participation, and access to information.

NORTH SLOPE OIL DISCOVERIES

A remnant of a much earlier and warmer age, oil lay in quantity under the North Slope. It seeped to the surface where Eskimos discovered it and burned it for fuel. Surveyor Thomas Simpson of Hudson's Bay Company found oil along the Canadian Arctic coast on his way to Barrow in 1836–1837. So did Ensign William Howard of Stoney's 1884–1886 Kobuk Valley Naval expedition, who made the first crossing of the Brooks Range by a Euro-American explorer. Also in 1886, whaler-trader Charles Brower reported surface oil 60 miles east of Barrow at Cape Simpson. Remoteness and climate deterred exploratory activity, and conservation policy fashioned by Theodore Roosevelt led to a withdrawal of federal lands from oil prospecting between 1909 and 1920. Gold prospector Sandy Smith, having seen oil seeps in 1917, returned in 1921 to stake claims for an oil company. Before the claims could be worked, President Warren Harding withdrew the region in 1923 as a fuel reserve for the navy, in the process of switching from coal to oil as ship fuel. Naval Petroleum Reserve No. 4 (known as "Pet 4" and renamed National Petroleum Reserve-Alaska in 1976) encompassed most of the northwestern corner of Alaska, 200 miles along the north coast by 250 miles inland.[1]

Navy teams and their contractors visited between 1944 and 1953 to investigate the oil production potential of the Indiana-sized petroleum reserve and some adjacent lands. Drilling in at least 20 sites, they appraised the western half of the North Slope coastal plain as a poor prospect for oil but a prolific source of natural gas. In the lower foothills of the western North Slope they found more oil and gas, most significantly an estimated 30 to 100 million barrels of recoverable oil at Umiat. No drilling and little evaluation occurred in the eastern half of the North Slope or in the higher foothills. The decade of exploration yielded extensive geological information and valuable experience in carrying out drilling operations under high Arctic conditions.[2]

Industrial and military strength relied on a heavy and increasing flow of oil, and crises involving Iran and the Suez Canal during the 1950s induced British and American attempts to lessen dependence on Mideast oil supplies. In 1962, oil companies obtained permits from the Bureau of Land Management for oil exploration on the North Slope east of the Petroleum Reserve. One of them, Atlantic Richfield (Arco, then Richfield Oil Company) had made the 1957 Kenai Peninsula strike that thrust Alaska into the oil era. In 1964, it entered a joint venture with Humble, a subsidiary of Standard Oil of New Jersey. Officials of the new state government, also aware of the evidence of oil, proceeded to make land selections guaranteed by the Statehood Act of 1958. The act, however, forbade selections contravening Native claims. Protests by Natives prompted Interior Secretary Stewart Udall in 1966 to "freeze" (halt the application process for) all federal lands in Alaska pending settlement of Native claims. Operating under tentative federal approval for ownership, the state had in early 1964 selected 2 million acres of the North Slope, intending to lease it to oil companies. Late in 1965, Arco-Humble bid successfully on the bulk of the acreage offered, including the vicinity of Prudhoe Bay. Most of the remaining leases went to British Petroleum–Sinclair.

Although observers widely assumed the North Slope held commercially viable oil, searchers had difficulty finding it. By 1967 only one drilling rig remained. Then came electrifying news of a major find. On December 26 Atlantic Richfield's wildcat rig *Prudhoe Bay State No. 1* struck evidence of oil, and later that spring *Sag 1* near the Sagavanirktok River and Prudhoe Bay confirmed the size of the discovery. Geologists estimated it to be nearly 10 billion barrels, by far the largest pool ever found in the United States.[3] It bore enormous implications for Alaska and for the financial world. Of all the invasions of Alaska—the fur seekers, whalers, salmon canners, gold seekers, and military— only the World War II-Cold War buildup would compare to the oil boom in its social and environmental impact.

In September 1968 the state opened bids for additional leases on its North Slope lands. In one day Alaska grew $900 million richer, reaping the further promise of at least $200 million per year in royalties. *US News and World Report* trumpeted the unrestrained optimism of Alaska's boosters. It cited the intention of Alaskan officials to use oil "as a wedge to open up and then develop riches in Alaska's Arctic region," and suggested that Rampart Dam might be revived. It cited real estate developer-Governor Hickel's vision of an extension of the Alaska Railroad to the North Slope, to be funded by the federal government. The railroad, Hickel projected, would stimulate the building of cities along the Arctic coast. Citing Russia's Arctic expansion, Hickel warned, "When Russia gains 15% of the Japanese market she will dominate Asia. This illustrates Alaska's importance to the free world. We must get moving quickly so that we can get more of a share of these markets."[4]

Walter "Wally" Hickel ranked as one of the dominant figures of Alaskan politics. Oldest of ten children born to Kansas tenant farmers, he arrived in Alaska at age 21 in 1940 carrying a proverbial 37 cents in his pocket. By 1953 he made a start in the hotel business and Republican politics; he won the governorship in 1966. He pictured himself as a conservation-

11.1. Prudhoe Bay State No. 1, *July 1968. Courtesy Alaska Resource Library and Information Services (ARLIS), Anchorage. This wildcat rig changed Alaska's place in the world.*

ist in the Roosevelt-Pinchot mold, counseling government management of natural resources for its maximally efficient use, and suspicious of the behavior of unregulated free enterprise. At the same time, he perceived Alaska as a land of abundance and opportunity, warranting aggressive entrepreneurship.[5] In his corporate and political behavior at the state level, he related government to business more as facilitator or subsidizer than as regulator. Hickel appealed to the public by demanding more state control over federal lands and resources, and by proposing grandiloquent infrastructure schemes. He believed that roads, railroads, pipelines, and port facilities, preferably paid for by federal funds, would catalyze economic growth in Alaska.[6]

By 1969, three large oil companies held most of the now-priceless North Slope leases: Atlantic Richfield (Arco), British Petroleum (BP), and the ironically-named Humble Oil and Refining Company (later Exxon). They resolved to get the oil out as soon as possible, through a buried pipeline designed in the standard manner, across central Alaska 789 miles to the port of Valdez, then to be loaded on tankers. The pipeline would be built and managed by Trans-Alaska Pipeline System (TAPS; later Alyeska Pipeline Service Co.), owned mostly by the big three. The oil companies wanted no delay and found government officials eager to comply. The companies proceeded to order $300 million of pipe from Japan months before asking for a permit for the pipeline. Then on June 6, 1969, they submitted their application, requesting a favorable response by the first of July.

11.2. Hickel Highway construction camp moving north of Anaktuvuk Pass, 1969. Courtesy Alaska Dept. of Transportation. The winter highway, carved in the tundra, turned into an embarrassment when it melted.

At the urging of trucking interests, Hickel had secured the approval of the legislature and the informal permission of the Bureau of Land Management to build a 390-mile winter road from Livengood across the Brooks Range to Prudhoe Bay. Without public hearings or environmental studies, the road went through during fall 1968 and winter 1969. State highway department crews bulldozed off the surface of the tundra. During the 1969 spring melt the permafrost thawed, transforming the "Hickel Highway" into the "Hickel Canal," and doing extensive damage to the land surface. The state spent $766,000 on the project. Not counting this expense, trucking costs approximated those of flying in the construction material and supplies by C-130 Hercules aircraft that moved nearly all the freight, leaving almost no impact on the land. Encouraged by Hickel's successor Keith Miller, the truckers pushed for a larger share of the project. Again in the fall and winter of 1969–1970 crews prepared a road. Unable to use some of the first roadbed, they gouged the tundra a second time. The road issue turned into an embarrassment for newly appointed Secretary of the Interior Hickel, who had approved it, and caused public apprehension about environmental degradation by Alaskan oil operations.[7]

Oil fever ran high in Alaska. More than a little pride accompanied the depiction of the 55-gallon oil drum as "Alaska's state flower." Fortune seekers of all kinds arrived or invested in Alaska, directing much of their attention to the North Slope. National Parks official Bob Belous discovered a place where a bulldozer carved into the tundra 450-foot-long letters

11.3. Geophysical Services, Inc. initials bulldozed in tundra. Courtesy ARLIS, Anchorage. Arrow points to Arctic Refuge, which oil companies hoped to open.

"GSI" (Geophysical Services Inc., an oil service company), underlined by an arrow pointing to the Arctic National Wildlife Range. Erosion cut as much as 10 feet deep; it would take hundreds of years to heal. Low-flying aircraft harmfully stressed caribou, Belous charged, and workers killed many caribou despite a prohibition of gun possession by oil workers.[8] Photographer Wilbur Mills reported from the North Slope that "countless miles of vehicle tracks and trails left by oil exploration crews criss-cross the tundra, causing thawing and erosion of the frozen soil. I have seen ruts deep enough to hide a man." He found trash voluminous and widespread, and "caribou have been seen hopelessly entangled in seismic wire, countless miles of which have been left behind by oil-exploration crews." Guide Bud Helmericks related, "The disturbing and hazing of game by helicopters is terrific. Pilots take turns running bears, wolves, and even moose and caribou."[9] Pilots allegedly marked on maps the nest locations of gyrfalcons and peregrine falcons, to be sold to falconers in the Lower 48.[10]

ENVIRONMENTAL CONFLICT

North Slope oil operations began just as the national environmental community experienced a rapid expansion in membership and public acceptance. New organizations and tactics, exemplified by the Environmental Defense Fund and its successful lawsuit over DDT, quickly made an impact. Acting on broadening definitions of ecological problems, environmentalists moved beyond wildland and wildlife protection per se and tackled such

11.4. Tundra scars left by tracked vehicles, west of Toolik River, North Slope, June 1969. By C. D. Evans. Courtesy ARLIS, Anchorage. Damage to tundra could last for decades.

issues as chemical pollution, human health, energy conservation, recycling, and population control. The January 1969 Santa Barbara oil spill spurred the movement and its public standing while casting oil companies in the role of public enemy. Similarly, the Hickel Highway and proposed pipeline, in addition to scars and debris left by the military, directed critical national attention to Alaskan oil activity. The Sierra Club's March 1969 wilderness conference focused entirely on Alaska, whereas the state had ranked sixth in priority at the 1967 conference. Delegates from the Alaska Conservation Society and other state groups attended, enhancing awareness and ties between Alaska and the outside.[11]

Oil industrialization threatened much that the environmentalists valued and labored for. But this project could not be stopped; it could only be modified in some degree. "The tide of petroleum discovery and development has raced ahead of our understanding of its implications, to say nothing of our ability to put that knowledge to work," mused Bob Weeden. Alaska Conservation Society leaders advocated slow growth in the context of comprehensive planning. They worried about oil's impact on subsistence and nonacquisitive lifestyles, damage to wildlife and wilderness values, and disruption of the state's economy. They preferred decisions made for and by the public rather than by private interests, in this case oil companies. They desired an honest choice of the route for transporting the oil, and strict measures to minimize environmental impacts. The society pressed these points in writings and conferences, and in resistance to Hickel's appointment as secretary of the interior.[12]

Pursuant to the oil companies' permit request for the pipeline, the Bureau of Land Management held hearings in summer 1969 in Fairbanks. Witnesses expressed anxiety about earthquakes, soil erosion, and melting of the permafrost by the warm pipeline. The companies planned to bury all but 30 to 50 miles of the pipe. Speakers raised questions about the routing to Valdez, located in a major fault zone and extensively damaged in the 1964 earthquake. They articulated fears about oil spills in Prince William Sound, through which the tankers had to pass on their way to the Lower 48 or Panama. Beyond these considerations, other possibilities existed for transporting the oil. Humble Oil explored a tanker route through the Canadian Arctic. Its icebreaker tanker *Manhattan*, specially reconstructed at a cost of $50 million, tested the route twice in 1969 and 1970 but stove a hole in its hull and could not demonstrate the route's cost-effectiveness. A Canadian company suggested a pipeline across the Arctic National Wildlife Range and south along the Mackenzie River Valley. Another scenario would pipe the oil to Fairbanks, then down the Alaska Highway. Each transport option entailed its own environmental and cost considerations.

Hickel's environmental credentials had become so suspect and his commitment to the Valdez pipeline so obvious that the Senate Interior Committee insisted he promise, as a condition of his confirmation, not to approve the pipeline without their concurrence. Unable to issue a permit, the Bureau of Land Management nevertheless allowed Trans Alaska Pipeline System to build eight large, completely equipped construction camps along the route. The Interior Committee decided in the fall of 1969 to leave the permit decision to Hickel, who in January 1970 lifted Udall's freeze on the transportation corridor. Before leaving office in January 1969, Udall had hardened his 1967 land freeze by stopping all transactions on unreserved federal lands until the end of 1971.[13]

The Bureau of Land Management prepared to issue the corridor permit, triggering lawsuits in March 1970. Five Native villagers claimed that TAPS had been given permission to cross Native lands as part of an agreement to hire Natives, and had reneged on the hiring. District court issued a restraining order against the crossing of 20 miles of land claimed by Stevens Village. The Environmental Defense Fund, Wilderness Society, and Friends of the Earth sued the Interior Department on grounds that the pipeline violated the environmental impact statement provisions of the National Environmental Policy Act and the 50-foot-wide access limit of the 1920 Mineral Leasing Act. District court accepted both arguments and granted a preliminary injunction, bringing the pipeline construction to a halt. In August 1971, Alyeska and the state of Alaska joined the Interior Department as codefendants. Several conservation parties also filed suit in 1971, seeking a permanent injunction: Natural Resources Defense Council, Center for Law and Social Policy, Cordova District Fisheries Union, Canadian Wildlife Federation (British Columbia chapter), and David Anderson, a member of the Canadian parliament. Of these, the last three cared particularly about tanker spills.[14] The lawsuits meant months or years before construction could begin.

Efforts by environmentalists and others to question or slow the pipeline touched off an angry reaction from the frustrated boosters. In fall 1969 Governor Miller termed the Senate Interior Committee's refusal to approve the pipeline "an unwarranted interference in the sovereign state of Alaska." A *New York Times* editorial suggested "The indignation is misdirected. It should be addressed, instead, to the Atlantic Richfield Company, the Humble Oil Company and the British Petroleum Company for the greedy haste with which they are prepared to endanger a vast territory—the land, its people and its wildlife—for the sake of a quick and enormously profitable return on their investment."[15]

Tension rose sharply in 1970. *US News and World Report* asserted, "Much of Alaska is beginning to feel a severe pinch, caused by the struggle between the conservationists on the one hand and the U.S. Government and private industry on the other. As a result of lawsuits and other activity, enterprise after enterprise in Alaska is grinding to a halt."[16] "Let the Bastards Freeze in the Dark" appeared on Alaskan bumper stickers. The Sierra Club, involved in an important Southeast Alaska logging lawsuit though not a plaintiff in the pipeline case, came under vigorous attack. An oil executive introduced a sober note in his private admission that "the conservationists are one of the best things that could have happened to us. We would never be taking the precautions we are if it weren't for the attention focused on us. After all, oil companies are very competitive. We like to think we're socially responsible but in the long run our aim is to make money. Until recently it was to our advantage to run a sloppy operation because no one was enforcing the rules."[17] Arco president Thornton Bradshaw publicly expressed a similar judgment.[18]

Congressional and environmental impact hearings focused on the where and how of transporting the oil. The state and oil companies insisted on the Prudhoe-Valdez line they believed would benefit them more than other options. They speedily initiated public relations efforts. A 1970 film *New For Tomorrow*, reportedly paid for by the state and oil companies, purported to show the benign effects of oil enterprises on wildlife of the North Slope. Sockeye salmon migrated upstream and a family of mallard ducks paraded among oil workers. Critics pointed out that no sockeyes existed on the North Slope and the ducks had been domesticated.[19] An Alyeska ad showing a cow caribou nursing her calf queried, "Will a pipeline ruin their Arctic? . . . In truth, what's good for the environment is also good for the safety and security of the pipeline."[20] The ad suggested design for environmental protection and the value of less dependence on foreign oil.

Economists scrutinized the cost-benefits of the Valdez route. The Midwest needed oil more than did the West Coast, and a gas line might go down the Alaska Highway anyway. Thus an Alaska Highway oil pipeline could be doubly advantageous. Canadians opposed an Arctic Ocean tanker route; Prime Minister Pierre Trudeau remarked, "We don't want it turned into a cesspool covered with oil."[21] They favored the Alaska Highway path, connecting to their own oil network in the north. But a Canadian throughway might subject the oil companies to unwelcome taxation and regulation, and a Valdez line could be constructed much more quickly. Weighing several alternatives involving ecological damage, the Alaska Conservation Society and most other environmental groups settled on Prudhoe-Fairbanks-Alaska Highway.[22]

Since Hickel's appointment, and after his replacement by Rogers Morton in 1971, the Interior Department and Nixon administration (a recipient of millions of dollars in campaign contributions from oil companies) appeared committed to the Valdez plan.[23] Interior's draft environmental impact statement did not address the pros and cons of Canadian options, despite the law's requirement to consider alternatives. Hearings held by the Interior Department in Anchorage in February 1971 focused on the adequacy of the statement. Speaking for the Alaska Conservation Society, Bob Weeden testified that the document "should have been a valuable aid in decision-making; instead it is an excuse for a decision already made. . . . Perhaps the most serious, and certainly the least comprehensible omission is the total lack of recognition of environmental risks along the marine portion of the Prudhoe Bay-Puget Sound-California route."[24] Celia Hunter also sensed the political dimension: "How often in the troubled years after the Second World War have we heard the well-worn riposte of national security used to justify a course of action and to shut off, as unpatriotic, further discussion. Let us not wrap ourselves in the flag on this one." She noted that while all local chapters of the Chamber of Commerce had been invited to testify, affiliates of the Alaska Conservation Society, though autonomous, had not.[25] Jack Hession of Sierra Club/Alaska warned of chronic low-level oil pollution in the marine segment, and emphasized that "major oil spill disasters can also be anticipated." "At stake is the coastal marine environment from South-Central Alaska to California." Regarding oil spill cleanup, Hession added that "evidence to date shows that the technology to effectively cope with massive marine oil spills does not exist."[26] Speakers representing commercial fisheries and other groups voiced similar concerns. Interior Secretary Morton testified he had directed the report drafters to address the tanker questions. However, the hearing moderator stated that the Bureau of Land Management, lacking expertise in marine matters, had asked the Coast Guard for information and did not want to hold up the hearings while waiting for it.[27]

Proponents of the tanker route either avoided the question of tanker accidents or gave assurances of safety. Alaska Chamber of Commerce director John Kelsey, a Valdez resident, indicated he foresaw no problem involving tankers in the Valdez vicinity.[28] Alaska's Commissioner of Economic Development Irene Ryan warned that going through Canada would entail greater costs, at least three years of delay, and (undefined) "political problems." She promised "not a drop of oil will be permitted to enter the pipeline until we are assured that no permanent damage to the environment will result from construction and operation of the pipeline."[29] Senator Mike Gravel cited the energy crisis and "opening of Interior Alaska" as reasons for the Valdez route.[30] Senator Ted Stevens urged rapid progress on the Valdez route, adding, "I fail to see any necessity for environmental extremists to close their eyes to the activities in their own backyards in order to focus on the north country of Alaska that they don't even know or understand."[31] Several federal agencies (Environmental Protection Agency, Army Corps of Engineers, and Departments of Commerce, Defense, and Transportation) questioned the adequacy of the impact statement in its treatment of Arctic ecology, alternative routes, and oil impact on marine ecology.

An emerging environmental movement needed symbols, and adopted the Alaska oil pipeline as its most visible focal point. In February 1971, conservation groups formed an Alaska Public Interest Coalition to act on the pipeline issue. Most influential national groups, but only one from Alaska, joined: Cordova District Fisheries Union, though not considering itself environmentalist, needed allies in its efforts to protect Prince William Sound fisheries. The coalition appeared in the public hearings and lobbied to minimize the pipeline's environmental impact. Convinced that a pipeline would be built, the coalition eventually took a stand favoring a Canada route.[32] Interior's nine-volume final environmental impact statement appeared in March 1972. It rated the Prudhoe-Mackenzie way (across the Arctic National Wildlife Range) as least damaging to the biotic environment, and Prudhoe-Fairbanks-Alaska Highway as least impactful on the marine environment. Prudhoe-Valdez would be superior only in doing the least damage to the abiotic (nonliving) environment, but this advantage would be insignificant if an additional line for gas were to be constructed along the Alaska Highway. The statement presented no analysis of a combined oil and gas Alaska Highway routing.[33]

For the tanker segment of Prudhoe-Valdez, the impact statement estimated that 140,000 gallons of oil would be spilled in an average year. It based its oil spill projection on a Coast Guard survey of accidents in U.S. waters in 1970, when no large spill occurred. It offered no estimate of the probability or likely biological effects of a large marine oil spill. It rated cumulative impacts of low-level spills as more serious than a major event.[34] Despite the dubious benefits of Prudhoe-Valdez, the document concluded evasively, "No single generalized route appears to be superior in all respects to any other."[35] A report by Interior's Office of Economic Analysis, withheld until permits had been granted for Prudhoe-Valdez, clearly indicated the superiority of the Alaska Highway alternative for combined oil and gas transportation.[36]

Resources for the Future economist Donald Cicchetti, in an in-depth analysis published in 1972, rated the Alaska Highway direction environmentally superior "principally because it would avoid the threat of earthquakes and avalanches in southern Alaska and, lacking tanker operations, would make no contribution to marine pollution." Pipelines, he noted, promised more safety than tankers. Cicchetti calculated, as had early oil company studies, that a trans-Canada route would be no more expensive to construct than a TAP-tanker route counting the cost of tankers and port facilities.[37] Why, then, should the oil companies and the state be so insistent on the Prudhoe-Valdez (TAP-tanker) idea? Cicchetti believed the companies had two contingency plans. One involved creating a glut of oil on the West Coast and getting permission to sell the excess Alaskan oil to Japan. By this means they would lower the royalties paid to Alaska, save on transportation costs to Japan by the shorter route and use of foreign vessels, and continue to sell other oil, shipped to the East Coast in foreign tankers, at high prices. The second plan involved shipping the oil to Panama and to the Virgin Islands in foreign vessels, selling it cheaply to their own refineries so as to lower the royalties to Alaska, then refining it and selling the finished products at high prices on the East Coast outside the limits of the oil import quota. By either arrangement, said Cicchetti, the oil companies would reap profits "at the expense of oil consumers, taxpayers, the U.S. maritime industry, and the state of Alaska. . . . The consequences of a TAP-tanker system for transporting Alaskan oil could haunt an entire continent for many years to come."[38] In congressional testimony, Cicchetti predicted that the excess supply of oil on the West Coast could reach 1 million barrels daily by 1985. "Finally," he said, "without quantifying the environmental savings expected of a Canadian route and possible economic savings for a joint gas pipeline, I conclude that national and state interests require the development of the economically superior and more urgently needed trans-Canadian pipeline even with delays up to 5 years." Thornton Bradshaw, in a letter to Senator William Proxmire, denied Arco had any intention of selling oil to Japan.[39]

Job seekers lobbied the state for an all-Alaskan land route, even though the in-state segment of a Prudhoe-Fairbanks-Alaska Highway pipeline would have been slightly longer (809 miles) than the distance to Valdez. More importantly, state officials had made ambitious spending plans and anxiously awaited the oil royalties.[40] They had spent 28 percent of the $900 million from the 1969 North Slope lease sale in fiscal year 1971 alone. To avoid possible royalty losses, in the late 1970s the state adopted a severance tax effective if the wellhead price should go below $2.65 a barrel.[41] The tax proviso afforded the state protection in case of oil sales to Japan at lower prices. A 1973 presidential directive halting import quotas had put an end to a possible Valdez-Panama-Virgin Islands arrangement.[42]

Interior's consideration of the Canadian pathways had been ordered by the U.S. Court of Appeals in its January 1972 ruling in the pipeline case, though the court lifted the injunction against a permit. A second opinion in February 1973 avoided the environmental impact statement issue and ruled the permit in violation of the 1920 Mineral Leasing Act. The Supreme Court refused to review the case, leaving the questions of pipeline routing and right-of-way to Congress.[43] May 1973 Senate hearings discussed three bills, two calling for examination of a Canadian route. Promoting his bill authorizing immediate construction of the Prudhoe-Valdez pipeline, Senator Stevens repeatedly cited the energy shortage and the danger of boycotts or blackmail by Mideast oil producers, warning, "America's dependence on foreign oil to meet our increasing energy needs is threatening our economic health, placing our national security in jeopardy and questioning America's role in the international community."[44]

Congress echoed the prevailing attitude that the question was not whether to build a pipeline but when, where, and how. The Nixon administration and its oil industry allies insisted the nation needed Alaskan oil to turn away from dependence on foreign sources in the interest of national security. Skeptics saw the motive as maintaining high prices and profits for the oil companies by keeping out cheap foreign oil. Appeals to patriotism and fear of the Middle East outweighed the dissent. Alaskan and western delegations and the oil companies backed the Valdez plan, in opposition to the eastern and midwestern delegations and environmentalists. Canada made a diplomatic plea for its route. A Senate amendment calling for investigation of a way through Canada fell short by a two-to-one margin. Then Senator Mike Gravel introduced a controversial amendment to accept the Interior Department environmental impact statement and prohibit further court challenges under the National Environmental Policy Act. Passage of the amendment would constitute a serious assault on the integrity of the new law. Vice President Spiro Agnew ensured passage of the amendment by breaking a 49-49 tie vote. As the bills went before the conference committee, the Arab oil embargo began, obviating any possibility of delay to assess a Canadian route. Nixon signed the Trans-Alaska Pipeline Authorization Act in November 1973, clearing the way for the pipeline after five years of legal and political strife.[45]

BUILDING THE PIPELINE

Construction of the oil pipeline started up in the spring of 1974. The oil companies turned the environmental issue to their advantage, adopting or at least publicizing protective measures. Embarrassed by revelations of North Slope offenses, they ordered cleanups and strict controls to conserve wildlife. Alyeska carried on the TAPS project of picking up

11.5. Barrels at DEW Line site, Camden Bay, 1960s. Courtesy U.S. Fish and Wildlife Service, Fairbanks. Debris left by government and private operations degraded the Arctic environment. Some cleanup occurred in the 1970s and 1980s.

hundreds of empty petroleum barrels left by Naval oil exploration and DEW Line construction of the 1940s and 1950s. It hired scientists to study environmental impact and design a reseeding program. It agreed to elevate nearly half the pipeline's length (380 miles) and quake-proof the terminal facilities at Valdez. Road-building specifications changed to avoid salmon spawning and peregrine falcon nesting areas.

Orders from the top did not always reach the bottom; damage occurred despite the environmental precautions. Oil spills happened: one incident, a leak caused by pipeline sagging after the subsurface ice melted, dumped 5,000 barrels into the Atigun River.[46] A front-loader struck a valve and 2,000 barrels flowed onto the tundra 23 miles south of Prudhoe Bay in 1977. A plastic bomb bore out fears of sabotage in early 1978 by tearing a hole in the pipeline east of Fairbanks, releasing 10,000 barrels.[47] Earlier, a state monitor had to threaten a lawsuit to force Alyeska to use welding rods designed for Arctic temperatures. Weld X-ray records were falsified and radiographer Peter Kelly fired for refusing to participate in the fraud. He sued, prompting congressional hearings. Following an audit, 3,955 welds had to be dug up and done over. Some game and river crossings had to be rebuilt.[48]

A joint Fish and Wildlife Advisory Team of federal and state biologists assembled, to recommend measures to minimize construction impact on wildlife. Notwithstanding the administration's emphasis on getting the oil out, this team (from the Alaska Department of Fish and Game, Bureau of Land Management, Fish and Wildlife Service, and National Marine Fisheries Service) set precedents in interagency and intergovernmental cooperation and rule making for environmental protection in large projects. In case of a conflict between wildlife needs and pipeline integrity, the latter received priority. The line crossed about 1,000 streams, and the team called for 500 sections of pipeline to be elevated for a distance of 60 feet at a 10-foot height to permit passage of large mammals. About 160 lacked the proper height; Alyeska corrected them by lowering the ground level beneath. Poorly done stream crossings sometimes waited two years for reconstruction.[49] The team's final report complained of lack of interest by engineers and inconsistent enforcement by monitors. The team believed the administrators wanted to get the job done quickly, not to protect wildlife.[50]

The Arctic Institute of North America set up an Arctic Environmental Council to encourage cooperation between oil companies and environmentalists in oversight of pipeline construction. Some environmental groups (the Alaska Conservation Society, Isaac Walton League, Natural Resources Defense Council, National Wildlife Federation, and Sierra Club) sent representatives; others declined. The Arctic Environmental Council organized pipeline inspection visits, but grew dependent on Alyeska funding. Its only Alaskan member, David Klein of the Alaska Conservation Society and director of the University of Alaska's Cooperative Wildlife Research Unit, resigned from the monitoring project because he felt used by the company for publicity purposes. The Alaska Conservation Society, Alaska Center for the Environment, and Fairbanks Environmental Center tried to sustain a separate monitoring effort but lacked adequate funding or cooperation from state, federal, or company officials. Fairbanks Environmental Center compiled

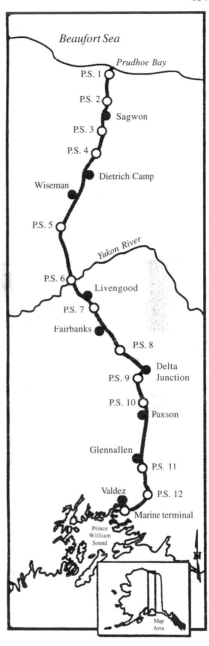

11.1. Trans-Alaska Pipeline Route. Courtesy Alaska Oil Spill Commission, Spill: The Wreck of the Exxon Valdez: Alaska Oil Spill Commission Final Report (Anchorage, 1990), 34.

11.6. Trans-Alaska oil pipeline section. Courtesy ARLIS, Anchorage. The oil pipeline became the nation's most prominent environmental issue.

detailed information about the performance of a federal monitor who allegedly accepted favors from a major contractor. The center's work resulted in the inspector's dismissal.[51] Overall, efforts by environmentalists to monitor the pipeline work achieved meager success.

Oil started flowing through the line in July 1977. The project cost, first estimated at $900 million, totaled nearly $9 billion. The summary report of the Alaska Pipeline Commission, an official monitoring group, cited "a minimum of $1.2 billion excess attributable to mismanagement of the pipeline and roads portion of the project alone," in addition to waste in the $2-billion cost of the Valdez port facilities. The project, it said, had been "poorly planned, mismanaged, and institutionally incapable of—and often indifferent to—effective cost control." [52]

THE HAUL ROAD

In environmental terms, the Haul Road (Dalton Highway) tendered problems distinct from those of the pipeline it paralleled. Dismayed at the construction of the road breaching the wilderness integrity of the Arctic, environmentalists anticipated the intrusion of trash, uncontrolled hunting, and other forms of degradation. Soon after he took office a year before the Prudhoe Bay oil strike, Governor Hickel had called for a road to open the North Slope to development. In July 1970 following the court injunction against the pipeline, Governor

Miller asked the legislature for $120 million to build the entire pipeline road, in hopes of circumventing the federal environmental impact statement requirement. The legislature agreed on the condition that TAPS would reimburse the state, an offer TAPS refused.[53] Following passage of enabling federal legislation, Alyeska built the road to state specifications.

Governor William Egan (1970–1974), who preceded Hickel and succeeded Miller, shared Hickel's goal of population buildup in the Arctic. The Bureau of Land Management proposed to open the Haul Road to the public; bus companies requested permits. Alaska Conservation Society testified against the plans, also opposed by the oil companies who wanted to avoid liability suits, damage to equipment, or related problems. Native groups concurred, anxious about loss of their lifestyles.[54] The state assumed control of the road in October 1979 and named it for James Dalton, an early Alaskan engineer. Fairbanks Environmental Center, Tanana Chiefs, and Rural Community Action Program met in December 1979 to work against a road opening. Through the Alaska Environmental Lobby, environmentalists assisted passage of a compromise state law limiting public access beyond the Yukon to three months a year, and only as far as Dietrich Camp at Mile 206 in the central Brooks Range. Throughout the 1980s and early 1990s, Native groups and the lobby resisted ongoing attempts to open the remainder of the highway. In 1992 the Hickel administration invited opening by ceasing to check for travel permits. By 1994 the annual total of visitors ascending the highway reached 12,000, about half in tour buses. In the wake of permissive court decisions, the state officially opened the road to the public effective January 1995.[55]

LEGACY OF THE PIPELINE

In the mid-1970s, Alaskan attitudes about oil underwent a change. Pipeline construction lured in a flood of aggressive workers, overloading social services. Fairbanks housing and supplies fell short, traffic jams proliferated, and the city periodically experienced one of the highest levels of air pollution in the nation. Crime increased, as did prostitution and pressure on fish and game.[56] Bumper stickers read "Happiness Is—10,000 Okies Going South With a Texan Under Each Arm." The new mood assisted the 1974 election as governor of an "environmental" candidate, fisherman and guide Jay Hammond. Another environmentally-oriented legislator, Lowell Thomas Jr., ran on the ticket for the lieutenant governorship. Hammond summed up public opinion about oil development: "Those who are intimately plugged into the pipeline construction program, and profiting handsomely, think oil is wonderful. Those who are not feel it has eroded their quality of life. So half of Alaska concludes that oil is the best thing that has happened to them. And the other half concludes that it's the worst."[57]

Alaska experienced an economic letdown and high unemployment as construction tapered off in the late 1970s; then it rebounded vigorously in the early 1980s. The state's Permanent Fund ballooned from its 25 percent of oil royalties, and 70 percent of the state budget came from oil by mid-1979. The operation of the pipeline itself fostered a sense of well-being. Except for the explosion of a pumping station, several oil spills of moderate size, and high winds occasionally halting tanker traffic, few apparent problems attended the oil flow. But many believed the pipeline should have been routed down the Alaska Highway. Governor Hammond's proposal to sell oil to Japan and replace it by Mexican oil imports got nowhere in Congress.[58] Alaska's boom-and-bust cycles, the inability to finance a gas pipeline, and debates over oil drilling and transportation, abided.

Beyond the short-term impact of the pipeline construction boom, North Slope oil activity had wide repercussions. It precipitated the land status settlement (Chapter 13) that assured Alaska Natives a land base, advanced the process of identifying state lands, and vastly increased the nation's acreage of national parks and wildlife refuges. Its prodigious outflow of cash speeded the process of modernizing and urbanizing Alaska, shifted social life further toward dependence on government, and swelled the population. An increasingly active host of regional, racial, generational, and economic groups, most prominently a newly powerful oil industry, competed against one another and demanded subsidies from the state government. While lifting material living standards, cash eroded Native social systems and furthered their alienation from the land.

Effects of the pipeline touched all levels, from local to international. The pipeline-enabling law stipulated that the oil could not be sold outside the country unless the president declared it to be in the national interest. The law accepted at face value company arguments that the nation needed the oil for domestic consumption, that the companies would not damage Alaska merely to make profits for themselves. Yet they may have intended from the beginning to sell to Japan.[59] Bad publicity for the oil companies during the OPEC oil crisis, and opposition from merchant marine interests and environmental organizations, helped deter presidential permission until Congress passed enabling legislation in 1995. '

Supplying one-fifth or more of the nation's production, North Slope oil slowed the growth of the nation's dependence on foreign oil and resultant balance-of-payment deficits, but functioned as an excuse for avoidance of conservation measures. It exacted a tangible price in the *Exxon Valdez* spill (Chapter 12), and intensified a national wilderness-versus-oil debate over the Arctic National Wildlife Refuge (Chapter 16). Directly and indirectly, oil production increased stress on wildlife and wilderness. The pipeline drama firmly implanted Alaska in the perceptions of the public as a natural heirloom threatened by industrial activity. It fortified the prestige and experience of the national environmental movement. And it powerfully stimulated an Alaskan environmental community and its outside colleagues to participate in land status issues and combat a proliferating array of negative ecological impacts. In doing so, it made the community a permanent supplement to the government regulatory process.

Prospects for far-ranging and permanent destruction of wildlands made environmental sustainability a central feature of the pipeline debate. The pipeline system failed the test of environmental sustainability and, from a long-term perspective, perhaps economic sustainability as well. Yet responsibility for wildlife protection received at least formal recognition, and critics managed to limit the damage done in the land segment of the project. Public participation and access to information through environmental impact statements succeeded in part. But evasive and manipulatory presentation of the impact statements, and congressional overriding of the Environmental Policy Act, weakened public influence at crucial points. Government and corporate accountability were only partly realized. It remained for the *Exxon Valdez* oil spill to reveal more fully the costs of the oil pipeline.

NOTES

1. W. Hunt, "Notes on the History," 8–10; Davis, *Energy/Alaska*, 197–199, 202–204.
2. J. Reed, *Exploration of Naval Petroleum Reserve*, 1–2.

3. Davis, *Energy/Alaska*, 204–207; Jones, *From the Rio Grande to the Arctic*, 328; Berry, *Alaska Pipeline*, 49, 68–69; Yergin, *The Prize*, 569–571; Chasan, *Klondike 70*, 6–10. Roderick, *Crude Dreams*, 168–169, 172, asserts that the state selected the North Slope acreage because determining the boundary line between offshore state lands and on-shore federal lands along the shallow-water coast could delay leasing for years. The state received 90 percent of leasing fees from federal lands, but would be part owner of the oil extracted from state lands.

4. *US News and World Report*, "Alaska Strikes It Rich," 48–53.

5. Hickel, *Who Owns America?* xi–xii, 38–41, 55–58, 68, 115–117.

6. *Anchorage Daily News*, December 9, 1990.

7. Berry, *Alaska Pipeline*, 95–104; Tom Brown, *Oil on Ice*, 43–46.

8. Belous, "Unsolved Problems," 16, 21.

9. East, "Is It TAPS for Wild Alaska?" 88–89.

10. Laycock, "Kiss the North Country Goodbye?" 72.

11. Coates, *Trans-Alaska Pipeline*, 165–166, 168, 171–174.

12. Weeden, "Alaska's Oil Boom," 3.

13. Marshall, "Bob Marshall," 31; Laycock, "Kiss the North Country Goodbye?" 72–74.

14. Coates, *Trans-Alaska Pipeline*, 189–190, 220, 235; *Wilderness Society v. Hickel* 325 F. Supp. 422 (1970).

15. *New York Times*, November 10, 1969, 46.

16. *US News and World Report*, "Why Alaskans Are Upset," 43.

17. *New York Times*, August 23, 1970, 42.

18. Manning, *Cry Crisis*, 108–109.

19. East, "Is It TAPS for Wild Alaska?" 88.

20. Berry, *Alaska Pipeline*, 145–146.

21. Laycock, "Kiss the North County Goodbye?" 74.

22. T.M. Brown, "That Unstoppable Pipeline," 99–100; *Alaska Conservation Society (ACS)* news release, mid-April 1971, 2–3.

23. Sherrill, *Oil Follies*, 158–163.

24. U.S. Department of the Interior (USDOI), *Trans-Alaska Pipeline Hearings*, Anchorage, February 16–18, 1971, vol. 2, 574–575.

25. USDOI, *Trans-Alaska Pipeline Hearings*, Anchorage, February 24, 1971, vol 1, 246; Washington, D.C., February 17, 1971, *Suppl. Testimony*, vol.1, Exhibit 5.

26. USDOI, *Trans-Alaska Pipeline Hearings*, Anchorage, February 24, 1971, vol. 1, 324–25; vol. 3, Exhibit 32.

27. USDOI, *Trans-Alaska Pipeline Hearings*, Washington, D.C., February 16–18, 1971, vols. 3, 5; February 24, vol. 1, 251.

28. USDOI, *Trans-Alaska Pipeline Hearings*, Washington, D.C., February 17, 1971, *Supp. Testimony*, vol.1, Exhibit 4.

29. USDOI, *Trans-Alaska Pipeline Hearings*, Anchorage, February 24, 1971, vol. 1 (Exhibits), Exhibit 2, 7–9.

30. USDOI, *Trans-Alaska Pipeline Hearings*, Washington, D.C., February 17, 1971, vol. 3, 62.

31. USDOI, *Trans-Alaska Pipeline Hearings*, Anchorage, February 24, 1971, vol. 1, 24. Stevens, an Alaskan attorney, served in the Interior Department during 1956–1961, the Alaska House of Representatives (1964–1968), and received appointment to the U.S. Senate following the death of Bob Bartlett in December 1968 (Barone and Ujifusa, *Almanac*, 33). He is known as an aggressive patron of Alaskan development and the most formidable opponent of the state's environmentalists.

32. Coates, *Trans-Alaska Pipeline*, 200, 205–206, 217–221, 244.

33. Berry, *Alaska Pipeline*, 277; U.S. Department of the Interior (USDOI), *Final Environmental Impact Statement: Proposed Trans-Alaska Pipeline*, vol. 1, 320–322.

34. USDOI, *Final Environmental Impact Statement: Proposed Trans-Alaska Pipeline*, i–c, vol 3, 431, 478; vol 4, 205.

35. USDOI, *Final Environmental Impact Statement: Proposed Trans-Alaska Pipeline*, vol 1, 320.

36. Coates, *Trans-Alaska Pipeline*, 230.

37. Cicchetti, *Alaskan Oil*, 117.

38. Ibid., 118–122.

39. U.S. Congress, Joint Economic Committee, *Natural Gas Regulation*, 217–118, 436.

40. G. Rogers, "A Comparison," 138–141.

41. Berry, *Alaska Pipeline*, 220, 239.

42. Manning, *Cry Crisis*, 193.

43. *Wilderness Society v. Morton* 479 F. 2d. 842 (1973).

44. U.S. Senate Committee on Interior, *Hearings: Rights-of-Way, Part 3*, 71–73, 81.

45. Berry, *Alaska Pipeline*, 215, 229, 234, 254–260, 269–272; 87 Stat. 576, November 16, 1973. Jack Roderick (*Crude Dreams*, 380) identifies Stevens as author of the amendment; Gravel employed it without Stevens's permission.

46. Coates, *Trans-Alaska Pipeline*, 183, 194, 255, 263, 268; Gilbert, "The Devaluation of Alaska," 67–68; Rearden, "Alaska Pipe Line," 136.

47. Naske and Slotnick, *Alaska: A History*, 262.

48. Hanrahan and Gruenstein, *Lost Frontier*, 157, 162–163; Lieberman, *Checks and Balances*, 80–81.

49. Morehouse, "Fish, Wildlife, Pipeline," 19–24.

50. *Bioscience*, "Biologists and the Alaskan Pipeline," 706.

51. Hanrahan and Gruenstein, *Lost Frontier*, 164–167; Coates, *Trans-Alaska Pipeline*, 249–250.

52. Lenzner, *Management, Planning and Construction*, xii–3.

53. Coates, *Trans-Alaska Pipeline*, 163, 191–192.

54. *Alaska Conservation Review (ACR)*, Summer 1970, 8; Wright, "Haul Road Puzzle," 3; *ACR*, Spring 1975, 10, 15; report by David Norton, *ACR*, Summer-Fall 1975, 4–7; G. Mayo, "Pipeline Overview," 11; Klein, "Monitoring the Pipeline," 21; Stonorov, "The Haul Road," 4–5; Stonorov, "Gumshoe," 12.

55. Coates, *Trans-Alaska Pipeline*, 307; Buskirk, "Haul Road," 3; report on lobby activity by Joe Geldhof; Steve Rinehart, "Dalton's As Ready As It Can Be," *Anchorage Daily News*, May 8, 1995, 1.

56. Hanrahan and Gruenstein, *Lost Frontier*, 167–174. Anthropologist Mim Dixon studied the social impact on Fairbanks. See *What Happened to Fairbanks*.

57. Roscow, *800 Miles to Valdez*, 140.

58. *Newsweek*, "Alaska's Pipeline: A Disappointment," 22.

59. Hanrahan and Gruenstein, *Lost Frontier*, 135–139; Naske and Slotnick, "Financiers, Workers and Saboteurs," 17–18.

12

Oil on the Oceans

Industrial civilizations's craving for oil spelled trouble for ocean ecosystems. Often discovered under continental shelves, oil frequently ended up in the water. Offshore extraction involved drilling and some form of transportation over or under the water. Supertankers appeared to be the cheapest way to move oil among separated continents. Spills great and small ensued, and Alaska received its share. Consequently, national opinion grew even more convinced of environmental abuse in Alaska, and environmental values further gained power and legitimacy. Alaskan environmentalists engaged in a mainstream effort to alleviate and respond to the effects of the momentous *Exxon Valdez* oil spill. They and other parties involved—state and federal officials, fishing and tourism interests, oil companies, Natives, and the Alaskan and national publics— acquired proficiency in the management of a deep-rooted and high-profile environmental crisis. The experience strengthened recognition of the need for government and corporate accountability, for public participation, and for ecological research.

Several national and international trends set the stage for an Alaskan oil disaster. By the 1980s the nation saw its oil production winding down and its dependence on imported oil increasing. Given the status of oil as the lifeblood of modern civilization, frightening possibilities accompanied a future decline of the oil supply. The OPEC embargo and the manyfold increase in the price of oil had heightened the anxiety. The nation reacted not by taking stock, planning, and conserving, but by searching farther and drilling deeper trying to find more. Not least, the Reagan administration's antipathy to government regulation and its fondness for the oil industry flashed a green light for corporate irresponsibility. Inevitably, a tanker found its way onto the rocks.

OFFSHORE OIL

Experts believed continental shelves—the least tapped being those off Alaska—held the greatest remaining potential for oil and gas production. The 1958 Statehood Act granted Alaska control extending three miles offshore, a total of about 40 million acres. Territory beyond three miles, termed the outer continental shelf, fell under federal jurisdiction. According to 1981 estimates, Alaska dominated the national list of offshore oil sources. But by the end of the decade, ill fortune in prospecting dramatically scaled back the projections.

Official figures set recoverable outer-continental-shelf Alaskan hydrocarbon reserves at 27 percent of the national offshore total of 8.2 billion barrels of oil, and 15 percent of the total of 74 trillion cubic feet of natural gas. Specifically, the Navarin Basin (Northern Bering Sea) and Beaufort Sea each held 0.89 billion barrels of recoverable oil, Chukchi Sea 0.54 billion, St. George Basin (eastern Bering Sea) 0.35 billion, and Gulf of Alaska and other areas, smaller amounts.[1]

Extracting oil from Arctic and subarctic waters would be much more difficult than from Prudhoe Bay. High waves and seasonal ice typified the Bering Sea. In the Arctic, cold and ice presented the most serious obstacles. Supply could be troublesome: in 1975 ice stopped a large flotilla of barges on its way to Prudhoe Bay and held them all winter. In 1981 the Coast Guard icebreaker *Polar Sea* embarked on a Seattle-to-Prudhoe trip to explore the feasibility of a tanker route. It sustained rudder and propeller damage, became icebound, and had to be evacuated. Pressure ridges of ice could be 50 feet high and scrape 10-foot-deep trenches in the sea floor, 150 feet below the ocean surface. Oil drilling would depend on gravel islands or stout refloatable platforms, and buried pipelines. A well blowout in winter could be disastrous; the currents might carry the oil for hundreds of miles under the ice. Such a spill could be partially cleaned up at best.[2]

Oil's toxicity to almost every living thing bode ill for Arctic and subarctic creatures— whales, walruses, polar bears, fur seals, sea otters, and seabirds—subjects of Alaskan environmental disputes extending over the previous century. Environmental defenders dreaded the prospect of offshore drilling in the Far North, anticipating damage to fish and wildlife, landscapes, subsistence economies, and Native culture. They urged more research on ecosystem impacts and toxic-spill control technology.

In December 1979 the state sold nearly a half-billion dollars worth of leases for drilling in its offshore territory along the Beaufort Sea. Trustees for Alaska, National Wildlife Federation, and other environmental groups and Native organizations sued in state and federal courts to forestall the drilling on grounds that it violated the Marine Mammal Protection, Endangered Species, National Environmental Policy, Alaska Coastal Zone Management, and Public Meetings Acts. They focused particularly on the safety of bowhead whale stocks. The Alaska Conservation Society declined to join the suits; it did not believe the bowhead whale to be endangered by the drilling, and took a moderate position advocating a coastal management plan for the North Slope Borough prior to a sale.[3]

In the state suit, the superior court issued an injunction in June 1980 pending more study of impact on Eskimos, but held that otherwise the sale violated no laws. The Alaska Supreme Court rescinded the injunction pending the expected research, and the sale proceeded.[4] In the federal suit, the Inupiat Eskimos and environmentalists persuaded the Washington, D.C., District Court to impose a supplemental environmental impact statement, but the circuit court reversed the decision. Trustees for Alaska (TfA) and the North Slope Borough sued in 1982 to prevent the weakening of seasonal drilling restrictions protecting the bowhead whales, and lost. However, the Interior Department agreed to safeguards for the bowheads—a 20-mile buffer zone around Barrow and limitations on construction of onshore facilities.[5] Eskimos contended in several federal suits that trusteeship responsibilities for Natives, and subsistence guarantees of the Alaska Lands Act (ANILCA), obliged the secretary of the interior to disallow offshore oil leasing. In 1987 the U.S. Supreme Court ruled the Interior secretary had no such duty because the outer continental shelf is not part of Alaska.[6]

In the northeast, the state prepared to lease its offshore lands along the Arctic National Wildlife Refuge. TfA brought a suit charging that the state leased 118,000 acres at Camden Bay in violation of the Alaska Coastal Management program. TfA interpreted the lease as a means of forcing open the Arctic Refuge to oil exploration, which by law should not happen prior to a congressional decision on the refuge. The Alaska Supreme Court partially upheld the plaintiffs in 1990, ruling that proper study and planning to avoid geophysical hazards and archeological sites had not been done.[7] Also in the late 1980s, TfA and others sued the state over an offshore sale at Demarcation Point, claiming that the plan failed to calculate the impact on the Porcupine caribou herd and on the subsistence practices of Kaktovik residents. A December 1993 Alaska Supreme Court decision ordered more examination of the risks posed by oil pipelines, roads, and other industrial activity, particularly for the caribou herd. In 1999, TfA challenged the state's impending sale of leases along the entire length of the Beaufort Sea coast, on grounds that it made no provision for prevention of oil spills. Underwater pipelines up to 150 miles long, in a harsh environment of moving ice, might be needed to connect the drill sites to the mainland.[8]

Several state leases resulted in viable oil finds. Of those partly or entirely in state offshore waters, the Alaska Department of Natural Resources estimated recoverable reserves in millions of barrels: Endicott 622, Milne Point 395, Niakuk 66, and Point McIntyre 358. The Point Thompson unit bordering on the northwest corner of the Arctic Refuge contained 300 million barrels, but lay 50 miles from the Trans-Alaska Pipeline, perhaps too far to be productively tapped. A 5-mile gravel causeway reached to Endicott's gravel drilling island, and a similar 2.5-mile causeway connected Prudhoe Bay to its boat dock.[9] Offshore and onshore operations in toto constituted a major industrial complex.

Before it left office, the Carter administration had set a schedule for federal Alaskan offshore leases: Gulf of Alaska, 1980; Cook Inlet, 1981; Norton and St. George Basins, 1982; Beaufort, Kodiak, and the Aleutian Shelf, 1983; and Chukchi Sea and the Hope and Navarin Basins, 1985. Environmentalists requested delays or deletions and more research on ecological and cultural impacts. To combat the leases they formed coalitions with fishing and Native groups. The state joined this effort; Governor Jay Hammond opposed any drilling in Bristol Bay, St. George Basin, and the Chukchi Sea.[10] Leasing proceeded aggressively during the Reagan administration, and differences among the interested parties came to a head over the North Aleutian area, in the eastern Bering Sea. Federal efforts to hold sales of leases met resistance from the state, Natives, and fishing and environmental groups. The parties called upon Robert Redford's Institute for Resource Management in 1985 to mediate the issue. In May 1987, negotiators agreed to a 48-million-acre lease area and enhanced safeguards for fish and wildlife, and chose a panel to develop regulations and oversee compliance.[11] Despite this achievement, no agreement emerged for Bristol Bay. Its billion-dollar-a-year fishery harvested five species of salmon, including the world's highest volume of sockeyes. Eight species of endangered whales, other marine mammals, and millions of seabirds frequented the region. The state asked for a delay until 1994, and more information about the impact on

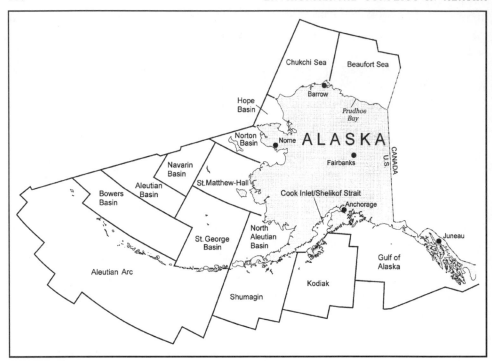

12.1. Federal Offshore Oil and Gas Leasing Areas, 1997–2002. Courtesy Minerals Management Service, Alaska OCS Office, Anchorage, 1999.

subsistence hunting and fishing. Insisting it had studied and compromised enough, the Interior Department initiated the sale. TfA, Natural Resources Defense Council, and the state filed suit on behalf of the coalition, alleging violations of endangered species acts and other environmental laws. District and appeals court decisions upheld the federal government in 1988 and the sale proceeded. The state planned an appeal to the U.S. Supreme Court, but in the wake of the 1989 *Exxon Valdez* oil spill, a congressional moratorium indefinitely postponed drilling in Bristol Bay.[12] Environmentalists then lobbied for buyback of the leases.

The Interior Department continued to lease offshore tracts through the 1990s, especially in the northern zones. Between 1976 and 1999, companies sank 83 holes in the outer continental shelf: Beaufort Sea, 30; Chukchi Sea, 4; Cook Inlet, 13; Gulf of Alaska, 12; Navarin Basin, 8; Norton Sound, 6; and St. George Basin, 10. By mid-1999 all had been abandoned as dry or economically unfeasible. Not a single federal offshore lease in this period had yielded a producing well. One field, Northstar, would require a six-mile undersea pipeline if it were to be tapped.[13] The Army Corps of Engineers estimated that over its 15-year projected lifetime, the pipeline would stand a 23–26 percent chance of creating an oil spill of more than 1,000 gallons.[14]

Notwithstanding the disappointments in federal waters, proliferating oil operations in the Arctic posed a formidable challenge to ecosystem integrity, and environmentalists expected weak enforcement of weak standards. The Environmental Protection Agency conducted no

Table 12.1—Wildlife Hazards From Alaskan Offshore Oil and Gas Development

Birds
— oil spill threat to large feeding flocks, especially diving birds
— added pressure on rare and declining species
— contamination or reduction of food supplies
— contamination of nesting sites or eggs
— disturbances of nesting sites, especially by helicopters

Fisheries
— pollution damage to eggs and larvae, especially near coast
— death or contamination of shellfish
— injury to crustaceans while molting

Marine Mammals
— contamination or depletion of food supplies
— oil spill threat to coastal whales, especially bowheads, grays, and belukhas
— disturbance of walrus haul-out sites
— disturbance or oil spills near sea lion or seal rookeries
— oil spill threat to sea otters and migrating fur seals
— disturbance of denning, and nuisance killing, of polar bears

Terrestrial Species
— displacement and disturbance by onshore development activities (most affected species: grizzly bears, caribou, and musk oxen)

Source: D. A. Bolze and M. B. Lee, "Offshore Oil and Gas Development: Implications for Wildlife in Alaska." *Marine Policy,* July 1989, 232–243.

inspections of offshore drilling operations between 1985 and 1990, then transferred its monitoring responsibility to the pro-industry Minerals Management Service. Lack of staff retarded the Alaska Oil and Gas Conservation Commission's ability to do safety tests of offshore well operations. A 1991 Alaska Ombudsman report judged that "Alaska falls far short of providing a viable regulatory presence in field safety . . . The commission's inspection program has slipped to the point of near non-existence."[15] In the 1990s, environmentalists called for a comprehensive environmental impact statement to estimate cumulative impact, and a "viable monitoring regime" to control it.[16]

TANKER SPILLS

Ocean transportation as well as drilling placed environmental integrity at risk (Table 12.1). For many reasons, crude oil and fuel got into the water. If happening constantly, small releases could do cumulative injury to harbor environments. Larger but unknown effects may have flowed from the practice of flushing out tanks at sea, prohibited in the 1980s. Such an incident may have caused the February 1970 spill fouling miles of shoreline in the Kodiak-Afognak region, killing an estimated 10,000 seabirds. Soon thereafter the navy upset 90,000 gallons of jet fuel in Womens Bay at Kodiak Island. The connection, if any, to the deaths of 86,000 murres and several sea otters went unresolved.[17] In 1973 the tanker *Hillyer Brown* grounded and lost 20,000 gallons of oil at Cold Bay. Conditions rendered cleanup impossible, and biological effects unknown.[18]

Oil spills occurred more frequently in the 1980s following the addition of Valdez traffic to that of Cook Inlet and elsewhere. In December 1985 the tanker *ARCO Anchorage* leaked 124,000 gallons of crude oil at Port Angeles, Washington harbor. Several hundred seabirds perished, and volunteers operated a cleaning station at a high school. A similar amount of oil escaped when the tanker *Glacier Bay* struck a rock at Cook Inlet in July 1987. Waves and currents impeded cleanup conditions; workers recovered only 10 percent of the oil after nine days. One boat reported catching 1,000 to 1,500 oil-contaminated salmon, and the fishing industry sustained an estimated $1.5 million damage in lost fish and gear.[19] Much larger spills of 23,000 and 15,000 barrels came from the British Petroleum tanker *Stuyvesant* in October. En route to Panama from Valdez, it ran into storms, causing leakage. Both incidents, the first in the Gulf of Alaska and the second off British Columbia, happened more than 200 miles offshore. Any injury to fish and wildlife or shorelines did not gain public notice.[20] In Prince William Sound, a near-disaster occurred in 1980 when the loaded tanker *Prince William Sound* lost power and drifted toward the rocks. Tugs had difficulty attaching lines to it. The tanker regained power 30 minutes before it would have grounded. Thereafter, the Coast Guard mandated quick-connect devices for tugs on all tankers.[21]

In and near the Arctic, a barge lost 68,000 gallons of heating oil near Flaxman Island in 1988 when ice broke through its hull. A cargo ship spilled 200,000 gallons of fuel oil after grounding on St. Matthew Island in 1989. Crews salvaged the ship and its remaining oil, but weather prevented cleanup or biological assessment of either Arctic spill. Four miles north of St. Paul Island in the Bering Sea, a collision occurred in February 1996 between a crab-processing ship and a freighter, the *M/V Citrus*. The *Citrus* spilled an unknown quantity of bunker oil and, two days later, oiled seabirds began to appear on the island. Scientists estimated that 1,765 dead birds came ashore, 1,609 of them king eiders. Searchers captured 165 live birds and sent them to a rescue facility. Additional oiled eiders flew to inland sites, and 96 birds, mostly king eiders, turned up dead on St. George Island, 50 miles from the spill site. The vast majority of affected birds may have died at sea. The incident illustrated the potential of oil spills to endanger uncommon wildlife species, and the near impossibility of preparing for and containing spills in such forbidding waters as the Bering Sea.[22]

THE *EXXON VALDEZ* OIL SPILL

In both magnitude and impact, the *Exxon Valdez* catastrophe of 1989 transcended previous Alaskan spills by a hundredfold. Hours before the event, Captain Joe Hazelwood and some of his crew spent an overcast afternoon in Valdez bars and restaurants awaiting their departure for Los Angeles. Shortly before 10 P.M. they cast off aboard Exxon's newest tanker, 987 feet long, carrying a cargo of 53 million gallons (1,264,000 barrels) of North Slope crude oil. As the ship passed through Valdez Narrows heading out into Prince William Sound, the harbor pilot departed. The captain notified the Coast Guard monitoring station that he planned to alter course to port (southward) to avoid icebergs calved off Columbia Glacier. Turning over the helm to Third Mate Greg Cousins, an officer not licensed to control the ship within the sound, the captain gave orders to correct to starboard at Busby Island Light, and retired to his quarters. On its southerly course, the ship passed along the eastern shoreline of the sound. Coast Guard radar, because of inadequate monitoring and technical

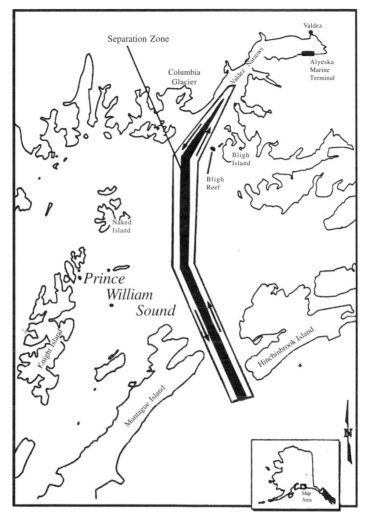

12.2. Prince William Sound Tanker Lanes. Courtesy Alaska Oil Spill Commission, Spill: The Wreck of the Exxon Valdez: Alaska Oil Spill Commission, Final Report *(Anchorage, 1990), 8.*

capability, took no note of its location. Six or seven minutes after the ship passed the light, the mate ordered the right turn. Responding slowly, the ship turned too late. The *Exxon Valdez* ground to a halt, perched precariously on Bligh Reef west of Bligh Island, 28 miles southwest of Valdez. Impact occurred at four minutes after midnight on March 24, the twenty-fifth Good Friday since the 1964 Alaska earthquake.

Whereas the ship drew 56 feet of water, the reef lay only 30 feet below the surface at low tide. Five hundred linear feet of the ship's hull tore open. Of the eleven cargo tanks, the impact ruptured eight, on the starboard side and in the center. Oil poured out of the vessel immediately, piling up thickly on the ocean surface. Nearly completed by mid-afternoon, the flow finally totaled 10,836,000 gallons (257,000 barrels). By losing one-fifth of its load, the *Exxon Valdez* precipitated the largest oil spill and one of the most memorable ecological disasters the nation ever experienced.[23]

Not many places could have been less suitable for such an event. Prince William Sound, a coastal region nearly enclosed by mountainous islands and mainland, lay largely unspoiled except for some logging plans by the Forest Service and Natives. Fish, seabirds, seals, sea lions, sea otters, porpoises, and whales richly endowed its cold waters. On its many islands and bordering mainland lived brown and black bears, wolves, mountain goats, Sitka deer, wolverines, river otters, porcupines, mink, and weasels. The unsullied beauty, known to few in winter, delighted summer sailors and cruise tourists.[24]

Prince William Sound's natural resources interested Alaska's earliest European visitors. Captain James Cook visited the sound in 1778 on his third voyage, on the way to his death by Natives in the Hawaiian Islands. His successor, Captain George Vancouver, later entered the sound and named it for a son of King George III, who became King William IV. He named Bligh Island for William Bligh, an earlier commander of one of Cook's ships who never visited Alaska, and who achieved immortality as master of the *Bounty*. Spanish explorers soon arrived at the sound, as did Russian fur seekers. Rivalry for territorial and sea otter hunting hegemony ensued, sometimes approaching international violence. Russians under Alexander Baranof established a presence and built a three-masted ship at Resurrection Bay in 1794. Slightly more than a century later, the Harriman Expedition toured the sound and named several glaciers for eastern colleges, one being Columbia.[25]

Five years into statehood, Prince William Sound experienced an environmental catastrophe—one caused by nature. The bay embraced the epicenter of the 1964 Alaska earthquake, one of the strongest ever in American territory. A tsunami 70 feet high washed away the buildings of Chenega Bay, drowning 23 of its 70 residents. Survivors rebuilt the town in 1984, 20 miles north of the original site. Valdez lost 32 people and many of its buildings, and relocated four miles away. In all, Alaska suffered 114 dead and missing, and $750 million in damages. A wave traveling at nearly 500 mph reached down into Crescent City, California, and drowned at least 10, leaving 15 others missing. A six-foot swell passed through the Gulf of Mexico at New Orleans. Cordova rose 6 feet, part of Montague Island near the epicenter lifted about 50 feet, and mountains on the Kenai Peninsula shifted 5 feet. The Kasilof River dried up and its salmon migration ended.[26] The quake did extensive damage to the beach ecology, though lack of research precluded assessment of the overall ecological effects. Such data would have proved useful in the *Exxon Valdez* oil spill aftermath.

North America's premier oil spill had solid roots in Alaska pipeline politics (Chapter 11). Alaskan politicians secured the Prudhoe-Valdez route through the backing of oil, construction, and commercial interests, and the Nixon administration. They overcame opposition from state and Lower 48 environmentalists and the fishing industry. A 1970 article by Bob Weeden and David R. Klein illustrated the critics' complaints: "Little attention has been focused on the problem of massive oil spills in the tanker lanes between Alaska and the west coast of the U.S., probably because the responsibilities for prevention and for assessing liability are scattered among many federal agencies, the oil industry and the shipping industry." Their conclusion: "To protect the resources of Prince William Sound serious obstacles must be overcome: fragmented government-business responsibility for preventing pollution; limited financial resources of public agencies; insufficient knowledge of the effects of oil pollution; and unsatisfactory technology for cleaning up spilled oil."[27]

Nearly 20 years later, Weeden and Klein's evaluation retained its validity, though political leaders and oil officials assured the public of thoroughgoing safety measures. In 1971 the state of Alaska had declared its intention to institute the following safeguards for Prince William Sound tanker traffic: (1) a pilot on board between Valdez and Bligh Reef; (2) a licensed officer on deck with the pilot at all times; (3) a pilot station in Knowles Bay; (4) one-way traffic and shore-based radar between Valdez and Bligh Reef; (5) ship-to-shore radio frequencies; and (6) control of fishing and pleasure boat activities.[28] Interior Secretary Rogers Morton announced in 1972, "Newly constructed American flag vessels carrying oil from Port Valdez to U.S. ports will be required to have segregated ballast systems, incorporating a double bottom." The Coast Guard would oversee the up-to-date oil spill contingency plans and "a continuing environmental monitoring system will be required during the lifetime of oil movement in American coastal waters."[29] Standard Oil (later Exxon) promised a congressional committee in 1973, "Each tanker will be equipped with modern navigation systems and all tanker traffic in the Prince William Sound and Valdez Harbor will be monitored by a traffic control system similar in concept to airport control systems. . . . Newly developed oil spill booms and skimming equipment will be readily available to put contingency cleanup plans immediately into effect in the event of an oil spill."[30]

Such safety devices as double hulls or double bottoms added considerably to shipbuilding costs. The Coast Guard, closely tied to the shipping industry, acknowledged the value of double bottoms. Objections from oil companies forestalled a proposed 1973 international agreement to prescribe double bottoms. A second attempt during the Carter administration yielded improvements in design standards but no accord on double bottoms or hulls.[31] Alaska state pipeline coordinator Charles Champion told a U.S. Senate committee in 1977 that tankers to be used on the Valdez route "don't meet minimum safety standards." He called for double bottoms, which Coast Guard sources had said would diminish oil spills from groundings by 87 percent. Only 10 of the 36 vessels to be used on the Valdez route had double bottoms.[32] The Exxon Valdez had none, thereby saving $12 million on its $125 million cost, and no double hull, saving $31 million. Instead, its oil and ballast tanks alternated on the front and sides, a measure intended to decrease damage in ship collisions. Such incidents occurred three times as often as groundings, but resulted in smaller spills. Coast Guard sources estimated that 25 to 60 percent less oil would have been released if the Exxon Valdez had had a double bottom.[33]

A moderate commitment to safety measures existed when tanker traffic got underway in 1977. As time passed and 8,700 tankers moved through Prince William Sound without an egregious accident, enforcement of standards grew lax. Coast Guard appropriations and environmental safeguards atrophied in the Reagan years. At Valdez the Coast Guard cut back its inspections and personnel, neglected to require adequate navigational radar on tankers, and installed only one ground radar station. Columbia Glacier began to recede in 1987 and increased its calving, and the Coast Guard routinely granted permission for tankers to leave the shipping lane to avoid icebergs. Exxon cut the size of tanker crews, causing them to work long and exhausting hours. Alaska state government and its poorly funded Department of Environmental Conservation did little to monitor oil spill prevention and cleanup provisions despite the warnings of its Valdez supervisor, Dan Lawn.

According to the state's understanding, responsibility for oil spill emergencies in Prince William Sound resided in the Alyeska Pipeline Service Company, a consortium of seven oil companies owned 50 percent by British Petroleum, 21 percent by Arco, 20 percent by Exxon, and the remainder by Phillips, Unocal, Mobil, and Amerada Hess. Alyeska compiled a lengthy record of willful violations of air and water pollution laws, almost entirely escaping punishment. Dan Lawn appraised Alyeska cynically: "I would characterize their attitude toward regulations as utter contempt."[34]

Alyeska's behavior eventually reaped a public-relations debacle for it and the parent oil companies. Charles Hamel, an oil shipper who felt cheated by Alyeska in the mid-1980s, began to collect evidence of environmental violations such as tanker flushing at sea and vapor emissions from Valdez tanks. He relayed the information to the Environmental Protection Agency and to Trustees for Alaska. Anticipating sanctions, Alyeska directed its security contractor Wackenhut to investigate the information leaks. During the seven-month life of its probe in 1990, Wackenhut spent $288,000 on monitoring phone records and other surveillance. Posing as environmentalists, its agents gained Hamel's confidence, and removed documents and recordings from his home. Impressed by Hamel, four of the investigators later sided with him. Wackenhut also gathered information on other critics: Dan Lawn, Cordova marine scientist Riki Ott, Trustees for Alaska, Fairbanks commentator Lewis "Frank" DeLong, and U.S. House Interior Committee chairman George Miller. Upon learning of the venture in September, British Petroleum, Arco, and Exxon put a stop to it but did not report it. In its summary of hearings on the scandal, the Interior Committee found that "Wackenhut agents engaged in a pattern of deceitful, grossly offensive and potentially if not blatantly, illegal conduct" and that "it was Alyeska which set the tone and the goals of the undercover operation." The hearings, following the August 1991 release of a General Accounting Office report critical of pipeline operations, helped defeat an attempt to open the Arctic Refuge to oil prospecting.[35]

Oil spill preparedness also reflected Alyeska's sense of social responsibility. A 1986 Alyeska computer analysis projected a large spill once in every 241 years.[36] In any case, it seemed expensive and perhaps unrealistic to keep a large work force in Valdez waiting for a major spill to occur. Alyeska disbanded its trained 12-person oil spill emergency crew in 1982, replacing it with workers doing other jobs and inexperienced in oil cleanup. It ended its lease on a 218,000-gallon cleanup barge in favor of one far smaller. Alyeska fired port manager James Woodle and spill coordinator Jerry Nebel; the two charged they had been terminated for complaining to the company about safety cutbacks. Alyeska president George Nelson attempted unsuccessfully to pressure Department of Environmental Conservation commissioner Bill Ross to fire Dan Lawn. The state assigned no full-time oil spill coordinator to Valdez after the mid-1980s.[37]

CLEANUP EFFORTS

Confusion over responsibility for the spill cleanup evidenced itself on the first day. Exxon claimed jurisdiction, maintaining it had agreed with Alyeska in 1982 to take over in case of a large spill, and had so notified the state, receiving no reply. Exxon's assumption of control on March 24 took state officials by surprise. Federal and state law specified a federal response team to take charge if the spiller proved incapable. But the federal government, even less prepared than Exxon or Alyeska, did not relish the burden.[38]

Exxon's earlier notification notwithstanding, state officials had relied on a contingency plan worked out with Alyeska and updated in 1987. A specific scenario envisioned an 8.4 million-gallon spill, 50 percent of it to be recovered. The plan lacked clarity about where the workers and equipment would come from. It called for Alyeska to place a cleanup team and oil-skimming equipment onsite within five hours of a spill. Practice oil-spill cleanups had been attempted by the inexperienced crews, showing poor results.

When the *Exxon Valdez* struck Bligh Reef, the jurisdictional uncertainty and lack of preparation paid their dividends. Alyeska supervisor Chuck O'Donnell, informed of the spill, assigned a subordinate to take care of it and went back to sleep. The hastily assembled crew had difficulty rounding up the equipment—the barge undergoing repairs, and the fenders needed for offloading the ship lost for hours under several feet of snow.[39] The barge arrived at the spill scene seven hours late, carrying 8,000 feet of containment boom and container capacity for 2,000 gallons of oil—1/5,000th of the amount already spilled. Workers needed far more equipment than that available during the crucial first three days, though the unusually calm water ideally suited skimming operations. The spill plan included possible use of chemical dispersants as a supplement, depending on spill conditions. However, it noted that state permission would be required and that the distance from the contracted aviation firm in Arizona would mean a delay of up to 72 hours. A brief application of dispersants yielded unimpressive results, and limited supplies of chemicals, lack of clarity of jurisdiction, and disagreement over the environmental impact hampered the operation. Another option involved igniting the oil by helicopter-based lasers. Following an experimental burn of 15,000 gallons, a shortage of fireproof boom and fear of setting the *Exxon Valdez* on fire prevented further burning.

On the fourth day after the spill, winds rose to 73 mph, frustrated skimming operations, and scattered the oil up to 40 miles from the spill site. Nevertheless, mariners successfully transferred the oil still on the *Exxon Valdez* to three other tankers. The operation began on the second day when the air force flew in pumps and hoses, and ended within two weeks, after the removal of all but 16,000 barrels of the load. This enabled the ship to be refloated and moved to Naked Island, where it received emergency repairs to prevent its breakup on the June 24 journey south to dry dock in Los Angeles.[40]

Open to charges of negligence on their own parts, Governor Steve Cowper and Department of Environmental Conservation commissioner Dennis Kelso acted aggressively to rouse the spill containment effort and win the upper hand in public relations. They attacked Alyeska and Exxon for misconduct, countered media statements by Exxon, demanded a speedup of spill response efforts, and participated in a multi-agency planning effort managing the cleanup until Exxon could effectively take over. Cowper ordered a slowdown in the oil flow through the pipeline and threatened to shut it off should adequate oil spill prevention measures not be forthcoming. He ordered enough oil booms placed in Valdez to contain a 10-million-gallon spill, and every loaded vessel accompanied by two tugs and a harbor pilot to Hinchinbrook Island entrance.[41]

12.1. Exxon Valdez *and offloading tanker, Bligh Reef, March 1989. By John Hyde. The nation's largest oil spill and most publicized environmental catastrophe.*

The scope of the cleanup project ranged far beyond the capabilities of any agency or corporation. The military transported more than 1,000 tons of equipment by C-5 and C-141 aircraft from points as far away as the East Coast, Finland, and the Black Sea. Within a month 58 vessels, including 42 skimmers, operated in the recovery effort. The Soviet oil skimmer *Vayda Ghubsky* reached Resurrection Bay a month after the spill. Its efforts ended in futility because the oil stiffened and mixed in other debris. As time passed, winds and currents dispersed the oil, evaporated some of it, mixed it with water creating a sticky mousse, and hardened it into tar balls. Eventually the oil spread over several thousand square miles, smearing wildlife sanctuaries including virtually all the shores of Katmai National Park, traveling nearly to the Shumagin Islands, and contaminating an estimated 1,244 miles of shoreline.[42]

As skimming grew more difficult, the emphasis shifted to cleaning the beaches. Exxon initiated cleanup operations a week after the spill. At first, workers wiped off individual rocks using absorbent pads, a hopelessly lengthy and expensive process. Public agencies rejected a kerosene-based chemical washing agent, proposed by Exxon, as potentially damaging to the biota. Jets of hot water, the most commonly used system, washed oil off the beach to be recovered by booms in the water. The use of fertilizer to stimulate oil-consuming bacteria appeared to improve the process of oil removal. Suction devices lost effectiveness as the oil hardened.

By early fall, workers had treated 1,089 miles of beach. However, the hot water tended to kill organisms that survived the oil, and it cleaned only the top few inches. Underneath lay a

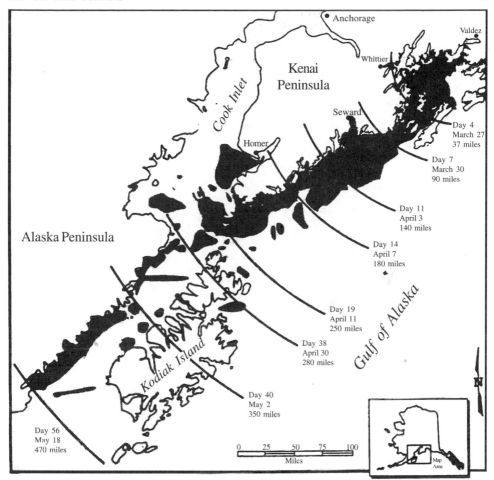

12.3. Exxon Valdez *Oil Spill Progression, May 18, 1989. Courtesy Alaska Oil Spill Commission,* Spill: The Wreck of the Exxon Valdez: Alaska Oil Spill Commission Final Report *(Anchorage, 1990), 62.*

zone saturated by oil that occasionally rose to the surface and recoated the beach. Some scientists argued that the beach-cleaning operation and its hot water, heavy machinery, human impact, and poor results did more biological harm than good. But Exxon, more concerned about public relations than ecology, felt irresistible pressure to do something visible, however actually useful it might be. At the peak of the operation Exxon employed nearly 11,000 workers, about 3,000 doing beach cleanup.[43] This extravagant effort recovered only about 14 percent of the total spill. National Oceanographic and Atmospheric Administration scientist Douglas Wolfe estimated that about 20 percent evaporated, 50 percent degraded, skimmers collected 8 percent, beach crews picked up 6 percent, and nearly four years after the spill, 12 percent remained in sediments underwater and 3 percent under beaches above the tide.[44]

Cleanup operations generated and gathered enormous quantities of toxic debris. Three small incinerators at Valdez and one mounted on a barge in Prince William Sound could not

12.2. Solid waste from oil spill cleanup, Valdez, July 1989. By Glenn Miller. Workers repackaged thousands of tons for shipment to Anchorage, then to an Oregon landfill.

handle the volume, and no adequate toxic materials dumpsite existed near the sound. Between 125 and 250 tons of excess material such as oil-soaked wood, earth, and cleaning equipment arrived daily in Anchorage to be transshipped in plastic bags to Oregon for landfill disposal. Removed oily debris totaled 30,000 tons by the end of 1990.[45]

Cold weather halted the beach cleanup in September, and parties debated what to do next. On the washed beaches, oil saturated the earth below the surface to a depth of several inches to two feet. Cut off from sun and air, it stayed viscous. Visits to sites of a 1970 oil spill in Nova Scotia and of the 1978 *Amoco Cadiz* spill off France revealed layers of asphalt on or below the surface, and some liquid oil beneath. The state, fearing that oil would be released for years into the water, wanted Exxon to return the following summer, dig up the beaches, and clean them. National Oceanographic and Atmospheric Administration scientists opposed further cleanup, contending that even the surface washing had been counterproductive. Exxon regarded deep washing as impractical and unsound.

Bioremediation efforts also involved controversy. Fertilizers used on 70 miles of beaches seemed to speed up by about 50 percent the oil consumption by naturally occurring bacteria. However, the process depended on oxygen and did not work well on solid oil masses or below one foot depth. Moreover, chemical solvents in the fertilizer could be toxic to wildlife, and may have caused some of the cleaning attributed to microbes. Thus the usefulness of fertilizers in Prince William Sound could not be confidently evaluated. Also, ecological variations among regions hindered the search for universally effective bioremediation measures.[46]

Table 12.2—Estimated Impacts of *Exxon Valdez* Oil Spill, 1989–1991

Sea Otters	— 3,5000–5,500 deaths; continued low reproduction and high mortality in young adults
Harbor Seals	— 200 deaths; reduced numbers
Killer Whales	— 20 deaths
Brown Bears	— No confirmed deaths; some hydrocarbon ingestion
River Otters	— A few deaths; reduced concentrations and body size
Bald Eagles	— 151–580 deaths; higher reproductive failure
Common & Thick- Thick-Billed Murres	— 172,000–198,000 direct deaths; complete reproductive failure 1989–1991 in several large breeding colonies
Harlequin Ducks	— Several hundred deaths; poor health; high reproductive failure
Marbled & Kittlitz's Murrelets	— High percentage of spill area population killed
Pigeon Guillemots	— 1,500–3,000 deaths
Birds (Total)	— 375,000–435,000 deaths
Pink Salmon	— Far higher egg mortality; reduced growth rates
Dolly Varden and Cutthroat Trout	— Far higher mortality in adults
Intertidal Zone	— Increased populations of smaller-sized and oil-laced mussels; significant reductions of other organisms
Subtidal Zone	— Concentrations of hydrocarbons, especially in clams
Archaeological Sites	— At least 35 damaged, mostly by cleanup activities
Subsistence Lifestyles	— Moderate to high disruption in several communities

Source: Exxon Valdez Oil Spill Trustees, *Exxon Valdez Oil Spill Restoration.* Vol. I: *Restoration Framework.* (Anchorage: *Exxon Valdez* Oil Spill Trustees, April 1992), 19–38.

Exxon ceased cleanup operations in mid-September, pronouncing the beaches "environmentally stable." It planned not to return in 1990, and gave money to communities for winter cleanup. The state and others protested, and the Coast Guard ordered Exxon to continue. A renewed effort began in the spring. A survey of spill-site beaches indicated 79 percent still had various degrees of oil contamination. Heavy sheens on the ocean and liquid pools under the gravel persisted in some spots. Cleanup methods included manual pickup of dried oil sediments, machines to scoop up and wash rocks and gravel, and conditions permitting, bacteria fertilizer.[47]

WILDLIFE IMPACT

Marine wildlife enjoyed special status among the concerns of the public, and the media focused intensely on bird and mammal deaths (Table 12.2). Of all the creatures affected, none achieved more prominence than the sea otter. Surviving in obscurity its near-demise in the nineteenth century, the sea otter ascended through nature films and the Amchitka controversy to near-heroic status. Caught in the oil spill, the otter became a media symbol of innocent wildlife victimized by a titanic, impersonal, arrogant, and powerful bureaucratic machine pursuing profit through modern technology. It evoked protective instincts in volunteers arriving from the Lower 48 to participate in the rescue. Thousands of cards poured in from schoolchildren, and tons of towels not needed; Alaskans had already donated more

12.3. Sea otter released at Simpson Bay, 1989. By Patrick Sousa. Courtesy U.S. Fish and Wildlife Service, Anchorage. The sea otter symbolized innocent wildlife victimized by the modern industrial machine. Otters cost nearly $80,000 each to rescue.

than enough. Contracting for a team from the Sea World Research Institute, Exxon set up otter rehabilitation centers at Valdez and Seward.[48] It funded a third built at Jackolov Bay by volunteer Nancy Hillstrand.[49]

Otters cost a great deal to rescue. Large quantities of live shellfish had to be purchased. Exxon spent a total of $18.3 million on 357 otters, and 234 initially survived at an average cost of nearly $80,000 each. Due to stress, loss of insulation, and inhalation or ingestion of toxics, 135 died in captivity and 876 turned up dead in the wild. Many others sank or otherwise escaped discovery. Prior to the spill an estimated 10,000 otters lived in Prince William Sound; the oil probably killed 3,500 to 5,500, mostly in the sound.[50] After treatment, wildlife officials released most of the survivors in safe waters, kept some to further research applicable to future spills, and sent a few orphans to aquariums in the Lower 48. Surveys in 1990 indicated lowered breeding success and increased mortality in oiled areas. Of 45 otters wearing radio collars, researchers counted 13 dead and 15 missing.[51]

Prince William Sound and the oiled regions to the west hosted hundreds of thousands of overwintering seabirds, and millions of shorebirds during the migration that began a few weeks after the oil spill. Water birds lost insulation through oiling of feathers, and ingested poison as they tried to clean off the oil. They could also be contaminated by feeding on oil-tainted organisms. Exxon immediately hired experts from the International Bird Rescue and Research Center, and located recovery facilities in Valdez, Homer, Seward, and Kodiak. Veterinarian Jim Scott organized a center for eagles and other raptors in Anchorage, funded by Exxon. At the peak of the effort, Exxon chartered 163 boats to retrieve injured birds to be cleaned by volunteers using detergents, then banded and released. Bird mortality and rehabilitation expenses ran high. Half the 1,589 treated seabirds died, and the cost of a survivor averaged $30,000. Rehabilitated eagles cost about $42,000 each. No followup study of released birds took place. Exorbitant financial outlays and scientific doubts about the ecological value of such efforts made the *Exxon Valdez* wildlife rescue operation the most expensive and controversial ever undertaken.[52]

About 31,000 dead birds showed evidence of oil. The vast majority that died probably sank or lay undiscovered on isolated beaches. Murres comprised the bulk of those killed; murrelets, sea ducks, cormorants, loons, and grebes also sustained large losses. A colony of 50,000 to 60,000 murres returning to breed at the Barren Islands nearly died out, and several colonies produced no young for three years. Researchers initially estimated total seabird mortality at 375,000 to 435,000. They found that gulls and shorebirds suffered few negative effects.[53] At least 151 bald eagles died, likely from eating oiled seabirds. Most of those fatally affected probably fell in the woods out of sight. Eagle nesting success dropped by two-thirds on islands in Prince William Sound affected by the oil. Biologists believed the cause to be oil brought to the nests on dead seabirds; a single drop could kill an embryo if deposited on the surface of an egg.[54]

Land mammals such as brown and black bears, wolverines, and foxes scavenged the bodies of oiled birds and mammals, and may have been poisoned. River otters, often foraging in salt water, showed signs of hydrocarbon intake. Deer believed to have died from eating oiled seaweed turned out not to have been harmed by oil. Of the sea mammals—harbor seals, sea lions, porpoises, and whales—some had contacted oil. An estimated 200 harbor seals and 20 or more of the 182 Prince William Sound killer whales died. Humpback whales evidenced no discernible effects, and impact on sea lions could not be determined. A few oiled or orphaned harbor seal pups recuperated in facilities in Valdez and Kachemak Bay.[55]

Behind the lavish outlay of money and effort to save wildlife, the cleanup exhibited a dark side. Veco, Exxon's main contractor for cleanup, consistently violated environmental protection guidelines, manipulated data to create favorable impressions, and fired workers who raised questions. Exxon similarly managed the cleanup with an eye to its corporate image and legal liability rather than to ecologically beneficial results. It imported arrogant and sometimes incompetent officials, ignored practical suggestions of locals, and used its money to control communities by rewarding cooperators and punishing dissenters. Immediately before the migration season, it severely constricted efforts to retrieve dead birds, perhaps to avoid the negative publicity attending larger finds. An Exxon official remarked in a public meeting, "We have to deal with birds, so we've got these tree huggers taking care of them. But we'll keep them in line . . . I'll kick their butts." Supervisors reportedly hired men to shoot oiled seals and otters at sea so they would sink and not be found.[56]

Politics affected government agencies as well. Officials permitted only 20 sick eagles at the Anchorage rehabilitation center; more might have undermined an effort to remove them from the endangered species list. Vern Wiggins, an Interior Department deputy undersecretary known for his pro-industry efforts in Alaska, strove to limit the Park Service's wildlife damage assessment in Kenai Fiords National Park. Superiors discouraged the Fish and Wildlife and Minerals Management Services from active investigation of spill damage. The Bush administration apparently sought to avoid publicity that might jeopardize offshore oil drilling or oil exploration in the Arctic Refuge. The Department of Environmental Conservation, like Exxon, tailored its moves—such as avoidance of directions to Exxon—to position the state for victory in negligence lawsuits.[57]

ECONOMIC, CULTURAL, AND POLITICAL ECHOES

Although Alaska depended on oil for 85 percent of its state funds, the oil spill caused alarm over the second and third industries, fishing and tourism. Fisheries in Prince William Sound earned $76 million in 1988. Negative consumer reaction could hurt sales of fish even from waters not affected by oil. Locally, fishing interests contemplated the possibility of being put out of business. To head off potentially damaging publicity of tainted fish, state officials closed fisheries—in Prince William Sound, Cook Inlet, and the Kodiak region— where any doubt existed. This policy, and the fact that most oil remained on the surface because few chemical dispersants had been used, helped prevent contaminated fish from reaching the market, which in turn showed no sign of panic. Preliminary surveys turned up scant evidence of oil in adult fish, though the continued presence of oil prompted closure of a few fishing areas as late as June 1990. Salmon and herring eggs sustained damage, and adult Dolly Varden and cutthroat trout declined. Bottomfish and intertidal organisms ingested hydrocarbons, but officials declared only clams and mussels inedible for humans.[58]

Exxon promised to compensate fishers for economic losses. It hired locals at $16.69 per hour for 84-hour-week cleanup duties, and rented boats at $1,500 or more per day. It asked some workers to sign statements agreeing not to talk to reporters.[59] High wages disrupted local economies as workers left regular jobs to do oil cleanup. Cordova Chamber of Commerce president Connie Taylor rated strains over money the most serious impact of the spill: "Long-term friendships have been destroyed by the money. And the guy who decided not to go to work with Veco just on principle isn't going to make the money, while people who did make enough money to put their kids through college."[60]

Native villages at Prince William Sound, Kodiak Island, and Kachemak Bay, reliant on fishing for subsistence, suffered greatly. Other Native villages and Exxon sent food, though not enough to meet physical needs. Neither could it restore the confidence of people accustomed to self-reliant harvest of nearby resources. Disturbances of family life related to the oil spill—anxieties over environmental damage, feelings of loss of control and identity, parents away working on cleanup, and the stress of inundations by outsiders—heightened levels of substance abuse and family violence. High cash influx introduced more competition and modern implements such as satellite dishes, accelerating the pace of social change.[61]

To protect the tourist industry, particularly cruise vessel tours, Governor Cowper headed an energetic effort to downplay the damage done to scenery. Exxon contributed $4 million to the state for an advertising campaign touting the unspoiled nature of Alaska. When *Alaska* ran a hard-hitting article in June titled "Paradise Lost," Princess Tours and Holland America Line cancelled $8,000 worth of ads in the magazine. Princess Tours president Ray Peterson commented, "It's the most asinine thing that I've ever seen a magazine like that do. That magazine is the voice of Alaska in terms of everything that Alaska stands for." Editor Ron Dalby responded, "I think the issue is that they have come to regard us as a house organ for the tourism industry . . . The spill is the kind of story that we can't ignore."[62] Tourism incurred no evident injury from the oil spill. Alaska's economy benefited more from cleanup expenditures than it lost in fishing revenues.

An outpouring of volunteerism followed the oil spill, even though Exxon initially took the position that volunteers would not be needed. Fishing and community groups in Valdez, Cordova, Homer, Seward, and Kodiak launched a variety of initiatives. Cordova District Fisheries United borrowed oil booms and saved four hatcheries from the advancing oil slick. State and federal officials worked far beyond normal hours. Hundreds of Alaskans and Lower-48 citizens offered their services. Alaskan environmental organizations occupied vital postions in the volunteer program. Governor Cowper, responding to offers of money and assistance, designated the Alaska Conservation Foundation (ACF) as the funding and information center for volunteer efforts. Using ACF funding, the Alaska Center for the Environment, Sierra Club/Alaska, and Greenpeace operated an Oil Spill Volunteer Response Center in Anchorage. By August 1 it processed 2,800 inquiries, received about 300 applications, and placed nearly 250 volunteers in federal, state, and private institutions and groups. Prince William Sound Conservation Alliance operated a second processing center in Valdez, and some volunteers went directly to government agencies. Approximately three-fourths women, the volunteers carried out a wide range of tasks including communications and public education, research and monitoring of damage, and retrieval and rehabilitation of wildlife. Many wanted to help birds, and even more, sea otters.[63]

The Alaska Center for the Environment (ACE) co-organized an Oil Spill Coalition, to provide information to the public and plan political action. Located at Cordova, the coalition consisted of fishing and community groups from Cordova, Homer, Seldovia, and Valdez. ACE and ACF set up a Prince William Sound Cleanup and Rehabilitation Fund to pool environmental defense efforts. About 70 percent of its donations came from outside the state. ACF established a Fund for Oil and Alaska's Future to address federal and state oil policy.[64] In June an Oil Reform Alliance formed to work on oil policy, its member groups representing fishers, Natives, environmentalists, and residents of small coastal towns.[65]

Given its notoriety and environmental significance, the oil spill created a battleground for public opinion. Cartoonists found an ideal subject: Ralph Dunagin featured a dead whale on the beach, metal rod protruding from its back and an onlooker explaining, "It isn't a harpoon, it's a dipstick." Exxon and the tanker captain served as the butts of jokes by comedians and talk show hosts. Several books emerged, ranging from the scholarly to a romance novel starring a captain wrongly accused of a spill and rescued by an insurance adjuster heroine.[66] Content analysis of the first two weeks of coverage by the *Anchorage Daily News* and *Boston Globe* revealed an initial emphasis on the "disaster" aspect, portraying the spill as a naturally or technologically inevitable occurrence. Second-week articles highlighted the "crime" aspect, pointing primarily to Joe Hazelwood, and the "environmentalist" theme, criticizing the oil companies and the Reagan and Bush administrations. *Tundra Times*, in addition to the "disaster" aspect, carried a "subsistence" theme, focusing on the injury to Native lifestyles through ecosystem damage. Government and industry officials, except Exxon to an extent, received favorable treatment. Few articles attempted to identify the underlying political and economic causes of the spill. A second study compared coverage of the 1969 Santa Barbara oil spill and 1989 *Exxon Valdez* oil spill by the *Santa Barbara News-Press*, *Anchorage Daily News,* and *New York Times*. It found much similarity between the 1969 and 1989 reporting. Emphasis on immediate ecological impact, where the oil went, and cleanup activities, increased. Reference to broader context, while prominent, declined.[67]

No subject had ever inspired so much mail to Anchorage newspapers, though the *Fairbanks Daily News-Miner* reported more reaction to the removal of the *Today Show* because of a weatherman's remark.[68] Many writers, such as Britt Johnston, expressed hurt and outrage at the damage: "Prince William Sound is the place where I discovered that the ocean is sometimes so clear that you can see 30 feet to the bottom when the surface is still. Prince William Sound is the place where I first saw ice calving off a glacier to become icebergs in the clear northern ocean. My heart is breaking this morning to hear that you have spilled more than 11 million gallons of crude into Prince William Sound."[69] Captain Hazelwood, tested nine hours after the accident and found legally intoxicated, received ample coverage: "Why didn't Exxon check out the captain's records before he boarded the ship? Why did they hire him if they knew he had a drinking problem?" queried fourth-grader Amy Baken.[70] Others such as Michelle Church saw him as a scapegoat: "I can't believe that the oil companies think we are so gullible that we'll allow them to redirect blame for the disaster in Valdez from themselves to Capt. Hazelwood. . . . we may actually owe Capt. Hazelwood our thanks. He has brought to light the truth about the oil companies' promises outlined in the glitzy, pristine environmental commercials. Maybe now we can protect the vital fisheries of Bristol Bay and the sanctity of ANWR."[71] The letters aired nearly universal censure of the oil companies and Exxon in particular: "Exxon's top pencil-pushers ought to be forced out to every beach and island on their knees to scrub every rock and piece of sand until it is spotless with no pay," suggested Mike Craig of Wasilla.[72] Grace Budka of Copper Center wrote: "Oil companies do not provide 85 percent of Alaska's annual revenue. Alaska's oil *fields* do. . . . If the oil companies think they are doing us a favor by pumping out our oil and hauling it away, we sure ought to replace them with someone who understands that it's a privilege to make millions of dollars in profits from our oil."[73] A rare defender, Lynn Langfield Jr. of Anchorage, wrote the *Anchorage Times* that "exploring for oil had nothing to do with the oil spill . . . Should we outlaw all gas stations because of the drunk drivers on the highway? That is the same thing that they are trying to do with ANWR."[74]

Alaskan politicians took a merciless thrashing: "The Alaska State Senate was one of the best investments the oil industry ever made. By pouring enough money into the election campaigns of a majority of the members of the Senate, the oil folks now own a controlling interest in that body" (Michael Coumbe).[75] Governors felt the heat from Toni Croft—"Jay Hammond was at the helm of the state when the events that led to this disaster started and he is to blame. At least the captain was drunk. What is Hammond's excuse?"[76]—and Garland Teich of Anchorage: "Where was the governor [Cowper] before the oil spill when Alyeska didn't have the cleanup barge and oil spill equipment ready and in place?"[77] None of the congressional delegation escaped criticism. Noting that Don Young had derided environmentalists before the Alaska legislature as "bunny huggers," Jeremy Seftor commented,

12.4. "Exxodus Valdeez" *in Fourth of July Parade, Seward, 1989. Courtesy U.S.Fish and Wildlife Service, Anchorage. The oil spill angered many Alaskans, and far more in the Lower 48.*

"Mr. Young takes pride in being a commercial fisherman. It is a good thing for him that his livelihood does not rest in fishing Prince William Sound."[78]

Many letters looked more deeply at the issue: "The Prostitution of Alaska would be an appropriate title for a book describing the self-destructive willingness of the Alaskan people and their government representatives to allow the oil companies to rape and plunder this beautiful state" (Jeanne Folan).[79] "Each one of us is responsible for the oil spill. Simply take a look at your own individual consumption of products that keeps the shipping lanes busy. And, of course, we *want* those shipping lanes to be busy, in *all* types of weather, so we may continue our 'feeding frenzy' of consumption and so our bloated state government will continue rolling along without an income tax" (Kathryn Dawson).[80] "For 10–20 years of oil development the earth will have eternal consequences. Is it possible for you and me, and for the leaders of our countries, to begin thinking ahead, at all? To begin thinking and creatively working on alternative sources of energy and to see that most of the development of natural resources is really the destruction of the earth?" asked Catherine Doss.[81] Several letters, like this from James Curtis, gave credit to environmentalists: "What role can we play in preventing such environmental catastrophes in the future? We can help support the experts who provide a check to those who abuse their power and pollute for profit. Put your money where your mouth is and join an environmental organization."[82]

Editorials in major newspapers, excepting the *Anchorage Times*, echoed the mood of the public. A week after the spill, the *Times* pleaded, "It's time to end all the hand-wringing and weeping over the Prince William Sound oil spill. It's not the time now for finger-pointing and oil company bashing. There's been more than enough wails and lamenting and we-told-you-sos from the professional environmentalists. . . . And it's time we all—from the governor on down—quit trying to relate what happened to the *Exxon Valdez* to . . . any kind of oil and gas development on the North Slope or elsewhere in Alaska."[83] The rival *Anchorage Daily News* judged, "No longer can we demand anything short of the most aggressive regulation from the state and federal governments. No longer can politicians trade their benevolence for campaign contributions. And no longer can Alaskans assume that some-one else—the oil industry, the state government, the Coast Guard—is looking out for their interests."[84] Uncharacteristically, the *Juneau Empire* commented, "We must take the responsibility and initiative to ensure the wilderness and way of life we prize remains intact. The spill has reminded us all that there is precious little untouched wilderness in the world—and what remains is priceless and should be protected at all costs. It is not just America's loss, it is a global loss." [85] Veco International, the primary oil service contractor for the oil companies, announced in November 1989 its agreement to purchase the *Anchorage Times*.[86]

Exxon officials apologized to Alaskans for the "accident," assuring them that cleanup would be expedited and "we also will meet our obligations to all those who have suffered damage from the spill."[87] They accused the state of denying them permission to use chemical dispersants in time to contain the spill. State officials retorted that use of chemicals had been preapproved for deep water, where the oil spread after the first two days; that dispersants did not work well in calm water that prevailed for the first three days; and that Exxon had nowhere near enough dispersants available to treat the spill. The exchange went on, souring relations between Exxon and the state.[88]

Environmentalists staged protests within and outside the state. Alaska Center for the Environment arranged a demonstration at the federal building in Anchorage, attended by a crowd of about 200, and a similar effort in Juneau drew 80. Earth First! activists climbed the building housing the Anchorage headquarters of Alyeska and unfurled a banner reading "Big Oil—Death of the Future," one member hanging suspended from either side, and pickets on the sidewalk below.[89] Both Alaskan and Lower 48 groups used the spill to increase membership and funds.

In the short run, public-relations efforts by the oil companies did not suffice to win over Alaskans. Opinion registered strongly negative toward the oil industry following the spill, particularly in the southern cities and coastal towns. A poll taken in August 1989 indicated people trusted the environmentalists more than they did the oil companies. Yet a November 1989 poll suggested the oil industry had recovered all but about 5 percent of the support it had lost.[90] Alaskan environmental organizations nevertheless acquired momentum, membership, and prestige. Seven groups, mostly oriented to coastal protection, originated in 1989–1990 as a direct result of the spill.[91]

Public opinion appeared more anti-oil in the Lower 48 than in Alaska. Possibly no environmental crisis had received such massive media coverage. It sharpened national awareness of the value and fragility of Alaskan marine life, and erected additional large barriers to oil intrusion in coastal zones. Spills on the East Coast in 1989 and 1990 boosted suspicion of oil companies. Building on the *Exxon Valdez* spill, these events helped force the passage of a 1990 bill prescribing double hulls for new tankers, increased liability for spills, and a national cleanup response center and regional citizen advisory councils to oversee oil industry activities. Within five years, the annual reported number of vessel spills over 100,000 gallons fell off by 66 percent, and the proportion of spills in the high range (more than 200,000 gallons) dropped by 60 percent.[92]

Alaska's congressional delegation maintained a subdued loyalty to the oil companies, but the state legislature, despite being under the influence of oil money since the late 1970s, shifted its position. Ten bills passed in the 1989 session, tightening regulations on handling of oil, enhancing state oversight capabilities, and requiring damage compensation. Most symbolic of the shift, the legislature amended the Economic Limiting Factor (ELF), a tax break meant to encourage the oil companies to utilize marginal fields. The tax increase would add $2 billion to the state treasury over the next 20 years.[93]

Results of the many studies, hearings, and investigations of the oil spill made clear the malfeasance of the parties responsible. In the final report of the Alaska Oil Spill Commission, Chairman Walter B. Parker wrote, "The original rules were consistently violated, primarily to ensure that tankers passing through Prince William Sound did not lose time by slowing down for ice or waiting for winds to abate. Concern for profits in the 1980s obliterated the concern for safe operations that existed in 1977." The document described the spill as the breakdown of a transportation system as well as elements of the system:

> The *Exxon Valdez* was an accident waiting to happen . . . for reasons of maritime tradition, economics, politics, public policy and modern practice, the maritime oil transportation system is relatively more error-prone than safety-inducing. Industry tends to measure success as operating the biggest vessel with the thinnest hull and the smallest crew at the highest speed with the quickest port turnaround consistent with meeting minimum government requirements.

Neither the industry nor the Coast Guard had displayed concern for environmental protection, said the commission. Industry fought every effort to strengthen environmental safety standards, and the Coast Guard chose not to exercise what regulatory powers it possessed, given limited personnel and budgets. More specifically, the spill could have been prevented by the promised radar coverage to Hinchinbrook Entrance, or by ceasing the routine practice of leaving the shipping lanes to avoid ice. The risk would have been lessened by slower tanker speeds or proper Coast Guard oversight of vessel manning practices. The state had attempted to regulate oil shipping through a 1976 law, but a court challenge by the oil companies succeeded on grounds that the act impinged on federal jurisdiction. Growth of oil company influence in state government resulted in weakening of oversight by the Department of Environmental Conservation. In the antiregulatory atmosphere of the Reagan years, neither state nor federal agencies undertook effective monitoring efforts.

As for the cleanup, the report observed,

> The federal government has relied on private industry to contain or clean up a major spill. The government provided no resources of its own to handle even moderate-sized spills adequately. Nor is there any indication that either the Environmental Protection Agency or the Coast Guard, the federal administrators of the [National Contingency

Plan], made any effort to determine whether the oil industry actually had the capability to clean up a catastrophic spill.

The summary outlined 59 recommendations for building an improved system of state and federal oversight, transportation technology, organization of cleanup operations, and research.[94] The state legislature responded in 1990 by passing six bills to improve oil spill prevention, increase penalties for hazardous waste spills and negligent tanker operation, and create an oil spill prevention authority and a citizen oversight council.[95]

LEGAL AND ADMINISTRATIVE RESULTS

By 1990 Exxon faced a maze of lawsuits. The state filed suit against Alyeska, Exxon, and the other members of the Alyeska consortium, seeking compensatory and punitive damages for injury to wildlife and the Alaskan economy. Exxon countersued, charging the state had impeded the cleanup by withholding permission for the use of chemical dispersants.[96] In February 1990 a federal grand jury indicted Exxon for neglecting to properly operate its ship and for violation of the Clean Water Act, Refuse Act, Migratory Bird Act, and other federal laws. Despite "intense pressure" from the Justice Department, state officials rejected a plea bargain proposed in 1990. The legislature voted down a second proposal, despite its backing by the new Hickel administration, in May 1991. In a final settlement reached in October, Exxon pled guilty to misdemeanor charges and accepted fines and restitution payments totaling $900 million to $1 billion, to be paid over ten years.[97]

Other lawsuits pressed on. Alaska Superior Court found Joe Hazelwood guilty on a minor charge of negligence, and the Coast Guard suspended his mariner's license for nine months. The state appeals court reversed Hazelwood's conviction on grounds that, in accordance with federal law, his reporting of the spill by radio rendered him immune to prosecution.[98] A 1994 federal jury found both Exxon and Hazelwood guilty of reckless behavior, leaving them vulnerable to damage judgments. Exxon agreed out of court to pay $20 million to the 3,500 Natives most affected. In August, the jury awarded $287 million to about 10,000 commercial fishers, and in September the same jury assessed Exxon a record-setting $5 billion in punitive damages. It required Hazelwood to pay $5,000.[99]

Separately from Exxon, Alyeska settled injury claims in 1993 for $98 million. Exxon's extraordinary $5 billion penalty equaled one year's profits, and it had spent about $2.7 billion in cleanup and injury compensation. Exxon stock went up immediately after the court decision. The company took no action against anyone except Hazelwood. Its lawyers succeeded in greatly narrowing the range of parties eligible for compensation. Exxon had also attempted to manipulate the jury and judge by making secret deals with seven seafood processors, whereby its payments to them would help it reduce damage payments to other parties. According to the court decision, 81 percent of the $5 billion would go to commercial fishers, 6.6 percent to Natives, 3.5 percent to property owners, 2 percent to municipalities, and the rest to other parties.[100] Exxon appealed the decision.

At the end of the 1990 season the state had declared half the oiled shoreline to be clean as feasible, and concentrated on monitoring and restoration after 1991. Pending resolution of criminal suits, secrecy impeded research; parties withheld any information that might be vital in a court case. Lack of access to oil-spill impact data hampered decisions about what research should be funded. The 1991 settlement agreement stipulated that $90 million be paid annually for ten years, to be administered by an *Exxon Valdez* Oil Spill Trustee Council of six state and federal officials, and spent on various aspects of restoration. In the first year, 1991–1992, most of the money went to reimburse federal and state agencies for oil spill cleanup costs.

Environmentalists worked for application of settlement funds to buy as parklands ecologically valuable habitat in the spill region. A bill to acquire forest lands in five locations passed in 1991, then fell to Governor Hickel's veto.[101] In 1993 Hickel signed a bill to purchase 24,000 acres of Native inholdings at Kachemak Bay State Park, and the Oil Spill Trustee Council approved purchase of 42,000 acres of Native lands near Seal Bay on Afognak Island. Both sites had been slated for logging. The Clinton administration committed an additional $25 million of Exxon criminal penalties to habitat acquisition.[102] As of mid-1999, 636,000 acres protecting 1,400 miles of shoreline had been protected. Of more than $900 million in settlement funds, $343 million had gone for habitat purchase, $173 million to cover expenses of state and federal agencies, and $40 million to Exxon for extra cleanup costs. Funds also underwrote research, monitoring, restoration projects, and a restoration reserve fund. Most of a $120 million endowment would fund a Gulf Ecosystem Monitoring program to further understanding and protection of the northern Gulf of Alaska.[103]

Ecological studies following the oil spill held potential to greatly advance understanding of the North Pacific marine environment, necessary for management of wildlife and commercial fisheries as well as oil transportation. Lack of baseline data, and the numerous biological and social aspects to be examined, made firm conclusions difficult. Regarding birds, three prominent articles agreed that nearly all species recovered by 1991.[104] Five years after the spill, some evidence of persistent oil contamination and long-term damage could still be found. Pink salmon and herring reproduction stayed below normal, and sea otter pup mortality remained high. Analyzing 32 key studies by government and Exxon scientists, marine scientist Riki Ott concluded that the wildlife losses "have seriously altered the structure, composition, and dynamic interrelationships in the affected coastal ecosystem. Indirect 'ripple' effects are just starting to appear. The time required for full recovery is unknown, but may take decades." In Native coastal communities, frustration over litigation and subsistence fisheries continued to cause stress and social breakdown. Ott noted that government studies tended to prematurely assume ecological damage, whereas Exxon studies downplayed long-term effects to lessen the company's liability. She recommended a federal law to institute a cooperative research system that would generate sound baseline data prior to oil lease sales, control the scientific quality of research, and guarantee public access to the results. Such information would enable the public "to press for social changes needed to prevent oil spills in the first place."[105]

A 1999 Oil Spill Trustee Council update identified two wildlife species—bald eagle and river otter—as recovered. Several others—killer whale (AB pod), harbor seal, common loon, harlequin duck, pigeon guillemot, and pelagic, red-faced, and double-crested cormorant—rated as not recovered. A middle category listed pink and sockeye salmon, herring, marbled murrelet, black oystercatcher, intertidal and subtidal communities including clams and mussels, and the sea otter. The report characterized some human services—recreation and tourism, passive uses, commercial fishing, and subsistence—as recovering.[106]

One analysis of the spill experience showed that it had been treated as a "technological" disaster, triggering a legal struggle over responsibility that delayed attention to the needs of injured parties. It did not qualify as a "natural" disaster, normally met by measures to speed recovery. Researchers J. Steven Picou, Duane Gill, and Maurie Cohen recommended a combined response system, and adoption of Coalition for Environmentally Responsible Economies principles whereby corporations would plan in advance to alleviate social and environmental effects of a disaster. They suggested the use of citizen oversight committees for both prevention and response to disasters.[107]

Several principles of environmentalism gained recognition in the *Exxon Valdez* spill crisis, albeit not in time to prevent the main debacle. Caution had been cast aside in the adoption of the pipeline-tanker route; environmental sustainability neither demonstrated nor planned for. Even after the spill, the state and national governments largely avoided accountability for their negligence. But both the Alaska legislature and the U.S. Congress passed oil-spill control legislation, and a federal court dealt Exxon by far the highest penalty ever ordered for environmental harm. The public participated in the spill cleanup, and in the process of overseeing the distribution of settlement funds. Purchase of lands for protection afforded a measure of sustainability, arguably outweighing the negative aspects of the spill. State and national legislation guaranteed a future public oversight role. The settlement paid for extensive research, part of which might lessen the chances of a future spill.

Rarely had an incident more clearly illustrated the trade-offs between environmental sustainability and exploitation than did the *Exxon Valdez* oil spill. It stood as a milestone in the ongoing contest over public values and policy. Optimistic environmentalists perceived a permanent shift in public opinion toward environmental values, both in Alaska and outside. Pessimists predicted a return to business as usual after the Exxon story left the TV screens. The crisis far outlasted the normal political attention span of the public, but conservation sympathy could expect a perpetual challenge from real or perceived national energy needs.

NOTES

1. Bolze, "Outer Continental Shelf Oil," 17–18, n. 4–6.

2. Weeks and Weller, "Offshore Oil," 371–377; C. Hunter, "This Our Land," May 1981, 32–33, 54.

3. E. Murphy, "Beaufort Oil and Gas," 4–5; E. Murphy, "Federal SIN Ecology," 4.

4. *Northern Line*, February 1980, 1, 3; *Anchorage Daily News*, June 13, 1980, 1; July 2, 1980, 1; *Hammond v. North Slope Borough* Alaska 645 P. 2d. 750 (1982).

5. Miller, Smith, and Miller, *Oil in Arctic Waters*, 7; *New York Times*, August 5, 1984, 27; *North Slope Borough v. Andrus*, 642F. 2d. 589 (D.C. Cir. 1980); *North Slope Borough v. Watt*, No. 84-3672 (9th Cir. 1984).

6. Bolze, "Outer Continental Shelf Oil," 55; 480 U.S. 531, 107 S. Ct. 1396, 94 LE 2d 542 (1987).

7. *Trustees for Alaska*, Summer 1987, 3; *Trustees for Alaska*, "Offshore Leasing Decision," 1; *Trustees for Alaska v. State Department of Natural Resources*, 795 P. 2d 805 (Alaska 1990). The Alaska Wildlife Alliance, American Wilderness Alliance, National Parks and Conservation Association, Northern Alaska Environmental Center, Sierra Club, Wilderness Society, and the village of Kaktovik joined TfA as plaintiffs.

8. Miller, Smith, and Miller, *Oil in Arctic Waters*, 7; Wilderness Society, "Exxon Valdez Plus Five; *Environmental Advocate*, "Postponed," 4.

9. Trustees for Alaska (TfA), *Under the Influence*, 21–26, 45.

10. Lowe, "Help Stop Offshore Drilling," 10; Cady, "Oil Overshadows," 1; *Trustees for Alaska*, Summer 1986, 4; *Alaska Report*, December 1988, 5.

11. Kizzia, "Feuding Groups," 76–77.

12. *New York Times*, September 8, 1985, 26; September 27, 1985, 37; December 13, 1985, 28; April 19, 1986, 16. *Northern Line*, April 1986, 12. *Trustees for Alaska*, Spring 1986, 1; Summer 1986, 4; *Alaska Report*, December 1988, 5.

13. U.S. Department of the Interior (USDOI), Minerals Management Service, "Sale Areas Offshore"; TfA, *Under the Influence*, 53; Stan Ashmore, interview by author, May 19, 1999.

14. Randall, "Conservationists Oppose Beaufort," 9.

15. Miller, Smith, and Miller, *Oil in Arctic Waters*, 81, 88–89.

16. TfA, *Under the Influence*, 45, 52, 56.

17. East, "Alaska's Agony," 33–35, 100.

18. Manning, *Cry Crisis*, 159.

19. *New York Times*, December 17, 1985, 19; *Northern Line*, August-September 1987, 12; *Fairbanks Daily News-Miner*, July 12, 1987, 1.

20. *New York Times*, October 15, 1987, 13.

21. *Anchorage Daily News*, March 27, 1989, E1, 4.

22. Miller, Smith, and Miller, *Oil in Arctic Waters*, 80–81; Flint, Fowler, and Rockwell, "Modeling Bird Mortality," 261–262, 264–267.

23. Skinner and Reilly, *Exxon Valdez Oil Spill*, 1–4, Appendix A, 1–3; Public Broadcast System, *The Big Spill*; *Anchorage Daily News*, July 19, 1989, 1; Keeble, *Out of the Channel*, 31–49.

24. Lethcoe and Lethcoe, *Cruising Guide*, 1–3.

25. *Alaska Fish and Game*, "What Areas Are Affected?" July-August 1989, 23–24; McCracken, *Hunters of the Stormy Sea*, 166–176.

26. *Alaska Fish and Game*, "What Areas Are Affected?" July-August 1989, 23–24; Crimmin, "One Year Later," 42–45.

27. Weeden and Klein, "Wildlife and Oil," 486, 488.

28. Alaska Dept. of Laws, *Comments*, 189.

29. U.S. Congress, Senate, Committee on Interior and Insular Affairs, *Hearings: Rights-of-Way*, pt. 4, 504–505.

30. Ibid., pt. 3, 18.

31. Walter B. Parker, interview by author, August 5, 1989.

32. Hanrahan and Gruenstein, *Lost Frontier*, 302.

33. Public Broadcast System, *The Big Spill*; Davidson, *In the Wake*, 96.

34. *Christian Science Monitor*, July 6, 1989, 1. For specifics on Alyeska's violations of regulations and treatment of dissenters, see Davidson, *In the Wake*, 28, 81–88, 225–228.

35. *New York Times*, September 23, 1991, 14, November 10, 1991, IV, 3; U.S. Congress, House, Committee on Interior and Insular Affairs, *Alyeska*, 1–5; *Anchorage Daily News*, July 24, 1992, 1.

36. *Anchorage Times*, May 3, 1989, 1.

37. Ibid., March 30, 1989, C1; Public Broadcast System, *Anatomy of an Oil Spill*.

38. Davidson, *In the Wake*, 34–35, 96–97.

39. *Christian Science Monitor*, July 6, 1989, 1.

40. Skinner and Reilly, *Exxon Valdez Oil Spill*, Appendix A, 1–10; Davidson, *In the Wake*, 49–53.

41. *Anchorage Daily News*, April 8, 1989, C1.

42. Skinner and Reilly, *Exxon Valdez Oil Spill*, 6–9, Appendix A; Alaska Department of Environmental Conservation, "Oil Spill Public Information."

43. Public Broadcast System, *The Big Spill*; *Anchorage Daily News*, September 12, 1989, C1.

44. Raloff, "*Valdez* Spill," 102.

45. *Anchorage Daily News*, June 27, 1989, 1; *Oil Spill Chronicle*, September 19, 1989, July 22, 1991.

46. *Anchorage Daily News*, September 12, 1989, 1; Public Broadcast System, *The Big Spill*; Lord, *Darkened Waters*, 41–42.

47. *Anchorage Daily News*, September 12 1989, C1, 3; *Oil Spill Chronicle*, October 10, December 12, 1989; March 13, April 3, May 1, 8, 29, 1990; U.S. Dept. of Commerce, National Oceanographic and Atmospheric Administration (NOAA), "Summary of Injuries," 14694.

48. *Oil Spill Chronicle*, August 1, 1989; *Anchorage Daily News*, May 3, 1989.

49. J. Hunt, "Making a Difference," 24.

50. Davidson, *In the Wake*, 160; *Oil Spill Chronicle*, October 17, 1989; NOAA, "Summary of Injuries," 14689–14690; *Exxon Valdez* Oil Spill Trustees, *Exxon Valdez Oil Spill Restoration,* vol. I, 20–23.

51. *Anchorage Daily News*, May 3, 1989, 2; *Alaska Fish and Game*, "What Are the Effects," July-August 1989, 29; NOAA, "Summary of Injuries," 14690.

52. *Oil Spill Chronicle*, August 1, 10; October 31, 1989; February 27, 1990; Lord, *Darkened Waters*, 44–47.

53. *Anchorage Daily News*, July 13, 1989, 1; *Oil Spill Chronicle*, October 31, December 12, 1989; Piatt et al., "Immediate Impact," 387; NOAA, "Summary of Injuries," 14691; Estes, "Catastrophes and Conservation," 1596; *Exxon Valdez* Oil Spill Trustees, Restoration, Vol. I, 25–30.

54. *Anchorage Times*, Jun 27, 1989, 1; *Oil Spill Chronicle*, Oct 31, 1989, Feb 27, 1990; *Exxon Valdez* Oil Spill Trustees, *Exxon Valdez Oil Spill Restoration,* vol. I, 27.

55. *Anchorage Daily News*, July 9, 1989; *Oil Spill Chronicle*, August 8, 1989; NOAA, "Summary of Injuries," 14689–14690; *Exxon Valdez* Oil Spill Trustees, *Exxon Valdez Oil Spill Restoration,* vol. I, 23–25. The estimate of 20 killer whales derives from the 1989–1990 disappearance of 24 whales, adjusted for natural mortality. Researchers conducted extensive study of orcas prior to the spill date; such baseline data existed for few other organisms affected by the spill.

56. Davidson, *In the Wake*, 141, 146, 188–190, 197–201, 208–209, 213–215, 229–234, 259–266, 302–303. Keeble's *Out of the Channel* presents another critical analysis of the oil-spill episode.

57. Davidson, *In the Wake*, 170–171, 176–177, 242–247, 253–254.

58. *Alaska Fish and Game*, "What Are the Effects," July-August 1989, 26; *Oil Spill Chronicle*, June 14, 1990.

59. *Anchorage Daily News*, July 25, 1989, 8; *Alaska*, "Paradise Lost," 24.

60. *Anchorage Daily News*, June 4, 1989, 1.

61. Ibid., June 6, 1989, H1; *Anchorage Times*, July 3, 1989; Lord, *Darkened Waters*, 30–33.

62. *New York Times*, May 28, 1989, IV, 5; *Anchorage Daily News*, June 13, 1989, 1.

63. Alaska Conservation Foundation (ACF), "ACF Oil Spill Update"; *Oil Spill Chronicle*, August 1, 1989; Pamela Brodie, interview by author, July 27, 1989.

64. ACF, "ACF Oil Spill Update;" Jim Stratton and Sue Libenson, interviews by author, July 18 and 20, 1989.

65. Hodson, "Oil Reform Alliance Meeting," 5.

66. *Anchorage Daily News*, July 6, 1989, E1.

67. Daley and O'Neill, "Sad's Too Mild a Word," 46–54; P. Miller, "Press Coverage of Oil Spills," iii–iv, 83.

68. *Anchorage Times*, April 3, 1989, 1, 8.

69. *Anchorage Daily News*, April 2, 1989, B4.

70. Ibid., April 23, 1989, E1–8.

71. Ibid., April 27, 1989, E11.

72. Ibid., April 23, 1989, E1–8.

73. Ibid., April 20, 1989, E11.

74. *Anchorage Times*, April 19, 1989, B5.

75. *Anchorage Daily News*, April 12, 1989, B7.

76. Ibid., April 20, 1989, E11.

77. *Anchorage Times*, April 19, 1989, B5.

78. *Anchorage Daily News*, April 2, 1989, B4.

79. Ibid.

80. Ibid., April 27, 1989, E11.

81. Ibid., April 1, 1989, B11.

82. Ibid., April 25, 1989, D7.

83. *Anchorage Times*, March 30, 1989, B4.

84. *Anchorage Daily News*, March 28, 1989.

85. *Juneau Empire*, April 13, 1989.

86. *New York Times*, November 29, 1989, B8.

87. *Anchorage Times*, April 4, 1989, 7.

88. *Anchorage Daily News*, April 29, 1989, 1; Steve Cowper, letter to Exxon Chairman Lawrence Rawl.

89. *Anchorage Times*, April 4, 1989, 6; Robinson, "EF! Alaska Task Force," 7.

90. *New York Times*, November 29, 1989, B8.

91. Alaska Conservation Foundation (ACF), *Alaska Conservation Directory*, 1989. The seven groups: Alaska Recovery Coalition, Alaska Wild Animal Recovery, and Balance of the Sea (Homer); Oil Reform Alliance and Stewardship Earth (Anchorage); Prince William Sound Science Center (Cordova); and Sound Renewal Project (Juneau).

92. *New York Times*, August 3, 1990, 12; 104 Stat. 484, August 18, 1990; Birkland, "Wake of the *Exxon Valdez*," 31.

93. Glude, *1989 Session Wrapup*; *Alaska Fish and Game*, "Assessment," July-August 1989, 36; Walter B. Parker, interview by author, August 5, 1989.

94. Alaska Oil Spill Commission, *Spill: Executive Summary*, ii–5, 16–17, 20–21, 32–34.

95. *Oil Spill Chronicle*, July 3, 1990; Glude, *1989, 1990 Session Wrapups*.

96. *Oil Spill Chronicle*, August 15, October 31, 1989.

97. *New York Times*, February 28, 1990, 1; March 1, 1990, 1; August 1, 1990, 7.

98. *New York Times*, October 9, 1991, 14; *Anchorage Daily News*, July 11, 1992, 1.

99. *New York Times*, June 14, 1994, 1; Keith Schneider, "$20 Million Settlement in Exxon Case," *New York Times*, July 26, 1994, 10; Schneider, "An Exxon Verdict of $286.8 Million," *New York Times*, August 12, 1994, 1; Schneider, "Exxon Is Ordered to Pay $5 Billion for Alaska Spill," *New York Times*, September 17, 1994, 1.

100. Hirsch, "Justice Delayed," 274–289; 302, n. 108. Lebedoff, *Cleaning Up*, presents an account of the trial process.

101. *Oil Spill Chronicle*, December 4, 1990; Busch, "Exxon Valdez Aftermath," 1134; Phipps, "Wally Kills Spill Restoration Project," 1–2.

102. *Center News*, "Council Approves First Habitat Acquisition," 4.

103. *Exxon Valdez* Oil Spill Trustee Council, *1999 Status Report*, 12–25; *Exxon Valdez* Oil Spill Trustees Council, *Gulf Ecosystem Monitoring*, 4–6.

104. S. Murphy et al., "Effects of *Exxon Valdez* Oil Spill on Birds," 310–311.

105. Ott, "Sound Truth," 1–5.

106. *Exxon Valdez* Oil Spill Trustee Council, *1999 Status Report*, 8–11, 27.

107. Picou, Gill, and Cohen, "Technological Disasters," 310–313.

13

Land Deal of the Century

One of the nation's paramount environmental contests unfolded in the 1970s. Many forces contended: the oil, timber, and mining industries; the Interior and Agriculture Departments; Congress and three presidents; outdoor sporting groups; Alaska Natives; Alaska's government and its business community; a newly powerful national environmental movement backed by Lower 48 public opinion favoring preservation of wildlands; and a small number of environmental activists in the state. Struggle filled the decade. It forged an outline for the future of Alaska's lands, and in the process helped shape an effective environmental community and national environmental values.

NATIVE CLAIMS

Oil exploration forced the lands issue by necessitating a settlement of Native land rights. Alaska Natives, like most Native Americans, had waited long to secure their lands. Two phenomena of the 1960s coincided to help them succeed: the civil rights movement and the oil strike at Prudhoe Bay. No oil could be extracted prior to a lands agreement, and Native claims could not be acted upon without a comprehensive disposition of Alaska lands.

While the United States purchased Alaska in 1867, the army fought Native Americans and Congress focused its energies on Civil War reconstruction and consolidating control over the western regions of the empire. Alaska Natives did not suffer defeat by the military, and lived on their aboriginal lands, most too remote and economically marginal for seizure by Euro-Americans. Yet their rights and control over lands lingered in uncertainty, pushed and pulled by the ongoing conflict among federal policies pursuing assimilation, federal stewardship, or tribal autonomy. The 1884 Alaska Organic Act stipulated that Natives "shall not be disturbed in the possession of any lands actually in their use or occupation or claimed by them," but left settlement to a future Congress. The 1906 Native Allotment Act allowed filing for 160-acre individual plots, but complicated procedures resulted in only 80 plots being registered in Alaska during the first half of the century. In 1891 Congress made Annette Island a reserve for the Metlakatla Indians. In the 1930s Karluk, Unalakleet, Venetie, Wales, and Little Diomede accepted reservation status, but other villages declined. The 1946 Indian Claims Act permitted Natives to sue the government over land claims; then a 1947 Tongass

Timber Sales Act preempted acquisition of commercially valuable forests by Natives in the Southeast.[1]

Between 1884 and statehood, the federal government recognized Alaska Native rights in principle, but not always in practice. Section 8 of the Alaska Organic Act dictated that "the Indian shall at least have as many rights after the passage of this bill as he had before." Nevertheless, the act permitted miners to stake claims and operate mines on lands tradition- ally used by Natives, and authorities seldom took legal action to defend Native land rights. The territorial government, established in 1912, extended social benefits to Natives but resisted large land grants to them.[2] The Statehood Act of 1958 authorized Alaska within 25 years to select 102.5 million acres of land not reserved by the federal government or claimed by Natives. In addition, the state could select 200,000 acres for schools and colleges, 400,000 for community expansion, and 400,000 from the Chugach and Tongass National Forests. Ultimately the state stood to hold at least 104,550,000 acres, more than all other western states combined. Alaskan Indian reservations occupied about 4 million acres in 1958, and private owners held or claimed 1.3 million acres. The Statehood Act and state constitution neither identified the Native lands nor spelled out procedures for identifying them. Settle- ment for the Natives still awaited federal legislative or judicial action.[3]

State officials designed their land selections in part to maximize ownership of mineral deposits. In choosing the potentially oil-rich 2 million acres around Prudhoe Bay, the state placed a notice in a newspaper seldom read by Eskimos. No one objected and the selection proceeded.[4] The state planned to offer "Wilderness Estates" for sale at the 1964 New York World's Fair until it became known the lots ran counter to Native claims, and some lay within the Tanacross village limits at Lake George. An employee of the Division of Lands reported being told by director Roscoe Bell to keep quiet about the conflicts, then being fired after leaking the story to the press.[5] The Bureau of Land Management assisted the state by transferring 6 million acres to it and processing 12 million more in 1966.[6]

As homesteaders, miners, the state, the military, and other federal agencies increasingly moved in on their lands, Natives also began making claims, eventually covering nearly the entire state. As early as 1961 the Bureau of Indian Affairs protested the state's selections of areas claimed by Natives of Northway, Minto, Tanacross, and Lake Aleknagik.[7] One group, the Tyonek Indians on the west side of Cook Inlet, won early satisfaction. Their Moquawkie Reservation, created in 1915, lacked clear mineral rights; Congress granted full title in 1962. The Bureau of Indian Affairs had leased part of the reservation to an oil company in that year, and the Tyoneks successfully sued the Interior Department. Earning $13 million in oil leases in 1964 and led by Emil Notti, the Tyoneks allocated much of the money to help other Natives pursue their land rights.[8]

Beginning in 1963, Natives appealed to Interior Secretary Stewart Udall to halt all selec- tions of federal acreage pending Native claim settlements. They rejected the modest land grants recommended by Udall's study committee. Building on their experiences in the Project Chariot, waterfowl hunting, and Rampart Dam controversies, and assisted by the Tyonek Indians and Howard Rock's *Tundra Times*, they organized the Alaska Federation of Natives in 1966 to press for a settlement. Anticipating a hopeless tangle of lawsuits, Udall an- nounced a halt in the processing of claims early in 1967.

Oil changed the picture. Following the North Slope strike in late 1967, both Congress and the state suddenly expressed an interest in consummating Native claims. All parties had taken notice of the victorious lawsuit by the Tyoneks. Natives threatened broader lawsuits that might take years for resolution. Most parties agreed on the necessity of a legislative conclusion.[9] Udall favored preservation of federal lands, but knew any attempt to get important measures through Congress would be blocked by Wayne Aspinall, chairman of the House Interior Committee and a powerful friend to western exploitative interests. Udall persuaded President Lyndon Johnson to use the 1906 Antiquities Act to name a 4.1-million-acre Gates of the Arctic National Monument, a 2.2-million-acre addition on the south side of Mt. McKinley National Park, and a 94,000-acre addition to Katmai National Monument. Under pressure from Aspinall, Johnson changed his mind on his final day in office and signed only the Katmai addition. He approved Udall's secretarial orders to establish a Cape Newenham National Wildlife Refuge and a million-acre addition to the Clarence Rhode National Wildlife Range.[10]

Momentum for resolution of state and Native claims pushed aside questions of the highest use of federal lands. Aware that the integrity of many of the nation's finest wild lands hung in the balance, Alaskan and Lower 48 environmentalists and some state and federal officials organized a February 1969 workshop in Juneau that gave birth to an Alaska Wilderness Council. The council sought to coordinate efforts for protection of prime wild areas as part of the land settlement. It operated through Sierra Club/Alaska, Alaska Conservation Society, and Fairbanks Environmental Center. It relied heavily on national park, fish and wildlife, and state park officials possessing extensive knowledge of Alaskan lands. The council's director, Sierra Club activist Mark Ganopole, organized a "Maps on the Floor Society" of experts who met for months to draft specific proposals for tracts of land. A regional network gathered suggestions, and nearly 200 Alaskans participated before the project terminated in 1972.[11]

A lawsuit by the state in response to Secretary Udall's land freeze produced a ruling mandating settlement of Native land claims prior to federal approval of state selections.[12] Bills appeared in Congress in 1969 and 1970. Environmentalists worked for language delineating parks, wildlife refuges, and wild and scenic rivers in the federal lands. The Audubon Society, Sierra Club, Wilderness Society, Friends of the Earth, National Wildlife Federation, and Wildlife Management Institute led the lobbying effort at the national level.[13] A mixed collection of groups opposed large land settlements for the Natives: Alaskan outdoor sporting groups (Alaska Sportsmen's Council, Territorial Sportsmen, and Tanana Valley Sportsmen's Association), who wanted hunting and fishing access; the Alaska Miners Association and the state, seeking mineral and political control; most newspapers, particularly the *Anchorage Daily Times*; and the Sierra Club and Wilderness Society, who feared corporate exploitation and loss of wild areas. By the late 1960s, Native organizations had grown adept at lobbying tactics, and initiated several lawsuits in support of their cause. While environmentalists sued the Interior Department over the oil pipeline in March 1970, five Native villages brought a separate suit contending that the pipeline crossed their land. The oil companies realized the essentiality of supporting Native claims to clear the way for oil development.[14]

As the lands-disposal bills neared passage, the modern national environmental movement coalesced. Sharing a strong interest in Alaska, activists organized an Alaska Coalition. In addition to national organizations, four state groups participated: the Alaska Conservation Society, Alaska Wilderness Council, Fairbanks Environmental Center, and Sierra Club/Alaska. Environmentalists and National Park Service and U.S. Fish and Wildlife Service officials attempted to insert wildlands protection guarantees in the bills in 1971. Amendments by John P. Saylor of Pennsylvania to do the same failed narrowly in the House. Morris Udall of Arizona introduced a substitute bill carrying similar provisions; it died 217-178, but showed enough strength to warrant an effort in conference committee. The Alaska Federation of Natives, the state, and commercial interests opposed the preservation measures. Alarmed, the environmentalists turned to chairmen Henry Jackson of the Senate Interior Committee and Alan Bible of the National Parks subcommittee. They also appealed to President Richard Nixon, to no avail.[15] One who went to see Jackson, Sierra Club representative Ed Wayburn, had accompanied Bible and National Park Service chief George Hartzog on part of a summer inspection tour of the Alaska lands, arranged by Hartzog to win Bible's support. "Scoop," said Wayburn, "you've done great things for the people of Alaska and you're about to do great things for the Alaska Natives. How about doing something for the people of the United States?"

"What do you mean?" replied the senator.

"Reserve areas for all Americans," said Wayburn.

"How much do you want?" replied Jackson.

"One hundred fifty million acres," said Wayburn.

"You want too much," said Jackson. "Will 80 million satisfy you?" Wayburn agreed.[16] Jackson consulted Bible, and Hartzog drafted an amendment ordering the secretary of the interior to review public lands in Alaska for possible status as "recreation, wilderness, wild rivers, or wildlife management areas within the national park and national wildlife systems," and to withdraw the lands for up to five years beyond the study period pending congressional action.[17] The amendment passed unimpeded by the Alaska senators, then survived the conference committee in a form modified by Morris Udall. Section 17(d)(2) of the bill empowered the secretary of the interior to set aside up to 80 million acres suitable for national park, forest, wildlife refuge, or wild and scenic river status; 17(d)(1) authorized temporary withdrawal of additional acreage that might fulfill other public purposes. Nixon, known to be sympathetic toward Native Americans, signed the Alaska Native Claims Settlement Act (ANCSA) on December 18, 1971.[18] No guarantee existed of protection for the wildlands. But the two "national interest lands" clauses, popularly known as "d-2," furnished the handhold enabling the environmental movement to realize one of its topmost achievements.

ANCSA, in addition to helping clear the way for the Alaska Lands Act and for oil expansion, engaged in grand-scale social engineering. It followed decades of ambivalence and policy shifts among forms of assimilation and tribal self-determination, and carried elements of both. It reflected a widely shared desire to avoid creating Native reservations, noted for isolation and dependency on government. At the same time, it recognized the value of ties to the land. Congress opted to terminate Native land claims by allowing Natives

13.1. Inupiat Eskimos plan ANCSA land selections, 1970s. Courtesy Arctic Environmental Information and Data Center, Anchorage. Unlike other Native Americans, Alaska Natives had a prominent role in the settlement of their land rights.

to select 44 million acres: about 28 million apportioned to 211 or more village corporations, at least partly for subsistence and other cultural purposes, and 16 million acres to 12 regional corporations to be utilized for profit. The law obligated each corporation to distribute 70 percent of its property-based profits to all others. Regional corporations held all subsurface mineral rights, including those on village lands. Only Natives born before December 19, 1971, received shares. Regional and village corporations and individuals divided a cash settlement of $962.5 million. Economic growth, proponents hoped, would raise the standard of living and move Alaska Natives into the modern economy.[19]

ANCSA authorized selection of Native lands from those to be reserved by the federal government. A Joint Federal/State Land Use Planning Commission, including Celia Hunter and Richard Cooley as federal appointees, would make recommendations for federal land disposal and management.[20] On January 21, weeks after ANCSA passed, the state filed for 77 million acres, before the federal government could conduct its withdrawals. Interpreting the law to give the federal government first choice, Interior Secretary Rogers Morton declined to recognize the state selections, and made the federal withdrawals in March. He chose 80 million acres under 17(d)(2), 45 million under 17(d)(1), 40 million for Native selection, and 35 million for immediate state selection. His proposals for federal parklands encompassed all areas identified by the "Maps on the Floor Society." The state then sued Morton, who settled out of court by permitting the state to select 600,000 acres that would have been added to the southern edge of McKinley Park, parts of the central Brooks Range, and a transportation corridor across the southern part of what became Gates of the Arctic National Park. For its part, the state relinquished its demand for immediate selection of the entire 77 million acres. A period of surveys, lobbying, and interagency rivalry followed; various federal agencies wanted to maximize their control of desirable lands. Morton's fall 1973 recommendations contained extensive park and wildlife refuge acreage, angering exploitation-oriented Alaskans.[21] Ernest Gruening accused him of doing the work of "conservationist extremists" who were "seeking to convert Alaska into a combination of wilderness and zoo."[22]

THE ALASKA LANDS ACT

In the 1972–1976 period, Alaskan groups of all persuasions seized the lands issue, though the Nixon and Ford administrations lacked interest and no momentum existed in Congress. The Federal/State Planning Commission held hearings and made recommendations reflecting its predominantly pro-development makeup. Of the Alaskan environmental units, Sierra Club/Alaska took the lead in preparing d-2 legislation. State and national environmental groups met in Fairbanks in February 1975 and later at Mount McKinley National Park to formulate their positions: (1) no mining in national interest lands; (2) no sport hunting in national parks; (3) regulated subsistence hunting and fishing in all units; (4) surface rights on national wildlife refuges to be controlled by the Fish and Wildlife Service; and (5) Petroleum Reserve No. 4 to be considered separately. A Sitka meeting focused on wilderness proposals for the Tongass National Forest.[23]

Fall 1976 brought an important forward step for the environmentalists: five Alaskan and several national groups met in Washington and revived the Alaska Coalition, to include all environmental organizations subscribing to a strong lands bill. Initially the new coalition had 16 members including 6 from Alaska; it grew to 53. The Sierra Club, Wilderness Society, Audubon Society, Friends of the Earth, and National Parks and Conservation Association made up its core. Laurance S. Rockefeller put together a group of 90 influential individuals titled Americans for Alaska to publicize and lobby for the coalition. The Alaska Coalition amassed endorsements from more than 1,500 groups, making it one of the largest and best-organized environmental lobbying forces ever assembled.[24]

Under the new president and Congress in 1977 the pace quickened. Morris Udall and Ohio's John Seiberling introduced a stout House Resolution (HR) 39 marking out 110 million acres of parks, refuges, and wilderness areas. Lee Metcalf of Montana sponsored a similar bill in the Senate. Hearings held in four major cities in the Lower 48 attracted overflow crowds overwhelmingly supporting it. In the Alaska hearings nearly half those testifying favored the bill.[25] Intense feelings poured forth. To environmentalists, the Alaska lands bill represented the last best hope for grand-scale preservation. Joe Vogler, a witness at the Fairbanks hearing, articulated the reverse: "I say Alaska must secede from the Union, become an independent country where men are free, not penned up behind yards of laws telling them they can't do here and they can't do there. No one is going to tell me when and where I can hunt. When I first came to this country I hunted when I damn well felt like it, where I damn well felt like it, and that's how it ought to be."[26]

HR 39 provoked opposition from virtually all Alaskan newspapers except the noncommittal *Anchorage Daily News*; from the legislators, who appropriated $5 million to promote a pro-industry agenda; and from Governor Jay Hammond, U.S. Senators Mike Gravel and Ted Stevens, and U.S. Representative Don Young. Young voiced the state's position in a letter responding to the *New York Times* endorsement of HR 39. Udall's bill, he said, would preclude hunting, public access, mining, timber harvest, and agricultural activity, and place 40 percent of Alaska in "a very limiting single-use management system—wilderness. . . . We should not set aside resource-rich areas which are likely to be off limits forever."[27]

An industry group named Citizens for Management of Alaskan Lands joined the state, National Rifle Association, and oil, timber, and mining interests to forward a bill guaranteeing their access to resources. Also challenging HR 39, the REAL Alaska Coalition spoke for 40 sport hunting and fishing groups and the Alaska Board of Game. The coalition sought hunting, fishing, and trapping rights and therefore wanted to minimize national park, wilderness, and wild and scenic river status for the lands. It rejected HR 39's subsistence provision allowing only Natives to hunt and fish on federal lands, and demanded state management of all wildlife in Alaska. Most sporting clubs had broken from their parent National Wildlife Federation which, though not an official member, assisted the Alaska Coalition of environmentalists. Their state organization, the Alaska Sportsmen's Council, later disaffiliated from the federation and reorganized under the name Alaska Outdoor Council in 1983. Alaska Sportsmen Inc. of Juneau, loyal to the federation, also went out of existence during the lands debate.[28]

Alaska Conservation Society leaders prepared for a painful decision. Unlike the days of Chariot and Rampart, they now had to choose between their preservationist and sporting friends. They occupied an uncomfortable middle ground, remaining in the Alaska Coalition but criticizing some parts of HR 39. They disapproved of hunting in parks but called for less park and wilderness designation, favored subsistence use if not defined ethnically, fought mining and transportation corridors, and urged cooperative federal-state game management. They viewed HR 39 as the best of inadequate alternatives. Alaska's Sierra Club and Friends of the Earth members strongly favored HR 39 and actively seconded the Natives on subsistence provisions disliked by the Alaska Conservation Society. These differences impelled the Alaskan environmental community close to a split, the most serious division in 40 years.[29] As the lands campaign moved to Washington, Alaskan environmental groups as such became less relevant, and their members operated primarily through the national organizations.

Under ANCSA, December 18, 1978, marked the expiration date for federal land withdrawals by the secretary of the interior. Alaska's delegation and its allies fought tenaciously. Representative Seiberling observed, "The problem is that developers don't want 95 percent of the resources; they want them all. The selfishness of the industries involved in the issue would blow your mind." "What would happen if there's a war or a world shortage of resources?" Don Young queried. "They'll go in and tear up the wilderness for copper and bauxite. There will be no controls and they will destroy the fish and pollute the air. A bill like HR 39 could be the worst environmental bill in history."[30] The House soundly defeated Young's weakening amendment and passed HR 39 in May 1978 by 277-31.

Senator Stevens preferred a prodevelopment bill to simply halting d-2 legislation, given the likelihood that Interior Secretary Cecil Andrus would execute the withdrawals anyway.

13.2. Sign protesting Jimmy Carter's designation of national monuments in Alaska, Anchorage, ca. December 1978. By Pete Robinson. Courtesy Alaska Center for the Environment collection, University of Alaska Anchorage Archives. Federal action setting aside lands provoked bitter resentment in many Alaskans.

Senator Gravel believed his chances for reelection depended on stopping the bill. He threatened to filibuster by reading the whole two-volume biography of Gerald Ford to "bring the Senate to its knees on the subject." After announcing in October that he would combat d-2 legislation, Gravel put forth last-minute demands for a Susitna dam, five transportation corridors in park and refuge areas, and a guarantee of no more federal land withdrawals in Alaska. He succeeded in stalling legislation until adjournment by thwarting efforts to reach a compromise acceptable to both houses. Gravel also filibustered a proposal to extend the withdrawal deadline for a year.

Sensing an opportunity to get out from under the ANCSA restrictions, on November 14 the state filed for selection of 41 million acres, 9 million lying in lands earmarked by the Carter administration for national parks and wildlife refuges. Two days later,

13.3. Sign endorsing Jimmy Carter's designation of national monuments in Alaska, Anchorage, ca. December 1978. By Pete Robinson. Courtesy Alaska Center for the Environment collection, University of Alaska Anchorage Archives. A strong minority of Alaskans favored reservation of federal parklands.

exercising his authority under the Federal Land Policy and Management Act of 1976, Andrus withdrew 111 million acres from mining or state selection for two years. President Jimmy Carter accepted a petition signed by members of Congress and over 1,000 citizen organizations, recruited by the Alaska Coalition, asking him to set aside national monuments from the withdrawn acreage. On December 1 he reserved through the Antiquities Act 17 national monuments totaling 56 million acres, most intended as national parks. Pursuant to the Federal Land Policy and Management Act, Andrus ordered 40 million acres withdrawn for national wildlife refuges and 4 million acres as potential national parks. Secretary of Agriculture Bob Bergland closed 11 million acres of the Tongass and Chugach National Forests to mining until evaluated for wilderness status.[31] When Andrus delimited the refuges two days before the deadline, he explained unofficially, "I wasn't going to let the rape, ruin and run boys exploit it before Congress could act again."[32]

Boosters again reacted irately, burning a Carter effigy in Fairbanks and throwing one off the dock in Ketchikan. The REAL Alaska Coalition staged a "Great Denali-McKinley Trespass" in Cantwell, featuring a horseback rider galloping down the street yelling, "The Feds are coming! The Feds are coming!" They entered the new monument, broke minor regulations to show their defiance, and conducted an unsuccessful "wolf hunt."[33] The state and Alaska Miners Association filed suit against Carter's withdrawals.

13.4. U.S. Reps. David Bonior (Michigan), left, and Andrew Maguire (New Jersey) at Gavia Lake, Kenai National Moose Range, August 1979. By Fran Mauer. Protective legislation drew wide public support in the Lower 48, and many members of Congress visited the state.

Meanwhile in Washington, the Alaska Coalition backed an even more pro-environment HR 39, now endorsed by the Alaska Federation of Natives. The state and its allies intensified their lobbying. HR 39 lost by one vote in the Interior Committee; a weaker bill emerged. On the House floor a substitute Udall-Anderson bill succeeded by a wide margin. No Senate bill reached the floor in 1979. Stevens, who had transferred to the Energy and Natural Resources Committee, dominated its proceedings; it passed a pro-industry bill. Early in 1980 Gravel and Stevens won an agreement from the majority leader to delay floor debate on the Senate bill for five months. In turn, they agreed not to filibuster, and each could introduce three amendments. The maneuver prompted Andrus to permanently withdraw 40 million acres for wildlife refuges and national park additions.[34]

As the time for floor action approached in July, environmentalists gathered to lobby the Senate. Carter, the most environmentally oriented president since Theodore Roosevelt, invited them to a rally at the White House and told them that "preserving Alaska's priceless natural resources is my number one environmental priority."[35] Presidential sympathy heartened the environmentalists, but the five-month Senate postponement did not. Gravel and Stevens resumed delay tactics in apparent violation of the spirit or letter of the agreement. Stevens threatened to introduce a list of 18 "second-degree" amendments to deter passage of a measure introduced by Gary Hart to improve wildlife refuge provisions. Despite evidence of strong Senate support for the amendment, Stevens succeeded in removing it from the floor. He then participated decisively in the crafting of a Senate bill containing more wilderness tracts and wildlife refuges than that passed by the Energy and National Resources Committee, but considerably weaker than the House bill. Gravel proceeded to obstruct the modified bill, and the Senate cut him off by a cloture vote. A few days later, in late August, he met defeat in the primary election.

Stevens threatened to filibuster any attempt to change the Senate bill in conference committee. He and Henry Jackson declared there could be no compromise; the House would have to take or leave the Senate bill. November events settled the question. Ronald Reagan won office and a half-dozen liberal senators lost their seats. House leaders and the Alaska Coalition by far preferred the Senate bill to what might happen under a Reagan administration. The Alaska National Interest Lands Conservation Act (ANILCA) became law on December 2, 1980.[36]

A potent sense of the decision's meaning pervaded the signing ceremony in the East Room of the White House. Carter announced, "Never before have we seized the opportunity to preserve so much of America's natural and cultural heritage on so grand a scale. . . . With this bill we are acknowledging that Alaska's wilderness areas are truly this country's crown jewels."[37] In a contrasting tone, Ted Stevens warned: "We're not finished, Mr. President. We're just getting started. The time will come when those resources being protected will be demanded by other Americans."[38]

ANILCA introduced or enlarged 13 national parks and 16 national wildlife refuges totaling 99 million acres (Table 13.1), more than half classified as wilderness. The act also named 25 wild and scenic rivers, 2 national monuments, and other preserves. Gates of the Arctic National Park materialized; most of Admiralty Island received wilderness status; the Arctic National Wildlife Range doubled in size and became a wildlife refuge. Mt. McKinley National Park (but not the mountain) changed to the Native name, Denali. The would-have-been Rampart lake bottom now bore the title Yukon Flats National Wildlife Refuge.[39]

At the end of more than a decade of strife the divide had finally been crossed. The Alaska Native Claims Settlement Act and ANILCA represented a historic achievement for environmental partisans, who accomplished the rare feat of passing a law despite the resistance of both senators from the state primarily involved. Through the aggressive if not duplicitous maneuverings of Gravel and Stevens they suffered serious losses. They lamented the omission of some favored wilderness and wildlife habitat in the Southeast, the termination of judicial review of RARE II (wilderness designation) decisions, and the mandated annual cut of 450 million board feet of timber in the Tongass National Forest.[40] Hundreds of thousands of acres that would have supplemented Gates of the Arctic and Denali National Parks went instead to the state for possible commercial purposes. Subsistence hunting and fishing rights in the preserves and wildlife refuges, necessary for obtaining Native assent, might be transformed into menaces by advancing population and technology.

Compared to the ideal of sustainable ecosystems, the land apportionment fell far short. As in the case of earlier American national parks, scenery received the highest degree of protection. Lands bearing potential for resource extraction tended to be excluded from park and wildlife refuge status or degraded by liberal rules of entry. Defenders of the preservation ideal, who had seen Alaska as the only large-scale opportunity for its realization in the

Table 13.1—Federal Conservation Lands in Alaska, ca. 1981

National Parks	Acres	Wildlife Refuges	Acres
Aniakchak National Monument	138,000	Alaska Maritime	3,549,000
Aniakchak National Preserve	376,000	Alaska Peninsula	3,500,000
Bering Land Bridge National Preserve	2,457,000	Arctic	18,055,000
Cape Krusenstern National Monument	560,000	Becharof	1,200,000
Denali Natl Park	4,366,000	Innoko	3,850,000
Denali National Preserve	1,330,000	Izembek	321,000
Gates of the Arctic National Park	7,052,000	Kanuti	1,430,000
Gates of the Arctic National Preserve	900,000	Kenai	1,970,000
Glacier Bay National Park	3,271,000	Kodiak	1,865,000
Glacier Bay National Preserve	57,000	Koyukuk	3,550,000
Katmai National Park	3,960,000	Nowitna	1,560,000
Katmai National Preserve	308,000	Selawik	2,150,000
Kenai Fjords National Park	567,000	Tetlin	700,000
Kobuk Valley National Park	1,710,000	Togiak	4,105,000
Lake Clark National Park	2,439,000	Yukon Delta	19,624,000
Lake Clark National Preserve	1,214,000	Yukon Flats	8,630,000
Noatak National Preserve	6,460,000		
Wrangell-St. Elias National Park	8,147,000		
Wrangell-St. Elias National Preserve	4,171,000		
Yukon-Charley Rivers National Preserve	1,713,000		

National Forests	Acres	Bureau of Land Management Units	Acres
Admiralty Island National Monument	900,000	Natural Petroleum Reserve—AL	23,000,000
Chugach National Forest	5,800,000	Steese National Conservation Area	1,200,000
Misty Fjords National Monument	2,136,000	White Mountains National Recreation Area	1,000,000
Tongass National Forest	16,700,000		

Sources: Alaska Land Use Council, "Alaska Lands" (undated); *The Alaska Almanac, 1983 Edition* (Seattle: Alaska Northwest, 1982).

United States, would have to engage in a perpetual struggle to maintain their partial success.[41] But environmental advocates would have achieved much less had there been no Carter administration or Democrat-controlled Congress when the issue peaked in the late 1970s.

Shaping of the Alaska lands settlement did much to reinforce environmental values, consolidate the national environmental movement, build Alaska's environmental community, and link the state and national efforts. Environmentalists pushed their Washington lobbying efforts to new heights, assisted by solid information about the nature of Alaskan lands. Public participation through open hearings in the Lower 48 and Alaska demonstrated the depth of nonconsumptive values involving the Alaskan environment. The lands fight empowered Native Alaskans, state government, and some federal agencies, in particular the National Park and Fish and Wildlife Services. Alaska became firmly fixed in the public mind as a priceless ecological resource in need of protection. These changes combined to guarantee permanent environmental strife over Alaska.

NOTES

1. 23 Stat. 26, May 17, 1884; W. Hunt, *Alaska: A Bicentennial History*, 154–159; Naske, *History of Alaskan Statehood*, 49, 251, 265–270.

2. Price, *Legal Status*, 153–155; 23 Stat. 26, May 17, 1884.

3. Williss, *"Do Things Right,"* 61–62; 72 Stat. 339, July 7, 1958.

4. *National Parks*, "Legal Battles," 31.

5. Berry, *The Alaska Pipeline*, 43–44; Chasan, *Klondike 70*, 76.

6. *National Parks*, "Legal Battles," 31.

7. Price, *Legal Status*, 156.

8. Roderick, *Crude Dreams*, 315–318; Durbin, *Tongass*, 49.

9. W. Hunt, *Alaska: A Bicentennial History*, 160–162; Williss, *"Do Things Right,"* 64–67; *New York Times*, January 3, 1969, 11; October 7, 1971, 18.

10. Cahn, *The Fight*, 9; Williss, *"Do Things Right,"* 57–58.

11. Cahn, *The Fight*, 10–11; Hickok, "Coalition's Creation," 10; *Alaska Conservation Review (ACR)*, Spring 1969, 12–13. Other leading participants in the "Maps on the Floor Society": Will Troyer and David Cline (Sport Fisheries and Wildlife), Bailey Breedlove and Richard Stenmark (National Parks), Richard Alman (State Parks), James Scott and Wayne Boden (Bureau of Land Management), and Walter B. Parker (former trapper and future member of the Joint Federal/State Land Use Planning Commission). According to Williss (*"Do Things Right,"* 71–72), the notion of a federal park complex in Alaska arose in the mid-1960s, conceived by Joseph Fitzgerald, chair of the Federal Field Committee for Development Planning in Alaska. Fitzgerald conveyed the idea to the Alaska Wilderness Council, and one of his staff members, David Hickok, specifically suggested the insertion of protection measures in the claims settlement bills.

12. Price, *Legal Status*, 156; *State of Alaska v. Udall*, 420 F. 2d 938 (9th Cir. 1969).

13. Cahn, *The Fight*, 12.

14. Berry, *The Alaska Pipeline*, 70–80, 108–110, 132, 196–214; Peirce, *The Pacific States*, 300.

15. Cahn, *The Fight*, 11–12; *New York Times*, October 3, 1971, 96.

16. Ed Wayburn, letter to author, October 3, 1989.

17. Hartzog, *Battling for the National Parks*, 213–214.

18. Allin, *Politics of Wilderness Preservation*, 211–218; Watkins, "Perils of Expedience," 28; Williss, *"Do Things Right,"* 73–77, 83–87; 85 Stat. 688, December 18, 1971.

19. Anders, "Social and Economic Consequences," 287–290; Berger, *Village Journey*, 20–25.

20. C. Hunter, "An Overview," 12.

21. Cahn, *The Fight*, 13–14; Cahn, "Alaska," 4; Williss, *"Do Things Right,"* 96–97, 103–104, 109–110, 122.

22. *New York Times*, January 14, 1974, 26.

23. *ACR*, Spring 1975, 12.

24. Cahn, *The Fight*, 15–16; Duscha, "How the Alaska Act Was Won," 8; Nash, *Wilderness and the American Mind*, 299. The 1976 Alaska group representatives: Tina Stonorov (Alaska Conservation Society); Jack Hession (Sierra Club); Jim Kowalsky (Friends of the Earth); and observers Dave Friday (Nunam Kitlutsisti) and Willie Goodwin Jr. (Northwest Alaska Native Association). Celia Hunter attended as president of the Wilderness Society and Peter Scholes as a member. Americans for Alaska included Cathleen Douglas, Lady Bird Johnson, Henry Cabot Lodge, Mrs. Rogers C. B. Morton, Paul Nitze, Theodore Roosevelt IV, and Elmo Zumwalt.

25. Cahn, *The Fight*, 16–19.

26. Weeden, "Where Does ACS Stand," 5.

27. *New York Times*, May 28, 1977, 18.

28. Cahn, *The Fight*, 19; *Alaska*, "Alaska Sportsman," October 1978, 64; Allen, *Guardian of the Wild*, 160–161; Grummett, *Territorial Sportsmen*, 122; Donald E. McKnight, interview by author, June 23, 1988.

29. Weeden, "Where Does ACS Stand," 4–5; Clifford Lobaugh and Richard Gordon, interviews by author, July 6, 1988.

30. Schiefelbein, "Alaska: The Great Land War," 16–17.

31. Cahn, *The Fight*, 20–23; Williss, *"Do Things Right,"* 205, 209–218; Allin, *Politics of Wilderness Preservation*, 223–238; Jimmy Carter, *Executive Order Nos. 4611–4628*, December 1 and 6, 1978, *CIS Presidential Executive Orders*, Microfiche, Washington, DC: GPO. Williss (p. 213) contends that although Gravel received the blame for stopping the bill, neither the state, Andrus, nor the Alaska Coalition liked the impending compromise.

32. Schiefelbein, "Alaska: The Great Land War," 17.

33. *New York Times*, January 15,1979, 8.

34. Cahn, *The Fight*, 26; Allin, *Politics of Wilderness Preservation*, 238–251; Williss, *"Do Things Right,"* 231–233; *Sierra Club Alaska Newsletter*, July 1980, 9; *Ravencall*, August 1979, 7. Alaskans active in the 1979–1980 effort included Peter Scholes (lobby leader and former Wilderness Society Alaska representative); Jack Hession, Mary Ellen Cuthbertson and David Levine (Sierra Club/Alaska); Richard Gordon (ACS); Dee Frankfourth (ACE); Paul Peyton (Sitka); Buster Doiron, Larry Edwards, and Theodore Whitesell (SEACC); James Barnett, Tim Sonnenberg, and Peg Tileston (Ed Wayburn's Alaska Task Force); and David Cline (Audubon Society).

35. *New York Times*, July 22, 1980, 12.

36. Cahn, *The Fight*, 26–29; *New York Times*, July 24, 1980, 12; July 25, 1980, 10; August 20, 1980, 17; August 26, 1980, 14; August 28, 1980, 12; Allin, *Politics of Wilderness Preservation*, 251–256; Williss, *"Do Things Right,"* 235–237.

37. Duscha, "How the Alaska Act Was Won," 4.

38. Cahn, "Paper Parks," 24.

39. Cahn, *The Fight*, 29; 94 Stat. 2371, December 2, 1980.

40. Wayburn, "Alaska: An Act of History," 5.

41. Runte, *National Parks*, 236–237, 255–257.

14

Managing Federal Lands

ANILCA, the Alaska National Interest Lands Conservation Act of 1980, may have been the most noteworthy piece of environmental preservation legislation ever adopted by Americans. Yet while setting down precedents in federal stewardship, it precipitated a seemingly endless contest among a multitude of government and private interests to define use of the Alaskan land. Oil, mining, timbering, and other extractive users, aided by the Reagan and Bush administrations, lobbied for rules permitting greater access. State and national environmental groups collaborated in often successful efforts, largely through court action, to ensure ecosystem sustainability in the parklands. In doing so, they compiled extensive experience in resource management, and strengthened principles of government and corporate accountability. ANILCA's formulation and implementation energized and lent direction to both the Alaskan and national environmental movements.

In physical scope ANILCA could never again be equaled; the frontier was no more. Public participation in ANILCA vastly exceeded that of less than a century earlier when a single personal contact from an influential figure could bring about presidential action. The act's preamble declared:

> It is the interest of Congress in this act to preserve unrivaled scenic and geological values associated with natural landscapes; to provide for the maintenance of sound populations of, and habitat for, wildlife populations of inestimable value . . . to preserve in their natural state extensive unaltered arctic tundra, forest, and coastal rain forest ecosystems; to protect the resources related to subsistence needs; to preserve historic and archaeological sites, rivers and lands, and to preserve wilderness resource values . . . and to maintain opportunities for scientific research and undisturbed ecosystems.[1]

ANILCA embodied a mixture of preservationist and utilitarian purposes, and left value-laden choices to the administrative process. Its preamble and its wilderness and park elements responded to public wishes for nature protection. Yet vested consumptive interests exercised a powerful influence. The act legalized subsistence hunting and fishing for rural residents, primarily for the benefit of Natives, on most federal lands. It facilitated industrial activity through (1) permission for the president to recommend to Congress the opening of any land unit (except national parks and the Arctic National Wildlife Refuge) for development in case of emergency; (2) direction of the secretary of the interior to examine Arctic Slope lands for oil and gas potential, and to initiate leasing in all other units not specifically prohibiting it; (3) permission to cross federal lands by roads, power lines, and pipelines; (4) guaranteeing rights-of-way to inholdings for state, Native, and other private owners; (5) allowing cabins owned prior to ANILCA in national parks; (6) permitting cabins, shelters, fish hatcheries, and other salmon enhancement measures in Forest Service wilderness areas; and (7) prohibiting presidential land withdrawals of more than 500 acres without congressional consent. ANILCA gave high priority to subsistence use of resources, and granted Natives and other rural residents a meaningful voice in subsistence policy. An Alaska Land Use Planning Council made up of state, Native, and federal-agency representatives exercised strong recommendatory powers for management of federal lands.[2]

ANILCA did not end the Alaska lands controversy; it only took a vital step in a long process. Critically important land-use plans, regulations, studies, and land exchanges had to be accomplished during the 1980s. Grave responsibility shifted to the federal land agencies and to environmental guardians in Alaska monitoring them. Environmentalists sought to limit oil operations, road building, logging, mining, off-road vehicles, and other actions diminishing the natural character of the lands. They tried to prevent private ownership of small parcels in remote and incompatible areas that would lead to increased traffic and social services, destroying wilderness integrity.

Ronald Reagan's assumption of the presidency foretold years of environmental strife. Reagan chose as chief steward of the nation's lands James Watt, a former lobbyist for the U.S. Chamber of Commerce and western economic interests. Watt secured a position in the Interior Department after spending five days coaching Walter Hickel for the 1969 secretary of the interior confirmation hearings. Watt strongly advocated full exploitation of resources as distinct from sustained-yield management. In a 1981 memo leaked to the press, he instructed Interior Department officials to find ways to "open wilderness areas."[3] The administration placed its highest natural-resource priority on maximizing private acquisition of oil, coal, and other minerals on federal lands, and minimizing protective federal regulations. In national forests it sharply increased funding for timbering and mineral extraction, and reduced funding for recreation, wildlife preservation, and soil and water conservation. It virtually halted additions to national parklands. However, congressional resistance forced the administration to conduct its resource policies through executive actions and budget cuts more than by changes in legislation.[4]

Upon taking office, Watt immediately made a series of decisions angering environmentalists: canceling U.S.-Canada caribou treaty negotiations, ordering the Bureau of Land Management (BLM) to cease studying lands for wilderness status, shifting funding from land planning and administration into mineral and timber production, reducing the time and budgets for oil impact studies, speeding up oil and gas leasing before proper investigations and oil spill plans could be made, allowing wolf hunts on federal lands, widening off-road vehicle use on lands, attempting to open BLM lands to homesteading and commerce, arranging land trades to maximize resource exploitation, ordering the Fish and Wildlife Service to facilitate oil drilling in national wildlife refuges, and giving the state additional control of wildlife in the refuges.[5] Sierra Club/Alaska joined a national attempt to remove Watt from

14.1. National Parks in Alaska. Courtesy National Park Service, Division of Realty, Anchorage.

office for "representing private economic interests" and "seeking to defy decades of legislation designed to protect our natural resources."[6] About 100 people picketed as Watt spoke to the Fairbanks Chamber of Commerce in 1981. While Watt visited the capitol, the Southeast Alaska Conservation Council staged a 21-chainsaw salute on the front steps. Watt cited the protest as the most creative he had encountered as Interior secretary.[7] None of the demonstrations appeared to sway Watt, though his tenure seemed to work wonders for membership rolls of environmental groups, many of which swelled in the early 1980s.[8]

LAND OWNERSHIP

Land selections under the Alaska Statehood Act, Native Claims Settlement Act, and ANILCA ended in 1994, though surveys, lawsuits, sales to private owners, and other transfers extended conveyances over decades. Alaska would contain about 225 million acres of federal lands, 105 million acres of state lands, 45 million acres of Native lands, and more than 3 million acres in other private ownership.[9] Federal units would be managed by the National Park Service, Fish and Wildlife Service, Forest Service, and Bureau of Land Management. ANILCA affirmed state jurisdiction over most inland fish and wildlife, providing it gave rural residents preference for subsistence.

Nationwide, the National Park Service is "dedicated to conserving unimpaired" more than 375 national parks, national monuments, national historic sites, national recreation

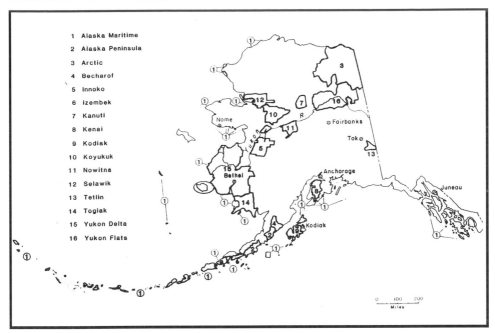

1 Alaska Maritime
2 Alaska Peninsula
3 Arctic
4 Becharof
5 Innoko
6 Izembek
7 Kanuti
8 Kenai
9 Kodiak
10 Koyukuk
11 Nowitna
12 Selawik
13 Tetlin
14 Togiak
15 Yukon Delta
16 Yukon Flats

14.2. National Wildlife Refuges in Alaska. Courtesy U.S. Fish and Wildlife Service, Division of Realty, Anchorage.

areas, and national seashores and lakeshores "for the enjoyment, education, and inspiration of this and future generations."[10] It assists state and local governments and private groups in related programs. It engages in land planning and management, public education, and provision of campground facilities. Of Alaskan federal lands in the mid-1990s, the Park Service maintained the most restrictive rules on its parks and preserves (Map 14.1), though permitting hunting and trapping on some preserves and allowing planes, helicopters, and motorboats on all preserves.

The U.S. Fish and Wildlife Service mission is to "conserve, protect, and enhance" migratory birds, endangered species, inland fisheries, and some marine mammals (sea otters, walruses, and polar bears in Alaska).[11] It operates through multiple forms of research, propagation, public education, and law enforcement. Of its more than 500 national wildlife refuges, Alaska contained 16 in the 1990s (Map 14.2). There, the service allowed the same activities as practiced in national parks and preserves plus timbering and, subject to some limits, off-road vehicles, snowmobiles, and dogs.

The U.S. Forest Service is responsible for 155 national forests including the Tongass and Chugach in Alaska, 20 national grasslands, and other tracts totaling 191 million acres in 2000. Lands are to be managed "under the sustainable, multiple use management concept to meet the diverse needs of people" and to sustain the health, diversity, and productivity of the land.[12] The service cooperates with other federal agencies, state and local governments, and private concerns through research, technical assistance, and operation of participatory programs. In addition to the activities permitted in national parks and wildlife refuges, mining

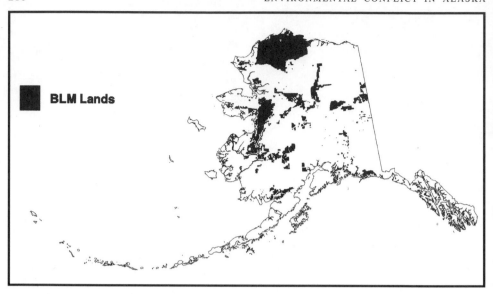

14.3. Bureau of Land Management Lands in Alaska, 1999. Courtesy Bureau of Land Management, Alaska State Office, Anchorage.

could be conducted almost anywhere in the Tongass and Chugach National Forests except for designated wilderness areas.

The Bureau of Land Management has jurisdiction over 264 million acres and over sub-surface mineral use in 300 million more acres of federal lands. It manages all resources—timber, solid minerals, oil and gas, wildlife, and habitat—for "protection, orderly develop-ment, and use . . . under principles of multiple use and sustained yield." Least restrictive of the federal land agencies in Alaska, it permits some form of mineral extraction in nearly all of its Alaskan lands (Map 14.3). Some segments of the Steese National Conservation Area and White Mountains National Recreation Area north of Fairbanks are closed to lode and placer mining, and oil and gas leasing.[13]

Environmental organizations took the lead for the preservation forces in federal land issues stemming from ANILCA. They systematized their efforts through an Alaska Lands Act Coordinating Committee, funded by the Alaska Conservation Foundation. The North-ern Alaska Environmental Center (NAEC) and Sierra Club/Alaska concentrated on the cen-tral and northern regions. NAEC monitored and publicized federal plans and regulations as they appeared, and tried to shape them. It strove to curtail unauthorized off-road vehicle use, road building through parks and wildlife refuges, excess construction of park facilities, and promotion of large-scale tourism in wild areas such as the Noatak.[14] In Gates of the Arctic National Park it opposed park buildings, roads, and requests by Natives for unlimited entry by all-terrain vehicles.[15] It backed the BLM in resistance to state demands for control of the corridor flanking the Haul Road between Gates of the Arctic and the Arctic National Wildlife Refuge. NAEC looked upon state ownership and its strong commercial orientation as a threat to the wilderness integrity of the central Brooks Range. The BLM reversed its stance in 1987, and shortly before the Reagan administration left office it granted the state permission to select 650,000 acres from the corridor.[16]

NAEC and Sierra Club/Alaska objected to the Alaska Land Use Planning Council's inclination to weaken control over trespassing cabins. The Alaska Lands Act permitted five-year renewable extensions for ownership of private cabins built on federal lands before 1973, and one-year nonrenewable extensions for those built later. The council voted to eliminate the requirement of proof of prior residency.[17] NAEC made its most visible effort in a leadership role in the national campaign to gain wilderness status for the coastal plain of the Arctic National Wildlife Refuge (Chapter 16).

A provision of ANILCA granted the Interior secretary "minor boundary adjustment" and "land exchange" authority. According to Morris Udall, Congress intended to enhance the value and integrity of federal lands by providing for acquisition of adjacent special features, and for trading outside land to eliminate inholdings jeopardizing the ecology of a given unit. Turning the intent around, Watt used the provisions to insinuate industry into the federal land units. In 1983 he approved a trade of 4,110 acres of St. Matthew Island National Wildlife Refuge in the northern Bering Sea to three Native corporations—Cook Inlet, Calista, and Sea Lion—for 14,175 acres of mainland property, most of it already designated as cemetery and historic sites and thus partially protected from development. The Natives intended to lease the 4,110 acres to oil companies as a base for operations in the Bering Sea. Plans called for a camp to house 250 workers, an airport capable of landing jets and helicopters, a deepwater port, and facilities for storage of oil piped ashore. St. Matthew Island had been a federal refuge for seabirds and mammals since 1909. Recognizing its unspoiled character, ANILCA specified the entire island as wilderness. Trustees for Alaska sued on behalf of the Audubon Society, Sierra Club, Wilderness Society, and other environmental organizations, contending Watt had no authority to conduct such a trade. They won their suit and set a legal precedent for challenges to other attempted land trades.[18]

Environmentalists deplored the impact of numerous inholdings (nonfederal ownership within the outer boundaries) in federal lands. Land acquisition by miners, the state, and Native individuals and corporations created many such land juxtapositions. These ownership rights could undermine the goals of agencies most oriented to environmental protection. Airports, roads, communication facilities, or tourist accommodations could damage aesthetic values or wildlife habitat. As of 1999, nonfederal interests controlled 3.5 million acres in National Park Service lands (Table 14.1) and, in 2000, 23 million acres in national wildlife refuges. Hundreds of millions of dollars would be needed to buy out the inholdings.

A particularly troublesome type of inholding, submerged lands, posed a grave danger to wilderness integrity. Federal law granted states ownership of lands under navigable waters. In response to requests by the state and its congressional delegation, Secretary Watt conveyed some land to the state and planned to continue. The Juneau-based Sierra Club Legal Defense Fund sued in 1984 on behalf of the Sierra Club and Wilderness Society, challenging the secretary's authority to transfer the land. Following a 1986 district court decision dismissing the suit for lack of standing of the plaintiffs, the appeals court reversed and returned it to the lower court for settlement.[19] In 1988 Congress passed legislation ceding 1.8 million acres of federal land to compensate for submerged lands. Of the total, 1.1

Table 14.1—Federal and Nonfederal (Inholding) Acreage Within Boundaries of National Park Units in Alaska, December 31, 1999

Park Unit	Federal Acreage	Nonfederal Acreage
Alagnik Wild River	26,366	4,299
Aniakchak National Monument	137,176	0
Aniakchak National Preserve	439,863	25,740
Bering Land Bridge National Preserve	2,537,912	159,727
Cape Krusenstern National Monument	594,409	54,773
Denali National Park	4,724,735	16,177
Denali National Preserve	1,304,132	29,986
Gates of Arctic National Park	7,263,774	257,795
Gates of the Arctic National Preserve	948,200	429
Katmai National Park	3,611,474	63,035
Katmai National Preserve	382,074	36,625
Kenai Fjords National Park	593,876	68,144
Klondike Gold Rush National Historic Park	2,419	10,772
Kobuk Valley National Park	1,669,808	80,924
Lake Clark National Park	2,226,630	393,103
Lake Clark National Preserve	1,999,999	201,087
Noatak National Preserve	6,276,055	293,849
Wrangell(St. Elias National Park	7,661,519	662,099
Wrangell(St. Elias National Preserve	4,000,873	851,880
Yukon-Charley Rivers National Preserve	2,183,133	343,379
Total	51,055,456	3,555,966

Source: U.S. Dept. of the Interior, National Park Service, Division of Realty, Anchorage.

million acres went to Native corporations, nearly 700,000 from wildlife refuges and 18,000 from national parks. State acreage and the remainder of Native acreage came from BLM lands.[20] Subsequently, a test case brought by the state resulted in district and appeals court rulings that the state could claim all land below high water in any river navigable even by canoe or kayak. These rulings left wild and scenic rivers as well as all others in federal lands open to forms of exploitation, including mining claims that in turn could be converted to other commercial uses. Environmentalists now faced a lengthy effort to persuade the federal government to buy back these new inholdings in parks and refuges, and to lessen the injury to public lands.[21]

A test case of the navigability issue arose in 1990 when the Alaska Department of Natural Resources (DNR) asserted jurisdiction over Moose Creek, the outlet of Wonder Lake in Denali National Park. Basing its claim on a trip made by a rubber raft in water six to eight inches deep, the DNR proceeded to issue three mining permits and allow 37 mining claims to be staked within the park. As work progressed on mining sites, negative public reaction caused the Hickel administration to suspend its claim of jurisdiction pending further study. Hickel's action left the mining permits in force and the matter unresolved until a 1995 Supreme Court decision affirmed federal jurisdiction over navigable waterways involving subsistence rights under ANILCA.[22]

ROADS AND DAMS

Almost no other projects held more potential to degrade the environment than did roads and dams; accordingly, environmentalists invested much energy in combating them. In south-central Alaska, Sierra Club/Alaska directed the drafting of a 200-page Citizens' Alternative to the Forest Service's inordinately logging-oriented Chugach National Forest plan. The Citizens' Alternative formed the basis for an appeal by the Sierra Club, Wilderness Society, National Audubon Society, and 14 commercial fishing and outdoor recreation groups. The final settlement, completing the first successful appeal of a Forest Service plan, doubled the acreage closed to road construction and halved the acreage for logging, requiring specific studies prior to each logging operation. Prominent protected tracts included most of the Copper River Delta, the Nellie Juan-College Fiords Wilderness study area, and Hinchinbrook Island in Prince William Sound.[23] Through the Sierra Club Legal Defense Fund, Alaska Center for the Environment and other parties filed an appeal of a Forest Service plan for a 35-mile road through a wild section of the Chugach National Forest on Montague Island in Prince William Sound. A Native group, the Chugach Alaska Corporation, wanted the road for access to one of its properties on Patton Bay, in order to facilitate logging. Appeal of the plan proved fruitless, and road construction proceeded in mid-1992.[24]

Logging in the Chugach sparked protests as it escalated on the Kenai Peninsula in the 1990s. The Forest Service increased the logging acreage more than tenfold despite losing money on the sales. Environmentalists objected vehemently to the roads, some violating areas slated for consideration as wilderness. Second largest of the national forests, the Chugach nonetheless contained no acreage protected as wilderness. Critics also pointed to the continuing loss of brown bear habitat on the Kenai. Represented by the Sierra Club Legal Defense Fund, they filed a 1997 suit against the plan for logging at Moose Pass north of Seward. In response to public complaints, in fall 1997 the Forest Service cancelled its planned cuts at Moose Pass and three other locations on the Kenai.[25]

Proposals for roads and dams imperiled the integrity of the scenic Stikine River valley, visited by John Muir in 1879. From its origins in the mountains of northwestern British Columbia, the Stikine dashes 400 miles to the Pacific. In Muir's words:

> It first pursues a westerly course through grassy plains darkened here and there with groves of spruce and pine; then curving southward and receiving numerous tributaries from the north, it enters the Coast Range, and sweeps across it through a magnificent canyon three thousand to five thousand feet deep, and more than a hundred miles long. The majestic cliffs and mountains forming the canyon walls display endless variety of form and sculpture, and are wonderfully adorned with glaciers and waterfalls, while throughout almost its whole extent the floor is a flowery landscape garden.[26]

The Alaska Lands Act set aside part of the valley, a popular recreation area, as the 443,000-acre Stikine-LeConte Wilderness. A U.S.-Canada agreement authorized a road through the valley to enable Canadian ore trucks to reach a shipping port. A tentative design by the British Columbia government and Alaska Department of Transportation worried residents of several small Alaskan towns, who preferred not to be connected by road to the Lower 48. In 1987 the Forest Service announced it would not endorse the road project for the time being, and planners took no more action. The issue lay dormant.

A much more serious menace to the Stikine appeared when BC Hydro and Power Authority, a provincial government unit, proposed to construct a series of five dams, filling the river's canyon. Southeast Alaska Conservation Council paid special attention to the project, monitoring and publicizing it in conjunction with the Sierra Club of Western Canada and local Alaskan towns. A number of reviews of the venture indicated a pattern reminiscent of Rampart and Susitna: in its other operations, BC Hydro had overbuilt: its costs and rates rose, customers cut back on power use, and it lost $18 million in 1982. Planners shelved the Stikine project in 1984.[27]

Many more mining and logging roads penetrated wild areas during the 1980s and 1990s, though no major highway had been built since 1972. A new threat emerged in 1992 federal legislation granting Alaska $1.4 billion in transportation funds to be spent during 1993–1998. The Hickel administration contemplated several road projects threatening wilderness: the Copper River Highway from Cordova to Chitina, through part of Denali National Park to Kantishna, westward from the Haul Road to Bettles, from Nenana to McGrath, from Juneau to Haines, from near Wrangell to the Cassiar Highway, from Portage to Whittier, and from Eureka to Rampart. Environmentalists challenged most of the road-building plans and the state's invocation of R.S. 2477 to gain rights-of-way across federal lands. The 1866 law, repealed in 1976 but bearing a grandfather clause, granted public roads the right to cross public lands. The state researched about 2,000 possibilities for rights-of-way. The federal government pursued regulations for processing claims, and the state sought court decisions to set precedents easing access across federal lands. In 1998, the state legislature claimed 602 routes thus far identified, and placed them under Department of Natural Resources jurisdiction. As of March 2000, the state had identified 667 routes.[28]

On behalf of several groups led by the National Parks and Conservation Association, Sierra Club Legal Defense Fund presented a brief in a case contesting R.S. 2477. In December 1996 the appeals court withdrew an earlier decision that encouraged states to file claims in national parks. The 1996 ruling invalidated ten claims by the State of Alaska in Denali and Wrangell–St. Elias National Parks.[29] Senator Stevens then placed a rider on a 1997 disaster relief bill to give the states power to determine the validity of their claims. President Clinton vetoed the bill, describing the R.S. 2477 rider as "an objectionable provision." Stevens settled for a promise by the Interior Department to submit a rights-of-way proposal to the Congress.[30]

MINING

Mining rights on public lands endured as a holdover from the pioneer era, in the Lower 48 as well as Alaska. Miners fancied their pursuits to be symbol and substance of a fast-disappearing ethic of individual freedom. Mining, they believed, had been largely responsible for Alaska's progress and would be vital to its economic future. Accordingly, they perceived restrictions on their activities as unfair and shortsighted interference in free enterprise. Ever fewer small miners, they argued, could afford the expense of meeting tightening regulations, and in the wake of the Alaska Lands Act most federal acreage in the state had been closed to mineral exploration. Although 90 percent of state-owned land could be mined, designation of state parks and other protected tracts progressively diminished mining opportunity.[31] Jamie Cox, a miner and officer in the Alaskan Independence Party on whose ticket Walter Hickel ran for governor in 1990, voiced the frustration of small miners: "You can't just mine anymore. You have to be a lawyer and wade a mass of bureaucratic jargon and paperwork. Most of us make just enough to get by; it's more the lifestyle. I don't know any rich miners. That's the really sad thing that's being lost. We don't hurt anything."[32]

Except for navigable waterways, and including preexisting claims in national parks, national wildlife refuges, and wilderness, a person or corporation could stake a claim and conduct mining on many federal lands. Along with the right to mine went the right to physical access, normally by road. Regulators commonly ignored the legal obligation to demonstrate the operation's economic viability. Aside from the roads, any type of mining resulted in considerable environmental impact. Shaft and open-pit mines generated great quantities of processed rock that could disfigure the land for decades or centuries. If dumped into water bodies, the tailings could alter local ecosystems through siltation, turbidity, and sometimes, hazardous pollution. Placer mining, a small-scale form of strip mining done in and near creek beds and riverbeds, could leave scars and disrupt the ecosystem for decades. By the end of the 1980s, federal and state regulations imposed restoration measures to follow all mining operations.

A common practice since the Gold Rush, placer mining rebounded as the price of gold climbed in the late 1970s. The more lucrative sites had been depleted by 1920, so miners introduced more powerful machinery to dig wider and deeper. An economically viable operation in the 1980s needed several pieces of heavy equipment such as bulldozers, backhoes, draglines, front-end loaders, and escalators. In large-scale operations, valleys disintegrated into gravel wastelands. Siltation and turbidity could disrupt fish feeding or reproduction, render water undrinkable, endanger canoeists, and otherwise lower recreational and wildlife values. Through their noises, roads, land impairment, and visual impact, placer and hard-rock mining harmed ecosystems and markedly reduced the quality of outdoor recreation.[33]

A provision of the Alaska Statehood Act of 1958 required payment of rents and royalties for minerals extracted from certain lands selected by the state. Whereas it could have meant substantial income, the state took no action regarding hard-rock minerals, including gold and silver. On behalf of several Native, fishing, and environmental units, Trustees for Alaska (TfA) sued in 1983 for enforcement of the law. Superior court denied the plaintiffs standing. TfA appealed successfully to the Alaska Supreme Court, whose 1987 ruling decreed that royalties be paid on minerals known to exist in the lands at the time of selection. The Alaska Miners Association and the state appealed to the U.S. Supreme Court, which refused to review the case in 1988, letting the ruling stand.[34] Backed by the Alaska Environmental Lobby, a state law enacted in 1989 imposed rents and royalties, proof of financial responsibility, and submission of reclamation plans prior to operation of mines.[35]

Mining in the South-Central and Southeast

Many clashes over mining plans busied environmental activists in the 1980s and 1990s. In 1982 the Forest Service issued permits for two mining roads in the Crescent Creek valley of Chugach National Forest. Sierra Club/Alaska appealed the permits and in 1983 the Alaska Center for the Environment, Alaska Sportfishing Association, and Kenai River Sportfishing

Association joined in the lawsuit. Declaring the mining claims invalid, their attorneys "topfiled" (made additional claims on the sites) to prevent land degredation in advance of legal examination. They won a restraining order halting the roads. Adoption of the Chugach land use plan settled the issue in 1985.[36]

In western Alaska, TfA sued the state (for failure to uphold coastal zone management) and BLM (for inadequate environmental statement) on behalf of Nunam Kitlutsisti and the Natives of Tuluksak. On the Tuluksak River, approval had been granted for a gold-dredging operation that plaintiffs regarded as a detriment to the fishing and drinking water of the Tuluksak Natives. An October 1988 district court ruling required the BLM to do a more complete analysis before allowing the dredge to continue. In 1990 the mining company abandoned the project.[37]

Southeast Alaska Conservation Council (SEACC) and Sierra Club Legal Defense Fund sought to curb the impacts of mines in Misty Fjords and on Admiralty Island. Misty Fjords, at the southern tip of Alaska, impressed visitors as an exceptionally beautiful corner of the earth, rich in forest and marine life in a setting of steep mountains, forests, bays, beaches, rivers, tundra, and glaciers. U.S. Borax staked a molybdenum claim in 1974 in the heart of the tract. Following issuance of a road-building permit by the Forest Service in 1977, eleven environmental groups (SEACC, Sierra Club, Alaska Conservation Society, Audubon Society, Wilderness Society, and Tongass Conservation Society) and fishing groups filed an administrative appeal of the environmental impact statement. The Forest Service denied Borax permission to build the road, determining that helicopters should be employed. It rejected a second Borax plan in 1979 on grounds that bulk sampling, a testing phase involving removal and crushing of large quantities of rock, would necessitate an environmental impact statement. Borax presented a third plan, not to include bulk sampling, and the Forest Service approved it.

Soon thereafter, ANILCA designated Misty Fjords a 1.5-million-acre wilderness national monument, but exempted a 153,000-acre section in the center for U.S. Borax operations. Borax then amended its plan to include bulk sampling in practice but not in name, and received Forest Service approval. The environmental coalition sued, winning district and circuit court decisions ordering an impact statement. The circuit court set an environmentally favorable precedent by affirming ANILCA's primary purpose as conservation rather than industrial activity.[38]

U.S. Borax planned one of the world's largest mines at Misty Fjords: a pit up to two miles long and 1,800 feet deep would be dug, 16,000 gallons pumped daily from nearby rivers, and 60,000 tons of tailings produced every day for the 70-year life of the mine. According to the original configuration, the tailings would be piped down into Boca de Quadra Fiord, following the Keta River. Environmentalists preferred to restrict damage to one river valley and fiord, and the deep Boca de Quadra Fiord could accommodate mine tailings much more easily than could the alternative, shallower Wilson Arm. But U.S. Borax changed its design and requested permission to run its pipeline down the cheaper Blossom River route to Wilson Arm, while using the Keta River valley for its access road. The Forest Service agreed, and the environmental coalition continued filing appeals and lawsuits. Aesthetics aside, environmentalists worried about the effects on fisheries and the marine ecological complex as a whole. They also contested a power line U.S. Borax wanted to run through a wilderness area.[39] Late in 1988, U.S. Borax submitted its impact statement for complete mine operation and received Forest Service assent. Sierra Club Legal Defense Fund then filed an administrative appeal to the Environmental Protection Agency (EPA), arguing that water quality standards would be violated and the ecology of Wilson Arm disrupted. As the legal process moved forward, the low price of molybdenum slowed the mine's progress. In fall 1990, the EPA refused permission to dump in Wilson Arm. U.S. Borax declined to appeal, and announced it would suspend the mine project indefinitely.[40]

At Greens Creek on northwest Admiralty Island, the Noranda company had staked a claim in the mid-1970s, seeking lead, zinc, silver, and gold. When ANILCA made the island a wilderness monument, it excluded the Greens Creek tract from wilderness status while retaining it as part of the monument. Congress stipulated that Noranda must complete the additions to its claims by 1985 or lose them. As the deadline approached, Noranda had not made ready, and to complete its claims it proposed a trade of 17,225 acres at Greens Creek (to be removed from monument status and conveyed to Noranda) for 18,174 acres in the Young Bay/Young Lake area, frequented by Juneau residents. The Forest Service recommended the plan. Taking the position that ANILCA had not intended trades to foster commercial development in federal land units, Southeast Alaska Conservation Council and Sierra Club Legal Defense Fund threatened a lawsuit. Congress passed a bill in 1985 granting a year's extension for Noranda, and encouraging a trade. Negotiations among the interested parties collapsed and Noranda (later British Petroleum) went on working its claim. Low metal prices caused the mine to discontinue operations in 1993. Two years later, Congress legislated a land exchange giving the new owner, Kennecott Greens Creek Mining Company, the right to mine underground on 7,500 adjacent acres. In return, the company would donate $6 million toward federal acquisition of private inholdings on Admiralty Island.[41]

Lynn Canal Conservation and other Alaskan and national environmental units joined Vancouver-based Tatshenshini Wild to work against a projected Windy-Craggy copper mine in British Columbia. Geddes Resources, Ltd. applied for a large-scale excavation in a wild region just northeast of the U.S. border at the juncture of the Tatshenshini and Alsek Rivers, the latter flowing through Glacier Bay National Park. New roads and bridges would enable ore trucks or a slurry pipeline to reach a port near Haines. Negative commentary on the mine venture by the British Columbia mines, tourism, and parks departments induced the provincial government to suspend the application in 1992 pending a more complete environmental review. Pressure from newly elected vice president Al Gore and 50 Canadian, American, and international environmental groups helped settle the issue. British Columbia premier Michael Harcourt reserved a 2.6-million-acre Tatshenshini-Alsek Wilderness Park in June 1993. The Glacier Bay-Kluane-Tatshenshini-Wrangell/St. Elias complex now spanned 27.2 million acres, the world's largest protected wilderness tract, most of it designated a World Heritage Site.[42]

PLACER MINING IN THE INTERIOR

The Northern Alaska Environmental Center (NAEC) in Fairbanks invested much of its energy in controlling the effects of placer mining on interior rivers and streams. Small-scale independent miners often treated hikers who wandered across their claims in national parks

14.1 Creekbed erosion caused by bulldozer transit, near Dalton Highway, 1989. By Ed Bovy. Courtesy Bureau of Land Management, Anchorage. A single passage by a bulldozer could leave a lasting impact on the northern environment.

as trespassers. Placer miners did not share the environmentalist attitude toward their impact on the land. Assuming that natural restoration would take place, Joe Bailey proposed, "Just give us ten good years to mine this country by any means we want, and we could get out most of the gold. Then you could make it a park or preserve without a complaint from us miners."[43]

NAEC director Randy Rogers described his experience as a 1980 summer employee for the BLM: "In my first trip into the field, my dreams of pristine Alaskan wild rivers were shattered. Driving out the Steese Highway to the Birch Creek put-in, I saw valleys being stripped of all vegetation and entire streams being traversed by heavy machinery and run through sluiceboxes. As we put in, the water was so heavily silted it appeared you could walk on it." When Rogers complained to the BLM staff, they blamed the state and EPA for lack of enforcement. An official in Alaska Department of Fish and Game confided in Rogers that whenever it tried to enforce the regulations, miners would go to their legislator who would threaten to cut the agency's budget. Later in the summer, Rogers witnessed a miner

> taking a cat train of heavy equipment right down the proposed wild river corridor, going from one bank to the other gouging ramps through the cutbanks and tundra with a bulldozer blade. Another miner working on a tributary creek drove a caterpillar down to Birch Creek and bladed a new airstrip on the edge of the river. Each time they went from the mine to the airstrip, a new path was cut through the tundra and black spruce, presumably so that the cat would not sink into the muck holes created by previous disturbances of the insulating tundra mat.

Rogers wrote out a detailed report, but the BLM area manager declined to take action. Neither of the mining operations, said Rogers, turned out to be economically successful.[44]

Placer mining created problems for state as well as federal agencies. Miners exercised a strong voice in Alaska's government even though they contributed very modestly to the economy. Their power centered in the Fairbanks region, and they engaged in numerous mining ventures in nearby federal lands. Birch Creek, a designated wild and scenic river northeast of Fairbanks, became so polluted by placer mining silt as to be useless for outdoor recreation. The Alaska Department of Environmental Conservation (DEC) felt pressured to weaken state water quality standards to accommodate the miners. And despite the mandate of the federal Clean Water Act of 1972, the EPA had issued no regulations for placer-mining effluents. Trustees for Alaska (TfA), Sierra Club/Alaska, Denali Citizens Council, and Northern Alaska Environmental Center (NAEC) sued the EPA in 1985 to obtain regulations. Pursuant to a consent decree, the EPA issued guidelines in 1987, mandating waste-water recycling by most placer mining operations.[45]

To assist miners in reducing harmful impacts, NAEC participated in the DEC Task Force on Placer Mining. While director of NAEC, Randy Rogers received a gubernatorial appointment to the Mining Water Use Review Committee. When the Miners Advocacy Council sued the DEC in 1985 for allegedly excessive enforcement, TfA and NAEC intervened in the case, calling the standards too weak. The plaintiffs won no relief.[46] TfA and NAEC later challenged a DEC decision allowing placer-mining discharges in excess of federal water-quality standards for fish, recreation, and drinking purposes. The Alaska Supreme Court upheld the plaintiffs' position in 1989.[47]

An investigation by NAEC of the economics of placer mining in Alaska revealed that between 1982 and 1985 the state spent $16 million on the industry but received only $562,000 in revenues from it. Placer mining accounted for less than half of 1 percent of Alaska's employment, 30 percent of the employees resided outside the state, and the smallest two-thirds of mining operations taken together generated only 10 percent of mining expenditures. The study directly contradicted small miners' claims to be vital to the economy. On the day following release of the report, Rogers found a death threat on his answering machine.[48] NAEC continued to investigate methods and technology for lessening impacts on land and water quality. Aided by the Alaska Environmental Lobby, it succeeded in blocking annual attempts at passage of the "Dirty Water Bill" submitted by miners to weaken state water-quality standards.[49]

14.2. *Aerial view of Ray Lester's mining operation, Birch Creek, 1989. Courtesy Alaska Department of Natural Resources, Division of Mining. The 1872 mining law permits gold-seekers to turn a river valley on public land into a gravel moonscape.*

NAEC invested most of its efforts in attempting to work cooperatively with the federal and state governments and the miners. Not infrequently, these endeavors broke down and legal action followed. Despite public opposition, and responding to requests from the Alaska Miners Association, the BLM proposed year-round entry for off-road vehicles in wild and scenic river corridors. NAEC tried unsuccessfully through the Freedom of Information Act to acquire a copy of the regulations, then it obtained a leaked copy.[50] Soon afterward, in 1984 the BLM proposed regulations for the Steese National Conservation Area and White Mountains National Recreation Area, permitting similarly free access by motorized vehicles and leaving only a small area untouched. NAEC argued that Congress had classified Steese and White Mountains primarily for wilderness recreation, not for mining. It organized a public workshop on the two land plans and sent a lobbyist to Washington to appeal the offending provisions.[51] The BLM regional office had overreached. Its plan met rejection by the state and the Citizens Advisory Council on Federal Areas, and even by the Reagan-appointed chief of the BLM, who observed that the provisions "do not reflect Congressional intent to manage the areas as national recreation and conservation areas" and embodied "the highest potential for adverse impacts on wildlife." The director's memo, not meant for release to the public, went on to warn that mismanagement of the lands could cause Congress to transfer them to the Fish and Wildlife Service or National Park Service.[52]

The BLM issued revised rules for the recreation areas, but disagreement soon arose over their enforcement. Randy Rogers observed that "BLM's on-the-ground management of placer mining did not appear to change significantly. Miners bladed a new unauthorized trail straight up over a hill in the White Mountains, leaving an erosion gully and scar visible for miles. Reclamation remained virtually nonexistent and water quality poor."[53] Sierra Club Legal Defense Fund brought a suit in 1986 for the Sierra Club, Wilderness Society, Northern Alaska Environmental Center, Nunam Kitlutsisti, and four other Native organizations against the BLM for failure to enforce protection standards or write an environmental impact statement for each placer-mining operation. Plaintiffs contended that fewer than 10 percent of sites showed evidence of reclamation, and that the BLM asked no bonding of miners as specified by law, and did not calculate impacts on subsistence users. Water quality laws went essentially unenforced; Native villages suffered deterioration of their drinking water, fishing, and trapping. Grayling apparently disappeared from some streams. Wild and scenic Birch Creek, naturally crystal-clear, flowed through 70 mining operations and gathered so much dirt as to obstruct mining itself. Most pollution came from mines of less than five acres; such operations comprised 80 percent of the 300 active placer mines in Alaska.[54]

While awaiting the court decision, the BLM agreed to execute many of the requested reforms beginning in 1986, and to provide enforcement data to the plaintiffs. In its May 1987 ruling, the district court halted all mining operations of more than five acres on three wild and scenic rivers after the 1987 season, pending individual environmental impact statements. "At the risk of belaboring the obvious," the court noted, "the transformation of the entire 126-mile length of Birch Creek National Wild River from a clean water stream to a silt-laden one is a significant environmental event" that "severely degraded the subsistence fishery. In short, the river appears to be practically barren." But the court upheld the BLM's practice of exempting small miners from regulation. The Sierra Club appealed the decision.[55] Draft impact

14.3. Placer mining, Kragness claim on Caribou Creek, Kantishna Hills, 1985. Courtesy National Park Service, Anchorage. This mining operation sparked a pivotal lawsuit by environmentalists.

statements by the BLM did not satisfy the environmentalists, and the conflict continued. In 1989 the BLM issued regulations mandating prior environmental evaluations of mine operations, stricter water quality provisions, and measures for reclamation of soil and vegetation.[56]

Environmentalists also targeted the National Park Service. Lacking staff and encouragement from the top, the service ventured almost no enforcement of mining regulations in the parks. Since 1978 the service had automatically issued approvals to applicants and written no site-specific environmental impact statements. Sierra Club Legal Defense Fund sued in 1985 on behalf of the Northern Alaska Environmental Center, Sierra Club/Alaska, and Denali Citizens Council. District court cited the mines as having "major adverse effects on fish habitat, water quality and scenic value." The court halted all mining operations in the parks pending impact statements for each. The Alaska Miners Association appealed and lost in 1986. The Park Service hired more than 30 additional employees to carry out enforcement. It presented its final impact statements in 1990, recommending that mining claims be bought out.[57]

The Park Service took miner/real-estate developer/secessionist Joe Vogler to court. To get to his claim on Woodchopper Creek, Vogler drove his bulldozer cross-country through the Yukon-Charley Rivers National Park and Preserve. Ruts up to two feet deep resulted from the one trip he made before being arrested. Vogler claimed precedence of R.S. 2477. Sierra Club Legal Defense Fund seconded the Park Service. It contended that if Vogler won, the state or other users could make a shambles of federal wildlands. A March 1987 district court ruling denied Vogler's claim, affirming the service's right to control lands by issuance or denial of permits. The circuit court upheld the Park Service in January 1989 and the U.S. Supreme Court refused to review.[58]

An interagency team (the Alaska Department of Fish and Game, BLM, EPA, and National Park Service) reviewed the status of placer mining in the mid-1990s. Owing in part to environmental lawsuits, some progress had been made in understanding the effects of placer operations and designing remedial measures. A state reclamation law had gone into effect in October 1991, and the BLM and the Park Service had enforced regulations and implemented a variety of experimental programs. Research showed that a placer operation typically disrupted a valley by changing the landforms, altering surface and groundwater flows, removing streamside vegetation and topsoil, silting fish habitat, reducing natural food supplies, and rendering the flood plain nonfunctional. Impacts could be lasting, and "many, if not most, miners and regulators believed that once a stream was disturbed it could not be reclaimed to a stable state." Effective remedial efforts needed to be interdisciplinary, taking into account the ecological characteristics of each stream valley. Involved parties should establish common goals, acquire training, and operate as working groups on both active and inactive sites. "Reclamation must be incorporated into the overall valuation of a mining project," said the team, and agencies should devote funding to public awareness.[59] In the late 1990s, a drop in the price of gold abated placer mining.

HUNTING IN THE PARKS

Alaskan resource issues returned to the national spotlight in the 1980s in a skirmish over hunting in the national parks. Alaska's congressional delegation introduced bills to open 12 million of the 32 million acres in Alaska closed to sport hunting. All but 8.5 percent of Alaskan lands, including national forests and national park preserves, national monuments, and wildlife refuges, already accommodated hunting.[60] James Watt saw the plan to widen hunting access as an opportunity to divide his enemies: "In a conflict between preservationists and sportsmen, we're going to the sportsmen. If there is a wedge to be driven between the conservation community, we'll help drive the wedge." Senator Stevens, who had vowed at the Alaska Lands Act signing ceremony to change its provisions, sponsored the hunting measure and promised, "The next bill I introduce will cover oil and gas and mining and timber and railroads . . . Hunters aren't going to help us with that . . . but eventually we'll win." Some observers interpreted the hunting legislation as an attempt to open more federal lands to commerce; others considered it a play for hunter votes in Stevens's reelection. Whatever the motive, it split the conservation groups. *Outdoor Life*, the National Wildlife Federation, and the National Rifle Association endorsed the bills, as did leaders of the newly formed Wildlife Legislation Fund who treated the issue as a national referendum on hunting and gun-ownership rights.[61]

Environmentalists regarded the proposal as an assault on the natural integrity of the parklands for the benefit of a small number of wealthy sport hunters. To fight it, the Alaska

14.4. National Park Service biologist Carol McIntyre studying gyrfalcon nest, Seward Peninsula, July 1992. By Layne Adams. American and Russian scientists conducted extensive research in the proposed Beringia International Heritage Park vicinity.

Coalition reactivated, enlisting 29 groups in 1983.[62] In Alaska the bill encountered opposition from Sierra Club/Alaska, Northern Alaska Environmental Center and other environmental groups, two Native corporations, the Tanana Chiefs, Alaska Association of Mountain and Wilderness Guides, and park concessionaires. Conditions favored the bill's opponents; Congress had no interest in an embarrassing, no-win fight to benefit the Alaska delegation. The Senate Energy Committee reduced the acreage from 12 million to 5 million acres and reported the bill without recommendation. Stevens did not pursue the issue in 1984, and it did not reappear.[63]

BERINGIA

The National Park Service worked for a Beringian Heritage International Park, linking lands on both sides of the Bering Strait to protect wildlife habitat, archaeological sites, and other elements of natural and cultural heritage. Acting on a 1972 U.S.-Soviet agreement on environmental cooperation, the service initiated the project in 1986. The 1972 agreement mandated a broad-based joint effort in pollution control and nature conservation. Its specific concerns included marine water quality and establishment of wildlife preserves in the Arctic and subarctic. Supported by Ford and Rockefeller Foundation funding, Audubon/Alaska engaged in research and planning for the Beringian park. Environmentalists from the two nations pressed for a marine biosphere component to safeguard surrounding ocean life, and to limit mining and drilling operations. Mining and oil companies sought access.[64] Presidents Bush and Gorbachev agreed on the park idea in June 1990, and in September the Soviet Council of Ministers ordered advancement of the plan. When the USSR dissolved, the succeeding Russian government reaffirmed the commitment.

In one early conception, the park would be comprised of a large segment of the Chukotka District on the western side of the Bering Strait, and Bering Land Bridge National Preserve and possibly others on the American side. Each nation would manage the segments of the park on its territory, and consult the other on matters of mutual concern. By 1994, nearly all Bering Strait villages on the U.S. side disapproved of the park plan, fearing restrictions on their subsistence activity. The nearby Northwest Arctic Native Association expressed interest in the Beringian park and joined the Park Service and Audubon Society in crafting a bill to include Cape Krusenstern National Monument, Kobuk Valley National Park, and Bering Land Bridge and Noatak National Preserves, but containing no marine component. The Beringian concept won endorsement by the Yeltsin and Clinton administrations, and awaited legislative action. No congressional vote had transpired by 2000, though the Chukotka government had instituted a Nature Ethnic Park-Beringia in 1993 and planned to extend it five miles offshore. Extensive cooperative research on both sides involved American, Russian, Japanese, and West European scientists, and the Park Service held an annual international Beringia Days conference in Anchorage.[65]

WILDERNESS

ANILCA, which set aside 57 million acres of wilderness, specified an Interior Department review and recommendation to Congress by 1988 of additional Alaskan lands to be classified wilderness. Of the 68 million acres in national parks and wildlife refuges identified by field staff as suitable candidates, Interior accepted only 8.1 million acres, but forwarded no recommendation to Congress.[66] By 1993, directors of the National Park Service and Fish and Wildlife Service had increased their accepted amounts to 7 million and 8.6 million acres, respectively. The Forest Service accepted 1.7 million acres. Responding to appeals by American Rivers and the national office of the Sierra Club Legal Defense Fund, the BLM modified its position in 1993 and agreed to review additional rivers for wild and scenic status.[67] BLM lands in Alaska contained an estimated 50 million acres qualifying for wilderness classification, and Forest Service lands another 7.2 million.[68] Yet by 2000, no proposals for wilderness designation had reached Congress.

A decade after the passage of ANILCA, environmentalists believed the federal government had not implemented it in good faith. Federal agencies holding responsibilities for wild lands lacked personnel to manage the vast tracts. Underfunding of personnel and research appeared to be part of a deliberate strategy of the Reagan and Bush administrations to maximize opportunity for private enterprise in national lands. Oil drilling, mining, tourism, logging, and hunting pressure impinged on wild areas. Little effort had been made to purchase inholdings threatening incompatible development. Permissive rules and decisions eased entry by motorized vehicles, utility transmission lines, and commercial activities. The Forest Service, BLM, and State of Alaska actively pursued road building and other intrusions.[69] Policies displayed more concern for the environment during the Clinton years, but Republican control made Congress an inhospitable environment for wilderness legislation.

Forces of exploitation got much of what they sought on federal lands in the 1980s and 1990s, but management practices evolved in the direction of sustainable use. Exercising their participation rights under the National Environmental Policy Act, water pollution laws, and other legislation, environmental advocates employed administrative and judicial procedures to prod government into action and force a modicum of agency and corporate accountability. Enforcement of protective regulations brought abuses to the land by mining and logging somewhat more firmly under control. Environmental guardians realized far less success in reserving wilderness and reducing inholdings, in large part because of counteraction by the Reagan and Bush administrations, the state, and its congressional delegation. The tug-of-war over use of national lands promised to go on indefinitely, expressing the conflicting interests of extractive industries, federal agencies, the state, Natives, hunters, tourists, environmentalists, and others.

NOTES

1. 94 Stat. 2371, December 2, 1980.

2. Cooley, "*Evolution* of Alaska Land Policy," 22, 37, 41, 44; 94 Stat. 2371, December 2, 1980, Sec. 802, 1501–1502, 1008, 1107, 1323, 1303, 1315, 1326.

3. Hession, " 'Good Neighbor' " 6–12; Wolf, "Interior Secretary," 7–8.

4. Leshy, "Natural Resources Policy," 17–19, 21–25, 31–32, 41.

5. Clusen, "Beyond Compromise," 14–17; Doherty, "Alaska: The Real National Lands Battle," 114–115; Watkins, "Perils of Expedience," 30–34.

6. *Sierra Club Alaska Newsletter*, July 1981, 3–5.

7. *Northern Line*, October 1981, 7; *Ravencall*, Fall 1981, 4; Jim Stratton, interview by author, July 21, 1988.

8. Dunlap, "Public Opinion on the Environment," 35.

9. Alaska Department of Natural Resources, Lands Information Office, personal communication, August 1993.

10. *U.S. Government Manual 1999–2000*, 309.

11. Ibid., 307–308.

12. Ibid., 136–137.

13. Ibid., 313–314; Alaska Land Use Council, "Alaska Lands"; Ed Bovy, personal communication, March 17, 2000.

14. *Northern Line*, September-October, 1983, 11; Reichardt, "1984 Issues," 4.

15. Kaye, "Paved or Pristine," pt. 1: 1, 8; pt. 2: 3.

16. *Northern Line*, August-September 1986, 1, 2, 8; McCargo, "The Front Burner," 2; E. Barnett, "Utility Corridor," 1, 8.

17. Hession, "Council Attempts," 1; *Alaska Report*, February 1985, 3–4.

18. Epler, "Judge Says No," 6–7; Hession, "Landmark St. Matthew Island Decision," 1–2; *New York Times*, August 11, 1983, 14; December 1, 1984, 24; December 2, 1984, 34; *National Audubon Society v. Hodel*, 606 F. Supp. 825 (1984).

19. *Alaska Report*, November 1984, 6–7; *Northern Line*, October-November 1986, 12; L. Adams, *Sierra Club Legal Defense Fund*, 1987, 12.

20. Hession, "House Passes Poor Bill," 1,7; Hession, "Committee Endorses Land Giveaway," 7; Public Law 100-395, August 16, 1988.

21. Hession, "Alaska's Protected Rivers," 6; *State of Alaska v. United States*, 662 F. Supp. 455 (1987).

22. T. Williams, "Alaska's Rush for the Gold," 52–53; *State of Alaska v. Babbitt* 72 F. 3rd 698 (9th Cir. 1995). Authority to identify applicable waterways would rest with federal agencies managing the respective lands.

23. L. Williams, "Comments Needed," 9; Finkelstein, "Chugach Forest Plan," 8; *Sierra Borealis*, Summer 1986, 4, 7; L. Adams, *Sierra Club Legal Defense Fund*, 1987, 5–6.

24. Phipps, "USFS Rejects Montague EIS Request," 2.

25. Stange, "Coalition Files Legal Challenge," 1, 8; Button, "Alaska Rainforest Campaign," 8.

26. Muir, *Travels in Alaska*, 44.

27. *Ravencall*, April 1979, 5; June 1980, 2–3; December 1980, 2, 16; Cuthbertson, "Stikine Update," 4; Cuthbertson, "Stikine-Iskut Dams," 1; Sisk, "Economics Undermine Stikine Dam," 10, 12; *Ravencall*, May-June 1986, 8.

28. Landry, "Alaska's Transportation Network," 8; L. Brown, "Road Schemes," 12–13; *Anchorage Daily News*, July 19, 1993, A1; Susan Peck, personal communication, March 22, 2000.

29. Heinrich, "Legal Decision," 19.

30. *Alaska Report*, "Alaska Bills in 105th Congress," 4–5.

31. McVee, "Issues Restricting Expansion," 5.

32. T. Williams, "Alaska's Rush for the Gold," 52.

33. Goodstein, "Placer Mining," 7, 9; D. Cook, *Placer Mining*, 7, 69–95; Robert B. Weeden and Jack Hession, interviews by author, July 12 and 15, 1988.

34. *Trustees for Alaska*, Fall 1985, 3; Spring 1987, 1–2; Summer 1987, 3; Spring-Summer 1988, 2; *Trustees for Alaska v. State* 736P. 2d. 324 (Alaska 1987). Other environmental plaintiffs were Alaska Center for the Environment, Friends of the Earth, and Southeast Alaska Conservation Council.

35. Glude, *1989 Session Wrapup*, 3; *Alaska Session Laws, 1989*, Chapter 101.

36. Kabisch, "View From Fourth Avenue," Fall 1982, 2; Parker, "Club Halts Invalid Mining Claims," 8.

37. Trustees for Alaska (TfA), *Summary*, 1988, 3; 1989, 2; Anna Phillip, interview by author, August 2, 1993.

38. *Ravencall*, November 1978, 15–16; Peale, "Borax Story," 6; Kueffner, "Southeast Alaska Conservation Council, Inc. v. Watson," 149–153, 172–173; *Southeast Alaska Conservation Council v. Watson,* 697 F. 2d 1305 (9th Cir. 1983).

39. L. Adams, *Sierra Club Legal Defense Fund*, 1987, 9; 1989, 8; Peale, "Borax: Which Misty Fjord?" 5, 7; U.S. Borax, *Fact Sheet*; Fuerst, "Playing Alaska's Natural Resource Hand," 25.

40. L. Adams, "U.S. Borax," 2, 7; Twitchell, "Borax Mine," 15.

41. Hession, "Noranda Mine," 3; Koehler and Peale, "Greens Creek Fate," 3; *Ravencall*, March-April 1986, 5; Spring 1996, 3.

42. *Alaska Report*, "British Columbia," 4–5; Enticknap, "Tatshenshini Wild, Forever," 1, 11.

43. Turner, "Of Gold Fever," 32.

44. R. Rogers, "Placer Mining in Alaska," 10.

45. Swan, "Placer Miners Run Amuck," 6; Flaharty, "Alaska Waters Threatened," 7–8; *Trustees for Alaska*, Fall 1985, 2; Spring 1987, 2.

46. E. Smith, "Placer Mining: A Threat," 6–7; R. Rogers, "Northern Center Involvement," 7–8; R. Rogers, "Where Did the Cooperative Spirit Go?" 2; *Trustees for Alaska*, Fall 1985, 3; *Miners Advocacy Council v. State Department of Environmental Conservation*, 778 P. 2d 1126 (Alaska 1989).

47. TfA, *Summary*, 1988, 3; *Trustees for Alaska*, December, 1989, 3.

48. *Northern Line*, January-February 1987, 2.

49. Blazer, "Water Quality and Mining," 12.

50. S. Cook, "Do Wild Rivers," 5; C. Hunter, "This Our Land," December 1985, 36.

51. Warren, "BLM Does It Again," 2; C. Hunter, "Do We Care," 1, 4.

52. Warren, "Public Outraged," 1, 10.

53. R. Rogers, "Placer Mining in Alaska," 11.

54. McGeye, "Steese and White Mountains," 5; R. R. Weeden, "Mining Regulations Go Unenforced," 6; R. Rogers, "NAEC Sues BLM," 1, 12; L. Adams, *Sierra Club Legal Defense Fund*, 1987, 7.

55. L. Adams, *Sierra Club Legal Defense Fund*, 1987, 7; R. Rogers, "Placer Miners Will Operate," 5; *Northern Line*, "Rivers Given New Lease," 1; R. Rogers, "Placer Mining in Alaska," 11; *Sierra Club v. Penfold* 664 F. Supp. 1299 (D. Alaska 1987).

56. R. Rogers, "Placer Mining: Comment Now," 6, 8; *Northern Line*, July-September 1988, 5; L. Adams, *Sierra Club Legal Defense Fund*, 1989, 7.

57. L. Adams, *Sierra Club Legal Defense Fund*, 1987, 6; C. Hunter, "This Our Land," December 1985, 36, 107; *New York Times*, October 25, 1986, 6; Watkins, "The Perils of Expedience," 68; *Northern Alaska Environmental Center v. Hodel* 803 F 2d 466 (9th Cir. 1986); Lauri Adams, interview by author, July 14, 1989.

58. L. Adams, *Sierra Club Legal Defense Fund*, 1987, 7–8; 1989, 7; *U.S. v. Vogler,* 859 F. 2d 638 (9th Cir. 1988); *Vogler v. U.S.*, 109 S. Ct. 1988.

5956. Zufelt et. al., "Aquatic Habitat Restoration," 79–83.

60. Wayburn, "Hunters Take Aim," 16–17.

61. Norris, "Alaska: Hunters Aim," 129–134.

62. *Wilderness*, "News, Notes," 39–40.

63. Finkelstein, "Decision Expected," 3; Kabisch, "View From Fourth Avenue," Fall 1983, 2.

64. W. Brown, "A Common Border," 18–23; Cline, *Work Plan for 1989–90*, 2; Graham, "U.S. and Soviet Environmentalists," 44, 49, 54–58; 23 UST 845, May 23, 1972.

65. *Beringian Notes*, June 26, 1992, 2–3; February 2, 1999, 1, 3–4, 7; John Quinley, interview by author, July 29, 1993.

66. Wilderness Society, *The Alaska Lands Act*, 1–7.

67. Pamela A. Miller, letter to author, April 7, 1994; Sierra Club Legal Defense Fund, *In Brief*, Autumn 1993, 15.

68. A. Smith, "Wilderness Management," 11.

69. Wilderness Society, *The Alaska Lands Act*, 1–7

15

Trouble in the Tongass

No Alaska federal land issue more clearly illustrated the collision of resource exploitation and sustainability values than logging in the Tongass National Forest. It pitted a determined group of environmentalists against a powerful agency and its client timber companies, competing for the favor of the local and national publics and legislatures. Critics of the Forest Service insistently raised questions of accountability for the social and environmental effects of clear-cut logging. Resolution of the issues depended on research and public involvement; thus the match progressed on both political and scientific grounds. At stake lay the ecological integrity of the world's most extensive temperate rainforest.

Alaska's southeast coastal region is mountainous and profusely forested; about 80 percent is in the 16.7-million-acre Tongass National Forest, largest in the national forest system. It is a drowned coast of large and small islands and a mainland infused by fiords. Above 1,800 feet, alpine tundra predominates and unmelted snow forms ice fields and numerous glaciers, rendering the scenery spectacular. As much as 200 inches of precipitation at sea level and 350 inches at higher levels sustain a temperate rainforest, one of the few remaining on earth. Sitka spruce, the highest-quality tree for building and crafts, comprised about 12 percent of the original forest trees, commonly reached a diameter of 7 feet and height of 200 feet, and could live 600 years. Western hemlock made up about 73 percent of the forest trees, grew to 3 or 4 feet in diameter, and could attain a height of 170 feet and an age of 800 years. The remainder of the trees consisted mostly of red and yellow cedar.[1] Marten, Sitka deer, mountain goats, wolves, river otters, black and grizzly bears, and bald eagles frequented these coniferous forests. In the coastal zone lived whales, porpoises, sea lions, harbor seals, sea otters, crabs, shrimp, and fish in abundance. By one count, 57 species of fish and shellfish, 83 species of mammals, and 303 species of birds inhabited or visited the region. In the 1970s, approximately 85 percent of U.S. salmon came from Alaska and 40 percent of these returned to rivers in the Southeast.[2]

Its rich store of resources destined Southeast Alaska for environmental turmoil. Many men died for sea otter pelts in the Russian era, and great nations jostled for geopolitical position. Sierra Club founder John Muir arrived in 1879—one year after the opening of the first salmon cannery and one year before the Juneau gold strike. Competing furiously, canners did their best to catch every last salmon, running roughshod over Native claims and public lands as well. With the canneries and the gold stampedes came waste of wildlife and accelerated disintegration of Native culture. Salmon catches fell off precipitously between the 1930s and 1950s, but the land remained relatively unaltered through the first half of the twentieth century. Efforts to designate Admiralty and other large islands as brown bear sanctuaries came to naught, though the bears suffered no appreciable loss of population.

Massive clear-cut logging in the Tongass National Forest, begun in the 1950s, represented a quantum leap in exploitative behavior in the Southeast. Yet Alaska could not escape the gathering national interest in wilderness protection. And few issues contributed more to environmental concern about Alaska, or the growth of the Alaskan environmental community, than Tongass logging. A combination of historical connections, local membership, and imperilment of wilderness motivated Sierra Club involvement. Its local chapters strengthened their organization, energizing the Alaskan environmental community. State and national environmentalists mounted an offensive against clear-cut logging. Southeast Alaska became the scene of one of the longest and most contentious of American environmental conflicts.

PRE-STATEHOOD FOREST USE

Humans left almost no mark on the southeastern forests before the twentieth century. Tlingit, Haida, and Tsimshian Indians used wood for houses, canoes, artwork, and fuel. Russians erected sawmills and built nearly 25 ships including a steamer in 1841, most at their capital of Sitka. They exported some charcoal and lumber to Mexico and China. The advent of canneries and gold mining under American rule in 1878 generated demand for wood used in building and mine construction, fish barriers, and packing cases. Eleven sawmills operated in the southeast in 1890, yet most lumber came from the States.[3]

Twentieth-century Tongass politics had roots in the Harriman Expedition of 1899, which numbered among its scientists former Division of Forestry chief Bernard Fernow. Scrutinizing the forests of the Southeast, Fernow judged them too far from markets for successful lumber commerce, but thought a pulp industry should be instituted. President Theodore Roosevelt ordered a feasibility survey carried out in 1901. Geographer Henry Gannett, also on the 1899 expedition, disagreed with Fernow. He saw the Tongass not as a pulp supply but as a recreation reserve: "Its grandeur is more valuable than the fish or timber, for it will never be exhausted. This value, measured by direct return in money received from tourists, will be enormous; measured by health and pleasure it will be incalculable."[4] Smoldering for over half a century, this difference over the value of the Tongass erupted into a dispute lasting for decades.

Alaska's forests soon came to the attention of Gifford Pinchot, Roosevelt's forestry chief. In 1905 Congress transferred the Forest Service, as well as the forest reserves, from the Interior Department to the Department of Agriculture. Roosevelt set aside as reserves parts of the Tongass National Forest (so named in 1907) between 1902 and 1909, and reserved the Chugach National Forest in 1907.[5] Pinchot wrote territorial governor John G. Brady on August 16, 1904, to explain his intentions:

> Forest reserves are not parks or game preserves, and the chief aim in their management is to provide for a practical, systematic, and conservative use of their various products.

15.1. Tongass National Forest, 1993. Courtesy U.S. Forest Service, Juneau.

In the administration of forest reserves the Government's policy is guided by the follow-ing general principles: All the land should be devoted to its most productive use. All the resources of forest reserves should be used, and so used as to make them permanent. The dominant industry should be considered first and with as little restrictions of minor industries as may be possible. . . . Timber, wood, and other forest products should be sold upon application at the market value and under such restrictions only as will insure a permanent forest growth. The establishment of forest reserves in Alaska will effectually prevent any individual or corporation from monopolizing the timber supply, and will remove the danger of extensive exploitation to the detriment of local industries. . . . I may add, the prosperity of the Indians will follow regular employment in logging.[6]

Industry-oriented Alaskans tended to regard Pinchot as a radical conservationist, a barrier to growth in Alaska. Yet Pinchot evidenced no concern for wildlife or outdoor recreation; he viewed forests as repositories of wood or minerals. Within a narrow utilitarian framework, he did his utmost to serve the public through sustainable use of resources. But he could not predict economics, political trends, or technology a half-century in advance, and his faith that the Forest Service could remain uncorrupted would later seem naive. Nor was he able to appreciate the growing interest in recreation and wildlife conservation, or the ecological principles that would throw his notions of utilitarianism into question.

Pinchot's plan nearly derailed in the 1920s when Interior Secretary Albert B. Fall proposed that jurisdiction over national forests be returned to the Interior Department. President Warren G. Harding favored the idea but Pinchot, by then out of government service, mounted strong opposition, as did Forest Service chief William B. Greeley. To dedicate the Alaska Railroad, Harding embarked on a fateful trip, the first to the territory by a U.S. president, in July 1923. Greeley and Secretary of Agriculture Henry Wallace accompanied Harding and persuaded him not to support the transfer. They may have been assisted by emerging Teapot Dome revelations, soon to envelop Secretary Fall. On his return trip in San Francisco, Harding died. National Forests remained under the Department of Agriculture.[7]

Designation of forest reserves followed by annual inspections put a damper on illegal commercial logging operations in the Southeast. Alaskans commonly regarded reserves as additional federal restrictions on their freedom to prosper, imposed on behalf of outside interests. In its first session in 1913 the territorial legislature resolved that the reserves should be abolished and the lands "thrown open to the general use of the prospector, miner, and settler." Reinforcing territorial suspicions, the Merchant Marine (Jones) Act of 1920 stipulated that ships operating between U.S. ports be U.S.-owned and operated. The act exempted Canadian ships except for Alaska ports. This exemption benefited the Seattle shippers, drove up costs, and shut down some Alaskan mills. However, a 1926 law prohibited the export of unprocessed logs, a measure intended to assist local economies.

Surveys of the Tongass aimed to employ its resources to facilitate economic expansion in the new territory. Pursuant to Fernow's vision, Forest Service officials placed their main bets on a pulp industry. Between 1913 and 1927, companies made five attempts to operate pulp mills; all fizzled out because of costs. The only operational mill existed briefly at Speel River south of Juneau and closed in 1923.[8] Sawmill activity persevered. The Ketchikan Spruce Mill, set up in 1898, sold wood to Britain, France, Italy, and Japan for construction of World War I aircraft. Before and during World War II, Sitka spruce supplied lumber, railroad ties, musical instruments, aircraft, and military construction in the Pacific.[9] Also, beginning in the 1940s, a swelling Alaskan population placed a greater demand on the forests.

Prime credit for progress of the timber industry belonged to one of the early Alaska surveyors for the Forest Service, B. Frank Heintzleman, who moved up to regional director for Alaska in 1937 and governor during 1953–1957. A strong proponent of economic growth through the pulp industry, he incidentally built a political base in the process. Following

World War II his plan encountered a series of changed conditions. Alaska sat in an economic slump, and adherents of statehood needed a growing population base and industrial foundation. One possiblility for the Southeast presented itself: at least temporarily, the nation experienced a severe shortage of newsprint. The timing seemed fortuitous for an effort to create a pulp industry.

Native land rights posed the main political barrier to an Alaskan timber industry. But a national debate pitted defenders of Native American land settlements against those favoring policies to assimilate Natives. A 1946 Indian Claims Act entitled Natives to sue the U.S. government for resolution of land claims. Interior Secretary Harold Ickes, a champion of land rights for Native Americans, left office in 1946. Another bill intended to provide a land settlement for the Southeast Alaskan Indians evolved into an authorization for Forest Service timbering nearly devoid of consideration for the Indians. The Tongass Timber Sales Act of 1947 empowered the secretary of agriculture to sell Tongass timber rights, and hold the money in escrow for possible compensation of Natives.[10] Tlingits from Southeast Alaska, believing much of the Tongass to be theirs, objected to the bill. In violation of a strict prohibition of lobbying by government employees, Heintzleman took action. By telegram he requested that his south Tongass assistant "have Bob Jernberg come to Washington, D.C. and represent the non-Indian sentiment. Tongass bill in trouble. Bob representing Chamber of Commerce can be of great help. Needed by Monday morning. Destroy this message." Jernberg and two others met Heintzleman, and the three went to see Senator Warren Magnuson of Washington, their main backer, and Senator William Langer of North Dakota, their main adversary. They persuaded Langer, winning the bill's passage.[11] The Alaska Native Brotherhood termed the Tongass Act "Alaska's Teapot Dome." Indians won a 1959 court of claims judgment, finally receiving payment of $7.5 million in 1965.[12] In 1971, Congress acted comprehensively on Alaska Native land claims (Chapter 13).

As regional director and as governor, Heintzleman played an instrumental part in arranging 50-year logging contracts for three major companies, two American and one Japanese. The Forest Service justified the extraordinarily generous terms, guaranteeing access to billions of board feet of prime timber, by citing the costs of investment in Alaska. Japan, having lost southern Sakhalin Island to the Russians, had approached the Americans after World War II in search of a wood supply for reconstruction. Another of its options might be to purchase wood from the Soviet Union, an option not favored by U.S. officials. The war had emphasized the strategic importance of Alaska and generated impetus for its settlement. Ketchikan Pulp Company signed a contract in 1951 and started pulp mill operations in Ketchikan in 1954, to cut a total of 8.25 billion board feet on Revillagigedo and Prince of Wales Islands. The Japanese-owned Alaska Pulp Company (also known as Alaska Lumber and Pulp) signed in 1953 and opened its mill at Sitka in 1959. It bought out the contract that Pacific Northern Timber Company signed in 1954. Alaska Pulp held rights to cut 5.25 billion board feet on Baranof and Chichagof Islands.[13] As the Forest Service executed its plan for commercial development, the Alaska Statehood Act of 1958 granted the state 400,000 acres to be chosen from the Tongass and Chugach National Forests. State selections began in the early 1960s. The act also allocated 25 percent of Forest Service timber sale receipts to the state,[14] an arrangement ensuring allies for the Forest Service in the emerging contest over logging.

15.1. Loggers taking down Sitka spruce, Southeast Alaska. Courtesy Alaska State Historical Library Archives, Juneau. More than half of the largest old-growth trees in the Tongass National Forest had been cut by the 1980s.

EARLY OPPOSITION TO LOGGING

Postwar construction demands intensified the cutting of national forests, shifting timber production to the top of the Forest Service priority list. Seeing that roads and clear-cutting increasingly endangered the existence of wild tracts, conservation groups began in the mid-1950s to work for a Wilderness Act, ultimately succeeding in 1964. Responding to the pressure, the Forest Service secured passage in 1960 of the Multiple Use-Sustained Yield Act. Forests would be managed according to the service's traditional principle of sustained yield, for timber, grazing, recreation, watershed protection, and fish and wildlife purposes. Power to define "sustained yield" and "multiple use" resided in the Department of Agriculture.[15] In the Tongass, large-scale changes took place. Compared to prewar outfits of a dozen or fewer hand-loggers wielding crosscut saws, the new logging camps housed a hundred or more families. Chain saws and bulldozers multiplied the impact on the environment. Clear-cut areas, normally limited to 320 acres, sometimes stretched for miles.[16] The logging left narrow strips of trees at recreation sites and along Alaska Marine Highway routes.

Conservationists reacted. *Field and Stream* editor Frank Dufresne and bear guides Ralph Young and Karl Lane, convinced of permanent damage to salmon streams, brown

15.2. Dixie Baade at Helm Bay, 1962. Courtesy Dixie Baade. One of Alaska's first and longest-active environmentalists.

bears, and other wildlife, protested in the 1950s. A division emerged among sportsmen; Territorial Sportsmen of Juneau led by A. W. "Bud" Boddy subscribed to the Forest Service argument characterizing clear-cutting impacts as minimal and temporary. Existing scientific data could not settle the question. Fish and Wildlife Service biologist David Klein and others studied logging effects on bears between 1957 and 1966, recommending that caution be exercised pending more evidence, and that interagency cooperation be enhanced. Forest Service studies indicated no harmful effects on salmon by stream silting, but other biologists did not trust the results. Beginning in 1962 the Alaska Department of Fish and Game, supported by Southeast Alaska Trollers and other groups, appealed to the Forest Service to set aside key watersheds for salmon protection. Partial compliance did not stem the growing dispute.[17]

Reflecting national trends, environmentalists began to add their voices to those of utilitarian conservationists. Nearly all environmental groups in the Southeast before 1989 originated in the logging controversy. Most initial leaders had connections to the preserva-

15.3. Jack Calvin, ca. 1980. Courtesy Margaret Calvin. An early Southeast Alaska environmental activist and author.

tionist Sierra Club, and several groups were affiliates of the Alaska Conservation Society. Their inspiration came from the 1964 Wilderness Act (detailing a process for wilderness designation), the advancing destruction of the forests, and air and water pollution from the pulp mills and logging operations.

One of the earliest leaders in the Southeast, Dixie Baade (1919–1991), had been a Sierra Club member since 1936. Working through the Southeast Alaska Mountaineers Association and other groups, she pursued wilderness status for outstanding areas including Misty Fjords and Tracy Arm/Ford's Terror. In a politically hostile environment, she sought to curb water pollution from the Ketchikan Spruce Mill.[18] Baade sensed a fundamental contradiction between the behavior of southeastern resource exploiters and the environmental quality that made it appealing to live in Alaska: "The history of the area is notable for the number who have 'made it' here and gone 'outside' to retire. With this general attitude of 'make it and get out' it is not surprising to find an apathy toward what is happening to the wildlife, the scenery and the wilderness. The wilderness exists to be conquered and there is nothing precious in the minds of these people other than the monetary gains from this conquest."[19]

Another of Alaska's original environmentalists, Jack Calvin (1901–1985), first arrived in the 1920s and made a 1932 canoe trip from Tacoma to Juneau, featured in *National Geographic*. A nature writer and tour guide, Calvin devoted his time to environmental protection. Assisted by the Sierra Club, he organized the Sitka Conservation Society in 1965. The

15.4. Richard J. Gordon, Juneau, 1977. Courtesy Richard Gordon. An activist in Alaska Lands Act proceedings, Gordon founded Southeast Alaska Conservation Council (SEACC), one of the most successful environmental organizations.

society called for forest planning and drew up an ultimately successful wilderness proposal for West Chichagof/Yakobi Island. In 1975 Governor Jay Hammond named Calvin "Alaskan Conservationist of the Year."[20]

A third activist in the southeast, Sierra Club member Richard Gordon, organized the forerunner of Southeast Alaska Conservation Council (SEACC) in 1969. The council set about drafting a coordinated set of proposals for wilderness tracts in forest areas.[21] SEACC survived to lead the campaign for preservation in the Tongass and become one of the most active and successful environmental organizations in Alaska. Gordon also spent 13 years writing about Admiralty Island and endeavoring to establish parks in Gates of the Arctic, Noatak, and other parts of the Arctic.[22]

An Alaska field office of the Sierra Club (Sierra Club/Alaska) originated in Anchorage in 1968, formed by the conservation committee of the Mountaineering Club. By 1970 affiliated groups existed in Fairbanks, Juneau, and Sitka. The Sierra Club had become the first national environmental organization to open a branch office in Alaska, concentrating mainly on wilderness and other land reservations.[23]

Georgia-born Ed Wayburn, a San Francisco medical doctor and former Sierra Club president, crucially facilitated Sierra Club success in Alaska. A 1967 visit to the state inspired Wayburn and his wife, Peggy, to invest their efforts in the preservation of its wilderness. Upon returning to San Francisco, Wayburn won approval for and assumed leadership of the

15.5. Ed and Peggy Wayburn, middle fork of the Koyukuk, 1989. Courtesy Ed Wayburn. Among the most influential private individuals in Alaskan environmental issues, the Wayburns became active in 1967.

Sierra Club's new Alaska Task Force, serving in that capacity through the 1990s. The Wayburns conducted a public campaign in the Lower 48, helped organize environmental groups in Alaska, and lobbied in Washington for land preservation bills, expressing special interest in Admiralty Island.[24]

LAWSUITS AND LOGGING PLANS IN THE 1970s

Central to the Tongass National Forest issue lay a difference in valuation of trees. Traditionally, foresters tended to regard a tree as so many board feet of timber, and a forest as a supply of trees. They judged old-growth (virgin) forests "overripe" or "rotten," and cutting them good for the "health" of the forest, an argument that persuaded many a private landowner to give over an ancient forest to loggers. The Forest Service's 1964 management guide for Alaska stated, "About 95% of the commercial forest of southeastern Alaska is occupied by overmature stands of hemlock, spruce and cedar. Silviculturally these decadent stands should be removed by clear-cutting methods as soon as possible to make way for new stands of fast growing second growth timber."[25] It was the "decadent" stands of large trees, however, that the industry most eagerly sought for their large, high-quality, readily accessible volumes of lumber and pulp.

Environmentalists perceived trees, particularly large old ones, as far more than isolated species of plant life and bundles of wood fiber. Trees in their view provided food, housing, and shelter to a community of plants, insects, fish, birds, and mammals. They formed integral

15.6. Old growth, near Kadashan River, Chichagof Island, Tongass National Forest, 1980. Courtesy John W. Schoen. Giant trees sustain a unique complex of wildlife.

and vital, often core, elements of natural ecosystems. Removal of the old trees in the Tongass would in large measure destroy the forest ecosystem of the Southeast. Thus environmental ists felt duty-bound to contravene Forest Service policy in the Tongass. Local groups, the national Sierra Club, and state and federal biologists led the drive for change in the 1970s.

Since the mid-1950s, events in Southeast Alaska had been building toward a grand confrontation. The first 50-year contracts committed hundreds of thousands of acres to clear-cutting, eventually raising protests from wildlife managers, sport hunters, sport and commercial fishing groups, small-town residents, and environmentalists. In 1965 regional forester W. Howard Johnson announced another 50-year timber contract for St. Regis Paper Company. Called the "Juneau Unit," it involved the biggest timber sale on record. It allowed for cutting 674,000 acres on the mainland near Juneau and Yakutat, and 416,000 on west Admiralty Island—a stronghold of the brown bears. A pulp mill would be constructed in the vicinity of Juneau. Added to the Ketchikan Pulp Company and Alaska Pulp Company contracts, it would commit 98.4 percent of the prime old-growth timber in the Tongass to logging. Each segment would be subject to harvesting every 100 to 120 years.[26] Johnson described the Tongass as "the last place in the country where substantial amounts of timber are available to support new industries."[27]

Unable to meet its contract obligations, St. Regis defaulted. In September 1968, without a public auction or public announcement, the Forest Service awarded the contract to U.S. Plywood-Champion Papers Inc.[28] When the company announced in December 1969 its

15.7. Clear-cut at Sitkoh Lake, Chichagof Island, Tongass National Forest, 1970s. Courtesy John W. Schoen. After clear-cutting, the rain forest requires 200 to 300 years to recover its ecological role.

intent to build a $100-million pulp plant at Echo Cove 40 miles north of Juneau, the Sierra Club sued. Because the case revolved around the definition of multiple use, it carried important implications for the future of all national forests. Four plaintiffs appeared in *Sierra Club v. Hardin*: the national Sierra Club, City of Angoon, Sitka Conservation Society, and bear guide Karl Lane. Sitka Conservation Society won standing based on its demonstrated interest in forest protection, and Karl Lane owing to his guiding business on Admiralty Island. Defendants included Secretary of Agriculture Clifford Hardin, Secretary of the Interior Walter Hickel, regional forester W. Howard Johnson, and Tongass forest supervisor Vincent Olson. U.S. Plywood and the State of Alaska joined the defense. Plaintiffs claimed violation of the multiple-use mandate and improper environmental studies and sale procedure. They argued the sale would create "an inflexible schedule of harvesting substantially all of the operable virgin growth timber in Southeast Alaska, to the exclusion of all other legitimate uses of such forests."[29]

District court convened at Juneau in February 1971. Ed Wayburn, representing the Sierra Club and its 400 Alaskan members, cited the club's interest, expressed as early as 1932, in making Admiralty Island a national park. Guide Ralph Young described the effects of clear-cutting on Admiralty Island's Whitewater Bay: "There used to be twenty-five to thirty bears there, when the salmon were in. Now the salmon waters are silted, the fish gone, and except for an occasional stray there are no bears in the area." Defendants denied the validity of all charges, claiming full authority of the Forest Service to conduct the sale. One statement justified the timber plan in part by the amount of "defective, old-growth timber" in the sale area.[30] Within a month the judge ruled against the plaintiffs on every count, suggesting they should have appealed earlier, and that Congress had in effect empowered the Forest Service to define multiple use. The case went to the appeals court, which remanded it to the district court for reconsideration.

A 1973 report by A. Starker Leopold, director of a team of seven ecologists hired by U.S. Plywood to conduct a wildlife impact assessment for the 50-year project, materially influenced the case. Rather than serving as an apologist for the plan, Leopold counseled that "the days of massive clear-cutting of whole watersheds have passed. Particularly on public lands, timber harvest schemes must take account of the full spectrum of social values." The proposed plan, he said, "seems to us to imply a level of timber removal in Southeast Alaska that is unrealistic by present day standards of ecologic acceptability." The team recommended that clear-cuts be restricted to one-third of a locality at a given time, and that 15 percent of commercially valuable timber tracts be retained for scenery and wildlife conservation.[31] The Leopold study precipitated the circuit court's remanding of *Sierra Club v. Hardin* to the district court.[32] Reduced acreage lowered the potential profit margin of U.S. Plywood, leaving the Juneau Unit less viable.

In 1976, U.S. Plywood and the Forest Service mutually canceled the Juneau venture. Company officials indicated that cost increases made it uneconomical.[33] Others believed the Forest Service had overcommitted the timber supply, that not enough existed to meet the demands of all 50-year contracts, the state, and the Natives.[34] The Alaska Department of Natural Resources had written to the Forest Service recommending cancellation of the sale.[35]

In part, the Juneau Unit folded because of changing national values. Appreciation of wilderness had grown steadily over the decade of the project's life, casting clear-cutting of public forests in a negative light. Under mounting pressure, the Forest Service made attempts to respond. It agreed to abstain from logging in West Chichagof/Yakobi from 1971 to 1976 pending review for possible wilderness status. Beginning in 1971 it invited citizen comments on management plans affecting their localities. It instituted eagle-protection measures on segments of Admiralty Island.[36]

Forest Service efforts fell short of satisfying the critics, and lawsuits persisted. The Sierra Club sued in 1972 to require environmental impact statements for cutting plans; the Forest Service agreed to do so in an out-of-court settlement.[37] In 1975, the Tongass Conservation Society headed a team of environmentalists and commercial fishing groups in a suit to prevent 60 clear-cuts at Point Baker-Port Protection on Prince of Wales Island. All logging operations were to take place within five miles of Port Protection, including construction of a camp for workers outnumbering the townspeople. In *Zieske v. Butz* the district court ruled for the plaintiffs, finding that no law authorized the practice of clear-cutting. As a result of several lawsuits, logging ceased on 800,000 acres across the nation for six months pending legalization of clear-cutting by the 1976 National Forest Management Act.[38] Responding to the nationwide controversy over clear-cutting and the dominant emphasis on timbering, the law also attempted to incorporate public comment in logging plans, reinforce the sustained-yield principle, and lay out more-explicit guidelines for management plans in each national forest.[39] Increasingly the Forest Service and timber industry came under attack from several quarters. Federal officials cited Ketchikan Pulp Company for water pollution in 1970. Storage of logs in Ward Cove, and discharge of sulfite waste into the cove and Tongass Narrows, endangered marine life. A similar investigation revealed a kill of 100,000 fish in Silver Bay near the Alaska Pulp Company plant in September 1970. Jack Calvin described the water as so foul that a boat passing through left a wake of foam lasting for hours. The fish kill resulted from hydrogen sulfide, probably from the plant. Alaska Pulp Company agreed to install a primary treatment facility.[40]

Competing ownership claims turned up the pressure on the forests. The Forest Service managed the Juneau Unit sale, as it had the three earlier long-term sales, exhibiting minimal regard for state or Native claims. The Alaska Statehood Act guaranteed the state a total of 400,000 acres to be chosen from the Tongass and Chugach National Forests, though not if precluding Native claims. Based on the Alaska Native Claims Settlement Act of 1971, Southeast Natives could ultimately take 564,000 acres of the Tongass. The state and Natives made some selections in the 1970s, but the process could not be finalized prior to passage of the Alaska Lands Act in 1980. Natives complained that the timber tracts they preferred had already been committed in Forest Service sales.[41]

Logging disputes also involved salmon and bald eagles. Southeastern Alaska Trollers requested in 1971 that logging along major streams be halted.[42] A poll of Alaska Department of Fish and Game (ADF&G) biologists rated logging as the main single peril for salmon populations. Surveys of eagle nesting on Admiralty Island revealed that despite the Forest Service–Fish and Wildlife Service agreement banning cutting within 330 feet of an eagle-nest tree, nesting actually dropped off within a mile of clear-cut areas.[43] The 1968 agreement had been engineered by Fish and Wildlife agent Fred Robards, who, in the words of a friend, "thought he could save more eagles this way than by trying to catch some hapless logger felling an eagle nest tree." Robards hoped to find enough eagle nests to create overlapping sanctuaries and save most of the beachfront old-growth forest. He spent so much time at the task that administrators transferred him out of the law enforcement division, thereby decreasing his pay and benefits.[44] Robards and fellow agent Jack Hodges estimated in 1979 that current plans for timber removal would degrade or eliminate 90 percent of eagle nesting and perching habitat.[45]

Research done in 1977–1978 by ADF&G biologists John Schoen and Olof "Charlie" Wallmo demonstrated that, contrary to previous notions, clear-cutting harmed Sitka black-tailed deer. A key species, the deer supplied food for humans as well as wolves, bears, and other wildlife. Stands of even-aged trees created by clear-cutting shaded out undergrowth for decades and sustained only one-fifth to one-seventh as many deer as did old-growth stands.[46] Fortified by such data, ADF&G attempted to redirect Forest Service logging policy.

15.8. Second growth, 147 years old (after burn), Admiralty Island, Tongass National Forest, 1978. By John W. Schoen. Dense and even-aged, second growth shades out understory plants, greatly reducing flora and fauna diversity.

Its requests dating back to 1962 had urged Forest Service cooperation in identification and protection of the most critically important wildlife habitat. The appeals bore hardly any fruit. In 1975 the Fish and Wildlife Service presented a list of places including Admiralty Island that it believed should not be logged. This too proved unsuccessful.[47] Such rebuffs prompted the Alaska chapter of the the Wildlife Society (the professional wildlife managers' association) to break from its apolitical tradition. It demanded that Forest Service policies be revised and that "finally, the Alaskan and U.S. public must be fully informed about the long-term and, from a practical standpoint, permanent and irreversible consequences for fish and wildlife of current forest practices in Southeast Alaska. Of critical importance is the concept that the coastal climax forest of Southeast Alaska is, under existing forest management policy, a nonrenewable resource."[48]

Environmental advocates strove to have lands preserved under the Wilderness Act. Pursuant to the act, the Forest Service classified 2.27 million acres of the Tongass as "wilderness study areas." Critics characterized the acreage as "rock and ice"—high and steep lands devoid of heavy timber and its aggregation of wildlife.[49] In 1975 the Forest Service presented a draft ten-year plan for management of the Tongass National Forest. Southeast Alaska Conservation Council drafted a "citizens' alternate" plan for consideration by the Forest Service. It identified 45 key habitat areas as needing safeguarding: 18 watersheds, 17 roadless recreation areas, 9 wilderness areas, and 1 wild river.[50] The Forest Service rejected virtually all the suggestions, and displayed a lack of solicitude for wildlife or wilderness. Jack Calvin expressed a widely shared view of the agency by environmentalist sypathizers in the 1970s:

> The new scourge of the land is the pulp and paper industry, aided and abetted in its depredations by the U.S. Forest Service. . . . Like all old bureaus, the once highly respected Forest Service has grown inflexible. It has been unable to comprehend or respond to the change in public attitude toward the environment. It feels heckled and angry. In spite of the bitter criticism that it must absorb every day, it plows doggedly ahead with its policy of helping a wealthy industry to get wealthier. The fact that the forest belongs to the people eludes it. The various uses of the forest mentioned in the enabling act besides logging get lip service, at most. The result of the present single-minded management is temporary prosperity for the industry and long-term disaster for Southeast Alaska.[51]

Admiralty Island stood out in the minds of conservationists and environmentalists, who for decades had sought protection for its brown bear population. Friends of Admiralty produced a film by Joel Bennett titled *Fortress of the Bears*, and presented their ideas for Admiralty Island in the summer 1973 issue of *Alaska Geographic*. They suggested creation of a "Wild Forest of Admiralty" under Forest Service jurisdiction, proscribing logging but not hunting, and specifying no definite ban on mining. The Juneau Unit contract would be bought back by Congress, or other timber substituted.[52] Other environmentalists preferred to seek wilderness status for Admiralty so as to preclude both logging and mining. President Carter fulfilled their wish by including the vast majority of Admiralty Island and Misty Fjords in the national monuments he named in 1978.

As the 1970s drew to a close, environmental defenders lost hope that the Forest Service would spare old-growth forest in the Tongass. National legislation seemed their best remaining avenue. Both sides appealed effectively to Congress. Abandoning its 1975 proposal, the Forest Service adopted a 1979 plan somewhat less completely oriented to timber production, apparently intending to influence the Alaska National Interest Lands Conservation Act (ANILCA). The Forest Service and industry triumphed when the Senate version became law, bearing lavish guarantees of federal patronage for timbering. ANILCA also specified millions of acres of wilderness in the Southeast: West Chichagof/Yakobi, most of Admiralty Island and Misty Fjords, Stikine-LeConte, Tracy Arm-Ford's Terror, Endicott River, South Baranof, Petersburg Creek-Duncan Salt Chuck, Tebenkof Bay, South Prince of Wales, and Coronation, Warren, and Maurelle Islands.[53] Environmental guardians got much of what they wanted, yet a high percentage of old-growth forest stood to be logged.

LOGGING IMPACT

By the 1980s, science had given biologists a deeper realization of what was happening in the Tongass National Forest. Forest Service policy implied not a temporary disruption but essentially permanent destruction of much of the Southeastern rainforest ecosystem. The agency planned to use clear-cutting to convert uneven-aged virgin forest to tree farms—even-aged stands of trees intended to yield more wood fiber per acre when harvested every 90 to 125 years. After being clear-cut, a forest needed 200 to 300 years to attain the structural characteristics of old growth necessary to sustain the interplay of wildlife native to Southeast Alaska. If cut every century the trees would, upon reaching 25 to 30 years of age, shade out the undergrowth and diminish the variety of forest life. They would be cut again long before the forest could recover its ecological integrity.[54] Paul Alaback, an ecologist studying forest response to clear-cutting, explained in botanical terms: "Large-scale disturbances, such as clear-cutting, create huge, uniform openings that only slowly, if ever, return to the complex primeval forest. The woody plants best able to exploit these catastrophic events capture most of the light by growing dense and tall. Such growth creates a stark and barren forest floor."[55]

Ongoing studies of Sitka deer by ADF&G and the Forestry Sciences Laboratory confirmed earlier evidence that deer depended on old-growth forests in winters of deep snows, and that "second-growth stands are, almost without exception, of limited value to deer in any season."[56] ADF&G biologists projected the loss of up to 90 percent of the most vital deer range in certain drainages if Forest Service logging schedules prevailed over the next century. ADF&G opposed the practice of entering many watersheds and taking out only the best old growth, and called for retention of selected watersheds as whole units. It attributed high deer populations in the late 1980s to years of mild winters, whereas the Forest Service cited the numbers as evidence of negligible logging impact.[57]

Less research had been done on other mammals, though biologists knew that wolf populations relied on deer, mountain goats depended on old-growth stands for shelter and forage in winter, brown bears frequented the woods in summer and early fall during the salmon runs, and black bears used logs and brown bears needed tree root structures for winter denning.[58] Studies affirmed general observations that brown bears avoided clear-cut areas and human-generated noise, roads, and other disturbances.[59] Clear-cutting and logging-road construction increased access, and bear-human encounters, added to the bears' weakness for logging-camp dumps, resulted in excessive legal and illegal kills of brown bears. On northeast Chichagof Island, bear losses forced an emergency season closure in 1988. Compared to 5.5 bears taken annually between 1961 and 1979, the 1985–1988 kill averaged 17.5 bears.[60] This occurred despite the environmental-impact-statement claim of the Forest Service that "there would be no noticeable changes in brown bear populations from timber harvesting." Other locales experienced similar overkill of brown bears.[61]

Scientific investigation documented reliance of otters, marten, bald eagles, and Vancouver Canada geese on old growth. Designation of Admiralty Island as wilderness secured much of the range of both birds, though removal of large trees along other coastlines continued to menace the population of eagles.[62] Studies by Jeffrey Hughes showed that birds—chickadees, creepers, hairy woodpeckers, and others—needed the holes in old trees for shelter during the winter, and at least 12 species nested specifically in old growth.[63]

Far more controversy swirled around logging impact on fish, especially salmon. Critics of Forest Service policy charged that logging cut down salmon populations by silting streams, altering water temperature, removing nutrients, and altering stream flow. Scientists found it difficult to produce unqualified indictments of clear-cut logging, or clear confirmation of the value of old-growth forest for fisheries. But by the mid-1990s, the weight of evidence from numerous studies in the Pacific Northwest led biologists to conclude that

> the most pervasive effect has been reduced habitat complexity due to loss of large woody debris, causing a widespread reduction in salmonoid abundance and diversity.

Despite improvements over the last 20 years, logging activities can still have multiple effects. Effects of timber harvest, road construction, and other activities anywhere in a watershed can be transmitted through hydrologic and erosional processes to affect salmonoid habitat. The most important changes result from sediment, stream flow, temperature and large woody debris.[64]

Suffering constant assaults by its critics, the Forest Service responded through a public relations effort and minor but gradually increasing measures to protect wildlife values. It continued to deny negative impacts of logging, proof of which necessitated lengthy and expensive research. It denied doing harm to fisheries and cited its success in increasing salmon production. The agency assisted ADF&G in construction of fishways, stocking and fertilization of lakes, stream clearance, and other operations. Annually during 1980–1987 the measures produced an estimated average of $7.2 million worth of salmon at a reported cost to federal and state governments of $6.7 million.[65] Thus the Forest Service could compromise the integrity of natural areas, for marginal economic gain, and display the results to divert attention from logging impact on forest ecosystems.

To facilitate logging, the Forest Service built roads to the stands to be offered for sale. Compared to 100 miles of permanent roads in the Tongass in 1950, 2,300 miles existed in 1988. Great numbers of temporary roads had also been constructed in the forests.[66] During the 1980s the Forest Service and timber industry added close to 300 miles of roads annually, more than 100 miles of it permanent.[67] Whereas the agency cited roads as multiple-use benefits, environmentalists regarded them as the tragic end of wilderness. Sources within the Forest Service reportedly confirmed suspicions about one motivation behind road building: an ADF&G memo stated, "The Forest Service is pre-roadbuilding areas in which no commercial interest has been expressed. Some Forest Service officials have even admitted privately that much of the work is designed to keep their staffs busy, and to prevent the area from being designated as 'Wilderness' in the future." A Forest Service forestry technician confided that the administration was "concerned that some lands would be excluded from timber harvest if they were designated as wilderness, so some mark needed to be made on the land."[68]

FOREST MANAGEMENT AND THE LAW

Federal law mandated that national forests be managed on a multiple-use, sustained-yield basis. These principles implied some sort of viable and equitable balance of uses of the forest lands that could be maintained indefinitely. Activities in the Tongass in the 1980s and 1990s included commercial and sport fishing, sport hunting, nature observation, preservation of wildlife habitat and populations, research, hiking, camping, winter sports, boating, sightseeing from aircraft and cruise vessels, logging, mining, and subsistence living. Of the incompatibilities among these values, none surpassed that between logging and almost all others. Yet by its vested interests and the training of its employees, expressed in its budgets and attitudes, the Forest Service favored timber extraction far above all other purposes combined.[69] All lands whose tree quality could support logging, including those legally protected as wilderness, bore the official label "commercial forest lands."

The Tongass Land Management Plan of 1979 bespoke the overweening logging-oriented priorities of the Forest Service, and undergirded the Tongass provisions of the Alaska

Lands Act (ANILCA) in 1980. Alaska's congressional delegation (Senators Ted Stevens and Mike Gravel and Representative Don Young) collaborated with the Forest Service and representatives of the two large timber companies, Japanese-owned Alaska Lumber and Pulp (or Alaska Pulp Company) in Sitka and American-owned Ketchikan Pulp Company (or Louisiana Pacific Ketchikan). Between them, the companies harvested about two-thirds of the Tongass timber offered for sale by the Forest Service. As part of the price for allowing ANILCA to pass the Senate, Stevens inserted an exceedingly benevolent consideration for the timber regime:

> The Congress authorizes and directs that the Secretary of the Treasury shall make available to the Secretary of Agriculture the sum of at least $40,000,000 annually or as much as the Secretary of Agriculture finds is necessary to maintain the timber supply from the Tongass National Forest to dependent industry at a rate of four billion five hundred million foot board measure per decade. . . . such funds shall not be subject to annual appropriation.[70]

Never before had such a timber sale law been enacted. In the perspective of resource economist Arlon R. Tussing, "The Forest Service . . . arranged a subsidy—largely unappropriated and largely off-budget—from the federal treasury to establish an industry that otherwise would have failed any test of market viability, and which would have been emphatically rejected in any analysis of nationwide economic costs and benefits." The agency had no incentive to conduct efficient timber sales, he explained, because the receipts went to the federal treasury. Similarly, it evidenced no concern that increased logging in Alaska caused reduced cuts on private land and resultant unemployment in small Washington and Oregon logging towns. Laid-off workers from those towns comprised a large percentage of the loggers in Alaska. In contrast to private logging in the Lower 48, the Tongass operation "required a small army of Forest Service employees to design and contract for road construction, supervise the logging spreads and scale the logs, and audit the lumber and pulp company books. At the same time, this policy won the Forest Service local acclaim, a permanent loyal constituency in each of the mill towns, and a responsibility for their continued survival."[71]

Forest economist Randall O'Toole observed a similar pattern in his analysis of the nationwide operation of the Forest Service: fundamentally, its goal is that of nearly all bureaucracies—to maximize its budgets. In the 1950s and 1960s, as postwar growth drove up demand for wood products, timber management furnished the prime means to the goal. Expanding the size and geographical range of timber cuts created constituencies who then lobbied Congress for increased appropriations for the Forest Service. Artificially lowering the prices charged for timber had the effect of stimulating demand and reducing competition from private timbering operations, thus creating the appearance of shortages that further induced appropriations. The Multiple Use–Sustained Yield Act of 1960 boosted funding for planning but did not alter the commitment to timbering. Notwithstanding the Wilderness Act of 1964, roadless areas became prime targets for road building to rationalize greater budget requests and, at least incidentally, to prevent their becoming off-limits to logging. Clearcutting increased the acreage and volume of timber cut per unit of preparation cost, satisfying more constituents. Because recreation fees went into the Land and Water Conservation Fund, forest managers felt no incentive to encourage recreation. Detailed planning called for by the National Forest Management Act of 1976 turned into a means of raising the number of Forest Service employees, while not affecting the dominant emphasis on timber production. Although not necessarily indicating conscious policies of the Forest Service, said O'Toole, the incentives to increase harvests and disincentives to balance costs against timber sale receipts produced the timbering priority, regardless of multiple-use directives by Congress. Meanwhile, the taxpayers lost $250 million to $500 million per year in addition to the unnecessary destruction of wildlife habitat and wilderness.[72]

The Alaska Lands Act's uniquely favorable arrangement for the Forest Service and the two corporations drew varying reactions from different interests. To SEACC attorney Steve Kallick, "the Forest Service has been given a blank check, the worst thing you can give to a bureaucracy."[73] To Senator Stevens, "the Tongass Timber Supply fund was the cost of taking the wilderness areas out of the harvest cycle." To change the law would be "to renege on that commitment to sustain Alaska's timber industry."[74] Jim Clark, vice president and general counsel for the Alaska Loggers Association, reasoned, "Why shouldn't taxpayers pay for timber sales? Why are they paying for farm subsidies, tobacco supports? It is to keep jobs in the American economy. Maybe Congress shouldn't do it—then let's undo it. But then let's take back the wilderness Congress created too."[75]

Wilderness and old-growth acreage lay at the core of the dispute. Virtually every attempt to save any of the Tongass as wilderness met vigorous resistance from the Forest Service and its allies; despite the adoption of the Wilderness Act of 1964, none of the West Virginia–sized Tongass received wilderness status until ANILCA passed in 1980. The Forest Service and the two large timber companies behaved as if the Tongass were a timber supply belonging to them, suggesting that the public should pay a high price to take it away from them, and the cost should be blamed on the environmentalists.

Critics of Forest Service Tongass policy labeled it "mining" (cutting at an unsustainable rate) and "highgrading" (taking the best timber at a disproportionate and unsustainable rate). The service denied both charges, in the face of contrary evidence. Prior to large-volume logging, the 16.7-million-acre Tongass contained about 186,000 acres of the highest volume (50,000 or more board feet per acre) old-growth forest. These stands encompassed the largest and oldest trees and thereby much of the most productive wildlife habitat in the region. By 1979, following state and Native selections and a quarter-century of clear-cut logging, only 89,000 of these acres remained (Table 15.1). Loggers had concentrated on the highest-quality, most accessible stands of timber, holding an average of 46,000 board feet per acre. According to the 1979–2079 plan, another 54,000 acres of highest-volume stands would be logged, leaving 35,000 acres or about 19 percent of the original.[76]

Responding to appeals from environmentalists, biologists, and others seeking to preserve old growth, ANILCA marked out 5.4 million acres of the Tongass as wilderness. This total contained 161,000 acres of prime wildlife habitat, but only about 9,000 acres of highest-volume old-growth. The remainder consisted of open and mountainous country and few trees. Wilderness status therefore preserved about 5 percent of the pre-1950 and 10 percent of the 1980 groves of the largest trees. The Forest Service set aside another 495,000 acres of commercially productive forest as roadless wildlands, without protection from future logging decisions.[77]

Table 15.1—Old-Growth Acreage in the Tongass National Forest, 1880–2080 (Projected)

Volume Class	1880	1980	Change	2080	Change
8–20 million board feet	2,966,850	2,950,800	-1%	2,203,300	-26%
20–30 million board feet	1,801,550	1,720,800	-4%	1,219,600	-32%
30–50 million board feet	702,800	573,600	-18%	360,400	-49%
50+ million board feet	186,200	89,300	–52%	35,100	-81%

Source: M.D. Kirchhoff, "Economic Boon or Ecosystem Ruin? Highgrading in Alaska's Coastal Rainforest." Presented at the Society for Conservation Biology, Toronto, August 1989.

Note: 2080 projections based on 1979–2079 Tongass forest plan

ANILCA guaranteed the two pulp companies access to timber of quality and quantity equal to any lost through wilderness classification. Alaska Pulp Company, the only one affected by the designations, received compensation.[78] Nevertheless, ANILCA and the state and Native selections left fewer acres of valuable timber for the Forest Service to offer for sale. Unless the market grew rapidly, more high-volume timber had to be cut to enable all parties to make profits. Congress intended ANILCA's $40 million Tongass Timber Supply Fund in part to relieve the pressure on high-volume forests by subsidizing the use of more marginal stands through construction of roads. However, the two large timber companies could choose from among Forest Service sale offerings, and opted for the higher-volume stands. Wildlife and recreational values therefore lost on both accounts: the best wildlife habitat continued to disappear at a disproportional rate in the 1980s, while roads increasingly violated other wild areas.

Limits on the supply of commercially important timber stepped up the tension between logging and competing values in the 1980s. If the Forest Service had consummated the Juneau Unit sale in the mid-1970s, virtually all of the highest-quality wildlife range would have been committed to logging. Even without the Juneau Unit, the ANILCA provision for cutting 450 million board feet per year put a great strain on forest resources. Stress on the forest intensified as the state and Natives made selections and commenced logging. Natives seldom attempted to preserve the best old growth; they sought profits and faced stiff competition from the two subsidized corporations protected by long-term contracts. In addition, the small size of village corporation holdings (averaging 23,000 acres) rendered sustained-yield commercial logging unfeasible.[79] From 22 percent of the regional harvest in 1980, Native timber production rose to a peak of 54 percent (530 million board feet) in 1989. Analysts projected a slide to less than 100 million board feet during the first decade of the twenty-first century.[80]

Indirectly, Forest Service policy accelerated the pace of destruction on Native-owned as well as public lands. Unable to compete against the two large companies and in some cases deep in debt, Native corporations clear-cut their forests at a rapid rate. Able to make profit only by selling sawlogs to Japan, they left much of the rest on the ground to rot. Alaska Department of Fish and Game field inspectors reported that loggers on Native lands clear-cut up to stream banks and on steep hillsides, causing landslides and excess stream siltation, and damaging wildlife habitat. Many clear-cuts exceeded 900 acres, and the logging eradicated what had been the largest trees and the highest-quality old-growth forest remaining in the Tongass. Natives ignored federal guidelines for environmental protection and sustained yield, and state biologists had neither the personnel nor the political backing necessary to curb the abuses. Despite the pace of cutting, few corporations realized profits. Senator Stevens inserted language in the 1986 Tax Reform Act permitting Alaska Native Corporations to sell their net operating losses to other corporations, who would receive tax breaks. By 1990 when Congress ended the benefit, it had cost taxpayers $716 million.[81]

The low price of logs encouraged waste everywhere in the Tongass; a 1982 Forest Service document estimated that 200 million board feet of logs lay on beaches. They had been lost from storage and transportation, and created a problem of clutter as well as a navigation hazard.[82]

Alaska's weak state forest management law prior to the 1990s did not construct an adequate legal basis for challenging destructive logging practices on the Native lands, and critics concentrated their fire on the Forest Service. The Alaska Board of Game, Alaska Department of Fish and Game, Wildlife Society, Territorial Sportsmen, and Southeast Alaska Conservation Council all protested and appealed Forest Service harvest plans.[83] In 1983, ADF&G asked that 72 critical habitat watershed areas be set aside pending the 1989–1999 Tongass Land Management Plan.[84] SEACC and other environmental groups engaged in public relations campaigns to combat those of the Forest Service. The Alaska Chapter of the Wildlife Society called on the Forest Service to comply with the fish and wildlife conservation measures of the National Forest Management Act of 1976. The chapter also asked for public education on the effects of logging, identification of sites critically important for wildlife, assessment of road-building impacts, cessation of disproportionate cutting of high-volume old growth, economic measurement of use values other than logging, accurate and open records, and planning and decisions taking account of the cumulative impacts of logging.[85] Debate continued on the effects of logging on fisheries and wildlife.

ENVIRONMENTAL LAWSUITS IN THE 1980s

Research on logging impact supplied powerful ammunition for public and congressional reform efforts, including lawsuits. SEACC, weak and nearly penniless after the passage of the Alaska Lands Act, recovered in the early 1980s. Led by Jim Stratton and John Sisk, it forged a coalition with commercial fishing groups, recreation interests, and local communities including Native villages. The coalition engaged perpetually in land-use disputes. In one case, a Sitka Native group calling itself Shee Atika applied for status as a village corporation. Congress specified in ANILCA that 23,000 acres of forest on the west side of Admiralty Island National Monument be assigned to Shee Atika in fulfillment of its claims. The conveyance transpired in January 1982. The corporation prepared to build a large log dump (storage area) and breakwater at Cube Cove, a stand to be clear-cut. Cube Cove served as an important hunting and fishing spot for the Angoon Tlingits, a community trying to retain elements of their traditional lifestyle. Anthropologist Kenneth Tollefson warned that the planned clear-cuts and roads might be "the last straw that could destroy the Tlingit way of life. . . . Tlingit subsistence and Tlingit culture . . . survive together or they become extinct."

15.9. Wasted logs on beach, Tongass National Forest, 1987. By Larry Edwards. Courtesy SEACC. According to Forest Service estimates, 200 million board feet of logs lay on the beaches in 1982.

Tlingit elder Lydia George explained, "To us, Admiralty Island is like a big dish; you are free to use it but not to break it. Our people are the guardians of the land."[86]

Shee Atika refused offers of trade for acreage on other islands. On behalf of the Angoon Tlingits, Sierra Club Legal Defense Fund (SCLDF) brought several lawsuits, and construction of the log dump ceased pending environmental impact statements. U.S. Circuit Court overturned the lower-court suspension and the operation went forward, but the Environmental Protection Agency ruled that impact statements be written for all log dumps.[87] The Sierra Club, SCLDF, Wilderness Society, SEACC, and Angoon residents entered into negotiations with Shee Atika to draft a compromise to be ratified by Congress. Legislation passed the House in 1986 but died in the Senate. The talks collapsed, Shee Atika logged Cube Cove and, subsequently, the bulk of its 23,000 acres. While the Angoon Tlingits lamented the loss of their traditional lands, their own corporation clear-cut part of Prince of Wales Island.[88] In

1990 the Tongass Timber Reform Act mandated negotiations for Shee Atika to receive other land in trade for the uncut portion of its 23,000 acres on Admiralty.[89] Negotiations again fell through, and Shee Atika logged the remaining prime timber sites.

SEACC fought what it considered unnecessary road construction in wild areas. One such case involved the Kadashan River, one of the outstanding salmon streams of Southeast Alaska, on Chichagof Island. The wild and beautiful Kadashan had been named for the Tlingit Indian who guided John Muir by canoe through the area in 1879. Despite protests by Tenakee Springs and an ADF&G request to defer harvest, the Forest Service approved Alaska Pulp Company plans to cut 30 square miles in the valley during 1981–1986. SEACC, the Wildlife Society, and three fishing groups appealed the decision and met rebuff by the Forest Service.[90] In 1984, SEACC and Tenakee Springs filed suit against a Forest Service attempt to bulldoze a 17-mile road into the heart of the drainage, on grounds of inadequate environmental impact statement. District court denied the plaintiffs relief and the road building proceeded. Circuit court reversed the decision, ordering a halt to the road construction and the preparation of a supplemental impact statement.[91] Plaintiffs gained permanent protection through the 1990 Tongass Timber Reform Act.[92]

Another logging-road engagement centered on Berners Bay, a wild tract 45 miles north of Juneau, extensively used for recreation and identified by ADF&G as one of the most valuable fish and wildlife locales in the region. In 1985 the Forest Service proposed to extend a road into the Sawmill Creek area to facilitate logging of old growth nearby, and to build a log transfer facility on the bay. The main purpose of the $5–$10 million project appeared to be to spend surplus funds; the Forest Service admitted it expected no bids on the timber. Vigorous local protest jelled into a 1,200-member Friends of Berners Bay, which joined SEACC, SCLDF, Sierra Club/Juneau, and Alaska Discovery (an outdoor-recreation business) in a lawsuit to demand an environmental impact statement. They won an injunction and a ruling requiring that impact statements be filed for each such plan; that the overall forest management plan did not exempt the Forest Service from doing site-specific studies. The Forest Service agreed to write an impact statement for Berners Bay but made no move to do so.[93] The Tongass Timber Reform Act prohibited logging on 46,000 acres at Berners Bay.[94]

Part of the Forest Service master plan for the Tongass had been to connect all major islands and population centers by a system of roads and ferries. Although the road plan entailed great social and environmental impacts, the service suppressed attempts to open it to public scrutiny. Tenakee Springs sought to defend itself by selecting lands lying astride the transportation route. But the Forest Service persisted. SEACC, SCLDF, the Wilderness Society, and the City of Tenakee Springs sued the service in 1986 to prevent a road in the nearby Game Creek sector. The road would come within two miles of connecting Hoonah to Tenakee, whose citizens wished to remain inaccessible by road. Plaintiffs won a ruling decreeing an environmental impact statement for the project.[95] In 1988 the Forest Service sued for condemnation of Tenakee's lands needed for completion of the road. The Tongass Timber Reform Act directed the service to reassess the road plan in consultation with the public.[96] Hoonah and Tenakee Springs stopped the road, but logging eventually went forward at Game Creek.

Environmentalists also challenged the 1986–1990 Alaska Pulp Company logging plan on environmental impact grounds. SCLDF and SEACC won a favorable ruling in 1987, resulting in a February 1988 settlement temporarily reserving 275,000 acres of roadless forest pending environmental studies.[97]

In 1988 Hoonah residents sued the Forest Service, contending the Alaska Pulp Company harvest plan violated subsistence guarantees of the Alaska Lands Act by removing old-growth deer habitat and facilitating intrusions by outside hunters through logging roads. By 1990, the plan called for cutting 7,000 acres and building 70 miles of new roads near Hoonah. SCLDF filed a second suit, challenging the plan's impact statement on behalf of environmental groups and other Native villages. A 1990 circuit court decision halted the cutting and set important precedents by ordering the Forest Service to do long-term and comprehensive planning, giving adequate consideration to subsistence and wildlife values.[98] Following completion of revised impact statements, however, logging proceeded near Hoonah and on other lands in the 1986–1990 plan.

The central achievement of the Tongass lawsuits lay in the requirement of separate impact statements for individual timber offerings. This enabled specific social and environmental impacts to be identified before irreversible changes resulted from clear-cutting and road building. When obliged to prepare a controversial impact statement, the Forest Service sometimes abandoned a project, knowing that pursuing it would mean an additional unpleasant fight against local residents and their environmentalist sympathizers. Considering the political difficulties it faced, the Forest Service did not desire more bad publicity. By carefully selecting their targets, SEACC and SCLDF bought time for 2–3 million acres of vital forest habitat, hoping that future legislation might safeguard them.

TIMBER INDUSTRY PROBLEMS

Beyond the direct ecological impacts of logging, several behaviors and circumstances combined to weaken the public standing of the timber industry. Water pollution in the Southeast continued to embroil it in controversy, as it had since the 1950s. The two large mills of Alaska Pulp Company and Ketchikan Pulp Company fouled the waters of Ward Cove and Silver Bay, respectively, by storage of logs, dumping of bark, and daily discharge of millions of gallons of mill effluent. The Environmental Protection Agency (EPA) granted extensions of variances from pollution regulations from 1976 until 1983, when it demanded compliance. Despite the installation of primary and secondary treatment facilities in the 1970s, emissions at the two plants exceeded legal limits. Senators Ted Stevens and Frank Murkowski held the national Clean Water bill hostage in 1984 in an attempt to win a third compliance extension for the mills. New York Times editors commented, "If Alaska wants to operate uneconomic mills, the state government can well afford to subsidize the mills out of the surpluses it's already been handing out to its citizens. But Senators Murkowski and Stevens are prepared to sabotage a bill that addresses the major outstanding sources of water pollution around the country."[99] The senators retorted that New York senators had secured extensions for New York City to dump sewage into the Atlantic, that no suitable spot existed for landfilling the mill sludge, and that burning it would only cause air pollution. The bill died a year later when Stevens and Murkowski introduced a measure, also unsuccessful, for a $7-million federally funded "demonstration" treatment plant for the Alaska Pulp Company mill in Sitka.[100] In 1986 the state legislature passed an $8.5-million loan guarantee to

Alaska Pulp Company for construction of an advanced wastewater treatment plant. Ketchikan Pulp Company agreed to purchase and install a $12-million treatment facility.[101]

Treatment plants did not end violations of water quality standards. Alaska Pulp Company paid $700,000 in fines between 1986 and 1991. When the EPA moved to put dioxin-laden Silver Bay on the Superfund List, all three members of Alaska's congressional delegation tried to prevent it. Murkowski's office threatened to cut the EPA's budget.[102] Toxic pollution at Ward Cove by Ketchikan Pulp Company persisted. During the early 1990s, the company illegally dumped 14.3 million gallons of toxic chemicals and metals in Ward Cove, and falsified its records. When chemical engineer Kevin James reported the activity to the EPA, the company fired him. In 1995, executives pled guilty to 14 criminal counts and the company paid a fine of $1.25 million. Ward Cove ranked as one of the nation's most polluted water bodies.[103]

Air pollution also plagued Sitka's Alaska Pulp Company, granted variances since 1976 by the Alaska Department of Environmental Conservation. Tests showed sulfur-dioxide levels had repeatedly exceeded twice the legal limit. Sierra Club Legal Defense Fund filed notice of intent to initiate a citizens' lawsuit, prompting the state to sue the company for the first time. When the state issued a consent decree in December 1986 giving the company another open-ended variance, SCLDF intervened. The court stiffened the variance to include deadlines for installation of equipment and provisions for fines if the deadlines should not be met, and granted SCLDF a role in monitoring compliance.[104]

Installation of air filters in 1989 raised the question of toxic fly ash disposal. Alaska Pulp Company used its private landfill until the Department of Environmental Conservation prohibited the practice. Next, the company got permission to put the ash in the city landfill, situated next to a grammar school, but public reaction forced a halt. Then the company flushed the ash through its sewage line into Silver Bay, but the EPA ordered it to cease. An EPA survey of 104 pulp mills showed the fly ash at Alaska Pulp Company contained 25 times as much dioxin as did the next ranking mill. Researchers found high levels of dioxin and other toxic chemicals and metals in fresh and saltwater sediments near Sitka, whose residents consumed large quantities of fish and shellfish.[105] For 30 years Alaska Pulp Company had attempted to avoid responsible treatment of local air and water.

Not least of the embarrassments visited upon the timber industry involved the bald eagle, a symbol of old growth in the Tongass. In 1987 the remains of two dozen eagles appeared in a Ketchikan Pulp Company logging camp at Labouchere Bay on Prince of Wales Island. Some had decomposed and others had been recently shot. A state court convicted camp manager John King of eagle killing and sentenced him to one year in jail, eleven months suspended. Thirteen dead eagles had been found at the same place in 1983, and in 1985 King had paid a $1,000 fine for eagle shooting.[106]

Monopoly practices added a dimension to the Tongass story. By the early 1970s, nearly all the small independent logging companies had gone out of business or become tied so closely by debt as to be subsidiaries of the two giants. Ketchikan Pulp Company had absorbed 16 companies, and Alaska Pulp Company at least 6. One of the survivors, Reid Brothers Logging Company, sued the two mills in 1975 for antitrust violations, and in 1981 the U.S. District Court ruled for the plaintiff. The court assessed the companies $1.5 million in compensation to Reid Brothers. It found the two big companies had secretly agreed not to bid against one another, sent disguised agents to outbid others, and kept log prices artificially low to keep small suppliers in debt to them. The Forest Service accused the two of maintaining false records of their sales to avoid taxes, at a loss to the public treasury of $63–$81 million. Illegal practices had occurred from 1959 through at least 1975. Eventually, in December 1982, the general counsel of the Agriculture Department formally recommended that the Justice Department initiate both antitrust and criminal proceedings, but Justice did not act. The Internal Revenue Service claimed a loss of $26.7 million and settled for $3 million. Notwithstanding its legal power to do so, the Forest Service declined to take administrative action.[107]

Economics raised the most truculent obstacles for the Tongass timber industry. In the early 1980s the market slumped. Japanese housing construction fell off, market demand for wood and for rayon and cellophane products made from pulp declined, and a strong dollar retarded sales. In addition, the rapid upsurge of harvest on Native lands helped saturate the market. The number of Tongass timbering jobs fell from 2,700 in 1980 to 1,280 in 1985. Alaska labor statistics revealed about 40 percent of the timber workers as nonresidents, a fact that undermined justification of the timber subsidies as being for the benefit of the local economy.[108]

ANILCA had not envisioned a market slump in its specification of a minimum $40 million timber supply fund and 450-million-board-foot annual cut. To help the companies harvest timber and to keep its own operations going, the Forest Service continued to spend the $40 million and prepare the 450 million board feet. It built roads to a large backlog of unsold timber, and sold less than half what it prepared during 1983–1985.[109] Retroactive to 1981, it cut the price it had charged Ketchikan Pulp Company for timber by 96 percent, and to Alaska Pulp Company, by 99 percent. The latter could buy Sitka spruce, appraised at $215 per thousand board feet, for $2.26.[110]

According to law, timber prices had to be determined by market price. Yet the Forest Service set highly concessionary prices in the absence of appropriate information. Since early in their operations, the two pulp companies had successfully hidden their costs so as to reduce their taxes and keep stumpage rates low. Their secrecy and near-monopoly status made it difficult to determine market values. An investigation conducted by the Forest Service in the 1970s uncovered much of the companies' illegal behavior, but the service kept the report from public view until environmental groups obtained it in 1989. An analysis released by the Wilderness Society in 1986 showed that in 1984 the Forest Service lost 93 cents on every dollar it spent on Tongass timber sales. Between 1977 and 1984 it lost a total of over $260 million, primarily by bulldozing roads into forests and realizing small amounts in timber sales. Each timbering job, in effect, received a taxpayer subsidy of $36,000 per year.[111] By 1986 the Forest Service lost 99 cents on the dollar, for an annual total of about $62 million. In that year it ceased the practice of building roads before making a sale. It also took steps to reduce costs to the timber companies by lowering road construction standards and permitting larger-sized clear-cuts. While the market price of Alaskan timber escalated by nearly 300 percent between 1986 and 1987, the rates the Forest Service charged the mills remained extremely low.[112]

A General Accounting Office investigation employing conservative accounting figures determined that $131 million had been spent unnecessarily during 1981–1986 to supply timber to the companies. Nevertheless, it found the Forest Service spending legally consistent with ANILCA.[113] Controversial expenditures included worker facilities featuring cable television and weight rooms, and an employee ballfield constructed in 1986 from sod carried by barge from Seattle.[114]

International economic recovery, a weakened dollar, and other market changes effected a rebound in the market for Alaskan pulp and sawlogs between 1986 and 1990. Most of the increase in employment occurred in Native logging. Alaska gained a larger share of a relatively flat market in pulp products, and increased its sales of saw timber to Japan, South Korea, Taiwan, and India. But Alaska competed in a complex and volatile world market. A shift in exchange rates could easily redirect Japanese purchases to British Columbia or other sources. Changes in rayon fashions, union-management relations, production and product technology, or other factors could reverse Alaska's advantage in the pulp market.[115]

Lumber generally fared better than pulp on the market. But Japan, the destination for 95 percent of Tongass sawed timber and 72 percent of its round logs in 1994, entered a recession in 1991. As a result, by 1994 the harvest dropped to its lowest level in a decade. In Southeast Alaska as a whole, logging employment fell to 1,177 from a 1990 high of 2,144. Native corporations, on their 600,000 acres of selected land taken out of Tongass National Forest jurisdiction, accounted for somewhat less than half the Southeast Alaska total. Their share represented a steady decline from the high in 1989. A downturn in Native logging and high prices in Japan suggested an ongoing market for Tongass sawlogs. But lumber sales to Japan could be influenced by environmental restrictions, trends in the Japanese housing market, or competition from Canada, Scandinavia, New Zealand, Chile, or elsewhere.[116] Moreover, distance from markets and high production costs inhibited Alaska-based manufactured wood products industries.

In contrast to lumber, pulpwood fortunes sank dramatically. In 1993, the Ketchikan pulp mill shut down for about four months and the Sitka pulp mill closed its doors indefinitely on September 30, laying off 400 workers. Mill officials attributed the moves to reductions of log supply by the Forest Service, and Alaska Pulp Company filed a lawsuit claiming breach of their 50-year contract. Forest Service officials blamed the shutdowns on a drop in world pulp prices. In April 1994 the Forest Service canceled Alaska Pulp Company's 50-year contract on grounds of failure to fulfill obligations to provide employment. The contract would have run to 2011, and the remaining noncompetitive Louisiana Pacific Ketchikan (LPK) contract would expire in 2004.[117] But world competition finally overwhelmed LPK, and it ceased operations permanently in the fall of 1996. Timber sales had become more indicative of true market conditions, and a miniscule Alaska timber industry precariously survived.

EFFORTS AT REFORM

Unfavorable economics, widening awareness of ecological impact, negative publicity, and resistance by local communities, commercial fishers, biologists, and environmentalists nudged the Forest Service toward policy change in the Tongass. Reform advocates exercised their main opportunity in congressional hearings. The Alaska Lands Act directed the

Forest Service to report to Congress within five years on its Tongass timber operations. Anticipating issuance of the first review, Southeast Alaska Conservation Council (SEACC) sent a team to Washington in early 1986 to seek oversight hearings, and to tour the nation and generate support for reform legislation. Grassroots organizer John Sisk arranged for testimony by Joe Sebastian, Joan Kautzer, and other residents of Southeast communities. They had to overcome the reluctance of Congress members to challenge the Alaska delegation, and the belief of national environmental leaders that reform would be impossible during the Reagan administration. Hearings held in May, in the context of growing national publicity, facilitated the introduction of a Tongass Timber Reform bill in July. The sessions lasted into 1987, and the National Audubon Society donated office space to SEACC. Lobbyists Jay Nelson and Scott Highleyman organized a national campaign to bring the Tongass to public notice. They won the cooperation of key members of Congress, and the enthusiastic sanction of the National Taxpayers Union.[118] The publicity and hearings rekindled the national debate over the Tongass without the distraction of the d-2 lands fight of the 1970s.

Contestants waged a protracted battle for the attention of Congress and the public. SEACC director Bart Koehler, a central figure in the reform campaign, branded the timber policy "a juggernaut grinding at wildlife" and declared, "We're not against a timber industry in Southeast Alaska, just this timber industry."[119] SEACC wanted a smaller harvest, more preservation of old-growth rainforest, and greater value assigned to tourism and recreation in multiple use. John Schoen expressed the view generally held in the Alaska Department of Fish and Game that "the harvest scheme will render the old-growth forest nonrenewable."[120] Gordon Williams testified for commercial fishing groups that "current logging practices are not providing the type of watershed and streamside environment that offers the needed protection against landslides, flooding, increased siltation, and destructive extremes of temperature."[121] Sylvia Geraghty, speaking for Alaskans for Responsible Resource Management (a small-scale timber and fishing group), charged that local Alaskan companies had been driven out of business by the large subsidized companies: "Instead of $2 per thousand board feet paid by LPK for prime old-growth spruce, a small operator recently bid $125 per thousand for all spruce on a sale, including those far from prime old-growth. This is some 6,000 percent over what LPK pays."[122] Bonnie Kaden, speaking for the Tongass Tourism and Recreation Business Association, contended that "the economic stability and future growth of Southeast Alaska depends on tourism, not logging; and . . . current Wilderness withdrawals cannot in large part support the visitor industry because they are biased toward preserving inaccessible icefields and mountains." She added, "The Forest Service now charges us more to take one person into the forest to look at trees for one day than it charges the pulp companies for 1,000 board feet of virgin timber. We are charged roughly $3 to take one visitor into the forest for nonconsumptive use, and we leave this forest completely intact."[123]

Angoon resident K. J. Metcalf reflected on his 20 years as a Forest Service planner: "During my years with the Forest Service I advocated an enlightened land ethic, and I trusted the Forest Service planning process and I worked hard to convince others to trust that. But today I am sickened at what I see happening on the Tongass. And I would like to publicly apologize to those people . . . I convinced them that the Tongass Plan would mean multiple use on the national forest."[124] Joe Mehrkens, who resigned as Forest Service senior regional economist and joined the Wilderness Society, disputed the agency's economic claims. Loggers extracted old growth at such a high rate, he said, that younger and much poorer-quality timber would have to be relied on after 1990. Thus "if the mills aren't highly profitable now, how can they be in the future?" Pointing to a Forest Service study showing that only 489 jobs would be lost even if both pulp mills closed, he concluded, "We are taking our most valuable land and cashing it in now, even though the wood will be far more valuable in the future, simply to protect 500 timber-related jobs. It just isn't a rational approach."[125] Mehrkens assumed directorship of the Southeast Alaska Natural Resources Center, opened by the Wilderness Society in Juneau in 1988 to work on Tongass issues.

Proponents of the timbering system viewed it differently. To Ketchikan Pulp Company manager Martin Pihl the 50-year contracts represented "a pioneering venture to utilize and renew a decaying forest through sustained yield forestry." It had succeeded in bringing "substantial year-around employment to Southeast Alaska" despite "the radical environmentalist forces pressing to shut down the timber industry in Southeast Alaska, by characterizing logging as 'mining' and the timber industry as a 'sunset' industry."[126] Forest Service official Daniel Hessel pointed to positive work the service did in the Tongass, such as "bringing tourists and providing recreation, providing jobs in Alaska, paying community taxes . . . We build roads that people use and produce a tremendous amount of salmon." Industry spokespersons denied harm to fisheries or the environment; deputy forest supervisor David Morton observed of formerly clear-cut areas that "nature here is pretty forgiving. What looked like god-awful places a few years ago are now pretty nice places."[127]

Timber industry partisans tried to focus the debate on jobs versus environment. Jim Clark, attorney and board member of Alaska Pulp Company, termed the subsidy to industry "a myth" in that the industry subsidized the government by building roads. He described the federal expenditures as "a net benefit of $49.5 million to the people of Southeast Alaska."[128] Wrangell mayor William Privet testified that without the contracts, the two pulp mills and the Wrangell sawmill would be forced to reduce production or even to close. "Our area cannot afford the loss, for whatever reason, of one more job," declared Ketchikan mayor Ted Ferry.[129] A group of loggers' wives named Alaska Women in Timber, organized in 1978, distributed material promulgating the industry–Forest Service position, and assisted the Alaska Loggers Association lobbying effort on Tongass timber reform legislation.

Conflict over logging policy reached well beyond words. Shortly after his testimony in favor of the Tongass Timber Reform bill, millwright Florian Sever lost his job at Alaska Pulp Company. Jess Cline, the company's personnel manager, admitted to a National Labor Relations Board examiner, and later at an NLRB administrative hearing, that Sever's testimony counted significantly in his dismissal. However, Cline told a House Subcommittee on General Oversight and Investigations that Alaska Pulp Company fired Sever not because of his testimony, but for writing a letter to the *Sitka Sentinel* in support of a workers' 1986 strike. The *Sentinel* did not publish the letter. Following a six-month investigation, the subcommittee referred the matter to the Justice Department for possible charges of obstruction of congressional proceedings and perjury. Representative Don Young opposed the action. Noting the magnitude of subsidies to the timber industry, subcommittee chairman Sam Gejdenson suggested, "This third of a billion dollars is not intended to pay only for employees who agree with the company's policy, nor is it intended to subsidize the squelching of free speech." Sever ultimately won reinstatement and back pay through the NLRB. The board also found Alaska Pulp Company guilty of unfair labor practices toward more than 200 strikers, and ordered compensation pay for more than 100, totaling $10 million. The company appealed and, more than a decade later, neither Sever nor the others had received the pay. Treatment of workers impaired the political standing of both pulp corporations.[130]

Numerous articles critical of Tongass policy appeared in national publications. A *Reader's Digest* story titled "Time to Ax This Boondoggle" commented, "The Forest Service, a 38,000-member bureaucracy, has staffed up with surveyors, road engineers and others who move up the ranks by putting lots of board feet on the scoreboard. Convincing them that it makes no economic sense is nearly impossible."[131] The *New York Times* editorialized: "The Forest Service, whose bureaucracy often fails to distinguish public interest from private, defends logging in the Tongass as a jobs program. . . . But the logging jeopardizes other jobs, in tourism and salmon fishing. In any case, what logic is there in asking the taxpayer to cover the wages of workers hired to chop down 500-year-old trees that hardly anyone wants to buy?" It termed the operation "so wrongheaded it's likely to provoke profanity from any fairminded person."[132]

Alaska's government officials felt obliged to take stands on the Tongass issue. Governor Steve Cowper, elected in 1986, at first cautiously rejected the "premature" Tongass reform proposals, preferring an administrative solution.[133] Unable to agree in 1987, the legislature passed a 1988 resolution calling for compromise to meet the needs of all interested groups.[134] Resolutions from the governing councils of 16 small Southeast communities appealing for Tongass reform weighed heavily, and belied claims of opponents that the impetus for reform came from outside Alaska. State politicians felt caught between the competing interests, and hoped to retain the income from salaried Forest Service employees and the 25 percent of timber-sale receipts guaranteed by law to local government.

Senator Murkowski argued that "more than 50% of the income entering Southeast from natural resources comes directly from the timber industry," and that Congress should not abandon the commitment it made.[135] Senator Stevens accused the environmentalists of seeking federal legislation "to remove the barriers to further wilderness designation in the Tongass," bringing on "another fight about how much of the forest will be left open to the people."[136] Senator William Proxmire awarded his monthly "Golden Fleece" award to the Forest Service and Congress for the timbering arrangement.[137] Citing losses of $365 million since 1982 and a possible $1 billion over the next 20 years, New York congressman Bob Mrazek introduced a strong reform bill. Don Young responded, "When an outsider comes into my backyard to try to change legislation of particular interest in my state, it's when I can stop being reasonable. There are a myriad of things I can do to stop that bill."[138] Many Alaskans looked upon Young as the outsider: "I'm proud of my Congressman Bob Mrazek" showed up on auto bumpers throughout the Southeast. One such van in Juneau had most of its windows smashed. A substitute reform bill by George Miller of California passed the Interior Committee, and later the House by a vote of 361-47.[139] Tongass reform fared worse in the Senate, where Murkowski placed a hold on the bill, preventing a vote before the close of the session in 1988.[140]

15.10. Tongass Timber Reform Act supporters, Sitka, April 1989. Courtesy SEACC. Environmentalists sought to change entrenched Forest Service policy favoring logging over all other national forest uses.

Results of a survey of public opinion in the Southeast, commissioned by Sealaska (Native regional) Corporation, appeared in 1989. Of the respondents, 91 percent claimed to be interested in the Tongass management question, though only slightly more than half indicated awareness of the Alaska Lands Act or the $40-million subsidy. Ratings of the Forest Service averaged 64 percent favorable compared to 62 percent for the Alaska Loggers Association, 53 and 55 percent for the large pulp companies, 54 percent for Southeast Alaska Conservation Council (SEACC), 50 percent for the Wilderness Society, and 39 percent for the Sierra Club. United Fishermen of Alaska tallied highest at 74 percent. Commercial fishing ranked as the most important area industry, scoring 46 percent compared to 19 percent for timbering. By a narrow 46 to 42 percent, respondents believed the Forest Service favored timber to the detriment of other industries, and by 41 to 44 percent they split on whether logging endangered fish and wildlife habitat. Forty-one percent favored modification of the 50-year contracts and 9 percent favored cancellation. Asked whether they wanted additional wilderness, 34 percent said yes and 64 percent no. But when asked whether more Tongass land should be designated wilderness, 48 percent agreed and 50 percent disagreed. Juneau exhibited the most openness to reform, Ketchikan the least.[141]

In June 1990 the Senate passed by 99-0 a Tongass Timber Reform bill containing no designated wilderness acreage. A compromise bill emerged in October and became law on November 28. Among its key contents: six new wilderness areas totaling 296,000 acres; 723,000 additional acres protected from logging; replacement of the mandated $40 million

15.11. Car of Tongass reform advocate, Sitka, April 1989. Courtesy SEACC. Activists on both sides held strong feelings about the Tongass National Forest.

and annual cut of 450 million board feet by market-related sustained-yield provisions; modification of the 50-year contracts to end highgrading and bring timber plans, management, and sales in line with other contracts; and 100-foot setbacks on salmon streams and their major tributaries.[142]

Rapidly growing tourism and ceaseless controversy over ecosystem damage suggested that Forest Service priorities would eventually shift from timber production toward recreational activities. Approximately 70 percent of the state's pleasure visitors came to the Southeast, and over 60 percent of these by cruise ship. Tourists on cruise vessels multiplied from 86,815 in 1980 to 248,428 in 1991. Nearly all these people wanted to see unspoiled natural beauty and wildlife. Visitor groups licensed to operate on land in the Tongass increased from 17 in 1980 to 77 in 1991. Forest Service research, conducted in cooperation with state and other federal agencies, broadened in the realms of wildlife habitat, basic ecology, logging impact, trends in demands of user groups, and other matters related to management of an ecosystem beset by ever-more-numerous influences and disputes. Survey objectives recognized the manifest trend of public demand for more protection of wildlife and ecosystems. As of 1991, 40 percent of the remaining old-growth high-volume forest of the Tongass lay in wilderness or similarly protected tracts.[143]

Environmentalists, initially elated by the Tongass Timber Reform Act, soon came to believe that the Forest Service did not intend to implement it in good faith. In its 1991 revision of the 1979 long-range plan, costing nearly $25 million to produce, the agency favored an insistently logging-oriented alternative. An examination of its plan, prepared for Southeast Alaska Conservation Council by Cascade Holistic Economic Consultants, identified a familiar list of shortcomings: inflated timber price and demand projections to justify unnecessary timber cuts and budget increases; a doubling of road construction mileage, especially in roadless areas, far in advance of most timber sales; failure to count $20 million to $30 million in road costs that would show an annual loss of at least $27 million rather than the claimed $3 million profit; continued highgrading, taking 40 percent of the top-quality timber in 20 years; faulty assumptions about timber inventory and effects on fisheries; and failure to mention losses of recreational potential in roadless areas. The authors asserted that "there are so many errors in the plan that the process can hardly be considered reasonable; nor is there any evidence that the agency attempted to use reasonable data."[144] Barring a thoroughgoing reform of Forest Service incentives, the agency and environmentalists in the Southeast could anticipate endless turmoil.

A 1993 analysis by forest economist Randal O'Toole calculated an average annual loss by the Forest Service in the Tongass between 1989 and 1992 of $38.8 million, including $64.1 million in 1992. In effect, for many years the taxpayers had been paying the two large timber companies to cut down the forest. Tongass losses would continue, O'Toole projected, because "no one involved in the process acts as a guardian of the U.S. Treasury. Members of Congress who allocate the funds have an incentive to waste money because it helps them get reelected. Forest Service officials have an incentive to waste money because it gets them larger budgets." The Forest Service received appropriations based on the amount of timber cut, regardless of the price charged for it. To eliminate the waste of money and trees, O'Toole recommended, forest management should be funded through profits from timber sales and recreation fees.[145] Cancellation of Alaska Pulp Company's 50-year contract moved Tongass economics a step closer to viability.

A 1997 General Accounting Office (GAO) review noted the gradual shift in emphasis of the Forest Service in Alaska from logging toward recreation and wildlife conservation. Internal division over its priorities, and resistance from the Environmental Protection Agency, Fish and Wildlife Service, and National Marine Fisheries Service, contributed to excessive delay in management plans. Insufficient scientific data had been gathered to settle disputes, and the Forest Service had neglected to adequately monitor the effects of logging. As a result, critics put up more and longer resistance to logging plans. To remedy the shortcomings, the GAO recommended that Congress give the Forest Service clearer guidelines for multiple-use priorities and interagency dispute resolution, and increase the agency's accountability for delay by application of the Government Performance and Results Act.[146]

Attempts to revise the Tongass management plan lasted through most of the decade. For the first time, the Forest Service put together an interagency team of biologists to draft safeguards for wildlife. The team judged prevailing logging practices to be unsustainable. They mapped out large tracts of old growth needed by nine species, some the subject of demonstrated concern by environmentalists: grizzly bears, Sitka deer, the Charlotte Island goshawk, and the Alexander Archipelago wolf. Superiors withheld their report for nearly two years; a journalist obtained it through the Freedom of Information Act. Democratic leaders in Congress then demanded a review by prominent scientists, who recommended even stronger wildlife guarantees. Under the Clinton administration, Tongass policy shifted in the direction of science-based management. The Biodiversity Legal Foundation successfully sued to list the Queen Charlotte goshawk and Alexander Archipelago wolf as threatened species, thereby forcing broader habitat protection measures in the Tongass plan.[147]

When Murkowski and Young took over the Senate and House natural resource committees in 1995, and Stevens later assumed the chair of the Appropriations Committee, the delegation intensified its maneuvers to increase logging and weaken preservation measures. Young introduced a bill to transfer the Tongass National Forest to the State of Alaska. Dozens of bills, riders, hearings, and other moves pressed their agenda. Murkowski, the most active, sought to dampen criticism by selling his Louisiana Pacific Ketchikan stock by mid-1995. The Alaska Rainforest Campaign and SEACC led the environmental defense against the delegation's attack, though they disavowed the attempt to list threatened species, which they feared would stir up more opposition than they could handle.[148]

Before the Louisiana Pacific Ketchikan pulp mill closed its doors in fall 1996, Senator Murkowski tried to hold hostage a parks bill in an attempt to secure a 15-year extension of its logging contract. The Clinton administration negotiated for a three-year close-out period and economic assistance to Southeast communities. In mid-1997 the Forest Service issued its ten-year Tongass management plan. It specified 500 miles of wild and scenic rivers, and otherwise shielded streams and shorelines. It also permitted an annual cut of 267 million board feet, a figure environmentalists regarded as far out of line with the 1996 cut of 120 million, and a rejection of the wishes of a majority of citizens commenting on the proposal. Neither did it satisfy the Alaska Forest Association, which sought larger cuts.[149]

Based on numerous appeals of the 1997 plan, Assistant Secretary of Agriculture Jim Lyons amended it in 1999. The annual harvest would be reduced to 187 million board feet, incorporating measures to discourage highgrading. Rotation intervals for harvest would double from 100 to 200 years. Land use would be based on 19 separate categories, and 18 areas totaling 234,000 acres formerly slated for logging would be protected as "mostly natural." Many tracts would be set aside for community recreation or biological research, and additional river corridors reviewed for wild and scenic status. Road building would be sharply reduced. The amendments brought the total of protected high-volume old-growth Tongass forest to 3.55 million acres, or 70 percent of what remained. A joint monitoring effort would involve the EPA, Fish and Wildlife Service, National Marine Fisheries Service, and the state, and would invite citizen participation. The new formulation sought to ensure a sustainable timber industry while maintaining the ecological integrity of the forest. Barring reversals by legislation or administrative decisions, the ten-year plan set Tongass policy firmly on a reform track.[150]

A 1999 economic analysis by Erickson & Associates, commissioned by SEACC, identified the rationale of the long-standing federal timber program as political, not viably economic. The congressional delegation, the two large timber companies, the Forest Service, and local leaders had insisted that subsidies must continue lest there be economic disaster. Yet the mill closings (at Sitka in 1993 and Ketchikan in 1996) had caused only minor and temporary losses of employment, population, and business activity. Fading fortunes of the timber industry had largely resulted from depletion of Native forests, higher prices for federal timber, and the low world price of pulp. Economic trends suggested that the remaining saw timber industry would more likely shrink than grow. Reliance on subsidies, said the report, "can make the community more, rather than less vulnerable to distant decisions over which the community in the future may have less control. Unless such decisions are based on sound economics, they are easily overturned when today's powerful senators no longer occupy the critical chaimanships."[151]

On one level, the struggle over the Tongass pitted interest groups—environmentalists and commercial fishers, subsistence advocates, and outdoor recreation people—against the Forest Service, organized loggers, and large timber companies. As a systemic issue, it involved those for and against the reform of a powerful bureaucracy and its legal, economic, and political underpinnings. At base it manifested in large part a clash between ecological and exploitation perspectives: people who wanted to save a rainforest because they perceived nature as inherently valuable and integral to human life versus those who treated it as an economic commodity to be consumed for short-term benefit.

Pressure from many sides—environmentalists and their allies, national media, Congress, and even dissidents within its own ranks—forced the Forest Service into a position of greater responsibility for the impact of logging. The widening array of critics made full use of the tools of modern environmental conflict, including numerous lawsuits and television, magazine, and newspaper articles. They managed to persuade many Southeast Alaskans of the dubious wisdom of clear-cut logging, and to put the state government in an equivocal position. Reformers made some headway by submitting proposals in the Forest Service planning process, though the agency rejected most of their suggestions.

Accumulating, increasingly broad-based research showed clear-cutting of old growth to be unsustainable in its effects on fish and wildlife, and objective analyses revealed the economic unsustainability of the large-scale timbering operation. Corporate accountability gained legitimacy but, excepting modest sanctions for water pollution, the big timber companies largely escaped accounting for their numerous abuses. However, closing of the pulp mills for economic reasons signaled the decline of the timber industry as the dominant Forest Service client, to be eventually replaced by the fast-rising tourism industry and other unsubsidized, primarily local users. If the Forest Service were to take seriously the directive to involve other agencies and the public in the management process, it would make a quantum change toward social and environmental responsibility. At minimum, in the pursuit of its own interest, the service in Alaska would have to adopt principles of environmental sustainability.

NOTES

1. Wilderness Society, *America's Vanishing Rain Forest*, 142; Harris and Farr, *Forest Ecosystem of Southeast Alaska*, 16; Matthew D. Kirchhoff, interview by author, July 14, 1989. Percentages of tree species in the coastal rainforest vary according to latitude and altitude.

2. Horton and Lobaugh, "Wilderness and Fisheries," 9; Ketchum and Ketchum, *The Tongass*, 9.

3. Evans, *An Historical View*, 507–511.

4. Rakestraw, *History of the U.S. Forest Service*, 15.

5. G. Rogers, *Alaska in Transition*, 73.

6. Alaska Governor, *Report, 1904*, 20–1.

7. Steen, *The Forest Service*, 148–152.

8. Evans, *Historical View*, 520, 526–533; 41 Stat. 988, June 5, 1920.

9. Buchanan, "History," 46–48.

10. Haycox, "Economic Development," 23–25, 29, 37–43; 60 Stat. 1049, August 13, 1946; 61 Stat. 920, August 8, 1947.

11. Buchanan, "History," 28–40.

12. Haycox, "Economic Development," 44–46; *Tlingit and Haida Indians v. U.S.* 177 F. Supp. 452 (Court of Claims, 1959).

13. Rakestraw, *History of the U.S. Forest Service*, 127–128; U.S. Forest Service, *Timber Supply, 1992*, 6; Joe Mehrkens, interview by author, July 12, 1989.

14. Evans, *An Historical View*, 555–556; 72 Stat. 339, July 7, 1958.

15. O'Toole, *Reforming the Forest Service*, 21–22; 74 Stat. 215, June 12, 1960; 78 Stat. 890, September 3, 1964.

16. Greenough and Johnstone, "Evolution of Timber Practices," 4–5.

17. Powers, "Public Involvement," 89–105.

18. Baade, Personal history, 1985; Kelly, "Dixie Baade," 2; *Ravencall*, Fall 1991, 1, 10; Dixie Baade, letters to author, September 15, 1988; May 15, 1989.

19. Baade, "Multiple Use in the Tongass," 13–14.

20. *Alaska Conservation Review (ACR)*, Spring 1976, 6–8; C. Hunter, "Legacy of Jack Calvin," 8–9; *Sitka Sentinel*, "Services Thursday for Jack Calvin, 83," undated, 1985; Margaret Calvin, letter to author, August 8, 1988; *Ravencall*, January 1980, 4. For story of canoe trip see Jack Calvin, "Nakwasina Goes North," 1–42.

21. Gordon, "Memo to Cooperators"; Gordon, "Early Alaskan Conservation Efforts," 1–2. Originally titled "Southeast Alaska Conservation Coordinating Committee," it had six member groups: Sitka/Sierra, Juneau/Sierra, Southeast Alaska Mountaineering Association, and Sitka, Tongass, and Petersburg Conservation Societies.

22. Gordon, "Proposal," 24–28; Gordon, interview by author, July 6, 1988.

23. Hensel, Spencer, and Hickok, "Willard Troyer"; Jack Hession, interview by author, August 6, 1992. Hession, a Californian, took an M.A. in political science at San Diego State College and interrupted doctoral work in natural resources at the University of Washington to do research and Sierra Club work in Alaska. He helped shape ANILCA and by the 1990s had become the longest continually serving environmental leader in Alaska.

24. Cohen, *History of the Sierra Club*, 124, 194–195, 399; Clepper, *Leaders in American Conservation*, 333–334; Wayburn, letters to author, October 3 and December 18, 1989.

25. *Ravencall*, February 1977, 5.

26. Powers, "Public Involvement," 76–77; Calvin, "Saws at Sitka," 37.

27. *New York Times*, July 4, 1965, 36.

28. Ibid., February 8, 1968, 66; Durbin, *Tongass*, 31.

29. *New York Times*, February 8, 1968, 66.

30. Ibid., 31, 50–52.

31. Leopold and Barrett, *Implications for Wildlife*, 48.

32. Cannon, "Heritage in Probate," 24.

33. M. Miller, "The Fight for the Trees," 16–17; *Sierra Club v. Hardin* 325 F.Supp. 99 (1971).

34. Schmidt, "Tongass Opportunity," 1; *New York Times*, June 15, 1976, 53.

35. Robert B. Weeden, interview by author, August 15, 1989.

36. Calvin, "Moratorium," 7; Powers, "Public Involvement," 80, 107.

37. *Sierra Club Alaska Newsletter*, January 1973, 2.

38. Stein, "Point Baker Law Suit," 9–10; *Zieske v. Butz* 412 F. Supp. 1403 (1976).

39. O'Toole, *Reforming the Forest Service*, 23; 90 Stat. 2949, October 22, 1976.

40. Reinwand, article in *Alaska Conservation Review*, Fall-Winter 1970, 14; M. Miller, "Alaska's Tongass Suit," 31.

41. Ketchum and Ketchum, *The Tongass*, 14.

42. Gordon, "History of Conservationists' Efforts," 1–2.

43. King, "Salmon Stream Destruction," 6–7, 11; Hession, "New Threat," 14.

44. James G. King, interview by author, July 13, 1989.

45. Wilderness Society, *America's Vanishing Rain Forest*, 170–171.

46. Wallmo and Schoen, "Response of Deer," 448.

47. Gordon, "History of Conservationists' Efforts"; Powers, "Public Involvement," 93–95.

48. *Alaska*, "Alaska Sportsman," September 1979, 30.

49. Evans, *An Historical View*, 558.

50. *Sierra-Juneau Newsletter*, June 1973; Whitesell, "Southeast Wildlands Study," 7–8; *Ravencall*, June 21, 1976, 1.

51. Calvin, "Saws at Sitka," 37.

52. Gordon, "Early Alaskan Conservation Efforts," 2; *Alaska Geographic*, "Admiralty: Island in Contention," 26–31.

53. Wilderness Society, *America's Vanishing Rain Forest*, 45–49; 94 Stat. 2371, December 2, 1980, Sec. 503, 703, 705.

54. Matthews and McKnight, "Renewable Resource Commitments," 575; K. Hall, "Second-Growth Forests," 10.

55. Alaback, "Endless Battles," 48.

56. Schoen, Kirchhoff, and Thomas, *Seasonal Distribution,* 9; Schoen, Wallmo, and Kirchhoff, "Wildlife-Forest Relationships," 538–541; Schoen and Kirchhoff, "Little Deer," 54–55.

57. Matthews and McKnight, "Renewable Resource Commitments," 575–579; Schoen, Kirchhoff, and Wallmo, "Sitka Black-Tailed Deer," 315–319; Kirchhoff, "Forest Cover," 32.

58. Wilderness Society, *America's Vanishing Rain Forest*, 149–156, 152–158; Schoen et al., "Denning Ecology of Brown Bears," 30, 36, 37.

59. Schoen and Beier, *Brown Bear Habitat Preferences,* 4–5.

60. Schoen, "Bear Habitat Management," 148.

61. *Ravencall*, "Bear Season Closed," September-November 1988, 1, 8; Rice and Robichaud, "Brown Bear Overharvest," 9.

62. Schoen, Wallmo, and Kirchhoff, "Wildlife-Forest Relationships," 539–540.

63. Hughes, "Winter Hideouts," 60–61.

64. M. Murphy, "Forestry Impacts," xvii.

65. U.S. Forest Service, *Status of the Tongass, 1987 Report*, 36–37.

66. B. Koehler, "You Don't Know," 8.

67. U.S. Forest Service, *Status of the Tongass, 1987 Report*, 15.

68. Ketchum and Ketchum, *The Tongass*, 84–85.

69. U.S. Forest Service, *Status of the Tongass, 1987 Report*, 12–14. For example, direct expenditures on recreation use and fish and wildlife totaled about $4 million of the $46 million budget in 1987.

70. Kallick et al., *Last Stand*, 20–24; 94 Stat. 2371, December 2, 1980, Sec. 705(a).

71. Tussing, "Alaska's Petroleum-Based Economy," 68–69.

72. O'Toole, *Reforming the Forest Service*, xi–xii, 104–110, 160–168, 183.

73. *New York Times*, June 14, 1987, 31.

74. Ibid., October 5, 1986, 38.

75. Ibid., July 11, 1987, 30.

76. U.S. Congress, Senate Committee on Energy and Natural Resources, *Tongass Timber Reform Act: Hearings*, 1987, 528–531.

77. U.S. Forest Service, *Status of the Tongass, 1987 Report*, 34–35; Wilderness Society, *America's Vanishing Rain Forest*, 4.

78. U.S. House Interior Committee, *Hearing: HR 987*, 1989, 60.

79. U.S. Forest Service, *Status of the Tongass, 1987 Report*, 5; Rae, "Alaska's Timber Industry," 6–9.

80. U.S. Forest Service, Alaska Region, *Timber Supply: Draft 1988 Report*, 3; *Fiscal Year 1991*, 5, 16.

81. *Juneau Empire*, October 29, 1987; Durbin, *Tongass*, 136–147.

82. Edwards, "Wasted Logs," 11–13.

83. Matthews and McKnight, "Renewable Resource Commitments," 575–581; Donald E. McKnight, interview by author, June 23, 1988.

84. Wilderness Society, *America's Vanishing Rain Forest*, 10.

85. Wildlife Society, Alaska Chapter, *Position Paper*.

86. Simel and Pyles, "Admiralty Island," 14–18.

87. Zaelke, "Admiralty Island Update," 2; Peale, "Shee Atika," 9; Kallick and Peale, "Log Dumps," 10; P. Barnett, "Appeals Court OKs Cube Cove Logging," 5.

88. Hellard, "New Proposals," 3; Wuerthner, "Natives—The First Ecologists?" 22.

89. 104 Stat. 4426, November 28, 1990, Sec. 502.

90. *Ravencall*, December 1980, 3–4; Stratton and Peale, "Kadashan," 1, 12.

91. Kallick, "SEACC and Tenakee," 1,9; Kallick and Peale, "Road Cuts Into Kadashan," 1, 4; *Ravencall*, December 1985, 1,8; *Juneau Empire*, November 4, 1987.

92. 104 Stat. 4426, November 28, 1990, Sec. 106.

93. *Ravencall*, Summer-Fall 1985, 3; Kallick, "Forest Service Agrees," 3; L. Adams, *Sierra Club Legal Defense Fund*, 1987, 4.

94. 104 Stat. 4426, November 28, 1990, Sec. 201.

95. Durbin, *Tongass*, 79–81; Sierra Club Legal Defense Fund, news release, September 30, 1986; McAllister, "Conflict Over Logging," *Juneau Empire*, November 4, 1987.

96. Kemp, "Tenakee Vows to Fight," 8; 104 Stat. 4426, November 28, 1990, Sec. 101, 103.

97. L. Adams, *Sierra Club Legal Defense Fund*, 1987, 4–5; Adams, "Memorandum to Dr. Edgar Wayburn."

98. Kallick, "Subsistence Users Sue," 1, 8; Waldo, "Court Blocks Logging," 7.

99. *Center News*, February 4, 1977; *New York Times*, September 28, 1984, 30.

100. *New York Times*, October 2, 1984, 26; October 8, 1985, 30.

101. *Ravencall*, May-June 1986, 8.

102. Romanoff, "Legacy of APC's Contract," 5; Jane Fritsch, "Threat to Cut EPA Budget Reflects a New Political Shift," *New York Times*, August 24, 1996, 1.

103. Durbin, *Tongass*, 234–239; *Amicus Journal*, "In Defense," 53. Plaintiffs included the Alaska Cleanwater Alliance, Alaska Rainforest Campaign, Natural Resources Defense Council, and Sierra Club.

104. Kelly, "Pulp Mill Violating," 6; Shepard, "Victory Against Alaska," 5; *Juneau Empire*, October 26, 1987; Shepard, "APC Violates Consent Decree," 15.

105. Romanoff, "Legacy of APC's Contract," 5; Durbin, *Tongass*, 228–231.

107. Kallick, "Eagles Massacred," 5; *Juneau Empire*, April 27, 1988, 1.

106. Barlow, "Mandate for Oblivion," 30–32; *New York Times*, June 12, 1983, 37; Drais, "The Tongass Timber Reform Act," 347; *Reid Bros. Logging Co. v. Ketchikan Pulp Co.*, 699 F. 2d 1292 (1983). See also Durbin, *Tongass*, chaps. 4 and 8.

108. U.S. General Accounting Office, *Tongass Timber Provision*, 31–32; U.S. Forest Service, *Timber Supply, 1987 Report*, 20; *Juneau Empire*, October 27, 1987.

109. U.S. Forest Service, *Timber Supply, 1987 Report*, 4.

110. U.S. Government Accounting Office, *Tongass: Timber Provision*, 38; Kallick et al., *Last Stand*, 18.

111. Durbin, *Tongass*, 121–128; Wilderness Society, *America's Vanishing Rain Forest*, 6–8.

112. Franklin, "Logging by Law," 52; U.S. Forest Service, *Status of the Tongass, 1987 Report*, 3; U.S. Forest Service, *Timber Supply and Demand, 1987*, 3.

113. U.S. Government Accounting Office, *Tongass National Forest: Timber Provision*, 33–36.

114. Skow, "Forest Service Follies," 80–82.

115. Rae, "Alaska's Timber Industry," 1–9; Kleeschulte, "Torrents Over Timber," 24–26; U.S. Forest Service, *Timber Supply and Demand, 1989*, 15–27; U.S. Forest Service, *Status of the Tongass, 1989 Report*, 2–1.

116. U.S. Forest Service, *Timber Supply and Demand, 1994*, 10–15, 20, 30.

117. *Anchorage Daily News*, July 12, 1993, B1–2; Brodie, "Tongass National Forest Victory," 1–2.

118. Fitzgerald, *Options for Conservation*, 29; Durbin, *Tongass,* 168–170, 173–175.

119. *New York Times*, October 5, 1986, 38.

120. Franklin, "Logging by Law," 51.

121. U.S. Congress, Senate Subcommittee on Public Lands, *Tongass Timber Reform Act: Hearings*, 253.

122. Ibid., 297.

123. Ibid., 309–310.

124. Ibid., 314–316.

125. *Juneau Empire*, October 30, 1987.

126. U.S. Congress, Senate Subcommittee on Public Lands, *Tongass Timber Reform Act: Hearings*, 432, 435.

127. *New York Times*, October 5, 1986, 38.

128. U.S. Congress, Senate Subcommittee on Public Lands, *Tongass Timber Reform Act: Hearing*, 469–471.

129. Franklin, "Logging by Law," 29.

130. *Ravencall*, "APC Fires Worker," 5; Finch, "House Committee Urges Prosecution," 3; Durbin, *Tongass*, 181–182, 186–187.

131. Beach, "Time to Ax," 103–105.

132. *New York Times*, June 25, 1987, 26.

133. U.S. Congress, Senate Subcommittee on Public Lands, *Tongass Timber Reform Act: Hearing*, 154.

134. Gatton, *1987 Legislation*, 6; Gatton, *1988 Legislative Session*, 8; State of Alaska, *Session Laws, 1988*, SJR 35.

135. Murkowski, "Commentary Southeast," 50.

136. U.S. Congress, Senate Subcommittee on Public Lands, *Tongass Timber Reform Act: Hearing*, 24–25.

137. *Ravencall*, July-Aug 1986, 4.

138. *Juneau Empire*, November 3, 1987.

139. J. Koehler, "Tongass Reform," 1, 8; Lawrence, "House Votes to Limit," 2112.

140. Finch, "Alaska Senators Block," 1, 8.

141. Decision Sciences, *Southeast Alaskans' Attitudes*, 17–20, 33, 42, 54–55, 65–66; *Juneau Empire*, March 7, 1989.

142. Finch, "Tongass Timber Reform Act," 1, 8–10; 104 Stat. 4426, November 28, 1990, Titles 1–4.

143. U.S. Forest Service, *Status of the Tongass, 1991* Draft, 2–5–7; 3-1,2; 6-1-5.

144. Cascade Holistic Economic Consultants, *Review*, iii–9.

145. O'Toole, *The $64 Million Question*, 1–2, 32.

146. US General Accounting Office, *Tongass National Forest: Lack of Accountability*, chaps. 0–0.41.

147. Durbin, "A Struggle for Science," 8–11; Durbin, *Tongass*, chap. 14, 277–278.

148. Durbin, *Tongass*, 267–278.

149. John H. Cushman Jr., "Senate Approves Bill to Preserve Parks Including Sterling Forest," *New York Times*, October 4, 1996, 1; Cushman, "US Clears New Cutting in Forest in Alaska," *New York Times*, May 24, 1997, 9; *Alaska Report*, "Forest Service Issues Plan," 6.

150. U.S. Department of Agriculture. *Record of Decision*, 4–5, 9–16.

151. Erickson & Associates, *Beyond Tongass Timber*, 6–16, 23–29.

16

Arctic Wilderness: A Question of Values

Hundreds of miles north of the Tongass National Forest, another federal land-use issue—a test of wilderness versus oil—matured by the 1980s into one of the salient environmental conflicts of North America. Oil companies and their allies in state and national government valued oil above the wilderness qualities to be sacrificed for it. Environmental advocates thought the sustainability principle especially applicable to a large and pristine ecosystem. For nearly half a century the two sides carried on the fight in the media, legislatures, courts, regulatory proceedings, and other forums.

Less than two years into statehood, Alaska had acquired one of its most controversial land designations: the Arctic National Wildlife Range (ANWR). National Park Service officials, aware of the ecologically diverse and unspoiled character of the region, had called on Wilderness Society director Olaus Murie in 1951 for help in its preservation. Murie, a wildlife biologist who had studied caribou in northern Alaska during the 1920s, responded. He and his wife Margaret had envisioned such a refuge since their 1924 honeymoon dogsled trip into the Brooks Range, as had Murie's Wilderness Society colleague and founder Bob Marshall. Overcoming opposition from Alaskan mineral interests and politicians, ANWR backers persuaded Secretary of the Interior Fred Seaton to reserve the refuge in December 1960. Their victory heartened environmentalists and called attention to Alaska, where far broader land decisions would soon be made. Within Alaska, ANWR and Project Chariot combined to launch an environmental movement.

Olaus and Margaret Murie's Arctic refuge success meant, like every other act of preservation, a step and not a destination. Secretary Seaton's order permitted mineral leasing contingent on the Interior secretary's authorization, a hint of future trouble. Alaska's attempts to pressure Secretary Stewart Udall to abolish ANWR failed. Senator Gruening blocked any funding for the refuge before his defeat in 1968, a few months after the oil discovery at Prudhoe Bay close to the western border of ANWR.[1]

Measured by oil profits, Prudhoe Bay wrote the outstanding success story on the North Slope. In the nearby National Petroleum Reserve-Alaska (NPRA), exploration by government agencies followed permissive 1976 legislation, and private companies gained entry in 1980. Fish and Wildlife Service recommendations resulted in some exemptions for tracts

16.1. Margaret Murie and Celia Hunter celebrate 25th anniversary of the Arctic Refuge, Fairbanks, 1985. By Alaska Conservation Foundation. Courtesy Northern Alaska Environmental Center (NAEC). Margaret and Olaus Murie led the 1950s effort to safeguard the refuge.

important for wildlife. Most of the drilling occurred in the northeast corner of the Petroleum Reserve near Prudhoe Bay where the navy had prospected in the early 1950s. Drillers had poor luck.[2] On a tract south of Barrow to the west, despite high expectations, Standard gave up after sinking 128 holes, finding virtually no oil. Similarly, Exxon and Diamond Shamrock spent $1.2 billion drilling northwest of Prudhoe Bay without success.[3] Prudhoe Bay itself peaked production at 1.6 million barrels a day in 1988; analysts expected it to taper off to about half that amount by the turn of the century.[4] Finds in nearby areas, and a possible gas pipeline and Arctic Refuge oil production, could extend North Slope oil operations well into the twenty-first century.

NORTH SLOPE GAS

Near its great reservoirs of oil, the North Slope held large quantities of natural gas. By the early 1970s, oil production on the North Slope had given rise to ideas for transporting gas to the Lower 48. In the aftermath of the pipeline issue, attention shifted to proposals for a gas line. But how best to get the gas south? Several possibilities existed: (1) pipe it to the west coast of Alaska, liquify it, and ship it south; (2) pipe it to Valdez and do the same; or (3) pipe it eastward across ANWR and southward through Canada's Mackenzie River Valley. Environmentalists found this last alternative unacceptable. Participating in Bureau of Land Management hearings and represented by Sierra Club Legal Defense Fund before the Federal Power Commission, they suggested a fourth route: south from Prudhoe Bay to Fairbanks, down the Alaska Highway to Edmonton, thence to the Lower 48. The Federal Power Commission split on the question, but the President's Council on Environmental Quality favored the Alaska Highway route. In 1977 the Arctic Gas Consortium abandoned the ANWR route and endorsed the Alaska Highway option.[5]

Canada helped quash the ANWR gas route. Its interest in the pipeline prompted the commissioning of retired British Columbia justice Thomas Berger to direct a feasibility study. Having completed an intensive survey involving hundreds of personal visits to Native homes in every village to be affected by a pipeline, Berger wrote a document most unusual in government management of natural resources. In the interest of maintaining the natural integrity of the area and its viability for Native subsistence, Berger recommended that no ANWR pipeline be constructed and that an international wildlife range be established, Canada matching the acreage of ANWR to double its size. In 1978 the Canadian government set aside 10 million acres corresponding to Berger's recommendation, and in 1984 it instituted a 3-million-acre Northern Yukon National Park along the U.S. border.[6]

In the wake of the 1978 Canadian land allocation, the United States and Canada discussed treaty options for protection of the Porcupine caribou herd. Conferees envisioned an international commission possessing power to conduct research and implement conservation measures. The Alaska Conservation Society approved the idea, as did the Tanana Chiefs (representing the regional Athabaskans) and the Kaktovik Eskimos. The state and North Slope Borough worked against a treaty, fearing it would limit their access to minerals and the state's authority over wildlife.[7] Soon after he took office in 1981, Interior Secretary James Watt cancelled the negotiations. The United States and Canada eventually signed a Porcupine caribou herd agreement in 1987, which lacked any authority superceding state or territorial powers. Environmentalists then sought full wilderness status for an international refuge.

Economics precluded attempts to build a gas pipeline in the 1970s and 1980s. Two major companies, Arco and Columbia Gas, lost interest, but efforts to realize a Valdez route persisted. By 1995, market conditions in East Asia indicated that Alaskan gas might be profitably sold shortly after the year 2000. Yukon Pacific Corporation secured permits for a gas line paralleling the oil pipeline from Prudhoe Bay to Valdez. Meanwhile, the North Slope oil companies investigated shipment of the gas through the Chukchi Sea by icebreaker tankers or by construction of a gas line westward through 500 miles of pristine land to the Chukchi coast. In a rare display of industry-environmentalist cooperation, the Alaska Conservation Foundation and Yukon Pacific jointly devised an environmentally sound Prudhoe-Valdez plan, and sided against oil company routing through the Chukchi Sea.[8]

As the turn of the century neared, parties moved toward resolution of the gas issue. Arco, British Petroleum, and Exxon, owners of nine trillion cubic feet of gas, reached a tentative deal with Yukon Pacific. A 42-inch buried pipe would carry the gas to Valdez, to be liquified for shipment to Japan. The $15 billion project would yield $400 million annually in royalties to Alaska, setting off another economic boom and influx of population. Anticipating greatly increased pressure on the land, Alaskan environmentalists called for thorough impact studies for the project. A pipeline might still be negated by competition for the Japanese market, or by delay past the point where oil companies could operate on the North Slope.[9]

ANILCA AND ANWR

In changing the Arctic National Wildlife Range to a wildlife refuge (also termed ANWR, or the Arctic Refuge) the Alaska National Interest Lands Conservation Act (ANILCA) cited four purposes: "(1) to conserve fish and wildlife populations and habitats in their natural diversity . . . ; (2) to fulfill the international treaty obligations of the United States with respect to fish and wildlife and their habitats; (3) to provide . . . the opportunity for continued subsistence by local residents; and (4) to ensure . . . water quality and the necessary water quantity within the refuge." Notwithstanding the commitment to conservation, the refuge bore an uncertain status. ANILCA registered the tension between preservation and mineral exploitation values in the Arctic Refuge. Although both House bills had prescribed full wilderness protection for the original portion of the refuge, the Senate's will prevailed. The refuge doubled to 18 million acres, 8 million in the northern half delimited as wilderness.[10] Abandonment of state selection of 972,000 acres in 1983 and addition of 325,000 acres by Congress in 1988 increased the total to nearly 19.3 million acres.[11] However, a 1.5-million-acre, 125-by-30-mile section of the coastal plain, bearing the highest potential for oil and gas production, did not receive wilderness standing. Popularly termed the "1002 area" or "coastal plain," it derived its status from section 1002 of ANILCA, directing the Interior Department to complete a survey within six years assessing the biological values, potential oil and gas reserves, and the possible impact of oil and gas operations on the wildlife of the coastal plain. Section 1002 also requested from the Interior secretary a recommendation on the advisability of permitting oil and gas activity on the plain.

All signs suggested the Reagan administration knew from the beginning what the research would conclude: it wanted oil and gas drilling, and treated wilderness as an impediment. After consulting the Alaska congressional delegation, Secretary Watt assigned the task to the U.S. Geological Survey, whose expertise related to mineral extraction rather than wildlife. Environmental groups represented by Trustees for Alaska won a federal court suit in 1981, ordering that the Fish and Wildlife Service carry out the study and monitor the activity of oil company prospectors. To avoid injury to the tundra, the service restricted surface vehicles to winter months and to land covered by six inches or more of snow, and directed that wildlife concentrations be avoided. The exploration took place in the winters of 1984 and 1985 amid arguments over snow cover and vehicle impacts. Light snows resulted in some gouges in the tundra, still visible 15 years later. On-site monitors complained that superiors ignored their recommendations for mitigation of damage, such as use of helicopters in place of ground vehicles. Biologists believed they lacked sufficient time to properly gauge the effects of potential development on wildlife.[12] Expressing the concerns of the environmental community, the Northern Alaska Environmental Center set up a volunteer field operation to monitor the study.[13]

Meanwhile, the administration attempted to open the Arctic Refuge by a different tactic. A little-noticed deal, made by the Interior Department in 1983, traded subsurface mineral rights of 92,000 acres of high-potential land on the coastal plain near Kaktovik to Arctic Slope Regional Corporation in return for its 101,000 acres of inholding at Chandler Lake in Gates of the Arctic National Park. Prior to finalization of the deal, Interior reduced the mineral land's valuation from $390 million to about $6 million—less than $50 per acre. The Native

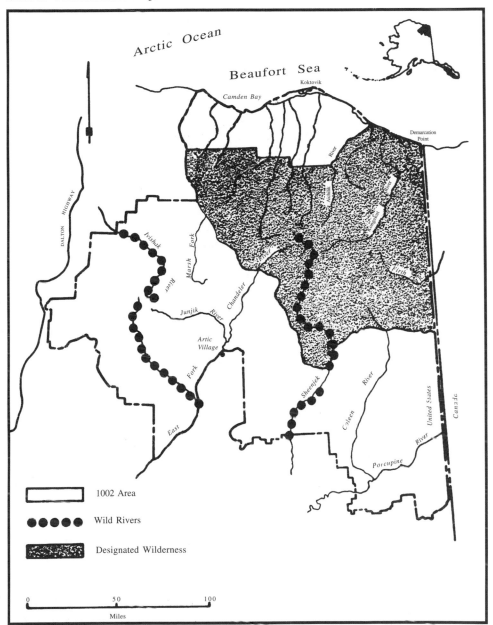

16.1. Arctic National Wildlife Refuge, 1992. Courtesy U.S. Fish and Wildlife Service, Division of Realty, Anchorage.

corporation had signed a contract with a group of oil companies headed by Chevron, who sank a well on the site and kept secret the results. The drilling appeared to violate the Alaska Lands Act. Risking a serious miscalculation, environmentalists chose not to challenge the trade in court lest it undermine their lawsuit over St. Matthew Island (Chapter 14).[14] In 1985,

Interior initiated a swap code-named "Project M" or "Megatrade"—891,000 acres of inholdings in national wildlife refuges to be exchanged by 18 Native corporations, all linked to oil companies, for subsurface rights of 168,000 acres on the Arctic Refuge coastal plain. As in the 1983 deal, Interior sought to trade away lands containing the highest potential for oil production. Natives would retain subsurface rights in the wildlife refuges, thereby leaving most involved lands open for mineral extraction. The parties signed Megatrade at an unannounced meeting in an Arlington, Virginia, motel in July 1987.[15]

Revelations of Megatrade and the 1983 deal provoked strong criticism. Environmentalists attacked Megatrade as a scheme to give away public resources to the oil companies, gain political support of the Natives, and further oil and gas activity in the Arctic Refuge without congressional permission. Speaking to the Alaska state legislators, Senator Frank Murkowski declared, "One thing the swaps would insure is that we get drilling in ANWR. If we're lucky, and something hits there will be that much more pressure to open up ANWR."[16] The state, originally involved in the trade negotiations, withdrew in early 1987. Oil companies not parties to the deal also repudiated it.[17] Trustees for Alaska sued in 1987 on behalf of six environmental groups, contending that Megatrade violated several federal statutes.[18]

A September 1988 General Accounting Office (GAO) analysis judged the trade not in the public interest. Of the 896,000 acres to be received from the Natives, it calculated, 349,000 already had protection from development and 270,000 other acres had been rated by Interior itself as low priority. Of the remaining high-priority lands, 53,000 acres would be vulnerable to subsurface mineral extraction. Moreover, the GAO charged, Interior had valued the Native land at $529 million as compared to its appraised value of $90 million. It characterized Interior's estimated values of the Arctic Refuge acreage as "highly uncertain," and noted that Interior sources acknowledged some of the lands could be worth up to 6.5 times the stated figure. Inadequate geological data and lack of information about the oil well at Kaktovik added to the uncertainty.[19] By overvaluing the Native land and undervaluing the mineral land, the administration intended to grant the oil companies mineral rights at a small fraction of fair value. Interior Secretary Donald Hodel eventually acknowledged the existence of Megatrade and relented, agreeing to file an environmental impact statement and not consummate the trade prior to congressional opening of the Arctic Refuge. A law passed in August 1988 forbade any trade in the refuge in the absence of congressional action.[20]

ENVIRONMENTAL IMPACT OF OIL OPERATIONS

Controversy surrounded the Fish and Wildlife Service projection of the impact of oil on the coastal plain. Interior planned to send the findings to Congress, bypassing public review. Trustees for Alaska, Northern Alaska Environmental Center, and three other Alaskan groups sued in 1985 and won a judgment ordering public hearings.[21] Interior's draft impact statement appeared in November 1986. It cited projections by biologists that full oil and gas production could reduce or displace populations of caribou by 20–40 percent and deplete other mammals and birds; the disruption would last 30 to 90 years. It expressed greatest concern for the welfare of the Porcupine caribou herd of 170,000, annually migrating up to 2,700 miles on its meandering journey between the Arctic coast and its wintering grounds on the south slope of the Brooks Range and in the Ogilvie Mountains of the Yukon. For the

16.2. Grizzly bear, Arctic Refuge. By Wilbur Mills. Along with the wolf and great caribou herds, the grizzly bear symbolized wilderness. Oil activity on the North Slope reduced populations of grizzlies and other animals.

calving season, the coastal plain provided food and relative relief from predators and insects. The statement noted that 82 percent of the cows gave birth on the coastal plain in 1985.

Interior's document admitted that "oil and gas development will result in widespread, long-term changes in wildlife habitats, wilderness environment, and Native community activities." It predicted the oil industry would convert local Eskimo culture to a cash economy. As for oil potential, it estimated a 19 percent chance of finding recoverable oil. If such oil should be found, it calculated a 5 percent chance of finding 9 billion barrels, a 95 percent chance of 600 million, and a median probability of 3.2 billion. By comparison, Prudhoe Bay held a known 12 billion. To be recoverable, Arctic Refuge oil would have to be priced at $33 per barrel in 1984 dollars; in 1987 it sold for about $10 per barrel. The secretary's recommendation described the coastal plain as "the most outstanding oil and gas frontier area in North America," and "In addition to reducing the dependence on foreign oil, contributions from the 1002 area would enhance the national security of the country, produce a more favorable balance of trade by saving $8.1 billion in the year 2005 on the cost of imported oil, and provide overall enhanced economic benefits to the Nation." It called for full oil and gas exploitation of the 1.55-million-acre coastal area.[22]

Interior issued its final impact statement and plan in April 1987, accepting the judgments of the preliminary report. It had deleted some first-draft wording including mention of the "unique and irreplaceable core calving grounds" and the projected 20–40 percent reduction or displacement of caribou. It conceded that losses of musk oxen, wolves, grizzly and polar bears, wolverines, waterfowl, and raptors could be expected; that "major effects on the Porcupine Caribou Herd could result if the entire area were leased and oil prospects contained economically recoverable oil"; and that "the wilderness value of the [coastal plain] would be eliminated." It went on to advocate full-scale oil activity, reciting the list of company claims about the compatibility of oil and wildlife preservation. On the page opposite the beginning of "Secretary's Recommendation" appeared a photo of grazing caribou cows and their calves against the backdrop of a large oil complex, captioned "production facility."[23]

Even though more than half the citizens commenting on the proposed alternatives preferred classification of the entire coastal plain as wilderness, the report recommended none. Boosters exuded pleasure and optimism about the prospects for oil.[24] Senator Ted Stevens, a firm supporter of Megatrade, depicted the Arctic Refuge as "the Saudi Arabia of North America."[25] The Resource Development Council of Alaska predicted that opening "would promote economic development, reduce our dependence on foreign oil, foster orderly development in the absence of an energy crisis, increase revenues from taxes and royalties, strengthen national security, restrain the national trade deficit, and create thousands of new jobs."[26] Representative Don Young asserted that based on Prudhoe Bay experiences, "we have shown not only that we can develop these areas but also that we can do it right."[27] Secretary Hodel characterized drilling in the Arctic Refuge as "vital to our national security." In the face of its decades-long record of championing Alaska's wildlife against commercial exploitation, the *New York Times* reasoned, "Ultimately, policy makers must weigh the dollar value of the oil against the intangible value of an unspoiled refuge. The most likely net value of the oil, after accounting for costs and assuming a future world price of $33 a barrel, is about $15 billion. How much an untouched refuge is worth is anyone's guess— but it's hard to see how it could realistically be judged worth such an enormous sum."[28]

Secretary Hodel echoed the industry view of Prudhoe Bay as an "environmental success story."[29] Claims of environmental success at Prudhoe Bay had been literally set in stone. A 3-by-4-foot bronze plaque in Golden Heart Park in Fairbanks, a public park adjacent to the tourist center, honored Arco Alaska. Titled "North Slope Oil Benefits All of Us," it declared, "Since beginning work on the North Slope, the producers, including ARCO, have demonstrated that oil development is compatible with wildlife and the environment"; the caribou herd "has more than tripled;" and "thousands of waterfowl continue to return to the fields each summer to nest and rear their young." Alluding to the Arctic Refuge, it suggested, "Just as North Slope oil has helped Fairbanks, the state of Alaska and the nation, so will development of other oil prospects in Alaska. These areas will play a key role in the energy future of Alaska and the nation. Thank you, people of Fairbanks for your participation in the development of northern Alaska's oil fields. You are the Golden Heart of a Great Land."[30]

Negative environmental impacts seemed inevitable given the scope of North Slope oil infrastructure (Prudhoe, Lisburne, Milne, Kuparuk, and Endicott oilfields). In the late 1980s

16.3. Part of Deadhorse complex, Prudhoe Bay, 1986. By Pamela A. Miller. The main supply base for Prudhoe Bay oilfields.

the operation ranked among the world's largest industrial complexes, composed of 1,056 active oil wells and thousands of other facilities spread out over hundreds of square miles, connected by 346 miles of roads and 1,123 miles of pipelines. A power plant, refinery, and sewage treatment plant served 1,500 people (down from a peak of 10,000) and their activities.[31] Drilling wastes containing toxic substances flowed into 264 unlined gravel pits, each covering 1,500 to 4,500 square feet, holding a total of 26 million barrels. Operations generated tens of thousands of tons of other waste, much of it toxic.[32] The entirety sat on a thin layer of fragile watery tundra, frozen except for a few months of the summer. While oversight responsibility for compliance with environmental protection laws rested in the Environmental Protection Agency and Alaska Department of Environmental Conservation, they had done no more than feeble monitoring.

As the Arctic Refuge issue heated in the 1980s, the oil industry cultivated a positive image of its doings in the Arctic. In the wake of cleanup efforts, in 1986 oil company officials invited environmental leaders to tour the facilities. Rather than being reassured, some of the guests reacted in dismay at what they saw. Concerning air quality, Wilderness Society president George Frampton noted, "Prudhoe Bay is emitting as many pollutants as the City of Chicago." Despite assurances by the hosts that drilling muds "do no significant damage to tundra or wildlife," National Wildlife Federation president J. D. Hair observed, "There are several examples of dead zones of vegetation around these pits—we need to know why."[33] Since 1972 there had been 23,000 recorded spills of fuel and other toxic substances not including drilling muds, the largest of them 200,000 and 658,000 gallons. One oil service company went bankrupt and left behind several thousand barrels of toxic fluids. At the abandoned Kaktovik drilling site, bush pilot Don Ross watched pink styrofoam panels, used to insulate drill pads, breaking into ever-smaller pieces as they blew across the tundra.[34] In 1988 a polar bear, stained fluorescent pink, died at Prudhoe Bay, apparently from ingesting chemicals.[35]

Following the 1986 visit to Prudhoe Bay, Trustees for Alaska, National Wildlife Federation, and Natural Resources Defense Council completed an extensive survey of the 1980–1987 environmental impact of oil extraction in the vicinity. Their report, *Oil in the Arctic,* appeared in January 1988. It cited "alarming environmental problems," "inadequacies of state and federal laws and regulations," and "absence of aggressive enforcement." Regarding water pollution: "Drilling and production wastes, oil spills and wastewater discharges are major sources of water pollution on the North Slope." It noted 953 recorded spills totaling 4,600 barrels of polluting liquids, over half oil and fuels, and evidence of injury to wildlife. Concerning air pollution: "Oil and gas facilities on the North Slope emit 9,000 to 27,000 tons of nitrogen oxides a year—or roughly the amount emitted annually by Washington D.C." Black smoke plumes "have been tracked for 100 miles." It stated that "lichens, an important food source for caribou, are especially sensitive to acidifying pollutants, particularly sulfur dioxide," that "hundreds of violations of state air quality regulations are documented in ADEC's files," and that "monitoring of air quality at Prudhoe Bay has been extremely limited." Regarding hazardous waste: "Serious contamination already has occurred on the North Slope due to improper hazardous waste management," and "just as there is no inventory of landfill wastes, there has been no comprehensive study of the fate of 20 billion gallons of industrial wastes and produced water that have been injected underground." Its assessment of impact on the environment: "Alteration and, in some cases, absolute elimination of substantial amounts of fish and wildlife habitat have resulted," and "enormous gaps exist in information about amounts and types of pollutants introduced on the North Slope and the effects these pollutants and other oil developments have on the region's biological system." On the prospects for restoration: "The Department of the Interior has . . . reported that successful rehabilitation techniques have not yet been developed for areas north of the Brooks Range. Moreover, industry predicts astronomically high costs for restoration, and there is no assurance that adequate monies have been set aside." The report concluded that "further oil development in the Arctic should not be considered until the consequences of such activity in the Prudhoe Bay region are fully understood and until the oil industry and responsible agencies demonstrate that they can operate in compliance with the environmental laws of the State of Alaska and the United States."[36]

Trustees for Alaska, Natural Resources Defense Council, Alaska Center for the Environment, and Northern Alaska Environmental Center sued Arco Alaska for discharging toxic wastes from pits onto the tundra in violation of the Clean Water Act, and for violating Army Corps of Engineers permit requirements that pits be leak-proof. Their action spurred the Environmental Protection Agency (EPA) to cite Arco for 43 spills. Trustees et al. also charged violation of law by the seawater plant at Kuparuk, and challenged its renewed and weakened EPA permits. Later they sued Arco for discharges from the Kuparuk sewage treatment plant. Years of legal sparring resulted in a 1988 cooperative settlement regarding drilling wastes.

Arco agreed to pay $1 million—$200,000 to the U.S. treasury, $400,000 for research on recycling and oil decontamination, and $400,000 to the Doyon Foundation to fund scholarships for Native students in natural-resource management. Arco also agreed to undertake a three-year review of disposal methods, monitored by the Natural Resources Defense Council, and a ten-year, $250 million cleanup of its nearly 200 drilling-waste storage pits.[37]

Lease agreements under state law dictated some measure of restoration of abandoned sites. Yet considerable doubt existed whether the oil companies would or could restore the damage on the North Slope, either during operations or after exhaustion of the oil pools. Chevron estimated a cost in excess of $200,000 to rehabilitate a single drilling-fluid pit. A Corps of Engineers source commented, "In light of industry's reluctance to develop and use compensatory mitigation and restoration techniques, none has been applied on the North Slope of Alaska, except to a very limited experimental extent. The technology has not been developed."[38] In 1988 British Petroleum and the state began work on a restoration plan for the Prudhoe Bay area to follow shutdown of oil operations.[39]

Oil companies revived their concern for environmental protection in the 1980s, to meet tightening restrictions on their new oilfields and to build public support for their bid to enter the Arctic Refuge. In the 1990s they made numerous efforts to lighten impact on the land. Department of Natural Resources literature claimed that technological advances made possible a 76 percent reduction in the size of drilling pads compared to Prudhoe, a 95 percent reduction in the space needed for service facilities, underground injection of drilling-fluid wastes, and 95 percent recycling of other wastes, and took away the need for gravel roads in pipeline construction.[40]

Research on environmental rehabilitation had been performed briefly by Arco in the early 1970s, and the National Science Foundation funded some baseline studies later in the decade. Accumulating experience proved that most types of environmental injury could be alleviated. Drilling muds could be recycled or injected deep underground. Drill cuttings could be washed and used in road construction, or injected. Underground waters produced by drilling could be injected for deep disposal or for extraction of more oil. Drilling wastes in reserve pits could be thawed, ground up, and injected deep underground. The lack of future need for reserve pits, closer spacing of wellheads, and other consolidation measures greatly decreased the necessary size and number of drilling sites. British Petroleum planned to end land disposal of all its onshore drilling wastes by 1994. The companies sought means to recycle or limit the need for other contaminant materials, including the ozone-depleting halons used in firefighting. Ice roads for winter and low-pressure wheeled vehicles for summer meant less gravel road construction. Lakes created by large gravel pits could be connected to natural waterways to serve as wintering sites for fish. All new pipelines would be elevated at least five feet because caribou preferred to pass under rather then climb gravel overpasses. The five- to seven-foot high gravel pads built for roads and drill sites might be left in place at the end of operations because wildlife sometimes took advantage of them for nesting and relief from insects. Researchers tested a variety of methods for reseeding and rehabilitating disturbed sites for erosion control and wildlife sustenance.[41] Engineering for wildlife enhancement entailed questions of what limits should be set on attempts to restore the land to its natural state.

A 1998 review by Trustees for Alaska found that, while some improvements had been made, the impact of oil activity on the North Slope had increased. Oil facilities covered 715 square miles, expected to soon increase to 1,085 square miles. In 21 years, permits for 3,331 oil, gas-injection, and water-injection wells had been issued. The Dalton Highway carried 45,236 trucks in 1996. Three airports could accommodate jet aircraft, the Deadhorse field handling 140,000 passenger arrivals and departures annually. Two refineries operated, one processing 1 million gallons of crude oil daily. Large numbers of drilling-waste pits had yet to be cleaned up. Environmental impacts of the vast system could not be easily measured because no coordinated means of oversight existed, and "baseline studies are notoriously lacking, a study of cumulative impacts does not exist, and no comprehensive EIS has ever been undertaken." The report recommended creation of a monitoring regime to evaluate the overall impact of North Slope operations.[42]

Environmentalists appraised Interior's 1987 final Arctic Refuge report as a political document whose recommendations ran counter to its projections of ecological damage. They contended that the Reagan administration wasted more oil by weakening auto fuel-efficiency standards and abolishing conservation measures than would be provided by the refuge's possible 3.2 billion barrels, an amount equivalent to only seven months of U.S. consumption. Pondering Alaska's Prudhoe Bay experience, Ginny Wood queried:

> This richest of oil discoveries ever made in North America is, after ten years, half depleted. Alaska, awash in its 90 percent of oil revenues spent about $23.4 billion of it, much for capital projects that local and state budgets can no longer afford to maintain. . . . Now, with unanticipated drops in the price of oil, Alaska is one of four states facing a budget deficit. Two of the others are 'oil' states. Where did it all go? And for what? And where and for what will more oil income go?[43]

Environmentalists rejected pleas that national security required immediate opening of the Arctic Refuge. Audubon/Alaska's David Cline opined, "What we should keep in mind is that if this oil exists, it belongs to all of us. It can figure into national security planning best by staying right where it is until *really* needed—not by the oil companies but by the U.S., which still owns it." Cline believed the true reasons for the push to open the refuge involved letting the oil companies purchase leases at low prices for future profits and to build support facilities for their drilling in the Beaufort Sea.[44]

Anthropologist Richard Nelson registered his stance on the Arctic Refuge by donating his annual Permanent Fund check of about $800 from oil revenues to the Southeast Alaska Conservation Council. Characterizing the fund as "a mix of welfare, blood money and bribery," he reasoned, "First of all, I didn't earn it. Second, it came to me only because the Arctic Slope—formerly one of the greatest wildlands in North America—has been subjected to wholesale industrial development. And third, accepting it would make me an accomplice to that environmental tragedy and to possible future tragedies such as violation of the Arctic National Wildlife Refuge."[45]

Additional research threw light on problems of oil industrialization. In fall 1987 a team of botanical scientists published a study of the effects of Prudhoe oil activity on soils and vegetation. They found that "(i) there have been major landscape impacts caused by the Prudhoe Bay Oil Field, (ii) indirect impacts, such as thermokarst [thawing and resultant erosion], may not develop until many years after the initial developments, and (iii) the total area covered by direct and indirect impacts can greatly exceed the area of the planned development." They cautioned that "a vast complex of roads, pipelines and service centers stretching across the Arctic Coastal Plain could have unpredictable long-term impacts on the total function of the coastal plain ecosystem." Because of differences in drainage, the Arctic Refuge might be expected to experience less flooding and more thermokarst than Prudhoe Bay.[46] An unpublished draft Environmental Protection Agency statement based on 1987 and 1988 visits indicated serious degradation from leaking chemical barrels, overflowing toxic-waste pits, and procedures violating federal regulations. It charged that the State of Alaska possessed neither the authority nor the committed resources necessary for proper enforcement.[47] A draft Corps of Engineers report released in 1987 indicated that British Petroleum's five-mile causeway to its two offshore gravel drilling islands diminished by 60 percent the productivity of near-shore habitat, by interrupting ocean currents.[48]

Representative George Miller of California, a pivotal legislative participant in the Arctic Refuge debate, requested that the Interior Department compare the biological effects of the Prudhoe Bay works to the 1972 environmental impact statement estimates. Interior produced a draft account in December 1987 but did not release it. Five months later, someone leaked a copy of the full text (Table 16.1) to the *New York Times*. In most cases, projections had been nonexistent or unquantified, and follow-up research inadequate. The comparison indicated that "fish and wildlife losses resulting from the construction and operation of the pipeline system were greatly underestimated in the environmental impact statement." Eleven thousand acres, double the original estimate, had been destroyed, including habitat that supported 20,000 birds. Companies sprayed large volumes of contaminated water onto roads, and pumped 200 million gallons of water daily from lakes and streams, neither procedure mentioned in the impact statement. Oil facilities in the Beaufort Sea had degraded water quality. Fewer Dall sheep and grizzly bears existed because of hunters attracted by the Haul Road. Nearly all species of birds and mammals had suffered losses of habitat and, in some cases, loss of population. Caribou gained at least in part because their predators, wolves and bears, had been killed or driven away.[49] Alaska Department of Fish and Game (ADF&G) caribou researcher Ray Cameron pointed out that aerial hunters shot most of the wolves in 1977–1978 when Alyeska permitted private individuals to transport fuel up the Haul Road to enable refueling and flying over the central North Slope.[50]

Oil boosters defended Prudhoe Bay by arguing that the resident central Arctic caribou herd had nearly quadrupled since drilling started; therefore oil production must not be harmful to caribou. ADF&G biologists considered the two areas not comparable. At Prudhoe a much smaller herd of about 12,000 roamed a 100-mile-wide plain, whereas on the Arctic Refuge a herd of 170,000 occupied a plain 30 miles wide. Beginning in 1974, biologists discovered that most caribou, especially pregnant cows, avoided human activity, pipelines, and other non-natural structures. Few would use the ramps and underpasses provided for them, and the pipeline seemed to be creating two separate herds. By the mid-1990s, gathering evidence demonstrated strong correlations between oil activity and reduced caribou calving, and a 23 percent shrinkage of the Central Arctic caribou herd over three years. Arctic Refuge manager James W. Kurth stated in 1995 that "the current decline of the

Table 16.1—Environmental Impacts of Construction and Operation of Prudhoe Bay Oilfields and Trans-Alaska Pipeline, North Slope

Air Quality	—pump station emissions unknown —short-term violations of standards at Prudhoe Bay
Freshwater Systems	—severe disruptions by siltation, diversion, impoundment —pollution by heavy metals, hydrocarbons, sewage —loss of habitat; changes in fish density/distribution
Marine Systems	—numerous small hazardous material or oil spills; impact unknown —causeways reducing carrying capacity of coastal waters —loss of polar bears through nuisance behavior, increased hunting, and reduced denning
Vegetation	—greater losses than expected; restoration minimal
Birds	—loss or displacement of 22,500 birds —increase in bird predators (foxes and glaucous gulls aided by human food); losses in most bird species
Mammals	—increase of caribou due partly to fewer wolves/bears —depletion of large mammals by increased hunter access and frequent killing of bears for safety or property defense (partly caused by feeding animals at construction sites)
Wilderness	—much greater impact and use of land than predicted

Source: U.S. Fish and Wildlife Service, *Comparison of Actual and Predicted Impacts of the Trans-Alaska Pipeline System and Prudhoe Bay Oil Fields on the North Slope of Alaska* (Fairbanks: USFWS, December 1987).

Central Arctic herd and its attendant relationship to oil development reinforces conclusions . . . which found major negative effects on the Porcupine Caribou Herd and other wildlife resources." A conflicting study concluded that caribou had become more accustomed to the oil facilities, and most fish and wildlife species in the Prudhoe Bay vicinity had maintained or increased their numbers.[51] Scientists continued to evaluate the effects of oil development on wildlife.

State biologists generally regarded the "core calving area" of the Arctic Refuge as vital to caribou survival, whereas oil industry biologists contended oil facilities would leave adequate room for calving. In 1987 and 1988, unusual snow conditions in Canada and the coastal plain kept most of the Porcupine herd outside the 1002 area.[52] Subsequent investigation demonstrated higher calf survival for cows in the coastal plain than for cows prevented by weather from reaching it.[53] Although oil boosters preferred to cast the issue as "caribou versus oil," biologists and environmentalists focused on a larger picture. University of Alaska researcher David Klein called attention to the coastal plain's "high productivity for wildlife" and the vital relationships among the caribou and other mammal and bird species and their migration routes.[54] "The complexity of any living system is many magnitudes greater than the most complex engineering projects that may affect them," said Klein. "The only responsible recommendation is to exclude from leasing those areas of known importance to caribou—that is, essentially all of the 1002 area."[55] Such an ecological perspective

16.4. Caribou crossing river, North Slope. Courtesy National Park Service and Arctic Environmental Information and Data Center. Debate over whether to permit oil drilling in the Arctic Refuge often centered on the Porcupine caribou herd.

had underlain visions of an Arctic Refuge since the beginning— to preserve a domain sufficiently large to maintain the natural, wide-ranging interplay of wildlife and habitat.

Fish and Wildlife Service wilderness specialist Roger Kaye examined the values that founders and subsequent visitors perceived in the Arctic Refuge. Beyond the commonly recognized benefits of wildlife protection, scenery, scientific study, and recreation, the refuge offered: (1) connections to the frontier experience, (2) mystery and exploration, (3) freedom and release from stress through solitude, (4) an example of nature uncontrolled by humans, (5) a connection to nature and the evolutionary past, (6) a source of humility and perspective on life, (7) nature as inherently valuable, (8) a gift to the future, (9) a place of voluntary restraint on technology, and (10) a sacred place. Because of the difficulty of measurement, Kaye noted, these values had not been accorded due weight in policy decisions. [56]

ATTEMPTS AT RESOLUTION

Interested parties pursued a range of solutions. Governor Steve Cowper and ADF&G sought a compromise on the Arctic Refuge, citing hazards to wildlife and the need for more information. They recommended limited leasing to avoid the core calving area. The legislature opted for extensive leasing. Native groups split; the Arctic Slope Regional Corporation favored drilling, as did the Inupiat Eskimo town of Kaktovik, though villagers displayed uneasiness at the prospect of losing their traditional culture. Alaska Federation of Natives could not agree on a position. The Canadian government, according to the Alaska Lands

*16.5. Cache at hunting cabin near Arctic Village. Courtesy NAEC.
Gwitch'in Athabaskans relied heavily on the Porcupine caribou herd
for food.*

Act a party to be consulted prior to any such undertaking, argued against opening of the
refuge, and wanted joint management of a protected international ecosystem.[57]

Residents of the nine Alaskan and five Canadian Gwitch'in Athabaskan villages consistently rejected drilling. They controlled no known oil lands, whereas wells at Kaktovik might
become a prolific source of funds for the North Slope Eskimos. The North Slope Borough, a
local government unit, could tax oil facilities anywhere on the North Slope. In the disagreement among Native groups, environmentalists took the side of the Gwitch'in, who also
enjoyed sympathy in the national press.[58] At a 1988 conference the Gwitch'in chiefs affirmed, "For thousands of years our ancestors, the Gwitch'in Athabaskan Indians of northeast
Alaska and Northwest Canada, have relied on caribou for subsistence, and [we] continue

today to subsist on the Porcupine caribou herd, which is essential to meet the nutritional, cultural and spiritual needs of the people."[59] Chief Trimble Gilbert of Arctic Village, a town that chose tribal control rather than corporation status under the Alaska Native Claims Settlement Act, articulated a traditional view of economic growth: "Money is not really good for native peoples. Here you don't see drugs and alcohol, or suicide and murder. Here people walk around proud that we have our land."[60] Anticipating the possibility of oil production in the Arctic Refuge, he reflected, "Our future is uncertain. We hurt because we see the land being destroyed. We believe in the wild earth because it's the religion we've been born with. After 10,000 years our land is still clean and pure. We believe we have something to teach the world about living a simple life, about sharing, about protecting the land."[61] Gwitch'in appeals weighed substantially in the resistance to legislation for opening the refuge.

Contestants introduced bills in both houses of Congress. Morris Udall's House bill, first appearing in 1986, bore the title HR 39 and specified complete wilderness protection for the coastal plain. Don Young's bill permitted full exploitation. Some hunting-fishing groups offered a third bill allowing restricted drilling but allocating one-fourth of the royalties to waterfowl enhancement. They hoped to counteract the disappearance of wetlands in the Lower 48, and the lack of funding for the 1980 Fish and Wildlife Conservation Act (for nongame wildlife) or for the 1986 U.S.-Canada Waterfowl Management Plan.[62] This third bill held potential for division among conservation groups, invited to choose between Arctic wilderness and Lower 48 wetlands. A Senate bill providing for waterfowl funding by Arctic Refuge royalties emerged from the Energy and Natural Resources Committee in 1988. An amendment requiring a national energy policy study before opening the refuge lost by 9–10 in the House Interior Committee.[63] Revelations of environmental impairment at Prudhoe Bay, the December 1987 impact report, controversy over Megatrade, and the ongoing low price of oil, prevented the passage of legislation in 1988.

At the national level, the Alaska Coalition including eight Alaskan groups addressed the refuge issue, lobbying for HR 39 and similar bills in the Senate. Northern Alaska Environmental Center, adopting a lead role, produced a 20-page brochure and a 25-minute film *Arctic Refuge: Treasure of the North* done by Larry Sutton.[64] The center worked for wilderness options in the Arctic Refuge comprehensive plan drafts of 1987 and 1988.[65] The National Audubon Society broadcast a *World of Audubon* television program in December 1990, the 30th anniversary of the refuge.[66]

Competition over access to oil-drilling information precipitated a falling-out among oil companies, several of whom sued Chevron-British Petroleum for information on the Kaktovik well. Chevron won its first round in superior court in May 1988,[67] and prevailed in the state supreme court. Exxon pursued federal legislation to bar Chevron from further exploration of the Arctic Refuge prior to a lease sale. All the companies wanted the refuge opened, partly because of the potential for offshore finds. Production of oil from wells off the shores of the refuge would necessitate onshore facilities, adding to environmental degradation.[68]

On its last day in office the Reagan administration bequeathed the oil industry a final gift: reduction of the rent oil companies paid for use of federal land (at a possible cost to the public of $35 million annually), and a formal recommendation by Secretary Hodel that Congress approve Megatrade and the opening of the Arctic Refuge.[69] Ignoring a petition by

16.6. Reaction to Walter Hickel's National Press Club plea for oil drilling in the Arctic Refuge, Washington, March 1991. Courtesy NAEC. No other single Alaskan land issue drew so much national media coverage, much of it favoring wilderness status for the coastal plain.

over 100 groups assembled by environmental organizations,[70] former oilman George Bush set out to open the refuge, aided by his Interior secretary Manuel Lujan who as a congressman had co-sponsored Don Young's bill to permit drilling in the refuge.[71] Lujan, however, disavowed any intention to finalize Megatrade.[72] At Anchorage on his way to Emperor Hirohito's funeral, Bush urged the refuge opening. A few weeks later the *Exxon Valdez* struck a reef in Prince William Sound, and the administration recessed its attempts to open the refuge. It revived the effort during the 1990–1991 Middle East crisis, when oil prices went up. Swift allied victory in the 1991 Gulf War soon returned the price of oil to a prewar level of about $20 per barrel.

Alaska's government participated in the national legislative drive to open the Arctic Refuge, though it stood to receive no more than 50 percent of the royalties compared to 100 percent on state land. The legislature appropriated $3 million for lobbying in fiscal year 1992, and Governor Hickel's Arctic Refuge coordinator Becky Gay argued, "Do we have to have another war before Congress lets Alaska supply the American people with oil?"[73] Hickel's Democratic successor, Tony Knowles, while generally solicitous of environmental values, also tried to open the refuge.

Citing a February 1991 Geological Survey estimate revising the probability of finding recoverable Arctic Refuge oil from 19 percent to 46 percent, the Bush administration put forth an energy bill featuring Arctic Refuge opening and containing slight provisions for energy conservation. A show of force by national environmental organizations struck down the bill in November.[74] Given the immediacy of the Alyeska-Wackenhut scandal and other indications of oil industry misbehavior in Alaska, timing favored the environment. The administration suffered an embarrassing defeat, and the environmental community demonstrated its abiding potency and the depth of public and congressional commitment to preservation of Alaskan wildlands. Lacking the votes to open the refuge, the administration omitted it from the energy bill that passed in spring 1992, again short of strong conservation measures.

After the Clinton administration assumed office in 1993, any congressional action to open the refuge faced a promised veto. Alaska's delegation made repeated attempts to authorize oil drilling in the 1002 area, and in 1995 the Alaska Federation of Natives took a stand for oil exploration in the refuge.[75] Resistance by environmental groups, lack of public approval outside of Alaska, and the prospect of Clinton vetoes, stymied Republican congressional efforts. Environmentalists sustained their effort to achieve wilderness status for the coastal plain, and for a national energy policy emphasizing conservation. Court cases involving the Arctic Refuge periodically added their verdicts. Champions of the refuge won an important legal victory in June 1997. For 18 years the state had claimed ownership of the shallow-water tidelands and lagoons along the full length of the Arctic Coast. State control would have enabled construction of facilities supplementing offshore drilling, thus increasing the pressure to open the coastal plain of the refuge. Alaskan and national environmental groups filed briefs seconding the federal government in the case. The Supreme Court ruled that the tidelands along the refuge coastline had been reserved prior to statehood and belonged to the nation.[76] Beyond the tidelands, the state retained ownership of a three-mile belt.

A second federal decree in March 1998 favored the Arctic Refuge. The Clinton administration deleted offshore continental shelf lands along the refuge from its Beaufort Sea oil-leasing program. Drilling would go forward off the National Petroleum Reserve to the west.[77] Like the Supreme Court tideland ruling, this decision lowered the chances of disturbance on the refuge mainland.

North Slope oil companies desired an early decision on the refuge to give them lead time to prepare for the inevitable shrinkage of Prudhoe Bay and Kuparuk River production. Economics and technology dictated a minimum pipeline flow of about 300,000 barrels per day. Arctic Refuge oil would keep the pipeline open longer, making greater use of Prudhoe area oil. Without the refuge oil, the companies would have to connect smaller fields to the pipeline, an expensive process requiring several years and dependent on oil prices for its profitability. Although finds at a half-dozen or more fields each contained at least 150 million recoverable barrels of oil, distance from the pipeline necessitated construction of processing facilities at several sites. A large reservoir of thick, low-temperature crude at the West Sak field called for alternative extraction technology. If no promising new sites could be added, companies projected that the pipeline could shut down sometime near 2010, leaving a billion barrels of recoverable oil on the North Slope and virtually ending the Alaska government's dependence on oil for 85 percent of its revenue. A large strike on the Arctic Refuge or elsewhere might extend the flow beyond 2025.[78]

By 2000, despite the ongoing drawdown of the Prudhoe Bay field, North Slope oil flowed steadily. Several other onshore or nearby offshore finds had gone into production, and Arco began to tap the huge supply of heavy crude at West Sak. Oil exploration proceeded apace, and the federal government initiated leasing in the National Petroleum Reserve to the west. The Alaska Department of Natural Resources expected the oilfields to be active at least until 2019.[79]

A three-year Geological Survey study estimated in 1998 that the 1002 area held an average probability of 2.6 to 3.2 billion barrels of commercially recoverable oil, and 7.7 billion barrels technically recoverable. More lay in adjacent Native lands and the state-owned waters within three miles of shore.[80] However, the 1998 failure of a much-publicized Arco well dubbed "Warthog" in Camden Bay off the refuge coast dampened faith in oil prospects. The debate continued, subdued in part by the continuing low price of oil.

The Arctic National Wildlife Range, having inspired Alaskans to create the Alaska Conservation Society and thereby the Alaskan environmental community, ultimately fired a national debate over wilderness protection and energy policy. No single Alaskan land issue had precipitated such an outpouring of interest on the part of the American public, who wanted both wilderness and oil, and hoped they would not be forced to choose. Oil companies sensed their final chance to penetrate an American land frontier, environmentalists their last opportunity to save wilderness on a grand scale.

At the onset of the twenty-first century, neither oil nor wilderness could claim more than temporary victory. Yet environmental principles of sustainability, accountability, and public access to adequate information had been applied and reinforced. While nonconsumptive use values gained little recognition in the planning process, their importance to millions in the Lower 48 who would never visit the refuge had been demonstrated. Court action and the press of public opinion, assisted by ecological research, caused both government and the oil companies to treat the Arctic ecosystem more carefully. Countering the power of the Reagan and Bush administrations and Republicans in Congress, environmental advocates elevated public awareness of the impacts of oil development and, for the time being, safeguarded the integrity of the Arctic Refuge.

NOTES

1. Jackson, "Floor of Creation," 16.

2. C. Hunter, "This Our Land," May 1981, 32–33.

3. Minard, "All Caribou," 44–45; Ritzman, "NPR-A Public Hearings," 7.

4. Berman and Hull, *Petroleum*, A19.

5. Kowalsky, "Another Arctic Pipeline," 4–7; *Alaska Conservation Review (ACR)*, Spring 1975, 8; L. Mayo, "Gas Transportation," 16; L. Mayo, "Conservation at Gas Hearings," 7–8; L. Adams, *Sierra Club Legal Defense Fund*, 1987, 11–12.

6. Jackson, "Floor of Creation," 16; C. Hunter, "International Caribou," 22; Laycock, "Wilderness by the Barrel," 115.

7. *ACR*, "International Caribou Treaty," Winter 1979, 5; L. Mayo, "Two Nations Cooperate," ll; Hession, "Controversial U.S.-Canada Treaty," 10; *Northern Line*, February 1981, 14; C. Hunter, "International Caribou," 22.

8. C. Hunter, "This Our Land," March 1982, 22; *New York Times*, December 15, 1987, 5; TAGS Environmental Review Committee, *North Slope Natural Gas Pipeline*, 2–8.

9. Callaghan, "Committee Reviews Gas Route," 5; Carey Goldberg, "Across Alaska's Tundra Yet Again," *New York Times*, April 26, 1997, 37.

10. Gould, "What Does 'Wilderness' Mean," 2, 4, 5; 94 Stat. 2371, December 2, 1980, Sec. 303.

11. U.S. Fish and Wildlife Service (USFWS), *Arctic National Wildlife Refuge: Draft River Management Plan*, 1993, 5.

12. 94 Stat. 2371, December 2, 1980; Jackson, "Floor of Creation," 18; D. Miller, "A Change of the Guard," 1, 6; *Trustees for Alaska v. Watt,* D.C. Alaska 524 F. Supp. 1303 (1981); Fran Mauer, interview by author, June 4, 1999. Plaintiffs were the Trustees for Alaska, Fairbanks Environmental Center, Alaska Center for the Environment, Village of Kaktovik, and two individuals.

13. Moran, "NAEC Completes Successful Field Season," 3.

14. Laycock, "Wilderness by the Barrel," 105; Farquhar, *Decision*, 14.

15. Kizzia, "Can Caribou and Oil Coexist?," 21; Laycock, "Wilderness By the Barrel," 111–112; Farquhar, *Decision*, 8, 17–19; *Fairbanks Daily News-Miner*, July 15, 1987, 7; Bill Kelder, "State Finds Auctions Disturbing," *Fairbanks Daily News-Miner*, July 15, 1987, 7.

16. Sutton, "Arctic Refuge," 6–7.

17. Farquhar, *Decision*, 9–12, 17–18.

18. *Trustees for Alaska*, Spring 1987, 4; Spring-Summer 1988, 5; Trustees for Alaska (TfA), *Summary* 1988, 4, 5–6.

19. U.S. General Accounting Office, *Federal Land Management*, 2–5.

20. Laycock, "Wilderness by the Barrel," 112.

21. Skilbred, "The ANWR," 8; TfA, *Summary*, 1; *Trustees for Alaska, et al. v. Hodel* 806 F. 2d 1378 (9th Cir. 1986).

22. D. Miller, *Midnight Wilderness*, 12; U.S. Fish and Wildlife Service (USFWS), *Artic National Wildlife Refuge (ANWR): Coastal Plain Resource Assessment, Draft*, pp. 3, 5–6, 28–29, 49–50, 72, 105–132, 166–170.

23. USFWS, *ANWR: Coastal Plain Assessment, Final*, 123–144, 184–192.

24. Livingston, "No Additional Wilderness," 1.

25. Udall, "Polar Opposites," 45–46.

26. Laycock, "Wilderness by the Barrel," 114.

27. *Fortune*, "A Compromise," 9.

28. *New York Times*, April 23, 1987, 26.

29. Laycock, "Wilderness by the Barrel," 114.

30. Among the commemorative plaques in the park, five are devoted to mineral extraction industries. None mentions the work of environmental groups.

31. Alaska Department of Environmental Conservation, *Water Quality in Alaska, 1988*, 40–41.

32. Trustees for Alaska (TfA), Natural Resources Defense Council (NRDC), and National Wildlife Federation (NWF), *Oil in the Arctic*, 1, 4, 32.

33. Lewis, "High Stakes," 8.

34. Laycock, "Wilderness by the Barrel," 114–115.

35. *New York Times*, April 23, 1989, 30.

36. TfA, NRDC, and NWF, *Oil in the Arctic*, preface, ii–vii.

37. *Trustees for Alaska*, Spring-Summer 1988, 1, 5; TfA, *Summary*, 1988, 3, 5; *Anchorage Daily News*, May 5, 1993.

38. Borrelli, "Oilscam," 25.

39. *New York Times*, April 23, 1989, 30.

40. Alaska Department of Natural Resources, "Evolution of Petroleum Development Technology."

41. McKendrick, "Arctic Tundra Rehabilitation," 30–37; Pacific Northwest Pollution Prevention Research Center, *Pollution Prevention*, 1–8; BP Exploration (Alaska) and ARCO Alaska, *North Slope Waste Management*, 4–11, 14–17.

42. Trustees for Alaska (TfA), *Under the Influence*, 36, 43–46, 51–53, 56.

43. Wood, "From the Woodpile," February-March 1988, 14.

44. Laycock, "Wilderness by the Barrel," 118–120.

45. *Ravencall*, December 1988-February 1989, 4.

46. Walker et al., "Cumulative Impacts," 757–760.

47. *New York Times*, March 4, 1989, 1, 35.

48. D. Miller, *Midnight Wilderness*, 203–204.

49. *New York Times*, May 11, 1988, 1.

50. Ibid., April 23, 1989, 30.

51. Cameron and Whitten, *Second Interim Report*, i; appendices 2 and 12; Cronin et al., "Northern Oilfields," 195, 203.

52. Farquhar, *Decision*, 14; *Arctic Reporter*, July 11, 1988, 3.

53. Whitten, *Movement Patterns*, 3.

54. Sutton, "Wildlife Biologist Speaks," 5.

55. Udall, "Polar Opposites," 46.

56. Kaye, "Perception, Experience, and Valuation," 9–22.

57. Sutton, "Refuge Future," 3; Minard, "All Caribou," 44; *Alaska Session Laws, 1988*, SJR 7.

58. Price, "Politics of Energy," 9.

59. Peale, "Beating the Drums," 36.

60. Linden, "A Tale of Two Villages," 62.

61. S. Reed, "Shadow Over an Ancient Land," 53.

62. Palmer, "Congress Considers," 47; Williamson, "Protecting Alaska's Wildlife," 44.

63. M. Matz, "Committee's Coastal Plain Package," 4.

64. *Northern Line*, December 1986, entire issue; Pendleton, "Udall Introduces Wilderness Bill," 1, 3, 6; *Northern Line*, May-July 1987, 1–2; D. Miller, "Miller Testifies," 1–3. Alaskan groups were the Alaska Center for the Environment, Audubon Society, Wilderness Society, National Parks and Conservation Association, Sierra Club, Southeast Alaska Conservation Council, Northern Alaska Environmental Center, and Trustees for Alaska.

65. *Northern Line*, October-November 1987, 3; March 1988, 3.

66. Cline, *Work Plan*, 1.

67. *New York Times*, May 16, 1988, IV, 12.

68. Smart and Melamed, "Big Oil's Blowout," 36.

69. *New York Times*, January 20, 1989, 1.

70. Ibid., January 25, 1989, 16.

71. P. Miller, "Arctic Refuge: Top Environmental Issue," 1.

72. *Alaska Report*, March 1989, 4.

73. Tyson, "Ardor for ANWR," 35–36; Becky Gay, interview by author, August 7, 1992.

74. *CQ Almanac*, "Arctic Plain," 208–209.

75. Alaska Federation of Natives, news release, June 15, 1995.

76. Callaghan, "Good News," 5; *U.S. v. Alaska*, No. 84, Orig., June 19, 1997. Trustees for Alaska filed on behalf of the Alaska Center for the Environment, Alaska Wilderness League, Audubon Society, Northern Alaska Environmental Center, Porcupine Caribou Management Board, Sierra Club, and Wilderness Society.

77. *Alaska Report*, March 1998, 7.

78. Tyson, "Missing Links," 53–57.

79. TfA, *Under the Influence*, 19–27.

80. Bird, *Arctic National Wildlife Refuge, 1002 Area, Petroleum Assessment, 1998*, 2, 4, 6.

17

Alaskan Environmental Organizations

Alaskan environmental groups participated—often minimally, sometimes decisively—in all major resource conflicts of the statehood period. Usually they served as the core of the sustainability side of the exploitation-versus-sustainability clashes, opposing extractive industry and, frequently, state or national government. Their early leaders had personal ties to national environmental organizations while maintaining a high degree of independence. They held largely preservationist values, but operated in a society permeated by staunch exploitation ethics. Small numbers and powerful adversaries worked to their disadvantage, but sound reputations and knowledge of the land stood them in good stead. As conflicts grew more national in scope, the leaders progressively relied on national organizations, which in turn gained local standing as their Alaska branch offices matured in age and experience. Alaska's environmental community has, in effect, functioned as a wing of the policymaking process, pushing reluctant governments to fulfill their legal and social obligations. It has measurably influenced the state's policies and contributed meaningfully to the national environmental agenda.

FORMATION OF AN ENVIRONMENTAL COMMUNITY

Before statehood, federal and territorial officials felt pulled one way by those eager to exploit natural resources, and another way by a few conservation-oriented groups and individuals. Impending land ownership and management decisions accompanying statehood vastly elevated the urgency of the debate. Natural resources received prominent attention in the Alaska Constitutional Convention, resulting in the adoption of significant if ill-defined principles of sustained yield, and multiple use when practicable. The constitution reserved surface and subsurface water rights to the public, guaranteed private mining claims, and prohibited exclusive fishing rights (later to be legalized). Attempts to settle Native claims fell by the wayside; the issue remained a responsibility of the federal government.[1] Disposal of nearly all Alaskan lands hung in the balance, also awaiting federal action.

Some Alaskan environmentalists realized that to shape the coming changes they must act swiftly to create an organization of citizens dedicated solely to environmental protection. For maximal success its leaders needed long residence in the state, wide knowledge of

17.1. Celia Hunter, right, at Republic Aviation, Farmingdale, Long Island, fall 1944. Others from left: Gertie Tubbs, Ruth Anderson, Josephine Pitz. Courtesy Celia Hunter. A Women Airforce Service Pilot during the war, Hunter became "Dean of Alaska's Conservationists."

Alaskan affairs, and firm social standing. They should be politically astute but moderate, and able to work easily within the Alaskan political system and communicate with all its groups, from business people and politicians to civil servants to hunters and nature defenders. Among their members and cooperators should be sympathetic officials in state and federal natural-resource agencies. Leaders should possess the skill and perspective necessary to deal with national government, media, and environmental groups, and be compelling speakers, writers, and political organizers. Channeling their devotion to protection of nature, they needed to build respect and influence rapidly through a reputation for clear and consistent stands tempered by caution and based on careful research. They also needed a statewide system of groups capable of addressing in a coordinated manner issues from local to national levels.

Such a tall order did not fully materialize, but in their first 20 years Alaskan environmentalists came close. A group of 12 people, mostly in university and government service, met in Fairbanks in February 1960 and organized the Alaska Conservation Society (ACS).[2] As they viewed the context, "Fortunately we came into statehood with our natural resources relatively intact and we have the chance to profit by the mistakes made by others. . . . With wilderness and wildlife resources, you don't get a second chance. When they are gone, they are gone." ACS would be "a truly Alaskan expression of concern in matters relating to the

17.2. Ginny Hill Wood, McGonagall Pass, Mt. McKinley National Park, September 1961. Courtesy Ginny Wood. A founding member of Alaska Conservation Society and activist for nearly 50 years.

disposition and use of Alaskan lands and resources . . . rather than yielding our right to speak for our beliefs to Outside conservation groups." As such it would accomplish more than by individual memberships in the national organizations. Outsiders could be members of the society, but only Alaska residents could have voting privileges. ACS would be "the only [Alaskan] organization with conservation as its primary concern." The choice of a log cabin for headquarters derived its inspiration more from the living style of early members than from public-relations consciousness.[3]

An array of talented people participated actively in ACS from the outset. Celia M. Hunter came to be the best-known of its leaders, and of the Alaskan environmental movement. A native of the state of Washington and veteran of the Women Airforce Service Pilots, she flew for Chuck West's Arctic Air Travel Service, the first tour company in the north. She built and for 25 years comanaged Camp Denali, a tourist facility at the Kantishna gateway to Mt. McKinley National Park, and one of the first two in Alaska to feature wilderness outings. In the 1970s she served as president and executive director of the Wilderness Society, the first woman to head a major national environmental organization. As a writer, activist, and "Dean of Alaska's Conservationists," she more than any other person facilitated the evolution of the Alaskan environmental community.[4]

Another founder and prominent member of ACS, native Oregonian Virginia "Ginny" Hill Wood, also flew for the Women Airforce Service Pilots and Arctic Air Travel Service, and

17.3. Robert B. Weeden, University of Alaska Fairbanks, 1989. Courtesy Bob Weeden. A founding member and leader of Alaska Conservation Society, and author of two books on Alaska's environment.

comanaged Camp Denali. As editor, columnist, activist, organizer, and president, Wood set the tone of ACS's image in Alaska."[5] She participated in environmental politics throughout the latter twentieth century.

A third dominant figure in ACS and Alaskan environmental history, Robert B. "Bob" Weeden, hailed from New England (Somerset, Massachusetts) as had many of the early naturalists in Alaska. Following a decade as wildlife biologist for the Alaska Department of Fish and Game, he taught wildlife management and natural resources at the University of Alaska Fairbanks. Weeden undertook a parallel career: an intense involvement in ACS from the beginning to the end as editor, president, and board member. In 1969 he pioneered full-time environmental lobbying in Alaska, operating in Juneau during the legislative session, encountering 20 registered lobbyists from the oil companies. He held a variety of state and national government advisory positions.[6] As an author, scientist, and government official, he lent scientific credibility to the Alaskan environmental movement and functioned as a link between it and government agencies.

By 1970 ACS had seven affiliate chapters. One of the most active, the Kenai chapter, sought to defend the integrity of the Kenai National Moose Range. Sierra Club member Will Troyer, cofounder of the chapter in 1967 and a federal wildlife biologist, had managed the Kodiak brown bear and Kenai moose refuges. Applying the 1964 Wilderness Act, the chapter strove for designation of parts of the Kenai Range as wilderness. Troyer wrote extensively on wildlife topics and participated in ACS from its inception, conducting surveys of

17.4. Refuge manager Will Troyer doing brown bear census, Kodiak Lake, Kodiak National Wildlife Range, 1960. Courtesy Will Troyer. A federal biologist and member of Alaska Conservation Society and Sierra Club, Troyer played a key role in identifying areas to be preserved under the Alaska Lands Act.

candidate wilderness areas in Alaska's wildlife refuges and identifying land categories for the Alaska National Interest Lands Conservation Act of 1980.[7]

As a credible local institution, ACS fostered the introduction of modern environmental values to Alaska. Through its part in prominent controversies, the society also helped mold the national environmental agenda. Many volunteers in and outside government participated in the work of ACS and its chapters as they built experience, organization, and public recognition in the 1960s. In the 1970s, Alaska's oil-based economy forced people to think about their values and take stands; environmental awareness spread rapidly. ACS gained over 1,000 members and 9 affiliates,[8] nearly all of which it had helped organize. The affiliates operated increasingly on their own, coordinating when necessary through ACS.

Their way of life and their wilderness under siege, Alaskan environmentalists stepped up their activity, supplemented by young outsiders who immigrated increasingly in the 1970s. National organizations joined the endeavor, working in Washington, D.C., and opening branch offices in Alaska. Nationals and locals represented a movement accelerating in size, breadth of perspective, and political activism. Technical and social perspectives such as pollution control, energy conservation, and public participation in resource decisions, some incubated in the Chariot, Rampart, and Amchitka controversies, supplemented the traditional conservationist agenda of wilderness and wildlife protection.

Alaska's geography and population concentrations necessitated regional environmental centers. Anchorage, Fairbanks, and Juneau, the three largest cities, lay in different ecosystems hundreds of miles apart. In 1971 the Fairbanks Environmental Center opened, assisted by ACS and by funds from Friends of the Earth (FOE) and the John Muir Institute for Environmental Studies. An outgrowth of the local Sierra Club chapter, the center adopted a more preservationist agenda than did ACS. During the 1970s it concentrated primarily on monitoring oil operations on the North Slope: pollution at Prudhoe Bay, plans for gas lines, construction of the Trans-Alaska Pipeline, and attempts to open the Haul Road to general traffic. The center worked on d-2 lands legislation, initiated a campaign to expose the cost-benefit imbalance of the proposed Susitna dam project, and embarked on a decades-long effort to control river valley degradation caused by placer mining.[9]

The Alaska Conservation Society, Wilderness Society, and Sierra Club/Alaska helped organize and fund the Alaska Center for the Environment (ACE) in Anchorage in 1971. Intended to be the coordinating agency for statewide issues, ACE initially functioned in that capacity. It shifted direction in 1973 toward urban-related concerns and public education. It organized workshops on d-2 hearings, energy conservation, air pollution, and public involvement, and set up a network of recycling centers. On a statewide level it tackled transportation planning, oil pipeline monitoring, and the acquisition and management of state parks. During 1974–1977 it sponsored annual "state of the environment" speeches by Governor Jay Hammond.[10]

Alaska's third regional organization, Southeast Alaska Conservation Council in Juneau, originated as an association of groups in 1969. Reorganized in 1976, it devoted itself to d-2 planning and logging issues in the Tongass.[11]

An early formulation of the Alaska Environmental Lobby, also instituted in 1976 on a continuing basis, functioned during the legislature's four-month sessions. It operated out of homes until 1981, when it took a more formal, statewide form. Early legislation influenced by environmentalists included the designation of Mendenhall Wetlands, Susitna Flats, and Trading Bay State Game Refuges (1976); repurchase of Kachemak Bay oil leases (1976); coastal resource management (1977); forest resources and practices (1978); subsistence hunting and fishing (1978); and Creamers Field Migratory Waterfowl Refuge (1979).[12]

Responding to the need for legal counsel, Anchorage-based Trustees for Alaska (TfA), beginning in 1974, served the growing community. TfA, aided by the Environmental Defense Fund, evolved from an oil-pipeline monitoring project. A second legal arm, the Sierra Club Legal Defense Fund, started up in Juneau in 1978.[13] These legal offices represented environmental groups and other parties in suits to implement state and federal laws.

Other environmental organizations came into being in the 1970s. Friends of the Earth, acting on preservationist values, opened an Anchorage office in 1971. It gave top priority to protection of land and sea mammals and their habitats. Nunam Kitlutsisti ("Protectors of the Land"), a Bethel-based arm of the 56 Yup'ik Eskimo and Athabaskan Indian villages of the Yukon-Kuskokwim Delta region, emerged in 1973. It sought to ensure Native ties to the land through oversight of natural-resource use.[14] Denali Citizens Council, created in 1974, addressed d-2 legislation and land-use management related to the Mt. McKinley Park region. Alaska Public Interest Research Group (AKPIRG), a Ralph Nader affiliate focusing on con-

sumer issues and good government, originated in 1974. Asbestos removal and energy conservation counted among its early activities. The National Audubon Society installed an
office in Anchorage in 1977. At that time mildly preservationist, it worked on lands legislation and local issues through its Anchorage, Juneau, and Arctic (Fairbanks) chapters. The
Alaska Chilkat Bald Eagle Preserve gave the society the most visibility of its early projects.
Greenpeace/Alaska, first appearing in 1978, adopted strong preservationist stands on
marine life and wolf control.

In the 1970s, Sierra Club/Alaska claimed about 400 members and 5 chapters: Knik (Anchorage), Denali (Fairbanks), Juneau, Ketchikan, and Sitka. In addition to d-2 and oil-related
matters, its chapters took on projects similar to those of the Alaska Conservation Society
affiliates: logging plans and preservation of the Mendenhall Wetlands in the Southeast, and
urban issues including transportation, air pollution, and state and city parks in the Anchorage
area.[15]

No environmentalist could escape controversy in the Alaska of the 1970s. Economic
boosters had their hopes high and strongly resented the delays caused by lawsuits. They
perceived the high-profile, preservationist Sierra Club as the epitome of hindrance to progress.
The Sierra Club presented a favorite target for newspaper commentators and politicians.
Being a member, or otherwise environmentally active, sometimes involved risk. Following
the 1970 Sierra Club logging suit, Southeast Alaska Conservation Council publicly protested
the firing of two of its sympathizers allegedly because of their environmental activities.[16]
Associated Contractors of Alaska distributed 10,000 "Sierra Club Go Home" bumper stickers. Pioneers of Alaska printed the statement: "We in Alaska are presently facing a deluge of
interference in our industry, commerce and land development, public works and business
affairs. This interference is generated by misinformed parties, however well-intentioned, in
the names of the Sierra Club, Friends of the Earth, Wilderness Society and other nonresident
groups." Legislators introduced a resolution requesting that the governor sue the "Sierra
Club and all other groups and parties seeking to thwart the orderly development of Alaska" for
a sum of "not less than one billion dollars."[17] The resolution failed and no suit materialized.

Counterbalancing the resentment, indications of official recognition appeared in the
form of honors and appointments. Alaskans gradually realized that environmentalists could
no longer be dismissed as naive outsiders; they had come to stay and could make valuable
contributions. Wasteful and destructive projects such as Chariot and Rampart had died in
part because of their efforts. Environmentalists had learned to influence state and national
government, showed themselves to be dedicated public citizens, and in general, established
a reputation for competence and integrity.

As the environmental community took shape, the Alaska Conservation Society grew
progressively less needed and less able to control events. It drifted to the side as the d-2
lands issue attracted national interest and the increasingly autonomous regional centers
gained momentum. Each Alaskan group tended to be more interested in nearby problems,
and resisted control by a faraway authority. Most importantly, the ACS had been weakened
by its own success. The separate units now could operate more effectively on their own
while cooperating through their lobby and legal arms. In 1981, ACS distributed its assets to
other units and passed out of existence.

17.5. Alaskan environmentalists and Governor Jay Hammond, Washington, December 1980. Courtesy Peg Tileston. Following passage of the Alaska Lands Act, environmentalists posed with their governor. From left: Roland Shanks, Sierra Club/Alaska; John Luther Adams and Cindy Marquette, Alaska Center for the Environment; Governor Hammond; Celia Hunter, Alaska Conservation Society; Peg Tileston, Alaska Center for the Environment.

Passage of the Alaska National Interest Lands Conservation Act (ANILCA) in 1980 enabled the environmentalists to redirect some effort toward state and local issues. At the same time, land-use plans for national parks and wildlife refuges called for intensive monitoring of pro-industry Reagan and Bush policies. Population increase, oil extraction, and other attempts to industrialize the state bred a new list of challenges. National media attention played a part, despite or because of the lack of protective action by the presidential administrations. Environmental sentiment also flowed from the growing encroachment on Alaskan lifestyles by such practices as clear-cutting of forests, mining of streams, and dumping of toxic waste.

Broadening public awareness of environmental problems in the 1980s translated into increased membership for Alaskan as well as national environmental bodies. A sample of eleven Alaskan groups and their affiliates claimed a total 1980 membership of about 10,300; by 2000 they numbered more than 19,000 (Table 17.1). Alaska Wildlife Alliance and Greenpeace, guardians of the wolf and the sea mammals, tallied the fastest growth in the 1980s, and Alaska Center for the Environment, the most diversified, multiplied its membership in the 1990s.[18]

National environmental organizations accelerated their involvement in Alaska, particularly regarding oil in the Arctic, logging in the Tongass, and the status of marine mammals. Nationals joined the more grassroots-controlled local units on these and other issues, yet remained somewhat aloof, not participating as full members of the Alaskan environmental

Table 17.1—Membership Growth in Selected Alaskan Environmental Organizations, 1980–2000

	1980	1990	2000
Alaska Center for the Environment	600	773	9,893
Audubon/Alaska	1,650	2,600	2,106
Denali Citizens Council	100+	160	130
Friends of the Earth	230+	200	n.d.
Friends of Glacier Bay	35	120	125
Greenpeace/Alaska	365	3,000	1,575
National Wildlife Federation/Alaska	4,500	8,000	1,300
Northern Alaska Environmental Center	437	650	1,200
Sierra Club/Alaska	700	1,900	1,333
Southeast Alaska Conservation Council	400–500	1,000	932
Trustees for Alaska	1,000	1,098	530
Totals	10,300	17,745	19,124

Source: Alaska Conservation Foundation, "Alaska Environmental Matrix," 1980, 1990; Ellen Maling, personal communication, March 27, 2000.

Note: Some 1980 and 1990 figures are rough estimates, and memberships may overlap.

community. This distancing hindered communications and strategy but helped to avoid a public perception of outside environmentalists as controlling Alaskan affairs.

By the early 1980s, Alaskan environmentalists had erected a comprehensive network of institutions. Much of their success stemmed from contributions by the Alaska Conservation Foundation (ACF, 1980), designed to strengthen, professionalize, and help coordinate the elements of the community. The ACF also served to legitimize and lend coherence to the appeals of Alaskan groups for funding by Lower 48 donors. Controlled by Alaskans, the foundation nevertheless received most of its grant money from outside the state. Not many wealthy families lived in Alaska, and of those, few embraced conservation. ACF assisted the community through publication of an *Alaska Conservation Directory*, shared mailing lists, office administration services, and funds. During its first 19 years the foundation dispensed $13.5 million in grants to Alaskan organizations, keeping some of them alive. Grants underwrote issue research, equipment, staffing, media presentations, workshops, organization, and legal action. ACF arranged and partially funded the 1986 visit of the "Group of Ten" top national environmental leaders, reinforcing their commitment to issues involving the Arctic National Wildlife Refuge and Tongass National Forest.[19] In 1997, ACF moved in a new direction, dispensing grants to assist local communities in creating environmentally sustainable economies.[20]

The annual Alaska Environmental Assembly (1981), held by turn in Fairbanks, Anchorage, and Juneau, soon took shape as a central element of the community. Taking no official stands so as to avoid splitting the movement, the assembly served primarily as a forum of communication and cooperation. It also possessed a public relations function; industry representatives and Governor Bill Sheffield spoke at its sessions, lending visibility and legitimacy to the movement. In 1997 the assembly became Alaska Conservation Alliance, given a wider role of assisting member organizations in public outreach.[21]

The Alaska Environmental Political Action Committee (AEPAC, 1981)[22] took part in the governmental process through elections. It donated money and volunteer time to candidates in the 1982, 1984, and 1986 elections. After termination of an income tax return checkoff provision that had supplied most of its funds, AEPAC ceased making monetary donations in 1988.[23] It continued to publicize environmental voting records of legislators.

Closest to a unified voice of the community, and only on legislative issues, was the Alaska Environmental Lobby (AEL). Reorganized in 1981, it evolved into a professional office.[24] Volunteers received intensive training in research, analysis, lobbying, and testifying, thereby augmenting the environmental leadership core in Alaska. By forming issue-based coalitions with interest groups (commercial fishers, Natives, small towns, tourism businesses), AEL grew to be an important player in state environmental legislation. On most such bills, it found greater sympathy among Democratic than Republican legislators. In the latter 1980s it could stop nearly all of what it considered the worst bills, and aided the passage of many (Table 17.2). Facing a conservative governor in the early 1990s and an even more conservative legislature throughout most of the decade, the lobby directed most of its energy against offensive bills. In 1997 the lobby absorbed the functions of AEPAC and became the Alaska Conservation Voters (ACV), a coalition of 31 member and associate chapters organized for public education and advocacy in Alaska and Washington, D.C. In addition to its lobby and election work, ACV initiated an effort to identify and publicize more sustainable forms of economic growth in Alaska.[25]

SOUTH-CENTRAL ALASKA

As they had in the 1970s, environmental bodies chose issues based on location and subject interest. At least 32 offices emerged in south-central Alaska during the 1980s. Most of the work relating to state lands involved Anchorage groups, concentrating on south-central and western Alaska. Alaska Center for the Environment (ACE), while occasionally engaging in lawsuits, functioned primarily as public educator and grass-roots organizer, and as a source of information and training. Largely through funding from the Alaska Conservation Foundation, it conducted studies and policy analyses, and offered workshops and other opportunities for public participation. It countered the Susitna power project, advocated limits on placer mining of streams, and resisted environmentally offensive activities on state lands in the Anchorage vicinity. It operated outdoor education camps for children, and a marine science residential camp at China Poot Bay.

Anchorage, containing 40 percent of the state's 1990 population of 550,000, experienced a much broader array of environmental problems than did other regions. ACE directed its attention to recycling, transportation, air pollution, pesticides, petrochemicals, and other urban matters. It sponsored annual statewide conferences on alternative energy technology until public interest waned in the mid-1980s. During the 1990s, ACE focused on state and city parks, wetlands and forest protection, *Exxon Valdez* oil-spill restoration, solid and hazardous waste, logging, road building and transportation planning, wolf control, and other primarily state and local subjects. Reacting to a permissive law passed by the legislature over the veto of Governor Tony Knowles, ACE organized a campaign for a 1998 ballot initiative to prohibit billboards on public roadways. The measure passed by 72 percent.[26]

Table 17.2—Alaska Environmental Legislation, 1980–2000

Lands and Wildlife		Pollution Control and Misc.	
1980	Haul Road Opening	1980	Energy Conservation Alaska Energy Center Litter Control & Recovery Oil Pollution Control
1981	State & Municipal Land Disposal	1981	Control of Nuclear & Radioactive Facilities & Materials
1982	Coal Surface Mining & Reclamation		
1983	Marine Parks Additions		
1984	Kenai River Special Management Area Matanuska Valley Moose Range Shuyak Island State Park	1984	Hazardous Waste Litter Control
1985	Anchor River/Fritz Creek Critical Habitat Area Nelchina Public Use Area Palmer Hay Flats State Game Refuge	1985	Asbestos Removal from Schools
1986	Hatcher Pass Public Use Area Marine Parks Additions	1986	Railbelt Energy Fund (Susitna) Oil & Hazardous Substance Cleanup Hazardous Waste Site Labeling
1987	Eagle River Greenbelt Land Exchange Willow Creek State Recreation Area	1987	Hazardous Agents in the Workplace Recycling and Reduction TBT-Based Paint Ban
1988	Anchorage Coastal Wildlife Refuge Minto Flats State Game Refuge Dude Creek Critical Habitat Area Tugidak Is. Critical Habitat Area Point Bridget State Park	1988	Hazardous Waste Materials/Placards Oil Discharge Control
1989	Kachemak Bay Park Additions Mining Rents & Reclamation Dump Bear Protection High Seas Interception of Salmon Ernest Gruening State Historical Park	1989	Hazardous Waste Whistleblower Protection Irradiated Foods Organic Foods Deferred Oil Drilling in North Aleutian Basin Oil spill Prevention
1990	State Land Leasing Reclamation Forest Practices Act Amendments Solid & Hazardous Waste Management Yakataga State Game Refuge Marine Park Additions	1990	Plastic Container Code Recycled Products Procurement Oil Spill Prevention Underground Storage Tank Control Heating and Lighting Standards
1991	McNeil River Sanctuary Add/ State Game Refuge	1991	Waste Reduction Awards Curbside Pickup Funding

continued on next page

Table 17.2—*continued*

Lands and Wildlife		Pollution Control and Misc.	
	Recreation Rivers Mgt Plan		
1992	Habitat Purchase with Oil Spill Funds	1992	Environmental Education
			Rural Drinking Water Cleanup
			Alyeska Responsibility for Oil Spills
1993	Kachemak Bay and Seal Bay purchases		
1997	Shuyak Island State Park Additions		
		2000	Milk and Meat Hormone Labeling

Sources: State of Alaska Session Laws and Resolutions, and Alaska Environmental Lobby/Alaska Conservation Voters, Anchorage.

Sierra Club/Alaska handled a wide spectrum of national, state, and local issues. Its Sitka (later deactivated) and Juneau groups challenged Forest Service logging policy in the Tongass; Denali Group concentrated on state land disposal and placer mining; and Knik Group (Anchorage) worked on Susitna, land use in Chugach State Park, state land disposal, petrochemical control, and urban transportation. Knik sponsored a 14-year run of Belle Dawson's Alaska Wilderness program at the Anchorage Museum. Other Sierra Club/Alaska activity in the 1980s involved Bristol Bay land use plans, wolf control, and subsistence questions. In the 1990s it addressed more wolf control, claims on submerged lands, mining, *Exxon Valdez* restoration priorities, defense of Glacier Bay National Park, road-building plans, and an unsuccessful effort to recall Governor Walter Hickel.[27]

The Audubon Society's five Alaskan chapters similarly tackled projects closest to their locales. More politically active than in the 1970s yet still relatively conservative, Audubon engaged wolf conservation and Chilkat eagles in addition to a range of federal land and wildlife issues including Yukon Delta geese and Beringia.[28] It joined several lawsuits to protect land and ocean wildlife and habitat.

Trustees for Alaska (TfA), the Anchorage-based legal arm of the community, operated in nearly every region of the state. TfA won suits to require state land-disposal planning, strip automatic funding from the Susitna project, stiffen state mineral-leasing policy, control toxic drilling mud on the Kenai Peninsula, and enforce EPA water quality standards on placer-mined streams. Achieving some of its objectives, TfA also sued to reduce oil leasing impacts in the Arctic and Cook Inlet. Other suits and actions involved air and water pollution, the *Exxon Valdez* oil spill, coal mining and gold dredging, park protection, access to federal lands, logging on state lands, road building in natural areas, hovercraft on interior rivers, wolf management, and walrus and polar bear protection.[29] TfA evolved into a prominent force in Alaskan public interest law in the 1980s and 1990s.

State parks turned into battlegrounds between entrepreneuers and preservationists. Sierra Club/Alaska and ACE monitored commercial activity and other park infringements. In one such case, plans by the Department of Natural Resources (DNR) to solicit bids in 1990 for a large resort in Denali State Park prompted a lawsuit by environmentalists. Part of the land conveyed to Alaska in 1972 by Interior Secretary Morton, it buttressed a southern flank of Mount McKinley and formed an integral part of the ecosystem that federal officials had intended to add to Denali National Park. The DNR projected a center including hotels, convention rooms, indoor tennis courts, running tracks, and swimming pools, and sought $14 million from the legislature to facilitate the project. Arguing that the resort would degrade both the state and national parks, TfA sued, joined by ACE, Northern Alaska Environmental Center, Sierra Club/Alaska, and Alaska Wildlife Alliance. The suit called for a halt to the project, alleging deficient evaluation of ecosystem impacts and economic feasibility.[30] The legislature refused funding, and a 1991 superior court decision mandating further study and hearings caused the DNR to shelve the project indefinitely.[31]

Environmentalists contested an ongoing series of proposals for state, federal, or private construction that threatened wilderness quality in and near the Denali parks. To accommodate the swelling crowds of visitors at Denali National Park, the Park Service and the state jointly planned a tourism center south of the park, to cost more than $50 million. It would extend more than 40 miles into wild areas of Denali State Park. Environmentalists, outdoor sporting clubs, and miners formed a coalition to press for placement of the facility closer to Parks Highway.[32]

Wetlands and water quality attracted the attention of activists. TfA perused Army Corps of Engineers permits for wetland filling, filed comments and objections to improper procedures, and published a *Guide to Wetlands Protection in Alaska*. The Alaska Environmental Lobby successfully advocated a popular Waterfowl Conservation Stamp to help fund wetland preservation. Responding to years of unwillingness by the state to enforce the Clean Water Act, TfA brought suit in 1980 to force the federal EPA to take action. A spring 1994 appeals court ruling required the EPA and the state to set standards based on cumulative pollution impact on water bodies, from both point and nonpoint sources. Adoption of the cumulative-impact principle would move the state toward holistic, watershed-wide ecosystem management.[33]

Anchorage organizations took the lead in toxic-waste monitoring. ACE produced a half-hour TV documentary on Anchorage hazardous waste, published a booklet on identified sites and problems in the state, and set up an information network.[34] Through TfA it sued under the Resource Conservation and Recovery Act to force the EPA to study ecological effects of oil- and gas-drilling mud containing toxic substances including lead, arsenic, benzene, and phenols. Federal law dictated that the EPA complete the study by 1982; nothing had been done by 1985. Drilling-mud disposal resulted in damage claims on the Kenai Peninsula and elsewhere in the state and nation. The EPA agreed to do the study, completed it in 1988, and made recommendations to Congress for legislation.[35] ACE lobbied for measures regulating toxic drilling wastes.

TfA and ACE organized a Citizens Hazardous Waste Education and Advocacy Project, funded by the Public Welfare Foundation. The project extended legal aid and advice, and provided training in public testimony, citizens' rights, and procedures of federal and state agencies. Through the program, Nome citizens took part in the first voluntary cleanup of a Superfund site in Alaska. TfA monitored state toxic-waste activities and filed comments on proposed regulations. Representing ACE, it successfully sued the EPA in 1987 to make public, under the Freedom of Information Act, data on toxic-waste sites in Alaska.[36]

In the late 1990s, more than 2,000 toxic sites existed in Alaska, six of them under Superfund. Many stemmed from 648 active or inactive military installations, leaving the remains of explosives, chemical weapons, fuels, and other hazardous materials. Mining and other industrial operations added pollutants to the air, water, and soil. About 500 sites involved contaminated drinking water. EPA surveys estimated 300 million pounds of toxic chemicals released in Alaska in 1998. The region tended to collect PCBs, pesticides, and other poisons carried by air and ocean currents from Asia, Europe, and North America. Moreover, the cold climate slowed the process of chemical breakdown. To address threats to public health and wildlife, Alaska Community Action on Toxics formed in 1997.[37]

Coal development also engaged TfA and ACE. Diamond Shamrock–Chuitna Coal Joint Venture planned one of the world's largest open-pit coal mines near Tyonek, 45 miles west of Anchorage. Anticipating loss of air quality and possible detriment to fish and wildlife, the two environmental groups sued to obtain denial of a Department of Natural Resources permit.[37] In a suit against the EPA, TfA obtained release of documents regarding air-quality impact of the proposed mine.[38] At a later stage, TfA won a 1992 Alaska Supreme Court decision directing an environmental impact study of all the mine's operations (mine, gravel pits, and port) prior to issuance of a permit.[39]

In 1991, newly elected governor Walter Hickel revived the Copper River Highway rejected in the 1970s. The route would run along the western edge of Wrangell–St. Elias National Park and Preserve, on the Copper River Railroad bed abandoned in 1938 when the Kennecott mines closed. Proponents wished to link Cordova by road to the outside through Chitina; others preferred to leave Cordova, or the Copper River, unspoiled. Unable to persuade the legislature to appropriate money, Hickel ordered construction without state or federal permits, using $250,000 of highway maintenance funds. TfA sued on behalf of ACE, Cordova District Fisheries Union, Northern Alaska Environmental Center, and Sierra Club/Alaska, calling for environmental impact statements.[40] Road construction ceased for the remainder of the 1990s.

INTERIOR ALASKA

Smaller human populations and a conservative atmosphere restricted environmental protection activity in the interior. The Northern Alaska Environmental Center (NAEC; formerly Fairbanks Environmental Center) addressed a variety of federal issues: oil in the Arctic, wilderness status for the Arctic Refuge coastal plain, rules for management of lands, power lines in natural areas, and very intensely, mining regulation. It countered the state over the Susitna dam project, land sales, pollution at Prudhoe Bay, wolf control, mining and water quality control, submerged land claims, and road-building plans. It worked for designation of the Tanana Valley State Forest in 1983 and participated in the management plan, seeking to curb road construction and logging of old-growth white spruce.

NAEC monitored toxic waste in the Fairbanks region and in 1989 drafted a hazardous-waste map of the interior. In 1991 it founded Camp Habitat, a three-week summer outdoor education experience for children. During the 1990s, NAEC monitored an open-pit gold mine

15 miles northeast of Fairbanks, deemed to be the largest gold-mining operation in North America. It worked through the permit process to minimize the project's impairment of water quality, aesthetics, and recreational values. It joined legal efforts to restrain expansion of the oil industry into the National Petroleum Reserve, and contested what it considered an unnecessary power line to run through wild sections of the Tanana Flats.[41]

SOUTHEAST ALASKA

In addition to Tongass National Forest logging, Southeast Alaska Conservation Council (SEACC) kept track of activities in the Haines State Forest and Chilkat Bald Eagle Preserve, a proposed Juneau-Skagway road through steep coastal mountains, road-building and dam threats to the Stikine Valley, and gold mining near Juneau. It led a successful effort to establish the Yakataga State Game Refuge. By 1990 it boasted 900 members and strong momentum. Of its 17 member groups in 2000, at least 7 sprang up after 1984 to resist Tongass logging impact on resources and lifestyles. Small communities, commercial and subsistence fishing groups, Native villages, and small loggers joined SEACC in lobbying and lawsuits.[42] More than any other major element in the environmental community, SEACC succeeded as a broad-based, inclusive organization.

The Sierra Club Legal Defense Fund (SCLDF) of Juneau (changed to Earthjustice Legal Defense Fund in 1997) focused on southeastern, central mainland, and ocean issues. It took legal action on Alaska Pulp Company mill pollution and, joining the TfA and eight other environmental groups, it sued to ensure Exxon's responsibility for damages and cleanup in the 1989 oil spill.[43] SCLDF went to court in 1993 over proposed gold mines in the Southeast. One suit challenged the Kensington mine plan to dump pollutants into the Lynn Canal near a prime salmon-fishing location 45 miles north of Juneau. Mine specifications contemplated a half-mile-long pile of tailings along Lynn Canal, and dumping of 20 to 30 million tons of spoils onto nearby lowlands. In 1994 the EPA disallowed the plan. A compromise among federal and state agencies and citizen groups paved the way for the company, Coeur Alaska, to open in spring 1999. But the low price of gold led Coeur to propose a new design. Cyanide would be used in the separation process, and measures taken to prevent its getting into the water. Eleven million tons of tailings would be piped into the bay and dumped at a depth of 750 feet, covering 900 acres. Fishing groups and environmentalists, expecting injury to the marine ecosystem, prepared for another round of debate.[44]

Another venture, the Alaska-Juneau, promised to be the largest underground gold mine in the Western Hemisphere. Blasting would take place in the hills as close as two miles from downtown Juneau. More than 400 acres of the valley of Sheep Creek, about four miles south of the city, would be filled by tailings behind a 345-foot dam. Water flow would be lowered by 80 percent, and 31 million gallons of wastewater containing cyanide and heavy metals would be dumped into the Gastineau Channel daily. Echo Bay, the mining company, ran into trouble in 1993 by releasing pollutants into Gold Creek, a stream running through Juneau. It settled a lawsuit by paying the city $250,000. Alaskans for Juneau, a citizen monitoring body, obtained an EPA document indicating that Echo Bay had continued to spill mud, oil, and hydraulic fluid into the creek in violation of the Clean Water Act. In 1997 Echo Bay declared the project economically unfeasible, and prepared to close it.[45]

17.6. Northern Alaska Environmental Center leaders, 1990. Courtesy NAEC. Left to right: Larry Landry, Glendon Brunk, Marie Beaver, Trudy Heffernan, Lou Brown, Rex Blazer. NAEC strove to protect the Arctic Refuge and other northern lands.

SCLDF represented environmental and outdoor recreation groups, commercial fishers, and local communities in a variety of legal undertakings. Like TfA, it achieved recognition as a vital element of Alaskan public-interest environmental law.

ENVIRONMENTALISTS AND STATE AGENCIES

As the state moved toward selection of its 105-million-acre total under the Statehood Act and the Alaska Lands Act, it assigned land to categories permitting varying degrees of intrusion. Environmentalists attempted to move the choices toward preservation, and to deter encroachment on protected tracts. In addition to interior lands, the state in 2000 held more than 40 million acres of tidelands, offshore lands, and acreage under navigable rivers. It maintained at least 118 park and wildlife refuge units.[46]

Environmentalists viewed the Alaska Department of Natural Resources (DNR), which manages nearly all state surface and subsurface holdings, as inclined to deliver public resources into the hands of private interests, especially timber, mining, agriculture, and oil. They worked for designation of state parks and sanctuaries, except those whose natural integrity had been too heavily compromised by rules of use. They criticized or attempted to curtail DNR projects they considered uneconomical or unnecessarily destructive. They endorsed creation of the Non-Game Section and the Habitat Division in the Alaska Department of Fish and Game, while seeing the agency as primarily representative of sport hunters

17.7. Southeast Alaska Conservation Council leaders John Sisk, Julie and Bart Koehler, and Steve Kallick, ca. 1989. Courtesy SEACC. Front-line activists in one of the longest-running American environmental conflicts.

and fishers. Environmentalists felt closest to the Department of Environmental Conservation, which regulates for protection of public health and the environment. DEC typically suffered from underfunding and intimidation by industrial interests. Environmentalists sought effective public participation in resource management decisionmaking processes, and intensified their activity in state and local concerns after 1980. These endeavors helped to cement their community and, perhaps more than their successes in national issues, won them acceptance in Alaska.

DETERMINANTS OF EFFECTIVENESS

Alaska's environmentalists have realized most of their success by helping to shape local, state, and national government policies. They affect state policy through temporary alliances with Natives, small towns, commercial fishers, tourist interests, and other resource user groups. Assistance from national environmental organizations enables the community to more effectively influence national policy.

The community is a loosely coordinated voluntary association, a network focusing on substantive issues, political and legal action, and information and education. It embraces general- and specific-purpose organizations, local and regional bodies, and national branch offices. In 2000 it included or maintained close ties to more than 90 units (Table 17.3). No binding statement of goals exists, and no governing body has the power to speak for all of

Table 17.3—Environmental and Related Organizations in Alaska, 2000

Organization	Location	Date of Origin
Alaska Action Center	Anchorage	1998
Alaska Boreal Forest Council	Fairbanks	1992
Alaska Center for the Environment	Anchorage, Palmer	1971
Alaska Clean Air Coalition	Anchorage	1986
Alaska Coalition	Washington, DC	1977
Alaska Community Action on Toxics	Anchorage	1997
Alaska Community Share	Anchorage	1985
Alaska Conservation Alliance	Anchorage, Juneau	1981
Alaska Conservation Foundation	Anchorage	1980
Alaska Conservation Voters	Anchorage, Juneau	1981
Alaska Forum for Environmental Responsibility	Fairbanks	1994
Alaska Friends of the Earth	Anchorage	1971
Alaska Inter-Tribal Council	Anchorage	1992
Alaska Lands Act Coordinating Committee	Anchorage	1981
Alaska Marine Conservation Council	Anchorage	1993
Alaska Natural Heritage Program	Anchorage	1989
Alaska Natural History Assn	Anchorage	1959
Alaska Natural Resources & Outdoor Education Assn	Anchorage	1984
Alaska Organic Assn	Palmer	1999
Alaska Public Interest Research Group	Anchorage	1974
Alaska Quiet Rights Coalition	Anchorage	1997
Alaska Rainforest Campaign	Anchorage	1993
Alaska Raptor Rehabilitation Center	Sitka	1980
Alaska Society of American Forestdwellers	Point Baker	1986
Alaska Waveriders	Anchorage, Juneau	1989
Alaska Wilderness League	Washington, DC	1993
Alaska Wilderness Recreation & Tourism Assn	Anchorage	1991
Alaska Wildlife Alliance	Anchorage	1983
Alaskans for Juneau	Juneau	1990
Alaskans for Litter Prevention & Recycling	Anchorage	1983
Alaskans for Responsible Resource Management	Tokeen	1983
Anchorage Waterways Council	Anchorage	1985
Arctic Network	Anchorage	1993
Bird Treatment & Learning Center	Anchorage	1998
Campaign to Safeguard America's Waters	Haines	1998
Center for Alaskan Coastal Studies	Homer	1981
Center for Marine Conservation	Anchorage	1993
Chichagof Conservation Council	Tenakee Springs	1985
The Conservation Fund	Eagle River	1994
Cook Inlet Keeper	Homer	1994
Copper Country Alliance	Copper Center	1992
Cordova District Fishermen United	Cordova	1935
Denali Citizens Council	Denali Park	1974
Denali Institute	Denali Natl Park	1999
Discovery Southeast	Juneau	1988
Earthjustice Legal Defense Fund	Juneau	1978

continued on next page

Table 17.3—continued

Organization	Location	Date of Origin
Eastern Kenai Peninsula Environmental Action Assn	Seward	1994
Friends of Chugach State Park	Anchorage	1986
Friends of Eagle River Nature Center	Eagle River	1997
Friends of Glacier Bay	Guatavus	1972
Friends of Kenai Natl Wildlife Refuge	Soldotna	1999
Friends of Kennicott	Anchorage	1989
Friends of Mat-Su	Palmer	1998
Friends of McNeil River	Anchorage	1990
Great Land Trust, Inc.	Anchorage	1995
Greenpeace Alaska	Anchorage	1978, 1983
Gwitch'in Steering Committee	Anchorage, Fairbanks	1988
Interior Alaska Land Trust	Fairbanks	1995
The Island Institute	Sitka	1984
Kachemak Bay Conservation Society	Homer	1975
Kachemak Heritage Land Trust	Homer	1989
Kenai Watershed Forum	Soldotna	1997
Kodiak Brown Bear Trust	N. Bethesda MD	1981
League of Conservation Voters Education Fund	Anchorage	1997
Lynn Canal Conservation, Inc.	Haines	1971
Narrows Conservation Coalition	Petersburg	1971
National Audubon Society	Anchorage	1977
National Parks & Conservation Assn	Anchorage	1985
National Wildlife Federation	Anchorage	1987
Native American Fish & Wildlife Society	Anchorage	1992
The Nature Conservancy of Alaska	Anchorage, Soldotna	1988
Northern Alaska Environmental Center	Fairbanks	1971
One/Northwest	Seattle	1995
Prince of Wales Conservation League	Craig	1991
Prince William Sound Science Center	Cordova	1989
Re-Group	Soldotna	1989
Research Information Center/Alaska Housing Finance Corp	Anchorage	1992
Sierra Club Alaska Chapter	Anchorage	1968
Sierra Club-Alaska Field Office	Anchorage	1970
Sitka Conservation Society	Sitka	1965
Southeast Alaska Conservation Council	Juneau	1969
Southeast Alaska Land Trust	Juneau	1995
Taku Conservation Society	Juneau	1976
Tongass Conservation Society	Ketchikan	1969
Training Resources for the Environmental Community	Burton WA	1998
Trans Alaska Gas System Environmental Review Committee	Anchorage	1990
Trustees for Alaska	Anchorage	1974
Valley Community for Recycling Solutions	Wasilla	1997
The Wilderness Society	Anchorage	1981
Wildlife Federation of Alaska	Anchorage	1985
Wrangell Mountains Center	Anchorage	1972

Source: Alaska Conservation Foundation, *Alaska Conservation Directory, 2000 Edition.* Anchorage, 2000.

the state elements. Most chapters approve of the work of Alaska Conservation Voters, and attend the annual Alaska Conservation Alliance assembly. They generally accept the semicoordinative role of the Alaska Conservation Foundation. Few divisive policy disputes have arisen since the passage of the Alaska Lands Act in 1980.

Although some Alaskan utilitarian conservationists openly identify with it, in general the environmental community is more preservation-oriented. To operate in the Alaskan context where "environmentalist" and "preservationist" are often pejorative terms, community members tend to refer to themselves as "conservationists." The utilitarian outdoor sportsmen and women also describe themselves as "conservationists." They have clashed with environmentalists on wolf control, hunting access to federal lands, and subsistence rights of Natives. Cooperation is normal and productive in curbing the destructive behavior of industries. This essentially positive relationship is useful to both parties; environmentalists rely on the clout of the outdoor sporting clubs, who sometimes need the expertise of the environmentalists. Considerable disparity in values and lifestyles, however, makes for uneasy and selective alliances.

Among the environmentalists and Native groups, some policy discord exists. The Alaska Wildlife Alliance and Southeast Alaska Conservation Council have vigorously disagreed over Native and commercial fishing in Glacier Bay National Park. Native sovereignty and related questions of subsistence use of state and federal lands could heighten tension among sporting groups, preservationists, and Natives. To the extent that environmentalists endorse Native preference in resource use, they weaken their ties to sporting groups. Environmentalists tend to disapprove of large-scale industrial projects involving Native corporations, as, for example, clear-cutting by several Southeast Alaska Native corporations of nearly all their timberlands. Some positions taken by animal-rights groups, such as opposition to trapping and snaring, have alienated environmentalists from Natives who feel their right to take wildlife is at risk. A wide cultural gap contributes to the distancing, and Natives are inclined to ally with environmentalists only on specific issues. Wilderness designation, which can protect wildlife populations needed for subsistence, is a matter of mutual concern. Yet limited potential exists for permanent or broad-based alliances of Native groups and environmentalists.

Alaska's economy vitally influences the environment and the fortunes of the environmental community. Prices of oil, gas, coal, lumber and pulp, gold and other metals, fish, agricultural products, and other resources are directly linked to stress on the environment. Higher prices for Alaskan products generally mean more work for environmental groups, far outnumbered and out-financed by economic interests. Expansion periods foster a boom psychology and momentum, forcing activists into a defensive position and branding them enemies of progress. Moderate growth allows environmentalists to limit their focal points and operate as relatively normal and accepted members of the body politic. Economic decline calls for the will to fight pork-barrel projects born of desperation, and to withstand accusations of being opposed to jobs, but it casts environmentalists in a relatively palatable role of rational planners and watchdogs of the public treasury. At the same time, recession tends to result in budget cuts for the Departments of Environmental Conservation and Fish and Game, weakening their capacity to protect natural resources.

Environmentalists in turn have to work harder and direct more of their energies toward fund-raising.

As oil companies withdraw from Alaska, their grip on public opinion and the legislative process will loosen. Poor prospects for increased oil revenues, and reductions of federal subsidies or other large income sources, would indirectly enhance environmental quality. Construction of a Prudhoe-Valdez gas pipeline might perpetuate oil company influence for years, generate another population boom, and put more pressure on natural resources through private and state-sponsored development.

Environmental protection may be expected to benefit from some aspects of the growth of tourism, especially the burgeoning interest in nature-related activities. Environmentalists will be able to build stronger political bridges to tourist-related interests, thus acting as patrons of qualitative economic growth. Environmentalists prefer small-scale, community-based tourism as distinct from "industrial-scale," mass-influx tourism that will demand more roads and facilities in wild areas. They resist proposals for transporting tourists into sensitive wild areas by such intrusive means as helicopter flights and hovercraft on rivers.

Modest potential lies in cooperation between environmentalists and their traditional adversaries, the extractive and polluting industries. A prime example is the Alaska Conservation Foundation–Yukon Pacific Corporation joint environmental planning of the Prudhoe-Valdez gas pipeline. Progress in such cooperation will be slow, and may be halted in trying economic times or if discouraged by conservative state or national administrations and legislatures. Yet gradual evolution of environmental responsibility in industry is likely to continue in response to the weight of public opinion.

Alaska's sociological makeup and population growth rate will affect the power of the environmental community and the quality of the environment. Whereas boom times attract both nature enthusiasts and aggressive exploiters, slack periods feature a higher percentage of long-term residents, who own a greater stake in environmental quality and tend to be more appreciative of environmental values. Transience among environmental activists is a mixed blessing; it instills freshness and enthusiasm but puts long-term stability of organizations at risk. Rising population will degrade the environment but not necessarily weaken the community; it will propagate an ever-greater number and variety of problems calling for evolving alliances with nonenvironmental groups.

Environmental protection has considerable support in Alaska. Whereas Alaskans comprised 0.22 percent of the U.S. population in the early 1990s, several national environmental organizations claimed a higher percentage of their membership in Alaska: Greenpeace (.026 percent), Sierra Club (.31 percent), Nature Conservancy (.34 percent), Audubon (.43 percent), Wilderness Society (.48 percent), and National Parks and Conservation Association (.49 percent).[47] Another indication of public endorsement has been the growth of membership in Alaskan groups (Table 17.1). A 1999 statewide opinion survey by the Alaska Conservation Alliance revealed significant shifts since 1996 toward environmental attitudes on a range of concerns including logging, air and water pollution, habitat protection, wildlife management, and growth and development. Respondents still favored oil drilling in the Arctic Refuge and other parts of the North Slope. In a list of eleven groups, they ranked scientists first, local environmental organizations third, and oil and timber companies last as sources of reliable information. Women indicated much stronger concern for the environment than did men, Democrats far more than Republicans, and "No Party" voters slightly more than Democrats.[48]

Issues of the 1970s placing the community at odds with the public, especially d-2 and the oil pipeline, have faded. Resolution of the main questions of land ownership, and completion of state and federal land-use plans, have enabled the community to concentrate more effectively on popular issues such as toxic-waste control and the selection and monitoring of state parks. Conflicts involving the poorly coordinated array of land units will, nevertheless, challenge environmental protectors for the foreseeable future. The gain in influence and readership of the *Anchorage Daily News* and the near-departure of its militantly industry-oriented rival the *Anchorage Times* (which retains a voice through an editorial page in the *Daily News*) have mirrored the changing environmental values and contributed to the community's more favorable image.

Essentially, the environmental community is a constructive element of the public policymaking process, dedicated to betterment of the quality of life. Its values of personal and social responsibility, openness and accountability by government and business, concern for public health and economic efficiency, care for one's surroundings, appreciation of nature, and science-based planning for the future are normal democratic traditions and aspirations. The public is reluctant to credit environmentalists, but often acknowledges the legitimacy of these values in principle if not consistently in practice.

Environmental matters have evolved into regular concerns of state and local government bodies, irrespective of the presence of "Greenie" activists. Paralleling the moderation of public opinion, administrative officials showed more tolerance of the environmental community in the 1980s and latter 1990s. Governors Hammond, Sheffield, Cowper, and Knowles recognized and enhanced the power of the community by their appointments of activists to positions of influence.[49] During the 1990s, however, environmental successes in state issues grew more scarce and difficult under the Hickel administration and a legislature dominated by conservatives. State courts have taken moderate stances in environmental cases.

Federal government policy will be a decisive variable in the future of Alaska's environment and the power of its environmental community. Many lands subject to disputes, as well as all ocean waters beyond three miles, are national. Federal actions can strain the resources of environmental defenders far beyond capacity, as they did during the Reagan and Bush years. Carter and Clinton administration policies, by contrast, generally favored the community. Loss of a major battle such as oil drilling in the Arctic Refuge would harm the prestige and standing of the community, whereas a victory like the Tongass Timber Reform Act can do the opposite. On the other hand, too little challenge could dampen membership growth, financial support, and volunteer enthusiasm. Crisis has a strong appeal for Alaskan as for other environmentalists.

In times of Democratic control, Congress may be expected to respond to environmental appeals. Under Republican control of Congress, especially if supplementing a Republican administration, activists are forced into rear-guard positions to defend a wide range of environmental values. Beginning in 1995, Alaska's delegation chaired key committees: Frank Murkowski—Senate Energy and Natural Resources; Ted Stevens—Senate Appropriations

(1997); and Don Young—House Resources. Powerfully positioned to mold federal policy, they actively sought to facilitate private exploitation of natural resources, especially in Alaska. Introducing numerous bills and riders to bills, they attempted to pass measures encroaching on natural areas. They displayed stoutly negative attitudes toward preservation values and the state's environmental community.[50]

Federal court decisions, especially at the appeals level, have been a fairly consistent source of accomplishment by the community. Several times, court orders originating in suits by Trustees for Alaska and Sierra Club Legal Defense Fund stopped the Reagan administration from making illegal intrusions into federal lands. Some court decisions—placing curbs on Japanese drift-netting, protecting killer whales from Sea World, and restricting oil leasing in Bristol Bay—won popular approval in Alaska. Legal action will continue to be a potent means to environmental protection, to political influence, and thus to heightened morale and prestige for the community.

Funding, quality of personnel, and organization will be vital ingredients of the success of the environmental community. Alaska has one of the highest percentages of environmental-group members of any state. At the same time, because most Alaskans have not lived long in the state, there is little "old money" available to fund the operations, still closely reliant on contributions from the Lower 48. Monetary aid is made possible by the exceptional national interest in Alaska, based on its history and its possession of most of the great relatively unspoiled natural areas in the nation. Personnel quality is high, often matching the complexities of the issues they address. Alaska attracts many talented young people who possess staunch environmental sentiments and willingness to devote their time for little or no pay.

Yet the structure and orientation of the community embody some weaknesses. Young, single, low-paid, and mobile activists often do not integrate well into the surrounding community. Their extensive education, upper-middle-class values, and largely preservationist philosophy present additional barriers. Their inclination, partly owing to lack of time and funds, is to try to win court cases and influence legislation or administrative decisions rather than to do fund-raising, membership recruitment, and public education. As a result, progress in forging alliances with potential allies has been marginal, and some groups have not grown in membership. More broadly, the piecemeal approach of targeting discrete issues is inherently reactive as distinct from a planned and holistic agenda. It functions as a holding action, checking some of the worst expressions of abuse while the quality of the environment continues to deteriorate from legal and normally accepted intrusions.

If the goal of sustainable use of the environment is to be achieved, a quantum shift in the perceptions, values, and behavior of the Alaskan public will ultimately be necessary. These changes will not automatically follow greater awareness of resource damage or the achievements of the environmental community. To some degree, environmental action may encourage a feeling of complacency, a belief that the problems are being taken care of. School systems and media can play a useful role in convincing the public that the quality of life depends on ecosystem integrity, but the environmental community may have to become more directly involved in the educational process. The Alaska Conservation Foundation's outreach program, launched in 1997, has attempted to improve the community's effectiveness in both public education and coalition building.

Piecemeal strategy also interferes with the ability of environmentalists to defend the environment. Saving a forest in one place may mean that logging is simply transferred to another of equal ecological value. Greater coordination of policy over wider geographical areas is necessary to maintain ecosystem viability and thus lifestyle sustainability. To this end, in 1993 the Alaska Conservation Foundation fostered the creation of three ecosystem-focused regional groups: the Alaska Marine Conservation Council, Alaska Rainforest Campaign, and Arctic Network. Regional cooperation among environmental and user groups can build more political clout, generate policy more responsive to ecosystem variations and complexities, and upgrade ecological education of the public.

Movement toward a more centralized and coordinated system, involving direct public education and more numerous and intimate ties to user groups, would mean some costs to the environmental community. Engineering a permanent shift in public opinion and behavior is an inordinately long, difficult, and costly task, and not very exciting. Choosing, fighting, and winning their own battles has given the disparate units pride, commitment, and membership gains. These benefits are likely to wane if the activists divert their energies to mundane membership activities, and as they compromise their values by joining broader alliances. Public approval may decline if environmentalists win fewer headline-making (and nonthreatening) victories. A more expensive and bureaucratic system would develop, mitigating some of the freedom and zeal that has been a driving force in the community.

The Alaskan environmental community has risen swiftly, compiling an enviable record of achievement. Collectively, it has embraced a wide range of concerns—government and corporate accountability, public involvement, adequate information, pollution control, nonconsumptive use values, ecosystem protection, and environmental and economic sustainability. It has regularly employed the tactics of modern environmentalism, especially legal challenges and media exposure. Its moderate acceptance by the Alaskan public is a measure of the incorporation of environmental values into public thinking. Indirectly and sometimes directly, the community has stepped up the pace of national environmentalism. Allied national and local groups have won consequential victories in contests over lands and wildlife. They have caught the public's attention and shifted the national conservation agenda northward, further confirming Alaska's environment as a valued national inheritance.

NOTES

1. Fischer, *Alaska's Constitutional Convention*, 130–140; *Constitution of the State of Alaska*, Art. VIII.

2. Founding members of the Alaska Conservation Society: Frederick and Susan Dean, Celia Hunter, Herbert and Hilda Melchior, William and Edna Pruitt, John Thomson, Robert B. and Judith Weeden, and Ginny and Morton ("Woody") Wood.

3. *Alaska Conservation Society (ACS) News Bulletin*, March 1960, 1–2; May 1960, 15; *Alaska Conservation Review (ACR)*, Spring 1976, 6–8.

4. Alaska Conservation Foundation (ACF), "Celia Hunter: Dean"; Hunter, "From My Corner," July–September 1977, 61; Nash, "Tourism, Parks," 18; S. Johnson, "Celia Hunter," 30–35.

5. Ginny Hill Wood, interview by author, July 28, 1992; Wood, "Back to the Woodpile," November 10, 1999, 16–17.

6. *ACR*, Spring 1976, 6–8; McCloskey, *Wilderness: The Edge of Knowledge*, 130; "Curriculum Vitae: Robert B. Weeden"; Weeden, interview by author, July 12, 1988. Weeden wrote two books on

natural resources and sustainable development: *Alaska: Promises to Keep* (1978) and *Messages from Earth* (1992).

7. Hensel, Spencer, and Hickok, "Willard A. Troyer"; *ACR*, Spring 1976, 6–8. Six ACS chapters existed before 1971: Kenai, Kodiak-Aleutian, Petersburg, Sitka, Tanana-Yukon (Fairbanks), and Upper Cook Inlet (Anchorage). Kachemak Bay, Taku (Juneau) and Tongass (Ketchikan) joined later.

8. C. Hunter, "This Our Land," April 1982, 21, 62; *ACR*, Winter 1979, 8. The 1979 ACS chapters: Kachemak Bay, Kenai Peninsula (Homer), Kodiak-Aleutian, Petersburg, Sitka, Taku (Juneau), Tanana-Yukon (Fairbanks), Tongass (Ketchikan) and Upper Cook Inlet (Anchorage).

9. *ACR*, Fall 1971, 8; Cissna, "Alaska Conservation, 1950–70"; Wright, "Northern Center," 7–13. Other founders of Fairbanks Environmental Center were Florence and Richard Collins, Jim Hunter, and the principal organizer, Gordon Wright.

10. *ACR*, Winter 1971, 10; Cissna, "Alaska Conservation"; *Center News*, June 15, 1979, 1. Chuck Konigsburg, Helen Nienheuser, Walter B. Parker and Ted Schultz also helped initiate ACE.

11. *Ravencall*, December 1977, 18–18; Whitesell, "Southeast Wildlands Study," 7–8.

12. Lobaugh, "Lobbyist in Juneau," 9; *Alaska Session Laws, 1976*, Chapters 45, 113, 140, 255; 1977, Chapter 84; 1978, Chapters 108, 151; 1979, Chapters 21, 39.

13. Peg Tileston, interview by author, July 14, 1988. Rod Cameron, Bob Childers, Walter B. Parker, and Peg Tileston organized TfA.

14. Nunam Kitlutsisti, "Nunam Kitlutsisti."

15. Denny Wilcher, interview by author, July 21, 1988.

16. *ACR*, Mid-April 1971, 4.

17. *ACR*, Spring 1973, 3, 6; *Sierra Club Alaska Newsletter*, October 1973, 3; *Alaska Session Laws, 1973*, SCR 44.

18. ACF, "Alaska Environmental Matrix," 1980, 1990; *Alaska Conservation Directory, 2000*; Denny Wilcher, interview by author, July 21, 1988; Ellen Maling, personal communication, March 27, 2000.

19. Perkins, "Alaska's Environmental Planning," 7; ACF, "Alaska Conservation Foundation: Helping Alaskans"; ACF, *Alaska Conservation Foundation Annual Report, 1997*, 12; Jim Stratton and Denny Wilcher, interviews by author, July 21, 1988, Deborah Williams, letter to author, June 1, 1999 Celia Hunter and former Sierra Club official Denny Wilcher cofounded ACF.

20. Konigsberg, "ACF Strategy," 3–5. The William and Flora Hewlett Foundation funded the initiative.

21. Marquette, "Strategies Planned," 6; Stanway, "Conservationists Gather," 6; Jay Nelson, interview by author, July 5, 1988; *United Voices, Year End Report, 1998*. Margie Gibson led the initiation of Alaska Conservation Alliance.

22. Early organizers of AEPAC: John Adams, David Benton, Bob Childers, David Finkelstein, Joe Geldhof, Margie Gibson, Roland Shanks, and Steve Williams.

23. Jay Nelson, interview by author, June 27 and July 5, 1988.

24. Larry Edwards, John Adams, Margie Gibson and Paul Lowe reorganized AEL.

25. Jay Nelson and Jim Stratton, interviews by author, July 5 and 21, 1988; Alaska Environmental Lobby, *How the Alaska Legislature Voted;* Shelton, "ACV Promotes Sustainable Economy," 1; *Conservation Voice* and *United Voices*, 1998–2000 issues.

26. Alaska Center for the Environment (ACE), *Annual Report, 1987; Center News*, 1980–2000 issues; Coelho, "We Did It!" 1, 5.

27. *Sierra Club Alaska Newsletter, Sierra Borealis*, and *Alaska Report*, 1980–2000 issues.

28. National Audubon Society, *News from Audubon*, 1980s issues; Cline, *Work Plan 1989–90*.

29. *Trustees for Alaska*, 1984–1993 issues, *TfA Environmental Action Report*, 1994–1998 issues; *The Environmental Advocate*, 1998–2000 issues; "Trustees for Alaska" brochure, ca. 1987; TfA, *Summary of Recent Activities*, 1991, 1–6.

30. Eames, "ACE Files Suit," 3; *Trustees for Alaska*, "Trustees Challenge DNR's Decision," 5; *Trustees for Alaska*, December 1990, 6.

31. Eames, "Celebrate Wild Denali," 4.

32. Michaelson, "Denali Development," 6.

33. TfA, *Summary of Recent Activities*, 1988, 7; *Alaska Session Laws, 1984*, Chapter 71; *TfA Environmental Action Report*, "Landmark Decision," 1, 3.

34. *Center News*, October–November 1982; March–April 1983; Pendleton, "Network Formed," 5.

35. Benson, "Delayed Study," 8; *Trustees for Alaska*, Fall 1985, 1, 3; Summer 1986, 1; TfA, *Summary of Recent Activities*, 1988, 1.

36. *Trustees for Alaska*, Spring 1987, 3; Fall–Winter 1988, 2; TfA, *Summary of Recent Activities*, 1988, 3, 7.

37. *Alaska Conservation Foundation Dispatch*, "Toxic Pollution in Alaska," 1–4. Pamela K. Miller organized Alaska Commuity Acion on Toxics.

38. *Trustees for Alaska*, Spring–Summer 1988, 3; *Center News*, August–September 1988, 5.

39. TfA, *Summary of Recent Activities*, 1988, 2, 6–7.

40. *Trustees for Alaska*, December 1990, 3; *Trustees for Alaska*, "Supreme Court Halts Diamond-Chuitna," 1.

41.*Trustees for Alaska*, "State Plows Over Laws," 4; *Trustees for Alaska*, "Copper River Highway," 1, 3.

42. *Northern Line*, 1980–2000 issues; Peale, "Tanana Forest Plan," 4–6; *Alaska Session Laws, 1983*, Chapter 91; Blazer, "NAEC 1988 Annual Report"; Stoltz "Camp Habitat," 14; Ward, "Mining on Fish Creek," 6–7; Groves, "Farewell to Sylvia Ward," 2.

43. *Ravencall*, 1980–2000 issues; Southeast Alaska Conservation Council, *SEACC: Operating Plan, 1988*; ACF, "Alaska Environmental Matrix," 1980 and 1990.

44. L. Adams, *Sierra Club Legal Defense Fund, 1987*; P. Barnett, "Victories in Alaska Litigation," 2.

45. *Ravencall*, "Coalition Works," 10; Sierra Club Legal Defense Fund (SCLDF), *In Brief*, Autumn 1993, 22–23; *Ravencall*, "EPA Finds Big Flaws," 12; Tom Morphet, "Coeur Touts Changes to Mine Plan," *Chilkat Valley News*, June 7, 1999.

46. *Ravencall*, "Massive Mine," 10; SCLDF, *In Brief*, Autumn 1993, 22–23; Ferguson-Craig, "Echo Bay Fined," 12; Dirk Miller, "Mine Company Dogged by Charges of Muddying Juneau Creek Water," *Ketchikan Daily News*, July 6, 1998.

47. Alaska DNR, Division of Parks and Outdoor Recreation, personal communication, June 13, 2000.

48. G. Matz, "Environmentalists," Table 1.

49. Alaska Conservation Alliance, "Alaska Statewide Opinion," ii–vii, 3–14.

50. Some appointments: David L. Allison, Alaska Power Authority, and North Pacific Marine Fisheries Commission; Rex Blazer, Project Analyst, Office of Governor; Joe Geldhof, Asst. Attorney General; Marilyn Heiman, Spec. Asst. to Governor; Jack Hession, Alaska Transportation Planning Commission; Dennis Kelso, Director, DEC; Sue Libenson, Spec. Asst. to Commissioner, DEC; Ernest Mueller, Commissioner, DEC; Jay Nelson, Spec. Asst. to Governor; Alan Phipps, Project Review Coord., Office of Governor; Roland Shanks, Director of Technical Services, DNR, and Spec. Asst., ADF&G; John Sisk, Spec. Asst. to Governor; Jim Stratton, Director, State Parks; Peg Tileston, Alaska State Water Resource Board; and Robert B. Weeden, Alaska Power Authority, DEC Environmental Advisory Board, and Director of Governor's Office of Planning and Policy Development.

51. John H. Cushman Jr., "Alaska Delegation Pushes Agenda of Development," *New York Times*, September 13, 1998, 46.

18

Trends and Prospects

At the core of environmental conflict in Alaska since it became a state in 1959 has been a struggle between forces sanctioning short-term exploitation and those counseling more sustainable use of natural resources. Each cause is grounded in philosophical convictions, for the most part sincerely held, about the meaning and value of life. Each employs a characteristic rationale for its positions, and each strives to promote compliant behavior by government and other social institutions. The contest between the two value clusters is central to the affairs of society, and a vital determinant of both the quality of human life and the fate of the natural world.

EXPLOITATION VERSUS SUSTAINABILITY

The exploitation or "development" ethic promotes immediate, often unsustainable, utilization of resources for the benefit of individuals, corporations, or society. It views nature as a store of resources to be taken by humans as needed or desired. It sees rapid resource consumption as a necessary steppingstone to, or byproduct of, progress. In turn, progress (implicitly defined in terms of comfort and material gain) is assumed to be a central goal of humans, who by nature or divine sanction have priority over other creatures. Competition among individuals, groups, or nations is viewed as a normal and beneficial aspect of resource appropriation. Explicitly or implicitly, resource stocks are assumed to be abundant or replaceable. Exploitation advocates in Alaska have promulgated their views and justified their patterns of resource use by one or more of the following means:

· Denying the unsustainability and pointing to the economic benefits, especially in dollar terms, of a project or enterprise;
· Appealing to the desire of individuals for personal gain, claimed as a right;
· Invoking the Manifest Destiny notion of natural and inevitable American progress;
· Claiming the sanction of "national security";
· Appealing to the desire for local as against "Outsider" control of natural resources (by the national government, public, media, or environmental groups).

The sustainability ethic assumes that resources are limited, and that their disposal has important consequences. It calls for much more restrained claims (sometimes no consumptive use) on a resource, and responsibility of users for environmental and social side-effects. The goal of sustainability may be understood as a condition of no significant deterioration in quantity or quality, a level of ecological integrity and economic well-being that can be maintained indefinitely. Advocates believe sustainable treatment of resources represents fairness and economic viability for present and future humans and for nonhuman creatures. They employ one or more of the following appeals:

· Attempting to show what has been or will be lost (wildlife, beauty, recreational opportunity, taxpayer dollars) by exploitation;
· Endorsing internalization of social and environmental costs incurred;
· Calling for research on ecosystems and environmental impacts;
· Requesting public access to information on uses and impacts;
· Encouraging public participation in decisionmaking on resource management.

Adherence to resource-management beliefs varies in degree and may be a mixture of values from both sides of the spectrum. Yet Alaska seems to have attracted unusually determined partisans of both perspectives. Forces aligned on the exploitation side have typically included the state government, majorities of the Alaskan public, the extractive industries, the commercial and construction interests, the Alaska congressional delegation, and most Republicans in the federal government. State and national environmental groups form the mainstay of the sustainability side. Often joining them are national media, national public opinion, and various national officials, disproportionately Democrats. Others may be neutral or join either side, depending on the issue: Native Americans, sport hunters, commercial fishers, local communities, the tourism industry, or elements of state public opinion and state government.

Three general categories of controversies have dominated Alaskan environmental politics in the statehood period: (1) taking of wildlife at levels that may jeopardize populations or raise questions of sustainability or equity of use (e.g., polar bears, bowhead whales, Yukon Delta waterfowl, and wolves); (2) experimental projects that take advantage of remote areas (Chariot and Amchitka nuclear testing); and (3) economic projects that endanger wildlife populations or wilderness values (Rampart and Susitna dams, oil drilling, pipeline and ocean transportation of oil, clear-cut logging, mining, and roads).

The outcome of a controversy is the product of interaction of many elements:

· What is the issue? What is the proposed or ongoing use of the land; who owns the land or controls the resources; which resources are threatened; who or what stands to gain or lose from usage?
· What is the time period? Which parties control the state and national governments, what is the state of the economy, what is the state or national public mood toward environmental protection?
· What are the rules of the game? What are the relevant state and federal laws and regulations; who has access to hearings, information, and courts?

· What is the quality of information on the issue? How adequate is baseline research and what is known about the particular use and its effects?
· Who will take part in the fight? What are their relative financial, organizational, reputational, motivational, and other strengths and weaknesses?

Promoters of exploitation operate at an advantage in most Alaskan conflicts, as elsewhere. Most can outspend their opponents in advertising, staffing, lobbying, campaign contributions, and legal proceedings. They can appeal to the short-term economic wants of current user groups and voters, whose influence completely outweighs that of future citizens and nonvoters, including wildlife. Their invocation of Manifest Destiny resonates in a state that has nurtured pioneer myths of progress through consumption of an endless supply of natural resources. Calls for local control please many who dislike federal restrictions or wish to obtain nationally-owned resources for themselves. During the Cold War, at least, pleas of "national security" (as in Project Chariot, Amchitka testing, Rampart dam, the Prudhoe-Valdez oil route, and the Arctic Refuge) helped rationalize ventures and taint opponents as disloyal.

Sustainability advocates have often succeeded in situations involving small economic stakes (e.g., polar bears, bowhead whales, Yukon Delta waterfowl, Chilkat eagles, Project Chariot). They have helped put an end to projects opposed by elements of the federal government (Rampart and Susitna dams), and lost the battle in others more clearly favored by the federal government (Amchitka testing, oil drilling and transportation). In most cases of resource extraction on federal lands (mining, oil drilling, logging, roads, inholdings) the outcomes have been mixed. Sustainability values have prevailed less frequently on state lands, and even less on Native owned lands. Owing in part to the major conflicts, a gradual trend toward acceptance of environmental values and sustainable consumption of resources has taken place in Alaska. It may be most unequivocal in the cases of subsistence harvest of particular species such as polar bears, whales, and waterfowl, and in preservation of the Chilkat eagles. For these species, at least, relatively noncontroversial and long-term arrangements attempt to ensure the survival of populations and their measured use by humans. For other species and for wildlife in general, swelling tourism has advanced the legitimacy of nonconsumptive wildlife values, as witnessed in the wolf-control controversy. Research, knowledge, and public awareness have slowly broadened in ecological perspectives. A proliferation of groups has focused on a wide range of aspects of environmental quality, and much protective legislation has been passed. To a degree, exploitative corporations and government agencies have moderated their behavior.

In the realm of economic sustainability, the termination of some big designs (Chariot, Rampart, Susitna) has represented at least a national reluctance to pay for economically nonviable ventures, especially when they undermine other values. This reluctance has extended to subsidized logging on federal lands, in particular the Tongass. It has not applied much to mining, which passes most of the external costs on to the environment. On Alaska state lands, mining and logging seldom pay either taxpayer costs or full environmental costs, and few such ventures are truly sustainable. They are tolerated or encouraged by a state government and public that have long enjoyed generous oil royalties and federal monies, and have felt little need to address problems of economic or environmental sustainability.

Oil drilling and transportation (by pipeline and tanker) may be economically unsustainable in that oil is nonrenewable and has no certain replacement. Alaskan oilfield production will ultimately decline and shrink state budgets. Alaskan oil operations are of questionable environmental and social sustainability, as indicated by the *Exxon Valdez* experience. The large amount that Exxon has been forced to spend, however, represents a clear statement of the principle of accountability, at least after the fact. But substantial gains in public commitment to sustainable consumption of oil may have to wait until the oil supply nears exhaustion.

Accountability of governments and corporations for the environmental and social effects of their actions has in large part flowed from the increasing participation of the public in resource issues. Alaska's state government has been forced to change course in the polar bear, Chilkat eagle, wolf control, and Susitna issues, among others. Public pressure altered federal policies or programs in Project Chariot, the Rampart Dam, placer mining, and Tongass logging. A measure of corporate accountability occurred in the design of the oil pipeline and in the *Exxon Valdez* follow-up. Alaska Natives had to become more accountable in their use of bowhead whales and Yukon-Kuskokwim waterfowl. The Endangered Species acts, National Environmental Policy Act, Clean Water Act, Marine Mammal Protection Act, and other federal and state laws, in part the result of Alaskan controversies, required increased consideration of environmental impacts. So did various international treaties and court decisions rendered in response to lawsuits brought under protection laws. The laws, treaties, and court decisions tended to require more public participation, which in turn reinforced accountability.

Openness of government and public participation have made large strides in Alaska. Polar bears, bowhead whales, Yukon Delta waterfowl, and several other exploited species are managed in part by panels of government agents, Native and sport hunters, environmentalists, or others. The state has involved advisory panels in the wolf controversy, though hunters, fishers, and trappers exercise a near-controlling influence in wildlife-management policy. Remedial work from the *Exxon Valdez* oil spill was overseen by a process involving citizens in advisory positions, and the crisis led to state and federal laws instituting citizen oversight of oil shipping. Environmental advocates have served on advisory bodies for mining and numerous other state and local matters. Modeled in part on Project Chariot, the environmental impact statement requires research and hearings, and the law permits citizen lawsuits, for most projects involving federal funds or lands. Environmentalists have successfully employed lawsuits to ensure citizen access to information and administrative processes. Conservative Congresses and Alaska legislatures have tried to limit public participation, which nonetheless appears to be an increasingly common element of disputes. Modern communications media have adopted environmental quality as a mainstream concern, and have helped to force openness of government by providing more information to a more interested public.

Valid scientific research, necessary for the identification and maintenance of sustainable conditions, has progressed by fits and starts. Some has been willingly undertaken by the state and federal governments; much has been forced on them by legislation or court orders. *Exxon Valdez* settlement funds have underwritten studies of marine ecology, as well as social and economic impacts of a large spill. Scientific data have figured prominently in nearly all the major conflicts, and ultimately won the day in several. Science has often been overridden by politics, as in Project Chariot and wolf control. Commonly, industry or agency pressures have impeded the flow of research, as in oil transportation and logging. Yet studies are increasingly accepted by the public as essential to the proper resolution of resource controversies. And, in large part because of the disputes, scientific investigation has broadened to include social effects and ecosystem functioning, gradually taking on a more holistic character.

DETERMINANTS OF ALASKA'S ENVIRONMENTAL FUTURE

A shift in environmental values does not guarantee a corresponding difference in environmental outcomes. Values are slow to change, whereas long-term ecological impacts, as by roads or clear-cut logging, can come swiftly. Values may be held by majorities, yet not reflected in the policies of governments, which tend to respond to highly focused or moneyed interest groups. Perhaps most important, the effects of at least two phenomena less directly related to normally perceived "environmental" values—population growth and global warming—may in the long run defeat all efforts to achieve sustainability.

Alaska enters the twenty-first century with a mixed environmental outlook. Multiparty conflicts over its resources persist in evolving forms. Exploitation versus sustainability remains the dominant theme, and subsistence-rights questions are usually present. Many factors—demographic, economic, and political— will influence the nature and eventual results of these conflicts. Among the leading elements will be human population growth; the state's economy; the activities of extractive industries; state and national public opinion; state, national, and foreign government policy; and environmental advocacy.

Growing at one of the highest rates in the nation, Alaska's population exerts evermounting pressure on natural resources through hunting and fishing, recreation, roads, housing, and other human activity. Maintenance of ecosystem integrity may not be possible under present conditions, let alone those created by future population growth. Alaska's image as a repository of boundless stocks of wildlife for the taking is not borne out in reality. Already, some of the best fisheries have been depleted, some species of birds and mammals have been diminished or removed from their habitats, and more than half the largest and oldest trees have been cut down. Wild areas undefiled by roads, machines, or other signs of civilization are increasingly scarce. Alaska is gradually losing its wilderness quality.

The Native American population, though only a sixth of the state's total, grows at three times the national average. In doing so, it stresses ecosystems by both subsistence and commercial use of resources. As Natives modernize, they may correspondingly weaken their claim to need state and federally owned resources for "subsistence." Yet their numbers beget rising levels of material consumption, some of which is paid for by exploitation of local resources. Ideally, subsistence is a limited form of resource consumption necessary for basic physical and social human sustenance, potentially consistent with the principle of sustainability. But there is not enough wildlife, timber, or any other limited natural resource to supply either a perpetually increasing number of consumers or ever-increasing economic expectations. Demographic and economic changes among both Natives and non-Natives are on a collision course with ecological reality, and with the original goals of subsistence rights. Unless an environmentally and socially viable resolution of the subsistence issue is reached, competition among Natives and non-Natives for fixed stocks of natural resources will probably intensify, and ecosystems will deteriorate.

In part dependent on the state of the economy, Alaska's population will experience another spurt if a Prudhoe-Valdez gas pipeline is built. But the boom would be temporary, and gas revenues could not replace the oil money that has fueled the economy and attracted many to the state through minimal taxes and annual payments to each resident. Notwithstanding declining revenues, natural population growth is likely to continue in a state that, like most others in the nation, senses no obligation to contain its numbers for the benefit of the ecosystem, the nation, or itself. Rarely do interest groups, including environmentalists, publicly suggest the need to limit Alaska's Native or non-Native population growth rates.

Extractive industries persistently seek access to state, federal, and Native-owned lands. By far the most prominent of these industries is oil, still the foundation of the state's economy. New discoveries may sustain the state for many more years, but eventually the resource must give out. By generating unsustainable infrastructure, population growth, and expectations, an extended period of oil wealth may prove to be a cumulative disadvantage for Alaskans.

Most of the controversy over oil drilling centers on federal lands. Low prices and high availability of oil make drilling in sensitive areas like the Arctic Refuge appear less urgent, easing the task of environmental defense. New finds worldwide may keep prices low for years to come. Yet an energy shortage might well induce the government to open the refuge, or permit more environmentally risky offshore oil production. In the meantime, the massive and expanding oil complex on the North Slope creates environmental impacts that are only partly understood.

Mining activity depends largely on fluctuating world prices of minerals. The boom-and-bust pattern is especially applicable to gold, the most sought-after metal in Alaska, which entered another slump in the 1990s. Regulation has gradually improved mining pollution control and restoration, but the prime determinant of mining impact is whether it happens in the first place, not how it is done. In the case of mining on federal lands, western senators have thus far blocked attempts to reform the easy entry granted by the 1872 Mining Law.

Distance from markets, and worldwide competition, have been and will be deterrents to economically successful industry in Alaska. They have caused the shutdown of large-scale logging and mining operations and discouraged manufacturing industries, and may forestall a gas pipeline. Tourism, a booming enterprise, is largely outside-owned and can deliver only a small fraction of the wealth that oil has generated. No major new source of revenue except gas is on the horizon, and the federal government seems unlikely to sustain the high level of subsidies it has granted Alaska for decades.

Some environmentally destructive enterprises, such as Alaska Pulp Company and Ketchikan Pulp Company, have operated through public funds garnered by Alaska's congressional delegation. Others, particularly in logging and mining, are subsidized by the state.

Congress has displayed a long-term trend toward ending support for economically dubious ventures, and often refuses the demands of its Alaska members. Falling revenues may eventually force the state be more prudent, though decades of oil revenues have encouraged influential groups to rely on a flow of largesse from government.

Public opinion is a fundamental determinant of environmental quality and the nature of environmental conflict. Numerous Alaskans have kept alive some cherished beliefs of the pioneer era: that natural resources are unlimited, and that national government, while providing economic aid, should not restrict the settlers' freedom to exploit the resources. Most Alaskans appear to want accessible wildlife, beautiful natural areas, economic prosperity, and a high-consumption lifestyle—values often mutually exclusive. They may favor protective measures, such as restrictions on wolf killing, that do not seem to interfere with the economy. They often back environmentally destructive proposals, such as road building in wild areas, that appear to boost the economy. They tolerate the state's environmentalists, but most do not see them as performing valuable public services except in particular instances such as the protection of local parks, local air and water quality, and popular animals.

The national public, in part because of escalating tourism, looks upon Alaska (at least the federal lands) as a parkland belonging to all Americans. As tourists, they may see it primarily as a playground, and demand intrusive access for themselves. But they do not take kindly to things like large oil spills, unnecessary killing of wildlife, and clear-cut logging in scenic areas. They are sympathetic toward national environmental groups, which in turn often join in Alaskan disputes.

Alaska state government policy both reflects and molds Alaskan opinion on natural resources. Its control over nearly a third of the land and over most terrestrial wildlife gives it broad power to shape the future. Its policies on environmental issues vary from moderate to resolutely conservative, depending on who is governor and who sits in the legislature. Democrats, more solicitous of environmental values, have opportunity to win the governorship in multicandidate, personality-oriented elections. In the 1990s the legislature moved insistently to the right, countervailing nearly all forms of natural-resource protection. Normally in resource conflicts, the state joins extractive or development interests against environmentalists and their coalition partners, and often against the federal government. This seems likely to continue at least as long as the petroleum industry dominates Alaskan economics and politics. The legislature has adopted some environmentally progressive measures (Table 17.2), but very few in the mid- to late 1990s, and no broad-based environmental protection law analogous to the National Environmental Policy Act.

National government policy turns mainly on who controls the Congress and presidency. Democratic leaders have usually worked for environmental protection in Alaska, in part because of their ties to influential environmental organizations. For decades, Alaska's congressional delegation has aggressively employed its influence to arrange subsidies and access to federally owned resources in Alaska on behalf of exploitative industries. In the late 1990s, the three Republican delegates chaired the committees holding the most power to direct natural resource policy. Republicans generally encourage exploitation of natural resources at the expense of environmental protection, but many do not believe in subsidies. Divided or Democrat-controlled governments have slowed the pace of degradation of nature in Alaska. A Republican president and Congress could be counted on to place the federal government's substantial weight on the development side of Alaskan resource conflicts.

Research on natural systems is basic to rational management and resolution of resource disputes. But scientific knowledge is seldom adequate for understanding of ecosystems, which requires a holistic perspective. And governments have reduced financial support for studies as they attempt to trim budgets. Moreover, research carries political implications: the less information available, the easier the access for an extractive industry, and the less it may have to spend on damage prevention or cleanup. Bias toward short-term economic production places the burden of proof on those who would question a project. Therefore, lack of data tends to shift the terms of environmental conflicts in favor of the exploiting parties. The potential effects of research make it an inescapable element of the tug-of-war between forces of exploitation and sustainability.

Just as Earth's ecosystems are interrelated, the status and treatment of Alaskan natural resources are determined in part by other nations, especially Russia, Japan, and Canada. Ocean currents and vessel routes affect the stocks of marine fish and wildlife. Air currents transport toxins from Europe and elsewhere, and birds and some mammals migrate across international boundaries. Competition for Alaskan resources has long been international, and efforts at dispute resolution have spawned a proliferation of treaties and cooperative agreements. This trend will endure worldwide as commerce and technology tie nations ever more closely to one another and continue to destroy remaining natural resources.

Associations working for environmental protection are a permanent fixture in Alaska. National organizations can be expected to intensify their activity, spurred in part by the public's high interest in the state. Together, state and national environmentalists will continue to form shifting coalitions with other interest groups to combat what they see as an ongoing series of abuses of natural resources. Some will enhance their effectiveness by increasing membership, as has Alaska Center for the Environment, or by forging close ties to local communities, and has Southeast Alaska Convervation Council. Their success as parties to disputes will parallel the approval or resistance they receive from government and the public. When current politics and opinion are against them, their best recourse is in the courts. When backed by national government and public opinion, in cases involving federal lands, they are likely to prevail. In state issues, they will realize their most consistent gains on such matters as parks, trails, local pollution, and urban issues, which offer the public immediate benefits and do not appear to limit economic growth.

Alaska's future will witness an endless series of environmental clashes large and small. Some of the leading tangible sources of damage to environmental quality, especially logging, mining, roads, and inholdings, will be shaped by government in response to the pressures of exploitative and conservationist pressure groups. Less tangible but no less menacing agents—population growth, the state of the economy, technological change, and global warming—will only in part be addressed through politics. For Alaska, the question is not whether its environmental integrity can be maintained, but how much of it will be retained.

On the surface, environmental issues are battles among interest groups; more fundamentally, they are collisions of value systems. Exploitation-versus-sustainability engagements pit those who want to make immediate and intrusive use of a resource against those who see development as destruction of the resource or depriving others of its benefits, or who see ecosystem integrity compromised. While judgment in value disagreements warrants caution and a measure of tolerance, reason suggests a working assumption that future generations are likely to value a resource as highly as do present generations. Reason calls into question the fairness of exhausting a resource that may be needed by others, and implies the validity of sustainable management. Matters of fact may best be decided by scientific investigation.

Sustainability as a core goal has important implications for the evaluation of resource conflicts. It leaves many questions open, such as the permissible length of time or degree of ecosystem disruption, and criteria for weighing of the benefits realized by different uses. But it argues against such extensive and long-term impacts as those of large dam projects, cutting of old-growth forest, and mining that tears apart entire stream valleys. Particularly suspect are ventures that are not economically viable in the narrow sense, much less when environmental and social side-effects are taken onto account. Many logging and mining operations appear to fall into this category. In the case of oil drilling and transportation, environmental sustainability entails the need for strict regulation of operations, and removal of infrastructure after completion. Viable cost-benefit calculations attempt to include fair measurement of environmental and social side-effects.

Sustainability connotes avoidance of significant or continued depletion of a species or other valued resources. Therefore it implies maintenance of the biodiversity of habitats in which species, including humans, interrelate for their mutual benefit. Loss of diversity will, directly or indirectly, diminish both human and nonhuman life. Sustainability cannot determine precisely how a limited stock of fish or game ought to be apportioned among claimants, as in the subsistence controversy. Nor may it be able to resolve the wolf-control dispute, which rests in large part on differences over quality as distinct from quantity. Given the expansion of technology and tourism, similar questions of apportionment and use values may be raised about other species. In any case, if wildlife stocks are to be maintained for the benefit of subsistence, sport, viewing, and existence valuers, or for the maintenance of ecosystem integrity, behaviors that permanently reduce populations must be discouraged. Among the most damaging and easily avoidable are clear-cut logging and building roads into wild areas. Also problematic in terms of sustainability or fairness is the employment of modern technology, such as aircraft and high-performance snowmobiles, in taking wildlife.

Environmental sustainability ultimately necessitates alteration of the present pace and direction of economic activity, of population growth, and of public attitudes toward the environment. In principle, all could be changed. Alaskans might well challenge the wisdom of such projects as a gas pipeline, which will temporarily boost the state's economy while attracting many more people and further eroding the environmental values that constitute Alaska's primary appeal. They might wonder at the viability of adding to their population at a high rate while the state's economic base is declining and no long-term means of reversing it is known.

Public attitudes in most modern societies reflect a meager sense of connectedness with the natural environment. Ecological thinking is intricate, requiring education and discipline. The public can react to the loss of favored resources, especially if they occur in such a tangible way as in the *Exxon Valdez* oil spill. But most deterioration of nature takes place quietly and bit by bit through the many encroachments of civilization. Progress toward acceptance of sustainability may be enhanced by education, media coverage, and the activities of environmental sympathizers. But evolution of ideas is seldom rapid enough to cope with the advance of destructive influences, particularly in a context so receptive to exploitation values as Alaska.

Notwithstanding the limitations of public ecological awareness, there is reason to encourage broad availability of information and opportunity to participate in decisionmaking processes related to publicly owned resources. Those proposing or implementing resource use are not necessarily more ecologically aware. More importantly, they may be expected to place agency, corporate, or personal advantage above the public interest. Project Chariot, Amchitka testing, the Rampart and Susitna dams, the Prudhoe-Valdez pipeline, and Tongass logging all illustrate the potential for unnecessary or harmful undertakings sanctioned by government and economic interest groups. The experience of Yukon Delta goose and eider duck management demonstrates the folly of leaving a wildlife resource entirely in the hands of consumers, whether Native Americans or Lower 48 sport hunters.

Consistent with democratic principles, those to be significantly affected by an action ought not have it imposed on them unilaterally. To defend themselves, people need adequate information and rights to intervene. The same applies to protection of the environment, whether nature be viewed as a public resource or as having rights of its own. Participation rights should include involvement in hearings, regulation-making, and judicial processes. Regulatory panels should reflect changes in public values, and not function as instruments of narrow spectra of interests. Wider public participation may slow decisionmaking and lead to ineffective or unfair results in particular cases, but it also creates broader understanding of the dimensions of a proposal, and can call a halt to a harmful scheme. If planning for resource use is to be holistic, it must hear from the public in order to incorporate economic and social cost calculations. Not least, sustainable management of resources must ultimately be based on public understanding and approval, both the products, in part, of public involvement in resource planning.

The inherent interconnectedness of elements of the environment implies that, ideally, resource management needs to be coordinated on an ecosystem-wide basis to achieve sustainability. Alaskan subsistence issues have been dealt with by cooperative management arrangements whereby officials and user groups regulate the taking of a species. These arrangements represent an improvement over the tradition of top-down regulation, which does not work well in rural Alaska. They may help maintain the pride and solidarity of indigenous culture while making progress toward resource sustainability. But they may exclude relevant interest groups, such as tourists or other viewers. Also, by focusing on a single species, they do not necessarily take ecosystem needs into account. Improved research could help ecosystem management, but politics is the main deterrent. The Alaska Lands Act created a maze of federal, state, Native, and non-Native private lands. The many inholdings on federal lands multiply the difficulties of planning and maintaining ecosystem integrity. Federal acquisition of inholdings, especially in national parks and wildlife refuges, needs to be a high priority.

Alaskan resource conflicts in the main illuminate the same types of issues as do those of other areas in the nation. Yet the state bears special significance for Americans; it is the last large relatively unspoiled region within the nation's jurisdiction. Its environmental future holds in trust the hopes of millions to touch the primeval wild, their dreams that some of Nature's masterpieces can live forever. Environmental guardians see much worth fighting for in Alaska, the more so as Earth's other wild treasures pass one by one into eternity. But the preservation of wilderness quality in Alaska is not enough; its survival cannot compensate or provide an excuse for the impoverishment of life on the remainder of the planet. For more than a century Alaska has exercised a molding influence on the national environmental agenda. As in the past, its most vital legacy may lie in the inspiration of efforts elsewhere to sustain a viable world, to create a shift of values.

ACE	Alaska Center for the Environment (1971)
ACF	Alaska Conservation Foundation (1980)
ACR	*Alaska Conservation Review* (1968-80). Formerly *Alaska Conservation Society News Bulletin* (1960–1965)
ACS	Alaska Conservation Society (1960–1981)
ACV	Alaska Conservation Voters (1997)
ADF&G	Alaska Department of Fish and Game
AEA	Alaska Environmental Assembly (1980–1997), became Alaska Conservation Alliance
AEC	Atomic Energy Commission
AEL	Alaska Environmental Lobby (1981–1997), became Alaska Conservation Voters
AEPAC	Alaska Environmental Political Action Committee (1981–1997), became Alaska Conservation Voters
ALP	Alaska Lumber and Pulp, or Alaska Pulp Company, Sitka
ANCSA	Alaska Native Claims Settlement Act (1971)
ANILCA	Alaska National Interest Lands Conservation Act (1980), or Alaska Lands Act
ANWR	Arctic National Wildlife Range (1960-80); Arctic National Wildlife Refuge (1980), or Arctic Refuge
Arctic Refuge	Arctic National Wildlife Refuge
APA	Alaska Power Authority
APC	Alaska Pulp Company, or Alaska Lumber and Pulp, Sitka
Appeals Court	Ninth U.S. Circuit Court of Appeals, San Francisco
Arco	Atlantic Richfield Company
ARLIS	Alaska Resources Library and Information Services, Anchorage
Audubon	National Audubon Society
Audubon/Alaska	Alaska Region of the National Audubon Society (1977)
AWA	Alaska Wildlife Alliance (1983)
BLM	Bureau of Land Management, U.S. Department of the Interior
Circuit Court	Ninth U.S. Circuit Court of Appeals, San Francisco

CITES	Convention on International Trade in Endangered Species of Wild Flora and Fauna (1973)
Coastal Plain	(or 1002 Area); 125-by-30-mile segment of the Arctic Refuge bordering on Beaufort Sea
Corps	U.S. Army Corps of Engineers
d-2	administrative and legislative efforts leading to the Alaska National Interest Lands Conservation Act (1980), stemming from Section 17(d)(2) of the Alaska Native Claims Settlement Act (1971)
DEC	Alaska Department of Environmental Conservation
District Court	United States District Court, Anchorage
DNR	Alaska Department of Natural Resources
EPA	U.S. Environmental Protection Agency
FOE	Friends of the Earth
GAO	General Accounting Office
GPO	Government Printing Office
Interior	U.S. Department of the Interior
IUCN	International Union for the Conservation of Nature and Natural Resources
IWC	International Whaling Commission
Juneau/Audobon	Juneau Chapter of National Audubon Society (1977)
Juneau/Sierra	Juneau Group of the Sierra Club (1968)
KPC	Ketchikan Pulp Corporation, or Louisiana Pacific Ketchikan
LPK	Louisiana Pacific Ketchikan, or Ketchikan Pulp Corporation
LRL	Lawrence Radiation Laboratory, Livermore, California
MMPA	Marine Mammal Protection Act (1972)
NAEC	Northern Alaska Environmental Center (1971)
NMFS	National Marine Fisheries Service, National Oceanographic and Atmospheric Administration, U.S. Department of Commerce
NOAA	National Oceanographic and Atmospheric Administration
NPS	National Park Service
NRC	National Research Council, an agency of National Academy of Sciences
SCLDF	Sierra Club Legal Defense Fund (1978)
SEACC	Southeast Alaska Conservation Council (1969)
Sierra Club	national Sierra Club, headquartered in San Francisco
Sierra Club/Alaska	Alaska Field Office of the Sierra Club (1968)
Superior Court	Alaska Superior Court
TfA	Trustees for Alaska (1974)
USDOI	U.S. Department of the Interior
USFWS	U.S. Fish and Wildlife Service, Department of the Interior (was Bureau of Biological Survey prior to 1940 and Bureau of Sport Fisheries and Wildlife, 1956–1974)
UST	U.S. Treaties
WOLF	Wildlife on the Last Frontier

Adams, Jacob. "The IWC and Bowhead Whaling: An Eskimo Perspective." *Orca*, March 1979: 11–12.
Adams, Lauri J. *Sierra Club Legal Defense Fund in Alaska: Case Digest*. 1987, 1988, 1989.
———. "Memorandum to Dr. Edgar Wayburn." Sierra Club Legal Defense Fund, Alaska Office, April 11, 1988.
———. "U.S. Borax: Battle Looms in Misty Fjords." *Alaska Report*, March 1989: 2.
Alaback, Paul. "Endless Battles, Verdant Survivors." *Natural History*, August 1988: 44–51.
Alaska. "Alaska Sportsman." May 1977, 38; November 1977, 28; August 1978, 32; October 1978, 64; December 1978, 94–96; September 1979, 30–31; December 1982, 94–96; August 1986, 58.
———. "Paradise Lost." June 1989: 21–29.
The Alaska Almanac, 1983 Edition. Seattle: Alaska Northwest, 1982.
Alaska Center for the Environment (ACE). *Annual Report, 1987*.
Alaska Conservation Alliance. "Alaska Statewide Opinion Survey." June 1999.
Alaska Conservation Foundation (ACF). "ACF Oil Spill Update." June 1989.
———. *Alaska Conservation Directory*, 1988–2000 editions.
———. *Alaska Conservation Foundation Annual Reports, 1993–2000*.
———. "Alaska Conservation Foundation: Helping Alaskans to Protect Alaska." Ca. 1985. Brochure.
———. "Alaska Environmental Matrix." 1980, 1990. Mimeo.
———. "Celia Hunter: Dean of Alaska's Conservationists." Ca. 1985. Pamphlet.
Alaska Conservation Foundation Dispatch. "Toxic Pollution in Alaska." Summer 2000: 1–4.
Alaska Conservation Review (ACR), 1968–1979 issues. Alaska Conservation Society.
———. "ACS Policy on Wolf Management." Spring 1976: 8–9.
———. "International Caribou Treaty." Winter 1979: 5.
Alaska Conservation Society (ACS) News Bulletin, 1960–1968. Continues as *Alaska Conservation Review*, 1968–1979.
Alaska Conservation Voters. "Description of 2000 Votes." May 2000.
Alaska Department of Environmental Conservation. "Oil Spill Public Information." September 12, 1989.
———. *Water Quality in Alaska, 1988*. Juneau, October 1998.
Alaska Department of Fish and Game (ADF&G). *Alaska Game Management Policies*. Juneau, 1973.
———. "Preliminary Results of Ground-Based Wolf Control in Game Management Units 20A, Winter 1993–1994: Report to the Board of Game." Juneau, April 1994.
———. "Questions and Answers Related to the Alaska Board of Game's June 1993 Action on Wolf Management." Juneau, July 2, 1993. Brochure.
———. "Subsistence in Alaska: 1998 Update." Juneau, March 1, 1999.
———. "Wolf Management Programs in Alaska, 1975–1983." Juneau, November 1983.

Alaska Department of Laws. *Comments on the Proposed Trans-Alaska Pipeline.* July 1971.

Alaska Department of Natural Resources. Div. of Oil and Gas. "Evolution of Petroleum Development Technology on Alaska's North Slope . . . Reduced Impacts and Enhanced Environmental Protection." September 1991. Brochure.

Alaska Economic Report. "Searching for a Future: Susitna in the Oil Squeeze." April 16, 1985: 3.

———. March 17, 1985, 3.

Alaska Environmental Lobby. *How the Alaska Legislature Voted on Conservation and the Environment: The 1987–88 Voting Chart.* October 1988; *1989–90 Voting Chart.* 1990; *1993–94 Voting Chart,* 1994.

Alaska Fish and Game. July-August 1989. Issue on *Exxon Valdez* oil spill.

Alaska Geographic. "Admiralty: Island in Contention." Summer 1973.

———. vol. 11, no. 3. "The Chilkat River Valley." 1984.

———. vol. 6, no. 1. "The Yukon-Kuskokwim Delta." 1979.

Alaska, Governor of. *Report of the Governor of the District of Alaska to the Secretary of the Interior, 1904.* Washington, DC: GPO, 1904.

Alaska Land Use Council. "Alaska Lands." Undated pamphlet.

Alaska Natives Commission. *Final Report, Vol. 3.* Anchorage, May 1994.

Alaska Oil and Gas Commission. "Alaska Production Summary by Active Fields for May 1995."

Alaska Oil Spill Commission. *Spill: The Wreck of the Exxon Valdez: Executive Summary.* January 1990.

———. *Spill: The Wreck of the Exxon Valdez: Alaska Oil Spill Commission Final Report.* Anchorage, 1990.

Alaska Report, 1984–2000 issues. Sierra Club Alaska Task Force.

———. "Alaska Bills in 105th Congress at Mid-Session." June 1977: 4–5.

———. "British Columbia Government Reviews Mine Proposal." September 1992: 4–5.

———. "Chilkat Eagles Threatened." July 1985: 5.

———. "Forest Service Issues Terrible Tongass Plan." June 1997: 6.

———. "Migratory Bird Treaty Amendments Announced." November 1999: 7.

Alaska, State of. *Session Laws and Resolutions.* Juneau, 1959–1999.

Allen, Thomas B. *Guardian of the Wild: The Story of the National Wildlife Federation, 1936–86.* Bloomington: Indiana University Press, 1987.

Allin, Craig W. *The Politics of Wilderness Preservation.* Westport, CT: Greenwood, 1982.

Amicus Journal. "In Defense of the Environment." Fall 1996: 53.

Amstrup, Steven C., and Douglas P. DeMaster. "Human Disturbances of Denning Polar Bears in Alaska." *Arctic,* September 1993: 246–250.

———. "Polar Bear." In Jack W. Lentfer, ed. *Selected Marine Mammals of Alaska: Species Accounts With Research and Management Recommendations,* pp. 39–56. Washington, DC: Marine Mammal Commission, 1988.

Amstrup, Steven C., Ian Stirling, and Jack Lentfer. "Past and Present Status of Polar Bears in Alaska." *Wildlife Society Bulletin* 14 (1986): 241–254.

Anders, Gary C. "Social and Economic Consequences of Federal Indian Policy: A Case Study of the Alaska Natives." *Economic Development and Cultural Change* 37, no. 1 (January 1989): 285–303.

Arctic Reporter. July 11, 1988: 1–3.

Association of Village Council Presidents. "Goose Conservation in Alaska." Ca. 1988. Brochure.

August, Robert M. "Political History of the Rampart Canyon Dam Proposal." In Stephen Spurr, ed., *Rampart Dam and the Economic Development of Alaska, Vol. 2,* pp. 1–9. Ann Arbor: University of Michigan School of Natural Resources, 1966.

AWA Newsletter, 1983–1990 issues. Continues as *The Spirit.* Alaska Wildlife Alliance.

———. "Kenai Wolf Louse Update." March-April 1984: 4–5.

Baade, Dixie. "Multiple Use in the Tongass." *Alaska Conservation Review,* December 1968: 10–14.

———. Personal history. November 1985. Typescript.

Ballard, Warren. "Bear Predation on Moose: A Review of Recent North American Studies and Their Management Implications." *Proceedings of 3rd Intl. Moose Symposium: Alces Supp. 1*. Syktyvkar, USSR, 1992, pp. 1–15.

———. "The Case of the Disappearing Moose." *Alaska*, Part I, January 1983: 22–25; Part II, February 1983: 36–39; Part III, March 1983: 38–42.

Barlow, Thomas. "Mandate for Oblivion." *Wilderness*, Spring 1984: 25–34.

Barnett, Emily. "Utility Corridor: BLM Surrenders to State Demands." *Alaska Report*, March 1989: 1.

Barnett, Phil S. "Appeals Court OKs Cube Cove Logging." *Ravencall*, Winter 1985: 3.

———. "Victories in Alaska Litigation." *Alaska Report*, September 1987: 2.

Barone, Michael, and Grant Ujifusa. *The Almanac of American Politics, 1992*. Washington, DC: The National Journal, 1991.

Bartonek, James C. *1992 Pacific Flyway Briefing Material*. Portland, OR: U.S. Fish and Wildlife Service. Office of Migratory Bird Mgt., July 15, 1992.

Beach, Bennett, "Time to Ax This Boondoggle." *Reader's Digest*, October 1986: 103–105.

Behnke, Stephen R. *How Alaska's Subsistence Law Is Working: Comparing Its Implementation Before and After 1992*. Alaska Dept. of Fish and Game. Div. of Subsistence. Juneau, March 1, 1996.

Belous, Robert. "Unsolved Problems of Alaska's North Slope." *National Parks and Conservation*, November 1970: 16–17.

Benson, Kristine. "Delayed Study on Drilling Wastes Coming Soon." *Center News*, July-August 1987: 8–9.

Berger, Thomas R. *Village Journey*. New York: Hill and Wang, 1985.

Beringian Notes. June 26, 1992; February 2, 1999. Anchorage: National Park Service.

Berman, Matthew D. "Renewable Resources." In Thomas A. Morehouse, ed., *Alaska Resouces Development: Issues of the 1980s*, pp. 105–133. Boulder, CO: Westview, 1984.

Berman, Matthew D., and Teresa Hull. *Petroleum: Sector Report*. Anchorage: Institute for Social and Economic Research, October 1989.

Berry, Mary Clay. *The Alaska Pipeline: The Politics of Oil and Native Land Claims*. Bloomington: University of Indiana Press, 1975.

Bioscience. "Biologists and the Alaskan Pipeline: Voices in the Wind." November 1979: 706.

Bird, Kenneth J. *Arctic National Wildlife Refuge, 1002 Area, Petroleum Assessment, 1998*. Washington, DC: U.S. Geological Survey Fact Sheet FS-040-98, May 1998.

Birkland, Thomas A. "Wake of the *Exxon Valdez*." *Environment*, September 1998: 4–9.

Blazer, Rex. "NAEC 1988 Annual Report." *Northern Line*, July 5, 1989. Insert.

———. "Water Quality and Mining: The Struggle Continues." *Northern Line*, February-March 1988: 12.

Bloch, Ivan, and Associates. *The Rampart Project: Yukon River, Alaska: A Handbook of Information*. Prepared for Yukon Power for America. Portland, OR: December 7, 1963.

Bockstoce, John. "Eskimo Whaling." *Alaska*, September 1977: 4–5.

Boeri, David. *People of the Ice Whale*. New York: Dutton, 1983.

Boertje, Rodney D., Patrick Valkenburg, and Mark E. May. "Increases in Moose, Caribou, and Wolves Following Wolf Control in Alaska." *Journal of Wildlife Management*, 60, no. 3 (July 1996): 474–489.

Bolze, Dorene. "Outer Continental Shelf Oil and Gas Development in the Alaskan Arctic." *Natural Resources Journal*, Winter 1990: 17–64.

Bolze, Dorene, and M. B. Lee. "Offshore Oil and Gas Development: Implications for Wildlife in Alaska." *Marine Policy*, July 1989: 231–248.

Borrelli, Peter. "Oilscam." *The Amicus Journal*, Fall 1987: 21–25.

BP Exploration (Alaska) and ARCO Alaska, *North Slope Waste Management: Minimization, Recycling, Disposal*. Anchorage: May 1993.

Braham, H. W., M. A. Fraker, and B. D. Krogman. "Spring Migration of the Western Arctic Population of Bowhead Whales." *Marine Fisheries Review* 42, nos. 9–10 (1980): 36–46.

Brandt, Herbert. *Alaska Bird Trails*. Cleveland: Bird Research Foundation, 1943.

Bratton, Paul. "Descent Into Devil's Canyon." *Sierra*, January-February 1981: 26–32.

Brelsford, Taylor. "A Meaningful Voice: Federal Regulatory Councils and Subsistence Management. *Cultural Survival Quarterly*, Fall 1998: 72.

Brodie, Pamela. "Tongass National Forest Victory." *Alaska Report*, June 1994: 1–2.

Brooks, James W. *The Polar Bear*. Juneau: Alaska Dept. of Fish and Game, 1965.

Brooks, Paul H. "The Plot to Drown Alaska." *Atlantic*, May 1965: 53–59.

Brooks, Paul H., and Joseph Foote. "The Disturbing Story of Project Chariot." *Harper's*, April 1962: 60–67.

Brower, Kenneth. *Earth and the Great Weather: The Brooks Range*. San Francisco: Friends of the Earth, 1971.

Brown, Lou. "Road Schemes Based on Century-Old Statute." *Northern Line*, March 26, 1993: 12–13.

Brown, Michael, and John May, *The Greenpeace Story*. London: Doring Kindersley, 1989.

Brown, Thomas M. "That Unstoppable Pipeline." *New York Times Magazine*, October 14, 1973: 34–35.

Brown, Tom. *Oil on Ice: Alaska Wilderness at the Crossroads*. San Francisco: Sierra Club Books, 1971.

Brown, William. "A Common Border." *National Parks*, November-December 1988: 18–23.

Buchanan, Robert K. "The History, Growth, Use and Future Development of the Timber Industry in Southeast Alaska." Master's thesis, University of Washington, 1969.

Buckheister, Carl W. "Duplicity and Destruction at Amchitka." *Audubon*, November-December 1965: 371.

Burch, Ernest S. *The Traditional Eskimo Hunters of Point Hope, Alaska: 1800–1875*. Barrow, AK: North Slope Borough, 1981.

Burns, John J., J. Jerome Montague, and Cleveland J. Cowles, eds. *The Bowhead Whale*. Society for Marine Mammalogy. Special Pub. No. 2. Lawrence, KS: Allen Press, 1993.

Burns, John J., Kathryn Frost, and Lloyd F. Lowry, eds. *Marine Mammals Species Accounts: Game Technical Bulletin No. 2*. Juneau: Alaska Dept. of Fish and Game, March 1985.

Busch, Lisa. "*Exxon Valdez* Aftermath: State Officials Slow Research on the Effects of the Spill." *Science*, May 22, 1992: 1134.

Buskirk, Lisa. "Haul Road: Natives/Conservationists Join Forces." *Center News*, March 21, 1980: 3.

Button, Karen. "Alaska Rainforest Campaign." *Center News*, October-November 1997: 8–9.

Cady, Norma Seneca. "Oil Overshadows Environmental Concerns." *Northern Line*, July-August 1985: 3.

Cahn, Robert. "Alaska: A Matter of 80,000,000 Acres." *Audubon*, July 1974: 2–13.

———. *The Fight to Save Wild Alaska*. New York: National Audubon Society, 1982.

———. "Paper Parks." *Audubon*, September 1981: 24–26.

Calkins, Donald G., and Karl B. Schneider. "The Sea Otter." In John J Burns, Kathryn Frost, and Lloyd F. Lowry, eds., *Marine Mammals Species Accounts: Game Technical Bulletin No. 2*, pp. 37–45. Juneau: Alaska Dept. of Fish and Game, March 1985.

Callaghan, Sara. "Committee Reviews Proposed Gas Route." *Northern Line*, October 25, 1996: 5.

———. "Good News for the Arctic Refuge." *Northern Line*, July 29, 1997: 1.

Calvin, Jack. "Moratorium on Logging." *Alaska Conservation Review*, Summer 1971: 7.

———. "Nakwasina Goes North." *National Geographic*, July 1933: 1–16.

———. "Saws at Sitka: A Citizen Protests." *Living Wilderness*, April 1976: 37–38.

Cameron, Jenks. *The Bureau of Biological Survey: Its History, Activities and Organization*. Baltimore: Johns Hopkins University Press, 1929.

Cameron, Raymond D., and Kenneth P. Whitten. *Second Interim Report on the Effects of the Trans-Alaska Pipeline on Caribou Movements*. Anchorage: Joint State/Federal Fish and Wildlife Advisory Team, 1977.

Cannon, Julie. "Heritage in Probate: Our Tongass Forest." *Sierra Club Bulletin*, April 1974: 4–8.

Carbyn, Ludwin N., ed. *Wolves in Alaska: Their Status, Biology and Management: Proceedings of the Wolf Symposium*. Report Series No. 45. Edmonton: Canadian Wildlife Service, 1981.

Carter, Luther. "Earthquakes and Nuclear Tests: Playing the Odds on Amchitka." *Science*, August 22, 1969: 773–776.

Cascade Holistic Economic Consultants. *Review of the Supplement to the Draft Revised Tongass Land Management Plan*. Oak Grove, OR: November 1991.

Caulfield, Richard A. "Alaska's Subsistence Management Regimes." *Polar Record* 28, no. 164 (January 1992): 23–32.

Center News, 1976–2000 issues. Alaska Center for the Environment.

———. "Council Approves First Habitat Acquisition." June-July 1993: 4.

Chance, Norman A. *The Eskimo of North Alaska*. New York: Holt, Rinehart and Winston, 1966.

Chasan, Daniel Jack. *Klondike 70: The Alaskan Oil Boom*. New York: Praeger, 1971.

Cicchetti, Donald. *Alaskan Oil: Alternative Routes and Markets*. Baltimore: Johns Hopkins University Press, for Resources for the Future, 1972.

Cissna, Sharon M., ed. "Alaskan Conservation 1950–70: Recognition Dinner, October 5, 1985." Alaska Conservation Foundation, 1985.

Clepper, Henry, ed. *Leaders in American Conservation*. New York: Ronald, 1971.

Cline, David. "Conflict on the Counciling Grounds." *Alaska Conservation Review*, Winter 1979: 6–10.

———. "To Band a Bald Eagle." *Alaska*, August 1981: 48–49.

———. *Work Plan for the Alaska-Hawaii Regional Office of the National Audubon Society for 1989–90*, January 30, 1989.

Clusen, Charles. "Beyond Compromise: ANILCA at the Mercy of Expedience." *Living Wilderness*, Spring 1984: 11–17.

Coates, Peter. "Project Chariot: Alaskan Roots of Environmentalism." *Alaska History*, Fall 1989: 1–31.

———. *The Trans-Alaska Pipeline Controversy: Technology, Conservation and the Frontier*. Bethlehem, PA: Lehigh University Press, 1991.

Coelho, Katy. "We Did It! Alaska Is Billboard Free." *Center News*, November-December 1998: 1,5.

Cohen, Michael P. *The History of the Sierra Club, 1892–1970*. San Francisco: Sierra Club Books, 1988.

Colt, Steve. "Devil Canyon Dam Rolls in Susitna's Grave." *Northern Line*, April 1986: 4.

Connors, Alex. "Corps Finally Takes Susitna Plans to Talkeetna." *Center News*, March 10, 1978: 1.

Conrad, Jon M. "Bioeconomics and the Bowhead Whale." *Journal of Political Economy* 97, no. 4 (August 1989): 974–987.

Conservation Voice, 1998–2000 issues. Alaska Conservation Voters.

Cook, Donald J. *Placer Mining in Alaska*. Fairbanks: University of Alaska Press, 1983.

Cook, Steve. "Do Wild Rivers and Placer Mining Mix?" *Northern Line*, April 1980: 5.

Cooley, Richard A. "Evolution of Alaska Land Policy." In Thomas A Morehouse, ed., *Alaska Resource Development: Issues of the 1980s*, pp. 13–49. Boulder, CO: Westview, 1984.

Cornwall, Peter G., and Gerald McBeath, eds. *Alaska's Rural Development*. Boulder, CO: Westview, 1982.

Corso, John. "Benefit-Cost Considerations in the Decision Against Rampart Dam." Master's thesis, University of Alaska Juneau, May 1974.

Cowper, Steve. Letter to Exxon Chairman Lawrence Rawl, April 28, 1989.

CQ Almanac. "Arctic Plain Was Legislative Battlefield." 101 Cong. 1 Sess. (1991): 208–209.

Crimmin, Eileen. "One Year Later: What Happened in Alaska." *Science Digest*, March 1965: 42–46.

Cronin, Matthew A., Warren B. Ballard, James D. Bryan, Barbara J. Pierson, and Jay D. McKendrick. "Northern Oilfields and Caribou: A Commentary." *Biological Conservation* 83, no. 2 (1998): 195–208.

Cuthbertson, Mary Ellen. "Stikine-Iskut Dams: Decisions Delayed, Studies Extended Two Years." *Ravencall*, Winter 1982: 1.

———. "Stikine Update." *Ravencall*, Spring 1982: 4.

Daley, Patrick, and Beverly James. "An Authentic Voice in the Technocratic Wilderness: Alaskan Natives and the Tundra Times." *Journal of Communications*, Summer 1986: 10–30.

Daley, Patrick, with Dan O'Neill. " 'Sad's Too Mild a Word': Press Coverage of the *Exxon Valdez* Oil Spill." *Journal of Communications*, Autumn 1991: 42–57.

Davids, Richard C. *Lords of the Arctic*. New York: Macmillan, 1982.

Davidson, Art. *Eskimo Hunting of Bowhead Whales*. Alaska Community Action Program, 1972.

———. *In the Wake of the Exxon Valdez*. San Francisco: Sierra Club Books, 1990.

Davis, Neil. *Energy/Alaska*. Fairbanks: University of Alaska Press, 1984.

Dean, Frederick C. "Amchitka." *Alaska Conservation Society News Bulletin*, March 1965: 2–4.

Decision Sciences, Inc. *Southeast Alaskans' Attitudes Toward the Tongass Timber Reform Act, the Future of the Tongass Forest, and Related Issues*. For Sealaska Corporation, Juneau, 1989.

Dittman Research Corporation. *Survey Among Alaska Residents Regarding Wolf Hunting*. Anchorage: Dittman Research, October 1992.

Dixon, Mim. *What Happened to Fairbanks: The Effects of the Trans-Alaska Oil Pipeline on the Community of Fairbanks, Alaska*. Boulder, CO: Westview, 1978.

Doherty, Jim. "Alaska: The Real National Lands Battle Is Just Getting Under Way." *Audubon*, January 1983: 114–116.

Dolitsky, Alexander B., ed. *Politics and Environment in Alaska*. Juneau: Alaska-Siberia Research Center, 1993.

Drais, Daniel G. "The Tongass Timber Reform Act: Restoring Rationality and Responsibility to the Management of America's Largest National Forest." *Virginia Environmental Law Journal* 8, no. 2 (Spring 1989): 317–372.

Drucker, James H. "Alaska's Upper Yukon Region: A History." Draft. Anchorage: Bureau of Land Management, 1982.

Dufresne, Frank. *My Way Was North*. New York: Holt, Rinehart and Winston, 1966.

———. "Rampart Roulette." *Field and Stream*, August 1964: 10–13.

Dunkel, Tom. "Eyeballing Eiders." *Audubon*, September-October 1997: 48–57.

Dunlap, Riley E. "Public Opinion on the Environment in the Reagan Era." *Environment*, July-August 1987: 6–11.

Durbin. Kathie. "A Struggle for Science on the Tongass." *Inner Voice*, March-April 1988: 8–12.

———. *Tongass: Pulp Politics and the Fight for the Alaska Rain Forest*. Corvallis: Oregon State University Press, 1999.

Durham, Floyd E. "A Historical Perspective on Eskimo Whaling and the Bowhead Controversy." *Orca*, March 1979: 5–6.

Durocher, Andrew E., Gerald W. Garner, Nicholas J. Lunn, and Oystein Wiig. *Polar Bears: Proceedings of Twelfth Working Meeting of IUCN/SSC Polar Bear Specialist Group, Oslo, Norway, February 3–7, 1997*. Occ. Pap. Of IUCN Species Survival Comm. No. 19. International Union for Conservation of Nature and Natural Resources, 1998.

Duscha, Julius. "How the Alaska Act Was Won." *Living Wilderness*, Spring 1981: 4–9.

Eames, Cliff. "ACE Files Suit Over South Denali Resort." *Center News*, April-May 1990: 3.

———. "Celebrate Wild Denali State Park." *Center News*, March-April 1991: 4.

East, Ben. "Alaska's Agony." *Outdoor Life*, January 1971: 33–35.

———. "The Angry Men." *Outdoor Life*, December 1970: 31, 119–122.

———. "Is It TAPS for Wild Alaska?" *Outdoor Life*, May 1970: 43–45.

Edwards, Larry. "Wasted Logs Prove Industry Over-Subsidized." *Ravencall*, January-February 1988: 11–13.

Enticknap, Peter. "Tatshenshini Wild, Forever." *Ravencall*, Autumn 1993: 1.

The Environmental Advocate, 1998–2000 issues. Trustees for Alaska.

———. "Postponed but Not Forgotten: Beaufort Sea Areawide Oil and Gas Lease Sale." Fall 1999: 4.

Epler, Patti. "Judge Says No to St. Matthew Land Swap." *Sierra Borealis*, Winter 1985: 6–7.

Erickson & Associates. *Beyond Tongass Timber: The Changing Role of the Tongass Timber Industry in the Economies of Southeast Alaska: A Local Perspective*. 2nd ed. Juneau: April 1999.

Estes, James A. "Catastrophes and Conservation: Lessons From Sea Otters and the *Exxon Valdez*." *Science*, December 13, 1991: 1596.

Evans, Sheila T. *An Historical View of Selected Alaskan Natural Resources*. Alaska Historical Commission and Alaska Department of Education, 1981.

Exxon Valdez Oil Spill Trustee Council. *Gulf Ecosystem Monitoring: GEM Science NRC Review Draft*. Anchorage, April 21, 2000.

———. *1999 Status Report*. Anchorage, 1999.

Exxon Valdez Oil Spill Trustees. *Exxon Valdez Oil Spill Restoration*. Vol. I: *Restoration Framework*. Anchorage: April 1992.

Farquhar, Ned. *Decision: The Future of the Coastal Plain, Arctic National Wildlife Refuge*. Fairbanks: Alaska State Legislature. House Resources Committee, November 1987.

Feazel, Charles T. *White Bear*. New York: Henry Holt, 1990.

Ferguson-Craig, Laurie. "Echo Bay Fined for A. J. Pollution." *Ravencall*, January 1995: 12.

Fienup-Riordan, Ann. *Eskimo Essays: Yup'ik Lives and How We See Them*. New Brunswick, NJ: Rutgers University Press, 1990.

———. *When Our Bad Season Comes: A Cultural Account of Subsistence Harvesting and Harvest Disruption on the Yukon Delta*. Anchorage: Alaska Anthropological Assn. Monograph Series No. 1, 1986.

Fikkan, Anne, Gail Osherenko, and Alexander Arikainen. "Polar Bears: The Importance of Simplicity." In Oran R Young and Gail Osherenko, eds., *Polar Bear Politics: Creating International Environmental Regimes*, pp. 96–151. Utica, NY: Cornell University Press, 1993.

Finch, Chris. "Alaska Senators Block Tongass Reform Bill." *Ravencall*, September-November 1988: 1.

———. "House Committee Urges Prosecution of APC." *Ravencall*, September-November 1988: 3.

———. "Tongass Timber Reform Act Becomes Law!" *Ravencall*, November-December 1990: 1.

Finkelstein, Dave. "Chugach Forest Plan Under Fire." *Sierra Borealis*, Winter 1985: 8.

———. "Decision Expected on Sport Hunting Bill." *Sierra Borealis*, Summer 1983: 3.

Fischer, Victor. *Alaska's Constitutional Convention*. Anchorage: Institute of Social, Economic and Governmental Research, 1975.

Fitzgerald, Sarah. *Options for Conservation: The Different Roles of Nongovernmental Convservation Organizations*. Washington, DC: World Wildlife Fund, 1990.

Flaharty, Jon. "Alaska Waters Threatened." *Center News*, June-July 1983: 7–8.

Flanders, Nicholas E. "Native American Sovereignty and Natural Resource Management." *Human Ecology* 26, no. 3 (1998): 425–449.

Flint, Paul L., Ada C. Fowler, and Robert F. Rockwell. "Modeling Bird Mortality Associated With the *M/V Citrus* Oil Spill off St. Paul Island, Alaska." *Ecological Modeling* 117 (1999): 261–267.

Flyger, Vagn, Martin W. Schein, Albert W. Erickson, and Thor Larsen. "Capturing and Handling Polar Bears—A Progress Report on Polar Bear Ecological Research." *Transactions of the 32nd North American Wildlife and Natural Resources Conference*, pp. 107–119. Washington, DC: Wildlife Management Institute, 1967.

Foote, Don C. "A Human Geographer Looks at Polar Bear Hunting." *Alaska Conservation Society News Bulletin*, May 1960: 5–6.

———. "Project Chariot and the Eskimo People of Point Hope, Alaska." Submitted to Atomic Energy Commission, March 1961. University of Alaska Fairbanks Alaska and Polar Regions Archives.

Fortier, Ed. "The Year of the Wolf." *Alaska*, July 1968: 6–9.

Fortune. "A Compromise the Caribou Will Like." May 25, 1987: 9.

Fox, M. W. *The Wild Canids*. New York: Van Nostrand Reinhold, 1975.

Franklin, Karen. "Logging by Law." *Alaska*, December 1987: 25–29.

Freeman, M. R., and Ludwig N. Carbyn, eds. *Traditional Knowledge and Renewable Resource Management in Northern Regions*. Edmonton: IUCN Comm. on Ecology and Boreal Institute for Northern Studies. Occ. Pap. No. 23, 1988.

Fuerst, Judith. "Playing Alaska's Natural Resources Hand." *Alaska Business Monthly*, June 1988: 24–29.

Gabrielson, Ira, and Frederick C. Lincoln. *The Birds of Alaska*. Washington, DC: Wildlife Management Institute, 1959.

Gambell, Ray. "The Bowhead Whale Problem and the International Whaling Commission". In International Whaling Commission. *Aboriginal/Subsistence Whaling (with special reference to the Alaska and Greenland fisheries): Special Issue 4*, pp. 1–6. Cambridge: International Whaling Commission, 1982.

Gasaway, William C., Rodney D. Boertje, Daniel V. Grangaard, David G. Kelleyhouse, Robert O. Stephenson, and Douglas G. Larsen. *The Role of Predation in Limiting Moose at Low Densities in Alaska and Yukon and Implications for Conservation*. Wildlife Monograph No. 120. Washington, DC: The Wildlife Society, 1992.

Gasaway, William C., Robert O. Stephenson, James L. Davis, Peter E. K. Shepherd, and Oliver E. Burris. *Interrelationships of Wolves, Prey and Man in Interior Alaska*. Wildlife Monograph No. 84. Washington, DC: The Wildlife Society, 1983.

Gatton, Gail. *1987 Legislation and the Environment*. Anchorage: Alaska Environmental Lobby, June 3, 1987.

———. *1988 Legislative Session*. Anchorage: Alaska Environmental Lobby, June 7, 1988.

Geldhof, Joe. Report on lobby activity. *Sierra Club Alaska Newsletter*, July 1980: 9.

Gilbert, Bil. "The Devaluation of Alaska." *Audubon*, May 1975: 64–80.

Gillelan, G. Howard. "Rampart Dam: A Wildlife Catastrophe for Nothing?" *Outdoor Life*, December 1964: 14–15.

Glude, Bill. *1989 Session Wrapup*. Anchorage: Alaska Environmental Lobby, May 26, 1989.

———. *1990 Session Wrapup*. Anchorage: Alaska Environmental Lobby, 1990.

Goodstein, Eban. "Placer Mining: How Big an Environmental Problem?" *Center News*, June-July 1983: 7.

Gordon, Richard. "Early Alaskan Conservation Efforts." Juneau, August 1985. Typescript.

———. "History of Conservationists' Efforts Regarding Tongass National Forest." Juneau, ca. 1975. Typescript.

———. "Memo to Cooperators, Re conservationist Meeting in Sitka, June 6–7, 1970." Typescript.

———. "A Proposal." In Kenneth Brower, *Earth and the Great Weather: The Brooks Range*, pp. 24–28. San Francisco: Friends of the Earth, 1971.

Gould, Laura. "What Does 'Wilderness' Mean for the Refuge?" *Northern Line*, May-July 1986: 2.

Graham, Frank, Jr. "U.S. and Soviet Environmentalists Join Forces Across the Bering Straits," *Audubon*, July-August 1991: 42–61.

Grahame, Arthur, "A-Test Alaska Threat?" *Outdoor Life*, January 1961: 10–11.

Grauman, Melody Webb. *Yukon Frontiers: Historic Resource Study of the Proposed Yukon-Charley National River*. National Park Service. Cooperative Park Studies Unit, Occasional Paper No. 8. Fairbanks: University of Alaska, November 1977.

Greenough, Jim, and Chuck Johnstone. "The Evolution of Timber Practices in Southeast Alaska." *Alaska Conservation Review*, Winter 1975: 4–6.

Greenpeace Examiner. "Fifteen Years at the Front Lines." October-December 1986: 8–12.

Greiner, James. "Tomorrow Came Too Soon." *Alaska*, May 1976: 4–8.

Groves, Pam. "Farewell to Sylvia Ward." *Northern Line*, November 10, 1999: 2.

Gruening, Ernest. "The Plot to Strangle Alaska." *Atlantic*, July 1965: 56–59.

Grummett, Karleen Alstead, ed. *Territorial Sportsmen, Inc.—1945–88: A Chronological History*. Juneau: Territorial Sportsmen, 1988.

Haber, Gordon C. "Biological, Conservation, and Ethical Implications of Exploiting and Controlling Wolves." *Conservation Biology*, August 1996: 1068–1081.

———. "Eight Years of Wolf Research at McKinley Park." *Alaska*, Part I, April 1973: 7–9; Part II, May 1973: 43–45.

Haggstrom, Dale A., Anne K. Ruggles, Catherine M. Harms, and Robert O. Stephenson. "Citizen Participation in Developing a Wolf Management Plan for Alaska: An Attempt to Resolve

Conflicting Human Values and Perceptions." Draft. Alaska Dept. of Fish and Game, August 18, 1993.

Hall, Kathryn. "Second-Growth Forests: All Timber, No Habitat." *Ravencall*, January-February 1988: 10.

Hall, Wayne. "Alliance Helps Commission Wolf Research by Dr. Gordon Haber." *The Spirit*, September-October 1993: 3.

———. "Kenai National Wildlife Refuge: Wolf Update." *AWA Newsletter*, May-June 1983: 3.

Hanna, G. Dallas. "Mammals of the St. Matthew Islands, Bering Sea." *Journal of Mammalogy*, May 1920: 118–122.

Hanrahan, John, and Peter Gruenstein. *Lost Frontier: The Marketing of Alaska*. New York: Norton, 1977.

Hansen, Andrew J., Erwin L. Boeker, John I. Hodges, and David R. Cline. *Bald Eagles of the Chilkat Valley, Alaska: Ecology, Behavior and Management*. Washington, DC: National Audubon Society and U.S. Fish and Wildlife Service, March 1984.

Harbo, Jr., Samuel J., and Frederick C. Dean. "Historical and Current Perspectives in Wolf Management in Alaska." In Ludwin N. Carbyn, ed., *Wolves in Alaska: Their Status, Biology and Management: Proceedings of the Wolf Symposium*. Report Series No. 45, pp. 51–64. Edmonton: Canadian Wildlife Service, 1981.

Harper, James. "Wolf Management in Alaska." In S. E. Jorgensen, C. E. Faulkner, and L. David Mech, eds., *Proceedings of a Symposium on Wolf Management in Selected Areas of North America*. Region 3, Chicago, March 24, 1970, pp. 24–27. Minneapolis/St. Paul, MN: Bureau of Sport Fisheries and Wildlife, 1970.

Harrington, Fred H., and Paul C. Paquet. *Wolves of the World*. Park Ridge, NJ: Noyes, 1982.

Harris, Arland S., and Wilbur A. Farr. *The Forest Ecosystem of Southeastern Alaska No. 7: Forest Ecology and Timber Management*. Portland: U.S. Forest Service. Pacific North-West Forest and Range Experimental Station, 1974.

Harrison, Gordon S. "Susitna Hydroelectric Project: Futile Quest for a Plan of Finance." *Northern Engineer*, Summer-Fall 1986, 22–31.

Hartle, John. "Summing Up the Juneau Story." *Northern Line*, June 1982: 9.

Hartzog, George B. *Battling for the National Parks*. New York: Moyer Bell, 1988.

Haycox, Stephen. "Economic Development and Indian Land Rights in Modern Alaska: The 1947 Tongass Timber Act." *Western Historical Quarterly* 21, no. 1 (February 1990): 21–46.

Hays, Samuel P. *Beauty, Health and Permanence: Environmental Politics in the United States, 1955–1985*. New York: Cambridge University Press, 1987.

Heinrich, M. Katherine. "Legal Decision Limits Road Claims." *National Parks*, January-February 1997: 19.

Hellard, Richard. "New Proposals for Admiralty Settlement." *Sierra Borealis*, Fall 1986: 3.

Henry, Daniel. "Allowable Cut: Fear and Transformation in a Tongass Timber Town." In Carolyn Servid and Donald Snow, eds., *The Book of the Tongass*, pp. 163–182. Minneapolis: Milkweed, 1999.

Hensel, Dick, Dave Spencer, and Mark Hickok. "Willard Troyer, Career Professional: A Biographic Sketch." Alaska Conservation Foundation. Mimeo; undated.

Herndon, Booton. *The Great Land*. New York: Waybright and Talley, 1971.

Hession, Jack. "Alaska's Protected Rivers Down the Drain?" *Alaska Report*, March 1990: 6–7.

———. "Committee Endorses Land Giveaway." *Alaska Report*, April 1988: 7.

———. "Controversial U.S.-Canada Treaty Proposed." *Sierra Club Alaska Newsletter*, October 1979: 10.

———. "Council Attempts to Weaken Trespass Cabin Regulation." *Sierra Borealis*, Winter 1985: 1.

———. " 'Good Neighbor' or 'Good Predator' Policy?" *Sierra Club Alaska Newsletter*, July 1981: 11–12.

————. "House Passes Poor Submerged Lands Bill." *Alaska Report*, September 1987: 1.

————. "Landmark St. Matthew Island Decision." *Alaska Report*, February 1985: 1–2.

————. "New Threat to Admiralty Island." *Alaska Conservation Review*, Spring 1975: 14.

————. "Noranda Mine Endangers Admiralty Island." *Alaska Report*, January 1984: 3.

Hickel, Walter. *Who Owns America?* Englewood Cliffs, NJ: Prentice-Hall, 1971.

Hickok, Mark Ganopole. "Coalition's Creation." *Sierra Club Alaska Newsletter*, January 1981: 10–11.

Highleyman, Scott. "Lobby Gears Up for Another Session." *Northern Line*, November-December 1985: 3.

Hill, P. S., D. P. DeMaster, and R. J. Small. *Alaska Marine Mammal Stock Assessments, 1996.* NOAA Technical Memo NMFS-AFSC-78. Seattle: Alaska Fisheries Science Center, September 1997.

Hinckley, Ted C. *The Americanization of Alaska, 1867–1897.* Palo Alto: Pacific Books, 1972.

Hirsch, William B. "Justice Delayed: Seven Years Later and No End in Sight." In J. Steven Picou, Duane A. Gill, and Maurie J. Cohen, *The Exxon-Valdez Disaster: Readings on a Modern Social Problem*, pp. 271–303. Dubuque: Kendall/Hunt, 1997.

Hodson, Marsha. "Oil Reform Alliance Meeting." *Center News*, August-September 1989: 5.

Horton, Alison, and Sharron Lobaugh. "Wilderness and Fisheries." *Alaska Conservation Review*, Winter 1977: 9.

Hughes, Jeffrey. "Winter Hideouts." *Natural History*, August 1988: 60–61.

Hunt, Joseph. "Making a Difference." *Philip Morris Magazine*, March-April 1990: 24.

Hunt, William R. *Alaska: A Bicentennial History.* New York: Norton, 1976.

————. "Notes on the History of North Slope Oil." *Alaska*, February 1970: 8–10.

Hunter, Celia. "The Big Wolf Witch Hunt." *Alaska Conservation Review*, Spring 1968: 1–3, 16.

————. "Do We Care About Saving Wilderness?" *Northern Line* (Special Ed.), February 1984: 1.

————. "From My Corner." *Living Wilderness*, July-September 1977: 61.

————. "International Caribou: The Argument Is Not Over." *Alaska*, June 1981: 22–23.

————. "Legacy of Jack Calvin Remains With Us." *Center News*, May-June 1985: 8–9.

————. "An Overview of the JFSLUP Commission." *Alaska Conservation Review*, Winter 1972: 12–13.

————. "This Our Land." *Alaska*, May 1981: 32–33; December 1981: 44; March 1982: 36; April 1982: 21; March 1983: 23; September 1985: 28; December 1985: 36.

Hunter, Jim, Article on wolf control. *Sierra Club Alaska Newsletter*, April 1974: 10–11.

Hunter, Robert. *Warriors of the Rainbow.* New York: Holt, Rinehart & Winston, 1979.

Ingersoll, Ernest, ed. *Alaska Bird-Life.* New York: National Association of Audubon Societies, 1914.

International Union for Conservation of Nature and Natural Resources. *Polar Bears: Proceedings of the Fifth Working Meeting of the Polar Bear Specialists Group.* 11 Morges, Switzerland: IUCN, 1976.

International Whaling Commission. "Report of the Cultural Anthropology Panel." In International Whaling Commission, *Aboriginal/Subsistence Whaling (with special reference to the Alaska and Greenland fisheries): Special Issue 4*, pp. 35–50. Cambridge: International Whaling Commission, 1982.

Ivan Moore Research. "Statewide Political Opinion Survey." Anchorage: Ivan Moore and Associates, Fall 1998.

Jackson, Donald Dale. "The Floor of Creation." *Wilderness*, Fall 1986: 12–20.

Johnson, Gerald W. "New Explosions in Science and Technology." *Bulletin of the Atomic Scientists*, May 1960: 155–161.

Johnson, Susan Hackley. "Celia Hunter: Portrait of An Activist." *Alaska Journal*, Autumn 1979: 30–35.

Jones, Charles S. *From the Rio Grande to the Arctic: The Story of the Richfield Oil Company.* Norman: University of Oklahoma Press, 1972.

Jorgensen, S. E., C. E. Faulkner, and L. David Mech, eds. *Proceedings of a Symposium on Wolf Management in Selected Areas of North America.* Region 3, Chicago, March 24, 1970. Minneapolis/St. Paul, MN: Bureau of Sport Fisheries and Wildlife. 1970.

Kabisch, Sally. "ADF&G vs. Wolves." *Alaska Report*, February 1985: 7.

———. "View From Fourth Avenue." *Sierra Club Alaska Newsletter*, Fall 1982: 2.

———. "View From Fourth Avenue." *Sierra Borealis*, Fall 1983: 2.

Kallick, Steve. "Eagles Massacred at LPK Camp." *Ravencall*, June-August 1987: 5.

———. "Forest Service Agrees to Full EIS for Berner's Bay." *Ravencall*, July-August 1986: 3.

———. "SEACC and Tenakee File Kadashan Suit." *Ravencall*, Spring 1984: 1.

———. "Subsistence Users Sue to Stop Hoonah Area Logging." *Ravencall*, June-August 1988: 1.

Kallick, Steve, Bart Koehler, John Sisk, and Ted Whitesell. *Last Stand for the Tongass National Forest*. Juneau: Southeast Alaska Conservation Council, January 1986.

Kallick, Steve, and Marty Peale. "Log Dumps Face Federal Permitting—En Masse." *Ravencall*, Summer 1984: 10.

——— "Road Cuts Into Kadashan While Court Hears Motions." *Ravencall*, Summer 1984: 1.

Kallman, Harmon, ed. *Restoring America's Wildlife, 1937–87*. Washington, DC: U.S. Fish and Wildlife Service, 1987.

Kancewick, Mary, and Eric Smith. "Subsistence in Alaska: Towards a Native Priority." *UMKC Law Review* 59, no. 3 (Spring 1991): 645–677.

Kawagley, A. Oscar. *A Yupiaq Worldview: A Pathway to Ecology and Spirit*. Prospect Heights, IL: Waveland, 1995.

Kaye, Roger, "Paved or Pristine Gateway to the Arctic?" *Northern Line*, pt. 1, April-May 1984: 1; pt. 2, June-July 1984: 3.

———. "The Perception, Experience, and Valuation of the Arctic National Wildlife Refuge as Wilderness." Unpublished paper, 1999.

Keeble, John. *Out of the Channel: The Exxon Valdez Oil Spill in Prince William Sound*. New York: HarperCollins, 1991.

Kelly, Julie. "Dixie Baade: Southeast's Spirited Conservationist." *Ravencall*, November-December 1985: 2.

———. "Pulp Mill Violating Clean Air Act." *Ravencall*, October-December 1986: 6.

Kemp, Molly. "Tenakee Vows to Fight Forest Service to End." *Ravencall*, September-November 1988: 8.

Ketchum, Robert Glenn, and Carey D Ketchum. *The Tongass: Alaska's Vanishing Rain Forest*. New York: Aperture Foundation, 1987.

Keziere, Robert, and Robert Hunter. *Greenpeace*. Toronto: McClelland and Stewart, 1972.

King, James G. *Alaska's Yukon Flats: An Arctic Oasis*. Juneau: Bureau of Sport Fisheries and Wildlife, April 1970.

———. "Refuge Narrative Report, January 1 to April 30, 1963: Clarence Rhode NWR, Alaska." Bethel, AK: Bureau of Sport Fisheries and Wildlife, 1963. Typescript.

———. "Salmon Stream Destruction." *Alaska Conservation Review*, Spring 1975: 6–7.

King, James G., and Dirk V. Derksen. "Alaska Goose Populations: Past, Present and Future." *Transactions of the 51st North American Wildlife and Natural Resources Conference*, pp. 464–479. Washington, DC: Wildlife Management Institute, 1986.

Kirchhoff, Matthew D. "Economic Boom or Ecosystem Ruin? Highgrading in Alaska's Coastal Rainforest." Presented at annual meeting of Society for Conservation Biology, Toronto, August 1989.

———. "Forest Cover and Snow: Implications for Deer Habitat in Southeast Alaska." *Journal of Wildlife Management* 51, no. 1 (January 1987): 28–33.

Kizzia, Tom. "Can Caribou and Oil Coexist?" *Sierra*, September-October 1986: 20–23.

———. "Feuding Groups Make an Oil Deal." *Sierra*, September-October 1986: 76–77.

Kleeschulte, Chuck. "Torrents Over Timber." *Alaska Business Monthly*, October 1988: 24–26.

Klein, David R. "Caribou: Alaska's Nomads." In Harmon Kallman, ed., *Restoring America's Wildlife, 1937–87*, pp. 190–207. Washington, DC: U.S. Fish and Wildlife Service, 1987.

———. "Monitoring the Pipeline." *Alaska Conservation Review*, Summer-Fall 1975: 20–21.

Koehler, Bart. "You Don't Know What You've Got 'Till It's Gone." *Ravencall*, January-February 1988: 8–9.

Koehler, Bart, and Marty Peale. "Greens Creek Fate in D.C. Hands." *Ravencall*, Fall 1984: 3.

Koehler, Julie. "Tongass Reform Sweeps Through U.S. House." *Ravencall*, June-August 1988: 1.

Konigsberg, Jan. "ACF Strategy Takes Long View." *Alaska Conservation Foundation Annual Report, 1997*, pp. 3–5. Anchorage: ACF, 1988.

Koski, K., and William J. Hauser, eds. *Aquatic Habitat Restoration in Northern Ecosystems*. Symposium on Habitat Restoration in Northern Ecosystems, Girdwood, Alaska, 19–22 September 1994. Anchorage: Environmental Protection Agency, 1997.

Kowalsky, Jim. "Another Arctic Pipeline." *Alaska Conservation Review*, Summer 1972: 4–7.

Kueffner, Eric A. "Southeast Alaska Conservation Council, Inc. v. Watson and the Future of the Alaska National Interest Lands Conservation Act." *Ecology Law Quarterly* 12 (1984): 149–173.

Landry, Larry. "Alaska's Transportation Network." *Northern Line*, September 28, 1992: 8.

———. "Wolves Lose at Game Board Hearings." *Northern Line*, November 20, 1989: 11.

Lawrence, Christine C. "House Votes to Limit Logging in Alaska Forest." *Congressional Quarterly*, July 30, 1988: 2112.

Laycock, George. "Alaska's Wildlife: An Abundance to Destroy." *Audubon*, July 1969: 60–87.

———. "The Beautiful, Sad Face of Amchitka." *Audubon*, November-December 1968: 8–12.

———. "Doing What's Right for the Geese." *Audubon*, November 1985: 118–133.

———. "How to Kill a Wolf." *Audubon*, November 1990: 44–48.

———. "Kiss the North Country Goodbye?" *Audubon*, September 1970: 68–75.

———. "Wilderness by the Barrel." *Audubon*, May 1988: 100–123.

Lebedoff, David. *Cleaning Up: The Story Behind the Biggest Legal Bonanza of Our Time*. New York: Free Press, 1997.

Lensink, Calvin. "The History and Status of Sea Otters in Alaska." Ph.D. diss., Purdue, 1962.

———. Memo to Wildlife Administrator, Bureau of Sport and Fisheries and Wildlife, Kenai, Alaska. "Observations on Amchitka Island, October 7 to November 7, 1965." November 23, 1965.

———. "Predator Control With the Bounty System." In *Alaska Dept. of Fish and Game Annual Report for 1958*, pp. 91–104.

Lentfer, Jack W. "Polar Bear Management and Research in Alaska." In International Union for Conservation of Nature and Natural Resources. *Polar Bears: Proceedings of the Fifth Working Meeting of the Polar Bear Specialists Group*, pp. 53–60. 11 Morges, Switzerland: IUCN, 1976.

———. "The Polar Bear." In John J. Burns, Kathryn Frost, and Lloyd F. Lowry, eds., *Marine Mammals Species Accounts: Game Technical Bulletin No. 2*, pp. 27–35. Juneau: Alaska Dept. of Fish and Game, March 1985.

———. "Solitary Sea Bear." *Oceans*, September-October 1979: 49–54.

———, ed. *Selected Marine Mammals of Alaska: Species Accounts With Research and Management Recommendations*. Washington, DC: Marine Mammal Commission, 1988.

Lenzner, Terry F. *The Management, Planning and Construction of the Trans-Alaska Pipeline System: Report to the Alaska Pipeline Commission by the Commission's Special Counsel*. Washington, DC: Alaska Pipeline Commission, August 1, 1977.

Leopold, A. Starker, and Reginald Barrett. *Implications for Wildlife of the 1968 Juneau Unit Timber Sale: A Report to U.S. Plywood-Champion Papers, Inc.* Berkeley: School of Forestry and Conservation. University of California, November 15, 1972.

Leopold, A. Starker, and Justin W. Leonard. "Alaska Dam Would Be Resource Disaster." *Audubon*, May 1966: 176–179.

Leshy, John D. "Natural Resources Policy." In Paul R. Portney, ed., *Natural Resources and the Environment*, pp. 13–46. Washington, DC: Urban Institute, 1984.

Lethcoe, Jim, and Nancy Lethcoe. *Cruising Guide to Prince William Sound, Vol. 1: Western Part*. Valdez, AK: Prince William Sound Books, 1984.

Lewis, Thomas. "High Stakes in a Land of Plenty." *National Wildlife*, June-July 1987: 5–11.

Lieberman, Jethro K. *Checks and Balances: The Alaska Pipeline Case*. New York: Lothrop, Lee and Shepard, 1981.

Liebhardt, Barbara. "Among the Bowheads: Legal and Cultural Change on Alaska's North Slope to 1985." *Environmental Review*, Winter 1986: 277–301.

Linden, Eugene. "A Tale of Two Villages." *Time*, April 17, 1989: 62.

Livingston, Steve. "No Additional Wilderness for Arctic Refuge." *Sierra Borealis*, May-June 1988: 1.

Lobaugh, Sharron. "Lobbyist in Juneau." *Alaska Conservation Review*, Spring 1976: 9.

Lord, Nancy. *Darkened Waters: A Review of the History, Science and Technology Associated With the Exxon Valdez Oil Spill and Cleanup*. Homer, AK: Homer Society of Natural History/Pratt Museum, 1992.

Lowe, Paul. "Help Stop Offshore Drilling." *Sierra Club Alaska Newsletter*, April 1980: 10.

Lowry, Cindy. "Ballot Measure Victory Under Attack." *The Spirit*, Spring 1997: 1.

———. "Fortymile Wolf Sterilization Plan Slated to Begin." *The Spirit*, Fall 1997: 1.

Macy, Mike, and Leonard Steinberg. "Conservationists Sue State Over Eagles." *Sierra Club Alaska Newsletter*, October, 1979: 13.

———. "A Feast of Eagles: Chainsaws vs. the Food Chain." *Sierra*, July-August 1980: 26–29.

Manning, Harvey. *Cry Crisis: Rehearsal in Alaska*. San Francisco: Friends of the Earth, 1974.

Margolis, Howard. "Project Chariot: Two Groups of Scientists Issue Objective but Conflicting Reports." *Science*, June 23, 1961: 2000–2001.

Marquette, Cindy. "Strategies Planned, Industry Reps Speak at EA." *Northern Line*, December 1982: 6.

Marshall, George. "Bob Marshall and the Arctic Wilderness." *Living Wilderness*, Autumn 1970: 29–32.

Matthews, John W., and Donald E. McKnight. "Renewable Resource Commitments and Conflicts in Southeast Alaska." *Transactions of the 47th North American Wildlife Conference*, pp. 573–582. Washington, DC: Wildlife Management Institute, 1982.

Matz, George. "Environmentalists: Who Are They?" Draft. *The Alaska Contractor*, Fall, 1994.

———. "Susitna Hydropower: These Two Dams Will Cost Too Much." *Northern Line*, January-March 1986: 4–5, 7.

Matz, Mike. "Committee's Coastal Plain Package." *Alaska Report*, April 1988: 4.

———. "Environmentalists Gather in Fairbanks." *Northern Line*, September-October 1984: 7.

Mayo, Gail. "Pipeline Overview." *Alaska Conservation Review*, Summer-Fall 1975: 11.

Mayo, Larry. "Conservation at Gas Hearings." *Alaska Conservation Review*, Winter 1976: 7–8.

———. "Gas Transportation From the Arctic." *Alaska Conservation Review*, Summer-Fall 1975: 16–19.

———. "Two Nations Cooperate on Caribou Conservation." *Alaska Conservation Review*, Fall-Winter 1978: 11.

McCargo, Dave. "The Front Burner." *Sierra Borealis*, Fall 1987: 2.

McCloskey, Maxine, ed. *Wilderness: The Edge of Knowledge*. San Francisco: Sierra Club Books, 1970.

McClung, Robert M. *Hunted Animals of the Sea*. New York: Morrow, 1978.

McCracken, Harold. *Hunters of the Stormy Sea*. Garden City: Doubleday, 1957.

McCutcheon, Steve. "Atomic Blast vs. Otter?" *Audubon*, November-December 1965: 376–381.

McGeye, D. T. "Steese and White Mountains Final Plans: Round 2." *Northern Line*, November-December 1984: 5.

McKendrick, Jay D. "Arctic Tundra Rehabilitation—Observations of Progress and Benefits to Alaska." *Agroborealis*, January 1991: 29–40.

McKnight, Donald E. *The History of Predator Control in Alaska*. Juneau: Alaska Dept. of Fish and Game, 1973.

McVay, Scott. "Another Perspective." *Orca*, March 1979: 13–14.

McVee, Curt. "Issues Restricting Expansion of the Mining Industry." *Alaska Action*, September 1989: 5.

Mech, L. David. "How Delicate Is the Balance of Nature?" *Alaska*, May 1985: 18–19.

———. *The Wolf*. New York: Natural History Press, 1970.

Merritt, Melvin L. *Physical and Biological Effects: Cannikin*. Las Vegas, NV: U.S. Atomic Energy Commission, Nevada Operations Office. October 1973.

———. *Physical and Biological Effects: Milrow Event*. Las Vegas, NV: U.S. Atomic Energy Commission, Nevada Operations Office. December 1970.

Merritt, Melvin L., and R. Glen Fuller. *The Environment of Amchitka Island, Alaska*. Washington, DC: Energy Research and Development Administration, 1977.

Michaelson, Nancy. "Denali Development Boondoggle: Opposition Strengthens." *Alaska Report*, September 1997: 6.

Miller, Debbie S. "A Change of the Guard." *Northern Line*, June 1981: 1.

———. *Midnight Wilderness: Journey in Alaska's Arctic National Wildlife Refuge*. San Francisco: Sierra Club Books, 1990.

———. "Miller Testifies on ANWR in D.C." *Northern Line*, October-November 1987: 1–3.

Miller, Mike. "Alaska's Tongass Suit—The 'Exercise' at Juneau." *American Forests*, March 1971: 28–31.

———. "The Fight for the Trees." *American Forests*, July 1971: 16–19.

Miller, Pamela A. "Arctic Refuge: Top Environmental Issue in Congress." *Northern Line*, February 24, 1989: 1–2.

———. "Press Coverage of Oil Spills and the Environment: From Santa Barbara to Valdez." Master's thesis, University of Oregon, 1991.

Miller, Pamela A., Dorothy Smith, and Pamela K. Miller. *Oil in Arctic Waters: The Untold Story of Offshore Drilling in Alaska*. Anchorage: Greenpeace, January 1993.

Miller, SuzAnne M., and Daniel W. McCollum. *Alaska Voters: Their Characteristics and Attitudes Toward Wildlife*. Anchorage: Alaska Dept. of Fish and Game, 1994.

Minard, Lawrence. "All Caribou Are Not the Same." *Forbes*, March 9, 1987: 43–45.

Mitchell, Donald C. "Native Subsistence Hunting of Migratory Waterfowl in Alaska: A Case Study Demonstrating Why Politics and Wildlife Management Don't Mix." *Transactions of the 51st North American Wildlife and Natural Resources Conference*, pp. 527–534. Washington, DC: Wildlife Management Institute, 1986.

Mitchell, John. "Fear and Loathing in Wolf Country." *Living Wilderness*, May 1976: 20–39.

———. "Where Have All the Tuttu Gone?" *Audubon*, March 1977: 2–16.

Mlot, C. "Wolf Hunts Resume in Alaska." *Sierra News*, November 3, 1984: 279.

Moran, Phil. "NAEC Completes Successful Field Season." *Northern Line*, September-October 1984: 3.

Morehouse, Thomas A., ed. *Alaska Resources Development: Issues of the 1980s*. Boulder, CO: Westview, 1984.

———. "Fish, Wildlife, Pipeline: Some Perspectives on Protection." *Northern Engineer*, Summer 1984: 18–26.

Morgan, Lael. *Art and Eskimo Power: The Life and Times of Eskimo Howard Rock*. Fairbanks: Epicenter, 1988.

———. "The Politics of Whaling." *Alaska*, May 1981: 8–11.

Motyka, Roman, and Terry Reichardt. "Concerns About the Susitna Hydro-Project." *Alaska Conservation Review*, Spring 1979: 6–9.

Muir, John. *Travels in Alaska*. Boston: Houghton-Mifflin, 1915, 1979 reprint.

Murkowski, Frank. "Commentary Southeast: An Economy Built on Compromise." *Alaska*, December 1987: 50.

Murphy, Edward. "Beaufort Oil and Gas Lease Sale Held." *Alaska Conservation Review*, Summer-Fall 1979: 4–5.

———. "Federal SIN Ecology." *Alaska Conservation Review*, Winter 1979: 4.

Murphy, Michael L. *Forestry Impacts on Freshwater Habitat of Anadromous Salmonoids in the Pacific Northwest and Alaska—Requirements for Protection and Restoration*. National

Oceanographic and Atmospheric Administration, Coastal Ocean Office. Coastal Ocean Program Decision Analysis Series No. 7. Silver Spring, MD, October 1995.

Murphy, Stephen M., Robert H. Day, John A. Wiens, and Keith R. Parker. "Effects of the *Exxon Valdez* Oil Spill on Birds: Comparisons of Pre- and Post- Spill Surveys in Prince William Sound." *The Condor* 99, no. 2 (1997): 299–313.

Myers, Eric. "Federal Commission Continues Review of Susitna Dam Project." *Center News*, October 1984: 10.

———. "Susitna Update." *Northern Line*, April-May 1983: 6.

Nash, Roderick. "Tourism, Parks and the Wilderness Idea in the History of Alaska." *Alaska in Perspective* 4, no. 1 (1981): 1–2.

———. *Wilderness and the American Mind,* 3rd ed. New Haven: Yale University Press, 1982.

Naske, Klaus-M. *A History of Alaskan Statehood*. Lanham, MD: University Press of America, 1985.

Naske, Klaus-M., and Herman E. Slotnick. *Alaska: A History of the 49th State*. Grand Rapids, MI: Eerdman's, 1979.

Naske, Klaus-M., and Herman E. Slotnick. "Financiers, Workers and Saboteurs: The Trans-Alaska Pipeline Story." *Alaskafest*, August 1979: 12–23.

Naske, Klaus-M., and William R. Hunt. *The Politics of Hydroelectric Power in Alaska: Rampart and Devil Canyon—A Case Study*. Fairbanks: University of Alaska, Institute of Water Resources, 1978.

National Audubon Society, *News from Audubon*, 1980s issues.

National Parks. "Legal Battles for Alaska." November 1970: 31–34.

National Research Council (NRC). *Wolves, Bears and Their Prey in Alaska: Biological and Social Challenges in Wildlife Management*. Washington, DC: Academy Press, 1997.

Nelson, Edward W. "The Emperor Goose." In Ernest Ingersoll, ed., *Alaska Bird-Life*, pp. 57–61. New York: National Association of Audubon Societies, 1914.

Nerz, Miriam. "Susitna Dam Proposal." *Center News*, September 1980: 8–9.

Newsweek. "Alaska's Pipeline: A Disappointment." June 11, 1979: 22.

Norris, Ruth. "Alaska: Hunters Aim Their Big Guns at America's New National Parks." *Audubon*, July 1983: 128–135.

Northern Line, 1980–2000 issues. Northern Alaska Environmental Center.

———. "Permanent Pennies." *The Northern Rag*. Reprint of April Fool's ed., 1982. April-May 1984: 3–4.

———. "Rivers Given New Lease on Life." August-September 1987: 1.

———. "Twenty Years of Alaskan Conservation." April 22, 1990: 11–15.

Norton, David. Report on Alaska Pipeline. *Alaska Conservation Review*, Summer-Fall 1975: 4–7.

Nunam Kitlutsisti. "Nunam Kitlutsisti." Bethel, AK, ca. 1985. Brochure.

Oil Spill Chronicle, 1989–1991 issues. Alaska Dept. of Environmental Conservation.

O'Neill, Dan. *The Firecracker Boys*. New York: St. Martin's, 1994.

———. *Project Chariot: A Collection of Oral Histories*, 2 vols. Anchorage: Alaska Humanities Forum, 1989.

———. "Project Chariot: How Alaska Escaped Nuclear Excavation," *Bulletin of the Atomic Scientists*, December 1989: 28–37.

———. "Project Chariot: Thoughts on History, Public Policy and Ethics." *Frame of Reference*, July 1989: 1, 7–11, 15–19.

Orca. "Editorial Perspective." March 1979: 18.

Orth, Donald O. *Dictionary of Alaska Place Names*. Washington, DC: U.S. Geological Survey Professional Paper No. 567, 1967.

O'Toole, Randal. *Reforming the Forest Service*. Washington, DC: Island, 1988.

———. *The $64 Million Question: How Taxpayers Pay Pulpmills to Clearcut the Tongass National Forest*. Portland, OR: Cascade Holistic Economic Consultants, March 1993.

Ott, Riki. "Sound Truth: Exxon's Manipulation of Science and the Significance of the *Exxon Valdez* Oil Spill: Executive Summary." Anchorage: Greenpeace, 1994.

Pacific Northwest Pollution Prevention Research Center. *Pollution Prevention Opportunities in Oil and Gas Production, Drilling and Exploration*. Seattle, 1993.

Palmer, Mark. "Congress Considers the Arctic Coastal Plain." *Sierra*, September-October 1987: 47.

Pamplin, W. Lewis, Jr. *Cooperative Efforts to Halt Population Declines of Goose Nesting on Alaska's Yukon-Kuskokwim Delta*. Juneau: Alaska Dept. of Fish and Game, 1986.

Parker, Jeff. "Club Halts Invalid Mining Claims." *Sierra Borealis*, Fall 1983: 8.

Peale, Martha (Marty). "Beating the Drums for Caribou." *Sierra*, May-June 1989: 32.

———. "Borax Story." *Ravencall*, Fall 1982: 6.

———. "Borax: Which Misty Fjord? *Ravencall*, May 1981: 5, 7.

———. "Shee Atika: Courts Defend Cube Cove." *Ravencall*, Summer 1983: 9.

———. "Tanana Forest Plan Reaches Critical Stage." *Northern Line*, September-October 1985: 4–6.

Peirce, Neil. *The Pacific States of America*. New York: Norton, 1972.

Pendleton, Kate. "Network Formed as Waste Hazards Surface." *Northern Line*, May-July 1987: 5.

———. "Udall Introduces Wilderness Bill." *Northern Line*, May-July 1986: 1.

Perkins, Joe. "Alaska's Environmental Planning Project Draws to End." *Sierra Club Alaska Newsletter*, October 1981: 7.

Perry, Richard. *The World of the Polar Bear*. Seattle: University of Washington Press, 1966.

Peter, Walter G., III. "Cannikin: A Compelling Necessity?" *Bioscience*, September 15, 1979: 955–958.

Peterson, Rolf O., and James D. Woolington. "The Apparent Extirpation and Reappearance of Wolves on the Kenai Peninsula, Alaska." In Fred H. Harrington and Paul C. Paquet, *Wolves of the World*, pp. 334–344. Park Ridge, NJ: Noyes, 1982.

Philo, L. Michael, Emmett B. Shotts Jr., and John C. George. "Morbidity and Mortality." In John J. Burns, J. Jerome Montague, and Cleveland J. Cowles, eds., *The Bowhead Whale*, pp. 275–312. Society for Marine Mammalogy. Special Pub. No. 2. Lawrence, KS: Allen Press, 1993.

Phipps, Alan. "USFS Rejects Montague EIS Request." *Center News*, June-August 1992: 2.

———. "Wally Kills Spill Restoration Project." *Center News*, June-August 1992: 1–2.

Piatt, John F., Calvin J. Lensink, William Butler, Marshall Kendziorek, and David R. Nysewander. "Immediate Impact of the *Exxon-Valdez* Oil Spill on Marine Birds." *The Auk* 107 (April 1990): 387–397.

Picou, J. Steven, Duane A. Gill, and Maurie J. Cohen. "Technological Disasters and Social Policy: Lessons From the *Exxon Valdez* Oil Spill." In J. Steven Picou, Duane A. Gill, and Maurie J. Cohen, *The Exxon Valdez Disaster: Readings on a Modern Social Problem*, pp. 309–315. Dubuque, IA: Kendall/Hunt, 1997.

Picou, J. Steven, Duane A. Gill, and Maurie J. Cohen. *The Exxon Valdez Disaster: Readings on a Modern Social Problem*. Dubuque, IA: Kendall/Hunt, 1997.

Portney, Paul R., ed. *Natural Resources and the Environment*. Washington, DC: Urban Institute, 1984.

Powers, Richard L. "Public Involvement and Admiralty Island, Alaska: Effects of Interest Groups on Natural Resource Allocations." Master's thesis, University of Alaska Juneau, May 14, 1972.

Prestrud, Pal, and Ian Stirling. "The International Polar Bear Agreement and the Current Status of Polar Bear Conservation." *Aquatic Mammals* 20, no. 3 (1994): 113–124.

Price, Robert E. *Legal Status of the Alaska Natives: A Report to the Alaska Statehood Commission*. Anchorage: Alaska Statehood Commission, 1982.

———. "The Politics of Energy and the Environment in Alaska." In Alexander B. Dolitsky, ed., *Politics and Environment in Alaska*, pp. 1–12. Juneau: Alaska-Siberia Research Center, 1993.

Public Broadcast System. *Anatomy of An Oil Spill*. March 20, 1990.

———. *The Big Spill*. February 27, 1990.

Rae, Brian. "Alaska's Timber Industry." *Alaska Economic Trends*, October 1988: 1–9.

Rakestraw, Lawrence. *A History of the U.S. Forest Service in Alaska*. Anchorage: Alaska Historical Commission, Alaska Dept. of Education, and Alaska Region, U.S. Forest Service, 1981.

Raloff, Janet. "*Valdez* Spill Leaves Lasting Oil Impacts." *Science News*, February 13, 1993: 102–103.

Randall, Bob. "Conservationists Oppose Beaufort Sea Lease Sale." *Environmental Advocate*, Spring 1999: 8–9.

Rau, Ron. "Valley of the Eagles." *Sports Illustrated*, February 25, 1980: 76–90.

Rausch, Robert A. "Progress in Management of the Alaskan Wolf Population." *Science in Alaska: Proceedings of the Fifteenth Alaskan Science Conference, 1964.* p. 43. Fairbanks: Alaska Division, American Association for the Advancement of Science, 1965.

Raveling, Dennis G. "Geese and Hunters of Alaska's Yukon Delta: Management Problems and Political Dilemmas." *Transactions of the 49th North American Wildlife and Natural Resources Conference*, pp. 555–575. Washington, DC: Wildlife Management Institute, 1984.

Ravencall, 1976–2000 issues. Southeast Alaska Conservation Council.

———. "APC Fires Worker After His Tongass Testimony." June-August 1988: 5.

———. "Bear Season Closed, Heavy Logging Blamed." September-November 1988: 1.

———. "Coalition Works to Protect Water and Major Fishery." Summer 1992: 10.

———, "EPA Finds Big Flaws in Kensington Mine Plan." January 1995: 12.

———. "Massive Mine Planned on Juneau's Doorstep." Summer 1992: 10.

———. "O'Haines!" November 10, 1980: 10.

Ray, Patrick Henry. *Compilation of Narratives of Explorations in Alaska*. Washington, DC: GPO, 1900.

Rearden, Jim. "The Alaska Pipe Line Five Years Later." *Outdoor Life*, April 1980: 57–61.

———. "The Arctic Caribou Herd: A Wild Life Disaster." *Alaska*, January 1977: 4–6.

———. "The Chilkat Miracle." *Audubon*, January 1984: 40–54.

———. "An End to Poisoning?" *Alaska*, May 1972: 13.

———. "Wolves, Moose, Airplanes and Man." *Alaska*, April 1975: 30–32.

Reed, John C. "Ecological Investigation in the Arctic." *Science*, October 21, 1966: 372.

———. *Exploration of Naval Petroleum Reserve No. 4 and Adjacent Areas, Northern Alaska, 1944–53: Part 1, History of the Exploration*. Geological Survey Professional Paper 301. Washington, DC: GPO, 1958.

Reed, Susan. "Shadow Over an Ancient Land." *People Weekly*, September 18, 1989: 48–53.

Reichardt, Paul. "1984 Issues." *Northern Line*, January-February 1984: 4.

Reinwand, Jerry. Article in *Alaska Conservation Review*, Fall-Winter 1970: 14.

Rice, Chuck, and Heidi Robichaud. "Brown Bear Overharvest Caused By Hunting at Logging Camp Dumps." *Ravencall*, December 1988-February 1989: 9.

Richter, Peter A. "A Comparative Study of the Conservation of Polar Bears in Canada, Denmark, Norway, Russia, and the United States." Master's thesis, Alaska Pacific University, May 1998.

Ricks, Melvin. *Melvin Ricks' Alaska Bibliography*. Anchorage: Binford and Mort, for Alaska Historical Commission, 1977.

Ritzman, Dan. "NPR-A Public Hearings Draw Crowds." *Alaska Report*, March 1998: 7.

Robinson, Michael. "EF! Alaska Task Force Storms North." *Earth First!*, September 22, 1989: 7.

Roderick, Jack. *Crude Dreams: A Personal History of Oil and Politics in Alaska*. Fairbanks: Epicenter, 1997.

Rogers, George W. "A Comparison of the Employment Impact of Alternate Routes on the State of Alaska." Appendix C, in Donald Cicchetti, *Alaskan Oil: Alternative Routes and Markets*. Baltimore: Johns Hopkins University Press, for Resources for the Future, 1972.

———. *Alaska in Transition: The Southeast*. Baltimore: Johns Hopkins University Press, 1960.

Rogers, Randy. "NAEC Sues BLM: Placer Mining Regs Unenforced for Too Long." *Northern Line*, January-March 1986: 1.

———. "Northern Center Involvement." *Northern Line*, April-May 1985: 7–8.

———. "Placer Miners Will Operate This Summer—And Do Reclamation." *Northern Line*, April 1986: 5.

———. "Placer Mining: Comment Now." *Alaska Report*, July 1988: 6.

————. "Placer Mining in Alaska: The Times They Are A-Changing." *Northern Line*, July 5, 1989: 10–11.

————. Where Did the Cooperative Spirit Go?" *Northern Line*, July-August 1985: 2.

Romanoff, Andy. "The Legacy of APC's Contract." *Ravencall*, Spring 1994: 5.

Roscow, James P. *800 Miles to Valdez: The Building of the Alaska Pipeline*. Englewood Cliffs, NJ: Prentice-Hall, 1977.

Runte, Alfred. *National Parks: The American Experience,* 2nd ed. Lincoln: University of Nebraska Press, 1987.

Scammon, Charles Melville. "Northern Whaling." *Overland Monthly*, June 1871: 548–554.

Schiefelbein, Susan. "Alaska: The Great Land War." *Saturday Review*, February 17, 1979: 14–20.

Schliebe, S., T. J. Evans, A. S. Fishbach, and S. B. Kalxdorff. "Summary of Polar Bear Management in Alaska." In Andrew E. Durocher, Gerald W. Garner, Nicholas J. Lunn, and Oystein Wiig, *Polar Bears: Proceedings of Twelfth Working Meeting of IUCN/SSC Polar Bear Specialist Group, Oslo, Norway, February 3–7, 1997*, pp. 115–123. Occ. Pap. Of IUCN Species Survival Comm. No. 19. International Union for Conservation of Nature and Natural Resources, 1998.

Schmidt, Lee. "Tongass Opportunity." *Alaska Conservation Review*, Winter 1975: 1.

Schneider, William. "Subsistence in Alaska: A Look at the Issue Over Time." In Peter G. Cornwall and Gerald McBeath, eds., *Alaska's Rural Development*, pp. 169–180. Boulder, CO: Westview, 1982.

Schoen, John W. "Bear Habitat Management: A Review and Future Perspective." *International. Conference on Bear Research and Management* 8 (1989): 143–154.

Schoen, John W., and Laverne R. Beier. *Brown Bear Habitat Preferences and Brown Bear Logging and Mining Relationships in Southeast Alaska*. Juneau: Alaska Dept. of Fish and Game, May, 1988.

Schoen, John W., Laverne R. Beier, Jack W. Lentfer, and Loyal J. Johnson. "Denning Ecology of Brown Bears on Admiralty and Chichagof Islands." *International Conference on Bear Research and Management* 7 (1988): 293–304.

Schoen, John W., and Matthew D. Kirchhoff. "Little Deer in the Big Woods." *Natural History*, August 1988: 52–55.

Schoen, John W., Matthew D. Kirchhoff, and Michael H. Thomas. *Seasonal Distribution and Habitat Use by Sitka Black-Tailed Deer in Southeastern Alaska*. Juneau: Alaska Dept. of Fish and Game, May 1988.

Schoen, John W., Matthew D. Kirchhoff, and Olof C. Wallmo. "Sitka Back-Tailed Deer/Old Growth Relationships in Southeast Alaska: Implications for Management." *Proceedings of Symposium, Juneau, 1982*, pp. 315–319. Juneau: American Institute of Fisheries Research Biologists, 1984.

Schoen, John W., Olof C. Wallmo, and Matthew D. Kirchhoff. "Wildlife-Forest Relationships: Is a Reevaluation of Old Growth Necessary?" *Transactions of the 46th North American Wildlife and Natural Resources Conf.,* pp. 531–544. Washington, DC: Wildlife Management Institute, 1981.

Science News. "FCC Stops Alaska's Aerial Wolf Hunt." January 26, 1985: 57.

Science News Letter. "High Alaska Fallout Risk." June 17, 1961: 375.

Scott, Sir Peter. *The World of the Polar Bear*. London: Hamlyn, 1978.

Servid, Carolyn, and Donald Snow, eds. *The Book of the Tongass*. Minneapolis: Milkweed, 1999.

Shelden, Kim, and David J. Rugh. "The Bowhead Whale: *Balaena mysticetus*: Its Historic and Current Status." *Marine Fisheries Review* 57, nos. 3–4 (1996): 1–20.

Shelton, Kirsten. "ACV Promotes Sustainable Economy for Alaska." *United Voices*, Mid-term 1999: 1.

Shepard, Fern. "APC Violates Consent Decree." *Ravencall*, January-February 1988: 15.

————. "Victory Against Alaska Pulp's Air Pollution." *Ravencall*, January-February 1987: 5.

Sherrill, Robert. *The Oil Follies of 1970–80*. Landover Hills, MD: Anchor, 1983.

Sherwood, Morgan. *Big Game in Alaska: A History of Wildlife and People*. New Haven: Yale University Press, 1981.

Sierra Borealis, 1983–2000 issues. Alaska Chapter of the Sierra Club.

Sierra Club Alaska Newsletter, 1973–1983 issues. Continues as *Sierra Borealis*.

Sierra Club Bulletin. "Project Chariot: The Long Look." May 1961: 4–17.

Sierra Club Legal Defense Fund. *In Brief.* Summer 1989: 1; Summer 1992: 22–23; Autumn 1993: 15.

———. News release on court decision requiring Environmental Impact statement for Hoonah-Tenakee Springs road. September 30, 1986.

Sierra-Juneau Newsletter, June 1973.

Simel, Nancy, and Tracy Pyles. "Admiralty Island: The Club Sues Over Logging Plans." *Sierra,* November-December 1983: 14–18.

Simmerman, Nancy Lange. *Alaska's Parklands: The Complete Guide.* Seattle: The Mountaineers, 1983.

Sisk, John. "Economics Undermine Stikine Dam Plans." *Ravencall,* Spring 1984: 10.

Skilbred, Amy. "The ANWR: USFWS Pursues Oil Option." *Northern Line,* January-February 1986: 3.

Skinner, Samuel K., and William L. Reilly. *The Exxon Valdez Oil Spill: A Report to the President.* Washington, DC: National Response Team, May 1989.

Skow, John. "Forest Service Follies." *Sports Illustrated,* March 14, 1988: 76–88.

Smart, Tim, and Dennis Melamed. "Big Oil's Blowout on the Hill." *Business Week,* June 27, 1988: 36.

Smith, Allen. "Wilderness Management in Alaska: Threats and Opportunities." Presented to 6th Annual Wilderness Conf., Santa Fe, New Mexico, November 14–18, 1994. Anchorage: The Wilderness Society, 1994.

Smith, Carl. "ACE Objects to Bowhead Ban." *Center News,* October 1977: 1.

Smith, Eric. "Placer Mining: A Threat to Streams." *Northern Line,* April-May 1985: 1.

The Spirit, 1990–2000 issues. Alaska Wildlife Alliance.

———. "ADF&G Appointed Citizen Planning Team for Wolves Holds First Meeting." October-December, 1990: 1–2.

———. "Always Cry Wolf." Summer 1995: 3.

———. "Gunning for Predators." Fall 1999: 1, 4.

Spurr, Stephen, ed. *Rampart Dam and the Economic Development of Alaska, Vol.1.* Ann Arbor: University of Michigan School of Natural Resources, March 1966.

Stange, Jay. "Coalition Files Legal Challenge to Forest Service Salvage Sale." *Center News,* May-June 1997: 1.

Stanway, Sondra. "Conservationists Gather." *Ravencall,* January-February 1987: 6.

Steen, Harold K. *The Forest Service: A History.* Seattle: University of Washington Press, 1976.

Stehn, Robert, Mike Wege, John Morgart, and George Walters. *Population Size and Production of Geese and Spectacled Eiders Nesting on the Yukon- Kuskokwim Delta, Alaska.* Anchorage: U.S. Fish and Wildlife Service. Alaska Fish and Wildlife Research Center, July 10, 1975.

Stein, Alan. "Point Baker Law Suit." *Alaska Conservation Review,* Winter 1975: 9–10.

Steinhart, Peter. "Can We Solve the Great Goose Mystery?" *National Wildlife,* June-July 1986: 4–11.

Stephenson, Robert O., Warren B. Ballard, Christian A. Smith, and Katherine Richardson. "Wolf Biology and Management in Alaska 1981–91." *Proceedings of 2nd International Wolf Symposium,* pp. 22–30. Canadian Wildlife Service Series. Edmonton: Canadian Wildlife Service, August 1992.

Stoker, Sam W., and Igor I. Krupnik. "Subsistence Whaling." In John J. Burns, Jerome Montague, and Cleveland J. Cowles, eds., *The Bowhead Whale,* pp. 579–629. Society for Marine Mammalogy. Special Pub. No. 2. Lawrence, KS: Allen Press, 1993.

Stoltz, Susan Grace. "Camp Habitat: A Rewarding Experience for All." *Northern Line,* September 30, 1991: 14.

Stonorov, Tina. "Gumshoe." *Alaska Conservation Review,* Winter 1977: 12.

———. "The Haul Road in Perspective." *Alaska Conservation Review,* Spring 1976: 4–5.

Stratton, Jim, and Marty Peale. "Haines Lawsuit: The 25,000 We Don't Owe." *Ravencall,* Summer 1983: 2.

———. "Kadashan: Longstanding Timber, Longstanding Controversy." *Ravencall,* Spring 1983: 1.

Sutton, Larry. "Arctic Refuge: The Saga Continues." *Northern Line*, March-April 1987: 6–7.

———. "Refuge Future in Hands of Congress." *Northern Line*, January-February 1987: 3.

———. "Wildlife Biologist Speaks on Caribou Biology."*Northern Line*, March-April 1987: 5.

Swan, Tom. "Placer Miners Run Amuck." *Center News*, June-July 1983: 6.

TAGS Environmental Review Committee. *North Slope Natural Gas Pipeline: The Western Route: New Threat to Northwest Alaska*. Anchorage: Alaska Conservation Foundation, May 1995.

Teller, Edward. "How Nuclear Blasts Could Be Used for Peace." *Reader's Digest*, May 1959: 108–110.

———. "We're Going to Work Miracles." *Popular Mechanics*, March 1960: 97–101.

Thomas, Clive S., ed. *Alaska Public Policy Issues: Background and Perspectives*. Juneau: Denali Press, 1999.

Thomas Jr., Lowell. "Giant State . . . Giant Resources . . . Giant Problems." *National Wildlife*, April-May 1969: 24–33.

Thornton, Thomas F. "Subsistence: The Politics of a Cultural Dilemma." In Clive S. Thomas, ed., *Alaska Public Policy Issues: Background and Perspectives*, pp. 205–219. Juneau: Denali Press, 1999.

Tileston, Peg. "New Susitna Report Out." *Center News*, June 15, 1979: 4.

——— –. "Temporary Restraining Order Stops Wolf Hunt." *Center News*, February 1976: 2.

Trefethen, James B. *An American Crusade for Wildlife*. New York: Boone and Crockett, 1975.

Tremblay, Ray, Milstead Zahn, Jim H. Branson, and Neil T. Argy. Memo to Regional Director, Bureau of Sport Fisheries and Wildlife, Juneau, May 12, 1961.

Trustees for Alaska (TfA). *Summary of Recent Activities*, June 1988; June 1989; November 1991. Annual case digest.

———. "Trustees for Alaska." Ca. 1987. Brochure.

———. *Under the Influence: Oil and the Industrialization of America's Arctic*. Anchorage: TfA, 1998.

Trustees for Alaska, 1984–1993 issues. Continues as *Trustees for Alaska Environmental Action Report*, 1994–1998, and *The Environmental Advocate*, 1998– .

———. "Copper River Highway Lawsuits Protect Habitat." August 1992: 1, 3.

———. "Offshore Leasing Decision Ruled Improper by Alaska's Highest Court." May 1990: 1.

———. "State Plows Over Laws in Building Copper River Highway." December 1991: 4.

———. "Supreme Court Halts Diamond-Chuitna Coal Mine." December 1992: 1.

———. "Trustees Challenge DNR's Decision." May 1990: 5.

Trustees for Alaska, Natural Resources Defense Council, and National Wildlife Federation. *Oil in the Arctic*. Washington, DC: Natural Resources Defense Council, 1988.

Trustees for Alaska (TfA) Environmental Action Report, 1994–1998 issues.

———. "Landmark Decision Forces New Procedures for Water Quality Standards in Alaska." October 1994: 1.

Turner, Tom. "Of Gold Fever and Brown Rivers." *Sierra,* July-August 1987: 30–33.

Tussing, Arlon R. "Alaska's Energy Policy in a Global Context." *Northern Engineer*, Summer 1984: 27–33.

———. "Alaska's Petroleum-Based Economy." In Thomas A. Morehouse, ed., *Alaskan Resources Development: Issues of the 1980s*, pp. 51–78. Boulder, CO: Westview, 1984.

Tussing, Arlon R., Lori S. Kramer, and Barbara F. Morse (prepared for the Alaska State Legislature). "Susitna Hydropower: A Review of the Issues." Anchorage: Arlon R. Tussing and Associates, April 15, 1980.

Twitchell, Marlyn. "Borax Mine Plan Shelved Following EPA Reversal." *Ravencall*, November-December 1990: 15.

Tyson, Ray. "Ardor for ANWR Fortifies Opposing Camps." *Alaska Business Monthly*, May 1991: 33–37.

———. "Missing Links Leave Oil Untapped." *Alaska Business Monthly*, July 1992: 53–57.

Udall, James R. "Polar Opposites." *Sierra*, September-October 1987: 40–48.

United Voices, 1998–2000 issues. Alaska Conservation Alliance and Alaska Conservation Voters.
————. *Year End Report, 1998*
U.S. Army, Corps of Engineers, Alaska District. *A Report on the Rampart Canyon Project, Vol. 1.* Anchorage, 1971.
————. *The Market for Rampart Power.* New York: Development and Resources Corp., April 1962.
————. *Rampart Study.* Anchorage, ca. 1962.
U.S. Atomic Energy Commission (AEC). *Background Information Regarding AEC Activities on Amchitka Island, Alaska.* Las Vegas, NV: AEC, July 30, 1969.
————. *Environmental Impact Statement: Cannikin, June, 1971.* Las Vegas, NV: AEC, 1971.
————. *Project Cannikin: D 30 Day Report: Preliminary and Operational Test Results Summary.* Las Vegas, NV: AEC, February 1972.
————. Nevada Operations Office. *Summary Report: Amchitka Demobilization and Restoration Activities.* Las Vegas, NV: AEC, June 1974.
U.S. Borax. *Fact Sheet: Quartz Hill Molybdenum Project Initial Plan of Operations.* November 4, 1982.
U.S. Congress, House. Committee on Interior and Insular Affairs. *Alyeska Pipeline Service Company Covert Operations. Draft Report. Part I.* 102 Cong., 2 sess., July 1992.
————. Committee on Interior and Insular Affairs. Subcommittee on Water, Power, and Offshore Energy Resources. Hearing: HR 987. 100 Cong., 1 sess., March 14, 1989.
U.S. Congress, Joint Economic Committee. *Natural Gas Regulation and the Trans-Alaska Pipeline: Hearings.* 92 Cong. 2 sess., June 1972.
U.S. Congress, Senate. Committee on Energy and Natural Resources. Subcommittee on Public Lands, National Parks and Forests. *Tongass Timber Reform Act: Hearings.* 100 Cong. 1 sess., November 3–5, 1987.
————. Committee on Interior and Insular Affairs. *Hearings: Rights-of-Way Across Federal Lands: Transportation of Alaska's North Slope Oil. Parts I–IV.* 93 Cong. 1 sess., May 2–3, 1973.
U.S. Department of Agriculture (USDA). *Record of Decision: Tongass National Forest Land and Resource Management Plan, Alaska.* Washington, DC: USDA, April 1999.
U.S. Department of Agriculture. Forest Service, Region 10. *Status of the Tongass National Forest, 1987 Report,* March 1988; *1989 Report,* August 1990; *1991* Draft, 1992. Juneau: U.S. Forest Service.
————. *Timber Supply and Demand, 1987.* Juneau, 1988; *Draft 1988 Report.* 1989; *1989 Report.* September 1990; *Fiscal Year 1991.* 1993; *Fiscal Year 1992.* September 1993; *1994.* March 1995. Juneau: U.S. Forest Service.
U.S. Department of Commerce. National Marine Fisheries Service (NMFS). *International Whaling Commission's Deletion of Native Exemption for the Subsistence Harvest of Bowhead Whales: Final Environmental Impact Statement, 1977, Vol. 1.* Washington, DC: NMFS, 1977.
U.S. Department of Commerce. National Marine Fisheries Service. Marine Mammal Commission. *Annual Report to Congress, 1999.* Bethesda, MD: Marine Mammal Commission, January 31, 2000.
U.S. Department of Commerce. National Oceanographic and Atmospheric Administration (NOAA). "Summary of Injuries to Natural Resources as a Result of the *Exxon Valdez* Oil Spill." *Federal Register* 56, no. 70 (April 12, 1991): 14687–14694.
U.S. Department of the Interior (USDOI). *Alaska Natural Resources and the Rampart Project.* Washington, DC: USDOI, June 1967.
————. *Field Report: Rampart Project, Alaska; Market for Power and Effect of Project on Natural Resources.* Washington, DC: GPO, 1965.
————. *Final Environmental Impact Statement: Proposed Trans-Alaskan Pipeline,* vols. 1, 3, and 4 of 9. Washington, DC: USDOI, March 20, 1972.
————. *Final Environmental Impact Statement: Proposed Yukon Flats National Wildlife Refuge, Alaska.* Washington, DC: Alaska Planning Group, 1974.

———. *Trans-Alaska Pipeline Hearings.* Vols. 1, 3 and 5 of 5; *Supplemental Testimony*, vol. 1 of 12. Anchorage and Washington, DC: USDOI, February 1971.

———. Alaska Power Administration. *Devil Canyon Project, Alaska: Status Report.* Juneau: Alaska Power Administration, May 1974.

U.S. Department of the Interior. Bureau of Land Management (BLM). *Hearings on Proposed Rampart—Upper Yukon Power Site*, Fairbanks, February 14, 1964; Fort Yukon, February 15, 1964. Anchorage: BLM, 1964.

U.S. Department of the Interior. Fish and Wildlife Service (USFWS). *Administration of the Marine Mammal Protection Act of 1972.* January 1, 1987–December 1, 1987. Washington, DC: USFWS, 1988.

———. *Aleutian Islands National Wildlife Refuge and Izembek National Wildlife Range: Narrative Report, January 1–December 31, 1969.* Unpublished report. Anchorage: USFWS.

———. *Amending the Migratory Bird Treaty with Canada.* (discussion paper). Washington, DC: USFWS, Office of Migratory Bird Management, July 1992.

———. *Arctic National Wildlife Refuge, Alaska, Coastal Plain Resource Assesment: Report and Recommendation to the Congress of the United States and Final Legislative Environmental Impact Statement.* Draft. November, 1986; *Final*, April 1987. Washington, DC: USFWS.

———. *Arctic National Wildlife Refuge: Draft River Management Plan and Environmental Assessment.* Fairbanks: USFWS, June 1993.

———. *Comparison of Actual and Predicted Impacts of the Trans-Alaska Pipeline System and Prudhoe Bay Oilfields on the North Slope of Alaska.* Fairbanks: USFWS, Fairbanks Fish and Wildlife Enhancement Office, December 1987.

———.*Conservation Plan for the Polar Bear in Alaska.* Anchorage: USFWS, Office of Marine Mammals Management. June 19, 1994.

———. *Environmental Assessment: The Yukon-Kuskokwim Delta Goose Management Plan.* Anchorage: USFWS, Office of Migratory Bird Management, March 1989.

———. *A Guide to the Yukon-Kuskokwim Delta Goose Management Plan.* Anchorage: USFWS, Office of Migratory Bird Management, 1988.

———. *A Report on Fish and Wildlife Resources Affected by Rampart Canyon Dam and Reservation Project, Yukon River, Alaska.* Juneau: USFWS, April 1964.

———. *USFWS Marking, Tagging and Reporting Program for Polar Bear, Sea Otter and Pacific Walrus.* Anchorage: USFWS, Office of Marine Mammals Management, January 1990.

———. *Yukon Delta National Wildlife Refuge Comprehensive Conservation Plan, Environmental Impact Statement, Wilderness Review and Wild River Plan (Final).* Anchorage: USFWS,January 1988.

———. *The Yukon-Kuskokwim Goose Management Plan (revised ed.).* Anchorage: USFWS, Office of Migratory Bird Management, March 1989; *1994 Addendum*, 1994.

U.S. Department of the Interior. Minerals Management Service. Alaska OCS Region. "Sale Areas Offshore Where Exploratory Drilling Has Occurred." Anchorage, May 19, 1999.

U.S. General Accounting Office (GAO). *Federal Land Management: Consideration of Proposed Alaska Land Exchanges Should Be Discontinued.* Washington, DC: GAO, September 29, 1988.

———. *Tongass National Forest: Lack of Accountability for Time and Costs Has Delayed Forest Plan Revision.* GAO/T-RCED 97-153. Washington, DC: GAO, April 29, 1997.

———. *Tongass National Forest: Timber Provision of the Alaska Lands Act Needs Clarification.* GAO/RCED 88-54. Washington, DC: GAO, April 1988.

U.S. Government Manual, 1999–2000. Washington, DC: GPO, 1999.

U.S. News and World Report. "Alaska Strikes It Rich." December 9, 1968: 48–53.

———. "Why Alaskans Are Upset About Conservation." October 4, 1971: 43–45.

Van Ballenberghe, Victor. "Forty Years of Wolf Management in the Nelchina Basin, Southcentral Alaska: A Critical Review." *Transactions of the 56th North American Wildlife and Natural Resources Conference*, pp. 561–566. Washington, DC: Wildlife Management Institute, 1991.

Van den Berg, David. "Center Condemns Wolf Control Programs." *Northern Line*, December 16, 1992: 3.
———. "An Improvement on Mayhem." *Northern Line*, November 26, 1997: 3.
Walden, Arthur Treadwell. *A Dog-Puncher on the Yukon*. Boston: Houghton-Mifflin, 1928.
Waldo, Tom. "Court Blocks Logging on Chichagof, Kuiu Islands." *Ravencall*, November-December 1990: 7.
Walker, D. A., P. J. Webber, E. F. Binnian, K. R. Everett, N. D. Lederer, E. A. Norstrand, and M. D. Walker. "Cumulative Impacts of Oil Fields on Northern Alaska Landscapes." *Science* 238 (November 6, 1987): 757–761.
Wallmo, Olof C., and John W. Schoen. "Response of Deer to Secondary Forest Succession in Southeast Alaska. *Forest Science* 26, no. 3 (1980): 448–462.
Ward, Sylvia. "Mining on Fish Creek: Then and Now." *Northern Line*, September 28, 1992: 6–7.
Warren, Bob. "BLM Does It Again." *Northern Line*, January-February 1984: 2.
———. "Public Outraged by BLM Plans." *Northern Line*, June-July 1984: 1.
Waste, Stephen. "A Gathering of Eagles." *Alaska*, November 1978: 4–6.
Watkins, T. H. "The Perils of Expedience." *Wilderness*, Winter 1990: 22–71.
Wayburn, Edgar A. "Alaska: An Act of History." *Sierra*, January-February 1981: 5.
———. "Hunters Take Aim At Alaska's National Parks: S49 and HR1493." *Sierra*, May-June 1983: 16–19.
Weeden, Robert B. "ACS and Western Arctic Wolf-Caribou Problem." *Alaska Conservation Review*, Fall 1976: 6–7.
———. *Alaska: Promises to Keep*. Boston: Houghton-Mifflin, 1978.
———. "Alaska's Oil Boom: From Swanson to Prudhoe Bay and Beyond." *Alaska Conservation Review*, December 1968: 3.
———. "Bowhead Hunting Stopped." *Alaska Conservation Review*, Summer 1977: 8.
———. "Curriculum Vitae." June 1989. Typescript.
———. "Fish and Wildlife Service Issues Another Favorable Report on Susitna River Hydro Complex." *Alaska Conservation Review*, March 1965: 5.
———. *Messages From Earth*. Fairbanks: University of Alaska Press, 1992.
———. "Where Does ACS Stand on (d)(2)." *Alaska Conservation Review*, Fall 1977: 4–5.
Weeden, Robert B., and David R. Klein. "Wildlife and Oil: A Survey of Critical Issues." *Polar Record* 15, no. 97 (1971): 479–494.
Weeden, Robert R. "Mining Regulations Go Unenforced by Some Agencies." *Northern Line,* July-August 1985: 6.
Weeks, W. F., and G. Weller. "Offshore Oil in the Alaskan Arctic." *Science*, July 27, 1984: 371–378.
Wells, Stephen. "Alaska Moves Ahead With Wolf Control Program." *The Spirit*, October-November 1993: 1.
Weltzin, Jeff. "Alaska Legislature Goes Home: A Major Loss." *Northern Line*, August 1981: 1.
———. "Susitna River: Energy Planning or Energy Promotion?" *Northern Line*, April 1980: 6–7.
Wentworth, Cynthia. "Subsistence Waterfowl Harvest Survey: 1992 Results and Comparative Data, 1985–92." Anchorage: USFWS, Division of Migratory Bird Management, February 1993.
———. "Subsistence Waterfowl Harvest Survey, Yukon-Kuskokwim Delta: 1994 Results and Comparative Data, 1985–94." Anchorage: USFWS, Div. of Migratory Bird Management, June 1995.
———. *Subsistence Waterfowl Harvest Survey: Yukon-Kuskokwim Delta, 1987–1997*. Anchorage: USFWS, Division of Migratory Bird Management, December 1998.
———. *Subsistence Waterfowl Harvest Survey: Yukon-Kuskokwim Delta, 1990–1999*. Anchorage: USFWS, Division of Migratory Bird Management, May 2000.
Wheeler, Polly. "State and Indigenous Fisheries Management: The Alaskan Context." In M. R. Freeman and Ludwig N. Carbyn, eds., *Traditional Knowledge and Renewable Resource Management in Northern Regions*, pp. 38–47. Edmonton: IUCN Commission on Ecology and Boreal Institute for Northern Studies. Occ. Pap. No. 23, 1988.
Whitesell, Edward A. "Southeast Wildlands Study." *Alaska Conservation Review*, Winter 1975: 7–8.

Whitten, Kenneth R. *Movement Patterns of the Porcupine Caribou Herd in Relation to Oil Development.* Alaska Dept. of Fish and Game, November 1992.

Wilderness. "News, Notes, and Comments." Summer 1983: 39–40.

Wilderness Society. *The Alaska Lands Act: A Broken Promise.* Hyattsville, MD: Wilderness Society, 1990.

———. *America's Vanishing Rain Forest: Executive Summary: A Report on Federal Timber Management in Southeast Alaska.* Washington, DC: Wilderness Society, April 1986.

———. *Exxon Valdez Plus Five: The Good News, The Bad News.* Washington, DC: Wilderness Society, March 23, 1994.

Wildlife Society, Alaska Chapter. *Position Paper: Old-Growth Forest Management in Coastal Alaska.* Juneau: Wildlife Society, June 1985.

Wilimovsky, Norman J., and John N. Wolfe, eds. *Environment of the Cape Thompson Region, Alaska.* Washington, DC: Atomic Energy Commission, 1966.

Williams, Larry. "Comments Needed on Chugach Forest Plan." *Sierra Borealis,* Fall 1983: 9.

Williams, Ted. "Alaska's Rush for the Gold." *Audubon,* November 1993: 50–54.

———. "Alaska's War on the Wolves." *Audubon,* May-June 1993: 44–50.

Williamson, Lonnie. "Protecting Alaska's Wildlife." *Outdoor Life,* October 1987: 40–44.

Williss, G. Frank. *"Do Things Right the First Time": The National Park Service and the Alaska National Interest Lands Conservation Act of 1980.* Washington, DC: National Park Service, September 1985.

Wolf, Ron. "Interior Secretary Watt's Religious Tradition Helped Shape His Public Life." *Sierra Club Alaska Newsletter,* July 1981: 7–8.

Wolfe, Robert J. "Subsistence and Politics in Alaska." In Alexander B. Dolitsky, ed., *Politics and Environment in Alaska,* pp. 3: 13–28. Juneau: Alaska-Siberia Research Center, 1993.

Wolfe, Robert J., and Robert G. Bosworth. "Subsistence in Alaska: 1994 Update." Alaska Dept. of Fish and Game, Division of Subsistence. Juneau: March 1, 1994.

Wood, Ginny Hill. "Back to the Woodpile." *Northern Line,* November 10, 1999: 16–17.

———. "From the Woodpile." *Northern Line,* February-March 1988: 11; September 28, 1992: 12; November 10, 1999: 16–17.

———. "Rampart: Foolish Dam." *Living Wilderness,* Spring 1965: 3–7.

———. "Where Have All the Caribou Gone?" *Alaska Conservation Review,* Winter 1977: 6–7.

Worl, Rosita. "Competition, Confrontation, and Compromise: The Politics of Fish and Game Allocations." *Indigenous Survival Quarterly,* Fall 1998: 77–78.

Wright, Gordon. "Haul Road Puzzle." *Alaska Conservation Review,* Winter 1973: 3.

———. "Northern Center Rooted in Individual Activism." *Northern Line,* April 22, 1990: 7–8.

Wuerthner, George. "Natives—The First Ecologists?" *Earth First!* May 1, 1987: 22–23.

Yergin, Daniel. *The Prize: The Epic Quest for Oil, Money and Power.* New York: Simon and Schuster, 1991.

Yould, Eric. "The Susitna Hydroelectric Project." *Northern Engineer,* Fall-Winter 1976: 14–23.

Young, Oran R., and Gail Osherenko, eds. *Polar Bear Politics: Creating International Environmental Regimes.* Ithaca, NY: Cornell University Press, 1993.

Yukon Power for America. "The Rampart Story." Ca. 1964. Brochure.

Zaelke, Durwood. "Admiralty Island Update." *Alaska Report,* February 1985: 2.

Zavaleta, Erika. "The Emergence of Waterfowl Conservation Among Yup'ik Hunters in the Yukon-Kuskokwim Delta, Alaska." *Human Ecology* 27, no. 2 (1999): 231–266.

Zimiski, Judy. "Bradley Lake Hydro Project Supported." *Center News,* October-November 1982: 1–2.

Zufelt, William, Robert F. McLean, Kenneth F. Karle, and Phillip A. North. "Aquatic Habitat Restoration for Placer Mining in Alaska: Past, Present, and Future." In K. Koski and William J. Hauser, eds., *Aquatic Habitat Restoration in Northern Ecosystems,* pp. 79–84. Symposium on Habitat Restoration in Northern Ecosystems, Girdwood, Alaska, 19–22 September 1994. Anchorage: Environmental Protection Agency, 1997.

Index

References to pages with illustrations, maps, or tables appear in italics.